THE JPS
GUIDE
TO
JEWISH
WOMEN

THE JPS
GUIDE
TO
JEWISH
WOMEN

600 B.C.E.–1900 C.E.

EMILY TAITZ, SONDRA HENRY, CHERYL TALLAN

The Jewish Publication Society
Philadelphia
2003 • 5763

The Jewish Publication Society
2100 Arch Street
Philadelphia, PA 19103

Design and Composition by Book Design Studio

Manufactured in the United States of America

03 04 05 06 07 08 09 10   10 9 8 7 6 5 4 3 2 1

Library of Congress Cataloging-in-Publication Data

Taitz, Emily.
  JPS guide to Jewish women 600 B.C.E. to 1900 C.E. / Emily
Taitz, Sondra Henry, and Cheryl Tallan.
     p. cm.
Includes bibliographical references and index.
ISBN 0-8276-0752-0
  1. Jewish women--Biography. 2. Women in Judaism--Biography. 3.
Jews--History. I. Henry, Sondra. II. Tallan, Cheryl. III. Title.
  HQ1172.T35 2003
  305.48'8924—dc21

                                   2002015263

Photo on page 139 courtesy of Richard Termine. Jenny Romaine in the Great Small Works production of *The Memoirs of Glückel of Hameln*, directed by Jenny Romaine, created by Romaine, Adrienne Cooper, and Frank London.
From a Performance at La Mama Etc. Annex Theater, February 2000, NYC.
Puppets by Clare Dolan. Costume by Alissandra Nichols.

Funding for this book is provided
in memory of my parents
the *inimitable* PHILIP SILVERSTEIN
and the *nonpareil* ESTHER K. SILVERSTEIN
Remembered with love
Harriet Seiler

This book is dedicated to our grandchildren.

CONTENTS

ACKNOWLEDGMENTS

Many people have helped us in the course of researching and writing this book. They include librarians, scholars, friends, and family. Although we cannot hope to name them all, we wish at least to thank the following people: the librarians at the Jewish Theological Seminary Library, especially Yisrael Dubitsky and Joshua Alan Gorfinkle; Barry Walfish, librarian at the Robarts Library, University of Toronto; the Hispanic Society of America; the Leo Baeck Institute; and Linda Fisher and Myrna Sloam of the Bryant Library in Roslyn, N.Y. Also, we thank librarian Rona Lupkin of Temple Israel of Great Neck for never calling back the books we borrowed, no matter how overdue they were.

Scholars with whom we corresponded and who shared data from their own research allowed us to include the most up-to-date material, sometimes even before it was published. Among them are Howard Tzvi Adelman, Carole Balin, Judith Baskin, Albrecht Classen, Don Harran, Yael Levine Katz, Ruth Lamdan, Rebecca Lesses, Joseph Tabory, Barbara Sparti, Frauke von Rhoden, and the scholars at the H-Judaica Listserv. Maria Baader, Sarah Taieb Carlin, Martin Lockshin, and Tirzah Meacham helped us to interpret information and suggested additional sources.

Dani and Rachel Blumenfeld, Linda Davidson, Christine Mielicke, Alice Morawetz, William Pinkus, and Isaac Taitz helped us with translations.

In addition, we want to thank Rabbi Renni Altman, Rabbi Marim Charry, Rita Gordonson, Adele Lobel, Rabbi Mordecai Waxman, and Natalie Zemon Davis for their help and for sharing valuable information.

We depended on Harold Fink for technical support and were always reassured by the knowledge of his readiness to help us through every computer disaster. Mark Deitch, Edward Henry, and Yaakov Taitz also gave technical assistance.

Emily Taitz, Sondra Henry, and Cheryl Tallan

INTRODUCTION

❖ Women's seals from biblical times indicate that women may have held appointed posts in ancient Israel.

❖ Archeological finds dating from the first to the sixth centuries (C.E.) reveal tombstones referring to specific women as heads of synagogues (*archisynagogissa*).

❖ Rashi's daughters and granddaughters were sought out by Jewish scholars in the twelfth century for their opinions on specific laws, and Dolce of Worms was a leader of the women in her community.

❖ Gracia Mendes Nasi, a woman of power and influence, was referred to as "the very magnificent lady" in the sixteenth century.

Such historical data represent real facts. And yet . . .

❖ Philo, a respected Jewish philosopher of Alexandria (c. 20 B.C.E. to 50 C.E.), wrote that women are always irrational, weak, and filled with "bestial passions."

❖ Beruriah, the scholarly woman mentioned in the Talmud, was portrayed one thousand years later as an adulterer in order to prove that even the best of women are sexually irresponsible and untrustworthy.

❖ When Rebecca Tiktiner's scholarly book of advice for women was published early in the seventeenth century, the printer felt it necessary to write: "Who had heard of or seen such a novelty within our time that a woman had, on her own, become a learned person!"

How can we explain this gap between stereotype and reality?

THE SOURCES

For centuries, history was written largely by men. Whether from ignorance or bias, most women's activities and accomplishments were overlooked; women's names, when mentioned at all, were buried in footnotes or old documents.

Recently, there has been a veritable explosion of interest in examining Jewish women's lives. In the last thirty or forty years, scholars and historians have searched out and analyzed literary, documentary, and archeological evidence that challenges the old stereotypes. However, such monographs, biographies, and journal articles are scattered and may be difficult to find.

In this comprehensive guide we have attempted to make both the old and the new data more accessible to interested readers. We have retrieved many of the older sources on Jewish women, organized much of the recent information, and examined and evaluated a variety of opinions. Notes consolidate and cite the sources clearly, and indexes list each woman by name to aid researchers in pursuing any individual woman or topic.

THE FORMAT

The format of the book is both chronological and geographical. We have divided Eastern Jewry from Western Jewry and marked out ancient, medieval, early modern, and Enlightenment periods, beginning in the late sixth century B.C.E. and ending at approximately 1900 C.E.

Each chapter covers a specific period or cultural context within this overall time frame and contains an overview explaining how historical events affected Jews in general and Jewish women in particular. This is followed by a section of biographical entries, in alphabetical order, of some of the women who lived during that time period. A third section, "The World of Jewish Women," is organized by topic, covering women's activities, interests, and issues. The names and subjects highlighted in bold letters (on first mention in each of these three sections) indicate that they have their own entries elsewhere in the book.

Spelling of names, especially when these are transliterated from another alphabet, sometimes varies. In all cases, we have chosen the variant that is used in the most current texts or in *The Encyclopedia Judaica*. When more than one spelling is accepted, a cross index is provided, or the second choice is in parentheses. If no last name is available, names are alphabetized by the first letter of the first name, not by a patronymic. (For example, "Sarah bas Tovim" would be listed under S.) When specific dates are known for any individual, they are included after the name. Sometimes only one date is available. Date of birth is preceded by "b." and date of death by "d." An "a." indicates that the person was active during that time, usually based on the existence of a document. Approximate dates are preceded by "ca." (circa).

CHOOSING THE WOMEN

We chose the women for a variety of reasons. The most obvious choices were the outstanding, well-known women such as rich moneylenders, prosperous and independent commercial traders, or the wives, mothers, and daughters of famous men. Others were chosen because they were unique. Women who assumed public roles, those who became teachers of men or religious mystics, for example, did not fit the traditional model. They serve to illustrate the broadest parameters of the society within which Jewish women might have found a place.

But we have also included a number of other women, chosen because they serve as examples of specific activities, occupations, or lifestyles. A will, a tombstone, a letter or other document may be the only marker that identifies them. While these markers were never intended to make them famous, these women should not be discounted as actors in history. They were often the backbone of the Jewish community and made important contributions to the family economy.

Of course, it is not possible to include every Jewish woman. For earlier periods, information is scarce or nonexistent. For later centuries, there is too much data to incorporate. Instead, we feature only a sampling of representative women.

CHOOSING THE TOPICS

Whatever their activities or accomplishments, all women in traditional Jewish communities functioned within a world of Jewish law and custom, and their lives can only be understood and appreciated within that framework. For this reason, each chapter's World of Jewish Women offers six basic themes that impacted on Jewish women's lives: **Economic Activities, Education, Family Life, Legal Status, Public Power,** and **Religious Participation.** Within these broad parameters, changing social values and differing rabbinical opinions are discussed, with sources cited for each.

GUIDELINES

In the course of compiling this book, we have consistently tried to avoid imposing our own contemporary views on other eras and to keep in mind certain general principles:

1. Women, even if they themselves were remarkable, rarely questioned a role that placed them in the home as guardians of their households, serving and subservient to husbands.

2. A challenge to tradition came about only recently, with the beginning of the Enlightenment in the late eighteenth century, and it evolved slowly.

3. While laws and practices remained on the books, women, without any overt rebellion, often seem to have gone beyond them, sometimes even forcing a reevaluation of the laws.

GOALS

Our goal here is to offer a guide to the evolving culture of Jewish women throughout history and to help bring their names and their lives into the mainstream. Ultimately, we hope this comprehensive volume will enable today's readers to know our Jewish foremothers, understand their past, and use it as a foundation for the future.

ALPHABETICAL GUIDE TO JEWISH WOMEN IN THE TEXT

In this guide to women mentioned in the book, the following abbreviations apply:
a = active during a specific year or range of years
b = year of birth
d = year of death
ca. = circa, denoting an approximate date or range of dates

Aberlin, Rachel (16th century)—respected mystic, consulted by R. Ḥayyim Vital; saw visions and advised other women.

Abrabanel, Benvenida (d. 1560)—community leader, respected scholar, and teacher in Naples (Italy); later, influential and rich businesswoman.

Aguilar, Grace (1816–1847)—educator, novelist, and religious essayist; author of eight books, including *The Women of Israel; or, Characters and Sketches from the Holy Scriptures and Jewish History* and *The Jewish Faith*; born in London of Sephardic ancestry.

Allegra of Majorca (14th century)—listed as owner of two books; one was a medical book on children's diseases, the other was listed as *Five Books of Genesis*.

Anna the Hebrew (a. 1508)—Italian cosmetician who sold cosmetics to the noblewoman Catherine Sforza.

Arnstein, Fanny Itzig von (b. 1757)—well educated, originally from Berlin; became a prominent salon hostess in Vienna after her marriage.

Ascarelli, Deborah (mid–16th century)—poet and translator of prayers into Italian; probably women's prayer leader of Catalan Synagogue in Rome.

Babatha (first half of 2nd century C.E.)—propertied woman who lived in the land of Israel during the Bar Kokhba rebellion; married twice; marriage contract, property deeds, and records of litigations show she was engaged in business.

Bacharach, Ḥava (1580–1651)—also known as Eva of Prague; learned woman, knowledgeable in Torah; granddaughter of R. Yehudah Loew of Prague.

Bat ha-Levi (12th century)—the unnamed daughter of R. Shmuel ben Ali, Gaon of Baghdad; reported to have taught the students in her father's academy.

Beila of the Blessed Hands (19th century)—trained midwife and *feldsher;* worked in small villages in Russian Pale of Settlement.

Bellina (mid–16th century)—singer and musician; entertained at the court of Venice.

Beruriah (2nd century C.E.)—talmudic scholar in the land of Israel; wife of R. Meir; mentioned in various tractates of the Talmud as a learned woman.

Brandeau, Esther (a. 1738)—disguised herself as Jacques La Frague and sailed as a cabin boy to Quebec (New France); imprisoned as a Jew; refused to convert and was returned to France.

Carvajal de Matas, Francisca de (d. 1596)—crypto-Jew of New Spain (Mexico); arrested and tortured under the Inquisition; burned at the stake together with her daughters Isabel, Catalina, and Leonor and her son Luis.

Cassia (9th or 10th century)—daughter of Shephatiah, from the family of Ahimaaz of southern Italy; mentioned in *The Chronicles of Ahimaaz.*

Caylar, Esther de (15th century)—community leader in Arles; member of prominent Nathan family; mother of Venguessone Nathan.

Çeti (14th century)—called rabbess in documents; probably tended the women's section of the synagogue and the ritual bath in Zaragoza (Spain).

Conat, Estellina (15th century)—first-known Jewish woman printer of books in Mantua, Italy.

Dahiya Kahina (7th century C.E.)—North African woman warrior; defeated the Muslims and ruled in the Maghreb for five years; may have been Jewish.

D'Arpino, Anna (16th century)—women's prayer leader in Rome; was paid by the Jewish community.

Daughter of Joseph (12th century)—unnamed woman of Baghdad (Iraq); believed by some of her contemporaries to be the Messiah.

De Lancey, Phila Franks (a. 1742)—oldest daughter of Abigail and Jacob Franks of New York City; secretly married Oliver de Lancey, a Christian; later baptized.

Dolce of Worms (d. 1196)—learned and pious woman; taught other women; led women's prayers in synagogue; wife of R. Eleazar of Worms; was killed by intruders, along with her two daughters.

Dunash ben Labrat's wife (10th century)—Hebrew poet; a sole remaining example of her work shows considerable talent.

Edel (18th century)—daughter of Israel ben Eliezer (the Baal Shem Tov); spiritual leader and mystical healer.

Eidele (19th century)—daughter of Malkah and Sholem of Belz; wife of R. Isaac Rubin of Sokolov; community leader among the Hasidim of Sokolov; delivered discourses on the Sabbath.

Ella bat Moshe (a. 1696)—printer in Dessau, Germany; daughter of convert Moshe ben Avraham, a printer, and Freide, daughter of R. Yisrael Katz; left a colophon in a Yiddish prayer book in 1696 indicating she was nine years old on that date.

Ellus bat Mordecai (a. 1704)—author and translator of kabbalistic prayers into Yiddish; lived in Slutsk, Russia.

Esterke of Opoczno (ca. 14th century)—legendary mistress of King Casimir the Great of Poland.

Falk, Bayla (16th century)—well versed in Jewish law; wife of R. Joshua Falk; issued a decision on when to light Sabbath candles.

Feige (18th century)—daughter of Edel and granddaughter of the Baal Shem Tov; considered to possess "divine inspiration"; mother of R. Naḥman of Bratislav.

Fishels, Roizel (a. 1586)—printer, teacher, and philanthropist; published a book of poems that she prefaced with an original poem in Yiddish.

Floreta Ca Noga of St. Coloma de Queralt (14th century)—prominent woman doctor of Aragon (Spain); treated the Queen of Aragon.

Francesa Sarah (16th century)—prayer leader and mystic; the only woman in Safed (land of Israel) known to have had her own *maggid* (imaginary spiritual advisor).

Frank, Eva (a. 1770–early 19th century)—daughter of religious rebel Jacob Frank; spiritual leader of Frankist movement after 1817; claimed to be a Romanov princess.

Frankel, Sarah (Sereleh) bat Joshua Heschel Teumim (1838–1937)—conducted herself as a rebbe among the Hasidim after the death of her husband, the *tzaddik* Ḥayyim Samuel of Chenciny; gave advice; known for her wise parables.

Franks, Bilhah Abigail Levy (b. 1688)—well educated; known for her correspondence with her son, Naphtali Hart Franks; wife of Jacob Franks; one of founding members of Congregation Shearith Israel, the first synagogue in New York City.

Freḥa bat Avraham (d. 1756)—learned Hebrew poet; member of the Bar Adiba family of Morocco; considered a holy woman; after her death her father built a synagogue in her name.

Frommet of Arwyller (15th century)—copied and inscribed a book to her husband (probably France or Germany).

Gela bat Moshe (a. 1710)—younger sister of Ella; wrote a Yiddish colophon in a book printed in her father's shop in Halle, Germany, when she was eleven years old.

Glikl of Hameln (1646–1719)—businesswoman; widely traveled for business and to arrange her children's marriages; authored the first Yiddish-language autobiography written by a woman; active in Hamburg, Germany.

Gnendel (d. 1672)—hardworking woman; distiller of brandy in Bohemia; remembered by her son after an early death.

Goldschmidt, Henriette Benas (1825–1920)—activist in promoting education for girls; leader in the early child-care kindergarten movement; encouraged higher education for women.

Goldschmidt, Johanna Schwabe (1806–1884)—author and educator in Hamburg, Germany; founded nondenominational kindergarten; helped establish a seminary for training teachers in the Froebel method.

Gratz, Rebecca (1781–1869)—noted Philadelphia educator and philanthropist; established first Hebrew Sunday school in the United States; active in creating social service institutions; noted letter writer.

Guta (d. 1306)—daughter of R. Natan; an early example of a woman prayer leader.

Gutman, Sarel (a. 1619)—businesswoman; with her husband ran a mail service between Prague and Vienna.

Ḥava/Ḥana (14th century)—surgeon of Manosque in Provence; member of a prominent medical family.

Handali, Esther *Kiera* (a. 1580–1590)—influential purveyor of goods to the women of the sultan's court in Istanbul; confidante to Sultana Safiyah Baffa; had great political power in 16th-century Turkey; believed to have been killed by rioters in Istanbul.

Hays, Esther Etting (a. 1779)—Revolutionary War patriot; smuggled food to American troops; member of pioneer Sephardic family of Philadelphia; wife of David Hays of New York.

Henndlein of Regensburg (15th century)—teacher; ran a school for young children; her official title was *di meistrin*.

Herodias (1st century C.E.)—daughter of Aristobulus and Berenice; married in defiance of Jewish law to her brother-in-law Herod Antipas, King of Galilee and Perea; mother of Salome by a previous marriage; exiled with her husband after his failed bid for power.

Herz, Henriette Lemos (a. 1780–1803)—talented linguist; early leader of the Berlin salons; married Markus Herz; was widowed in 1803; became a translator; converted to Christianity in 1813.

Homburg, Blümele (a. after 1759)—widow of Issahar Homburg; became court factor in Mainz, Germany, after her husband's death.

Horowitz, Sarah Rebecca Rachel Leah (b. ca. 1720)—exceptional scholar and noted writer of *tkhines*; born in Bolekhov, Poland; daughter of Yaakov Yokel ben Meir Horowitz and Rayzel bat Heschel; wrote "Tkhine of the Matriarchs," which contained sections in Hebrew and Aramaic.

Hurwitz, Bella (17th century)—printer in Prague; wife of a cantor; believed to have written a history of the house of David.

Ima Shalom (1st century C.E.)—outspoken, clever women who lived in the land of Israel; wife of R. Eliezer ben Hyrcanus, sister of R. Gamliel, head of the Sanhedrin.

Jamila (16th century)—wrote a letter to her son, R. Abraham, detailing family matters; probably lived in Salonika.

Jehoishma (5th century B.C.E.)—daughter of Tamet and Ananiah; lived in Elephantine, lower Egypt; records show that she received a bride-price *(mohar)* and dowry.

Johanna (2nd century B.C.E.)—poor woman who lived in Egypt; accused of beating a pregnant woman.

Joseph, Rachel Solomons (18th century)—pioneer to Canada; observant Jew who taught Judaism to her children; married to Henry Joseph, the first ritual slaughterer in Canada.

Kandlein (14th century)—moneylender and powerful community leader in Regensburg, Germany.

Katz, Hannah (17th century)—wrote religious verse in Yiddish in Amsterdam.

Kaulla, Madame (1739–1809)—court factor in Wurttemberg, Germany; member of the influential Kaulla family; first name not known.

Laza of Frankfurt (a. 1692)—editor and translator of book of Hebrew prayers written by her husband, Jacob ben Mordecai; wrote introduction in Yiddish; lived in Schwerin, Germany.

Lazarus, Emma (1849–1887)—scholar and poet in New York; authored many poems, a novel (*Alide: An Episode of Goethe's Life*), and a play (*The Dance of Death*); active in helping Russian-Jewish refugees; famous for her poem "The New Colossus" inscribed on the pedestal of the Statue of Liberty.

Leah Dreyzl (early 18th century)—*firzogerin*; writer of *tkhines*; wife of R. Aryeh Leib Auerbach of Poland.

Licoricia of Winchester (d. 1277)—rich and successful moneylender in England; lent money to English nobility; killed by robbers.

Liebmann, Esther Schulhoff Aron (d. 1714)—court Jew; born in Prague, lived in Berlin; supplier of jewelry to the court in Berlin in the seventeenth century; in charge of the mint; had considerable influence with Frederick I of Prussia.

Luxemburg, Rosa (1871–1919)—active Socialist leader in Poland and Germany; died in prison.

Malchi, Esperanza (a. 1599)—*kiera* in the court of the Turkish sultan in Istanbul; wrote a letter to Queen Elizabeth at the request of the sultana.

Malkah (19th century)—Hasidic spiritual leader active in the court of Belz (Galicia); prominent men were counted among her devotees; wife of R. Sholem Rokeaḥ.

Malkeleh the Triskerin (19th century)—Hasidic spiritual advisor; active for charitable causes; daughter of R. Abraham of Trisk, founder of the Trisk dynasty; granddaughter of R. Mordecai Twersky.

Mansi, Paula dei (a. 1288–1293)—scribe and scholar; lived in Verona, Italy; translated Bible commentaries from Hebrew into Italian; from a learned family variously known as Anau, dei Mansi, Piatelli, Pietosa, or Umani.

Maria the Hebrew (2nd or 3rd century C.E.)—legendary chemist/alchemist; credited with the invention of hydrochloric acid; believed to have lived in Egypt.

Mariamne (d. 29 B.C.E.)—Maccabean princess; second wife of Herod I, King of Judea; executed by him for adultery.

Mariamne (1st century B.C.E.)—daughter of Simon ben Boethus, third wife of Herod I, King of Judea.

Marion (a. 10 B.C.E.)—daughter of Isakios of Alexandria; borrowed money with her husband and brother-in-law.

Marion (2nd century B.C.E.)—daughter of Jakoubis; listed as owner of large amounts of livestock in Egypt.

Markel-Mosessohn, Miriam (a. 1868)—well-educated Russian-Jewish writer; composed original Hebrew poetry and translated German works into Hebrew.

Meisel, Frumet (16th–17th century)—moneylender; wife of Mordecai Meisel of Prague.

Mendelssohn, Dorothea (see Schlegel).

Mendelssohn, Henriette (late 18th century)—daughter of Moses Mendelssohn; became governess in Vienna; converted to Christianity.

Mendes, Brianda (16th century)—sister of Gracia Mendes Nasi; had a falling-out with her sister who controlled the family money.

Mercado, Judith (a. 1654)—one of the first twenty-three Jewish refugees from Recife, Brazil, to arrive and settle in New Amsterdam (later, New York); probably a widow.

Merecina (15th century)—Hebrew poet of Gerona, Spain; referred to as *rabbiness*.

Mibtahiah (5th century B.C.E.)—daughter of Mahseiah. Lived in Elephantine, lower Egypt; owned considerable property; married twice and had the right to initiate divorce; her two sons inherited her wealth.

Mibtahiah (5th to 4th century B.C.E.)—daughter of Gemariah; involved in independent property transactions.

Minis, Abigail (1701–1794)—tavern-keeper and businesswoman in Savannah, Georgia; Revolutionary War patriot who helped supply the Continental army; among the earliest settlers to Savannah in 1733.

Minna (d. 1096)—martyr who chose death over conversion in Worms during the first Crusade.

Minna (14th century)—wealthy moneylender in Zurich; in partnership with her two sons; murals from her house have been rediscovered.

Miriam (11th–12th century)—daughter of Rashi, wife of R. Yehudah ben Natan and mother of R. Yom Tov of Falaise and a daughter, sometimes referred to as Alvina (northern France).

Miriam (11th–12th century)—second wife of Rashi's grandson, R. Yaakov ben Meir (Rabbenu Tam); after R. Tam's death she was consulted by his colleagues about his rulings and traditions.

Miriam (12th century)—sister of Maimonides; wrote a letter to her brother requesting help in contacting her son.

Miriam/Mariamne (2nd century C.E.)—mother of Babatha and owner of considerable property in the land of Israel.

Miriam bat Benayah (15th–16th century)—scribe in San'a, Yemen; part of a family of scribes.

Mizraḥi, Asenath Barazani (16th–17th century)—scholar and teacher; ran a yeshivah in Mosul, Kurdistan; daughter of Rabbi Shmuel ha-Levi Barazani; her name was revered by Kurdish Jews long after her death.

Modena, Fioretta/Bathsheva da (16th century)—scholar; grandmother of well-known scholar Aaron Berekhiah, who credited her with his education; died on her way to the land of Israel.

Moise, Penina (1797–1880)—poet and teacher; ran a girls school; composed about 190 hymns for Temple Beth Elohim in Charleston, South Carolina; cultural leader; first Jewish lyric poet to publish in the United States.

Montagu, Lily (1873–1963)—leader of Liberal Judaism in England.

Montefiore, Judith Cohen (1784–1862)—English philanthropist for Jewish causes; diarist and traveler, respected by the Jewish communities of England and Palestine; wife of Moses Montefiore (1784–1885), a wealthy philanthropist and prominent Jewish leader.

Morgenstern, Lina Bauer (1830–1901)—organizer and social activist in Berlin; organized kindergartens; set up soup kitchens for soldiers during Franco-Prussian War; founded association for homemakers, providing for employment and pensions.

Morpurgo, Rachel Luzzatto (1790–1871)—scholar in Jewish and secular subjects; mystic and noted Hebrew poet; born in Trieste, Italy; her poetry was reprinted in 1890 as *Ugav Raḥel* (Rachel's harp).

Al Mu'allima (The Teacher) (11th century)—learned wife of the Karaite Abu l-Taras of Toledo; after his death, his followers came to her for authentic traditions; her name is not known.

Murada, Madame (a. 1542)—woman doctor in Günzburg, Bavaria.

Myers, Rachel (a. 1776–1780)—British loyalist, widow with nine children; fled to Canada and settled in Gagetown, New Brunswick, during the Revolution.

Nasi, Gracia Mendes (1510–1569?)—influential business leader and philanthropist; born into a *converso* family in Portugal; returned to Judaism in Italy; invited into Turkey by the sultan; Doña Nasi was also known as Beatrice de Luna, Hannah Mendes, and La Signora.

Nasi, Reyna (16th century)—daughter of Gracia Nasi, married to her cousin João/Joseph Nasi in Istanbul; ran a publishing house in Turkey that printed Jewish books.

Nathan, Venguessone (15th century)—successful businesswoman and money-lender; owned a shop in Arles; left bequests to all her relatives in her will, including money and books in Hebrew and Latin.

Nissim, Diamante of Pisa (a. 1524)—daughter of R. Asher Meshullam of Venice; follower of and hostess to pseudomessiah David Reubeni.

Nuñes, Ricke/Rachel (a. 1654)—one of the first twenty-three Jewish refugees from Recife, Brazil, to arrive and settle in New Amsterdam (later New York); probably a widow.

Pan, Toibe (17th century)—wrote a historical poem in Yiddish in Prague.

Pappenheim, Bertha (1859–1938)—noted social worker and activist for women's causes; founder of Der Jüdische Frauenbund.

Perele (18th century)—ascetic with her own disciples; daughter of Israel ben Shabbetai of Kozienice; said to have worn tzitzit.

Perna (a. 1460)—physician licensed in Fano, Italy.

Pulcellina (d. 1171)—powerful woman of Blois, France; possible lover of Count Theobald V of France; burned at the stake together with other Jews, the result of a blood libel charge.

Qasmuna (11th or 12th century)—poet; possibly related to Samuel ibn Naghrela (Shmuel ha-Nagid); lived in Granada, Spain. A few of her poems are extant.

Rachel (2nd century C.E.)—name attributed to wife of R. Akiva by post-talmudic writers; supposedly accepted poverty and gave her husband permission to be absent for twenty-four years while he studied.

Rachel/Belle Assez (11th–12th century)—daughter of Rashi; married briefly to Eliezer/Vasselin and then divorced; purported to have helped her father write a responsum while he was sick (Troyes, northern France).

Rachel/Rashka (16th century)—businesswoman of Krakow, Poland; active in community affairs.

Rachel of Mainz (d. 1096)—martyr during the first Crusade; killed her children and then herself.

Rakowski, Puah (1865–1955)—Jewish educator and Hebrew scholar; established the First Hebrew School, an all-girls institution, in the 1890s in Warsaw, Poland.

Rappoport, Serel (18th century)—wrote "Tkhine of the Matriarchs for the New Moon"; daughter and wife of rabbis.

Raquel of Toledo (12th–13th century)—legendary mistress of King Alphonso VIII of Castile.

Rashi's granddaughters (11th–12th century)—Rashi had at least two granddaughters, variously called Alvina, Hannah, or Miriam in different manuscripts; known to have taught women the Commandments.

Reynette of Koblenz (a. 1372)—successful moneylender who dealt in large amounts of cash.

Richa (a. 1525)—member of the wealthy Meshullam family of Venice; owned property independently; signed her own will in Yiddish and the Venetian dialect.

Richenza of Nürnberg (d. 1298)—prayer leader of women; died as a martyr.

Rivka of Ferrara (late 16th century)—daughter of the scholar Yeḥiel ben Azriel Trabot of Ascoli (Italy); publicized her father's teachings after his death.

Rivkah bat Yisrael (early 18th century)—printer; daughter of Yisrael ben Moshe, a printer in Frankfurt; niece of the sisters Ella and Gela; left a colophon in a book she printed "with my own hands" when she was quite young.

Rivkah Sarah Merele (d. 1679)—ascetic, pious woman; remembered in an obituary notice.

Rose, Ernestine Potowski (1810–1892)—public speaker and reformer in the United States; activist for women's rights and against slavery; born in Poland; rebelled against tradition; married a non-Jew in England; emigrated to the United States in 1836.

Rossi, Europa di (16th century)—known as Madame Europa; singer and musician for the court in Mantua, Italy.

Rufina of Smyrna (2nd century B.C.E.)—influential woman of Asia Minor who was head of a synagogue and owned property and slaves.

Saker, Maria (a. 1869)—writer; authored the first article written by a woman in the Russian language.

Salina Alexandra (2nd century C.E.)—wife of Aristobulus, Hasmonean king of Judea; often confused with Salome Alexandra.

Salome (1st century B.C.E.)—sister of King Herod I; inherited property from him at his death.

Salome (1st century C.E.)—daughter of Herodias and stepdaughter of Herod Antipas; reported to have requested the death of John the Baptist to please her mother.

Salome Alexandra (139–67 B.C.E.)—wife of Alexander Jannai, king of Judea; ruled Judea for seven years after the death of her husband; known as an ally of the Pharisees.

Salomon, Rachel Franks (b. 1762)—married patriot Ḥaym Salomon in 1777 at the age of fifteen; left penniless with four children when her husband died in 1785; remarried to David Heilbrun and settled in Holland.

Sambathe (1st or 2nd century C.E.)—name of a Greek sibyl; poetry foretelling the future once attributed to her; now believed to be legendary.

Sarah (a. 1654–1674)—refugee from Polish massacres of 1648; married Shabbetai Zevi, the false messiah in Cairo in 1554; converted to Islam with Zevi.

Sarah (ca. 13th century)—known as Donna Sarah; wife of Solomon the Scribe; wrote a letter to her husband entreating him to return to the family; probably Italian.

Sarah (7th century C.E.)—Yemenite poet, probably Jewish; wrote about the historic defeat of the Banu Qurayza, an Arabian-Jewish tribe.

Sara de Sancto Aegidio (14th century)—doctor in Marseilles; taught medicine to a male apprentice.

Sarah bat Tovim (18th century)—noted, popular writer of *tkhines*; author of *Shloyshe Sh'eorim (Three Gates)*; born in Podolia, Ukraine.

Sarah of Turnovo (14th century)—also known as Queen Theodora; converted to Christianity to marry Tzar Ivan Alexander of Bulgaria.

Schlegel, Dorothea/Breindel Mendelssohn Veit (b. 1765)—one of the Berlin salon women; organized Jewish Lecture Society; daughter of Moses Mendelssohn; well educated; married Simon Veit in 1783; left Veit for Friedrich Schlegel, a Christian; converted to Christianity in 1804.

Schwerin, Jeanette Abarbanell (1852–1899)—one of the founders of the German Society for Ethical Culture in 1892; saw social work as a path to women's emancipation; organized and led Girls' and Women's Groups for Social Service Work.

Segal, Shifrah (a. 1770)—writer of *tkhines*; author of "New Tkhine for the Sabbath"; used kabbalistic texts; advanced her own theory of women's rituals.

Shabazi, Shama'ah (17th century)—believed to be a poet; daughter of Yemenite poet Shalem Shabazi; died young with no extant work known.

Shapira Luria, Miriam (ca. 15th century)—scholar and teacher; a daughter in a family of scholars.

Sheftall, Frances Hart (1740–ca. 1792)—resourceful pioneer woman of Georgia; corresponded with her husband and son in a British prison.

Shelamzion (2nd century C.E.)—daughter of Judah Khtusion, stepdaughter of Babatha; lived in the land of Israel.

Shoḥat, Manya (1880–1961)—Russian revolutionary; emigrated to Palestine in early twentieth century; a founder of the kibbutz movement.

Shondlein (mid–15th century)—learned woman who wrote a response on ritual purity in Yiddish; wife of R. Israel Isserlein of Austria.

Sophia of Gortyn (4th–5th century C.E.)—was referred to as both an elder and head of the synagogue on inscriptions from Crete.

Soreh (mid–18th century)—early follower of Hasidism; widow who directed her son Leib to study with the Hasidim; Leib adopted his mother's name in acknowledgment of her influence and was known as Leib Soreh.

Sullam, Sara Copio (1592–1641)—accomplished and recognized poet in Venice; corresponded on philosophical and religious matters with Ansaldo Cebà, a monk and diplomat; was accused of denying the immortality of the soul; wrote a manifesto in her own defense.

Sussman, Rachel (a. 1546–1567)—Ashkenazic woman living in Jerusalem; wrote letters in Yiddish to her son in Fustat, Egypt, containing historical details about Jerusalem and her family.

Tamar (14th century)—daughter of Sarah/Queen Theodora and Tzar Ivan Alexander; wife of the Ottoman emperor Murad I.

Tamet (5th century B.C.E.)—handmaid of Meshullam ben Zaccur of Elephantine, lower Egypt; granted a dowry and right of divorce.

Theodote (a. 13 B.C.E.)—contracted to be a wet nurse for a slave child in Alexandria.

Tiktiner, Rivkah bat Meir (d. 1605)—also known as Rebecca Tiktiner of Prague; scholar and educator of women; author of pedagogic and ethical work *Meneket Rivkah* and a poem for Simḥat Torah, both in Yiddish.

Twersky, Ḥannah Ḥava (19th century)—Ḥasidic spiritual leader and advisor to women; daughter of R. Mordecai Twersky; active in her father's court in Chernobyl, Ukraine.

Urania of Worms (13th century)—woman prayer leader; daughter of a cantor; she sang hymns to the women.

Varnhagen, Rahel Levin (1771–1833)—brilliant, self-educated woman; leader of the Berlin salons; encouraged the poet Goethe; converted to Christianity in 1806 and married Karl Varnhagen von Ense.

Virdimura (a. 1376)—physician in Catania, Sicily; given a license to treat the poor.

Wengeroff, Pauline Epstein (1833–1916)—Russian diarist and writer; kept detailed diary in German recording the assimilation of Russian Jewry; later published the diary as *Memoirs of a Grandmother*.

Werbermacher, Ḥannah Rachel (1815–ca. 1895)—mystic and spiritual leader in Ludmir, Poland; built her own synagogue; preached sermons on Sabbath; emigrated to Jerusalem where she concentrated on kabbalistic studies until her death.

Wolf, Frumet/Fani Beilin (d. 1849)—composed a controversial political tract in Eisenstadt, Hungary; wrote an ethical will for her children in 1829.

Wuhsha of Egypt (11ᵗʰ–12ᵗʰ century)—successful banker and moneylender; involved in divorce and scandal; lived in Fustat, Egypt; her will stipulated an expensive and elaborate funeral.

Yente (18ᵗʰ century)—spiritual leader; early follower of the Baal Shem Tov who declared her a prophet; wore tallit.

Yoḥeved (11ᵗʰ–12ᵗʰ century)—daughter of Rashi, wife of R. Meir ben Shmuel and mother of the famed Tosafists R. Shmuel ben Meir (the Rashbam) and R. Yaakov ben Meir (Rabbenu Tam) and a daughter sometimes referred to as Ḥannah; lived in Ramerupt (northern France).

Yoḥeved/A'isha (a. 1674–1676)—from a prominent family in Salonika; married Shabbetai Zevi in 1674; converted to Islam after his death in 1676; promoted a new post-messianic movement with her brother who was proclaimed to be Zevi's reincarnation.

CHAPTER 1

Buried Treasures

Archeological Evidence from the Ancient Near East

OVERVIEW

The history of Judaism does not really begin until the late sixth century B.C.E. when many of the people of Judea were exiled from their own land and sent to Babylonia (present-day Iraq). Before the exile, they were a loose confederation of tribes with a central religious focus. After the return of some Jews from Babylonia, approximately seventy years later, a new pattern began. A Jewish state now "co-existed in a symbiotic relationship" with active Jewish communities in the Diaspora.[1]

Much of what can be proven about these formative years comes from archeological discoveries. Archeology offers the most dependable

---

THE EARLIEST DISCOVERIES

In ancient times seals were used instead of signatures to give legitimacy to any document issued by an official. In the 1970s, a cache of seals was discovered dating from the period of Jeremiah (seventh century B.C.E.) until shortly after the return of the exiles from Babylonia. Included in this collection of seals were a small number belonging to women. "Abigayil, wife of Asayahu" and "Shelomit, maidservant of Elnatan the Governor" are two examples of women with Hebrew names who possessed seals of their own. Such ownership suggests that despite female subordination—a given in many of the biblical and post-biblical books—some women did have **public power** and could sign contracts and documents even after marriage.[2]

FIG. 1. This seal, for Ma'adana, daughter of the King, dates from approximately the seventh century B.C.E. It is one of a group of West Semitic stamp seals belonging to women. (Courtesy of the Israel Museum, Jerusalem)

evidence available, because it is untouched by later civilizations. Such tangible remnants of the past continue to be unearthed both in the land of Israel and in the Diaspora and account for some of our expanding knowledge of early Jewish communities and the women who lived in them. The evidence used in this chapter is based solely on archeological findings dating from the sixth century B.C.E. to the sixth century C.E.

Elephantine, an Early Diaspora Community

Shortly after the Babylonian exile, a small number of Jews fleeing from the war and destruction of their homeland made their way south to Egypt. They settled on an island in the southern part of the Nile River called Elephantine. By the last quarter of the sixth century B.C.E., a large and developed Jewish community existed there. These Jews remained in Elephantine even after the temple was rebuilt.[3] When Cyrus's son Cambyses conquered Egypt in 525 B.C.E., he found a thriving community of Jews. They had their own temple and their own communal structure. Because of past Persian policies encouraging the resettlement of Jerusalem, the Elephantine Jews were well disposed toward these conquerors. From that time on, Elephantine functioned as a Persian military colony known as *Yeb the Fortress* and remained a Persian stronghold in

Egypt even after the rest of the country became independent. The Jewish community was a dynamic component on the island until the end of the fifth century B.C.E.

Evidence of this early Jewish community was first uncovered in 1901. Among the hundreds of papyri unearthed on Elephantine, many expanded our knowledge of Jewish women's lives, suggesting different interpretations and new possibilities. A number of scrolls concerned a Jewish woman named **Mibtahiah,**[4] who owned property independently, both by gift and inheritance; contracted marriages that carefully safeguarded her rights; and was free to initiate divorce. In light of what we know of biblical law, such options do not seem probable. Yet, since they were untouched for almost two thousand years, the scrolls were unaffected by subsequent rabbinic decisions and interpretations and are true witnesses to Jewish **family life** at that time.

The Spread of Greek Culture

After the Jews returned from Babylonia to rebuild and resettle Jerusalem in 537 B.C.E., the population of Judea gradually increased. Temple sacrifices were reestablished and land reclaimed. There was a high degree of Jewish self-government that continued even after Persia and its territories were taken over by Alexander the Great in 332 B.C.E. and large parts of the Jewish population became hellenized.[5]

Following Alexander's death in 323 B.C.E., his empire was divided into two parts, and from 320 to 198 B.C.E. Judea was ruled together with Egypt by the dynasty of the Ptolemies. Many Jews moved to Egypt to avoid war or to improve their economic position.[6]

By the first century C.E., Jewish communities could be found along the coasts of the Black Sea and in Egypt, northern Africa, Greece, and the nearby islands. It is in this Diaspora of late antiquity that we find different sorts of archeological evidence about women. There are inscriptions on tombstones, carved writings on synagogue remains, and fragments of stones,[7] all offering clues to women's **religious participation** in the communities of a growing Jewish Diaspora.

Events in the Land of Israel

The steady growth of the Diaspora was spurred mainly by the hardships encountered by the Jews living in Judea and the surrounding areas. After the Maccabean revolt and the short period of independence under the Hasmoneans from 152 until 63 B.C.E. (see chapter 2), the Roman Empire began to exert a stronger influence in the Middle East. Eventually all of Palestine, including the lands of Judea and Samaria, the Galilee, and north into Syria, came firmly under Roman rule.[8]

In the years that followed, Rome's power became harsher and less sympathetic to Jewish interests. Many Jewish rebellions were attempted, but failed. The most devastating of these began in 66 C.E. Four years later, when it was over, Jerusalem lay in ruins. The Holy Temple had burned to the ground, and the Roman general Titus carried the Temple's treasures to Rome together with a large number of Jewish captives, both men and women.[9]

Jewish rebels, inside and outside Palestine, continued to fight hopeless battles against Rome. All were ruthlessly put down. When Emperor Hadrian came to power in 117 C.E., he reintroduced Hellenistic policies into the Middle East and forbade traditional Jewish practices. This resulted in a final confrontation, in which the Jews were led by a young man named Simon Bar Kosiba, or as his followers dubbed him, Bar Kokhba (son of a star).[10]

For a short time Bar Kokhba was successful. He ruled an independent state from 132 to 134 C.E., but the new Jewish army could not hope to defeat the powerful Roman legions. Bar Kokhba's last stronghold was destroyed in 134/135 C.E.

In 1961 a series of caves and underground passages used during the Bar Kokhba period were rediscovered. One of them, given the name "Cave of Letters," contained artifacts and fragments of scrolls including thirty-five documents that had belonged to a woman named **Babatha**.[11] These scrolls reveal the **legal status** and family life of this woman and her female relatives. Historians and archeologists continue to study them for further evidence concerning women's lives in this period.

Babylonia: A Refuge for Jews

When the Bar Kokhba revolt ended with the final destruction of the Jewish state by Rome, more Jews fled from the land of Israel. This time many turned toward the northeast, to Babylonia. Babylonian Jewry enjoyed a considerable amount of power in the first centuries of the Common Era. By 60 to 80 C.E., a Jewish exilarchate was in place and Jewish nobles ruled their own large and growing community.[12] They were in a good position to welcome refugees from the devastated Jewish state to the south.

There is much written evidence concerning the strong and well-developed Jewish community of Babylonia (see chapter 2), but fewer archeological finds. Among them are magic bowls and amulets. These ancient objects give us a glimpse into the reality of women's existence and offer clues to women's religious participation at a time when they were being progressively excluded from organized, public religion.

BIOGRAPHIES

BABATHA OF MAHOZA, PROPERTY OWNER

(2nd century C.E.)

Babatha, a woman of property, is known only through a cache of thirty-five papyrus documents found in 1961 in a cave in the Judean desert.[13] From these documents we know that she engaged in business and litigation regarding her own interests and those of her son. She lived in Mahoza, a town on the southern end of the Dead Sea, in the Nabatean region of the land of Israel.

Included in the collection of documents were five deeds dealing with the custody of Babatha's son by her first husband, Joshua. Also included were

FIG. 2. These items were found in the Cave of Letters, although they were not specifically identified as belonging to Babatha. (Courtesy of the Israel Museum, Jerusalem)

the marriage contracts of both Babatha and her stepdaughter, **Shelamzion**; two deeds concerning Shelamzion's property; five claims made by members of her second husband's family against Babatha; and six deeds of property dated from 110 to 122 C.E.[14] The latest date on any of the documents was 132 C.E.

These documents, most likely hidden away for protection during the Bar Kokhba rebellion (132–135 C.E.), reveal that Babatha was the daughter of Shimon and Miriam (Mariamne). Probably an only child, Babatha inherited lands and possessions after her mother's death. The properties had originally been transferred from her father to her mother while both parents were still alive.

Babatha was married twice. Her first husband was Joshua, son of Joseph. After his death, Babatha was not named as one of her son's guardians. She later brought a legal action against the two legal guardians in an effort to increase the money used to provide for the care of her son, "orphan Joshua, son of Joshua."[16]

Babatha's second husband was Judah ben Eleazer Khtusion of Ein-Gedi. He died three years after the wedding, bequeathing to Babatha considerable property. In 131 C.E. members of Judah's family, including a first wife, Miriam, contested the will. The determination of this suit is not known, but Babatha did have to hand over some property to Khtusion's family.[17]

As a widow, Babatha remained involved in the business and legal affairs of her stepdaughter, Shelamzion. This may have been the result of a loan made to her husband for Shelamzion's dowry that was not yet repaid at the time of Judah's death.

Whether Babatha survived the Bar Kokhba rebellion or its aftermath is not known.

JEHOISHMA OF ELEPHANTINE, FREE WOMAN
(5th–4th century B.C.E.)

Jehoishma, daughter of **Tamet** and Ananiah, lived in the Jewish colony of Elephantine. Her mother had been a slave but Jehoishma was born free, a fact that was reflected in the large amount of her dowry and bride-price. As a free virgin, she received the standard bride-price of ten shekels. After her marriage, Jehoishma also received a grant of property from her father.

JOHANNA OF EGYPT, DEFENDANT
(2nd century B.C.E.)

Johanna lived in a small village in Egypt. She was a defendant in a complaint lodged against her by another Jew who claimed that she had beaten

---

A COMPLAINT AGAINST "THE JEWESS JOHANNA" BY AN UNKNOWN JEW OF EGYPT

In consequence of the blows and fall she is suffering severely; she has had to take to her bed, and her child is in danger of miscarriage and death. I present you this petition in order that, when you have visited the spot and observed her condition, Johanna may be secured until the result is apparent and that it may not happen that Johanna in case of any untoward event go scot-free.[15]

and injured his pregnant wife. He wanted Johanna taken into custody until his wife gave birth and it could be determined if the child was unharmed. The outcome of this lawsuit is not known.[18]

JULIA CRISPINA OF EGYPT AND JUDEA, LANDOWNER AND OVERSEER
(2nd century C.E.)

Julia Crispina is believed to be a descendant of King Herod. Two documents indicate that she was an important woman. She was the owner of an estate in Egypt and an overseer and law guardian for two orphans in Judea. In a document found among Babatha's papers, Julia Crispina was designated as one of two guardians representing the nephews and heirs of Judah Khtusion in a suit against his widow Babatha. Since women were not allowed to serve as guardians according to Jewish law and did not routinely appear in Roman courts, historians have assumed that she was chosen for this role because of her important connections.[19]

MARION, DAUGHTER OF ISAKIOS, DEBTOR
(1st century B.C.E.)

Together with her husband, Lysimachos, son of Theodotos, and Tryphon, son of Theodotos (probably Marion's brother-in-law), Marion borrowed the small sum of 140 drachmas in the spring of the year 10 B.C.E. in the city of Alexandria. The three borrowers needed fourteen months to repay the amount, in installments of ten drachmas each, suggesting that they were people of very modest means.[20] Nothing else is known of Marion, but she is one of the rare cases of poorer women whose names appear in ancient documents.[21]

MIBTAHIAH OF ELEPHANTINE, PROPERTY OWNER
(5th century B.C.E.)

Mibtahiah was a prosperous woman who lived on Elephantine, a small island in the Nile River with a thriving Jewish community. Born in 476 B.C.E. to a well-to-do family that owned property and slaves, the meager facts of her life are contained in eleven papyri, discovered by diggers near Aswan, Egypt. These documents, written in Aramaic, clearly show the amount of property Mibtahiah owned and how it was legally protected.

Mibtahiah had two brothers, Gemariah and Jedaniah. Probably in order to bypass the biblical ruling that daughters cannot inherit if there are sons, her father, Mahseiah, gifted property to her at the time of her marriages.

Mibtahiah's first husband was Jezaniah, the Jew who owned the plot of land next to her father's house. The marriage, which took place in 460 or 459 B.C.E. when she was approximately sixteen years old, was marked by two transfers of a deed for a building plot: one by Mahseiah to his daughter, granting her title to the property, and the second to Jezaniah giving him the income only. This was a typical dowry arrangement at that time. Jezaniah died shortly after the marriage, and there was no record of any children.

Eshor the Egyptian was Mibtahiah's second husband, whom she married in 449 B.C.E. For this marriage there is an existing contract called a "document of wifehood," stipulating that either party could initiate divorce, a right that was not common to Jewish women in later periods.

MIBTAHIAH'S DOCUMENT OF WIFEHOOD

[Mibtahiah] is my wife and I am her husband from this day and forever. I gave you as mohar for your daughter Miptahiah *[sic]* 5 shekels . . . Your daughter Miptahiah brought in to me in her hand: silver money, 2 shekels; 1 new garment of wool, striped with dye; another garment of wool, finely woven; 1 mirror of bronze; 1 bowl of bronze; 2 cups of bronze; 1 jug of bronze. All the silver and the value of the goods: 6 karsh, 5 shekel, 20 hallurs . . . 1 bed of papyrus-reed . . . 2 ladles; 1 new box of palm leaf; 5 handfuls of castor oil; 1 pair of sandals.

Tomorrow or the next day, should Eshor die not having a child, male or female, from Miptahiah his wife, it is Mibtahiah who has right to the house of Eshor and his goods and his property and all that he has on the face of the earth, all of it. Tomorrow or the next day, should Miptahiah die not having a child, male or female, from Eshor her husband, it is Eshor who shall inherit from her her goods and her property.

Tomorrow or the next day, should Miptahiah stand up in an assembly and say: "I hated Eshor my husband," silver of hatred is on her head. She shall place upon the balance-scale and weigh out to Eshor silver . . . and all that she brought in her hand she shall take out, from straw to string, and go away wherever she desires, without suit or without process.

Tomorrow or the next day, should Eshor stand up in an assembly and say: "I hated my wife Miptahiah," her mohar will be lost and all that she brought in in her hand she shall take out, from straw to string, on one day in one stroke, and go away wherever she desires, without suit or without process . . . And I shall not be able to say: "I have another wife besides Miptahiah and other children besides the children whom Miptahiah shall bear to me. . . ."[22]

The union of Mibtahiah and Eshor produced two sons, Jedaniah and Mahseiah. When Mibtahiah died in 416 B.C.E. at the age of sixty-four, she left a considerable estate to her sons, including both real and personal property.

Mibtahiah emerges as a woman who had considerable control over her own life. She was guaranteed status as an only wife, was free to divorce at will, and acted independently in business.

RUFINA OF SMYRNA, HEAD OF A SYNAGOGUE
(2nd century C.E.)

Rufina was an established and respected citizen of Smyrna (Turkey) who owned property and slaves. She is known only by an inscription on a tombstone that she had built for her freed slaves. This inscription specifically identifies her as a Jew and head of a synagogue (archisynagogissa). Hers is one of nineteen Greek and

Latin inscriptions referring to Jewish women in the Mediterranean area over several centuries.[23] Many of them were listed as "head of synagogue."

The inscription contains a threat to impose a fine on any person who dares to bury another body in that spot. The proceeds of the fine were to be split between the Jewish community and the "sacred treasury" (possibly the Imperial treasury or the treasury of a pagan temple, suggesting that Rufina may have been a convert from paganism). The fact that a copy of this warning was filed in the public archives indicates that Rufina was an influential woman. There is no mention of a husband and no evidence that her title was derived from a husband or other male relative.[24]

SHELAMZION OF SOUTHERN ISRAEL, PROPERTY OWNER
(2nd century C.E.)

Shelamzion was the daughter of Judah Khtusion and Miriam. Her marriage contract and other documents concerning her were found, together with documents belonging to her stepmother, Babatha, in the Cave of Letters in the Judean Desert.

These papers, undoubtedly placed there for safekeeping during the Bar Kokhba rebellion, reveal a few facts about Shelamzion's life. Her marriage contract with Judah Cimber, written in Greek, followed Hellenistic rather than Jewish law. The dowry stipulated in the contract included silver, gold, and clothing. There was a promised future payment of three hundred dinars by Judah to Shelamzion.

Shelamzion also owned property in her own name, deeded to her by her father eleven days after her wedding. Her wedding dowry may have been secured by means of a loan from Babatha to her father.[25]

THE INSCRIPTION CONCERNING RUFINA

Rufina, a Jewess, head of the synagogue, built this tomb for her freed slaves raised in her house. No one else has the right to bury anyone [here]. If someone should dare to do so, he or she will pay 198 dinars to the sacred treasury and 1000 dinars to the Jewish people. A copy of this inscription has been placed in the [public] archives.[26]

SOPHIA OF GORTYN, HEAD OF A SYNAGOGUE
(4th or 5th century C.E.)

Only Sophia's tombstone, found in Kastelli, Kissamou, on the island of Crete, marks her as "elder and head of the synagogue." As is the case with **Rufina**, there is no mention of a husband, nor any reason to assume that her title was derived from him as some historians have suggested.[27]

TAMET OF ELEPHANTINE, FORMER SLAVE
(5th century B.C.E.)

According to documentation from the Elephantine papyri, Tamet was the slave of Meshullam ben Zaccur. Her status, translated as "handmaid," changed when Meshullam gave her in marriage to Ananiah, son of Azariah. Although she received no bride-price, she came to her husband with a small dowry, probably provided by her former master. Her marriage contract explicitly grants her the right of divorce, indicating that this right was common in

Elephantine and not merely a privilege of rich women.[28]

Tamet and Ananiah had at least one child, a daughter **Jehoishma** whose marriage contract was also found among the Elephantine papyri.

TATION OF KYME, PHILANTHROPIST

(3rd century C.E.)

A single inscription concerning Tation was found in Kyme, a city in western Asia Minor (Turkey). She paid for an assembly hall and the enclosure of a courtyard with her own funds. As a reward for her donation she was given a gold crown and a seat of honor in the synagogue. Because the inscription says that the hall and the courtyard were given "as a gift to the Jews," some historians suggest that she herself may not have been Jewish, but there is no other evidence of her identity.[29]

THEODOTE OF ALEXANDRIA, WET NURSE

(1st century B.C.E.)

Theodote lived in the early part of the first century B.C.E. in Alexandria, Egypt. Although she was married, she earned money as a wet nurse. A contract between Theodote and a Persian man, Marcus Aemilius, detailed an agreement she made to nurse a slave child for eighteen months in return for a set fee.[30]

During the time of the contract, Theodote was to bring the baby to Marcus once a month for inspection. She also committed herself to abstain from sexual intercourse during this period, since sexual activity would put her at risk of pregnancy and might decrease her milk supply. If she defaulted from the contract for any reason, she would have to pay a heavy fine. In the event that this infant slave died while in her care, she was obligated to replace him with another child.

Theodote's contract is one of the very few extant documents that offers information concerning the **economic activities** of poor women who owned no property.

THEOPEMTE OF MYNDOS, PHILANTHROPIST

(4th, 5th, or 6th century C.E.)

Theopemte lived in Myndos, Caria, a district on the southwest coast of Asia Minor. Her large donation to the synagogue, given together with her son Eusebios, was acknowledged on a white marble post retrieved from the ruins in that area. The inscription, tentatively dated from the sixth century, names her as head of the synagogue.[31]

THE WORLD OF JEWISH WOMEN

ECONOMIC ACTIVITIES

Most archeological evidence relating to the economic activities of Jewish women in this early period teaches us about women who were prosperous. Because deeds, donations, and ownership lists were most often what was recorded in ancient societies, it is this kind of information that remains. Such records, preserved either in stone or on papyrus, reveal women as property owners, philanthropists, and buyers and sellers of real estate or large amounts of movable goods. Some women owned herds of livestock, either alone or together with a husband.

Poor women, since they owned no property, rarely required the use of official documents, and fewer details about their lives have been recorded. This fact gives a skewed image to history, since most people, whether Jews or gentiles, were not wealthy property owners and thus have left little evidence for future generations. There are a few exceptions, however. These include **Marion, daughter of Isakios,** who borrowed money, and **Theodote,** the wet nurse from Alexandria, Egypt.

It is certain that most women worked, usually together with their husbands on farms and in workshops. Cloth making was everywhere the work of women, and women routinely spun thread and wove textiles for the use of their own families. The Book of Proverbs (31:19) refers to a woman who "puts her hand to the distaff and her hand holds the spindle." Sometimes women, usually unmarried, spun and wove as a skilled occupation. Gynacea were large factories in Alexandria where Greek women worked weaving cloth. Such institutions were an accepted part of the community.[32] Women with no specific skills could be laundresses, servants, or wet nurses.

Wet-nursing was one of the few ways that a poor woman could earn money without an initial investment or an education. Although not a high-prestige occupation, it usually gave her at least the means to eat well. The contract between the wet nurse Theodote and Marcus, the owner of the slave child she contracted to nurse, was not very favorable, either to her or to her husband, Sophron, who was involved as her co-signer. However, it did give her half her wages in advance and assurances that she would receive the remainder "if she duly performs everything."

THE RESPONSIBILITIES OF A WET NURSE

[This contract, written in Greek, is dated 13 B.C.E.]

Theodote agrees that she will for eighteen months . . .bring up and suckle in her own house in the city with her own milk pure and uncontaminated the foundling slave baby child Tyche which Marcus has entrusted to her, receiving from him each month as payment for her milk and care 8 drachmai of silver besides olive oil, and Theodote has duly received from Marcus by her guarantor Sophron for the agreed eighteen months wages for nine months adding up to 72 drachmai; and if the child chances to die within this time, Theodote will take up another child and nurse it and suckle it and restore it to Marcus for the same nine months, receiving no wages, since she has undertaken to nurse continually, providing her monthly care honestly and taking fitting thought for the child, not damaging her milk, not lying with a man, not conceiving, not taking another child to suckle. . . .[33]

Contracts binding other Jewish wet nurses were found in the same collection, although Theodote's is particularly well preserved.[34]

EDUCATION

Archeological evidence in the form of scrolls and other ancient documents casts little light on how Jewish women were educated. Rich women, or those

---

WOMEN LIVESTOCK OWNERS

Lists of livestock owners from the second century B.C.E. from a village in Egypt include many women. Among them were:

- Marion, daughter of Jakoubis, owned 80 head of cattle and 30 sheep.
- Theoxena, daughter of Leukias, owned 30 cattle, 15 sheep, 2 she-goats and 2 kids.
- Sambathion, daughter of Jonathas, was the owner of 15 cows, 5 sheep, she-goats and one kid.
- Apollonia owned 925 head of cattle, 399 sheep, 45 she-goats, 32 lambs, and 3 he-goats, or a total of 1404 animals.[35]

---

from learned families, were certainly taught more than those from peasant families, where the education of men was also limited. Records such as deeds and contracts may indicate little more than the fact that a woman could sign her name.

Mibtahiah of Elephantine owned considerable property and married twice, but only her husband and her father signed each of her marriage contracts. We do not know whether she, or any of the women of Elephantine, could read or write.

Some six hundred years later, evidence of Jewish women's literacy is still scanty or nonexistent. Only one of the thirty-five documents pertaining to **Babatha** found in the Cave of Letters in Israel actually contained her own signature. This does not constitute proof that she was able to read and write. In fact, scholar Tal Ilan who studied

women in ancient Judaism states definitively that Babatha was illiterate.[36]

FAMILY LIFE

Betrothal and Marriage

Dowry and bride-price were an accepted part of marriage in the Bible, and as early as the fifth century B.C.E. archeological remains give evidence that these practices continued. Mibtahiah received a piece of land from her father immediately preceding her first marriage in 460 or 459 B.C.E. On the same date, the usufruct (income and use) of that land was transferred to her future husband, Jezaniah.

When she married a second time in 449 B.C.E., she brought a dowry consisting of two shekels and an assortment of clothing and other goods for her personal use, all carefully itemized in her "agreement of wifehood." Such an itemized dowry was common for the women of Elephantine and also appears in the marriage contract of both the slave woman **Tamet** and her free-born daughter, **Jehoishma**.

Mibtahiah's husband, Eshor, gave a bride-price of five shekels, the standard amount for a widow, while Tamet, because she was a slave at the time of her marriage, received none.

Such practices were already institutionalized in Elephantine, and appropriate amounts were set for virgins, widows, and freed and unfree women. They reflected the customs of Egypt as well as ancient Israelite tradition. Later marriage conventions in the hellenized world and in Roman Palestine show a similar blend of Greek, Roman, and Jewish elements.

Judah ben Eleazer Khtusion of Ein-Gedi, Babatha's second husband, was a man of some means. His marriage contract with Babatha, dated

February 2, 127 C.E., was written in Aramaic but followed the practice of Judea, which included Ein-Gedi. The word *ketubbah* appears on the face of the document in Hebrew letters, and the contents refer to a sum of money pledged to Babatha in the future.

Such a clause, promising money to the bride if the marriage was dissolved by divorce or death, replaced the bride-price and later became the official definition of ketubbah. The ketubbah clause, together with the phrase stating that "the marriage is according to the Law of Moses and the Jews" may make this one of the earliest marriage documents that can officially be called a ketubbah.[37] The formula "according to the Law of Moses and Israel" (rather than ". . . Moses and the Jews") probably was introduced during Bar Kokhba's time.[38] Babatha's contract, therefore, predates the crystallization of rabbinic marriage law.

Unlike Babatha's ketubbah, **Shelamzion**'s marriage document was written in Greek and followed Hellenistic rather than Jewish law. The two traditions had some commonalities, however. Judah Cimber, Shelamzion's husband, acknowledged the receipt of her dowry, which included silver, gold, and clothing and promised future payment of three hundred dinars to her. This constitutes additional evidence that the practice of pledging money to a wife in the future was already becoming an accepted part of Jewish marriage agreements,[39] although it was not yet universal.

A marriage contract written to "Salome Komaise of Maoza by Jesus son of Menaḥem" in 131 C.E. suggests other traditions as well. It includes the words: " [he] has taken Salome . . . to live with her as heretofore," suggesting that the couple had previously lived together as husband and wife before an official marriage had taken place and without the benefit of either a contract or a payment of any kind.[40]

Children

Small amounts of archeological information about children in the ancient world offer a very sketchy picture. Parents cared for young children in the home, although wet nurses were often used for the children of the well-to-do or for orphans. Evidence of this practice can be seen from the contract of Theodote, who was hired to nurse a slave child in the first century.

Early marriage, especially for female children, was routine. Shelamzion may have been a minor when she was married. Her age is not indicated in her marriage contract, but the wording: "I have given my daughter in marriage to this man . . ." was a formula often used for a minor, suggesting that she may have been under twelve.[41] The marriage of minor daughters was not uncommon even in later periods, although the Rabbis of the Mishnah frowned on it. Rabbinic sources give several instances where girls were married before puberty.[42]

Divorce

The biblical standard for divorce stipulates that if a husband no longer wants to be married, he must give his wife a bill of divorcement. Although no procedure is stipulated if the wife no longer wants to remain married, evidence from ancient documents makes it clear that such procedures were in place in many communities.

A recurrent stipulation in Elephantine marriage contracts was that both parties had an equal right to divorce. The formula for this was monetary. If the wife demanded the divorce, she had to pay a penalty but took back all the property she brought to the marriage. The accepted legal language for this was: "all that she brought . . . from straw to string."[43] If the husband wanted the divorce, he would forfeit the bride-price.

A legal document from the second century C.E. may also be evidence that women could initiate a divorce. The document, issued by "Shelamzion, daughter of Joseph Qebshan to her husband Eleazar, son of Ḥananiah" stipulates "this is for you from me a bill of divorce and release."[44] The wording here is identical to similar documents issued by men and was found in a cave in southern Israel.

Although there is no clear evidence that such a right to divorce created an unbroken tradition for Jewish women, similar formularies were known in Egypt at a later date and were considered legal options by the Rabbis who compiled the Palestinian Talmud[45] (see **Divorce**, chapter 2).

Family Purity

Archeological remains of ritual baths dating from early centuries have been uncovered both in the land of Israel and in neighboring Diaspora communities. These finds suggest that the laws of *niddah*, requiring women to immerse in a *mikveh* after menstruation, were widely practiced by the Jews even before being officially outlined in rabbinic law.

Monogamy

In spite of the Roman standard of monogamy, the practice of polygyny persisted among Jews.[46] Not only very wealthy men, as was commonly claimed, but ordinary men could and occasionally did have more than one wife.[47] Sometimes this caused complications.

Papers concerning one possible problem were found among Babatha's documents in the Cave of Letters. Judah Khtusion died three years after his marriage to Babatha,[48] leaving her a large amount of property. But Babatha was a second wife, and Judah's first wife, Miriam, was living in Ein-Gedi when he died. Thus Judah left two widows, both claiming the right to his possessions. In 131 C.E. Babatha and Miriam accused each other of "unlawful acts regarding the estate of their deceased husband."[49] The outcome of these claims is not known, but Babatha was sued by members of Judah's family as well, and had to surrender several pieces of property.[50]

Violence Against Women

Fights and violence were certainly not unheard of among Jews. While no specific evidence of wife beating is available, there is some suspicion of it from examining the contents of ossuaries discovered in caves in Jerusalem.[51] The prevalence of women who died from blows to the head or face or from other violent injuries suggests that family violence was probably as common then as in later periods. There also exist some traces of violence against women by those outside the family. One incident involved a pregnant woman who was beaten by **Johanna** and feared for the safety of her unborn child.

Philo, in his rebuke of women aiding their husbands in street quarrels, gives a vivid picture of the kind of violence that could occur, this time by women. He wrote: "[It] is a shocking thing, if a woman is so lost to a sense of modesty, as to catch hold of the genital parts of her opponent."[52]

Incidents such as these were not commonplace, but they suggest that even in peaceful times, Jewish women's lives included stress and the risk of violence.

LEGAL STATUS

Women As Heirs

In the ancient world women sometimes received considerable amounts of property in wills from fathers and husbands. A document from Elephantine, dating from the fourth century B.C.E., involved an exchange of inherited shares by two sisters, Salluah and Jethoma, daughters of Kenaiah.[53] There may have been no sons to inherit in this case, or the biblical law may simply have been ignored. In later centuries, both Babatha and Shelamzion inherited land from their fathers.

More often, however, we see evidence of property gifted to daughters while the fathers are still living. This was an acceptable way to compensate for the biblical ruling that daughters cannot inherit when there are living sons (see chapter 2). So Mibtahiah received a gift of property from her father when she married her first husband, Jezaniah, and another at the time of her marriage to her second husband, Eshor.

Centuries later, in the land of Israel, we see hints of another attempt to circumvent biblical law. Babatha's father, Shimon, gave to her mother, Miriam (Mariamne), all of his possessions, although he retained the right of usufruct for himself during his

lifetime. His deed of transfer is full of legal formulae designed to protect Miriam and her heirs from all claims.[54]

Although Yigael Yadin (the archeologist who discovered this archive) believes that the purpose of such deeds was to avoid the payment of taxes,[55] they may also have been a useful method of circumventing the Jewish law that excluded wives from inheriting their husbands' property. After Miriam's death the lands and possessions passed to Babatha, who was probably an only child.[56]

Women As Testators

While women may technically not have been able to inherit, they could bequeath what they owned, especially if they outlived their husbands. All Mibtahiah's property was bequeathed to her two sons, Jedaniah and Mahseiah. The inheritance was considerable. Besides the houses she owned, she claimed additional possessions, including silver, grain, clothing, bronze items, and iron vessels.

Control of Money and Property

There are enough papyrus scrolls and other archeological evidence to confirm that a woman could often function independently and control her own money and property. The ownership of seals by individual women in the ancient Jewish kingdom (7th–6th centuries B.C.E.) suggests that despite female subordination, women did have some legal rights and could seal contracts and documents (the equivalent of a signature) even after marriage.

In 446 B.C.E., in an independent business arrangement, Mibtahiah acquired a house from her father several years after her marriage to Eshor. This was in exchange for some unspecified goods of considerable value. Another scroll, this one a quitclaim granted by a different Mibtahiah, the "daughter of Gemariah, a Jewess of Elephantine" to "Isweri, daughter of Gemariah, a Jewess" offers a glimpse of other women who were also making independent property settlements.[57]

Certainly, Mibtahiah and her female contemporaries and descendants did not enjoy the status or the privileges of men in that society. However, they did have considerable freedom to act independently, be parties to litigation, take an oath in court, and contribute money in their own names.[58] In general, they seem to have had more latitude than later Roman or rabbinic law allowed.

In the second century C.E., in Roman Palestine, Babatha and Shelamzion possessed similar property rights. They owned property in their own names, mostly deeded to them by

---

AN ANCIENT TRANSFER OF PROPERTY

Eleven days after her wedding, Judah Khtusion, Shelamzion's father, transferred to his daughter:
. . . all his possessions in Ein-Gedi, viz. half of the courtyard across from the synagogue . . . including half of the rooms and the upper story rooms therein, but excluding the small old court near the said courtyard, and the other half of the courtyard and rooms Judah willed to the said Shelamzion [to have] after his death.[59]

---

their fathers, and could presumably sell it, but in the Roman courts they had to be legally represented by male guardians.

Babatha was engaged in litigation regarding her own interests and those of her minor son, who had two male guardians. Official clerks of the Roman Empire had drawn up most of the papers; it is uncertain whether Babatha herself ever appeared as a witness in any of her litigations. She did testify in the Roman court at Petra to declare her ownership of specific properties for the record, but her husband, Judah, accompanied her.[60]

Other documents from the Cave of Letters reveal Babatha's business dealings. On February 21, 128 C.E., she lent her husband, Judah Khtusion, the sum of 300 dinars. Subsequently, this sum was given over to Shelamzion's husband, Judah Cimber, for Shelamzion's dowry.[61]

PUBLIC POWER

While women may have had a certain amount of power in the home, public power was traditionally closed to them from earliest times. For this reason, any tangible evidence of women who held some form of official rank or influence, no matter how minor, is noteworthy. This is the case for the most recent discovery of seals dating from the preexilic and postexilic Jewish kingdoms.[62]

For the most part, only royal officials or their deputies—people who held power—possessed seals. For this reason, it was particularly intriguing to discover, among a hoard of such seals, thirteen that belonged to women. Most of these thirteen seals identify the woman merely as "daughter of" or "wife of," as for example "Abigayil, wife of Asayahu," or "Yeho'adan, daughter of Uriyahu." A few give names that have been connected with the ruling families of Judea, although not all are from royal families.

An interesting seal found together with a collection of official documents names the owner as "Shelomit maidservant of Elnatan the governor."[63] The meaning of the word "maidservant" is not clear in this context. It may have been used as the female equivalent of servant (*eved*) to designate a high official, or it may have meant the governor's wife. In either case, it is assumed that she held an appointed position of some import in Judea.

Other hints that a few women enjoyed some form of public power many centuries later have also been uncovered. These are in the form of nineteen Greek and Latin inscriptions written in stone and dating from 27 B.C.E. to the sixth century C.E. These inscriptions were found in areas extending from Italy to Turkey, Egypt, and the land of Israel and include women's names and titles. Notable among the titles are "head of the synagogue" (archisynagogissa), "elder," "leader," and "mother of the synagogue."

Until recently, historians and archeologists have dismissed such labels as honorific, assuming that women could not possibly have held positions of leadership in ancient synagogues or Jewish communities. In the last decades of the twentieth century, however, women scholars began to challenge those old opinions.[64] They claim that there is no evidence from ancient Judaism that wives or widows routinely took on their husbands' titles. Their continuing investigations suggest that women such as **Rufina** of Smyrna, **Sophia** of Gortyn and **Theopempte** of

Caria, all holding the title of archisynagogissa, were important functionaries in the Jewish community.[65]

When the archisynagogue title applied to men, the position assumed wealth. The men were usually from families of high status and were responsible for assigning people to the reading of the law, inviting preachers to the synagogue, and collecting money from the congregation for synagogue building and restoration. There seems no reason that women holding that title in their own right would not have done the same. While their administrative and fund-raising duties may have been directed especially to the women, there was no clear sign indicating that even this was so.

RELIGIOUS PARTICIPATION

Involvement in Synagogues

As early as the fifth century B.C.E., there is evidence that women were involved in religious life. Lists of contributors to the Jewish Temple in Elephantine make it clear that many women made regular donations in their own names. These women were financially independent and had the legal right to dispose of their own money and goods.

Centuries later, the engravings on stone monuments found in Mediterranean lands attest to similar participation by women both as donors and lay leaders. In the eastern Mediterranean region, Sophia of Gortyn (4th or 5th century C.E.) was an elder (*presbytera*) in her synagogue as well as an archisynagogissa. Several other examples of women with the title of "elder" have been recorded in the early centuries of the Common Era. These include Rebekka of Thrace, Beronikene of

Thessaly, and Mannine of Italy. Peristeria of Thessaly is referred to as "leader."

Veturia Paulla (date unknown) held the title "mother of the synagogue" for two separate synagogues in Rome. While this title may have been honorary, it most probably was accorded to women (and men) who gave sizable donations. Veturia Paulla was a gentile who converted to Judaism at the age of seventy.[66]

Tation and Theopemte had no religious titles, but they too were generous donors to synagogues. The same can be assumed for the nine women whose names are preserved on the mosaic floor of a synagogue in Apamea, Syria. Other women's names also appear as benefactors in that same mosaic, but they are listed in groups together with men, so they may not have controlled their own money.[67]

Such inscriptions—and there may be more as yet undiscovered—stand in stark contrast to written rabbinic sources that claim women should be secluded and were uninvolved in the activities of the synagogue or the study hall. However, these inscriptions do not suggest that women were prayer leaders, either. Nor do they show that women were active in any of the ritual activities that rabbinic law demanded of men. The Greek inscriptions referring to a few

---

TWO MAGICAL TEXTS

This bowl text directed against Lilith is reminiscent of the Hebrew formula for divorcing a wife. It was written for a woman named Komish bat Maḥlafta, but the formula for protection was credited to Joshua bar Perohia, a rabbinic leader who lived in the first century B.C.E.

"This day from among all days, years, and generations of the world, I Komish bat Maḥlafta have divorced and dismissed and banished you— you Lilith, Lilith of the desert, ghost and kidnapper.

You, the three of you, the four of you, the five of you, are sent out naked and not clad. Your hair is dishevelled, thrown over your backs.

It is announced to you . . . Hear and go away and do not associate with her, with Komish bat Maḥlafta in her house. Go away, come from her house and from her dwelling and from Kalleta and from Artashriat her children.

I have decreed against you, with the curse which Joshua bar Perohia sent against you. I adjure you . . . receive your gets and your divorces . . . Hear and go away and do not lie with her, with Komish bat Maḥlafta, not in her house and not in her dwelling. . . ."[68]

The typical text below, from a fragment of an amulet, was written on bronze. Such amulets were believed to protect women in childbirth.

". . . by and/or for Surah, daughter of Sarah: . . . the foetus of Surah, daughter of Sarah, that it should not emerge except in its proper time . . . the four holy angels . . . I have been revealed and have spoken with him that placed the foetus in my belly . . . she should not give birth . . . until her time comes. I invoke you, holy angels and good names."[69]

Jewish women (Marin from lower Egypt, Gaudentia of Rome, and Lady Maria of Beth She'arim) as "priest" (*hierissa*),[70] describe no specific religious function.

Women and Folk Religion

Before rabbinic law was firmly established as normative Judaism, much of Jewish practice was syncretistic and changeable, blending biblical precepts with local custom. So Mibtahiah of Elephantine, in filing a quitclaim in a business arrangement with Pia the builder, an Egyptian, took an oath by the Egyptian goddess Sati. Even after rabbinic practice became Jewish law, whenever a Jewish minority lived within another culture, they always adopted some of the customs of the host country.

A small number of intriguing magic bowls and amulets discovered by archeologists point to a shared belief by Jews and gentiles in a world filled with spirits and demons who could be controlled only by means of magic. Such beliefs were firmly implanted in Jewish culture.[71]

Magic bowls came from Babylonia. They were fashioned from metal or clay and were placed facedown in strategic positions in the home or building to be protected. Amulets from Babylonia were written on clay, bone, or papyrus and were often inscribed for use by a specific person.[72] In Syria and the land of Israel, amulets were made to be worn, carried, or affixed to a house like a *mezuzah*.

Written in Aramaic using the Hebrew alphabet, the inscribed texts, all dating from the fourth to the seventh centuries C.E., almost always contained variations of the name of God

---

THE LEGEND OF LILITH

Evil spirits were often female, and the most prominent among them was Lilith. The name Lilith originated in Babylonia as a generic term for all flying spirits. Over the centuries, a legend arose about Lilith as the first wife of Adam. According to this legend, Lilith and Adam fought and she flew out of the Garden of Eden. God sent three angels to bring her back, but she refused, threatening to take her revenge by killing all newborn infants. In order to escape death by the hands of the angels, Lilith agreed to stay away from any home that displayed their names as well as her own names. Although the earliest written version of this story in Hebrew dates only from the seventh century C.E., earlier versions of it have been discovered in other cultures. The names of the three angels, given as Sanvi, Sansanvi, and Samengalef, appear in older amulets and bowls in a multiplicity of forms.[73]

---

as well as the names of angels, both evil and good.

Although the individuals who inscribed the magical formulae on the bowls and amulets are not known, it is probable that they included more men than women, simply because men were more likely to be literate. What is sure, however, is that many of the recipients of these magical safeguards were individual women. By means of such amulets, women sought defense against demons or malevolent spirits that could cause illness, danger to their unborn children, or death in childbirth.

In their use of amulets and other magical practices, women were neither defying nor ignoring Jewish custom. On the contrary, incantation texts represent a long tradition. They illustrate how all people in the early centuries attempted to cope with fear, find a measure of protection, and control the dangers that confronted them in their daily lives.

CHAPTER 2

A Written Legacy:
Literary Evidence from the Ancient Near East to 600 C.E.

OVERVIEW

Ancient Literature

Archeological discoveries indicate that women were active participants in ancient Jewish society. But literary evidence has had a much greater impact than archeology on how we view the position and status of Jewish women. Because women's activities have scarcely appeared in ancient Jewish literature, people assume that women played only a minor role. When texts such as the Apocrypha, the Mishnah, and the Talmud are analyzed carefully, however, they suggest that women had a greater role than was originally assumed. Even though much of ancient literature has been altered by defective transmissions, cultural misunderstandings, and faulty translations, detailed examination and analysis yields considerable data previously overlooked. This chapter will concentrate on such literary evidence.

The Hasmonean Dynasty

Following the final defeat of the Ptolemaic Empire in 198 B.C.E., the Seleucids ruled in Syria and Judea. Antiochus IV (175–164 B.C.E.) enforced a policy of Hellenization and suppressed Jewish practices. This ultimately resulted in the Jewish uprising of 165 B.C.E. led by Mattathias, a priest of the Hasmonean family, and his five sons.

After Mattathias's death, his middle son, Judah (nicknamed "the Maccabee") led a small but determined Jewish army into battle against the

Syrians and succeeded in overcoming a combined force of Syrian-Greeks and Jewish assimilationists.[1] Once in control of Jerusalem, the Jews cleansed the Temple of any signs of pagan worship and rededicated it. The festival of Hanukkah commemorates this victory.

Judah the Maccabee continued fighting for several more years, however, as Antiochus's successors attempted to regain control and reimpose Greek culture on the area. When Judah died, his brothers succeeded him and established the Hasmonean, or Maccabean, Dynasty.[2]

The Hasmoneans dominated the land of Israel from 152 until 63 B.C.E. The main literary sources for this period are the apocryphal books 1 and 2 Maccabees, and Josephus's works, from the first century of the Common Era.[3] These accounts concentrate on dynastic and military actions, and women are almost completely absent from the narratives. When they are mentioned, the facts about them mainly concern their relationships to the principal male protagonists.

Simon, the last Maccabean brother, was killed in 134 B.C.E. by his son-in-law and was succeeded by his son John Hyrcanus. As each generation of the Hasmonean family ascended the throne, the dynasty became more hellenized and increasingly corrupt. Fighting between the different factions of the family increased, resulting in a series of civil wars. In addition to these dynastic struggles, two political/religious parties had emerged in Judea: the **Sadducees**, the party of the ruling class, and the **Pharisees**, supported by the people. Contention between these two parties resulted in a brutal civil war in which approximately 50,000 Jews died before the Sadducees, led by King Alexander Jannai (103–76 B.C.E.), triumphed.[4]

When Alexander Jannai died in 76 B.C.E., his wife, **Salome/Shelamzion Alexandra,** succeeded him, becoming the only Hasmonean woman to hold power in Judea. She ruled for nine years, a period of relative peace. Following her death, her two sons, Aristobulus II and Hyrcanus II, fought over the succession and invited Rome in to mediate their claims. Rome

---

SADDUCEES AND PHARISEES: TWO COMPETING FACTIONS IN JUDEA

The Sadducees were more nationalistic, were willing to use force to spread Judaism, and adhered to a literal reading of biblical law. They represented the ruling class in Judea.

The Pharisees disagreed with the expansionist policies of the Hasmonean rulers and believed in a more liberal interpretation of the Torah, incorporating the oral law. They were considered the party of the common people.[5]

gradually took control of the Jewish state and the surrounding areas, and the Hasmonean Dynasty weakened and finally disappeared.

King Herod I

After a series of attacks on Jerusalem and the brutal execution of forty-five members of the Sanhedrin, Herod, the son of the Idumean governor Antipas, took control of Judea (by then incorporated into greater Palestine). He was granted the title of king by the Roman Empire and reigned from 37 to 34 B.C.E. During those years he built major public buildings, palaces, and fortresses, and some of the ruins remain as landmarks today. However, his rule was marked by cruelty and murder as well as by serial marriages. He took ten wives in all (see **Herodian Women**), divorcing each in turn to marry the next. After many rebellions by his sons, he divided his kingdom among his three remaining heirs, Archelaus, Herod Antipas, and Herod Philip. None ever achieved the power of their father.

The Hellenistic Diaspora

While the Jews in the land of Israel were enduring troublesome times, those in Alexandria and the other Greek cities of Egypt were living relatively well. By the last century before the Common Era and up until the Greek/Jewish wars of 115–117 C.E., their communities were large and prosperous. They were well respected by the local population of Egyptians and Greeks, and many Jews were rich and successful.

The style of Judaism practiced in this hellenistic Diaspora was a blend of Jewish law and Greek philosophy. It fit in well with the ideas espoused in other Jewish communities, and some Greeks were attracted to Judaism. One female prophet (sibyl) was known as Sambathe. Her prophecies focused on monotheism, sexual purity, and social justice, and she was one of many popular sibyls whose words have been preserved.[6] It was long believed that Sambathe was a Jewish woman, although most modern historians now acknowledge that the collection called *The Sibylline Oracles* is a composite work, compiled from many folkloric sources, and cannot be attributed to any individuals.

Philo, one of the leading Jewish philosophers of the Hellenistic world, lived in Alexandria between 25 B.C.E. and circa 50 C.E. His allegorical interpretations of the Bible were well known and respected. His opinions on women, however, reflecting the prevailing views of Greek culture, were mostly negative. Philo praised only one particular group of learned women. These were the Therapeutrides, women who belonged to a community of Therapeutics (see **Religious Participation**).[7]

The Growth of Rabbinic Judaism

The characteristics and mores of rabbinic Judaism, while they have their roots in biblical law, are revealed in all their diversity in the Talmud, a compilation of books including most of the chapters of the Mishnah with accompanying explanations (the Gemara).

A codification and commentary on the laws of the Bible was begun by the Pharisees during the first century B.C.E. under the Hasmoneans and continued for some three hundred years. At the end of the second century C.E., Yehudah ha-Nasi, the chief religious leader (patriarch) in the land of Israel, edited the work and closed it to further changes. It was called the Mishnah and was divided into six orders, each containing many sections dealing with different topics.[8]

Through the centuries, as new interpretations proliferated, each generation added its own thoughts and customs to the original Mishnah. Eventually, all these layers were codified and edited by two different groups of scholars, one in the land of Israel and one in Babylonia. The result was two compilations: the Palestinian (often called the Jerusalem) Talmud, and the Babylonian Talmud, the larger and more comprehensive of the two. The Mishnah is still published as a separate series of books, without the Gemara, and citations from the Mishnah by itself are considered more authoritative.

The Babylonian Diaspora

Once a place of exile, Babylonia gradually became the strongest and most influential Jewish community in the Diaspora. The two Babylonian academies, first established by Jewish scholars from the land of Israel in the earliest centuries of the Common Era, produced and edited the most definitive and authoritative version of the Talmud. It was here that the *Resh Galuta* (Exilarch) reigned over one million or more Babylonian Jews.[9]

A LIBRARY OF RABBINIC JEWISH LITERATURE

- The Mishnah: original explanations of the biblical laws, closed in 200 C.E.
- The Tosefta (Additions): a separate compilation of rabbinic conversations, stories, legends, and legal rulings assembled during the time of the Mishnah but not included in the Mishnah itself.
- The Gemara: explanations and discussions based on the Mishnah and combined with it to form the Talmud. This compilation was edited in the mid–fifth century and completed in approximately 500 C.E.

In the sixth century, when the Babylonian Talmud was closed to further additions, the compilation consisted of sixty-three complete tractates, a collection that has had an overreaching effect on Jewish life.

A few women historians have recently conjectured that these written rabbinic sources became more significant to later generations than they ever were to their contemporaries. These scholars suggest that talmudic standards may reflect only the social realities of a handful of Jewish communities in the land of Israel and in Babylonia. Rather than representing the reality of those centuries, they may simply be the ideals of a small, elite group of influential men.[10] Whether or not these recent analyses are correct, the Talmud had and still has a profound effect on the lives of Jewish women.

BIOGRAPHIES

BERURIAH OF PALESTINE, SCHOLAR

(2nd century C.E.)

Beruriah's name is mentioned in the Babylonian Talmud and in various ancient and medieval writings, and she has become legendary. Although possibly fictional, the following anecdotes convey a typical account of Beruriah's life.[11]

Beruriah, a daughter of the great Palestinian sage R. Hananiah ben Teradion, was an accomplished scholar. Even as a young girl, her intelligence surpassed that of her brother. It was said she learned "three hundred laws from three hundred teachers in one day" (B. *Pesaḥim* 62b). She married R. Meir, the miracle worker and one of the great sages of the Mishnaic period.

Tragedy stalked Beruriah and her family. Her father was martyred by the Romans, and her mother and brother also died violently. Her two sons died suddenly in a single day, and her sister was carried off into exile.

Beruriah could be loving and gentle, as she was with her husband, Meir, and also arrogant and biting, even to great scholars. She ridiculed a sectarian (B. *Berakhot* 10a), derided an erring student (B. *Eruvin* 53b–54a), and made a fool of R. Jose the Galilean when he met her on the road (B. *Eruvin* 53b).

When she mocked the sages' belief that women are weak and easily seduced, she challenged the prevailing wisdom of her time and came to a shameful end, proving the contention of the Rabbis that any woman who studies excessively, like Beruriah, is vulnerable to sexual sin.

These accounts concerning Beruriah are made up of different components, most written much later by many different men. In the Babylonian Talmud she is called the wife of R. Meir, pupil of R. Akiva. In the two passages about her in the Tosefta (an earlier, Palestinian compilation) she is referred to once by name with no association to any male relative (Tos. *Kelim, Bava Metzia* 1:6), and the second time as the unnamed daughter of R. Hananiah (Tos. *Kelim, Bava Kamma* 4:17). Because of these variations, it has been suggested that perhaps two or even three historical women became incorporated into a single persona.[12] One is Beruriah the scholar, another is the wife of R. Meir, and a third is the daughter of R. Hananiah ben Teradion.

THE WISDOM OF BERURIAH

There were once some robbers in the neighborhood of R. Meir, and Meir prayed that they should die. His wife, Beruriah, said to him: "How do you make out that such a prayer should be permitted, because it is written 'Let *hatta'im* (sins) cease?' Is it written *hot'im* (sinners) cease? It is written *hatta'im*! Furthermore, look at the end of the verse: and let the wicked men be no more. Since the sins will cease there will be no more wicked men. Rather pray for them that they should repent and they will be wicked no more." He did pray for them and they repented.

—*B. Berakhot 10a*

In the stories from the Babylonian Talmud that portrayed Beruriah as a scholar, her name was mentioned alone, without reference to husband or father. In these reports she was quick, sarcastic, and knowledgeable in areas beyond domestic issues.

In the stories that refer to Beruriah as R. Meir's wife, she is compassionate, gentle, patient, and understanding as well as wise. She quoted Bible passages to her husband in order to improve the quality of his prayer (B. *Berakhot* 10a), and comforted him when their children died.

But these examples of Beruriah's emotional strength and intellectual ability are not the sum total of her story. In the Middle Ages, a plot of seduction and shame was superimposed on the heroic character of Beruriah. The shocking account was first written down by Rashi in the eleventh century as part of his commentary to the Talmud (B. *Avodah Zarah* 18b). The passage itself alludes to the fact that R. Meir had to flee from the Romans because he had rescued his wife's (Beruriah's) sister from a Roman brothel. Rashi adds his own postscript to this passage: "But some say [he had to flee] because of the Beruriah incident."

According to Rashi's explanation, Meir arranged the seduction of his wife by one of his pupils in order to prove the validity of the talmudic claim that women are light-minded. After many refusals, Beruriah finally yielded to the student's sexual advances. When she realized that her husband had set the trap for her, she hung herself and Meir ran away out of shame.

This incident, while not part of the original talmudic composite, raises some disturbing questions: Could a

---

THE DEATH OF BERURIAH'S SONS

This legend from a post-talmudic source illustrates Beruriah's strength and religious faith.

"Some time ago a man came and gave me a deposit in trust, and now he comes to claim that deposit. Shall we return it or not?" He answered her: "My daughter, whoever has a deposit in trust, must he not return it to its owner?" She said to him: "Had you not said so, I would not have returned it." Beruriah then took his hand and brought him up to the room [where their sons were lying] and drew him near the bed and drew down the sheet, and he saw the two of them dead and collapsed on the bed. He began to cry . . . at the same time she [Beruriah] said to R. Meir: "Did you not say we must return the deposit to its owner? It is said, the Lord has given, the Lord has taken away. Blessed be the name of the Lord."
—*Midrash Proverbs 31:16–29*

---

woman such as Beruriah have existed in the land of Israel in the second century? If the **education** of women was rare, then Beruriah was more likely an exception or a legend. Whether she was fictional or historical, why did Rashi feel obliged to damage the reputation of a righteous and learned woman by writing down these stories?

Despite the unanswered questions associated with her, Beruriah's name continues to resonate in women's history and she remains an exemplary heroine for scholarly Jewish women.

HASMONEAN / MACCABEAN WOMEN

(134 B.C.E.–57 B.C.E.)

The women in the Hasmonean line rarely enjoyed power. They were more often than not pawns in the vicious cycle of internecine strife and murder. Although information about these women is fragmentary, we know of a few. One was the wife of Simon, the last Maccabean brother, and mother of John Hyrcanus, successor to the throne.

When John Hyrcanus was attacked by his brother-in-law Ptolemy, he desisted from retaliating because Ptolemy held John's mother as hostage. According to Josephus, she was tortured on the ramparts so her son would be able to watch. She begged John not to hold off the attack on her account and called out to him: "It would be pleasant . . . to die in torment if the enemy who was doing these things . . . paid the penalty."[13]

Despite his mother's pleas, John held back from a full attack, but his decision did not have the desired result. This unfortunate, unnamed woman was killed by her son-in-law.[14] Ultimately, John Hyrcanus managed to defeat Ptolemy and reigned as both ruler and High Priest.

John Hyrcanus's wife also remains unnamed in the sources, but when John died, he willed to her total control of the secular government while granting the post of High Priest to his oldest son, Aristobulus. But Aristobulus wanted the complete power that his father had enjoyed. He quickly imprisoned his mother and his younger brothers and took for himself the double title of king and High Priest. His

mother was allowed to die of hunger in prison; the brothers were released only after Aristobulus' untimely death in 103 B.C.E. Then Alexander Jannai, the next in line, assumed leadership of the Judean state and married **Salome/Shelamzion Alexandra**.

The Maccabean line continued until Aristobulus II and Hyrcanus II, the sons of Salome Alexandra, invited the Romans into Judea to mediate their quarrel over the succession. After that, the Maccabean family persisted, but no longer held official power.

Salome Alexandra's granddaughter Alexandra was the mother of **Mariamne** (Herod's second wife) and was widowed at a young age. She attempted to take an active role in her son-in-law Herod's government. Despite many secret plots and several appeals to Queen Cleopatra VII (69–30 B.C.E.) of Egypt, she failed in her efforts to either influence or overthrow him. She was killed by Herod one year after Mariamne's execution.

Other Maccabean women do occasionally appear in the history books, most often as wives of the Herodian kings.

HERODIAN WOMEN

(57 B.C.E.–1st century C.E.)

Herod I (the Great) had many wives. Some, like Mariamne, the Maccabean princess, are well known. Others are known only as mothers of famous or infamous sons.

Herod's first wife was Doris of Jerusalem, mother of Herod's oldest son, Antipater. Herod divorced Doris in order to marry Mariamne, and Doris's son Antipater was eventually killed by his father after he plotted to take the throne for himself.

Herod's second and third wives, Mariamne the Hasmonean and

The Hasmonean Dynasty

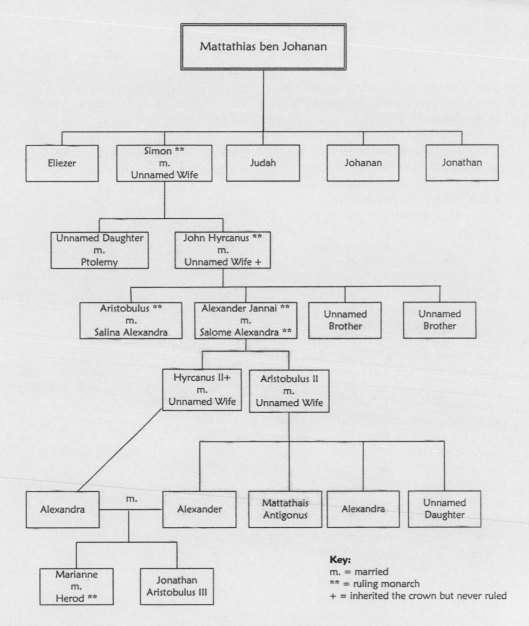

FIG. 3. Although many of the Hasmonean daughters and wives are not named in the history books, they often played crucial roles in the events of the time.

Mariamne, daughter of Shimon ben Boethus, were followed by seven other wives, but none played important roles in the government. Malthace the Samaritan, Herod's fourth wife, had two sons, Archelaus and Herod Antipas, who inherited parts of his kingdom after their father's death. The third son to inherit was Herod Philip, son of his fifth wife, Cleopatra of Jerusalem. Most of his fifteen other sons and daughters were murdered for plotting against their father.[15]

HERODIAS OF NORTHERN ISRAEL, QUEEN

(1st century C.E.)

Herodias, a daughter of Aristobulus and Berenice, and granddaughter of King Herod I and Mariamne, had two husbands, both from the Herodian line. Her first husband was her uncle Herod, son of Herod I with Mariamne bat Shimon ben Boethus. With this husband, she had a daughter, **Salome**. Some years later, she met Herod's half-brother, Herod Antipas.

Shortly after she and Herod Antipas met, they determined to marry. Herod Antipas's first wife, an Arabian princess, was to be sent back to her father. The couple ignored the political risks created by the repudiation of a king's daughter. They also refused to consider the fact that Jewish law forbade marriage to a brother's wife unless he had died childless.[16] Their disregard of the law was condemned by John the Baptist. It was later suggested that he was imprisoned because of this disagreement (Matt. 14:3–5; Mark 6:17).

Years later, when Herod Antipas antagonized the new Roman emperor Caligula, he lost his title and was exiled to Gaul. After the sentence was handed down, Caligula gave Herodias permission to remain in the land of Israel and stay with her brother Agrippa instead of following her husband. She refused this offer, saying: "My loyalty to my husband is a bar to my enjoyment of your kind gift, for it is not right when I have shared in his prosperity, that I should abandon him when he has been brought to this pass."[17]

IMA SHALOM OF PALESTINE, PROMINENT WOMAN

(1st century C.E.)

Ima Shalom is one of the few women named and quoted in the Talmud. The facts about her that have been pieced together portray a woman from a prominent and powerful family, born in approximately 50 C.E. She was supposedly the daughter of Shimon ben Gamliel, a descendant of Hillel, and the sister of Rabban Gamliel, head of the Sanhedrin.

Ima Shalom was married to R. Eliezer ben Hyrcanus, chief of the academy at Lydda. Although Eliezer expressed negative views about women, Ima Shalom herself was a woman of superior intellect. She offered her opinions freely in men's discussions and gained a reputation for cleverness and wit.

More recently, stories concerning Ima Shalom have been analyzed anew, and scholars suspect that rather than being a single personage, Ima Shalom, like **Beruriah,** may be a construct of several different women.[18] In certain passages Ima Shalom is mentioned only as the wife of R. Eliezer, in others only as the sister of R. Gamliel, and in still others she is named without reference to any family members.

Only one early Palestinian source refers to R. Eliezer's wife, but her

The Herodian Dynasty

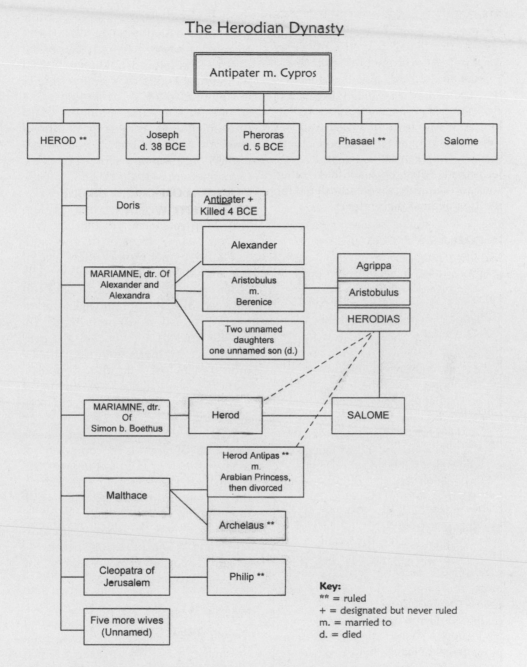

FIG. 4. The women of the Herodian Dynasty frequently tried to influence husbands and fathers but most often failed.

THE BEAUTIFUL CHILDREN OF IMA SHALOM

While discussing sexual relations the Rabbis contended that a child is born deaf when his parents converse during cohabitation, and blind if the parents look at "that place." The definition of the word "converse," used by Ima Shalom as a euphemism for sexual intercourse, is at the core of the ensuing segment of the Gemara, which seeks to disprove the majority's view by using Ima Shalom as an authority. Her husband is not named.

Ima Shalom was asked: "Why are your children so exceedingly beautiful?" She replied: "[Because] he [my husband] converses with me neither at the beginning nor at the end of the night, but [only] at midnight; and when he converses he uncovers a handbreadth and covers a handbreadth, and it is as though he were compelled by a demon. And when I asked him: 'What is the reason [for choosing midnight]' he replied, 'so that I may not think of another woman, lest my children be as bastards.'"

—*R. Yohanan ben Dahabai, B. Nedarim 20b*

The Rabbis reject R. Yohanan's proof, claiming that the conversation pertained specifically to conjugal matters, but the quotation from Ima Shalom does indicate that her experience and her opinion were valued.[19]

name is not given, suggesting that this was not Ima Shalom (Tos. *Niddah* 6:8). In another passage, the scholars of the Babylonian Talmud link Ima Shalom with a husband, although this time *he* is not named (B. *Nedarim* 20a–b). A source linking Ima Shalom to R. Eliezer simply relates a comment made by the rabbi but offers no information on his wife beyond her name (*Sifra* Shemini *Mekhilta de Miluim* 99:5).

Only two anecdotes in the Babylonian Talmud connect Ima Shalom with both husband and brother. One concerns a ban placed on her husband, R. Eliezer, by her brother, then head of the Sanhedrin (B. *Bava Metzia* 59b). The other passage tells of a lawsuit between Ima Shalom and her brother over a question of inheritance (B. *Shabbat* 116a–b). In this case, she contested her brother's sole right to the inheritance of family property. Although she lost the case, the report demonstrates her ability to confront authority.

Whether we accept the new thesis that Ima Shalom is a composite of many women or hold to the older tradition that she was a historic figure, the written record exists. It tells us that Ima Shalom, either as one person or many, exhibited cleverness, self assurance, and a sharpness of speech not usually reported in a woman of the first century.

MARIA HEBREA OF EGYPT, ALCHEMIST
(2nd or 3rd century C.E.)

Maria the Hebrew (*Maria Hebrea* in Latin) was famous for her invention of the *balneum Maria* or "Maria's water bath" (a type of double boiler). She also devised a specific model of still or oven, sometimes called "Maria's oven" (*kerotakes* in Greek), and was believed to have discovered hydrochloric acid, a secret supposedly passed down from the time of Moses' destruction of the golden calf.[20]

Maria left no writings of her own. The earliest references to her work are from Zosimus the Panopolitan, a writer and alchemist of the third or fourth century. Zosimus assumed that Maria was Jewish. He wrote that Jews had learned alchemy directly from the Egyptians, and attributed to Maria the belief that only the descendants of Abraham could understand and practice alchemy.

An early legend identifies Maria, supposedly an Egyptian herself, as the sister of Moses.[21] Another work associated with Maria (probably from a later Hellenistic period) shows clear evidence of a belief in one God as the Creator of the Universe. Such allusions to monotheism and Judaism may have led to her characterization as "the Hebrew."

In both chemistry and cooking Maria's association with the double boiler persists until today. In French a vessel that fits into a larger vessel is called a *bain Marie;* in German it is a *marienbad.* Despite all the existing information, some writers question Maria the Hebrew's authenticity as a historical figure and insist there is no basis to the legend.[22]

MARIAMNE OF JUDEA, HASMONEAN PRINCESS
(1st century B.C.E.)

Mariamne was a direct descendant of the Maccabees (also called the Hasmoneans), the priestly family that dominated the land of Israel from 152–63 B.C.E. She was the daughter of Alexander and Alexandra

---

IMA SHALOM'S LOYALTY TO HER HUSBAND

In a dispute over a legal interpretation, Ima Shalom's brother, R. Gamliel, had excommunicated her husband R. Eliezer. This ban remained in effect until Gamliel's death. From the time of the excommunication, Ima Shalom did not permit her husband to "fall on his face," a practice by which a Jew might address God with personal pleas to remedy an injustice. The Talmud reported the incident to show that God listens to the appeals of those who have been wronged, but it also illustrates Ima Shalom's conflicted loyalties.

"Now a certain day . . . a poor man came and stood at the door [of Ima Shalom's house], and she took out some bread to him. On her return she found [R. Eliezer] fallen on his face. 'Arise!' she cried to him, 'You have slain my brother!' In the meanwhile an announcement was made from the house of R. Gamliel that he had died. 'How did you know It?' [Eliezer] questioned her. 'I have this tradition from my father's house,' Ima Shalom answered: 'All gates are locked, except the gates of wounded feelings.'"
—*B. Bava Metzia 59b*

In his dispute with Rabban Gamliel, R. Eliezer had appealed to God to judge between them. Ima Shalom, accepting the justice of her husband's cause, assumed that if his appeal was granted, her brother would die. The results affirmed her belief.

DEATH OF A QUEEN

[Mariamne] went to her death with a wholly calm demeanor and without change of color, and so even in her last moments she made her nobility of descent very clear.
—*Flavius Josephus*[23]

(granddaughter of Salome/Shelamzion Alexandra) and became the second wife of King Herod I (Herod the Great).

The Romans appointed Herod I king of the Jews in 37 B.C.E. He divorced his first wife, Doris, to marry Mariamne in the hope that an alliance with a Hasmonean princess would legitimize his rule. Some believed that he nevertheless loved Mariamne and that her beauty, combined with her scorn at his less than royal descent, fueled his jealousy. Desperate for her love, Herod left orders with his brother-in-law Joseph that if he should die, Mariamne was to be murdered so she could never belong to another man.

Ultimately, Herod did have Mariamne killed. When he left on a diplomatic mission to Rhodes, he ordered his loyal friend Soemus to secretly act as her bodyguard and assure that she would remain faithful. On his return, he accused Mariamne and Soemus of adultery and Soemus was immediately executed.

Mariamne was indignant and fought with Herod. Cypros and **Salome,** Herod's mother and sister, disliked "the proud Mariamne" and encouraged the quarrel. Salome plotted with a servant to accuse Mariamne of attempting to poison King Herod. This proved to be the final provocation

for Herod, and Mariamne was put on trial. Josephus reported two conflicting stories concerning this event. In one version she was accused of adultery; in another version the charge was attempting to poison her husband.[24]

Before her death, Mariamne bore Herod five children, three sons and two daughters. Six years after their mother's execution, the sons were sent to Rome to be educated, and the youngest died there. The other two, Alexander and Aristobulus, remained in Rome until King Herod sent for them and arranged their marriages. Eventually, they were also accused of treason and their father had them killed in 7 B.C.E.[25]

MARIAMNE BAT SHIMON BEN BOETHUS OF ALEXANDRIA, WIFE OF KING HEROD
(1st century B.C.E.)

Mariamne was the daughter of Shimon ben Boethus, a well-known priest from Alexandria, Egypt. She became the third wife of King Herod I. The year the marriage took place, 24 B.C.E., Herod appointed her father, Shimon, as High Priest in Jerusalem. In spite of this auspicious beginning, Mariamne was implicated in a plot to kill Herod and was quickly sent away.[26] She died in approximately 20 B.C.E.

Mariamne bat Shimon had only one son, also named Herod. He was later excluded from the succession after having been implicated in a plot to kill his father.

RACHEL OF JERUSALEM, IDEAL WIFE
(1st century B.C.E.)

Rachel[27] was the daughter of one of the wealthiest men in Jerusalem. Over her father's objections, she married Akiva, then a poor, uneducated shepherd, and devoted her life to enabling him to study. With Rachel's blessing and encouragement, he left their home for the academy at Lydda and remained away from her for many years while she lived in poverty with their children. When he became a great scholar he credited his wife for making it possible.[28]

Rachel herself never aspired to scholarship or greatness. Her sacrifices, most of which fall into the realm of legend, are held up as an ideal for other women. She was a contemporary of **Ima Shalom,** whose husband, R. Eliezer ben Hyrcanus, was one of R. Akiva's teachers at Lydda.

SALOME, SISTER OF A KING
(1st century B.C.E.)

Salome was the sister of Herod I (the Great). Together with her mother, Cypros, she actively encouraged enmity between her brother and his second wife, Mariamne. Upon Herod's death in 4 B.C.E., she was rewarded for her loyalty with a generous inheritance. It included the cities of Jamnia (Yavneh), Azotus, and Phasaelis and 500,000 pieces of silver.[29]

SALOME OF NORTHERN ISRAEL, DANCER AND DESCENDANT OF NOBILITY
(1st century B.C.E.)

Salome came from a long line of aristocrats. She was the daughter of **Herodias** (by her first husband) and stepdaughter to Herod Antipas, her mother's second husband. Herod Antipas was Tetrarch of the Galilee and son of Herod I.

Salome's fame stems from her beauty and her ability to dance. According to a legend repeated in the New Testament, she danced so beautifully at her stepfather's birthday celebration that he promised as her reward to grant any wish she had. Allegedly, at the instigation of her mother, Salome requested the head of John the Baptist, then in prison. Herod Antipas reluctantly agreed, and the popular religious leader was beheaded.[30]

SALOME/SHELAMZION ALEXANDRA OF JUDEA, QUEEN
(139–67 B.C.E.)

Salome Alexandra, whose Hebrew name was Shelamzion, was a descendant of the Hasmonean family.[31] Some historians have claimed that she was the first wife of Alexander's older brother Aristobulus and became Alexander's wife through the laws of the levirate (see **Family Life**).

Whatever her previous marital status, however, Salome Alexandra was most certainly the wife of Alexander Jannai, with whom she had two sons, Hyrcanus II and Aristobulus II. Before her husband's death he willed the secular government to her and the high priesthood to his oldest son, Hyrcanus. It was not the first time a Hasmonean ruler had designated his own wife as his successor. However, this time the succession was not contested, either by her sons or any other faction, and Salome Alexandra became the first Hasmonean woman to rule Judea as its queen.

During her nine-year reign, Queen Salome Alexandra completely reversed her late husband's hostile policy toward the Pharisees and brought them into her government. Even while Alexander Jannai was alive she had invited Shimon ben Shetah, leader of the Pharisees, to her palace. Now she appointed him joint head (with Yehudah ben Tabbai) of the Great Assembly

TWO WOMEN OR ONE? SALOME AND SALINA

According to most historians (who base their conclusion on Josephus's account), when Aristobulus died, his wife, Salome Alexandra, released his brothers from prison and appointed a younger brother, Alexander, as his successor. If this is true, Salome Alexandra followed the proper Jewish procedure for levirate marriage *(yibbum)* which demands that the brother of a dead man must marry his childless brother's widow (Deut. 25:5–10). However, this seems unlikely for several reasons:

1. Josephus made no mention of a marriage to Salome Alexandra.
2. She was only named as Alexander's wife in the course of reporting the King's death twenty-seven years later.
3. In his history of the Jews, Josephus called Aristobulus's wife Salina Alexandra and not Salome Alexandra, suggesting that there may have been two different women.

pharisaic policy opposing foreign conquests, she dispatched an army to Damascus, headed by her son Aristobulus. That military operation was a failure, but Salome Alexandra retained full power and lost no territory.

Her diplomatic skills proved more successful, and her timely gifts to the Armenian ruler, Tigranes, who was marching toward Judea, warded off an attack.

Under Salome's rule and probably with her tacit approval, Diogenes, a Sadducee who had been Alexander's counselor and thus an opponent of the Pharisees, was executed. She did help to protect her son Aristobulus and other prominent Sadducees from the revenge of the Pharisees, but at the end of her life Salome was forced to stand against her younger son.

When Aristobulus II contested the claims of his older brother, Hyrcanus II, and began capturing key positions, she approved a military action to stop him. This set off yet another civil war, but Salome Alexandra did not live to see her sons destroy the peace she had established in Judea.

Queen Salome Alexandra died at the age of seventy-three, loved by the Pharisees and hated by their opponents. Josephus criticized her harshly, suggesting that she was power hungry.

The Talmud, a rabbinic (and therefore a pharasaic) source, praises her as an intermediary between her husband, Alexander, and the Pharisee Shimon ben Shetaḥ, and credits her with rescuing seventy elders who were condemned to death. Another talmudic passage reports that during her reign the harvests in Judea were "miraculously bountiful."[32]

(Sanhedrin). She also allowed the oral law, espoused by the Pharisees, to be incorporated once again as the law of the royal court. By these acts, Queen Salome Alexandra maintained the support of the people.

Although she is credited with establishing a period of comparative peace and restoring national unity in Judea, the Queen did not flinch from difficult and even brutal decisions. In spite of

SERVANT OF YEHUDAH HA-NASI
(early 3rd century)

This unnamed woman lived in the land of Israel in the late second and early third centuries, but was referred to by the Babylonian sages several hundred years later in their writings. She is mentioned a few times in the Talmud as one who was knowledgeable but unobtrusive, most especially helping the Rabbi's students by making significant observations as she went about her work.[33] One passage relates that she knew Hebrew and that sages learned the meaning of rare Hebrew words from her.[34]

It was reported that when the great Patriarch, R. Yehudah, was ill, she prayed for him, but seeing how painful and difficult his last days were, she changed her prayer. Instead of praying for his life, she prayed: "May it be the will [of the Almighty] that the immortals may overpower the mortals" (i.e., that he be taken up to Heaven). When she saw that his disciples continued praying for his life, "she took up a jar and threw it down from the roof to the ground. They ceased praying [for a moment], and the soul of the Rabbi departed to its eternal rest."[35]

THE WORLD OF JEWISH WOMEN

ECONOMIC ACTIVITIES

Women always worked, and their contribution to the household economy was vital. Besides child care and household management, women's most important activities were spinning, weaving, and sewing clothing for the family. In talmudic discussions, the Rabbis noted that women worked, especially at weaving and spinning,[36] and were apparently present in the streets, necessitating constant warnings to men not to engage in conversation with them (B. *Nedarim* 20a).

Women also might own property or work the land. The biblical Book of Proverbs (31:16) praises the capable wife who "sets her mind to an estate and acquires it" and "plants a vineyard by her own labors."

The Mishnah and Talmud also mention women who are property owners and assume that most women are working. They explain that the proceeds of a married woman's labor go to her husband unless he has failed to

provide maintenance according to her *ketubbah*. In that case, she may use her earnings for her own support.[37]

EDUCATION

Children's Education

The Bible states that the laws of God must be taught to one's children (Deut. 6:8). Written in Hebrew, a language that has no neuter words, the verse can be read in two ways: "... you will teach it to your children" (assuming that the male noun includes the female) or "... you will teach it to your sons." There is some evidence that early Palestinian sources believed women could also acquire merit from studying Torah,[38] but the Babylonian scholars strongly disagreed. For those who lived in societies that never questioned women's inferiority, this ambiguous verse was not likely to be interpreted as a mandate to teach daughters, and the education of girls was always inferior to the education of boys.

Commandments for Women

An important limitation placed on women by the sages was the decision that most of the time-bound, positive commandments *(mitzvot)* were binding only on men, and therefore girls did not need to learn them. Barred from communal learning, young girls were taught at home and were expected to know only the commandments for which they were obligated. These included the laws of tithing, family purity *(niddah)*, candlelighting, and the ritual of setting apart some dough for an offering when baking bread (the commandment of *ḥallah*). The Rabbis warned that a woman's failure to follow these rules would result in her death during childbirth (M. *Shabbat* 2:6).[39]

Rabbinic Standards and Their Results

When the standards of rabbinic Judaism became well established and spread throughout the Diaspora, the disparity between the education of men and women widened further. The sages whose words are included in the Mishnah as well as those who compiled the Talmud glorified learning as an ideal activity. It became a means of attaining closeness to God, but it was an activity reserved for men.

Exclusion from the formal process of education created an even more severe limitation on women than is immediately apparent. Through the course of many centuries, the study of Talmud became the most respected and valued occupation in which a Jew could engage. Since women, by definition, had no obligation to be taught, to learn, or to teach,[40] they were usually barred from that group of persons who ranked highest in the community.

Women's "light-mindedness" and unstable judgment were invoked as reasons for not educating them. Their lack of education, in turn, resulted in further evidence of women's inability to deal with serious matters of law[41] and caused their lower status in rabbinic society.

Scholarly Women

Scholarly women were clearly exceptions and made their way into historical reports only as anomalies. Most often these educated women were from the ranks of elite, learned families, and especially from families who had no sons. In those cases, the wish to obey the commandment to teach one's children spurred fathers to teach their daughters by default.

In communities dominated by rabbinic culture, women seem to have accepted all the restrictions placed on them with no visible protest. Because they were not routinely educated the way men were, they had little recourse to the law and could hardly refute rabbinic decisions. Yet even those who were educated never seem to have reached out to other women.

There are a few examples of scholarly women mentioned in the Talmud. One source (B. *Sanhedrin* 8b) discusses the fact that theoretically, a scholarly woman could be accused and executed for a crime without warning, but the woman in this example is merely hypothetical. In another instance, the two scholarly women seem to represent a real case that came before R. Akiva (50–135 C.E.), thus placing them in the land of Israel (Palestine) in approximately the late first or early second centuries (B. *Ḥagigah* 20a).[42]

The Babylonian Talmud also reports on another unnamed woman in

Palestine who came to consult R. Eliezer ben Hyrcanus, the husband of **Ima Shalom** (first century C.E.) on a matter of scriptural interpretation. This question, coming from such an unexpected source, led R. Eliezer to resort to stereotypes: "A woman's wisdom is at the spindle," he answered scornfully (B. *Yoma* 66b).[43]

R. Eliezer made other, similar statements about women. He is quoted as saying: "He who teaches his daughter the Law teaches her frivolity" (B. *Sotah* 20a). He also was reported to have said: "Better the Torah be burned than to be studied by a woman" (P. *Sotah* 3:4).

Although a survey of the full range of talmudic opinion about women would probably result in a slight advantage on the positive side,[44] R. Eliezer's negative statements concerning women's education are among the best known and most frequently quoted.

FAMILY LIFE

Betrothal and Marriage

The sages who compiled the Mishnah and the Talmud accepted the fact that marriage was desirable for both men and women, but they carefully stipulated the conditions under which it was to be arranged, carried out, and maintained. No aspect of betrothal or marriage was left to chance.

TWO TALMUDIC WOMEN

Beruriah, a daughter of the great Palestinian R. Ḥananiah ben Teradion, represents one extreme of talmudic possibility: the truly educated woman. Beruriah was an accomplished scholar. As a young girl, her intelligence surpassed that of her brother. Beruriah even became a teacher herself, and one talmudic report (B. Eruvin 53b–54a) illustrates her exacting standards.

Recently, scholars have begun reexamining these stories, questioning the likelihood that a learned woman like Beruriah could exist in the land of Israel in the second century. Some historians accept the possibility while admitting she must have been an exception. Others assert that she was a composite of several women, and as a scholar, she could only have existed at a much later time, in Babylonia and not in Israel. They point out that only in the Babylonian Talmud is Beruriah transformed into a scholar. Still others dismiss her as a legendary character.[45]

Rachel, the wife of R. Akiva, who allegedly devoted herself to enabling her husband to study, makes an interesting contrast to Beruriah. The story of Rachel's self-sacrifice and devotion has never been subjected to the kind of criticism that later attached itself to Beruriah, and Rachel's example, unlike Beruriah's, has been held up as a traditional role model.[46] It was clear to most people of this period (and later) that a woman's ideal role was not to be a scholar but to enable her husband or son to be one.

According to the Mishnah, a father was required to arrange a marriage for his daughter (with or without her consent) and to provide her with a dowry and a trousseau.[47] By the rabbinic period, bride-price had been completely eliminated and succeeded by a promise of payment directly to the bride if the marriage ended. The Talmud stipulated that this promise of payment was a requirement for a Jewish marriage.

Children

The Rabbis of the Mishnah established a father's obligation to maintain and educate his sons but not his daughters. Legally, a daughter could be sold into slavery, although we can assume this was done only in times of severe financial need. A father was not required to provide for a child's maintenance after the age of six, but he was required to provide his daughter with a dowry from his estate, even after his death.[48]

Divorce

Obtaining a divorce *(get)* according to biblical law simply involved the man giving the woman a bill of divorcement (Deut. 24:1–4). In fact, it was relatively easy for a man to divorce his wife.

The biblical statement that he can divorce her if he finds something unseemly in her could be interpreted loosely or strictly. The school of Shammai limited the definition of "unseemly" to sexual misconduct, but the school of Hillel broadened the definition to include even the smallest infraction. A man could divorce his wife if she burned his dinner or if he found someone else that he preferred (M. *Gittin* 9:10).

If a married woman went out with her hair uncovered, spoke to other men, or sat in the street to spin, she could theoretically be divorced without the return of her *ketubbah* (M. *Ketubbot* 7:6). As for what should happen if a woman wanted a divorce but her husband did not want it: This scenario was never discussed in biblical writings, and the Mishnah assumed that a woman could not initiate divorce (M. *Yevamot* 14:1).

In the Babylonian and the Palestinian Talmuds, the rulings and suppositions differed slightly from each other because each was based on local practice. Yet both assumed that they were following biblical law. The Palestinian Talmud recognized the tradition of Egypt and Palestine, already evident in the early marriage contracts of Elephantine (see chapter 1). This tradition allowed either party in a marriage to initiate a divorce if such a condition was written into the marriage contract.[49] The appropriate clause was: "if she hates [her husband] . . ." or "if he hates [his wife] . . ." The initiating party would lose the original monetary investment in the marriage but would be completely free to remarry. Josephus reports that King Herod's sister **Salome** sent her husband a bill of divorce.[50]

The Babylonian Talmud, based on traditions prevalent in Babylonia and the surrounding areas, confirmed a man's sole right to grant a divorce,[51] although there are traces of evidence that acknowledge the alternative tradition even here.[52] A woman could request a divorce and could even appeal to the rabbinic court if she had reasonable grounds, mainly impotence or an extreme distaste for his profession,[53] but in the event that the husband refused to issue the legal

---

TAMAY AND TAHOR

The word *impure (tamay)* has no associations with cleanliness or dirt as we understand it and should not be interpreted as such. It is a word that implies only a fitness to approach God or to participate in certain ritual obligations. Biblical law defines impurity as proximity to a dead person or animal, the appearance of open or running sores associated with certain skin diseases, a discharge of pus or semen, or the flow of menstrual blood. If any of these occur, the person affected must exclude himself or herself from the community for a set amount of time or until the condition disappears, and then ritually purify himself or herself in a body of water *(mikveh)*, thus returning to a state of purity *(tahor)*.

---

documents necessary, she had no recourse.[54] If the community's sympathy was with the woman, they might pressure the husband to act honorably, but if he continued to refuse or if he simply disappeared, she was trapped. Over the course of centuries, the stipulations of the Babylonian Talmud became normative for all Jews.

Family Purity

The laws of purity for women, also known as *niddah* (literally, "one who is excluded"), were a topic of concern among the talmudic sages, and their decisions were based on biblical law. It states very clearly in the Bible (Lev. 12–15) when a person is considered ritually impure *(tamay)*. During the time of the impurity, the impure person was not allowed to come in contact with any other member of the community or to approach the Holy of Holies, which was the dwelling place of God in the Jerusalem Temple.[55]

After the Temple was destroyed, the laws of *niddah* changed and only purity between husband and wife was emphasized. By the time the Talmud was being written, the rule that menstruating women may not touch their husbands (Lev. 15:19–28) had grown stricter. This change was noted in Tractate *Ketubbot:* "R. Ḥananiah stated [in the name of] R. Ḥuna: 'all kinds of work which a wife performs for her husband a menstruant also may perform . . . with the exception of filling his cup, making ready his bed, and washing his face, hands, and feet'" (B. *Ketubbot* 61a).[56]

Levirate Marriage

According to biblical law (Deut. 25:5–10), a woman whose husband died without an heir, male or female, was expected to marry her deceased husband's brother. It was his obligation to father a child in his brother's name. The law of the levirate *(yibbum)* was outlined and expanded in the Mishnah, extending the responsibility to all the brothers of the deceased and not just the oldest.[57]

Although there is no specific evidence that the Hasmoneans followed the laws of levirate marriage, it was later assumed that King Alexander Jannai was a *levir* and his wife, **Salome Alexandra,** had previously been the wife of his late brother, Aristobulus. If this is what happened, it was in accordance with the proper Jewish procedure for levirate marriage, but recently this assumption has been questioned.

Outside of the levirate arrangement, a man was strictly forbidden to marry his brother's wife. One recorded instance of such a marriage became a source of criticism and even bloodshed in Judea in the first century C.E. This was the case of Herod Antipas and **Herodias**, his half-brother's wife.

Ignoring Jewish law, Herodias and Herod Antipas married while her first husband was still alive. The disapproval of John the Baptist, a local preacher who openly spoke out against Herod Antipas and his illegal marriage, angered Herodias. She used her considerable influence with her husband to have John the Baptist imprisoned and later killed.[58]

Monogamy

Ancient Israelite society was polygynous, as were most ancient societies, and laws about women and marriage were based on that presumption. Under Greek and then Roman influence, however, most Jewish men seem to have limited themselves to one wife at a time (but see chapter 1 for an example of polygyny in the land of Israel). There is no evidence that the Hasmoneans practiced polygyny, and Herod, living under the aegis of Rome, took care to divorce each wife before marrying another.

A generation later, Herod Antipas, who also held office with Roman

---

> ## WOMEN'S VOICES
>
> Women's voices were considered indecent and shameful *(ervah)* according to R. Yosef, a talmudic sage. He was quoted as saying:
>
> "If men sing and women respond [i.e., by singing after them or joining in the chorus] it is a breach of law, but if women sing and men respond it is as if a fire was raging in a field of flax."
>
> — *B. Sotah 48a*

---

approval, followed the same custom. When he met and fell in love with Herodias, he sent his first wife, an Arabian princess, back to her father before marrying again. Although this caused a great deal of enmity between Judea and Arabia, Herod Antipas does not appear to have considered polygyny as an option.[59]

Most of the talmudic sages did not practice polygyny, either, and limited themselves to one wife at a time.

Women's Sexuality

Assuring a daughter's virginity until marriage was deemed important in all cultures, and rabbinic opinion was no different. It was considered desirable to isolate unmarried daughters within their homes so they would incur no risk of losing their virginity before marriage. Once married, no matter how young, a girl could move about more freely, but even a married woman's freedom of movement was limited in the interests of propriety. Women were even told not to go out into the fields alone "lest they be taken for harlots."[60]

Paternity and paternal inheritance were vital for the maintenance of the social order, and it was these concerns that determined rabbinic views on women's sexuality. Because patriarchy stresses the legitimacy of offspring, adultery was considered a serious crime. Adultery was addressed originally in the Bible, then elaborated on and interpreted in the Mishnah and the Talmud. The Bible states that adultery occurs when a woman *who is married* is sexually intimate with any man except her husband (Lev. 20:10). The man is not considered to be an adulterer unless the woman is someone else's wife. Therefore, if a married man had a sexual encounter with an unmarried woman, he was required either to marry her (if she gave her consent) or to pay damages to her father for the loss of her virginity (Deut. 23:28–29). Since biblical society was polygynous, it was a simple matter for him to marry her, even if he had several wives.

Only when the woman was already married was this not possible. A definition of adultery, therefore, was dependent on the marital status of the woman and not the man. Her biological function belonged to her husband exclusively. Neither the other man's status nor his faithfulness to an existing wife was at issue. The main concern was paternity.[61]

A man, on the slightest suspicion of unfaithfulness on his wife's part, could bring her to the rabbinic court to undergo a shameful ordeal involving the drinking of "bitter water" (*mey hamarim*). This was water mixed with earth from the tabernacle floor, into which the priestly words of admonition to the woman regarding faithfulness had been washed off from a scroll (Num. 5:11–31). The assumption was that if she was guilty, this infusion would ultimately kill her. If innocent, she would remain unharmed. The biblical ceremony of bitter water and the rituals surrounding it were included in the Talmud (Tractate *Sotah*)[62] but never practiced after the destruction of the Second Temple.

Despite all these unfavorable laws, the Rabbis assumed that women had sexual rights in marriage. Conjugal rights, the accepted translation of the Hebrew *onah*, were variable and depended, at least in part, on the husband's work. The guidelines were outlined in the Mishnah (M. *Ketubbot* 5:6), and it was clear from the text that a man might not deny sexual satisfaction to his wife for any reason without her permission. If he was a laborer, he was obligated to lie with his wife twice a week; a caravan driver did not have the same obligation, but was nevertheless expected to return monthly to his wife's bed, while a sailor was required to make one visit every six months.

LEGAL RIGHTS

Women had few legal rights in public life, but in private transactions they had considerable rights. A woman could own property, but if married, her husband had control of it. She could sue in court, although usually she did not testify herself and was generally regarded as an unfit witness. She did not inherit from her father but was entitled to maintenance by her father's heirs until her marriage. If there was only a small amount of money, her maintenance took precedence (M. *Ketubbot* 13:3).

The Babylonian Talmud reports on a lawsuit between **Ima Shalom** and her brother, Rabban Gamliel, over a

A SISTER'S INHERITANCE

This talmudic story describes a legal suit between Ima Shalom and her brother over a familial bequest.[63]

"Ima Shalom, the wife of R. Eliezer, was Rabban Gamliel's sister. There was once a [Christian] philosopher who had a reputation for not accepting bribes. They came to mock him. She [Ima Shalom] brought him a golden lamp, property that she claimed to have inherited from her family. The philosopher said to them: 'Divide it.' Gamliel said to the philosopher: 'It is written . . . "where there is a son, a daughter shall not inherit."' The philosopher said: 'From the day that you have been exiled from your land, the law of Moses has been withdrawn and another book introduced in which it is written: "A son and a daughter shall inherit equally."' Next day he [Gamliel] brought him an ass and quoted (from Matthew 5:7): '"I have not come to add to the Law of Moses." And it is written there: 'Where there is a son, a daughter shall not inherit."' She [Ima Shalom] said to him [the philosopher]: 'Your wisdom shines like a lamp.' The philosopher answered: 'An ass came and kicked the lamp.'"

—*B. Shabbat 116a–b*

question of inheritance. In this court case, Ima Shalom contested her brother's sole right to the inheritance of family property but lost the case.

While a wife had no legal right to initiate a divorce, she had the right to appoint an agent to accept the divorce (M. *Gittin* 6:1). Following a divorce, she could sue her husband for her marriage portion (*ketubbah*).

An unmarried woman, whether single, divorced, or widowed, was legally autonomous. She could dispose of her own property, sue or be sued in court, and bequeath her property to others.

PUBLIC POWER

Public power was rare for women and was always viewed with suspicion, even if legitimate. When he died, John Hyrcanus, son of Simon the Maccabee and King of Judea, willed total control of the secular government to his unnamed wife (see **Hasmonean Women**). In choosing her, John Hyrcanus followed the Hellenistic model already well established in Ptolemaic Egypt,[64] but she was never allowed to hold that power. Her son Aristobulus, designated as High Priest by his father, imprisoned her along with his younger brothers and allowed her to starve to death while he took total control of the kingdom.

Salome / Shelamzion Alexandra (139–67 B.C.E.), the wife of Alexander Jannai, was more fortunate. Before her husband's death he willed the secular government to her, and the high priesthood to his oldest son, Hyrcanus II. She managed to reign for nine years but not without being constantly challenged by her younger son, Aristobulus II.

Although Salome Alexandra enjoyed some popularity among her people, she did not escape the stereotypes prevalent at that time. Josephus described her as "a woman who showed none of the weakness of her sex," a woman who was "inordinately desirous of the power to rule" and thus had "no consideration for either decency or justice."[65]

Queen Salome Alexandra, the only post-biblical woman to be acknowledged as a ruler, lived long before rabbinic norms were well established. From those early centuries until the time the Talmud was closed, women's right to power in rabbinic Judaism became increasingly restricted.

The Talmud stipulated a clear delegation of function for men and women, with public roles going to the men. This must have seemed reasonable to the Babylonian and Palestinian scholars, who, like most of the men in Mediterranean cultures, viewed women as intellectually inferior, "light-minded," and extremely sexually oriented.[66] Thus women's activities were limited. They were barred from public activities and from the study house, and their exclusion from public life was taken for granted.

RELIGIOUS PARTICIPATION

Women and Communal Religion

While the apochryphal literature of the early centuries does mention some pious women, apochryphal characters are generally believed to be fictional. There is almost no discussion of women's religious activities in the historical literature written during the Hasmonean period or afterward.

The Rabbis of the Talmud considered women less spiritual than men. They were excluded from study and public prayer and could not be counted in a *minyan* of ten or even in a group of three to recite grace after meals. However, outside the rabbinic centers of Babylonia and the land of Israel,

---

THE THERAPEUTIC SOCIETY

In his treatise *On the Contemplative Life* Philo discussed the Therapeutic Society, a monastic sect located on the shore of Lake Mareotis near Alexandria. It included both men (Therapeutae) and women (Therapeutrides). Each member of this ascetic community lived separately in a simple house, praying daily and studying the Bible. They assembled on Sabbath and holidays for a meal and a religious service and used a common sanctuary. A wall extending partway up to separate the men from the women functioned to protect the women's modesty while allowing them to hear the speaker.[67]

Both men and women participated equally in all the activities of the group. In describing the women, Philo stressed that they were "aged virgins,"[68] well educated and devoted to the philosophical life. This leaves open the question of whether they were postmenopausal women who had previously been married and left their families for a life of seclusion, or whether they had never married.[69]

---

there is some evidence that women did participate and even mingle with men in synagogues. The third-century C.E. excavations of the synagogue at Dura-Europos, an ancient city on the Euphrates River, indicate that there was no separate women's section, not even divided benches. The remains of the synagogue at Masada show only a single entrance, suggesting that men and women mingled together there.[70] While this information does little to show the extent of women's participation in synagogue ritual, such evidence, combined with scattered comments from early post-biblical texts,[71] does prove that they were often present in the synagogue.

The only example we have of women fully participating in communal religion is in the case of the **Therapeutic Society.** This group, described by the Alexandrian Jewish philosopher Philo, kept the men (Therapeutae) and women (Therapeutrides) separate but both had equal religious status in the community. However, there is no evidence of their actual existence other than in Philo's writings.[72] If they did exist, they were most certainly a tiny, elite group and functioned well outside the experience of the majority of women.

Women and Folk Religion

Many women did practice a kind of folk religion that combined popular magical practices with aspects of Jewish law. In fact, there was a general belief among both Jews and gentiles that women possessed special talents in the area of magic and that many women were sorceresses.[73] Often, women (and men as well) made use of mystical names and numbers to sum-

> ### A MAGIC INCANTATION FROM THE TALMUD
>
> Abaye said: Mother told me, All incantations which are repeated several times must contain the name of the patient's mother, and all knots must be on the left [hand?].
>
> Abaye also said: Mother told me, Of all incantations, the number of times they are to be repeated is as stated: and where the number is not stated, it is forty-one times.
>
> — *B. Shabbat 66b*

mon divine powers. Charms, amulets, and magic bowls were commonly used to invoke special protections (see chapter 1).[74]

The Bible and the Talmud frowned on the use of magic, and thus the ancient sages' assumption that magic was a part of women's nature was a negative one.[75] Yet despite rabbinic protests, the Talmud itself offers examples of the use of charms and spells and accepts magic as reality,[76] suggesting that the difference between "magic" and "religion" was a matter of who was defining it and who was practicing it.

CHAPTER 3

Jewish Women under Islam:
The Near East, North Africa, and Spain to 1492

OVERVIEW

The Growing Jewish Diaspora

Egypt, Syria, and Babylonia had large and well-established Jewish communities by the seventh century C.E. Smaller settlements could also be found throughout the Middle East, North Africa, and west along the northern Mediterranean coast. The Jews in these communities lived in diverse situations with varied lifestyles, but the position of women tended to be relatively similar everywhere.

Women could attend synagogue and were allowed a degree of **religious participation.** There was as yet no consistent separation of the sexes for prayer—at least not in the land of Israel.[1] However, much evidence points to Jewish women's continued isolation from public life. As can be seen below, even women who gained some degree of fame because of their accomplishments or through a propitious marriage were routinely left unnamed in contemporary reports. This was totally consistent with the position of gentile women in the societies of the Near East and North Africa and represented little change from earlier centuries.

The Rise of Islam

Women's status was hardly altered even after the middle of the seventh century, when Muhammad, an Arabian from the Hashemite clan (571–632 C.E.), created a new religion: Islam. Based partially on the monotheistic teachings of Jews and Christians, Muhammad's new religion recast first the Arabian Peninsula, then the entire Middle East, and would ultimately affect most of the Western world.[2] Although Muhammad did establish some legal protections for women, the new Muslim culture made their isolation in the home and their subservience to men a matter of Islamic law.

After Muhammad's death in 632, his followers crossed the borders of Arabia, conquering and converting the peoples of the neighboring lands. Once Islam controlled the Middle East, Arab culture and trade began to flourish, first under the unified rule of the Umayyad Caliphate (661–750) and then the Abbasid Caliphate (750–1258). The scattered and diverse Jewish communities of the Diaspora also became more unified and enjoyed a parallel cultural growth. Widespread improvements raised the economic position of the Jews, giving them specific rights. Under Arab rule, Jews along with all other minority groups became *dhimmis*, restricted but also protected.[3]

Babylonia

In the eighth, ninth, and tenth centuries, under Muslim rule, Babylonian Jewish power reached its highest level. Muslims allowed the Babylonian Jews almost complete self-government, although the *Resh Galuta* (Exilarch) had to have the formal approval of the sultan after being chosen by the Jewish community.

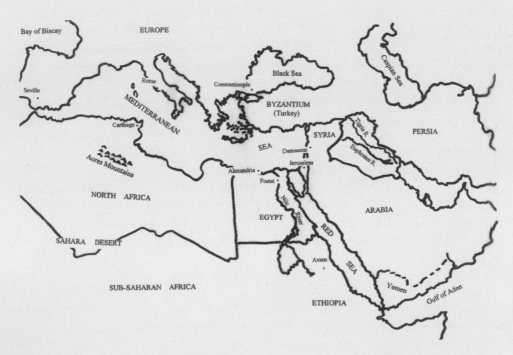

FIG. 5. After the rise of Islam, the Jewish communities of the Middle East became more united.

The *Resh Galuta* appointed judges and collected taxes from the Jews, but he shared his power with the two most important scholars *(geonim)*. The *geonim* headed the major academies in Babylonia and answered queries put to them by Jews and Jewish communities throughout the Diaspora. Because they used the new compilation, the Talmud, as the basis for their legal decisions, they spread knowledge of talmudic law to communities all over the world. The *geonim* did not make any radical changes in the customs of the times, but because they actively worked toward consistency of Jewish practice, the laws and standards they imposed affected all Jews living in the lands of the Diaspora.

By the mid–eleventh century, the influence of the *geonim* had already begun to wane. Jewish immigration to Egypt, North Africa, and other Diaspora communities increased, and Babylonian Jewry went into a decline from which it never recovered. But the geonic rulings, made over the course of four or five centuries, remained standard practice throughout most of Europe and the Middle East.

Arabia and Yemen

Jews had been living in northern Arabia and Yemen from the period of the Second Temple. Like the Arab population, they were organized according to clans and tribes. Despite a high degree of assimilation, including a common language and culture, the Jewish tribes were considered a separate group.

Jews seem to have influenced some Arab tribes to accept monotheism and to observe the Sabbath. Therefore, it was not always clear whether monotheistic tribes or individuals were Jewish. Assumptions were sometimes made by non-Jewish historians with little factual evidence beyond the knowledge that these groups or individuals worshiped a single God or celebrated one or two Jewish rituals. **Sarah,** the Yemenite poet, may fall into this category.

In northern Arabia, most of the Jewish tribes lived in or near the oasis city of Medina and were prosperous date farmers.[4] When Muhammad first began his major proselytizing campaign in Medina, the first Jewish tribe to be conquered was the *Banu Qaynuqa*, who were quickly defeated and allowed to emigrate to Syria. Shortly after, the *Banu l'Nadir* were forced to surrender, but the Arabs allowed them to leave for Khayber, another Jewish stronghold in Arabia, with all their movable goods except for weapons.

The last Jewish tribe to be defeated by the Muslims was the *Banu Qurayza*. All the *Qurayza* men were slaughtered and the women and children sold into slavery or traded for weapons. This event is referred to in the Koran as the victory of Muhammad over "those who have received the Scriptures" (Koran, 33:26). The place in Medina where they were killed is still called "Market of the Qurayza."[5]

WOMEN OF THE BANU L'NADIR

Instead of going off humbly, as a conquered tribe was expected to do, the *Banu l'Nadir* "paraded through the heart of Medina to the music of pipes and timbrels. Their women unveiled their faces to flaunt their renowned beauty and sported all their finery."[6]

This description gives us one of the earliest glimpses of the Jewish women living in tribal Arabia in 622. Those same women, who were reported to have proudly marched off with their tribe, had the misfortune of being captured and enslaved two years later when the men of the *Banu l'Nadir* were slaughtered in Khayber by the Muslims.

North Africa

From the second century B.C.E. North Africa (called the Maghreb in Arabic), had been part of the Roman Empire. When Rome became Christian in the mid–fourth century, all other religions were outlawed. This persecution created a natural alliance between the pagan Berber tribes and the Jews who lived there as seminomadic farmers and warriors. In those formative years, when the development of talmudic or rabbinic Judaism was in its infancy, the identity of Jews was less exact and sometimes problematic, as can be seen in the case of **Dahiya Kahina.** Although it is unlikely that any Berbers were converted according to Jewish law, many were heavily influenced by Jewish practices and beliefs.[7]

After the death of Muhammad and the conquest of Syria, Babylonia, and Egypt, the army of Islam turned to North Africa. Prince Ḥassan, the leader of this military campaign, was told that the *Jerawa*, a judaized tribe led by Dahiya Kahina, was the strongest in the region. He determined to destroy them in order to secure the rest of North Africa. It took him five years to accomplish that goal.

After the defeat of the Jerawa, Jews continued to live in the Maghreb, and especially in the new Arab city of Kairouan,[8] but resentment of the Arab occupation by the local North African population continued. The Arabs were finally driven out in 909 and replaced by an indigenous dynasty: the Fatimids.

Egypt

Although part of North Africa, Egypt was an entity unto itself, with a long history that began at the dawn of civilization and a tradition of strong women who ruled, most commonly as co-regents, but often independently. The famous Cleopatra was only one of the Egyptian queens.

After gaining power in Egypt in 909, the Fatimids built a new capital city not far from Fustat, the original capital, and named it Cairo. Jews, who had lived in Fustat in large numbers, now began moving into the newer, more prosperous center, and Cairo eventually overshadowed Fustat. This population transfer created an unplanned archive: the Cairo Genizah. The Genizah preserved a great deal of evidence about Fatimid culture, including letters and papers showing a wide range of activities of both Muslim and Jewish women. In fact, one of the important discoveries to come out of studies of the Genizah documents was the significant position that some Jewish women held in Egypt.

THE CAIRO GENIZAH

The Cairo *Genizah* (hiding place or storage place) was an attic storeroom in the Ibn Ezra synagogue in Fustat, an ancient town that had once been the center of Jewish life in Egypt. Such a storehouse developed because it was (and remains) Jewish practice never to deliberately destroy any document that might contain the name of God, but to store the papers until they could be properly buried in the ground.

But as the old Ibn Ezra synagogue deteriorated, the contents of its storeroom were gradually forgotten and remained unburied. In 1752, still intact, the storeroom was rediscovered but no one realized what a treasure it held until the 1890s, when it was brought to the attention of Solomon Schechter, a famous Jewish theologian and talmudist.[9] Schechter identified a centuries-old fragment of the Hebrew text of Ben Sira's *Ecclesiasticus* from the papers that were brought to him and decided to travel to Cairo. There, the heads of the Jewish community permitted him to transfer a large portion of the contents from the Ibn Ezra synagogue back to England for serious study. The archive contained documents and manuscripts dating from the tenth to the sixteenth centuries.[10]

Maimonides: Egypt's Most Famous Jew

R. Moshe ben Maimon, popularly known as Maimonides, lived in Fustat, Egypt, during the twelfth century and is generally considered one of the most illustrious figures in Judaism since the closing of the Talmud. He was born in 1135 in Cordova, Spain, but as a result of anti-Jewish persecution, his family left that city when he was thirteen years old. Moshe's formative years were spent wandering through Spain and North Africa.

Moshe, with his parents, brother David, and sister Miriam, finally settled in Fustat in 1165.[11] There, he devoted himself to study and writing until his brother, who had supported him, died at sea. Maimonides then became a doctor and eventually was appointed personal physician to members of the royal court.

Maimonides seems to have married shortly after his brother's death. It was a second marriage, to the sister of Ibn Almali,[12] one of the royal secretaries. The couple had one son, Abraham. Neither this wife nor his first wife, who apparently died young, are known by name, and they played no part in his public life. In fact, Moshe ben Maimon disapproved of any **public power** for women and stipulated in his writings that women should not be appointed to any communal office.[13]

In his replies (responsa) to the questions addressed to him by members of the Jewish community, Moshe ben Maimon revealed many aspects of his attitudes toward women, much of it more restrictive than the prevalent custom. Because Maimonides came to be such an influential figure, both during his lifetime and after, his strict interpretations became accepted tenets in Judaism. They remained valid long after the more relaxed customs of Fatimid Egypt were forgotten.

Muslim Spain

The Iberian Peninsula was invaded and conquered by the Arabs in 711. From that time, Spain and its small Jewish population came under the rule of the Arab caliphate, strengthening its ties with the Muslim East.[14]

Jews fared better under the rule of Islam than they had under Christianity. After Spain broke away from the East to establish its own caliphate in 929, the Jews enjoyed a period of prosperity and creativity that exerted considerable influence, both positive and negative, on the women of the community.

By 975, the now large Jewish community of Muslim Spain was united and relatively strong. The study of Torah and Jewish law was widespread,

---

MAIMONIDES: LEADER AND AUTHOR

Besides his work as a doctor, Moshe ben Maimon was head of the Jewish community of Fustat for many years and was also a prolific writer. His best known works are:
- *Mishneh Torah*, completed in 1180
- *Guide of the Perplexed*, completed in 1190
- *Sefer ha-Mitzvot (Book of the Commandments)*
- *Iggeret Teiman (Letter to the Jews of Yemen)*
- *Ma'amar Tehiyyat ha-Metim (Treatise on the Resurrection of the Dead)*
- Numerous letters and responsa

and Arabic literature and poetry were popular. The Jews of Spain created Hebrew laws of grammar; wrote poetry in Hebrew, some of it in direct imitation of Arabic poetry; and translated the most important literary and scientific works of the period from Greek and Arabic into Hebrew.[15]

But by the twelfth century, Muslim Spain, having lost substantial territory to Christian invaders, was taken over by the Almohads. The Almohads were Muslim Berbers who tolerated neither Christians nor Jews. To escape their brutality, many Jews migrated north, where expanding Christian governments were ready to utilize their financial skills. Other Jews fled to the lands of the more tolerant Muslim east as had Maimonides' family. Large numbers were converted or killed in the pogroms of 1391 and later. As Christian Spain conquered more Muslim areas, Muslims either converted or emigrated and most Jews lived under Christian domination.

Finally, in 1492, the Christians captured the city of Granada, the last bastion of Muslim power in Western Europe. With the fall of Granada, Muslim rule in Spain came to an end. Later that same year, the new Christian rulers, King Ferdinand and Queen Isabella, expelled all Jews who refused to convert.

BIOGRAPHIES

BAT HA-LEVI OF BAGHDAD, SCHOLAR
(12th century)

This unnamed woman, referred to in documents only as *Bat ha-Levi* (daughter of the Levite), was the child of the Gaon of Baghdad, Shmuel ben Ali. Writings about her relate that she lived in Baghdad in the twelfth century and was well educated in Bible and Talmud. Travelers reported that she lectured the students at her father's academy from behind a screen or from an adjoining room, so that the young men would not be distracted from the law by her lovely appearance.[16]

A lamentation, written after her death by R. Eleazar ben Yaakov ha-Bavli, described her as a woman who was distinguished by her many virtues and her rare wisdom.[17]

BIBLE TEACHER OF FUSTAT
(12th century)

This woman, who remained unnamed in the documents, is known from two separate queries, both addressed to R. Moshe ben Maimon (Maimonides).[18] The first letter, from her husband, described her as a wife who had been working outside the home as a teacher (*mu'allima*) without her husband's consent. She began teaching in her brother's school while her husband was away on business for almost four years. When he returned, he informed her that he felt her work was improper. As he explained: "I fear that their [the pupils'] fathers . . . will come to visit the children, and you will be in an embarrassing position because of them, and I do not want this, neither for my sake nor for your sake."

EULOGY FOR BAT HA-LEVI

Heartfelt sorrow brought forth
A sigh that broke the heart of all the
* universe*
On the death of the precious lady
A source of wisdom and pride to the
* nation.*
And for the humble people who were
* protected within her shadow,*
The sons of man and all the chil-
* dren of the womb,*
Was she not like eyes to the blind
And as a tongue to the mute.
And the eyes of the universe were
* lighted by her light*
And there were tremendous visions
* of evil.*
Did not her fragrance spread to the
* far corners of the land,*
Like cinnamon and all the best per-
* fumes.*
And she brought mysteries to light
And uncovered the hidden.
*   —R. Eleazar ben Yaakov*[19]

According to the letter, the Bible Teacher became angry and "refrained from doing her duties—those which the daughters of Israel must perform for their husbands—but she persisted in teaching the children at her brother's from morning until evening." In other words, her husband described her as a recalcitrant wife, a *moredet*, someone whom he could divorce without paying her *ketubbah* money.

The teacher's husband, however, did not want a divorce, perhaps because his wife owned the home in which they lived. Instead, he wanted to marry a second wife and bring her into their home even though the Bible Teacher's marriage contract stipulated that he must pay her *ketubbah* if he took another wife or concubine.

The answer Moshe ben Maimon gave to the Bible Teacher's husband is clear: He could not take a second wife without the permission of his first wife unless he divorced her and paid her *ketubbah*, but he could prevent her from working.

The Bible Teacher did not agree to this decision, however, and had her own letter sent to Maimonides.[20] It told a different story and filled in a few more details of her life.

She was orphaned as a young child and had inherited property from her parents that she owned jointly with a relative who also became her guardian. At the age of nine, she was married to one of the sons of this relative/guardian. At sixteen, with a young son, she had no support either from her husband, who had been traveling through the Middle East for three years, or from the guardian. After her husband's return, he still failed to support her, although the couple had another son. Then he disappeared once again, leaving the young mother penniless.

It was at this time that she "asked her brother to let her teach the children Bible with him, so that she would have a means of sustaining herself and her sons, since she was already near to death from the misery in which she was enveloped, and he [the husband] was absent."[21]

The woman's letter ended by asking whether she had to leave her profession and return to what she had in the beginning. "Does she have to fulfill his needs and serve him," inquired the letter writer, "when he does not provide her with food or drink or clothes and does not do a thing for her that is said in the Torah?"

Moshe ben Maimon's brief answer to this query conceded that the Bible Teacher was entitled to teach, but showed little sympathy for her position. His reply suggested that she employ one of the few marginal methods available to a woman who wanted a **divorce** but sheds no light on the final outcome of her dispute.

DAHIYA KAHINA OF NORTH AFRICA, TRIBAL PRINCESS AND WARRIOR
(early 8th century)

Named Dahiya or Kahiya bint (daughter of) Thabitah ibn Tifan, this woman warrior was called the *Kahina*, a word meaning prophet or soothsayer.[22] She was the leader of the *Jerawa*, considered by some to be a Jewish tribe although most historians label them as "judaized" rather than Jewish.[23] Reports about Kahina, the Jewish woman warrior, developed and spread throughout North Africa and beyond. Because her name was later confused with the Hebrew *kohen* (priest), it offered still another reason to connect Dahiya with the Jews.

According to the traditional story related by Arab historians, Dahiya Kahina united many of the Jewish, Christian, and pagan tribes of the Maghreb into a single army that successfully drove back the Muslims. This victory made her the virtual queen of the region, and she ruled for five years. Her reign was harsh and difficult, and when the Muslims attacked again, they had already managed to divide the early alliance. Kahina was killed in battle, and her sons, along with most of the Berber population, eventually converted to Islam.[24]

A JEWISH FOLK SONG ABOUT
KAHIYA

An old ballad sung by the Jews of
the Maghreb recalls Princess
Kahiya's bloodthirsty reputation.

O! Sons of Yeshurun!
Do not forget your persecutors
The Chaldeans, Caesar, Hadrian,
*   and Kahiya —*
That accursed woman, more cruel
*   than*
All the others together
She gave our virgins to her warriors,
She washed her feet in the blood of
*   our children.*
God created her to make us atone
*   for our sins.*
But God hates those who make His
*   people suffer.*
Give me back my children so that
*   they can mourn me.*
I left them in the hands of Kahiya.[25]

Whether Dahiya Kahina was a Jew,
a Berber convert to Judaism, or a
monotheist practicing a combination
of religious traditions cannot be confirmed.[26] Like many of the North
African tribes, the *Jerawa* very likely
followed syncretistic practices and
were not considered Jews by the standards of the more sedentary, established Jewish communities. This
would explain the total absence of any
mention of this woman warrior in
Jewish records, while the Arabic
sources claim she was a Jew.

DAUGHTER OF JOSEPH OF BAGHDAD, MYSTIC
(early 12th century)

Information about the Daughter of
Joseph is available to us only through a

single letter, written on the back of an
old deed and addressed to a recipient
in Fustat, Egypt. It tells a curious story
concerning an unnamed woman from
Baghdad known only as "the daughter
of Joseph, the son of the physician."[27]

The letter describes a young woman
believed to be the Messiah but does
not give her name. It was sent in
approximately 1121, sometime after
the event itself, in the years when the
power of Babylonian Jewry was
already seriously diminished.

The writer explained that during a
period of trouble between the Jews
and the Muslim caliph over taxation,
an attempt was made to reactivate the
rules concerning the special clothing
that Jews were required to wear. As a
result of this dispute, the entire male
Jewish population of Baghdad (probably numbering no more than two or
three hundred by this time) was
imprisoned.

Suddenly, the daughter of Joseph, a
pious young woman who had led an
ascetic life and had only married under
pressure, saw a vision of the prophet
Elijah. The appearance of Elijah has
always been accepted as the forerunner
of the Messiah, and the Jewish community became convinced that this
woman herself was their redeemer.

The caliph, after threatening to have
her burned, had a dream that caused
him to change his mind. He ordered
the Jewish prisoners released and
withdrew his demand for additional
taxes. Here, the letter breaks off and
we know nothing more about the fate
of this young woman.

MIRIAM BAT MAIMON, SISTER OF MAIMONIDES
(12th century)

Miriam was the only sister of the
great Rabbi Moshe ben Maimon

(Maimonides). She left Spain in the mid–twelfth century together with her family, settled in Fustat in 1165, and was married to a royal secretary of the caliph's court, referred to as Ibn Almali in documents of the period.

Only one letter, written in her name and found in the Genizah collection, gives us any clues to her personal life. The letter is an appeal to her brother, begging him to search out her son, who had disappeared and had not written to her. Miriam begged Moshe to contact him and convince him to write.

Since Miriam had the letter written by a scribe, it is clear that her own education did not equal her brother's. Furthermore, it was written only in her name rather than together with

---

A MOTHER SEARCHES FOR HER SON

. . . And if you saw me you would not recognize me because of my rotten condition and [lack of?] strength . . . And the reason is the matter of the disappearance of my son. My knowledge of him is as one who lives in a pit. No letter has come from him to me. . . . And I think that you can help me in this matter, because your status is all-encompassing and your right is the greatest. Let me know how he is and where he lives. If he is in the place graced by your presence tell me please. And if he is absent in another place send him my letter and a letter from you with words of reproof. Please write me and tell me what you know about him.[28]

—*Miriam, Sister of Maimonides*

---

her husband, and thus we can assume that she was either a widow or was divorced.[29]

AL MU'ALLIMA OF TOLEDO, TEACHER
(11th century)

Al Mu'allima (the Arabic word for teacher) was a Karaite, unknown except for a single mention in the work of R. Abraham ibn Daud, a Spanish-Jewish writer of the twelfth century. She was the wife of the Karaite leader Abu l-Taras and lived in the city of Toledo between 1050 and 1090.

Al Mu'allima was learned in the Karaite version of Jewish law, and Abu l-Taras's followers relied on her for authoritative tradition after his death. According to Ibn Daud: "They would ask each other what the Mu'allima's usage was, and they would follow suit."[30]

In spite of the Mu'allima's knowledge, she is referred to as the "accursed wife" of Abu l-Taras. This pejorative term is most certainly due to the fact that Ibn Daud was a Rabbanite and she was a Karaite, a sect that was in opposition to rabbinic Judaism.

QASMUNA OF GRANADA, POET
(11th or 12th century)

Qasmuna is one of very few women poets known from the period of Jewish cultural expansion in Spain. Only three of her short poems, all in Arabic, have been preserved. They suggest that she was quiet and gentle but with a lively intelligence. She tended to be melancholy and often felt lonely.

One scholar, who believes that Qasmuna's father trained her in the art of poetry, offered the following anecdote: Qasmuna's father would compose two lines of a rhyming poem and have her complete them with another rhyming couplet. One example of that method shows the father's two lines:

I have a friend whose [woman] has repaid good with evil,
Considering lawful that which is forbidden to her.

Qasmuna's answering lines were:

Just like the sun, from which the moon derives its light
Always, yet afterward eclipses the sun's body.[31]

In this poem, Qasmuna deftly turned a complaint about a woman into an astronomical metaphor, revealing her cleverness and a good foundation of knowledge in the natural sciences as well as in literature. Her father was allegedly delighted with Qasmuna's lines. It was reported that he embraced her, showered her with kisses, and declared: "You are a greater poet than I!"[33]

Qasmuna never married. Some writers have suggested that she was the daughter of Shmuel ha-Nagid (Samuel ibn Naghrilah) and that she died in June 1044, during an epidemic of smallpox.[34] More recently, Dr. Norman Roth gives the date of her writings as post-1100. This precludes any possibility of her being the daughter of Shmuel ha-Nagid, although Roth concedes the remote possibility that she may have been his great-granddaughter.[35]

SARAH OF YEMEN, POET
(7th century)

Partly because of the questionable origins of many Yemenite Jews in those early centuries, there is some doubt as to whether this seventh-century poet actually was a Jew. Sarah may have fallen into the category of persons who were judaized rather than Jewish,[36] but despite doubts about the legitimacy of her Jewish ancestry, the few details of her life suggest an involvement with Jews and Judaism.

In addition to being a poet, Sarah reputedly participated in a guerrilla action against Muhammad before a Muslim agent killed her.[37] The subject of her one extant poem, which eulogizes the *Banu Qurayza* and relates their history, suggests that she herself may have been a member of that tribe. Only one small segment of that poem remains. It is the earliest example of a long legacy of Yemenite Jewish women's poetry.

WIFE OF DUNASH BEN LABRAT
OF SPAIN, HEBREW POET
(10th century)

This poet was not only literate in the Hebrew language—a skill not routine-

---

TWO POEMS BY QASMUNA

A garden whose harvest time has come,
No harvester can be seen to extend a hand to you.
Alas! Youth passes and is wasted, while one remains—
I will not name him—who is alone.

Oh deer, you who graze constantly in the meadows,
I resemble you in wildness and in blackness of the eye.
Both of us are alone, without a friend; and
we heap blame always on the decree of fate.[32]

ly taught to women—but she could write in Hebrew as well. Her name has not been preserved, but she left a single Hebrew poem that attests to her ability, her sensitivity, and her love for her husband.

Dunash ben Labrat was one of the great masters of Hebrew letters. Although he was a scholar of North African origin, the couple lived in Spain. Dunash helped to establish a system of Hebrew grammar and was also an innovative and well-respected poet writing on religious and secular themes. The first to apply the form of Arabic poetry to Hebrew, he created a poetic style that was adopted and used throughout the Middle Ages.[38]

A controversial man, Dunash ben Labrat was forced to flee Spain, perhaps at the suggestion of Ḥasdai ibn Shaprut.[39] His wife was not pleased with the prospect of being left alone with a baby. She wrote her poem in approximately 950, probably right after his departure, while the details of their farewell were still fresh.

The tone and words display a high level of talent, and the poem, part protest and part love song, is a unique example of a Hebrew poem authored by a woman.

WUHSHA OF EGYPT, BROKER
(11th–12th century)

Wuhsha began life as Karima (the Dear One). She was the granddaughter of the head of the Alexandrian Jewish community and daughter of Ammar (*Amram* in Hebrew) of Alexandria, a banker.

The earliest Genizah document concerning Wuhsha is her marriage contract to Arye ben Yehudah. Because she was one of at least three daughters and two sons, her dowry was modest

---

SARAH'S POEM MOURNING THE BANU QURAYZA

Sarah's poetic style is typical of Arabic poetry of the time. It is based on an intricate system of rhyme, meter, and syllable length that is very difficult to maintain in translation. Nevertheless, Sarah's feelings of loss and sadness over the *Banu Qurayza*, "obliterated by the wind," still come through.

*By my life, there is a people not
    long in Du Ḥurud,
obliterated by the wind.
Men of Qurayza destroyed by
    Khazraji swords and lances,
We have lost, and our loss is so
    grave, it embitters for its people
    the pure water.
And had they been foreseeing, a
    teeming host would have
    reached
there before them.*[40]

The recitation of oral poetry was common among the mostly illiterate Jewish women of Yemen. Their poems relied heavily on well-established themes and literary conventions, intertwined with Hebrew quotations and stories to which they added their own political commentary.[41] It is the one strong, female tradition that has persisted in Yemen until modern times.

---

and so was Arye's marriage gift.[42] The couple had a daughter, Sitt Ghazal, but their marriage was relatively brief and in a different document, only a few years later, Wuhsha was referred

A RARE EXAMPLE OF A
WOMAN'S POETRY

*Will the beloved remember his
graceful gazelle
as on the day they parted, while she
held the boy on her arm?
He put the ring from his right hand
on her left while she put the
bracelet on his arm.
When he took her cloak as a keep-
sake and also took her chain as
a token.
Will there remain in the entire land
of Spain its lord Dunash,
Even if he takes one half of the kingdom with him?*[43]
—*Wife of Dunash ben Labrat*

to as "the divorcée of Arye ben
Yehudah."

The exact dates of this marriage and
divorce are unknown, but clues are
available from other documents. Arye
ben Yehudah remarried and in 1095
divorced his second wife. In that same
year, records indicate that Wuhsha
gave birth to a son from what was
referred to as "an irregular liaison."

The details of this relationship are
revealed in an undated document that
came to light only after Wuhsha's
death. It attests to the fact that "al-
Wuhsha, the broker" came before a
certain cantor and said: "Do you have
any advice for me? I had an affair with
Ḥassun and conceived from him. We
contracted a marriage before a Muslim
notary, but I am afraid that he may
deny being the father of my child."[44]

The cantor advised her to arrange a
tryst with Ḥassun and prepare witnesses to catch them in the act. The
witnesses were named in the docu-

ment, and it was presumably filed
away for the future.

By means of this official text,
Wuhsha's son, Abu Sa'd, was assured
that his birth was not the result of any
illegal union that might mark him
officially as a *mamzer* and thus unable
to marry a Jewish woman. Wuhsha's
marriage to Ḥassun was legal only in
a Muslim court but had not been performed according to Jewish law. The
probable reason for this was that
Ḥassun's first wife would not agree.

Wuhsha's actions in this matter
must have been a scandal in the community. Her notoriety caused her to be
expelled from the Babylonian (Iraqi)
synagogue on that Yom Kippur of
1095. Her wealth and prominence,
however, seem to have offset her reputation and given her more license than
most women of her time could expect.

Wuhsha never married again, and
when she died, she was in possession of
a large estate, including property, movable goods, and cash, some of it in gold.
In her will, she bequeathed large sums
of money to Fustat's four synagogues,

WUHSHA'S WILL

In her will, Wuhsha left these
detailed instructions concerning her
son's education:

"The *melammed* (teacher), Rabbi
Moses, shall be taken to [my son]
and shall teach him the Bible and
the prayer book to the degree it is
appropriate that he should know
them. The teacher shall be given a
blanket and a sleeping carpet so
that he can stay with him. He shall
receive from the boy's estate every
week five dirhams."[45]

the Jewish cemetery, and the poor. Her relatives and their children received token amounts, but Wuhsha left instructions that "not one penny shall be given" to Ḥassun , the father of Abu Sa'd.[46] The bulk of Wuhsha's estate was set aside for this son, still a minor, who was to get proper Jewish training.

In addition to providing for her son's education and the maintenance of his teacher, Wuhsha's will stipulated detailed instructions for her own funeral, an exorbitantly expensive affair for which she set aside fifty dinars. She estimated the price of a new burial outfit for herself and the cost of the coffin and pallbearers, and ordered "cantors walking behind me and chanting, each in accordance with his station and excellence."[47]

Wuhsha is certainly not typical, but rather an exceptional example of the extent of power and freedom a Jewish woman could gain in Egypt.

THE WORLD OF JEWISH WOMEN

ECONOMIC ACTIVITIES

Marriage and a quiet life, away from the public eye, remained the fate and the desired goal for women, both Jewish and Muslim. Most female roles were limited to managing households and helping husbands in their work. Yet women, especially in Egypt, did have opportunities for a working life outside the home.

While Jewish women certainly did not enjoy equality, and their professional opportunities were much narrower than those available to Jewish or other minority men, they did often function in a variety of occupations. Women might be doctors, midwives, undertakers, or textile merchants. They were also valued as professional mourners, to follow the funeral bier wailing.[48] Bride comber was another possible occupation. The skills of the bride comber were needed to help with the elaborate dressing and combing of the bride before her wedding.

Some women also worked as textile brokers, visiting the homes of other women to buy and sell their wares or trading the material in bazaars. The bazaars of medieval Egypt were busy markets, and many working women depended on them for freshly cooked foods when they could not afford to keep a servant and lacked the necessary time to prepare meals.[49]

A small number of the better-educated women might work as teachers, as was attested by Maimonides' response to the **Bible Teacher.** As we see in his responsum, however, the husband would need to agree to any economic activity in which his wife was involved, and had the power to prevent her from working outside the home.

Sometimes, a marriage contract stipulated that a wife might work for her

---

A RULING ON MOURNING CUSTOMS

Maimonides stipulated that when a man's wife dies, he is obliged to arrange, as the minimum funeral, "a eulogy and lamentations . . . including two flute players and one wailing woman." This must be done even if the family is very poor.[50]

own money or to provide herself with clothing, but in general, a husband was required to support his wife.

Poor Women

Cases of neglected, abandoned, or otherwise destitute women show up often enough in the Genizah collection, indicating clearly that these were not a rarity. In cases of great need, women petitioned the head of the community for support. During the first half of the twelfth century a poor woman claimed: "I hereby inform your excellence and greatness that I am a blind woman with a blind child . . .They demanded from me the poll tax and we two do not even have bread. . . ."[51]

AN APPEAL FROM A CAPTIVE WOMAN

During the twelfth century the Crusades resulted in many captives who were held for ransom. Since it was a commandment *(mitzvah)* to redeem captives, the Jewish community regularly raised money for this cause, and no captive was left unransomed. But for women, the ransom was often only half the battle, as this letter indicates:

". . . I hereby inform the holy congregation—may God enhance its splendor—that I am a woman who was taken captive in the Land of Israel. I arrived here a week [ago] from Sunbat and have no proper clothing, no blankets, and no sleeping carpet. With me is my little boy, and I have no means of sustenance."[52]

Turayk, daughter of Avraham, a woman with no resources of her own, lived in the home of a certain merchant in Fustat for over ten years, entirely at his expense. Another woman had been maintained by the community and given a home on the synagogue grounds.[53] Still others were the victims of war or various misfortunes. According to the Genizah records, a fairly large number of Jewish women received alms from community funds.[54]

EDUCATION

Some girls received a partial education during this period. Although the Talmud did claim that "he who teaches his daughter the law, teaches her *tiflut* (frivolity/obscenity)" (B. *Sotah* 20a), Rav Hai, a tenth-century Gaon, was concerned with the education of girls as well as boys.[55] While girls were not educated in depth, they were required to know the laws and their meanings so that they could follow the commandments and be "kosher women of Israel."[56] This education was mainly the responsibility of the girl's mother and usually ended when the daughter left her parents' home to be married, sometimes as early as nine or ten years old as was the case with the Bible Teacher.

Occasionally, reports surfaced concerning young women who were well educated. A Jewish convert to Islam wrote about his mother and her two sisters, natives of Basra, who were "proficient in the scriptures and in Hebrew calligraphy."[57] They were certainly exceptions, as was **Bat ha-Levi,** the daughter of Shmuel ben Ali, Gaon of Baghdad in the twelfth century.

Stories of learned women, repeated throughout the centuries, only served to highlight the rarity of such women and were not presented as role models. Most women married young and had little time for the formal learning of traditional texts.

It was apparently more common for women to be educated in Egypt than in some other parts of the Middle East or North Africa, and women, especially poorer women who had to support themselves, could sometimes work as teachers of children in either boys or girls schools.

There is evidence that teaching was an accepted occupation for women— even for married women. Most female teachers, like the anonymous Bible Teacher, taught only the rudiments of literacy, perhaps some Bible stories, and the reading of a few prayers. Some instructed girls in embroidery and needlework.

One Arabic source from eleventh-century Cairo refers to female teachers (*mu'allimat*) in the plural and mentions a school called the "Synagogue of the Women Teachers" where reading and writing were taught to children between the ages of four and thirteen.[58]

A few female teachers might have been as well educated as men, but they were always exceptional. A teacher in Fustat was sufficiently literate to be able to write her own query to a rabbi, something that was unusual, even for learned men.[59] Maimonides own sister, **Miriam,** used a scribe to write a letter to her brother.

Other letters reveal that ordinary women, although disadvantaged in education themselves, were often deeply and sincerely concerned with their children's education and proper upbringing in Jewish values. Such concern was sometimes extended to female children also.

In Muslim Spain, educated women were relatively uncommon and even

---

A LETTER FROM A DYING MOTHER

In a letter from a dying young mother, addressed to her sister in Fustat, we read the following words:

"My most urgent request to you, if God the Exalted indeed decrees my death, is to take care of my little daughter and make efforts to give her an education, although I know well that I am asking you for something unreasonable, as there is not enough money for maintenance, let alone for education. However, she had a model in our mother, the saint."[60]

Jewish women born into learned or rich families, those most likely to be learned themselves, rarely gained prominence. The poets, **Qasmuna** and the **wife of Dunash ben Labrat,** as well as the Karaite woman teacher in Toledo **(Al Mu'allima)**, were among the very few who gained any public attention.

FAMILY LIFE

Betrothal and Marriage

The *geonim* dealt with many issues relevant to Jewish communities, but among the most vital were the laws of betrothal and marriage. Many of their rulings still survive today as models and remain the standard for the behavior of Jewish women in traditional communities.

Geonic rulings attempted to standardize the marriage vow as well as the minimum amount of money that might be given to the woman in her *ketubbah*. They also tried to set the procedure for betrothal and marriage.

Rav Hai Gaon (939-1038) ruled that no matter where a Jew lived, he could not be married without a *ketubbah* (the required sum of money) and a *ketubbah* document. This was the custom of the Jews of Babylonia. If someone did not follow that practice and married without benefit of a *ketubbah* document, ". . . they will punish him until he fixes the matter."[61]

Men were expected to be able to support a wife before they committed themselves to marry,[62] and it would

---

THE ROLE OF A GOOD WIFE

The role of a good wife was spelled out very specifically by Rav Yehudai (Gaon at Sura in 757), who wrote:

"Women are obligated to honor their husbands, nurse their children, and feed their husbands even with their own hands; to launder and cook, as the sages said: 'a woman grinds [flour] and bakes, etc.' And when her husband enters she must stand up and is not permitted to sit down until her husband sits, and she is not permitted to raise her voice to him, and even if he beats her she is to keep still, as modest women do. And they are obligated to make themselves attractive for their husbands, to put blue color on their eyes and anoint themselves with perfume so that his heart will turn to her and she will be beloved to him as she was on the day she came to the *ḥuppah* [marriage canopy]."[63]

---

seem that most did so. Before the marriage, the groom pledged a set amount of money or goods to his wife (the *tosefet*) in the event that the marriage was dissolved, either by death, divorce, or abandonment. A father was expected to pledge a more or less equivalent amount for his daughter at the time of her marriage.

The bride's family's contribution was referred to as the dowry (*nedunya*). It was available for the use of the husband but always belonged, technically, to the wife, and together with the principal payment (*ikkar*), established from biblical times, acted as a kind of insurance policy.

Both the bride's dowry and the groom's payments, part paid in advance (*muqdam*) and part promised in the future (*muḥar*), made up the *ketubbah*. These sums would be returned to the wife in case of death or divorce.

Children

The rights of fathers in the marriage arrangements of their daughters, first stipulated in the Mishnah and Gemara, were reiterated and elaborated on by the *geonim*. For example, the *geonim* confirmed the absolute right of fathers over their daughters' marriage arrangements and allowed a father to marry off a minor daughter (a girl under twelve years) by acting on her behalf even at the ceremony itself.[64] The Bible Teacher, who lived in Fustat, Egypt, was orphaned as a young child and married at the age of nine to the son of her legal guardian.

Young women, including those up to twenty years old (well beyond the average age of marriage), were expected to follow their fathers' wishes in choosing a marriage partner. "There is no such thing as rebelling, or *ḥutzpah* among the daughters of Israel, that she may reveal her opinion and say 'I want so-and-so.' Rather, she depends on her father."[65]

Divorce

Divorce remained solely a male prerogative in Babylonia and its area of influence during this period, and it was generally easy for a man to obtain a divorce. Rav Hilai (Gaon at Sura in 896) decreed that if a married man wanted to marry a second wife and his first wife would not agree, he could simply divorce her provided he sent her off with her *ketubbah* money.[66]

Moshe ben Maimon's preliminary advice to the husband of the Bible Teacher confirmed this husband's right to divorce his wife if she did not perform her duties, namely "kneading and cooking and making the bed and cleaning the house; washing clothes and fulfilling her duties to her children. . . ."

He further insisted that "the court is required to admonish her and to deter her from [working outside the home]." In fact, he makes it clear that "if she sues for divorce because her husband prevents her from teaching, her request will not be granted. On the contrary, all doors are locked before her and all paths are to be obstructed, and her affairs will be delayed for as long as it takes until she withdraws and agrees to behave properly toward her husband."[67]

There is still scattered evidence from the Genizah that the right of a woman to sue for divorce could be included in her marriage contract. This tradition was found among Jews originating in the land of Israel, but such examples are not numerous.[68] A Jewish woman

---

A STANDARD DIVORCE CLAUSE IN A PALESTINIAN *KETUBBAH*

If this Sa-id, the groom, hates this Maliha, does not desire her, and wants to separate from her, he shall pay her all that is written and specified in this marriage contract completely. And if this Maliha hates this Sa-id, her husband, and desires to leave his home, she shall lose her *ketubbah* money, and she shall not take anything except that which she brought from the house of her fathers alone; and she shall go out by the authorization of the court and with the consent of our masters, the sages.[69]

---

could also obtain a divorce by going to the gentile courts. The Jewish community always frowned on this method, but documents attest to the fact that it was often used.

Another alternative was for the wife to become a *moredet*, a rebellious woman. A *moredet* signified a woman who did not obey her husband. She might act in unbecoming ways such as wandering about the streets, talking with men, or gossiping. Such a woman might not make herself available to her husband for sexual intercourse or refuse to perform the household duties required of a wife.

The original talmudic ruling stipulated that a *moredet* must be warned of the consequences of her actions once a month over a period of twelve months. Each week that she did not comply, her *ketubbah* payment was reduced by a set amount until none was left. Then, if she did not alter her behavior, her husband could divorce her, paying nothing except her dowry.[70] Later on, Rav Sherira (Gaon at Pumbeditha in 968) adjusted this law to eliminate the waiting period.[71]

When Maimonides advised the Bible Teacher to accept the label of *moredet* and let the courts grant a divorce without any *ketubbah* payment, he was, in effect, explaining how she could obtain a divorce without her

---

A DESPERATE PLEA

This query, written in Egypt and found in the Genizah, was addressed to a rabbi. It related a story of nonsupport as well as a campaign to malign the reputation of a simple *mu'allima* (teacher). The letter, written by the woman herself, reads in part:

"I hereby inform your Excellency, our Gaon . . . that I am a lonely orphan girl whom they have married to a man with no means of support. I have been with him for ten years, and he has always taken what I earned. Finally, when I was in shreds with nothing to cover me properly, I said to him: 'I shall not give you a thing anymore. I'll buy myself clothing with what I earn.' He is not worth a thing, not even one dinar. For a year or more he has given me a bad name. I went to the judges and offered to buy myself free with everything due me from him to save my honor. But they did not grant me a divorce. By God, my honor is worth something to me!"[72]

---

husband's specific agreement. In most instances of divorce found in the Genizah, if the wife is repudiated and labeled a *moredet*, it is because she has initiated the divorce against her husband's wishes.[73]

Besides becoming a *moredet*, a woman could initiate a "ransom divorce," called in Arabic an *iftida*. This involved the woman simply giving up the *ketubbah* payment promised in the original marriage contract in order to obtain a divorce.[74] Women, it seems, were often willing to give up this promised payment if it would enable them to be rid of husbands who failed to support them, or beat them, or were impossible to live with in other ways. Moshe ben Maimon agreed. ". . .She is not like a captive," he said, "to be forced to engage in intercourse with someone she hates."[75]

The Laws of Levirate Marriage

The only area in which the law seems to have acted directly in the service of women was in the case of the "unfortunate widow," left alone with her husband's debts and little money besides her *ketubbah*. If that happened, her late husband's debtors could not collect until her *ketubbah* was paid. In other words, her *ketubbah* constituted a previous lien on her husband's property that superseded any other debts he had incurred.

Moreover, if her *ketubbah* was small, the burial expenses were to be paid by the community and not from her own resources unless she specifically wanted to pay them.[76]

If the widow was childless, however, and her husband had a surviving brother, the issue was more complicated. She was then expected to marry her brother-in-law, who had the obligation of fathering a child as a proxy for his dead brother so the name of the deceased relative "may not be blotted out in Israel" (Deut. 25:5–10).

This custom of levirate marriage, called *yibbum* in Hebrew, was upheld in varying degrees throughout the ages. In biblical times it was the preferred solution. If the dead man's brother refused, he was forced to perform a ceremony called *ḥalitzah* officially releasing the widow, who was then free to remarry. During Mishnaic times (200 B.C.E.–200 C.E.) the tendency was to prefer *ḥalitzah* over levirate marriage, and if either party did not want to marry, that person's wishes were followed and no penalty was inflicted.

In Babylonia, opinion on this issue was divided, but while the *geonim* never explicitly forced the woman into an unwanted levirate marriage, some did declare that if she refused, she would be considered a *moredet* and would not be entitled to the *ketubbah* payment. This ruling was issued in separate cases by Rav Netronai, who ruled that she might nevertheless retain her dowry, and by Rav Sherira (Gaon of Pumbeditha).[77] Rav Aharon (Gaon of Pumbeditha in 943) made a more favorable ruling. He insisted that the woman receive her *ketubbah* whether or not she agreed to *yibbum*, for "she is no different from the rest of the widows in the matter of the *ketubbah*, though the levir must give her permission to [marry] others."[78]

Clearly, geonic decisions varied over the centuries. Beyond Babylonia, other communities tended to favor one or the other option, depending on the custom in each place.

THE SAGES' VIEWS ON WOMEN

The Babylonian sages and the *geonim*, like the earlier sages of the Mishnah, believed that one of women's most important purposes was to serve men and that this traditional arrangement was most conducive to household peace. Such ideas represented a mind-set that guarded, first and foremost, the well-being of the family but also assumed that the interests of the family and the interests of the man of the family were identical.

Monogamy

After the rise of Islam, polygyny became more common and women now had even fewer protections from divorce, mistreatment, or their husbands' sexual liaisons. These changes in the status of women were part of the cultural transformation engendered by the new Islamic religion.

In some marriage agreements, especially those contracted in Egypt during the Fatimid period, a first wife did have limited control over a husband's subsequent marriages. This was highlighted in the case of **Wuhsha** and Hassun. It can also be seen in Moshe ben Maimon's answer to the husband of the Bible Teacher, stating that he might not take a second wife without the permission of his first wife unless he divorced her and paid her *ketubbah*.

Violence Against Women

A well-known ruling stipulates that if a woman fails to perform the minimum

BLESSING FOR A NEW BRIDE

The *geonim* mandated a special ceremony following the consummation of a marriage to a virgin. This ceremony, probably originating in the land of Israel,[79] required proof of the bride's virginity and the recitation of a blessing.[80] It was never included in the Talmud but was widely practiced throughout the Middle East and parts of Europe. The custom was confirmed by a responsum offered by Rav Hai, who called it "a received tradition among the sages."[81]

The ceremony was full of biblical references to the Song of Songs and Proverbs and was conducted following the consummation of the marriage, when the bridegroom brought out the bloodstained sheet. It included a blessing to God "who placed the walnut in the Garden of Eden, the lily of the valley, so that no stranger shall have dominion over the sealed spring." The blessing ends with an additional allusion to fertility: "Blessed are You, Lord, who chooses the descendants of Abraham." This ceremony is closely connected to the biblical and talmudic concern with a wife's infidelity and the legitimacy of offspring.

the wife was unquestioned and widely accepted within both the Jewish and Muslim communities.

Women's Sexuality

Men who married young women expected them to be sexually pure, and fathers guarded their daughters' virginity with great care, keeping them close to home as much as possible. An unchaste woman brought dishonor to her family, and if evidence of sexual indiscretion was discovered on her wedding night, her bridegroom was entitled to send her back to her father's house.

The sages saw any break with the traditional ideal of female modesty and chastity as a threat to the husband and to family continuity and well-being. Thus, a girl who was not a virgin at marriage, as well as a rebellious or recalcitrant wife, a *moredet*, represented major dangers that had to be addressed with special laws.

Occasionally, women managed to circumvent the laws. This was the case with Wuhsha of Egypt, a divorcée who scandalized the Jewish community by giving birth to a son without benefit of a Jewish marriage. She later established the child's paternity by arranging for witnesses to surprise the father in a potential sexual encounter with her.

Documents from Muslim Spain also show sexual activity by women that did not meet the normative standards set by the *geonim*. The "Jewess" with whom the Arab leader Sa-id ibn Djudi was said to have been "dallying" when he was killed remains nameless and unknown.[83] Other women who had lovers or were sexually promiscuous are known only from responsa, where specific names are never mentioned.[84]

wifely duties—washing her husband's hands and feet and serving him his meals—she can be chastised with rods.[82] This physical chastisement of

As the Jewish population flourished, Jewish-gentile contact increased. A few Jewish women became concubines to Muslim or Christian men, and Jewish prostitutes were not unknown.[85] A still more common occurrence was for Jewish men to seek the company of Muslim women as mistresses and concubines.[86]

Most Muslim women involved with Jewish men were servants or slaves, but some were not.[87] If children resulted from these unions, the woman might be converted to Judaism so the children would be Jewish. Although the Spanish rabbis disapproved of this practice and of concubinage in general, claiming that it led to the "abuse of lawful Jewish wives," the practice continued.[88]

LEGAL RIGHTS

In the Fatimid Empire, Jewish women appear generally to have had more rights than in other areas of the Middle East such as Babylonia and the land of Israel. For example, in contrast to the older, Roman custom requiring women to have a male guardian in court, women in Fatimid Egypt could appear in court on their own recognizance. An outstanding example of such a right is evidenced in documents concerning Wuhsha, a prosperous Jewish woman who lived at the height of Fatimid rule.

Interacting with both women and men, Wuhsha was well known by court officials and several records of her lawsuits remain. In one, dated June 30, 1104, she held a share in a business deal worth 800 dinars and sued for her

---

A LETTER TO A WIFE

In one of the rare personal letters found in the Genizah, a husband pleaded with his wife to join him in the capital where he had an opportunity for an appointment. He addressed her with the utmost love and respect and with the understanding that she had the right to refuse his request.

"I am writing to you, my lady, my dear, crown of my head and my pride—may I never be deprived of you, for you cannot imagine how I yearn for you. May the Creator, the Exalted, make easy what is difficult and bring near what is far away, for He knows what is in my heart.

Of late, my yearning has become so strong that I am not able to bear it any more. I want you to know this.

Therefore, put your trust in God and come to me, solely because you rely on Him and for no other reason. For I am confident that God, the Exalted, will not forsake me, even when I am alone, far less when I shall be accompanied by a pious and valorous woman such as you. Therefore, do not tarry, but come. A woman who has a husband whom she knows is religious and God-fearing and loves her is expected to assist him. I spare you by saying no more. . . .

Please do not neglect me. . . . In short, there remains no one who loves and encourages me except you."

Despite his pleas, this wife would not give in and later documents find him back in his provincial town, where he became a judge.[89]

share. In another venture, the total of goods involved amounted to twenty-two camel loads, of which only 11,000 pounds had arrived at the time the court recorded her claim. Some of her holdings consisted of loans for which she held collateral.⁹⁰

Married women also had many rights in Egypt that were not routinely accepted in the geonic culture of Babylonia. For example, a first wife often had specific safeguards written into her marriage contract. One was the woman's right to refuse permission for her husband to take a second wife. Another right was the right of choice of residence granted to many brides. This protected them from being carried off to another town or even a foreign land in the interests of a husband's business.

Occasionally, a woman chose to live in the town where her own birth fami-ly resided even if this was in opposition to her husband's wishes. Such disagreements could, of course, end in **divorce** if the husband was insistent, but if the right was written into the marriage contract, obtaining a divorce would be more difficult.

Women's Wills

In Fatimid Egypt, women commonly made their own wills. An outstanding example of this is the will of Wuhsha the broker. Wuhsha bequeathed large sums of money to Fustat's synagogues, the Jewish cemetery, and the poor. The bulk of her estate was set aside for her son, and provisions were made for relatives and their children.

Wuhsha's will gave detailed instructions for an expensive funeral but omitted any bequest either to her

---

A SISTER'S LETTER

The unknown writer of this eleventh-century letter offered no apology for her sisterly advice; nor did she relate anything about the family that might indicate their discontent with her decisions. Her power within the family is evident.

". . . Now, what you wish to know, dear brother: Your family is in the best of circumstances. Najiya is as you like her to be and more than that, and so is Maulat.

May God fulfill all the hopes you have for them and may He let me see a son of yours in the very near future. . . . Najiya never ceases to speak about you—may God unite you with her and fulfill your hopes for her—but Maulat is prettier than Najiya.

Dear brother, although you need not be reminded, send [your children] all that is fit for them and likewise to their mother.

To Abu l-Fadi—may God preserve him—another girl was born, and I called her by the name of my mother, Surura (Happy). May she come into a happy and blessed home and may the two [girls] be happy and blessed and may God give you and him whatever will make you proud [i.e., sons]. Abu l-Surur (Isaac) became a father and called his son Barhun (Abraham)—may God keep him alive and let his father witness his wedding. . . . Bring an appropriate present for him [the newborn], a prayer book or a part of the Bible. . . ."⁹¹

daughter, Sitt Ghazal, or to Hassun, the father of her son.

Daughters commonly received their inheritance in the form of a dowry at the time of marriage rather than at the death of a parent. However, there was often a token amount left in the will itself, sometimes to a daughter's children.

PUBLIC POWER

Women in the Muslim world had almost no public presence. Even noblewomen remained secluded, and any influence they might have exerted was indirect. Perhaps because women lacked public power, historians in subsequent eras may have dramatized **Dahiya Kahina**'s military victory and her atypical accomplishments as a leader. Even though she ruled for only five years, she was later referred to as "Queen of the Maghreb."

Within the family, however, Jewish women sometimes held esteemed places and played influential roles. One such example was an unnamed woman living in Kairouan in the eleventh century who seems to have been the unofficial matriarch of her extended family. She advised her brother about personal relationships, recommended gifts he should bring back to family and friends, and had the privilege of naming the female children in the family (see p. 70).

RELIGIOUS PARTICIPATION

Documents give us few clues as to the reality of women's religious experiences. Although we know from the

> ### A CHARM FOR PROTECTION
>
> This charm, found among the Genizah treasures, appeals to the forces of the zodiacal sign Leo:
>
> ". . . to prevail against all harmful spirits and those which cause pain and sickness to the woman Ḥabibah bint Zuhra . . . to drive away all kinds of demons and demonesses . . . and every sort of fear and trembling. . . ."[92]

Cairo Genizah that women commonly dedicated Torah scrolls, contributed large sums of money to charity, and headed committees for building and repairing synagogues, there is as yet little evidence of their involvement in public prayer or their personal spirituality.[93] The meager reference to the vision of the **Daughter of Joseph** describes a rare event and is certainly not typical of women's religious participation.

More commonly, women worried about the dangers to which poverty, disease, and calamity could lead. Despite official male criticism, they continued to protect themselves with a variety of charms and amulets. Many such artifacts were found among the Genizah's treasures. Often written on pieces of parchment, amulets invoked the spirits and demons on behalf of the supplicants, most of whom were identified by the names of their mothers.

CHAPTER 4

Farther from Home:

Jewish Women in Christian Europe to 1492

OVERVIEW

The First Jewish Communities in Western Europe

From the population centers of the Middle East and North Africa, Jews slowly migrated to the northern shores of the Mediterranean. Italy, Spain, and Provence were the first to receive Jews. From there they spread into northern Europe. What began as a trickle grew into a steady flow, and by the ninth and early tenth centuries Jews were moving into Europe in larger numbers.

In European towns and cities Jewish families usually lived close to one another. By the late tenth century the number of Jews in some areas was sufficient to enable them to form small, self-governing communities, many with a local sage to interpret Jewish law. The information we have about women during this period comes mostly from rulings and responsa written by these sages.

The Jewish communities issued their own rulings and created their own courts, administered individually by local Jewish leaders who managed all the community's religious, political, and financial affairs. After the feudal lord had imposed his tax on the Jews as a group, the local leadership assessed and collected it, taking an assigned amount from each head of household. Once the obligation of taxes was met, the Christian secular government was rarely involved in internal Jewish concerns during this early period.

Jewish Learning and Jewish Sages

Serious scholarship among the Jews of northwestern Europe lagged behind that of the Middle East and Italy, but by the tenth century, there were some recognized sages in northern Europe. The most noted among them were R. Gershom (960–1028) of Mainz (Germany), referred to as "the light of the exile" *(me'or hagolah)*, and R. Shlomo ben Yitzḥak (Rashi) (1040–1105) of Troyes (northeastern France). R. Gershom made many rulings favorable to women that still remain part of Jewish law. Rashi, after studying in Germany for many years, returned to Troyes and set up his own school.[1] From that time, eastern France began to vie with western Germany as a center of Jewish scholarship.

Rashi became one of the most noted and prolific teachers of his day. He wrote commentaries on the Hebrew Bible and on the Talmud, and his collected responsa laid out the problems and solutions of his time and offered precedents that are still in use today.

Although Rashi had no sons, two of his three daughters, **Yoḥeved** and **Miriam,** married their father's disciples. Their sons became famous in their own right as scholars and as commentators on Jewish law. They were included among the *Tosafists* (meaning "those who added"). The Tosafists' commentaries (the *Tosafot*), written during the course of the twelfth to fourteenth centuries, are included in most editions of the Talmud.

The Crusades

Outside of a few isolated attacks, Jews lived relatively undisturbed in Europe until Pope Urban II launched the first Crusade in 1096. This Crusade engaged a large part of the noble classes of northern Europe and their armies. Fired by religious zeal, crusaders marched eastward to liberate the Holy Land from the hands of Muslim infidels. On the way, they killed hundreds of German Jews or forced them to convert.

A large number of Jewish women martyrs are connected with these anti-Jewish actions. Some women not only killed themselves but also their own children, preferring their children's deaths to the possibility of their conversion.

The crusading armies conquered Jerusalem in 1099 and established a short-lived Crusader kingdom there. In later attempts to win back the Holy City, several other major Crusades were launched, each less successful than the previous one. The Crusade of 1291 led to disaster for the Christians. After that, Crusades continued to be called, but they were never as large or as organized as the earlier ones. Nevertheless, many took their toll on the lives of Jewish women, men, and children.[2]

In many ways, the Crusades established the tone of Christian-Jewish relations in the high and late Middle Ages. Jews looked on Christians with more suspicion and hatred. Christians considered Jews different and evil, people to be shunned and punished, and anti-Jewish violence escalated. However, the Crusades did have some positive results. A brisk trade developed in the wake of the continual traffic between East and West, and Jews as well as gentiles benefited from it. With this increase in trade, commercial activity involving women also increased considerably.

The exchange of goods brought with it a cultural exchange as well, introducing to the West the more developed civilization of the East. Hebrew translations of the works of Greek and Arabic philosophers, doctors, mathematicians, and poets found their way into Europe. Subsequently, some of these works were translated from Hebrew into Latin, and knowledge of them became more widespread.

Anti-Jewish Rulings

Despite the economic benefits resulting from the opening of trade and the beginning of a commercial revolution in Europe, the position of the Jews in the northern part of the continent became increasingly unstable. With the expansion of the Jewish population and their growing participation in the economic life of European towns and cities, Christians began to resent Jews. Debtors begrudged the amount of interest they had to pay Jewish lenders. Such economic and social intolerance, encouraged by the Church's anti-Jewish policy, precipitated unrest among the population and often led to violence. The unrest, in turn, became a convenient tool to further a government's economic policy, or simply cancel out a ruler's debt to his Jewish subjects.

When the presence of Jews in certain areas of northern Europe became too difficult or too controversial, the Jews were expelled. England sent

---

THE JEWS OF GERMANY AND THE BLACK DEATH

The spread of the bubonic plague throughout Germany in the mid–fourteenth century precipitated the false accusation and subsequent murder of Jews as poisoners of wells and spreaders of the Black Death. There were anti-Jewish riots in Augsburg and Munich in 1348 and in the Rhineland in 1349. Jews experienced the worst massacre in Strasbourg, then part of western Germany, when 2000 men, women, and children were burned. One document reported:

"On Saturday—that was St. Valentine's Day—they burnt the Jews on a wooden platform in their cemetery. There were about 2000 people of them. Those who wanted to baptize themselves were spared . . . many children were taken out of the fire and baptized against the will of their fathers and mothers. And everything that was owed to the Jews was cancelled. . . ."[3]

away their Jews in 1290; parts of northern France did the same on several occasions during the fourteenth century. Thus, the European Jewish population moved eastward. The spread of plague through central Europe in the mid–fourteenth century precipitated still more killing of Jews and more scattered expulsions.

The largest and most tragic of the expulsions was the order issued by King Ferdinand and Queen Isabella in 1492. This decree demanded that the Jews of Spain either convert or leave the country.

By the end of the fifteenth century the European Jewish population was centered primarily in parts of Germany, Italy, Poland, Bohemia, and Austria. Many of the *Romaniot*, the Greek-speaking Jews of the Eastern Empire (Byzantium), pressured by repeated wars and persecutions, migrated into the Balkans and southern Russia.

BIOGRAPHIES

ALLEGRA OF MAJORCA, BOOK OWNER
(14th century)

Allegra of Majorca (Spain), wife of Abraham Crespi the shoemaker, was one of the few non-noblewomen in medieval Europe to own a medical book. In a modern survey of records for book ownership (from 1229 to 1550) in Majorca, Allegra is listed in a 1388 entry as the owner of two books. One was the "Five Books of Genesis," and the other was a book referred to in the same list as *Catonim,* which is thought to be *Me-hanhagat ha-ne'arim haqetannim,* a Hebrew translation of al-Rāzî's book on children's illnesses. Allegra may have been a doctor who specialized in the diseases of children.[4]

ÇETI OF SARAGOSSA, SYNAGOGUE OFFICIAL
(14th century)

Çeti of Saragossa (Spain) was referred to as "rabbess of the female Jews" in documents of the period. She had held this post for twenty years or more. Çeti probably tended the women's section and the ritual bath in the Saragossa synagogue, a position that would have been highly regarded by the community.[5]

DOLCE OF WORMS, PRAYER LEADER
(12th century)

Dolce was a learned and pious woman. She had no official position in the Rhineland Jewish community of Worms, but as the wife of R. Eleazar of Worms, a prominent rabbi, she would have been an authority for other women even beyond her own town. Dolce supported her husband and children as a moneylender but also

---

R. ELEAZER'S EULOGY FOR HIS WIFE DOLCE

[The words in bold type indicate quotes from the biblical passage in Proverbs 31, on which his poem is based.]

. . . **Her husband trusts her implicitly,** she fed and clothed him in dignity so he could sit among the elders of the land, and provide Torah study and good deeds . . . Zealous in everything (she did), she spun (cords) for sewing tefillin and *megillot,* gut for (stitching together) Torah scrolls; quick as a deer she cooks for the young men and attends to the students needs; . . . She freely did the will of her Creator, day and night; **Her lamp will not go out at night**—she makes wicks for the synagogue and schools, and she says Psalms; she sings hymns and prayers, she recites petitions; daily (she says) confession, "*nishmat kol ḥai*" and "*ve-khol ma'aminim*"; She says "*pittum ha-qetoret*" and the ten commandments; In all the towns she taught women (so they can) chant songs; she knows the order of the morning and evening prayers, and she comes early to the synagogue and stays late; she stands through Yom Kippur, sings, and prepared the candles (beforehand). . . .[6]

FIG. 6. The Worms Synagogue, where Dolce led the women in prayer, was one of the earliest synagogue structures that had a separate room for women. Destroyed during World War II, the synagogue has been carefully rebuilt, using the original stones and materials wherever possible.

acted informally as a teacher and conducted prayers in the women's section of the synagogue.

Dolce died a violent death in 1196. In a report following the murder, her husband related:

> . . . I was sitting at my table, two marked men came to us, and they drew their swords and struck my saintly wife, mistress Dolce. . . . And they wounded my head and my hand, on my left side, and they wounded my students and my schoolmaster. Immediately the saintly woman jumped up and ran out of the winter quarters and cried out that they were killing us. The wicked ones went out and cleaved her in the head from the windpipe to the shoulder and from the shoulder to the waist, across the width of the back and her front, and

the righteous woman fell dead. And I secured the door, and we cried out, until help should come to us from heaven.[7]

Although the house was full of men including students, a schoolmaster, and Dolce's husband, it was Dolce who ran out to call for help. R. Eleazar locked himself in the house and prayed.

After Dolce's death, her husband wrote a poetic eulogy in her honor that was modeled after the biblical passage "A Woman of Valor" (Prov. 31). Based on information about her in this poem, we can surmise that Dolce may have been an early precursor of the Jewish woman prayer leader (*firzogerin*) who functioned in the women's section of the synagogue. Several other *firzogerins* from this period are known from records or tombstones.

ESTHER DE CAYLAR OF ARLES, JEWISH COUNCIL MEMBER
(15th century)

Esther de Caylar, the granddaughter of Bonjues Nathan, head of a prominent Jewish family, lived in Arles, in southern France. Probably because of her important family connections, she was authorized to participate in the general assembly of the heads of families in Arles in 1407, a post usually held by the male head of family. During that time, she shared in a decision to select a schoolmaster.[8] Her daughter **Venguessone Nathan** was a successful businesswoman.

FLORETA CA NOGA OF ARAGON, DOCTOR
(14th century)

Na Floreta Ca Noga, a prominent Jewish woman doctor of St. Coloma de Queralt, was physician to the Queen of Aragon (Christian Spain). A record shows that in 1381 she was paid fifteen gold florins "for the successful treatment of the queen."[9] ("Na" is the version of "Doña" in the local dialect; Floreta's name is always preceded by this form of address in the literature about her.)

FROMMET OF ARWYLLER, SCRIBE
(15th century)

Frommet of Arwyller copied a Hebrew code of laws for her husband. Little is known of Frommet's family or of Frommet herself; only that she was literate in Hebrew and had a fine handwriting. The inscription in her book reads: "This copy has been executed by Frommet, daughter of Arwyller, for her husband, Shmuel ben Moshe, 1454."[10]

ḤAVA / ḤANA OF MANOSQUE, SURGEON
(14th century)

Ḥava or Ḥana was a surgeon and part of a prominent medical family. Among the documents of Manosque (Provence), one record reports that a certain Ḥava (or Ḥana) intervened to rescue a wounded Christian gentleman by the name of Poncius Porcelli. He had been hit in the most intimate organs of his body and the court wanted to know whether Fava [sic] had actually palpated the wound. Luckily, she could answer in the negative because her son Bonafos had assisted her during the treatment. She gave instructions and assigned the necessary medicines, while her son did the actual handling.[11]

HENNDLEIN OF REGENSBURG, TEACHER
(15th century)

Henndlein of Regensburg (Germany), active in approximately 1415, was called *di meistrin* in official documents.[12] Although this term could mean rabbi, in this case she was probably a teacher and ran a school for girls or for young children of both sexes. There is no evidence of other female teachers, or of girls being taught outside the home during this period.

KANDLEIN OF REGENSBURG, COMMUNITY LEADER
(14th century)

Kandlein was a widow whose family was among the largest taxpayers in the town of Regensburg (Germany). She was a prominent moneylender and, after her husband's death, became one of the appointed leaders of the Regensburg Jewish community, a post she held for at least two years. She was also a member of the council that set the taxes for all the Jews in the town, regulating which Jews should be allowed to settle in Regensburg and how much they should pay for the privilege.

Kandlein obtained her authority from the Council *(Rat)* of Regensburg and wielded her power especially among newly settled Jews. In lists of community leaders, her name was always mentioned first and her son was known by his mother's name: Yoslein, the son of Kandlein.

Neither the exact date of her birth or her death are certain, but records indicate that she was murdered shortly after October 8, 1358, when she was last mentioned in a Regensburg record. By January 3, 1364, loan documents refer only to Yoslein, the son of Kandlein, but not to Kandlein herself.

Her murder is reported in a plea about missing documents that came before the *Rat* of Regensburg in

August of 1365. In that claim, Friedrich der Schikchenberger and his brother Hans testified that their documents had been lost with others in Kandlein's possession "when that Jewess was murdered a fair while back in her house among the Jews."[14]

LICORICIA OF WINCHESTER, MONEYLENDER
(13th century)

Licoricia was already considered the richest Jew in Winchester by the late 1230s, when she was still quite young. This would imply either an inheritance from her natal family or a large *ketubbah* after the death of her first husband. A document indicates that by 1239 she was an active moneylender.[15]

In 1242, Licoricia married again, this time to David of Oxford, one of the richest Jews in England. But within two years of the marriage, David was dead. His goods and money were sent to the Exchequer for evaluation, and Licoricia herself was placed in custody. This was to ensure that she would not flee with her husband's wealth before taxes were paid.

She was released only after several prominent Jews pledged security for her obligations, but she had to pay a vast amount in death duties to Henry III. A significant portion of that money was used for the rebuilding of Westminster Abbey.

For the next thirty-three years, Licoricia continued as a prominent moneylender. She was active in much of southern England, mainly lending on her own, sometimes in partnership with one of her sons. She handled large sums of money and made loans to members of the royal family. Licoricia's "direct relationship with the King and the Court, her extensive and successful transactions, her coop-

---

CREDIT FOR A JEWISH LENDER

Licoricia, a Jewess of Winchester, is to receive credit [at the Exchequer] for the ten pounds that was owed her by [the monks] of St. Swithin's, Winchester, whose pledges [for payment of that debt] she delivered to Brother Geoffrey of Winchester in 1239, and which Brother Geoffrey then delivered to the monks of St. Swithin's.

—*Calendar of the Liberate Rolls, 1240*[13]

eration with the principal Jewish bankers of the day—mark her as an outstanding personality. "[16] She was at least fifty-three years old when she died.

Licoricia and her Christian maidservant, Alice, were murdered during a robbery in 1277. Both women were killed "by a blow to the chest made by a knife to the heart."[17] The bodies were discovered by Belia, Licoricia's daughter. Although the secular authorities conducted an investigation and Licoricia's belongings were locked for safekeeping, a few men subsequently "broke the doors and locks" of the house. They then "seized and carried off the goods and chattels of the aforesaid Licoricia and other Jews, which chattels were of the king and amounted to £10,000."[18]

MERECINA OF GERONA, POET
(15th century)

Merecina of Gerona (Spain) is a Hebrew poet whose single poem, dated prior to 1492, is still extant. It is prefaced with the words: "This song was made by 'a woman of virtue,' the lady Merecina, the Rabbiness from Gerona." The title Rabbiness may indicate that Merecina was the wife of a rabbi or, like Çeti, the caretaker of her synagogue.

We have no other information about Merecina and do not know the date of the writing itself. However, a line such as "Keep slander far away from me" suggests that it may have been written during the fourteenth century, when forced conversions were commonplace in Christian Spain, and the Inquisition was watching every move of the newly converted Jews in an attempt to prevent them from backsliding.[19]

A WOMAN'S POEM FROM MEDIEVAL SPAIN

Merecina of Gerona's poem, written in Hebrew, draws on several biblical passages, especially Psalms, and also shows some knowledge of later rabbinic literature.

Blessed, majestic and terrible
  you established the Torah in Israel;
happy are they who seek your
    shelter,
  they do not forget the Lord's will.
Salvation is far from the evil . . .
  though they've known of your
    Learning and Law;
the sowers in tears will soon exult
  they trust in Him who enables.

It has spread abroad—
  quickly plead, O Lord, my cause
with those who say from Gehenna:
    Give . . .
  Our God determines who will
    prevail.

He is seen, he strikes, and then
    heals,
  applies the balm before what
    comes;
exhausts alike the weak and strong,
  and restores well-being to Israel.

I will say what I must, and tell
  the truth to him who taunts me.
Keep slander far away from me;
  Grant peace to the people of
  Israel.[20]

MINNA OF WORMS, MARTYR
(11th century)

The chronicler of the pogrom at Worms that occurred during the first Crusade described Minna as an important and worthy woman, not only in the Jewish community but in the general community as well. She entertained the nobility in her home and was respected even by the men who threatened her life. She, along with many other women, chose to die rather than convert to Christianity.[21]

THE MARTYRDOM OF MADAME MINNA

A worthy woman lived [in Worms] and her name was Madame Minna. She hid in the cellar of a house outside the city. And there gathered unto her all the people of the city and said to her: "Behold you are a woman of valor—know now that God no longer wants to save you. The dead lie naked in the street and there is none to bury them. Defile yourself (a pejorative expression for baptism)." They fell on the ground before her as they did not want to slay her since her name was known far and wide since at her house were found all the great ones of the city and the nobles of the country. And she answered and said: "Far be it for me to deny God in Heaven. For His sake and for His sacred Torah slay me. Delay no more."

—*Crusade Chronicles*[22]

MINNA OF ZURICH, MONEYLENDER
(14th century)

In the middle of the fourteenth century, Minna, the widow of Menaḥem from Zurich, lent money in partner-

ship with her two sons. Theirs was one of the richest families in town, and Minna owned a house on *Kleine Brunnengasse* with a grand salon and murals painted on the walls.

She also raised substantial amounts of money, and one of her loans had the value of eight to ten large town houses. The bilingual seals that Minna's sons used were indicative of their high social position.[23]

NATHAN, VENGUESSONE, MERCHANT AND MONEYLENDER
(15th century)

Venguessone Nathan, daughter of **Esther de Caylar** of Arles (Provence), was a very rich woman. Her property included a house, a vineyard, and a shop where she sold drapery and crockery. She also owned books in both Hebrew and Latin. Venguessone was an active moneylender, and when she died, the money owed to her from debts and pledges was included in her will.

Venguessone's son, Isaac, had a great deal of money of his own, and so her largest bequests went to her grandsons. Her unmarried granddaughters received money for their dowries (probably in addition to what their father would contribute). Her married granddaughters, having already been given Venguessone's contributions to their dowries, received twenty-five florins for clothes for their first birthing, probably a layette.

Outside of family legacies and after stipulations concerning her place of burial and her tombstone, Venguessone made several charitable bequests. These included money for the cemetery, a light for the synagogue, ten florins for the crown of the Torah scroll, and money for dowries of poor brides.[24]

PULCELINA OF BLOIS, PROMINENT WOMAN
(12th century)

Long believed to be the lover of Count Theobald V of Blois (1152–1191), Pulcelina may be one of the few Jewish women whose place in history rests on a possible sexual liaison with a man. She lived in the northern French town of Blois, and her name appears in several records attesting to some relationship with the count.

The Hebrew report that involved Pulcelina tells of a blood libel charge precipitated by a Christian servant who mistakenly assumed that an untanned hide was a dead child. The servant ran to tell his master, who, according to the Hebrew document, said: "Now I can wreak my vengeance on that person, on that woman Pulcelina."[25]

When Count Theobald was informed of this event, "he became enraged and had all the Jews of Blois seized and thrown into prison. But Dame Pulcelina encouraged them all, for she trusted in the affection of the ruler who up to now had been very attached to her."[26]

Historian Susan Einbinder is presently questioning whether or not Pulcelina and Theobald were actually lovers. Einbinder's theory is that the word *ohev* in the document means "favor" and not, as commonly assumed, "sexual love." She believes that Pulcelina lent money to the count and possibly to the countess and other nobles and that this accounts for her arrogance "to all who came to her."[27]

Whichever theory is accepted, however, there is no doubt that Pulcelina had some power in the community. One of the documents reported: ". . . with her rested the authority of the ruler like a rock, and she behaved

proudly with everyone . . ."[29] Pulcelina was bitterly resented by both the local lord and the count's wife, Alix, who "swayed [Count Theobald], for she also hated Dame Pulcelina."[30]

EXCERPTS FROM VENGUESSONE NATHAN'S WILL

- . . . to Crescas, her house with its well, free of all taxes and, in addition, two hundred florins.
- . . . to Bonjues, a vineyard in St.-Medard, all her books in Latin, one hundred florins to buy Latin books if he continues to study Latin, and two hundred florins.
- . . . to Crescas and Bonjues . . . all her jewels (of gold, silver, and pearls), and all her silver-plate (vases, goblets, etc.).
- . . . to Astrug and Salomon, her two other grandsons, all debts, pledges, and claims [owing to her] . . .
- . . . to all the male children of Isaac (born or to be born) all her books in Hebrew to be divided [among them], her drapery shop, and all the business matters, debts, and claims pertaining to it.
- . . . to Serena and Regina, in addition to their dowries which have already been provided, twenty-five florins to use for clothing on the occasion of the first birthing.
- . . . to Bonadona and Bonosa, two hundred florins on the occasion of their marriage.[28]

TWO POPULAR LEGENDS

Two accounts concerning Jewish women, one from Spain and one from Poland, probably stemmed from a single popular legend. Although there is no proof that these women existed, stories about them have been retold in many different forms.

One story concerns Raquel, variously known as "La Fermosa," "La Hermosa," or "The Jewess of Toledo." She was said to be the daughter of the Jewish finance minister to King Alphonso VIII of Castile (1155–1214) and became Alphonso's mistress. It was claimed that Alphonso's ardor enabled Raquel to exert a positive influence on the king's policies toward the Jews. A poet, quoted in one of the later chronicles, wrote about Raquel: "For her the King forgot his Queen / His kingdom and his people." Raquel was ultimately murdered in the palace that Alphonso had built for her.[31]

The other story, also with no historical basis, tells of Esterke of Opoczno, Poland, who had a long relationship with King Casimir the Great (1310–1370). The king built two palaces for Esterke and presumably visited her regularly. She bore him several children; their sons, Pelka and Niemera, were given grants by the king and became Christians. The daughter (or daughters) were raised as Jews.[32]

While the Jews remained in prison and in shackles, Pulcelina herself was not placed in chains. But she was prevented from speaking to the count for fear that she might convince him to change his mind and release the Jews. A second document claimed that she was unaware that she had fallen out of favor with the count.

Other Jews from outside Blois did come and try to arrange for a ransom to free the prisoners, but the amount offered was rejected as too small. Ultimately, the priests proved to be the most influential while Pulcelina's influence, whatever it had once been, quickly disappeared. Despite the fact that no corpse was ever found and no child was reported missing, thirty-one Jews of Blois were burned at the stake in 1171. Pulcelina and her two daughters were among them.[33]

RACHEL OF MAINZ, MARTYR
(11th century)

Rachel is perhaps the most famous of the martyr mothers of the first Crusade. Faced with the threat of her children's capture and forced conversion, she decided that their deaths were preferable. The youngest son was killed by her companions. She herself cut the throats of her two daughters and her son Aaron before being murdered by the oncoming Crusaders.[34]

RASHI'S DAUGHTERS AND DESCENDANTS, LEARNED WOMEN: YOḤEVED, MIRIAM, AND RACHEL
(11th–12th centuries)

The daughters of Rashi—Yoḥeved, Miriam, and Rachel—are among the few women known by name from that early period. Rashi's two older daughters both married his students.

Yoheved's husband was Meir ben Shmuel (1060–1130). Yoheved and Meir had four sons: Shmuel, Yitzhak, Yaakov, and Shlomo; and at least one daughter, Hannah. Hannah's teaching concerning the lighting of the Sabbath candles was quoted by her brother R. Yaakov (Tam).[35] She married R. Shmuel of Dampierre and gave birth to a son, Yitzhak, who also became a great and respected scholar.

Miriam married R. Yehudah ben Natan (Rivan) (dates unknown). Their son was the scholar R. Yom Tov of Falaise. Miriam's daughter Alvina is said to have taught some of Rashi's customs, learned from her mother, to her cousin Yitzhak (of Dampierre).

Rashi's youngest daughter, Rachel, was also known by the name of Belle Assez. She was divorced after a brief marriage to Eliezer (known also as Vasselin or Jocelyn) and spent a good deal of her life in her father's house. It was long believed that as Rashi grew older and became ill, Rachel wrote a legal ruling and/or a responsum in his name. If she did so, she must have had some knowledge of Hebrew and of Jewish law.[37] However, there has been recent disagreement on this point, which was based on a misreading of an older text.[38]

RASHI'S FEMALE DESCENDANTS

Female descendants of the great sage Rashi (R. Shlomo ben Yitzhak) appear from time to time in a variety of texts.

- One of Rashi's granddaughters (unnamed) is credited with having taught the women of her community how to perform the commandments for which they were obligated.
- *Rabbenu* Tam's second wife, Miriam (Rashi's granddaughter-in-law), was asked to explain her husband's customs after his death.
- The wife (b. 1305) of R. Yosef ben Yohanan Treibish, another of Rashi's descendants, clarified obscure passages in the Talmud and explained difficulties [in the works] of the Ba'alei Tosafot.[36]

REYNETTE OF KOBLENZ, MONEYLENDER
(14th century)

During the fourteenth century, Reynette of Koblenz (Germany), was an active moneylender. The business activities of her first husband, Leo, were the initial source of her assets, but as a widow and then during her second marriage to Moses Bonenfant, her business prospered. Eventually, Reynette surpassed both Leo and Moses in the size of her financial dealings. Her most successful year was 1372, when she raised the exceptional sum of 8,000 guldens to meet the demands of the Andernacher city fathers.[39]

RICHENZA OF NÜRNBERG, PRAYER LEADER
(13th century)

Richenza was one of the early women prayer leaders (*firzogerins*) active in Germany about one hundred years after Dolce of Worms. She was murdered in a pogrom in Nürnberg along with 728 other Jews on August 1, 1298.[40]

SARA DE SANCTO AEGIDIO (ST. GILLES), DOCTOR
(14th century)

Sara of Sancto Aegidio lived in Marseilles. She was the widow of the physician Avraham and contracted with a student, Salvetus de Burgonoro of Salon de Provence, to instruct him in medicine. The contract referring to this apprenticeship was found in the records of Marseilles (France) and dated August 28, 1326. The document states that "Sara agreed to teach Salvet *artem medicine et phisice* for the period of seven months; and she further agreed to board, lodge, and clothe Salvet. In return, the pupil was to relinquish all fees which he might receive during his apprenticeship and turn them over to his instructress."[41]

SARAH OF TURNOVO / QUEEN THEODORA OF BULGARIA
(14th century)

In 1346, Tzar Ivan Alexander of Bulgaria, part of the Byzantine Empire, "thrust out his former wife who was still living and substituted a Jewess whom he straightway led to divine baptism for, so they say, he loved her for her beauty."[42]

This woman, from the capital city of Turnovo, was reputed to be both beautiful and intelligent. Although she converted and became Queen Theodora, she did influence Ivan Alexander to institute a more liberal policy regarding the Jews. Anti-Jewish legislation adopted by the Christian Church in 1352 was never implemented in Bulgaria, and this was attributed to Theodora, who had considerable influence on state affairs. Her efforts ultimately resulted in tragic consequences, however. The Jews were later accused of fostering the revival of heresy in Bulgaria and the neighboring territories.

Theodora and Ivan Alexander's daughter, Tamar, married the Ottoman Emperor, Murad I. This fact was probably the source of a much later report of a Jewish woman in the sultan's harem as well as a claim that Mehmed II, the son of Murad II, was born of a Jewish mother.[43]

THE WORLD OF JEWISH WOMEN

ECONOMIC ACTIVITIES

Economic Contributions of Women

All medieval women worked. Whether Jewish or gentile, married or unmarried, women began working at a very young age. The sources show that in addition to household management, the majority of Jewish women were involved in the economy, as was the case for women everywhere. This fact is evidenced by R. Meshullam ben Kolonymos (early tenth-century Germany) who wrote: "it is the custom of men to appoint their wives as masters over their possessions."[44]

Later, in one of his explanations of a talmudic passage, Rashi wrote that a woman can do four things simultaneously: "watch the vegetables, spin flax, teach a song to a woman for a fee, and warm silkworm eggs in her bosom."[45]

Women might work with their husbands, with other relatives, or alone; for cash, board, or as part of a family enterprise. Some may have worked for their own satisfaction, most to

A MEDIEVAL JEWISH FARMER

This document from an eleventh-century letter offers a rare example of a Jewish widow who worked her lands alone with the aid of sharecroppers. Her problems were catalogued in an appeal to Jewish communal leaders for a reduction of taxes.

"She sweats a lot and eats a little. Sometimes the fruit is burnt or becomes decayed or injured. . . . The sharecroppers take half the profit. Sometimes there are reverses, such as too much sun or too much cold, too little rain or too much rain, or hail, or several kinds of locusts that are impossible to get rid of."[46]

could, however, act as local agents for long-distance traders, who were not always their husbands. Women might have earned money by supplying goods on a fixed commission, allowing the men to keep whatever excess profits they might be able to receive.

Women also traded locally. In Exeter in 1287, "Comitissa [the widow of Bonefant the Scribe] who lived in High Street, dealt in corn to the value of thirty-three pounds, six shillings, eight pence for 100 quarters."[47]

Some Jewish women combined commercial and financial activities. A twelfth-century French widow began by trading and went on to moneylending. It was stated to the rabbi: "There only remained from her husband nine *gav* of grain. She sold it and worked to make her nest egg grow and also borrowed from others and [lent

contribute to the family income. But overall, their work was an integral part of the economy of the Jewish community.

Until the twelfth century, European Jews, both men and women, could own and work agricultural holdings, most often as a family enterprise. By the twelfth and thirteenth centuries, however, many European rulers had forbidden Jews to own land and they became increasingly urbanized. From that time on, the source of the earned income of Jewish men and women came primarily from different types of commerce and moneylending.

Commerce

While Jewish men traded throughout Europe as well as in Muslim lands, sometimes traveling great distances, Jewish women traveled less often. They

TWO JEWISH BUSINESS-WOMEN: EXCERPTS FROM TWO RESPONSA OF THE ELEVENTH CENTURY

- Reuben, your husband, obtained his supplies from me and gave me from his assets silk equal to a value of half a pound of silver. . . .
- My brother said to me, "I don't want to make any *riysala* (Arabic for a business contract) for you, but if you want I will accept your merchandise on commission. If you have anything more, give it to me [also] on commission." I did so and I gave him the merchandise and due to my illness I also sold some gold and gave [the money from the sale] to him. . . .[48]

that money] out and made a profit with that also and now she has approximately thirty pounds."[49]

In the latter part of this period, Jewish women owned shops. **Venguessone Nathan** of Arles, in addition to being a prominent moneylender, had a shop in which she sold dishes of wood, earthenware, and glass.

Doctors

Historical sources mention Jewish women doctors throughout medieval Europe. Like Jewish men, women were barred from studying medicine at universities. They learned through apprenticeship, usually with members of their immediate families. After this training they might receive a license to

---

A JEWISH WOMAN EYE DOCTOR

When I was an infant about three months old, my eyes were affected and were never completely restored. A certain woman tried to cure me when I was about three years of age, but she added to my blindness to such an extent that I remained confined to the house for a year, being unable to see the road on which to walk. Then a Jewess, a skilled oculist, appeared on the scene. She treated me for about two months and then died. Had she lived another month, I might have recovered my sight fully. As it was, but for the two months' attention from her, I might never have been able to see at all.[50]

—*Yehudah ben Asher's Ethical Will*

---

practice medicine from the communal authorities. Although official licensing was rare and happened in only a few localities, these women were usually considered legitimate doctors or surgeons just like their fathers, husbands, and brothers.

Many Jewish women doctors treated men and women, Christians and Jews. If Jewish women did have a specialty, it was likely to be ophthalmology. In Frankfurt am Main, between 1428 and 1450, of seven women doctors mentioned in the archives, all were Jewish and four were eye doctors.[51] A Jewish woman eye doctor treated the eye diseases of Yehudah, son of Rabbi Asher, in Cologne around 1350. He wrote about her in his ethical will. (An ethical will, generally drawn up by a parent, outlined the standard of moral behavior to be followed by the children after the parent's death.)

A few women doctors specialized in treating the poor, but most practiced for pay. In a tax roll of 1292 and again in 1296–1297, a woman doctor is listed as one of four Jewish doctors in Paris. Other lists of Jewish women doctors included in license records mention Sarah, Serlin, and Hebel; many others are listed as Jewish women without mention of their names.[52] In Aragon in 1381, **Floreta Ca Noga** received fifteen gold florins for treating the queen.

One Jewish woman taught medicine. A contract found in the records of Marseilles, dated August 28, 1326, is between **Sara de Sancto Aegidio**, widow of the physician Avraham, and her disciple Salvetus de Burgonoro.

Money lending

The expansion and development of the Christian populations of northern Europe during the later Middle Ages

FIG. 7. This double tombstone from the Worms cemetery marks the graves of a man and a woman. The woman's grave, on the left, is inscribed to "an important woman," the daughter of the *Parnas* (head official) Abraham. She gave much money to charity and "was quick to offer medicines."

led to an increase in their economic needs, and especially to a demand for money and experienced financiers. The Christian Church condemned usury, basing their prohibition on the biblical tenet "thou shalt not lend upon interest to thy brother" (Deut. 23:20–21). But Jews and Christians were not considered brothers, and thus Jews, who were almost always literate and often formed international commercial networks, were allowed to fill that need, at least for a while.

In the twelfth century many Jewish men and women became moneylenders, at first mainly to the gentry and church officials. Later, with the increased use of money by all classes, they also dealt with poorer Christians.

Because they were experienced traders, Jews were used to handling money and granting credit. Individual Jewish families were sometimes even imported to fill the banking needs of a town or a particular ruler and his household.

Many of the Jewish moneylenders were women, either married or widowed. Evidence of Jewish women moneylenders can be found throughout *Sefer Hasidim*, an ethical work produced by a small group of Jews in Germany in the twelfth and thirteenth centuries. A variety of entries show women actively lending money, sometimes with pledges.[53] In England and France, Jewish women lent out money until the Jews were expelled. They continued to lend throughout the Middle Ages in other lands.

SOME PROMINENT
MONEYLENDERS OF MEDIEVAL
ENGLAND

Avigay of London
Belassez of Oxford
Belassez, widow of Leo
Belia of Winchester
Belia, the widow of Pictavin of
    Bedford
Bella and her granddaughter
    Pucell
Chera of Winchester
Comitissa of Cambridge
Floria, widow of Bonevie of
    Newbury
Floria, widow of Master Elias
Henne, widow of Aaron of York
Henne, widow of Jacob of Oxford
Milka of Canterbury
Mirabel of Gloucester, her
    daughter[54]

The most prominent of the women moneylenders of England was **Licoricia of Winchester,** but there were a large number of other Jewish women, many of them widows, who lent out money.

Records from thirteenth-century Perpignan show that in Spain and Provence, "[l]oans by Jewish women—mostly widows—were not uncommon; twenty-five such women were involved in a total of sixty-one loans recorded in the registers."[55] Thus women were principals in about forty per cent of the loans found in those records. The frequency is even higher in medieval Picardy (France). It has been stated that "the Jewish creditors of the Picard documents, as elsewhere in Europe, were women about half the time."[56]

In thirteenth-century Vienna, Jewish women moneylenders organized themselves into an informal network. One example involves a young man whose father had died. He gave his money (probably an inheritance) to his aunt to keep for him, since he was afraid that the duke might otherwise claim it. She, in turn, gave over part of it to other women for investment purposes without keeping careful records. When she died, her nephew tried to reclaim his money. The writer of the letter explained: "She [his aunt] told him that she gave twelve pounds of money to one Jewess for half the profit and such and such an amount to another Jewess. Afterwards she died and she had not instructed her daughter [as to the whereabouts of the money]."[57]

Occupations of the Poor

Since most medieval sources deal only with the elite, it is difficult to find information about the occupations of poorer women. One query from the eleventh century discusses two women, a mother and daughter, who earned money by sewing and embroidering. They made gold-embroidered gloves and sold them through a third party[58] In the later Middle Ages, sources are more plentiful and records reveal Jewish women working in domestic service (see chapter 6), in the production of agricultural materials such as cheese, and in textiles. Well before that time, however, a ruling attributed to *Rabbenu* Gershom offers clear evidence that sizable numbers of Jewish women lived marginally or were left destitute while their husbands were away. *Rabbenu* Gershom reiterated the talmudic law that if a husband was gone for more than eighteen months, his wife could demand her maintenance from the court. The court would then sell a portion of her husband's property in order to insure her support until his return. Two centuries later, *Rabbenu* Tam reiterated that decree.[59] Despite these seemingly favorable rulings, the appearance of Jewish women beggars and prostitutes point to the community's inability to provide help for all women.[60]

EDUCATION

Early Education of Girls

Although one of Peter Abelard's (1079–1142) students claimed that the Jews were so zealous for learning that "they even taught their daughters,"[61] there is no evidence that Jewish girls were routinely educated more than was absolutely necessary. A 1388 record from Goerlitz, Germany, offers the earliest evidence of a school for Jewish children,[62] but most girls learned at home. They were taught primarily by their mothers, learning basic domestic skills and the commandments that applied to women.

In cases where it was thought important that a young woman learn to read Hebrew (especially the liturgy) and to write (for business reasons or to aid members of her family), her father usually taught her.

In some cases a tutor was hired for young women. R. Eliezer of Mainz (thirteenth century) wrote in his ethical will: "Even if compelled to solicit from others the money to pay a teacher, they must not let the young, of both sexes, go without instruction in the Torah."[63]

Women of Scholarly Families

Once women married, their education usually stopped except in cases of scholarly families. R. Israel Isserlein of Germany (1390–1460) took a male tutor, an older man, for Raidel, his daughter-in-law.[64] It is not known whether Isserlein's wife, Shondlein, was taught by her father, her husband, or by a tutor, but she was learned enough to have passed on a legal decision. It was a reply to a woman who had sent her a query directly, concerning matters of ritual purity. The answer was written in Yiddish.[65]

In general, the more learned the men were, the better educated their wives, daughters, and daughters-in-law were likely to be, and women were sometimes depended upon for evidence of a late father's or husband's rulings or practices. In addition to **Rashi's daughters and granddaughters**, Bella, a sister of R. Yitzḥak ben Menaḥem (eleventh century) is mentioned in the *Maḥzor Vitry* as an educated woman whose opinions were considered authoritative.[66]

A BAD NEIGHBORHOOD IN SARAGOSSA

In 1283 the famous Muça de Portella complained to the Infante that Jewish courtesans had set up a brothel in a building near his house in Saragossa. From the same source we learn that the Jewish prostitutes did not usually reside within the Jewish quarter. The Infante accordingly ordered the communal leaders, the *adenantados*, to expel all prostitutes from the *juderia*. In Barcelona, Jewish prostitutes were permitted to operate in Castel Nou, adjacent to the Call. . . .[67]

THOUGHTS ON THE EDUCATION OF DAUGHTERS

If they [his daughters] do not know how to write, they will be forced to request men to write their receipts for pledges when they lend money. They will be alone with those men who write for them and they may sin, and this will be my fault, for whenever it is in one's ability to construct a fence for sin and one does not do it, it is as if one has caused it, as it is written in Hosea 4:13: "I will not punish your daughters when they commit harlotry, nor your daughters-in-law when they commit adultery," because it is the fathers who have been the cause. And even if they do not sin, they may think about it. Moreover, he did not want them to acquire a bad reputation, and thus he taught them to write receipts for their pledges. . . .

—*Sefer ha-Kavod*[68]

Educating Women for Business

Many women needed to read and write, at least in the vernacular, to enable them to conduct their business affairs without being cheated or robbed. Another reason for teaching women—especially young girls—was to keep them from lustful behavior. As one pietist explained, an illiterate woman might be forced to call in a man to help her in a business transaction and thus create a climate for sin.

SOME REASONS FOR CHILD MARRIAGE

A man is forbidden to marry off his daughter when she is a minor . . . Nevertheless it is our custom to betroth our daughters even if they are minors because day after day the [oppression of] Exile increases and if a man has the possibility of giving his daughter a dowry now [he betroths her] lest he not have it later on and she will remain an *agunah* forever.

—*Tos.* Kiddushin *41a, s.v. "asur"*

FAMILY LIFE

Betrothal and Marriage

Women in the medieval period usually married young. While the talmudic authorities stated that a marriage was not to take place until the bride and groom reached maturity—thirteen for boys and twelve and a half for girls (B. *Yevamot* 112b)—fathers frequently married off their daughters while they were still minors. Nor was it uncommon for brides and grooms to be betrothed in early childhood.

Such early marriages sometimes caused severe problems for young people. Records from *Romaniot* (Greek-speaking) Jewish communities suggest that the stresses of matrimony could lead to much unhappiness, especially because the *Romaniot* allowed cohabitation before the marriage ceremony had taken place. Many of these marriages ended in divorce, always an option for both young and old.[69]

Children

In the Jewish family, sexual relations between husband and wife were obligatory and children were consid-

הר עריי לובשי ׳התב

FIG. 8. This bride and groom were pictured in an illuminated manuscript from the Worms Maḥzor (prayer book for holy days and special events). Completed in 1272, it shows the couple joined by a tallit. The bride, completely veiled, is on the left. (Courtesy of Hebrew National and University Library, Jerusalem)

ered a blessing. However, this did not preclude strict discipline when necessary, especially for girls. *Rabbenu* Tam stated unequivocally that "boys and girls should be separated and kept from joint play and merriment."[70] In his will, Eliezer of Mainz stipulated: "I ask, I command, that the daughters of my house be never without work to do, for idleness leads first to boredom, then to sin."[71]

Desertions

R. Ḥayyim Or Zarua, a Viennese rabbi of the fourteenth century, recorded a decree *(takkanah)* that had been in

effect since the time of R. Meir ben Barukh of Rothenburg (1215–1293). Quoting from R. Meir's letter, R. Ḥayyim explained that "a wife deserting her husband should lose her rights, not merely to the *ketubbah* but also should forfeit whatever property she brought to her husband."[72] This ruling was issued at a time when the number of women who deserted their husbands had increased.

According to later explanations, this ruling did not apply across the board, but only to a woman who might leave her husband "because of the persuasion of relatives." But however narrow the parameters of the decree, it hints at

FIG. 9. The remains of a twelfth-century *mikveh* (ritual bath) in Cologne, an ancient Rhineland town. Modern steel rods shore up the recently excavated stones.

an ongoing problem and the solution was certainly not favorable to women.[73]

Divorce

In approximately 1000 C.E., *Rabbenu* Gershom decreed that a man was prohibited from divorcing his wife against her will. This ruling could not be suspended "except by one hundred men from three countries and from three communities."[74] Despite this loophole,

the ruling had important ramifications for women. Although it did not apply to Jews in Muslim lands, it was incorporated into Jewish law among European Jews and continued to be reaffirmed.

Such a ruling gave a wife a little more stability in her marriage than was available to her previously, but it was still primarily the husband who could initiate divorce and there is some evidence that many did. A manuscript of

Seligmann Bing (1395–1471), a rabbi in the Rhineland, condemns "the rapid turnover of marriage partners facilitated by hasty divorces." He alludes to "erotic attraction" as the main reason for this development and sets out prohibitions against hasty remarriages.[75] There is no evidence that any specific ruling was passed during this time to stem this trend, and the available numbers were high. In Nürnberg, for example, during the years 1416 to 1442 thirty divorces were recorded among a population of seventy adults.[76]

According to these documents, women were also guilty of easy divorce and quick remarriage, and this might partially account for the increased numbers of divorces granted. However, women who sought divorce through the Jewish courts remained at a distinct disadvantage. They could not initiate a divorce themselves, and Jewish law recognized only a limited number of circumstances that would be acceptable on appeal to a Jewish court, mainly if her husband was a habitual gambler, had a loathsome disease, beat her unnecessarily, or was impotent.

Family Purity (Niddah)

The rules concerning *niddah* were strictly adhered to in the Jewish communities of Christian Europe, and when there was any deviation from the norm, the rabbis were quick to point it out. In the twelfth century, a bitter rabbinical exchange took place between *Rabbenu* Tam and his contemporary, R. Meshullam of Melun (France). The dispute involved the amount of time a woman should wait after her menstrual period before she immersed in the ritual bath (*mikveh*). The more lenient R. Meshullam had ruled that a woman could go to the *mikveh* on the morning of the seventh day instead of waiting until night, when a trip to the ritual bath might involve danger. *Rabbenu* Tam insisted that this was not according to Torah law, and those who followed R. Meshullam's ruling were threatened with excommunication.[77]

Among the *Romaniot* Jews it was the custom for women, after their period of menstrual separation, to use the public baths for their immersions instead of the usual drawn water of the *mikveh*, but this practice too was widely criticized by northern European Jewish scholars.[78]

Monogamy

Following the older, Eastern tradition, the Jews who lived on the southern shores of the Mediterranean could and sometimes did have more than one wife. Among northern European Jews, however, there is almost no evidence of polygynous marriages except in cases involving the marriage of a man to his childless brother's widow

---

THE BAN AGAINST PLURAL MARRIAGES

The *ḥerem* [writ of excommunication] according to the ruling of our communities declared by *Rabbenu* Gershom Me'or Ha-Golah that it is forbidden to marry two wives, may only be revoked by one hundred rabbis from three regions and three different communities.

—R. Meir ben Barukh of Rothenburg[79]

(**levirate marriage**), when a second wife was permitted.[80]

It was *Rabbenu* Gershom of Mainz who incorporated the tradition of monogamy among northern Europeans into Jewish law. Sometime around the year 1000, he issued a decree forbidding plural marriages for Jews on pain of excommunication. This ruling remained in force for all Jews in Christian Europe. In the thirteenth century, R. Meir ben Barukh of Rothenburg confirmed the already-established decree, citing the single exception allowed. Just as a man could divorce a wife without her consent by calling on one hundred men, so he could take a second wife using the same method.

Violence Against Women

By the late Middle Ages, excessive wife beating was one of the major reasons for trying to persuade the husband to grant a divorce. Wife beating was common in all areas of Europe, and by the twelfth century R. Shmuel ben Meir (the Rashbam) and *Rabbenu* Tam had been called upon to rule on such matters. Although *Rabbenu* Tam had written "this is a thing not done in Israel," and R. Meir of Rothenburg claimed "Jews are not addicted to the prevalent habit of ill-treating their wives," it continued to be a problem for some.[81]

In Spain, wife beating was so prevalent that ultimately the Jewish courts had to rule that if a woman fled to her father's house because her husband continually abused her, she could not be labeled a rebellious wife and would not need to forfeit her *ketubbah*.[82]

In France, R. Peretz of Corbeil (d. 1295) decreed that a man who habitually beat his wife must accept forced separation but continue to support her. The wording of this ruling suggested that large numbers of women themselves had complained. It began: "The cry of the daughters of our people has been heard concerning the sons of Israel who raise their hands to strike their wives."[83] Based on the absence of any clear evidence, it is assumed that this decree never became official, although many scholars followed its recommendations.

Women's Sexuality

Even at a very young age, a girl was viewed principally as a sexual being, and concern for her chastity dominated all instruction she might receive. Modesty was equally important, since immodesty would likely lead to unchastity. A Jewish polemic writer of the mid–twelfth century praised Jewish girls, who "behaved with modesty and were not wanton like the daughters of the gentiles who go out everywhere to street corners."[84]

In the following century, a Jewish writer echoed the same opinion. "Jews," he wrote, "get [their daughters] used to keeping themselves away from men. Debauchery is unknown among them."[85]

This last statement was not completely true. In Christian Spain especially, adultery among Jews was a fairly common occurrence in the thirteenth century, and complaints about wives' immoral conduct "were so numerous that they cannot all be ascribed to the jealousy of husbands."[86]

LEGAL STATUS

Married Women

Married women encountered legal barriers not faced by widows or single women. Since, according to Jewish law, all of a married woman's property and earnings was controlled by her husband, she technically had no assets of her own. Therefore, if she lost or damaged someone else's property she was not liable to pay compensation, as that would mean she was paying from her husband's assets (B. *Bava Kamma* 87a). Although this lack of liability might appear to be an advantage for married women, in reality it was not always so.

Married Women and Business Law

A married woman's lack of liability created serious problems. People might hesitate to deal with a business in which a woman was an active partner, because she was not obligated to pay for loss or damage even if she had caused it deliberately. However, a wife's labor was often indispensable in a family enterprise.

One of the earliest solutions to this dilemma was a proposal offered by R. Yosef Tov-Elem (d. 1040). He suggested that even though it was not an obligation, the husband or father should pay the damages caused by the woman in the interest of goodwill. One generation later, Rashi, in his clarification of the original talmudic text, explained that the debt remains valid and if the woman is divorced or widowed and acquires property of her own, she has to pay the damage.

By the twelfth century, however, when both the Jewish population and Jewish commercial activities had increased substantially, a solution dependent on goodwill, or postponed for an indefinite period, was no longer realistic. Finally, late in the twelfth century, R. Eliezer ben Natan (d. ca. 1170) of Mainz gave a two-part solution. First, he insisted that the right of a husband to the fruits of his wife's labor

---

> ### WOMEN IN BUSINESS
>
> In these times . . .women are guardians and shopkeepers; they conduct business and borrow and lend and pay and get paid and receive and make deposits. . . .
> —*R. Eliezer ben Natan*[87]

---

does not excuse the wife from responsibility for her own actions.

This decision was controversial, and many scholars felt it went against Jewish law. But that was only one part of R. Eliezer's ruling. He also suggested that the wife, no matter in what activities she was engaged, was always acting as an agent for her husband. This was more consistent with Jewish law and also protected the customer. The husband was now responsible for his wife's losses and damages even if she administered her own business or profession independent of his supervision. R. Eliezer's ruling was definitive and was widely accepted. It allowed businesses to function more smoothly but did little to advance a married woman's status.

R. Avraham ben Nahman later stressed R. Eliezer's claim that a woman acted as her husband's agent at all times. He thus removed the more controversial aspect of the ruling that originally granted women full responsibility for their own actions.[88]

Widows

Widows had a larger range of opportunity than married women, because after a husband died, his widow became a legal entity in the community and in the courts. From that time on she was obligated to pay her own taxes and was responsible for her own debts. If she remained unmarried, she would most likely have to become the breadwinner, with the legal right to make all her own decisions. Once she remarried, those rights reverted to her husband.

Women As Heirs

According to Jewish law, daughters were not permitted to inherit from fathers or mothers, but already in the Mishnah (M. *Ketubbot* 13:3), modifications of that prohibition were being made.

By the early Middle Ages it was accepted that sons inherited from the father's estate but daughters received a dowry during their father's lifetime. If a father died before his daughters were married, they were to be maintained from their father's estate even at the expense of the sons' inheritance. Wives did not inherit from their husbands and had to be maintained from the estate during their lifetimes or until they remarried.[89] In some cases, however, Jews managed to bypass these laws either by giving gifts during their lifetime or by registering their wills in the secular courts.

Women's Wills

Wills involving bequests by women sometimes challenged the limitations of law concerning women since, technically, their property belonged to their husbands. In several communities, women may have circumvented Jewish legal restrictions by filing their wills through the Christian courts. This is suggested from the recent discovery of collections of fourteenth-century wills of women from France, Provence, and Spain, including the Kingdom of Majorca.

From a study of four of these wills, drafted between June 24, 1306, and June 24, 1307, and a fifth will from a widow in Valls (Catalonia) in 1336, it was concluded that "[w]omen's wills have a strong philanthropic element, at times startlingly generous. They include bequests to other women, relatives or friends, more usually than men's wills."[90] Such generosity and concern is also evident in the will of Venguessone Nathan, who bequeathed money to grandchildren and to a variety of charitable organizations.

PUBLIC POWER

Power can be defined as "the ability to act effectively, to influence people and decisions, and to achieve goals."[91] In the Middle Ages, both in Christian Europe and the Muslim East, there were only a few ways that people could acquire such power. For men, power came through birth, conquest, or money. An eldest son born into wealth, trained in the skills of war, or heir to ample lands had the ability to control his world. Jewish men acquired power through lineage and wealth, and also through Torah knowledge. Male power was public and visible and accepted without question.

Female power was much rarer and harder to achieve because women were not often permitted a public role in society. The requirement that women be modest and chaste, the assumption that their intellect was weak, that they were irrational and untrustworthy, permeated all classes and all religious groups. For the most part, societal norms were successful in keeping women secluded in their homes under the jurisdiction and control of fathers, husbands, or other male relatives.

Some women, however, did find ways to influence their world, if only for a short time. One example may have been **Minna of Worms** (eleventh century), who was described in a chronicle as an important woman who entertained "the nobles of the city and the princes of the land"[92] in her home. Although she may have been famous at the time, her influence was transitory, as she was murdered by Crusaders.

A handful of women managed to hold on to real power and to exercise that power in the public arena. Such women were most often widows who stepped into a late husband's leadership role. Usually they were from families who already enjoyed prominence in the community, such as **Kandlein of Regensburg** and Chera of Winchester. In 1241, Chera was elected to be "the Winchester hostage." This meant that she was the Jewish official responsible for collecting the taxes of the Jewish community for that year.[93] There were a handful of others as well, including a few women from Provence who represented their families in Jewish councils. They were: Rosa and Baceva, Jewish widows in Manosque at the turn of the fourteenth century;[94] **Esther de Caylar;** and Regina, "widow of the doctor Abraham Avicdor," both of Arles.[95]

Occasionally, a woman might gain power briefly because her beauty or charm was able to influence a powerful man. This may have been the case with **Pulcelina of Blois** or **Sarah of Turnovo,** who became queen of Bulgaria. Such occurrences, however, were rare and often had negative results.

RELIGIOUS PARTICIPATION

Observance of the Commandments

Religious activities for women were limited, as it was assumed that their time would be taken up with childcare and household management and income-producing labor. There were a few documented cases, however, where women were allowed to participate in certain commandments (*mitzvot*) usually reserved for men.

In the twelfth century, *Rabbenu* Tam approved of the practice of women wearing phylacteries (*tefillin*) and, in general, allowed women to perform certain commandments from which they were exempt. His reasoning was based on a talmudic passage that reported how Mikhal, daughter of King Saul, used to put on phylacteries. Among the Tosafists the question arose: Could she also recite the appropriate blessing? Yes, said *Rabbenu* Tam. It was indeed legitimate to recite the blessing, and not merely "to please the women."[96] It was acceptable to say a blessing even on acts that were not obligatory[97] Later, Maimonides (1135–1204) disagreed with this opinion, but *Rabbenu* Tam's ruling remained in force in the Jewish communities of Europe.

Another example of women's participation in religious ritual was their role in the ceremony of circumcision (*brit milah*). In the twelfth to fourteenth centuries in Germany, it was not uncommon for a woman to be honored by being named as a sponsor (*sandeket*) at the birth of a son or grandson. The sponsor was responsible for holding the baby during the circumcision itself, which took place in the synagogue. A responsum quoting R. Meir of Rothenburg disapproved of this practice since a woman, alone with the men in the congregation, would be arrayed in fine clothes, wearing jewels and perfumes. "It doesn't seem to be a kosher tradition at all,"[98] complained R. Meir. His students agreed, and eventually the practice was discontinued.

FIG. 10. This tombstone, from the thirteenth century in the Worms cemetery, is inscribed: "My teacher, Lady Krinkhova," who "attended the synagogue every day" and gave charity "to all who held out their hands."

In Mainz in the late fourteenth century, a woman named Bruna was reported to have placed fringes on her garments, and a century later in Paris, R. Yehudah Sir Leon permitted his wife to do the same.[99] A few other isolated instances suggest that some women were pushing the boundaries of their activities beyond the accepted norm. In the *Tosafot*,[100] R. Avraham is used as an example of someone who encouraged his daughters to form their own prayer group to recite the introduction to the grace after meals. Some women were granted the right to recline at the seder table on Passover, sit in the sukkah, and, in general, recite the blessings over time-bound commandments. The Spanish sage, R. Nissim bar Reuben (1290–1375), in his commentary on the Talmud, wrote that women are obligated to hear the *Megillah* read on Purim and therefore they may read and fulfill the commandment for men also. They may even be counted in a minyan for that purpose.[101]

R. Meir ben Barukh of Rothenburg's well-known opinion allowing women to be called up to say the blessing on the Torah does not make a significant positive addition to the rulings concerning women's religious activities. He did write that in a specific case where all the inhabitants of a town were *kohenim* women might be called to fulfill the remaining *aliyot* to the Torah, but there is no evidence that this was actually ever done.[102] The mishnaic precept claiming that women were not called up to the Torah because of "the honor of the community" *(kavod hatzibbur)* (B. *Megillah* 23a) may have been suspended in this specific case, but was never seriously questioned and seems to have remained in place.

Personal Prayer

A single prayer book, dating from the fourteenth or fifteenth century and written in Judeo-Provençal (the language of the Jews of Provence), may be an example of women's slightly improved status during this time. The book was inscribed: "to my sister, be the mother of thousands of ten thousands." Clearly intended for the use of a woman, it contains a variation of the morning blessing. Instead of thanking God "who made me according to His will" (the accepted, traditional version), the blessing reads: "Blessed art Thou, Lord our God . . . who has made me a woman." This small change may indicate a greater pride in being a female than the more common version would suggest.[103]

At about the same time, the mother of the renowned R. Israel Isserlein

(1390–1460) was reported to have replaced that same morning prayer with a blessing thanking God "for not making me an animal."[104] The use of such a prayer was discussed by a disciple of R. Isserlein and suggests that the wording accepted in our times: ". . . who has made me in His image," may have been introduced only in the early fifteenth century and was still rather flexible until that time.

Prayer Leaders

Evidence of women who functioned as prayer leaders first appeared in the Rhineland (Germany) in the twelfth century, although it does not seem to have been an official post until much later. The earliest example of a woman who held this informal position is **Dolce of Worms**. Several others are known from records or tombstones, including Urania of Worms (d. 1275), **Richenza of Nürnberg,** and Guta bat Natan (d. 1306). Guta is remembered as "the important young woman who prayed for the women with gentle prayers."[105] These women later came to be called *firzogerins*, the Yiddish word meaning prayer leader.

URANIA OF WORMS: AN EARLY EXAMPLE OF A WOMAN PRAYER LEADER

Urania's gravestone reads:
"Urania, the daughter of the chief of the synagogue singers. His prayer for his people rose up to glory. And as to her, she, too, with sweet tunefulness officiated before the women to whom she sang the hymnal portions."[106]

Religious Status of Women

R. Yitzḥak of Dampierre (1120–1200) wrote: "If they [women] are not prophets, they are the daughters of prophets and [among] the great ones of the generation and we ought to depend on their practices."[107] Mordecai ben Hillel of Germany (1240–1298), in his compendium to the Talmud, called simply *The Mordecai*, repeated that assertion, claiming that in his time all Jewish women were "daughters of prophets and important women" and thus had earned the privileges enjoyed by men.[108] This implied the privilege to perform time-bound *mitzvot*.

Despite such broad statements, there is little evidence that large numbers of women moved beyond their accustomed place in society. Rather, these small changes were more in the nature of privileges bestowed on deserving women and were not written into law.

By the late fourteenth century, R. Yaakov ben Moshe, known as the Maharil (1365–1427), was less certain about women's right to recite specific blessings than the earlier sages had been. He had two learned sisters, Bunlin and Simḥa, and although he conceded that women who were educated and obeyed all the commandments were allowed to recite the prayers, he claimed that most did not fall into that category.[109]

Synagogue Officials

Women officials were always necessary for synagogue life. They were needed to oversee the ritual immersions at the *mikveh* and maintain the facility. Often women sewed the Torah covers and wall hangings for the synagogue and cared for them. Although official titles for such work are difficult to recover, one woman, named **Çeti of Saragossa** (Spain), was called "rabbess of the female Jews." She had held this post for twenty years or more.

The difficulty in understanding this unusual document lies in the definition of *rabbess*. Certainly she was not a female rabbi, and there is no evidence of women prayer leaders in Spain as there was in France, Germany, and Italy. It is likely that Çeti took care of the women's section of the synagogue and the ritual bath. Such a position was probably held by women in many Jewish communities and would have engendered considerable respect.

CHAPTER 5

A Separate Community:
Jewish Women in Italy until the 1800s

OVERVIEW

Early Settlement

Jews originally came to Rome as slaves, the result of the first Roman conquest of Jerusalem in 63 B.C.E. Most were soon ransomed or liberated, and a small number of them remained in that city, eventually settling on the banks of the Tiber River.[1] Thus Rome became the oldest Jewish community in Europe. About one hundred years later, after the Roman general Titus destroyed the Holy Temple and burned the city of Jerusalem, Jews were again transported to Rome as prisoners or slaves, adding to the Jewish community.

The level of education among Roman-Jewish men benefited from their continuing ties to the land of Israel and the Palestinian centers of learning. By the time those centers closed down, sometime in the fifth century C.E., there was already a strong foundation of Jewish scholarship on the Italian peninsula, concentrated mostly in the port cities of the south.

The Writings of Ahimaaz

The history of those early communities is, for the most part, unrecorded, and almost no names have come down to us outside of one family history written in 1054 by Ahimaaz ben Paltiel. In a work called *The Book of Genealogies*, Ahimaaz traced his family back to first-century Jerusalem where they were taken captive and brought by ship to Rome. "They came to Oria," relates Ahimaaz; "they settled there and prospered through remarkable achievements."[2] This document records the history of all of Ahimaaz's large family over several centuries, and includes incidental reports about a few women, including the young girl **Cassia**.

As Ahimaaz's book confirms, the tenth and eleventh centuries saw a marked growth in the population of Jews in southern Italy, as well as in the number of scholars and institutions of learning. Not only were Jews tolerated in those few hundred years traced by Ahimaaz; if his account is to be believed, they prospered and gained positions of political power. Their numbers were not large, but their growth was continuous and they lived in relative security, even during the troublesome years of the Crusades.

The Beginning of Diversity

During the thirteenth century, most established Jewish communities were found in the southern part of the Italian peninsula, and the Jewish population was relatively homogeneous. Then, beginning in 1348, Jews were expelled from some of the German cities[3] and began migrating into northern Italy, settling mostly in towns where they could establish themselves as pawnbrokers. In 1387, a few German Jews requested the permission of the Count of Milan to enter his land for purposes of trade. This privilege, granted and affirmed by means of a written *condotta* (charter),[4] became the mark of legitimacy for native Italian Jews as well as those from Germany. A *condotta* guaranteed them the right to live in a specific area and engage in loan banking, moneylending, pawnbroking, and trade. Under the regulation of the reigning duke or noble, Jews opened banks, collected high interest, and shared their profits with the rulers in the form of taxes.

Some of the Jews fleeing the fourteenth-century persecutions in Spain also sought asylum in Italy. After the decrees expelling all Jews from Spain in 1492 and the forced conversion of Portuguese Jews in 1497, many more, such as the family of **Benvenida Abrabanel**, found havens in Italian cities.[5] By the early 1500s, large numbers of Jews of Spanish and Portuguese origin had expanded the once homogeneous Italian-Jewish population even more. Congregations of Sephardic Jews appeared within almost every community. Eventually the Jewish mix included the original Italianate Jews, Ashkenazim (German Jews), Sephardim (Spanish and Portuguese Jews), and Levantine (Middle-Eastern) Jews, all with their own synagogues.

The geographic and political divisions of the peninsula itself added to the diversity of experience for Italian Jews. Although there were certainly intervals of oppression throughout the Middle Ages and into the early modern period, large numbers of Italian Jews enjoyed a degree of tolerance. A few even assimilated into the general population. Because a different duke or merchant family ruled each city-state or island, Jews might be welcomed into some areas, given protection (usually under a *condotta*), and permitted to work and practice their religion in relative peace and safety, while in other areas they were expelled. The Jews of Perugia, Vicenza, Milan, Lucca, and Florence all experienced temporary expulsions in the last two decades of the fifteenth century, but simultaneously, Jews were flourishing in other areas and were receiving large numbers of Jewish immigrants.

The Renaissance

By the time that Jews were establishing a strong financial presence in the north of Italy, the Renaissance had begun. The Italian Renaissance spanned slightly less than two centuries, from approximately 1375 to 1527.

By the late 1300s, the Jewish inhabitants of Italian towns and cities, estimated at 50,000 (out of a total population of eleven million),[6] began to feel the affects of Italy's cultural, political, and intellectual rebirth. Many Jews contributed to this exciting cultural growth, adding their own literary and musical works and even participating in public performances. A few of these participants were women, such as **Madame Europa** and **Madonna Bellina.**

Some historians claimed that during the Renaissance period, women stood on an equal footing with men. This evaluation was endorsed and repeated by Jewish historians, but it is certainly an overstatement.[7] As the fourteenth century gave way to the fifteenth, however, there is evidence that some Jewish women, particularly in the upper classes, received a better **education** than they ever had before.[8]

The New Ghetto Communities

It was toward the end of this thriving and creative period in Italy, and on the heels of increased immigration, that the Jewish ghetto was established. Conceived as a reaction to pressures by the new Protestant religion, the first ghetto was built by closing off the original Jewish quarter of Venice in 1516.[9] It was assumed that the area was called *ghetto* because it was near an iron foundry (*geto* or *ghetto* in Italian), but recent reevaluation of this word suggests other derivations.[10]

By the mid–sixteenth century, Martin Luther and John Calvin had established new forms of Christianity in northern Europe, and the Catholic Church, threatened by their success, instituted the Italian Counter-Reformation. This was a policy aimed at renewing interest in religion by suppressing the secular art and literature that had enjoyed so much popularity. Jews, already living in ghettos and beginning to feel the effects of harsh anti-Jewish legislation, nevertheless continued to participate as fully as possible in the cultural life of their communities and sometimes mingled freely with Christians.[11] There were Jewish writers, entertainers, musicians, playwrights, and poets in many of the Italian cities. Among them were a few women. **Deborah Ascarelli** was a poet active in the mid–sixteenth century. **Sara Copio Sullam,** another example of that humanistic tradition, felt free to write both religious and secular poetry and for a while was well known and respected within her community, but she was one of the last.

The Decline of Italian Jewry

In 1553, Pope Julius III ordered all copies of the Talmud to be burned throughout Italy. In 1555, the Jews in the Papal State, which included Rome, were prohibited from any commercial activity except for the sale of rags and old clothes. By the end of the sixteenth century, Jews had virtually disappeared from the south, were confined to ghettos in the central and northern cities, and suffered from severe discriminatory legislation. The oppressive policies could not help but affect family life, and women's and men's economic and social status deteriorated. Only a few families rose to a high economic level.

Male scholars did continue to study, write, and publish, but from the middle of the seventeenth century, among the approximately 30,000 Jews still remaining in Italy, there is no longer any evidence of outstanding, learned, or talented Jewish women. Influential women such as Benvenida Abrabanel and **Gracia Nasi** (see chapter 7) or even less public figures like the scholar **Fioretta da Modena** were no longer a visible part of Jewish life in Italy. Rabbis, increasingly conservative, insisted that women remain in their primary domestic role.[12]

The Italian ghettos were opened for a brief time when the French Revolution spilled into Italy in 1796 and again under Napoleon's rule in 1800. No lasting changes were made, however, until after the first quarter of the nineteenth century, when, in one community after another, the ghettos were finally abolished.

A POET'S THOUGHTS ON WOMEN

"A woman's movements should be free only three times," wrote the Italian rabbi and poet Immanuel Frances (1618—ca. 1710). "The first at birth, and then when she is led beneath the canopy. The third and last—and this the best—when she is led to her final rest."[13]

BIOGRAPHIES

ABRABANEL, BENVENIDA OF SPAIN AND NAPLES, SCHOLAR AND COMMUNITY LEADER
(16th century)

Benvenida was well educated in both Jewish and secular subjects. She was the daughter of Jacob Abrabanel and a niece of Don Isaac Abrabanel (1437–1508), who had been financial advisor to King Ferdinand of Spain. Following the expulsion of Jews from Spain, Benvenida emigrated to Naples together with the entire Abrabanel family. While still young, she was married to Isaac's youngest son, Samuel. For Samuel, born in 1473,[14] it was a second marriage. The couple had three sons and three daughters.[15]

Samuel inherited his father's skill at finance, and after his father-in-law Jacob died, he succeeded him as the leader of the Jewish community of Naples. Because of the family's associations with the royal court, Benvenida met Don Pedro of Toledo, Spanish viceroy to the kingdom of Naples, and became the teacher of his daughter, Eleonora. This relationship led to a lifelong friendship between the two women. Many years later, when Eleonora married the Grand Duke of Tuscany, that friendship enabled the Abrabanel family to continue to prosper in the face of renewed persecution.[16]

In 1532, after years of warfare in which the kingdom of Naples was being squeezed between Spanish and French ambitions, the government of Naples moved to expel the remaining Jews from southern Italy. Neither Benvenida's appeals to her friend Eleonora nor Samuel's attempt to stop the expulsion by bribery succeeded.

Although Emperor Charles V, then in control of Naples, had agreed to a ten-year postponement, he did not abide by his promise, and Samuel and Benvenida were forced to move in 1541.[17] This time they accepted the invitation offered by the Duke of Ferrara, a duchy in the northern part of the Italian peninsula, where they lived peacefully and prospered.

When Samuel died in 1547, he left full control of the family enterprises to Benvenida[18] and she expanded them. She worked with two of her sons,

---

WORDS OF PRAISE FROM DAVID REUBENI

Benvenida Abrabanel befriended the traveler and pseudo-messiah David Reubeni, on whom she lavished expensive gifts. When Reubeni came to Pisa, he wrote in his diary that he had received from Signora Benvenida, wife of Samuel Abrabanel, "a banner of fine silk on which the ten commandments were written . . . with gold embroidery" and "a Turkish gown of gold brocade . . . besides having sent me money three times when I was in Rome."

Reubeni also wrote about his benefactor that she "fasts every day." He reported that he had already heard of her fame in Alexandria and Jerusalem and "how she used to ransom the captives, and had ransomed more than a thousand captives and gave charity to everyone that asked of her. . . ."[19]

Jacob and Judah, and possibly a son-in-law and became a successful businesswoman, obtaining important commercial privileges through her connections with Eleonora, Duchess of Tuscany.[20]

Benvenida Abrabanel was known as a sincere and pious Jew, a philanthropist who gave generously to charity and supported scholars. When she died in 1560, she was described as one of the "most noble and high-spirited

---

BEAUTY ADVICE FROM THE SIXTEENTH CENTURY

"To begin with . . . a black salve which removes roughness of the face, and makes the flesh supple and smooth. Put this salve on at night, and allow it to remain on till the morning. Then wash yourself with pure river water; next bathe your face in the lotion that is called *acqua da Canecare*; then put on a dab of this white cream; and then take less than a chickpea grain of this powder, dissolve it in the lotion called *acqua dolce* and put it on your face, the thinner the better. . . .

Now if your illustrious Highness will apply these things, I am quite sure that you will order from us continually."

Following her signature, Anna the Hebrew added:

"The black salve is bitter. If it should happen to go into the mouth, you may be assured that it is nothing dangerous; the bitterness comes from the aloes in it."[21]

This warning served to assuage any possible fear by Catherine that the cosmetics would be used to poison her.

---

matrons who [has] existed in Israel since the time of the dispersion . . . a pattern . . . of chastity, of piety, of prudence, and of worth."[22]

ANNA THE HEBREW OF ROME, COSMETICIAN
(late 15th to early 16th century)

Anna sold face cream to the noblewoman Catherine Sforza in 1508 and described other lotions and powders that she sold, with prices for each. She wrote an accompanying letter explaining the use of each item and signed the letter "Anna the Hebrew."

D'ARPINO, ANNA OF ROME, PRAYER LEADER
(16th century)

One extant record names Anna d'Arpino of Rome as a cantor or precentor (*shaliaḥ tzibbur* in Hebrew; *firzogerin* in Yiddish). For two and a half years, she led the women in the synagogue on Saturdays and holidays and was paid indirectly with an interest-free loan.[23]

ASCARELLI, DEBORAH OF ROME, POET AND TRANSLATOR
(16th century)

Deborah Ascarelli may have been a prayer leader for the women of the Catalan Synagogue in Rome, the congregation headed by her merchant husband, Joseph Ascarelli.[24] She knew Hebrew and translated many important works from the original Hebrew into Italian for the benefit of women.

Among Ascarelli's better-known translations were the Sephardic version of the Yom Kippur *avodah* service, and the "Great Confession" of Rabbenu Nissim. She also translated *Me'on Hashoalim*, parts of *Mikdash*

Me'at (two works by Moses Rieti), and the *Tokeah*, the admonition for the High Holy days that was composed by the popular Spanish moral writer, Baḥya ibn Pakuda (11th century).[25]

In addition to her translations of literary pieces, Deborah Ascarelli translated important hymns that were sung regularly in the synagogue and wrote original poems in the Italian language. She is believed to have been one of the first Jewish women to have her work printed in Italian. Her poetry was written in approximately 1537 but first appeared in print in 1601.[26]

As the Jews' economic and social position declined and emigration out of Italy increased, Deborah Ascarelli's poetry was forgotten. Pellegrino Ascarelli, a descendant of Deborah's, discovered and personally republished her work in 1925.[27]

MADONNA BELLINA OF VENICE, MUSICIAN
(16th century)

A document of the period praised Madonna Bellina lavishly, saying "she wondrously played, sang, and composed, much to the delight of the city."[28] Besides praise for her musical skills, nothing is known of her life.

CASSIA, DAUGHTER OF SHEPHATIAH OF SOUTHERN ITALY
(9th or 10th century)

The only information available about Cassia is from *The Book of Genealogies*, a chronicle in which the Italian Jew Ahimaaz ben Paltiel (b. 1017) related his family history. According to Ahimaaz, Cassia, daughter of his ancestor Shephatiah, was "of rare beauty, of genial and charming disposition," and her father loved her dearly. He was anxious to arrange for her marriage, but her mother turned every

---

A POEM BY DEBORAH ASCARELLI

Although Ascarelli was primarily a religious poet, she did write several poems on topics that were popular among Italian writers and artists. One of these was the apocryphal story of "Susannah and the Elders." In this poem, Deborah Ascarelli described Susannah as a righteous woman who is miraculously saved from a false accusation of adultery. She offered a brief physical picture but concentrated on the inner beauty and spiritual excellence of this popular fictional heroine.

Although a beautiful shock of golden hair swings across her forehead
And love finds nourishment in her eyes
The chaste Susannah never strays from the right path
And harbors not one thought without the Lord.
Hence those who, casting caution aside, ogle her
And see beauty in her, and grace, and worth,
Finally notice that in a chaste heart
There is no place for deception, flattery, or suspicion.
Whatever in me is of heaven
Is born because from your blossoms
I collect the gentle honeydew
And find delight and satisfaction
In feasting eagerly on your Ambrosia.
From you comes the sweet liquid
From you issues the true Love
And your thoughts and your words
Awaken the soul to the Creator of the Sun.[29]

potential suitor away, insisting that Cassia's husband must be as accomplished and learned as Shephatiah himself, and possessing "every good quality."

One night when his daughter brought water to Shephatiah, he noticed that "she had arrived at the time of maturity for marriage."[30] Feeling ashamed that he had not done his duty by her, he quickly summoned his brother and arranged Cassia's marriage to Ḥasadiah, his brother's son. Once Cassia was safely married, her name was never mentioned again in Ahimaaz's chronicle.

CONAT, ESTELLINA OF MANTUA, PRINTER
(15th century)

Estellina Conat, together with her husband, Avraham ben Shlomo Conat of Mantua, and Ferrara, a physician and printer of books, established one of the first Jewish printing presses in Mantua in 1475. Estellina knew Hebrew and worked independently on the family press, as her husband attested in a Hebrew letter, saying: "she wrote the book with many pens, without the aid of a miracle."[33]

GAUDIOSA OF PALERMO, BOOK OWNER
(15th century)

Gaudiosa of Palermo, Sicily, was the widow of Nissim de Randagio. At her death in 1478, she left seventy-two Hebrew books and manuscripts to her nine-year-old son. His guardian was an aunt. The books were identified in the inventory as Bibles, Talmuds, and Commentaries.[34] Although we cannot assume that Gaudiosa used these books or even that she could read them, they were in her possession rather than in the care of a male relative and she was free to dispose of them as she wished.

DEI MANSI, PAULA OF VERONA, SCHOLAR AND SCRIBE
(13th century)

Paula, one of the earliest female scribes known to historians, was the daughter of Abraham Anau and a member of a distinguished family of scribes.[35] Members of the family were variously known as *Dei Mansi, Piatelli, Pietosa,* or *Umani,* and all traced their roots back to Yeḥiel ben Avraham and his famous son, Natan ben Yeḥiel (Baal ha-Arukh).

Paula was Yeḥiel's great-granddaughter. She first married Shlomo de Rossi, with whom she had three sons, Immanuel, Yekutiel, and Shlomo. Shlomo, the youngest, was named after his father, who died before the birth in 1285. There were no children

---

A HEBREW INSCRIPTION

Estellina added the following Hebrew colophon to a book printed in 1476:

"I, Estellina (wife of my master, my husband, the honored Rabbi Abraham Conat, may he be blessed with children, and may his days be prolonged, Amen), wrote* this book, *Investigations of the World,* with the aid of the youth Jacob Levi de Provence, of Tarascon, may he live."[31]

*The accepted Hebrew word for the process of printing was not developed until Abraham the Dyer of Ferrara adopted the term *difus* in 1477. Until that time both Abraham and Estellina Conat used the Hebrew word *kotev* (write).[32]

from a second marriage to Yehiel ben Shlomo dei Mansi, probably a cousin.

The first evidence of Paula's scribal and intellectual skills was her translation of a collection of Bible commentaries in 1288. Her father wrote the original work and Paula added her own explanations, translating the whole manuscript from Hebrew into Italian.[36] In the front of the manuscript, she signed her name and included her full genealogy. The Hebrew colophon reads: "This book, the commentary on the prophets, was written by the hand of Paula, daughter of R. Avraham the Scribe, son of R. Yoav, from the son of his son, of R. Yehiel, father of Rabbenu Natan."[37]

The Dei Mansi family continued to produce many generations of scholars. Although the official family tree records only the names of the male members, Paula was part of this distinguished line of copyists.

DA MODENA, FIORETTA / BATHSHEVA, SCHOLAR
(16th century)

Fioretta was a disciplined and dedicated scholar. She was the wife of Shlomo da Modena, and her husband's nephew was Yehudah Arye (Leon) Modena (1571–1648), a famous and controversial rabbi, scribe, lecturer, and historian. It is from this nephew that we have information about Fioretta and her equally well-educated sister, Diana Rieti.[38]

Fioretta's grandson, Aaron Berekhiah da Modena (d. 1639) who later became a noted kabbalist, remembered his grandmother as "the one, above all others, who raised me like a son from the time I came out of my mother's womb, and I owe her the honor due a father or mother."[39] She was an expert

---

BY THE HAND OF PAULA DEI MANSI

A prayer book with explanations was dedicated by Paula to her son, then eight years old. In it she wrote:

"This was completed . . . in the year 1293 by the hands of Paula, the daughter of R. Avraham the Scribe, the son of Yoav, and I wrote it in the name of my son Shlomo, the son of my honored teacher, R. Shlomo" (her first husband). She added: "May He Who has made me worthy to write this, make me worthy to see [my son] great in Torah, in wisdom, and in fear of God."[40]

Menahem ben Benyamin the *Tzaddik* was another recipient of Paula's scribal efforts. The book was a collection of laws. A lengthy inscription acknowledged:

"My dear relative came to me and entreated, begged, and compelled me to write this holy book for him . . . With the help of God I made a great effort in this work and finished it . . . on Wednesday, the second day of the first month [Tishrei] in the year 1293."[41]

---

in Torah, Mishnah, Talmud, Midrash, and Zohar, and Aaron related how, when he was a young boy, his grandmother ("the mother of my mother, the important and wise elder *Marat* Fioretta") would try to get the best possible teachers for him.[42] It was not unusual for mothers and grandmothers to be concerned with the religious education of children, particularly the boys in the family.

When Fioretta was seventy-five years old, she left Italy for Safed, a city in northern Palestine noted for its kabbalistic scholars. She hoped to end her days there but died before she reached the land of Israel.

NISSIM, DIAMANTE OF PISA, HOSTESS
(16th century)

Diamante Nissim of Pisa entertained the pseudo-messiah David Reubeni in her home in approximately 1524. In his travel diary, Reubeni reported: ". . . Diamante, the daughter of R. Asher Meshullam of Venice, and the mother of R. Yeḥiel, Signora Laura, and her mother, Signora Sarah, and other young women used to dance in the room where I was and the wife of R. Yeḥiel played the harp, and they said to me, 'We are come here for your honor's sake and in order that the sorrow may go from the fast and that you may rejoice.'"[43]

PERNA OF FANO, PHYSICIAN
(15th century)

In 1460, the "Jewess Perna" applied for a permit to practice medicine in Fano, a town known to be favorable toward Jews.[44]

RACHEL OF VENICE, SINGER
(17th century)

Rachel, the daughter of Jacob, was a well-known Jewish woman singer in early seventeenth-century Venice. She was gifted with a voice of unusual beauty and was a familiar figure in the salons of the nobility, having obtained special permission, along with her father and brother, to leave the ghetto at night in order to sing in the homes of "nobles, citizens, and other honor-able persons." Later that permission was rescinded, apparently because she had not limited her visits to the nobility. In 1613, she was accused of "singing around the city at night by gondola without express permission."[45]

RICHA OF VENICE, PROPERTY OWNER
(16th century)

Richa was a rich Ashkenazic woman from the powerful Meshullam family.[46] Her will, drafted in 1525 in Venice, revealed that she had substantial property at her disposal. She signed the will both in Yiddish and the Venetian dialect and, following tradition, left her entire estate to her husband. The couple was childless.

RIVKAH OF FERRARA, EDUCATED WOMAN
(late 16th century)

Records mention Rivkah of Ferrara as the daughter of Yeḥiel ben Azriel Trabot of Ascoli (d. 1591). Rivkah brought her father's teachings to the attention of his colleagues, who then recorded them for posterity.[47]

DI ROSSI, EUROPA OF MANTUA, MUSICIAN
(16th century)

Europa di Rossi was the first female Jewish singer to gain substantial fame beyond the Jewish world. She was the daughter of Bonaiuto di Rossi and the wife of David ben Elisha. Her brother Salomone was a well-known Jewish composer, instrumentalist, and singer at the Mantuan court. He was also famous for his Hebrew sacred works, performed by Jewish singers in synagogues and at Jewish social functions throughout the seventeenth century.[48]

Europa di Rossi was well known and admired in Mantua's musical circles, and her name appears in two salary rolls of the Mantuan court.[49] In 1592–93 she was listed along with her brother, Salamone di Rossi, and several other musicians; and a modest salary was specified for her.

Europa's most famous performance may have been *The Rape of Europa*, a drama set to music, part of a series of theatrical events produced at court in 1608. The occasion for this musical extravaganza was the marriage of Crown Prince Francesco Gonzaga to Margherita of Savoy. Some historians incorrectly assumed that Europa adopted her name after performing the role, but records indicate that her name predated the production.

DONNA SARAH OF ITALY, ABANDONED WIFE
(ca. 13th century)

A single letter written to her husband, Solomon, and preserved in the Cairo Genizah offers evidence of the life and concerns of this Italian-Jewish wife and mother of several daughters. The dates of Sarah's birth and death are not known, but based on the style of the handwriting and her use of the title "Donna," scholars have concluded that she was an Italian-Jewish woman of the thirteenth century.[50]

We know that Sarah's husband traveled to Egypt in search of relief from taxes. The letter expressed her worries, her need for reassurance that she had not been abandoned, and her indignation at her husband's long absence.

DONNA SARAH TO HER HUSBAND SOLOMON

May ample peace and welfare be with my master and ruler . . . my master and husband, the learned Rabbi Solomon, the scribe, may he live long. . . .

We are all longing to see your sweet face . . . and we are wondering that you have not answered the numerous letters we have sent you. We have written you often begging you to return, but—no answer at all. If you can manage . . . to obtain release from taxes it will greatly be to your profit. . . .

We are all assembled, your wife, your daughters, and your son-in-law Moses, to implore you from the bottom of our hearts not to go further either by sea or by land, because we have heard that you have the intention of leaving for Turkey. I swear to the Lord that if you do this, you must not speak with us anymore; and if you do this, which will make the world despise us . . . you will inflict pain upon your daughter and perhaps she will suffer a miscarriage. And you will also endanger the happiness of your beautiful daughter Rachel.

. . . People will talk scandal and say: "Here is a respectable old scribe, who left his wife and daughters and has been missing for many years. Perhaps he is mad. . . . "Beg the physician, Rabbi Solomon, therefore to provide you a confirmation about the release from the taxes; otherwise come home [in the name of] the Blessed one! . . . Do nothing else. And Peace."[51]

It is not certain whether Donna Sarah wrote this letter herself or if a scribe or a relative wrote it on her behalf. Since R. Solomon was a scribe, his wife might also have possessed such skill, but there is no confirmation for this.

It is impossible to know what happened to R. Solomon, but Donna Sarah had good reason to be concerned. If he did not return, she would have become an *agunah,* a wife abandoned by her husband. She would have no possibility of getting a legal divorce and would never be able to remarry unless there was a witness to prove that her husband was dead (see **Divorce** on p. 122).

SHAPIRA-LURIA, MIRIAM, SCHOLAR (15TH CENTURY)

Miriam Shapira-Luria was mentioned in an old document attributed to Yoḥanan Lurie and reprinted in a work of Yosef ben Gershom of Rosheim (1478–1554). Yoḥanan traced his family tree back to "Rabbanit Miriam," daughter of Shlomo Shapira, reporting that she "sat in the yeshivah behind a curtain and taught the law to some outstanding young men." The probable dates for this are between 1425 and 1450, but there is no confirmation for the report.[53]

SULLAM, SARA COPIO OF VENICE, POET AND SCHOLAR (17th century)

Sara Copio[54] was born in Venice in 1592 into a prosperous merchant family. She was the oldest of two or three daughters[55] and received an extensive humanistic education that included training in Hebrew, Spanish, Latin, and Greek as well as her native Italian. She was also taught philosophy, music, and rabbinic literature.

At a very early age, Sara began to write verse and became known in Italy as a poet and singer who accompanied herself on the lyre. She continued writing poetry even after her marriage, in 1613 or 1614, and her home became a meeting place for Jewish and Christian poets, artists, and scholars. Her husband, Jacob Sullam, was himself a patron of the arts in addition to being a moneylender.[56] In 1615 the couple had one daughter, Rebecca, who died at the age of ten months.[57] There is no evidence of any other children.

Sara Copio Sullam's writings displayed her knowledge of the Hebrew language as well as the texts of the Hebrew Bible and the New Testament. There were references to Josephus, Aristotle, and Dante. Over the years, she became known for her poetic improvisations, a sort of literary dueling match between participants that, unfortunately, was never written down. She also wrote sonnets and numerous letters.

Sullam's most famous correspondent was the aged Christian poet, Ansaldo Cebà. Thirty years older than she, Cebà was a retired diplomat who

---

AN EARLY POEM BY SARA COPIO SULLAM

*For some time now what was once
  my lyre has been silent,
Hence the fame I sometimes
  enjoyed has departed.
Bothersome cares have cut the
  wings of beautiful desire,
From which song rises and seeks
  life.*[52]

had an illustrious career as a writer and translator of the classics. Among his works was a play in verse entitled *La Reina Ester* (Queen Esther) that Sara read early in 1618 while recovering from a miscarriage. Moved to write to him to express her admiration, that first letter began a long-distance relationship that lasted for four years.

Cebà and Sullam never met. She remained in the Venetian ghetto and he in Genoa where he had retired to a monastery, but their correspondence is full of intimate, sometimes even physical allusions and metaphors. Besides letters, they exchanged books, portraits, and gifts.[58] Cebà's avowed goal was to convert Sara to Christianity. In spite of her open admiration for him, she steadfastly refused to consider it and suggested in one letter that she might pray for *his* conversion.[59] This daring proposal, coupled with what appears to be misplaced trust and extreme naïveté, ultimately led to trouble.

Desiring to perfect her many skills, Sullam took lessons from some of the poets, painters, and scholars who frequented her salon. In return, she offered them sponsorship and financial support. At first, her benefactors wrote flattering poetry to her, alluding to her blond beauty, her charm and pleasant disposition.[60] Many, however, seem to have taken advantage of her kindness and gone on to betray her trust.

One example of such betrayal came from the Italian scholar and prominent cleric, Baldassare Bonifaccio, who had often been a guest at Sullam's home. In 1621, in his "Discourse on the Immortality of the Soul" *(Discorso sull'immortalita dell'anima)*, Bonifaccio accused her of deny-

---

EXCERPTS FROM SULLAM'S MANIFESTO

The title of her work was: "Manifesto by Sara Copio Sullam, Jewess, in which she condemns and deprecates the opinion denying the immortality of the soul, falsely attributed to her by Signor Baldassare Bonifaccio." It was dedicated to the memory of Simon Copio, her "beloved father," who died when she was sixteen. The dedication reads, in part:

"This little but necessary work could not be dedicated to anybody else than to him who has passed the threshold of this transient life, because it confirms the thesis which I prove in this work, namely that I undoubtedly believe in the immortality of the soul. . . .

I should like to continue to contribute to the increase of thy heavenly pleasures by the modest fame I was able to acquire, which, I trust, will be not less dear to thee because it was produced by a woman most desirous but unable to do as much for the perpetuation of thy name as a son would have done. . . . Accept, therefore, this humble token of the unlimited devotion of thy daughter [who] will live for the honor of thy name, no less than for her own."[61]

---

ing immortality, an accusation that amounted to heresy, and a serious crime in the Venice of her day. Sara Copio Sullam was quick to reply with

A PRAYER FOR VINDICATION

Some of Sara Copio Sullam's bitterness and disappointment comes through in this sonnet, in which she appeals to God to protect her from "the lying tongue's deceit."

O Lord, You know my inmost hope and thought,
You know when e'er before Thy judgement throne
I shed salt tears, and uttered many a moan.
It was not for vanities I sought.
O turn on me Thy look with mercy fraught,
And see how envious malice makes me groan!
The Pall upon my heart by error thrown,
Remove: illume me with Thy radiant thought.
At truth let not the wicked scorner mock,
O Thou, that breathed in me a spark divine,
The lying tongue's deceit with silence blight.
Protect me from its venom, Thou My Rock,
And show the spiteful slanderer by this sign
That Thou dost shield me with Thy endless might.[62]

Sara Sullam sent her friend Cebà a copy of her manifesto, hoping for his support on her behalf, but Cebà was old and ill. After many months he replied, but only to comment once again on her failure to convert. Ansaldo Cebà died in 1623, shortly after this last correspondence.

The accusation by Bonifaccio and the failure of Cebà and her other friends to rally to her defense constituted real danger to Sullam should the Inquisition decide to investigate the charges. In addition, they were serious personal disappointments. This difficult period in her life continued for some years. Many of her friends and teachers left her, and others played cruel jokes or tried to trick her out of her money. She was even accused of plagiarizing.

Not until after 1625 did someone come to Sullam's defense. In a manuscript called *Codice di Giulia Soliga*, her anonymous defender described an imaginary trial against

SARA COPIO SULLAM'S TOMBSTONE

This is the headstone of the modest Signora Sara, wife of the living Jacob Sullam.

"The afflicting angel shot an arrow, in the holy service; the angel removed and killed her.

Sage among women, crown of the poor, she was a true companion to the wretched.

If today she is unredeemed, with the hope only of the worm and the moth, the time of redemption will come, when the Lord will say to her, 'Return, return, oh my Shulamite.'"[64]

a manifesto of her own, defending herself against this dangerous charge. She accused Bonifaccio of not knowing Hebrew, and he retaliated, alleging that she herself had not written the manifesto.[63]

her accusers and denigrators and compared her to some of the most famous Italian women writers of the fifteenth and sixteenth centuries.[65]

After this work, which included some of her unpublished sonnets, nothing much was written about this most celebrated woman of her time. She died of "a continual fever lasting three months."[66] Although the date of her death is in doubt, her death certificate gives February 15, 1641.[67]

VIRDIMURA OF SICILY, PHYSICIAN
(14th century)

Virdimura was tested by the physicians of the royal court and obtained permission to practice throughout the kingdom of Sicily in 1376. The document stated that she was granted this right "in consideration of praise universally given her."[68] Virdimura was the wife of the physician Pasquale of Catania, and she was particularly interested in treating the poor who could not afford the high fees charged by doctors.

WIFE OF R. ḤAYYIM OF SICILY, MYSTIC AND PROPHET
(12th century)

Rabbi Ḥayyim's wife was nine months pregnant when her activities were brought to the attention of the community. In front of a group of male spectators from the synagogue, she went into a trance and prophesied about the end of the world, admonishing all to repent of their sins. She called for a tallit to cover herself, and when it was put over her, Hebrew letters miraculously appeared on it.

A similar incident occurred the next day. At that time, a sweet-smelling liquid ran from her hands. The men tasted it and declared it to be like honey. The woman then urged the men to go to the synagogue and pray, and two of them subsequently saw visions as well.

One of the witnesses to this event was a traveler in Catania, Sicily. He was greatly impressed by the mystical powers of this unnamed woman and reported her activities in a letter that ultimately was discovered among the documents of the Cairo Genizah.[69]

THE WORLD OF JEWISH WOMEN

ECONOMIC ACTIVITIES

For the earliest Jewish settlers in southern Italy the preferred occupation was agriculture, and many bought farms as soon as they could afford them.[70] However, the various prohibitions against Jews owning land or employing Christian servants[71] altered this situation, and women's traditional household and farm work began to change. Besides those women who directly served the Jewish community as midwives, bathhouse attendants, prayer leaders for women, or occasional scribes or teachers,[72] a majority worked as artisans, peddlers, and merchants. A few extant licenses indicate that some Jewish women also practiced medicine, as did **Virdimura of Sicily** and **Perna of Fano**.

Women in Business

By the late thirteenth and fourteenth centuries, Jewish women and men began to be involved in the financial trades. Women usually worked alongside their husbands, but they also could be found as independent moneylenders and businesswomen.[73]

Italian-Jewish businesswomen have left behind many records that confirm their activities in the developing world of finance. Besides acting as moneylenders and pawnbrokers, women functioned as financial agents for their husbands, especially if the men were traveling. Widows often continued the family business alone, or together with their children. Many women were experienced and capable of accessing funds and paying damages for claims.[74] One of the businesses in which Jewish women might engage was the making and selling of cosmetics. **Anna the Hebrew** counted the noblewoman Catherine Sforza among her clients in 1508.

In the late 1500s and early 1600s, women's participation in business increased. There are records of women such as Stella Sacerdote and Chiara Sciunnach, who engaged in the silk business; Dulcia bat Ḥanniah who raised buffalo; and Gioia di Montalto, a manufacturer and seller of buttons.[75] Women traveled for business purposes, going unescorted to trade fairs and markets. In the sixteenth century, this precipitated the harsh judgment of R. Katzenellenbogen (1482–1565), who strongly disapproved of such behavior,[76] but his condemnation seems to have had little effect on women's activities.

Women Printers

The invention of printing in 1455 opened up yet another occupation for women. Johannes Gutenberg's press produced the first printed edition of the Latin Bible in 1457. Just twenty years later, in 1475, one of the first Jewish presses appeared in Mantua operated by **Estellina Conat** and her husband Avraham.

By the end of the fifteenth century many Jewish printing presses were operating. With printing carried on in home workshops, it was natural that women would become involved in the production of books together with the men in the family. In addition to Estellina Conat, other women printers and editors produced works or were involved with printing. In many cases the women were the authors as well as the printers and publishers and filled an important function in the early production and publication of Hebrew books in Italy.[77]

Work in the Arts

Italy was rare among Christian European lands in permitting secular music and entertainment, and Jews followed suit, participating in a variety of musical activities. Between 1450 and 1650, music thrived in the Jewish communities, especially in northern Italy, and many gala presentations were created, from instrumental performances to operas, dances, and even an occasional pageant. To be a music or dance teacher was an accepted Jewish occupation, although less acceptable when women engaged in it or when Jews taught Christians. In 1433 the government of Venice decreed that "no Jew was to operate a school for teaching games, skills, sciences, dancing, singing, playing instruments . . . subject to a fine of five hundred ducats and six months in jail."[78] The ruling was repeated in 1644. But even here there were exceptions. In the late sixteenth century a special dispension was given to a

Jewish musician and dancer to teach dancing, singing, and music to the children of a small number of noble families.[79]

In Mantua, where musical entertainment was highly valued by the ruling nobility, a handful of Jewish women were regularly employed as singers and instrumentalists in the royal court. Some records of this employment have survived, among them the notation for a salary for Madame **Europa di Rossi,** who was one of several official court entertainers. In the first half of the seventeenth century, **Rachel** was a well-known Jewish singer in the courts of Italy.

Jewish women occasionally participated in more public entertainments as well. One of the most famous was the wedding of Costanzo Sforza with Camilla d'Aragona at Pesaro in 1475. The extravagant production involved many Jewish performers. The procession of Jewish women and men, lavishly dressed in gold and silver costumes, featured an unnamed young woman who played the role of the Queen of Sheba. Garbed in gold and riding on a wooden elephant maneuvered by men hidden inside, she descended from her throne to give an address to the bridal couple in Hebrew. She then presented a wedding gift from the Jewish community.[80]

EDUCATION

Basic Education of Girls

In Italy, as everywhere among Jews, the most important aspect of a Jewish girl's education was learning to manage her household. This included the proper customs for holiday and Sabbath celebrations, the careful observance of the laws of family purity, and the intricate demands of kashrut.

WOMEN BUTCHERS AND RITUAL MEAT SLAUGHTERERS

Ritual slaughtering, killing an animal according to the laws of kashrut, was a rabbinic invention without biblical precedent. Because of this, women were technically allowed to act in the capacity of ritual slaughterers *(sheḥetot),* usually performing these functions only when no qualified man was available. A few widowed women with children, living in isolated towns, possibly left to run a loan bank, needed to learn this skill so they could eat meat. In other instances, rich women who spent long periods of time in their country homes, far from their husbands, had to depend on themselves for the availability of fresh, kosher meat.[81]

To date, only a few written authorizations for women who qualified to practice ritual slaughtering have been found, all issued between the years 1556 and 1624 in the area of Mantua. The wording of the licences granted them indicates that they were subject to a rigorous examination, concerning both the ritual aspects and the physical stamina required,[82] but it is not clear whether any women ever depended on this skill for an income.

Porging *(nikkur),* the removal of fat, veins, nerves, and sinews from the meat before it was cooked, was one of the tasks that young women had to

FIG. 11. This illustration of northern Italian-Jewish couples dancing together, with accompanying lute players, is from a fifteenth-century manuscript. (Courtesy of Rothschild Misc. 246v., Israel Museum, Jerusalem)

learn before they married. This skill implied knowledge of talmudic sources concerning the rules of kosher slaughtering and was expected of women as part of their household chores.[83]

Girls in Italy never participated in the formal Jewish education offered to boys in yeshivot, but many were educated at home, perhaps learning to read the more important Hebrew prayers.[84] Some read the Bible and prayed daily in Italian. The Jews of Italy also considered dancing an important component of a well-rounded education. Jewish dance masters, some of them rabbis and scholars themselves,[85] taught music and dance to young men and women. Several fifteenth-century miniatures from the Mantua-Ferrara area attest to

women's participation in dance. One shows a wedding scene with a well-dressed couple being married by a rabbi and then dancing together.[86] Another depicts three couples, simply dressed, dancing to the music of lute players.[87]

Higher Education

As the standards of the Italian Renaissance became more widespread, there is evidence that some Jewish women, particularly in the upper class, received a better secular education than Jewish women ever had before.[88] A document of the sixteenth century reports that rich young women, both Christian and Jewish, studied poetry; learned Boethius, Ovid, Cicero, Dante, and Petrarch; and discussed these writings among themselves, making jokes and allusions to them.[89]

The stricter authorities regularly condemned this sort of education for women. In the early years of the sixteenth century, R. David ben Yehudah Messer Leon (ca. 1470–1526) took issue with a verse in the Jerusalem Talmud attributed to R. Yoḥanan that allowed women to be taught "Greek wisdom." He insisted that since women were light-minded, surely R. Yoḥanan meant only the Greek language and not Greek philosophy.[90] As late as the seventeenth century, R. Asael ben David del Bene of Ferrara was warning Jews that the instruction of girls in the Italian national literature was a danger to morality. "Female youth," he asserted, "become corrupted and poisoned by a premature awakening of impure thoughts and the excitation of love."[91]

Notwithstanding the disapproval of the rabbis, some women, especially during the sixteenth century, clearly achieved intellectual excellence according to the new standards and with it, a more prominent public role.[92] One example of an educated woman who earned some degree of fame—perhaps even notoriety—was **Sara Copio Sullam**. Sullam was well educated in languages, including Hebrew, Greek, and Latin, as well as in literature and philosophy; and **Paula dei Mansi** knew enough Hebrew to translate her father's writing into Italian.

Women occasionally became learned even in areas of Jewish law from which they were traditionally excluded. **Miriam Shapira Luria** was said to have taught the law to male students. **Fioretta / Bathsheva da Modena** was expert in Bible and Talmud as well as in the Zohar, a mystical work rarely made available to women. However, most learned women would have been well aware of the stipulation of female modesty and thus would have been reluctant to display their erudition in public.

FAMILY LIFE

Betrothal and Marriage

In the early Jewish communities of southern Italy, women were expected to play a relatively passive role and had little control over their own lives. This is evident in the case of **Cassia**, the young daughter of Shephatiah referred to in a work called *The Book of Genealogy* or the *Chronicle of Ahimaaz*. Apparently having just arrived at puberty, Cassia was neither consulted nor informed about her betrothal to her cousin. Moreover, her mother, who had attempted to postpone her daughter's marriage, was "rebuked" and "shamed" by Shephatiah. He complained: "I have followed your advice and have not found happiness for her; I have violated the ordinance of the Scripture and disregarded the words of the sages."[93]

Marriage within families, especially between cousins, was very common at this time. Not only did Cassia marry her cousin; many hundreds of years later, Paula dei Mansi and **Benvenida Abrabanel** also married cousins. This was often considered the best arrangement for a daughter, as it kept her safely within the family.

As for the duties demanded of a wife, these differed little from expectations of earlier years and followed mishnaic rulings. In 1456, R. Moshe ben Yoav warned an assemblage of Jews at a betrothal ceremony that married women who rebelled against traditional behavior would give birth to defective children.[94] He repeated the old assumptions that women were naturally passive, lacked imagination, and were incapable of understanding the spiritual. R. Moshe also told his audience that the proper activity of a wife was to serve her husband and be helpful to him. He quoted R. Eliezer's comment: "He who teaches his daughter the Law, teaches her *tiflut* (obscenity)" (B. *Sotah* 20a).

Despite such attitudes, repeated in subsequent centuries by others, traditional restrictions that had limited the roles of women in Italian-Jewish society did slowly change. By the fifteenth and sixteenth centuries, many of the older laws were relaxed, overlooked, or sometimes blatantly ignored by large segments of the Jewish population, and considerable numbers of Jewish women acted independently of their husbands. R. Katzenellenbogen railed against women who worked and traveled, calling them gadabouts and likening them to prostitutes.[95] He insisted that women be modest and obedient to their husbands, because "they are simple-minded and have a tendency to trivialize."[96] But despite these opinions, legal documents suggest that women were more assertive than the rabbis would have liked, and there was a frequent discrepancy between the religious ideal and the social reality.[97]

Divorce

According to Jewish law, a woman could initiate divorce only in very specific circumstances, and even in these instances the court could not grant her a divorce without her husband's consent. This standard, stipulated in the Babylonian Talmud and reiterated by the *geonim* (see chapters 2 and 3, **Divorce**), was not altered in Italy, and

Italian-Jewish men were sensitive to the problem. When men traveled great distances, they routinely provided their wives with conditional divorce documents. If a husband did not return within a stated period of time, the divorce (*get*) would become effective, and the wife would be saved from the status of *agunah*, literally, chained woman.[98]

This was precisely the problem faced by the twelfth-century woman **Donna Sarah**. We will never know if or when this woman's husband returned, but if he did not, Donna Sarah would have been left in the unfortunate legal position of an *agunah*, a deserted wife, never able to remarry unless there was a witness to prove that her husband was dead. Such abandoned women were common among the Sephardim who immigrated to Italy after the expulsion from Spain in 1492. Families were separated, and many people died far from their loved ones with no witnesses to report the event (see also chapter 7).

Monogamy

Italian rabbis, living in the shadow of the Church, did not feel free to allow plural marriages for Jews, and most Jewish men had only one wife. However, there was no strong feeling against it, especially among Sephardic Jews who were never bound by R. Gershom's ruling (see chapter 4), and there are some cases of plural marriage. Chiara, the daughter of Abram Salom, denounced her husband, Jacob Bueno, because he ignored their marriage agreement and took a second wife.[99]

Another instance where plural marriage might occur was in the case of *yibbum*, levirate marriage. There was much disagreement among Italian rabbis on this issue during the six-teenth century. Most Italian and Ashkenazic rabbis favored the release of the woman by her brother-in-law in the traditional formal ceremony (*halitzah*). Rabbi Leon Modena insisted that this issue had always been a matter of local custom, and in Italy *halitzah* was the custom. Among the Sephardim, however, marriage to the levir, the late husband's brother, was regularly practiced as there was no prohibition against plural marriage. The problem of whose tradition would prevail in Italy was never definitively resolved.[100]

Men who took concubines or mistresses outside of marriage circumvented the standard of monogamy but never actually challenged it. Many of these concubines were Jewish. This seems to have been the case for Isaac Abrabanel, the husband of **Benvenida Abrabanel**. A challenge to his will revealed that he had a Jewish mistress by whom he had fathered a child.[101]

Violence Against Women

Wife beating was an inherent part of Christian and Jewish culture, and this was echoed in Italian-Jewish literature. Azriel bar Shlomo Diena (d. 1536) insisted that "every man should rule over his women in his house and be firm with his helpmate."[102] "Firmness" often included physical beatings, and many rabbis, like their Christian counterparts, assumed that it was a man's right and responsibility to beat his wife in order to correct her.[103] Italian rabbis consistently refused to rule that wife beating was sufficient reason to force a man to divorce his wife, except in extreme cases of violence.[104]

There was no question that wife beating was permitted if the wife failed to obey her husband. In Rome, Anna di

---

> ### HOW TO HANDLE A WIFE
>
> [A poem written by Moshe ibn Habib, a refugee from Portugal to Italy, advised his male readers]
>
> *If your wife is evil and does not obey,*
> *Or serve you, and evil plots she does lay,*
> *Know that with a strong stick to a rebellious cow,*
> *You can straighten her furrows and she will plow.*[105]

Signori was ordered to listen to her husband "like modest females do," and if she didn't, he was allowed to beat her "as permitted by the Torah."

Likewise, Shabbetai ben Rafael Duriel declared that he would beat his wife when she returned home from her father's house "in the manner in which one beats women."[106]

Women's reactions to such routine violence is rarely recorded, although one testament from the early seventeenth century, written by Rachel, daughter of Manuel Valensin, accused her late husband, David Crespin, of beating her.[107]

Women's Sexuality

Ultimately, a woman's modesty was her only protection against the dangers her sexuality posed to herself and to men, and immodest behavior was always suspect. Prohibitions directed at women were often reactions to what was perceived by men as immodesty. Rulings prohibiting "more than three ladies and two maids to walk together in the streets" or limiting the number of women and girls invited to a banquet are examples of such restrictive laws guarding women's modesty.[108] Sumptuary laws, prohibiting excessive exhibition of luxurious fabrics and ostentatious jewelry, are another example (see **Sumptuary Laws** below).

The social mingling of males and females was a continual concern of the rabbis. Both men and women were repeatedly warned against being alone with a member of the opposite sex, and any kind of contact between Jewish women and men who were not their husbands was especially perilous. This

---

MODESTY AND HIGH FASHION

It was a tradition among Jewish women everywhere to keep their heads covered, and Italian-Jewish women were well aware of this. However, their interest in keeping up with the latest fashion prompted them to use wigs, often blond, instead of the traditional head covering. This, in effect, placed Jewish law in the service of high fashion, defeating the proscription for modesty while following the letter of the law.[109] The rabbis legislated against the practice but never succeeded in wiping it out. Eventually, the use of wigs spread from Italy north into Germany and then into the communities of Eastern Europe. Rather than a way to circumvent the laws of modesty for women, the wig eventually became the head covering of choice for traditional Jewish women and had the full approval of the rabbis.

---

was not simply a theoretical concern; specific cases of improper sexual behavior often came to the attention of Italian rabbis. Rabbi Azriel Diena answered a query dealing with unwed mothers and discussed what category of children were illegitimate *(mamzerim)*. At least one of the women he dealt with in his responsum had been a Jewish servant, working in the home of the man who fathered her child.[110]

In Modena in 1534, R. Diena also noted several instances of women who made personal complaints against men concerning sexual matters. He did not question the legitimacy of the women's complaints but did condemn them for loudly cursing the men while the Torah was being removed from the ark.[111] Although a condemnation of men who practiced casual sex was implicit in R. Diena's writing, there was special concern to eliminate any question of inappropriate behavior by Jewish wives and daughters.

LEGAL RIGHTS

Legally, everything a wife earned was the property of her husband, who was the head of the family. He was recognized as the family spokesperson in all secular as well as religious affairs. He paid the taxes and usually represented his wife in court. Even if she ran a business of her own, she was considered his agent (see chapter 4, **Economic Activities**).

Wills

Jewish law also assumed that a woman was maintained by her husband's property after his death, but a wife could not inherit or bequeath property, as her earnings and property technically belonged to her husband. Women's wills, however, indicate that they often ignored this precept, bypassing the general rule and leaving bequests to relatives and friends. They were able to do this either by going to the secular courts or by making a deathbed will.

Wills notarized in secular courts were technically frowned on by Jewish law but were so common in Italy that it was impractical to challenge them. The rabbis rationalized their acceptance of this practice with the talmudic opinion that *dina demalkhut dina* (the law of the land is binding). Often, men drew up notarial wills in order to leave bequests to wives and daughters. This was the case with Benvenida Abrabanel's husband, who left her his entire estate, bypassing his sons.[112]

Deathbed wills were often made before the birth of a child or when the woman was ill. As long as some mention of her health was included, a woman could give testamentary gifts to anyone she chose. Some women also included specific instructions to husbands and children in their wills.[113] Several wills belonging to Jewish women from the fourteenth and fifteenth centuries have been found in Crete, then under Venetian rule. They were written and registered by official Latin notaries.[114]

Many women left their property to children or husbands, but some added special requests. For example, in 1340, Esther, the wife of Lingiachus, left her goods to her husband but reminded him of their promise to their daughter Henregine.[115] Anastassia named her husband, Judah Balbi, and her brother as executors and specified that her money should go to her husband and, at his death, to her three sons. However, if her husband took a second wife, he would no longer be permitted to keep the inheritance. In that case, Anastassia stipulated that the money

---

> ### WOMEN'S WILLS FROM CRETE
>
> - Eudhochia, wife of Rabbi Peres, left "all my goods, movable and immovable" to Nacium, the son of Sanbathei Vlimidhi, a relative.
> - One woman named "Moses, my dear brother" as her beneficiary.
> - Another woman named "Helias, my dear friend" as an heir.
> - Cheranna, the widow of Curtesus, bequeathed her valuables to her sister and brother-in-law in a will dated 1347. She asked that they pay all her debts and give money to charity in her name.[116]

---

would be placed in trust by the other executor and invested until each of her sons reached the age of twenty years. She reminded Judah that permission to make such arrangements had been written into her marriage contract.[117]

Outside of Venetian Crete similar examples are available. **Gaudiosa of Palermo,** Sicily, bequeathed Hebrew books and manuscripts to her young son, while Rosa Cara of Venice left her small bequest to the people who cared for her before her death.[118] It was common for women to leave money to house or clothe the poor, to dower indigent brides, or to finance the study of Torah.

Rights of Widows

When a husband predeceased his wife, the widow was considered a legal entity in the community and in the courts. She was now obligated to pay her own taxes and was responsible for her own debts. If she remained unmarried, she would have to step into the role of breadwinner, usually continuing a family business but with the legal right to make all her own decisions.

Widows often controlled the family finances and arranged their children's marriages without the supervision of a male relative or guardian.[119] Some women became legal guardians of children. When Gaudiosa died, her nine-year-old son passed to the guardianship of an aunt. Another example of a female guardian is Dolcebella, who was responsible for the orphans of Mordecai di Rossetto in 1560. Rachel Corcos, widow of Salamone Benafri, acted as executor of her husband's will. Both Rachel and her husband were from banking families, and Rachel became executor and administrator of the family property at her husband's death in 1626.[120] Benvenida Abrabanel also took over the family holdings after her husband's death, even though there were several living sons.

Sumptuary Laws

While the sumptuary laws promulgated by Italy's Jews often applied to both men and women, those attempting to put limits on ostentatious dress were directed more often against women.[121] Early laws attempting to put limits on the type of clothing worn by women can be found in records from an early conference in Forli. In this 1418 ruling, women were told that they must not wear "open or silk-lined sleeves, linings of ermine, sable, marten, or other kinds of costly fur, jackets and dresses of silk or velvet, gold necklaces and gilt hairnets . . . belts with silver buckles

weighing more than ten ounces." An exception was made for "newly married brides [who] may wear golden hair nets unconcealed for thirty days after the wedding." In this ordinance, men also had restrictions placed on them, and the main impetus for the law is given: ". . . with a view to bending hearts to behave humbly and not to attract the attention of the Gentiles."[122]

More often, it was Christian laws that limited styles for Jewish women. At a time when Jews and Christians mingled freely, differences in dress served the purpose of distinguishing one from the other, so that a Christian would not inadvertently have sexual intercourse with a Jew. That was the avowed purpose of the original legislation of the Fourth Lateran Council of 1215, but it was not consistently enforced. In 1480 in parts of Italy, Jewish women were required to wear earrings.[123] Beginning in the late fifteenth century, in the Venetian Republic, Jewish women had to wear yellow badges or yellow headgear (the same as prostitutes) to differentiate them from Christians. This was considered a humiliating social distinction, and occasional exemptions were granted to individuals or families.[124] Eventually, the color of the headdress was changed to red for Ashkenazic Jews while Jews from the East wore yellow.[125] By 1566 in Milan, Jewish women were exempt from the badge simply because their hairstyles and earrings apparently were unique and enabled them to be distinguished from Christians.[126]

PUBLIC POWER

Examples of women who could exercise real influence in the public realm are hard to find. Specific conditions had to exist before women might act as leaders: Their families had to have been among the most prominent in their communities, or the women themselves had to perform certain roles within the structure of their families, roles for which no men were available or suitable. Even then, women rarely assumed visible, public power unless the family or community was in crisis.

In Italy this combination of conditions appeared in the later centuries, after the influx of Jews from Spain. At this time, persecution and expulsion of Jews from various Italian cities sometimes forced families to reorganize and depend on the strongest among them regardless of sex.[127] Benvenida Abrabanel took on a leadership role, attempting to influence events revolving around the expulsion of the Jews from Naples, and **Gracia Nasi** (see chapter 7) was involved in communal decision-making concerning the boycott of Ancona while living in Italy. These two are the only known examples of women who succeeded in wielding some public power on the Italian peninsula.

RELIGIOUS ACTIVITIES

Women in the Synagogue

Women's religious participation in Italian synagogues seems consistent with that of their counterparts in other European lands. Women attended prayers with enough regularity that it was necessary to formalize and institutionalize the practice of women precentors here as had been done in Germany. One extant record names **Anna d'Arpino** of sixteenth-century Rome in this role. **Deborah Ascarelli,** from the same century, was very likely a prayer leader also.

Women seem to have felt at home in the synagogue. Not only did they attend public prayer, but they also worked to enhance the synagogue interior. The devotion of some Italian-Jewish women is evident in the form of Torah ark curtains and Torah covers skillfully sewn and embroidered, often dedicated in honor of children or parents. Some of these have been preserved in museums.

Despite women's involvement in synagogue life, the service was not translated into Judeo-Italian until 1596. This development may have been encouraged by the increased immigration of Ashkenazic Jewish women, who often had their own Yiddish prayer books (see chapter 6), but it also attests to Italian women's continuing lack of a classical Hebrew education. Although there were men who did not read Hebrew either, it was usually assumed that such translations were done for the benefit of the women. Women themselves translated some prayers. Deborah Ascarelli translated hymns into Italian that were sung regularly in the synagogue.

It can be assumed that women prayed regularly at home as well. One woman's prayer book from 1480 contains a slightly altered version of the morning blessing for women, hinting at a female assertiveness rarely found, even in early modern times. Instead of thanking God "for making me according to Your will," it praises God "who made me a woman and not a man."[128] It is impossible to ascertain whether this wording was according to the wishes of the woman herself or was simply written as the mirror image of the man's prayer thanking God for not making him a woman. But even if freely chosen, the independent ideas of this unnamed woman were almost certainly kept between the covers of her daily prayer book.

Alternative Religious Expression

Although always in the background, women's religious and spiritual activities rarely came to the attention of the male community. One manuscript, found in the Cairo Genizah and dating from the twelfth century, does report on the pregnant **wife of R. Ḥayyim of Sicily** who had visions and prophesied. The woman then spoke the words of God, predicting that "the end is near" and urging the people to repent.

Besides this document, nothing is known about R. Ḥayyim's wife. Like **the daughter of Joseph** (see chapter 3), she is mentioned only in a single letter and never became famous. Fioretta/Bathsheva da Modena, a scholar of Jewish texts including the Zohar, concentrated on kabbalistic teachings in her later years. But such involvement, as well as the more common practices used to enhance spirituality, were frowned on for women. Women's first responsibility was not to God but to their husbands and households. In the sixteenth century, the Italian R. Avraham Yagel of Reggio (ca. 1553–1623) was very explicit about that point, rebuking women who were "involved in ascetic practices such as daily prayer, fasting, placing ashes on their heads, wearing sackcloth, or denying themselves earthly pleasures." The reason he gave was that their single-minded devotion to God was a dereliction of their duties to their husbands and homes.[130]

Other men found other reasons to discourage women's religious instincts. In the seventeenth century, Immanuel Frances of Italy (1618–1710) wrote that "to teach the religion of God to a female / Is like putting a treasure in the furnace."[131] Nevertheless, women's religious activities held great significance for some and were a legitimate path to spirituality.

PRAYER FOR A WOMAN
IN CHILDBIRTH

[The following prayer, originally translated from Hebrew into Italian for an Ashkenazic Jewish woman, is by an unknown author. It was to be recited at the hour of childbirth.]

"Remember me. Do not forget Your humble servant. Give Your devoted one a child. God of Israel, grant me my desire. Like a deer yearns for the flowing waters in the hour that she comes to give birth; as her labor gets harder, she reaches for You with her antlers. . . .

Open the wall of my womb so that I may at the proper time bear this child who is within me. . . . May I not struggle only to achieve emptiness, may I not labor in vain, God forbid. Because You alone hold the key to life, as it is written, "And God remembered Rachel and listened to her and opened her womb."

Therefore, take pity on my entreaty. From the very depths of my heart I call to You. I raise my voice to You, God. Answer me from the heights of Your holiness."[129]

CHAPTER 6

European Jewry Moves East:
The Early Modern Period (1492–1750)

OVERVIEW

The Growth of Eastern European Jewry

Murder, expulsion, or forced conversions were prominent components of Jewish life in western Europe throughout the fourteenth and fifteenth centuries. This was the time when England, France, and parts of Germany "witnessed the near-destruction of Jewish religion, learning, and life."[1] From 1470 to 1570, most of the remaining Jewish communities in the West, including the Sephardic community, were destroyed. Even in Germany and parts of Italy, where the last remnants persisted, Jewish life suffered a drastic contraction.[2] Such unrest had major effects on family life and often meant that women took on new roles, either as substitutes for men or alongside them to help deal with impending or existing crises.

As the politics and policies of Europe changed, more Jews began migrating eastward, especially into Poland and Lithuania. Although after 1570 they were readmitted into Germany, Austria, and Bohemia,[3] their status remained uncertain. Caught in the middle of a religious struggle between the established Catholic Church and the new Protestants, the Jews were considered suspect by both groups. They had to seek specific permission to live in most German, Austrian, and Bohemian cities and everywhere were confined to ghettos. Nevertheless, their numbers grew.

The Jewish settlements in Vienna and Prague increased in size and importance. Jews also migrated to the smaller towns of Bohemia and Moravia, and scattered centers appeared in western Poland and Silesia.[4] The culture of Ashkenaz, previously predominant in France and Germany, now spread through central and eastern Europe, and Jewish communities flourished.

129

Court Jews

Most Ashkenazic Jews lived quiet lives, making a modest living in the money trades (as lenders, tax collectors, or agents of local lords), as merchants, or through work inside the Jewish community. A small number, however, offered financial services to the rulers of the many independent duchies and principalities of central and eastern Europe. In return, they obtained some privileges from the ruling Christian powers. They were called court Jews.

Court Jews functioned as creditors and provisioners. They offered credit or cash advances to the ruler, provisioned his army, supplied metal for the mint, found luxury goods for his household, and developed opportunities for trade and industry. In return, the court Jew usually obtained the privilege of living outside the ghetto and he (or she) was recognized as an official of the state.[5] This put him in the unique position of being able to ask for favors for his family or for the Jewish community. The person who held this unofficial position was called a *shtadlan*. Although the *shtadlan* was almost always a man, it could be a woman as well. **Esther Liebmann** held this post in Berlin in the seventeenth century.

War and Persecution

The Thirty Years' War began in 1618, and until 1648 central Europe saw continuous fighting. This war opened with a Protestant rebellion in Prague against Ferdinand, the new Catholic king of Bohemia and heir to the Holy Roman Empire (see map on page 131). The rebellion quickly spread and drew in all the tiny city-states and duchies of the Holy Roman Empire, as well as France, Denmark, and Sweden.[6] At one time or another, all of these areas were involved either directly or indirectly in the war.

When the Thirty Years' War finally ended in 1648, the long, drawn-out battle had solved very little. The middle European lands of the Holy Roman Empire were still divided among feuding factions of Catholics, Lutherans, and Calvinists. The Treaty of Westphalia allowed the ruler of each land to choose the religion of its own people. But everywhere, the Jews still remained the outsiders.

In Poland, where Jews had prospered since the fifteenth century, 1648 was a time of disaster. During that year, a dissatisfied member of the lower aristocracy named Bogdan Chmielnicki revolted and fled from the Polish authorities to the Cossack center below the Dnieper River. Here, he organized the Cossacks and fought against Polish rule in the Ukraine, launching an orgy of killing, raping, and looting that destroyed Poles and Jews indiscriminately. Many Jews were murdered during this rebellion, but many more succeeded in fleeing across the borders. Streams of Jewish refugees turned north and west, moving back into the fortified German cities.[7]

FIG. 12. During the sixteenth and seventeenth centuries, the borders of central European lands were constantly changing. The dark line represents the borders of the Holy Roman Empire after the Thirty Years' War.

Messianic Hopes

In the wake of the persecutions and hardships of those tumultuous years, Jews searched for a ray of hope. They found it in the new elaboration of Kabbalah expounded by Isaac Luria of Safed (1534–1572). Throughout the sixteenth century, Lurianic Kabbalah had been confined to a small, esoteric circle of men. Luria's ideas spread slowly from the Middle East into Europe. Then, with the advent of the Chmielnicki pogroms in 1648, a large segment of eastern European Jews began to embrace the kabbalistic idea of repair of the world (*tikkun olam*) and the hope for the imminent coming of the Messiah. The result was an increased susceptibility to all sorts of imposters and fanatics.

The appearance of Shabbetai Zevi in Turkey and his claim that he was the Messiah (see chapter 7) confirmed the idea that *tikkun olam* would lead to redemption.[8] Many Ashkenazic Jews were so convinced that the Messiah had come that they packed their belongings in anticipation of the call to the Holy Land. When Shabbetai Zevi converted to Islam in 1666, disillusionment spread throughout the Jewish world. Many of his followers, however, remained convinced that the kabbalistic theories of Isaac Luria and the Safed school were still relevant.

The Development of Hasidism

Less than a century after Messianism had declined, a new mystical movement within Judaism developed in southeastern Europe. This movement, called Hasidism (Piety), overlapped with Sabbatianism and was contemporaneous with the Haskalah (Enlightenment) movement in western Europe (see chapter 8) but offered very different opportunities to Jewish women and men.

Hasidism began in approximately 1736 as a revivalist, anti-intellectual movement. It rejected the emphasis on scholarship and scholarly legalisms that had become such a central part of Rabbinic Judaism among the Ashkenazim, preferring instead more charismatic, prophetic types of lead-

---

MEMORIES OF A FALSE MESSIAH

When Shabbetai Zevi, a Jew from Smyrna, Turkey, announced in 1648 that he was the Messiah, word quickly spread to all the Jewish communities. In her memoirs, **Glikl of Hameln** reported these events in detail, speaking of the messianic excitement in Hamburg where she lived, and then the disappointment when the supposed messiah proved to be an imposter. Years later, her words allow us to share the intensity of feeling surrounding those events in the Hamburg community.

". . . About this time, people began to talk of Sabbatai [*sic*] Zevi, but *woe unto us, for we have sinned,* for we did not live to see that which we had heard and hoped to see. When I remember the penance done by young and old—it is indescribable, though it is well enough known in the whole world. O Lord of the Universe, at that time we hoped that you, O merciful God, would have mercy on your people Israel and redeem us from our exile. We were like a woman in travail, a woman on the labor-stool who, after great labor and sore pains, expects to rejoice in the birth of a child but finds it is nothing but wind. . . . We did not merit to see the longed-for child, but because of our sins we were left neither here nor there—but in the middle."[9]

ers.[10] The early Hasidim insisted that even unlearned Jews could come close to God.

The principal founder of Hasidism, Yisrael ben Eliezer (1700–1760), known widely as the Baal Shem Tov,[11] was not well educated in the classic texts. The Baal Shem Tov practiced mysticism and taught it to his followers, borrowing heavily from the mystical philosophy of Lurianic Kabbalah. A charismatic who used magical methods to heal people, the Baal Shem Tov's reputation and following quickly grew among Jews living in the small towns of southern Poland and the Ukraine.[12]

Hasidism was certainly not developed with a female audience in mind,[13] but during its early years it did invite the poor, the powerless, and the uneducated to enter into God's presence. Such ideas were bound to attract some women, especially those who were pious and had spiritual inclinations. Scattered throughout Hasidic literature and legends are reports of women such as **Edel**, the Baal Shem Tov's daughter, who gained a following of their own.

There was often bitter dissension between the Hasidim, concentrated in southern Poland, and the mainstream Rabbinic Jews, centered in Lithuania in the north. The Rabbinic Jews, called *Mitnagdim* (those who are against), mistrusted the Hasidim and sharply criticized their interpretation of law, their use of magic, and their charismatic style of leadership. In a few instances the two groups actually came to blows, although they ultimately made peace with each other, joining to combat what they saw as the evils of the Enlightenment.

The New Demographics of Ashkenazic Jewry

Although small numbers of Jews were slowly returning to the West, filtering back into England and into southern and eastern France by the late seventeenth century, the vast majority of European Jews now lived east of the Rhine River. In Germany, they populated the larger cities; in Bohemia, Poland, and Lithuania they lived in smaller communities. The Polish monarchy developed large and vibrant Jewish centers with a varied economic life,[14] while in the western Ukraine many Jews became representatives of the Polish landlords to the Ukrainian peasants and formed the middle class.[15] There was still no important settlement of Jews in Russia. This would only begin after Russia's annexation of parts of Lithuania, Poland, and the Ukraine under Catherine the Great in the late eighteenth century.

The women in these Ashkenazic communities continued to live traditional lives, ruled by Jewish law and Jewish men. This would change only very slowly, as the Enlightenment, the intellectual and philosophical movement away from tradition, permeated the Jewish communities of Germany and gradually moved east.

BIOGRAPHIES

BACHARACH, ḤAVA OF PRAGUE, SCHOLAR
(16th to 17th century)

Ḥava or Eva Bacharach (1580–1651) was one of the few woman who entered the more erudite culture of learned men. She was the grand-daughter of the eminent Rabbi Yehudah Loew (the Maharal) of Prague, and daughter of Rabbi Shimshon and Vogele Cohen. Her son was elected Rabbi of Moravia, and her grandson, Yair Ḥayyim Bacharach, continued the family's tradition of serious scholarship.[16] Although Ḥava left no writings of her own, she has been immortalized in the introduction to her grandson's book of responsa, named *Ḥavvot Yair* after his illustrious grandmother.

REMEMBERING A GRANDMOTHER

Yair Bacharach describes his grandmother Ḥava as:

". . . unique of her kind in her generation in Torah. She had an original explanation of Midrash Rabbah. She taught . . . through her comprehension and knowledge . . . and she explained in such a manner that all that heard her understood that she was correct. These things I wrote in my book in her name. She explained the festival and petitionary prayers and Rashi's commentary on the five books of Moses, and the whole Bible, and *Targum* [Aramaic translation], and Apocrypha."[17]

In her knowledge of Jewish sources, Ḥava Bacharach of Prague was comparable to some of the learned women in Italy such as **Fioretta da Modena,** the aunt of Leon Modena (see chapter 5). Bacharach was also a skilled teacher, and the extent of her learning was an inspiration to her grandson, Yair Ḥayyim.

EDEL BAT YISRAEL BEN ELIEZER OF SOUTHERN POLAND, MYSTIC AND HEALER
(18th century)

Historians agree that Edel was the only daughter of Yisrael ben Eliezer, the Baal Shem Tov, founder of the Hasidic movement. She married one of her father's disciples, Yeḥiel Ashkenazi, and had two sons and one daughter, **Feige,** whom she supported by running a small store. Edel was said to be a charismatic herself who shared a special bond with her father. She learned his mystical methods for healing and was allowed to visit patients on her own.

There are many fables and folktales about Edel that attempt to fill in the details of her life. The Baal Shem Tov's followers believed that the *Shekhinah* (the presence of God) rested on Edel's face, and they honored her as a rebbe. Even her name, associated with the phrase *Esh daat lamo* (EDL), translated as "a fiery law unto them," was given mystical significance.[18]

Edel's children became famous in their own right. Her first son, Moshe Ḥayyim Ephraim, was a respected scholar and writer. The younger son, Barukh, succeeded his grandfather as the leader of Hasidism. Her grandson, Naḥman of Bratislav, is quoted as saying about Edel: "All the *tzaddikim* (righteous ones) believed her to be endowed with Divine Inspiration and a woman of great perception."[19]

ELLA BAT MOSHE OF DESSAU, PRINTER
(late 17th century)

Ella, daughter of the convert Moshe ben Avraham, set type in her father's printing house in Dessau, Germany. She was the oldest girl in a large family in which all the children, and eventually the grandchildren, learned printing skills from a very young age. Ella was literate in both Hebrew and Yiddish, as attested by a colophon she wrote. It was inserted in the prayer book *Tefilah leMoshe* (Prayer to Moses) that she printed in Dessau in 1696 when she was only nine years old. *Tefilah leMoshe* also included a group of *tkhines* (petitionary prayers), and Ella added a few lines of her own here as well, praising "a pious lady" who paid for the printing.

ELLUS BAT MORDECAI OF SLUTSK, SCHOLAR AND TRANSLATOR
(18th century)

Ellus bat Mordecai was a learned woman who translated some of the newer, mystical works into Yiddish in order to introduce them to women. Her first translation was of the work *Maavor Yabbuk (Crossing the Yabbuk)*, written by the kabbalist Aaron Berekhiah da Modena, the grandson of Fioretta da Modena (see chapter 5). The work dealt with rules and traditions concerning the sick and dying and was published in 1704 in Frankfurt an der Oder. Her second collection, published that same year, was *Shomrim laBoker (Dawn Watchers)*, a book of prayers translated into Yiddish to be recited at sunrise.

Ellus's book gained the endorsement of three rabbis. One of them, R. Hillel Levi Mintz of Leipnik, praised Ellus as "the chaste, wise woman of rabbinical family, the *dabranit* [woman's prayer leader]." As Ellus explained, these translations were her attempt to help women comprehend the new type of prayer and recite with understanding. Although originating in Slutsk, then part of Lithuania, Ellus and her husband, Aaron ben Eliakum Goetz (author of *Even HaShosham*), decided to settle in the land of Israel. However, it

---

NOTES FROM A YOUNG WORKING WOMAN

These Yiddish letters I set with my own hand—
Ella the daughter of Moses of Holland,
My years number no more than nine;
The only girl among six children fine,
So, if you should find a misprint wild,
Remember, this was set by a mere child.[20]

As an introduction to a group of *tkhines* that had been added to the same prayer book, Ella wrote:

These beautiful new prayers have not appeared before.
They are entitled Minḥat Ani, prayers of the lonely and the poor.
Added at no cost to the reader, they are proffered
As the gift of a pious lady who has offered
To pay their cost. Almighty, smile on her evermore![21]

appears that they stopped in Moravia, where Aaron became a preacher. It is not clear whether they ever resumed their journey to Palestine.[22]

FALK, BAYLA OF LEMBERG, EDUCATED WOMAN
(16th century)

Bayla was the daughter of Israel Edels and the wife of the prominent rabbi Joshua Falk (1555–1614). Her sons praised her, saying that she was "the first to arrive at the synagogue every day . . ." and that "she would occupy herself with learning Torah. . . ."[24] She was well versed in Jewish law and was said to have ruled on a decision concerning when to light holiday candles.[25]

FEIGE OF SOUTHERN POLAND, MYSTIC
(late 18th century)

Feige was Edel's only daughter and a granddaughter of the Baal Shem Tov. She was famous for divine inspiration, and her contemporaries reported that she had inherited many of her mother's attributes. She was a woman of unusual ability and understanding and is said to have seen a vision of the Baal Shem Tov at her granddaughter's wedding.[26] Her own son was the beloved Hasidic spiritual leader and storyteller, R. Naḥman of Bratislav, who holds an important place in Hasidic history.

FISHELS, ROIZEL OF KRAKOW, PRINTER AND TEACHER
(16th century)

In 1586, Roizel Fishels printed a book of psalms that had been translated into Yiddish by R. Moshe Standl. As a preface to that book she wrote her own Yiddish poem. Its content suggests that Fishels was more than a simple printer. She was also a teacher and a philanthropist who probably understood some Hebrew.

GELA BAT MOSHE OF HALLE, PRINTER
(early 18th century)

Gela, Ella's younger sister, also set type on her father's press, now moved to Halle, Germany. In a prayer book print-

---

WITH THE HELP OF GOD

*With the help of God, blessed be
    His name,
With the help of God, I will endure
    the same.
In time, the holy psalms will prove
    to all
That Jews who praise God will
    never fall,
These psalms, whether by woman
    or man begun,
And, as King David, blessed be he,
    had done.
I never discouraged, and where I
    did go,
Taught to all who wanted to know;
Until they began to come, one and
    all, to me,
I also gave psalms to Moshe Vondri,
Here, to the holy city of Hanover,
    the psalms I donated;
At the same time, by Rev. Moshe
    Standl they were translated.
Now songs from the book of
    Samuel could be sung
By all as well in our own mother
    tongue,
And reading them, easier and pleasant to do,
For men and women and young
    girls, too.[23]*

—Roizel Fishels

A YOUNG GIRL'S POEM

Of this beautiful prayer book from beginning to end,
I set all the letters in type with my own hands.
I, Gela, the daughter of Moses the printer,
and whose mother was Freide, the daughter of Rabbi Israel Katz,
may his memory be for a blessing.
She bore me among ten children;
I am a maiden still under twelve years.
Be not surprised that I must work;
The tender and delicate daughter of Israel has been in exile
for a long time.
One year passes and another comes
And we have not yet heard of any redemption.

We cry and beg of God each year
That our prayers may come before Him, Blessed be He,
For I must be silent,
I and my father's house may not speak much.
As will happen to all Israel,
So may it also happen to us,
For the biblical verse says,
All people will rejoice,
Who lamented over the destruction of Jerusalem,
And those who endured great sufferings in exile
Will have great joy at the redemption.[27]

—Gela the Printer

---

ed in 1710 she wrote an extensive poem from which we learn that she was one of ten children. Her father, Moshe ben Avraham, originally from Amsterdam, was assumed to be a convert to Judaism because of his name[28] and because she does not name his ancestors. Her mother, Freide, was the daughter of a rabbi, R. Yisrael Katz. Gela wrote the poem when she was twelve years old.

GLIKL BAT YEHUDAH LEIB OF HAMELN, BUSINESSWOMAN
(17th century)

Born in Hamburg in 1646, Glikl was the first woman to write a Yiddish-language autobiography. In her book, published after her death, she reported: "I was not yet three [August 16, 1648] when the Jews were driven thence [i.e., out of Hamburg] and went to Altona, which then belonged to the King of Denmark."[29]

Although they lived in Altona, the men continued to trade in Hamburg,

---

GLIKL REMEMBERS

I have undertaken to write as much as I can remember of my childhood, not because I wish to present myself as a pious woman or to pretend I am better than I am. No. My sins are too heavy to bear. I am a sinner. Every day, every hour, every minute, every second—full of sins, and unfortunately am shut out from very few sins. *For these I weep and mine eyes runneth down with water* (Lam. 1:16). I would rejoice to do penance and weep for all my sins but the anxieties and sorrow for my orphaned children do not let me do penance as I should like.[30]

—Memoirs of Glikl of Hameln

about a quarter of an hour away. Eight years later, Glikl's father received permission to resettle there, the first German Jew to return.[31] Glikl's family prospered in Hamburg, and at the customary age of twelve, she was betrothed and then married to Ḥayyim of Hameln.

After a brief stay in Hameln with her in-laws, the young couple moved to Hamburg. They built up a thriving business, and Glikl bore thirteen children (one died as an infant). While bearing and raising her children, she also actively worked with her husband.

When Ḥayyim died, the result of an accident, it was a great personal loss to Glikl. Nevertheless she continued working, managing their trading business herself.

Despite a busy life, Glikl was lonely without her husband. To occupy her evenings and in order to enable her children to know about their origins and understand her view of the world, she decided to write as much as she could of her life.

In Glikl's time, the expectation that the Messiah would come was pervasive. She reported matter-of-factly about Shabbetai Zevi, a Jew from Smyrna, Turkey, who announced in 1648 that he was the Messiah. Even after he was revealed as an imposter, Glikl still wrote: "Therefore, put your trust in God. Pray that He should not desert us, nor all Israel—but bring us good tidings soon and send us our Messiah speedily, in our own time. Amen."[33]

The marriage of Tzipporah, one of Glikl's daughters, to the son of the rich and powerful Reb Elia Cleve, was a high point in her life, and Glikl enthusiastically recounted the details. Such costly celebrations were not that common, and Tzipporah's lavish wedding is a reflection of the financial success of Glikl's family (see also **Family Life**).

Glikl remained a widow for many years. She only reluctantly agreed to marry again, in hopes of gaining a secure old age. Her second husband was a prominent and rich financier from Metz, and Glikl lived in that city after her marriage to him in 1700. Although she admits that he was kind to her, Glikl never loved him as much as her first husband, and when he lost his own and her money and died bankrupt, she was left both widowed and penniless.

Refusing to take charity from others, Glikl lived in hardship for many years

---

A BRIDE AT FOURTEEN

Before I was twelve years old I was betrothed and the betrothal lasted two years. My wedding was celebrated in Hameln. My parents, accompanied by a party of twenty people, drove there with me. . . .

In the evening we had a great feast. My parents-in-law were good, honest people, and my father-in-law, Reb Joseph, of blessed memory, had few to equal him. At the feast he toasted my mother with a large glass of wine. . . .

After my wedding my parents returned home and left me, a child not yet fourteen, in a strange town, among strangers. I was not unhappy but even had much joy because my parents-in-law were respectable, devout people and looked after me better than I deserved.[32]

—*Memoirs of Glikl of Hameln*

MOURNING FOR A HUSBAND

Writing of her experiences during the period of mourning for Ḥayyim, Glikl struck a universal chord that will be familiar to anyone, in any age, who has suffered the death of a loved one:

"What shall I write, my dear children, of our great loss? To lose such a husband! I who had been held so precious by him, was left with eight orphaned children [the others had already married] of whom my daughter Esther was a bride. . . . I shall have to mourn my friend all the days of my life. . . .

The whole community mourned and lamented him; the unexpected blow had fallen so suddenly.

Surrounded by my children, I sat the seven days of mourning, a pitiful sight, I and my twelve children thus seated. . . . All our friends and acquaintances, men and women, came every day of the week of mourning, to console us. My children, brothers, sisters, and friends comforted me as well as they could. But each one went home with a loved one, while I remained in my house in sorrow with my orphans. . . .

My dear mother, sisters, and brothers comforted me, but their comfort only increased my sorrow and poured more oil on the fire. . . . These comfortings lasted two or three weeks; after that no one knew me. . . ."[34]

FIG. 13. The life of Glikl of Hameln was portrayed in a recent theater production, *The Memoirs of Glückel of Hameln.* Jenny Romaine played the role of Glikl, shown here with some of her twelve children, depicted as paper puppets.

until she was persuaded to make her home with her daughter Esther. After Glikl's death in 1724, it was Esther's son Moses, then chief Rabbi of Baiersdorf, who found her memoirs and copied them. More than a century later, in 1896, they were published in Judeo-German by David Kaufmann. Now translated into many languages, this document still offers historians important clues to daily life in the seventeenth century.

GNENDEL OF BOHEMIA, DISTILLER OF BRANDY
(late 17th century)

In the late seventeenth century, an unknown author recounted his childhood in Bohemia. He reported that his mother, Gnendel, a pious, intelligent woman, supported the family by manufacturing brandy out of oats while his father studied. "This was very hard labor," he wrote, "but she succeeded." Later, one of Gnendel's relatives gave some money to her husband and he also became active in business. Within a few years he was granted a large distillery from the count with "servants to do the work and grain to prepare brandy." However, Gnendel must have continued working with him, and her son reports that "she fell sick in consequence of the heat and the fumes from the brandy, and she died in 1672 at the age of thirty-four years."[35]

GUTMAN, SAREL OF PRAGUE, BUSINESSWOMAN
(17th century)

In business together with her husband, Sarel Gutman ran a mail service out of the Prague ghetto to Vienna, 160 miles away. It was set up mostly to facilitate the Gutman's own communication with each other, since her husband,

Loeb, was often in Vienna on business. One letter from Sarel to Loeb is preserved in the collection of Prague ghetto letters. It was written on November 22, 1619, the eve of the outbreak of the Thirty Years' War, and is one of the few Jewish letters in the collection that relates the political developments of the day (see p. 141).

HOROWITZ, SARAH REBECCA RACHEL LEAH OF BOLEKHOV, SCHOLAR AND WRITER
(mid-18th century)

Perhaps one of the most learned and intelligent among the women who wrote *tkhines* was Sarah Rebecca Rachel Leah, usually known simply as Leah Horowitz. Leah was born in Bolekhov, Poland in approximately 1720, the daughter and granddaughter of rabbis. Her father was Yaakov Yokel ben Meir Horowitz and her mother, Rayzel bat Heschel. She married into another elite rabbinical family, becoming the wife of Aryeh Leib.[36]

Leah probably married young, as one of her older brother's pupils, Ber of Bolekhov, remembered that she and her husband were boarding with her brother, R. Mordecai. Ber recalled that Leah often explained passages of the Talmud to him while her brother, his teacher, napped. She would say: "What are you puzzled about?" After he told her, "she would begin to recite the words of Talmud or Rashi by heart, in clear language, explaining it well as it was written there and I learned from her words."[37]

Leah Horowitz believed that tears were one of the most efficient paths that women could use to come close to God. Tears were symbolic, and women's tears, especially, had the power to bring about redemption. In eastern Europe, crying was an important part of women's prayer culture and it enhanced their spiritual life. By urging them to cry, Leah Horowitz was interpreting the various kabbalistic symbols and concepts concerning the *Shekhinah* and translating them into a form that ordinary women could understand. A woman might direct her tearful prayers to the matriarchs Sarah, Rebecca, Leah, and Rachel, in the hope that they would use their merit to engage the mercy of God and bring about the desired redemption.[38]

Leah Horowitz's most popular piece of writing, "Tkhine of the Matriarchs," beseeched God: "For the sake of the merit of our mother Leah, who wept day and night . . . until her eyes became dim."[39]

Although she urged women on to more spirituality, Leah Horowitz

---

A WIFE'S LETTER TO HER HUSBAND

Although there is some evidence to suggest that Sarel Gutman did not write this letter herself,[40] her words have a ring of authenticity to them and show her to be an astute and caring woman.

"Many good, blessed, and pleasant years, may they surely come to you and to your head and hairs! To the hands of my lovely, dear, beloved husband, the pious and prudent, worthy Rabbi Loeb . . . I have been ever grieved because I have not heard a word from you for seven weeks, where you are in the world, especially in such a situation as that which we have now. . . . I was indeed at my wits' end, and did not know what I should think about all that. Honestly, I do not know how I live in my great distress. The Lord be He praised, knows how I feel. I do not eat, I do not drink, I do not sleep, my life is no life for me. For in good days, if I did not have two letters a week, I thought that I should not be able to live longer. . . . And now I do not at all know for such a long time where you are in the world. . . .

I had much to write you about horrible things, but I cannot write, about the affliction we had to endure here when riots almost occurred in our streets. It was like at the destruction of the Temple. . . .

Besides, you should know that they have crowned the King here with great honors, and her too. . . . Write, too, what is going on, so that one may know what is happening. . . . You may know that just as we were writing, people arrived from Vienna and did not bring me a letter either. This has frightened me even more, and they told me that you have sent a letter through a messenger and are looking forward to my answer. But I have not seen any letter at all. Therefore, do not upset me any longer and write me certainly about all things and thoroughly. I have no rest in my heart. They told me that you were having quite a nice time there. I, too, should like to enjoy it. But I do not blame you. You have never become entirely settled, and thus you think; out of sight out of mind. . . .

And thus, good night from your loving wife. . . ."[41]

TKHINE OF THE MATRIARCHS

Leah Horowitz's *tkhine* was divided into three parts. Parts one and two included an introduction, written in Hebrew, and a liturgical poem in Aramaic with a Yiddish paraphrase. Part three was the *tkhine*. The first two parts were found in the early editions but were dropped in subsequent printings as few women could understand them. In that introduction she urged women not to pray solely for their own personal concerns and material benefits, but also for the *Shekhinah*, who was still in exile. Criticizing prayers for selfish requests, Horowitz wrote: "They bark like dogs, give us life, etc. There is no one who repents for the sake of the *Shekhinah*, but all the good that they do, they do only for themselves."[42]

Despite this criticism, though, Horowitz did not totally exclude personal requests in the prayers that she composed. She ended a prayer for Rosh Hodesh with these words: "And we pray You to grant to us . . . worthy, living, and healthy offspring. May they be scholars, and may they serve God with perfect hearts and with love, together with all the pious ones, Amen."[43]

HURWITZ, BELLA OF PRAGUE, PRINTER
(17th century)

Bella was the wife of a cantor, Yosef he-Ḥazan of Prague. In addition to her work as a printer, she is believed to have written a book outlining the history of the house of David.[44]

KATZ, HANNAH OF AMSTERDAM, YIDDISH POET
(17th century)

Only one poem written by Hannah Katz is extant.[45] Printed in Amsterdam during the seventeenth or eighteenth century, its theme is the forbidden fruit in the Garden of Eden. Although it is written principally for an audience of women, some of the verses are addressed to both men and women.

HANNAH'S PARABLE ON EVE

Dear men and women today I am going to tell you
That the snake spoke in a human voice and came [to Eve].
She approached Eve.
Eve, why did you sin so?
You ought not eat from that tree
You had enough to eat
Just like God, may His name be blessed, you will know everything.

—*Hannah Katz*[46]

never encouraged them to study. It was quite clear to her that an educated woman was an anomaly, and in her own comments she, like many male writers, lumped women together with the ignorant.

LAZA OF FRANKFURT, EDITOR AND TRANSLATOR
(late 17th century)

Laza, the wife of Yaakov ben Mordecai of Schwerin (*ca.* 1690), was an educated woman. In 1692, she translated her husband's work, *Tikkun Shalosh Mishmarot (Prayers for the Three Night Watches)*, from Hebrew into Yiddish, adding her own introduction to the Yiddish translation.[47]

LEAH DREYZL OF STANISLAV, COMPOSER OF PRAYERS
(18th century)

Leah Dreyzl, who lived in the first half of the eighteenth century, came from a distinguished family that included rabbis and scholars associated with the early Hasidic movement (approximately 1736). Leah Dreyzl, wife of R. Aryeh Leib Auerbach, the rabbi of Stanislav (Poland), wrote two *tkhines* that were passed on to her own daughter-in-law Hena, who subsequently had them published.

Both prayers, containing mystical overtones, were written for the holiday season of Rosh Hashanah and Yom Kippur and deal with sin and repentance. In one passage, she pleads: "... I beg my own limbs, don't stand against me, I want to go into God's house and pour out my heart, and confess my sins with bitter tears."[48]

Leah Dreyzl's writing is filled with biblical references and quotes from the prayer book, indicating that she knew Bible and Hebrew liturgy. This leads us to assume that she was a *firzogerin* in her husband's synagogue in Stanislav.

LIEBMANN, ESTHER SCHULHOFF ARON
(17th century)

Esther Schulhoff came from a learned and distinguished Prague family. She married Israel Aron, a Jew from Poland[49] who was the first Jew to obtain the right of residence in East

Die Jüdin nach der Synagog gehend.
Chr: Weigel excudit.

FIG. 14. A typical German-Jewish woman on her way to synagogue. Her clothing reflects the style of the seventeenth century. (Courtesy of the Leo Baeck Institute, New York)

Prussia in 1655. In October 1657, he was given permission to conduct business in Berlin and by 1665 was appointed court Jew. He did not accumulate much money for himself and died in 1673.

Esther was still young when she became a widow and found herself the sole provider for her own two small children. In addition, she was expected to support Israel's children from a first marriage, her elderly parents, and her mother-in-law and sister-in-law. Israel Aron's family demanded their share of the inheritance, even though debt made it basically worthless. Esther had to request a two-year moratorium on her late husband's debts, but this served only to postpone her problems. Her dowry was contested, and at one point her creditors removed even her furniture, beds, and clothing. Eventually, the debts were so large that she was forced to give up her entire inheritance. Nevertheless she managed to survive.

With very little capital and many mouths to feed, it is not surprising that just a few years later, Esther married again. Her second husband was Jost Liebmann, Israel Aron's successor to the post of court Jew.[50] Esther's dowry was not substantial, but she did bring to Jost something even more important: her first husband's business connections, the right to live in Berlin, and her contacts with Frederick I, the Prussian king, and his court.[51]

Esther Liebmann was a strong person, gaining the reputation of a tyrant. She dominated her sons, stepsons, and other family members and intimidated officials. She managed to obtain letters of safe conduct for doing business in other cities, win trade concessions, and even influence rabbinical appointments.[52] Among her important privileges was exemption from the restrictions imposed on Jews by a Jewish commission.

After Jost died in 1702, Esther continued his business, supplying precious gems to King Frederick. Because the royal family owed her so much money for all the jewelry she had supplied after her husband's death, she was given the right to mint and distribute coins.[53]

Esther Liebmann was known to have had a very close association with Frederick I. There were even suggestions that the relationship between them may have been intimate as well, since she could enter his chambers at any time, unannounced. She remained influential and successful until Frederick's death in 1713. After that, the King's debt to her, said to be somewhere between 106,000 and 186,000 talers, was denied by his successor. Her books were examined by the state, and she was forced to pay high penalties for defrauding the court.[54]

Although Esther was subsequently allowed to resume her business selling jewels to the new king, Frederick William I, and she remained a wealthy woman, she resented the injustice done to her. Just one year later, in 1714, she died. At her request, she was buried with a gold chain that had been a gift from her friend King Frederick I.

MEISEL, FRUMET OF PRAGUE, MONEYLENDER
(16th to 17th century)

Frumet was the second wife of the wealthy Mordecai Meisel (1528–1601) of Prague. She was described as "a fine person, the crown of her husband."[55] The Meisel family's success can be partly attributed to King Rudolf II (1576–1612), who in 1577 issued a charter to Bohemian Jews expanding their economic opportunities. It was during this period that Meisel lent large sums of money to the king.[56]

Whether Frumet lent money independently or simply aided her husband in his business is not clear, but when Mordecai died, she hid the bulk of his money and treasures from officials. A nephew was arrested and tortured until he gave away information that led to the subsequent confiscation of 516,250 florins from Frumet's home by the emperor's representatives.[57] Frumet lived for twenty-four more years after her husband's death.

PAN, TOIBE OF PRAGUE, YIDDISH POET
(17th century)

Toibe Pan wrote a historical poem about a plague, one of the many outbreaks of that disease that occurred in Prague throughout the sixteenth and seventeenth centuries.[58] Her writing serves as additional evidence of the charitable work women performed in caring for the sick and dying.

IN PRAISE OF PIOUS WOMEN

One verse of a Yiddish poem by Toibe Pan describes those who care for plague victims:

The whole time, pious women do
*   a great deal of good for the sick.*
The whole time, numerous soci-
*   eties are prepared to do many*
*   admirable deeds.*
May God watch over them for all
*   the sufferers.*
Father King.[59]

RACHEL/RASHKA OF KRAKOW, BUSINESSWOMAN
(16th century)

Rachel (also called Rashka) of Krakow, Poland, was a widow who became active in her husband's business and also in communal affairs. She was granted an honorary position in the king's court and was the only Jew to be given the right to own a house in Krakow after the expulsion of Jews from that city in 1495 to nearby Kazimierz. Through her influence at court she was able to advance the careers of her two sons-in-law, R. Jacob Polak and R. Asher Lemel.[60]

RIVKAH BAT YISRAEL OF FRANKFURT, PRINTER
(early 18th century)

Rivkah represented the third generation of a large family of printers. Her father, Yisrael ben Moshe, was the older brother of **Ella** and **Gela**. He set up his own print shop in Frankfurt, and for a while Ella helped him there. After he had his own family, his daughter, Rivkah, learned the trade and worked with him. She, too, began when she was very young and left her mark in several of the books published by her father. At the end of the first part of a prayer book, she inserted in Yiddish: "I did this with my own hands, Rivkah, daughter of Yisrael, the owner of the printing press. Dear reader, if you find any mistakes, please excuse them, for I am only a child."[61]

REMEMBERING
REBBETZIN RIVKAH

An obituary notice in the communal records of Metz, Germany, recognized Rivkah Sarah Merele with the following notice:

"The distinguished and pious *rebbetzin*, Rivkah Sarah Merele, daughter of the trustee, the Ḥaver Yaakov, who deprived herself of numerous things to live in piety and asceticism and to mortify herself. For many years she fasted three or four days and nights consecutively each week. Even in her old age she did not give it up. . . . Her children gave a gift to charity in her name. . . . The *rebbetzin* of the community of Bingen . . . died and was buried at Bingen on Sunday the 26th of Elul, 5439 (3-9-1679)."[62]

RIVKAH SARAH MERELE OF BINGEN, ASCETIC WOMAN
(17th century)

Rivkah was the daughter of Yaakov, a trustee of the congregation in Bingen (Germany). Her obituary called her "the *rebbetzin* of Bingen," a title that usually refers to a rabbi's wife. At a time when asceticism was frowned on for women, Rivkah was respected as a pious woman who fasted and deprived herself of material comforts. She died in 1679 (see p. 145).

SARAH BAT[63] TOVIM, OF PODOLIA, PRAYER LEADER AND WRITER OF PSALMS
(18th century)

Sarah, a learned woman, stands out as a prolific writer of *tkhines* (personal, petitionary prayers).[64] Known only by her pen name, Sarah bat Tovim (daughter of distinguished men), she became a legendary figure in eastern Europe. Because of her popularity, her name was placed as author on a variety of *tkhines* even after her death.

Sarah bat Tovim, born in Podolia, Ukraine, came from an illustrious family of rabbis. Her father was alternately referred to as Mordecai, Yitzḥak, or Yaakov of Satanov; her mother was named Leah.[65]

A selection of Sarah bat Tovim's writings continues to be reprinted today. Most well known among them is the prayer pamphlet *Shloyshe Sh'eorim (Three Gates)*. It includes prayers for the three commandments (mitzvot) that women were required to perform (see **Religious Participation**), a penitential prayer for the High Holy Days, and a prayer for Rosh Hodesh (the new month). A lengthy introduction to *Shloyshe Sh'eorim*

describes Paradise, imagined as a six-chambered area. Each chamber houses an honored female ancestor as well as "several thousand righteous women who have never suffered the pains of Hell."[66]

A WOMAN'S PARADISE

In Sarah bat Tovim's description of Paradise, she wrote:

And the chambers of the matriarchs cannot be described; no one can come into their chambers. Now, dear women, when the souls are together in paradise, how much joy there is! Therefore, I pray you to praise God with great devotion, and to say your prayers, that you may be worthy to be there with our Mothers.[67]

Sarah bat Tovim's prayers echoed the emotions of the early kabbalists and evidenced a personal striving for communion with God in the everyday rituals of women. In her prayer for candlelighting she wrote: "May my mitzvah of candle lighting be accepted as the equivalent of the High Priest lighting the candles in the Temple."[68]

Sarah bat Tovim also hinted at her own life in this pamphlet. She was born into a prosperous home but later suffered a reversal of fortune, perhaps as a result of becoming a widow. Sarah attributed her present homelessness to her sin of talking in the synagogue and admitted: "I used to come into the beloved synagogue, all decked out in jewelry. I would do nothing but joke and laugh." She entreated women not to do what she did: "When you enter the beloved synagogue, a great terror should overcome you; you should know before whom you have come and to whom you pray and to whom you must answer for your life."[69]

TIKTINER, RIVKAH BAT MEIR OF PRAGUE, SCHOLAR AND WRITER (16th century)

Rivkah bat Meir Tiktiner,[70] referred to most frequently as Rebecca Tiktiner, was first and foremost an educator of women. Her book of ethics, *Meneket Rivkah* (Rebecca's nursemaid), was the first book written in Yiddish by a woman, and its main purpose was to teach ethical behavior.

Much of the book is taken up with advice concerning the care and education of children. She instructed mothers on how to encourage their sons to learn. Although the education of girls is not totally overlooked, daughters were placed firmly in the role of enablers. It is interesting to note that despite her own superior education, Rivkah does not advocate serious study for girls.

Rivkah cautioned mothers not to expect too much from their children. She included a proverb, heard even today, advising the women: "One mother can bring up ten children but ten children cannot feed one mother."[71]

In addition to being a writer and educator, Rivkah bat Meir was probably a preacher who may have traveled to other cities to lecture, teach, and preach. She may also have been a *firzogerin*, a leader of prayer for the women in the synagogue. It has been suggested that her book is made up of a collection of her lectures to women.

Although Rivkah's work gives no personal information about husband or children, an item in the *Sefer Hazkarot*, a book of records from Prague, listed her husband as a donor to the synagogue. (Scholar Frauke von Rohden discovered this record in 2001 but could not decipher his name.)[72]

Rivkah died in 1605 and is buried in Prague. Her book, *Meneket Rivkah*, survives in two copies, both published posthumously. A copy of the first edition, printed in Prague in 1609, is preserved in the library of the university at Erlangen, Germany.[73] A second edition, printed in Krakow in 1618, can be found in the library of the Jewish Theological Seminary in New York. Its title is a reference to the biblical story of Rebecca who brings her nurse

---

RIVKAH BAT MEIR'S GRAVESTONE

Rivkah, daughter of our teacher, the rabbi, R. Meir Tiktiner, died on the 25th of Nisan, in 1605, Rivkah . . . may her soul be bound in the bond of life. "Many daughters have done well but you surpassed them all (Proverbs 31: 29)": "We put our confidence in her (Proverbs 31: 11)" as Abigail in her life, may her merit protect her: She is given as an atonement in death, a perfect offering as a ram: She preaches day and night to women in every faithful city: Let the eye fill with tears of all that go out and come in when she is hidden and buried.[74] (See figure 15.)

FIG. 15. This tombstone marked the grave of Rivkah bat Meir Tiktiner, who was buried in Prague in 1605.

(personal governess) with her when she leaves home to join Isaac, her new husband (Gen. 24:59, 35:8).

Rivkah bat Meir was familiar with both Hebrew and Yiddish literature. Her writing reflects her knowledge of many religious sources. These include Bible, Talmud, Midrash, and *Yalkut Shimoni* (a medieval midrashic anthology), as well as Hebrew ethical writ-

ings and Rashi's commentaries.[75] She used these sources in her own style, transforming them into poems, sayings, and stories that provided ethical advice and a general behavioral guide for women.

The printer of her book was astonished at Rivkah's knowledge. In the preface to *Meneket Rivkah* he stated, "Who had heard of or seen such a novelty within our time that a woman had, on her own, become a learned person. And she read biblical verse and homiletical commentary. That is why I printed her book."[76] The book was known to Christian scholars for several centuries after her death.[77]

Rivkah bat Meir Tiktiner gave the following advice to mothers:

- Sit in the house in order to hear how they [the boys] pray and say the blessings, and don't depend on the rabbi. . . . Also, the lessons that the mother learns [together] with her son are much more successful than what he learns later, as it says in the verse: "Listen, my son, to the tradition of your father and do not blot out the teaching of your mother." And they ask in the Gemarah, why is it written the teachings of your mother and the tradition of your father? Because the father is involved in his business and is not found in his house except occasionally, and if he sees his son does not behave appropriately he disciplines him and teaches him moral lessons, but it is the responsibility of the mother, who is always in the house, to supervise her children and she has it in her hands to do many good deeds. . . .[78]
- When he begins to learn one should arrange that he learn with joy. One time he should be given sugar, one time nuts, or bread spread with honey so that he should learn

happily. . . . When he becomes more intelligent he is told, "Child, live, be pious, and learn. [Then] I will make you fine clothes." When he becomes even more clever he is told, "if you'll learn happily then you will become, God willing, an important young scholar and then they will give you a prominent scholar's daughter with a great deal of money [to marry]. And you will become the head of a yeshivah [rabbinical academy]." When he achieves his complete intelligence he is told, "dear son, learn for the sake of God. Then you can have this world and the world to come."[79]

• . . . Now I will speak about the education of daughters. Our sages said "if a daughter comes first, it is a good sign for sons." [This is] because she will be able to help the mother in the education of the children who will come afterward. Thus, every woman should try to educate her daughter to good deeds. . . . and don't think "why does my daughter need to work, since I have enough money."' But no man knows what the day will bring, as our eyes see. . . .[80] [This advice originates in the Talmud: B. *Bava Batra* 141a.]

THE WORLD OF JEWISH WOMEN

ECONOMIC ACTIVITIES

Women had always been active in the economic sphere, and the Jewish women in central and eastern Europe were not exceptions. In the towns and villages of Ashkenaz it became even more common for a woman to gain favor in God's eyes by supporting her family and enabling her husband to study.[81]

In the course of business, women routinely went outside their homes to the marketplace and some traveled long distances. They bought and sold on their own accounts or for a family business, they owned property in their own names,[82] and their activity, both inside and outside the home, made an important contribution to the family economy.

Jewish wives were involved in a wide variety of trades and professions. A few were trained and skilled; others earned in whatever way they could, living by means of "an economy of makeshift."[83] Records show women working as cheese-makers, goose-herders, bar-

maids, washerwomen, veil makers, weavers, embroiderers, milliners, and seamstresses.[84] Poor Jewish women often worked as street vendors.[85] In late medieval Germany many did domestic work as cooks, kitchen maids, and maidservants.[86] Jewish women filled all, or almost all, of the economic niches available to Jews in late medieval Ashkenaz. In the sixteenth century, R. Shlomo Luria (1510?–1574) wrote: "Our women now conduct business in the house [and] represent the husband."[87]

Money Lending and Trade

In the early part of this period, money lending was still a common way for Jews to earn a living. In certain cases the rights of residence in a community would only go to a select number of Jewish moneylenders. The number was set by the Christian leaders of each government, based on how many Jews they thought would be required to serve their economic needs. All others had to be members of the moneylenders' households or their employees, and some of those were certainly female. In addition to wives and daughters, Jewish women unable to gain the right of residence in any other way lived "in the shadow of the privileged, serving in a Jewish household."[88] In one extant document, dated from 1750, the list of tolerated communal Jewish officials in Berlin included a female bath attendant and eight attendants for the sick, a few of whom were presumably women.[89] Although this particular document was issued at the end of the period in question here, such a list was a prototype of earlier charters granting the right of settlement to individual families.

Women were often important moneylenders also. In late medieval Germany, about twenty-five per cent of the Jewish moneylenders were women.[90] In Poland, R. Shlomo Luria made at least one ruling concerning a woman moneylender who was independent of her husband.[91] In Prague, where there were many Jewish moneylenders, wives often participated in the business and eventually, as widows, they took over the entire enterprise, as

did **Frumet Meisel.** In Germany, **Glikl of Hameln** and **Esther Liebmann** did the same.

There were many active businesswomen in the Jewish communities of central Europe during the two hundred and fifty years from 1492 to 1750. Both the wife and the daughter of Levko of Krakow were active in his business before his death and assumed full control after he died. Records show widows and also wives of toll farmers or businessmen who received various privileges and tax exemptions through their connections at court,[93] although not all were as prosperous as **Glikl** or **Rashka.**

Doctors

Jewish women doctors appear in the archival records of some German communities, especially in the fifteenth and sixteenth centuries. Among the women doctors listed in the archives of Frankfurt am Main for the late fifteenth century, most were Jews.[94] A Jewish "doctoress" is mentioned in the records of 1494–1499. She was relieved of paying the *Schlafgeld*, a tax paid by strangers sojourning in the city, "in order to induce her to remain" (*damit sie hie bliben moge*).[95] In 1542, we find mention of another woman doctor, Madame Murada, in the *Zitn-Bukh*, a Yiddish translation of the Hebrew ethical work *Sefer Middot.*

In Metz, in northeastern France,[96] several obituary notices in the *Memorbuch* for that town show women practicing popular medicine. These women were probably herbalists and midwives, functioning in the community without licenses. By the sixteenth century, most women had been effectively closed out of the established medical profession. They continued to practice, however,

---

AN ACTIVE BUSINESSWOMAN

Glikl of Hameln (1646–1719) aided her husband in his trading business in Hamburg. After his death she continued the business he had managed. She wrote:

"At that time I was still quite energetic in business, so that every month I sold goods to the value of 5000 to 6000 *reichstaler.* Besides this, I went twice a year to the Brunswick Fair and at every fair sold goods for several thousands. . . ."[92]

FIG. 16. A sixteenth-century Jewish working woman from Worms. Attached to her cloak is a *rouelle,* the circular mark that Jews were required to place on their clothing during this period. (Courtesy of Hessische Landes-und Hochschulbibliothek, Darmstadt)

concentrating especially in midwifery and the treatment of women's and children's illnesses. According to one noted historian, the *Memorbuch* "testifies . . . to the survival of a popular medicine carried on without payment by worthy women who attended the sick and the women giving birth, preparing and distributing dressings and lint [bandages] and not hesitating to give out amulets. . . . Their number seems to have been quite large in comparison with that of the doctors. . . ."[97]

A DEDICATION TO A LADY DOCTOR

At the end of the *Zitn-Bukh* there is a special supplement that begins with the following lines: "Honor to God the Almighty alone. To all women and maidens we extend our warm greeting, and, above all, to the honorable and modest Madame Murada, lady doctor of the liberal art of medicine, resident in Ginzburg [probably Günzburg in Bavaria]. Kind lady! After I understood that you desire and long for the *Sefer Middot,* I ventured with the aid of Almighty God and published it."[98]

Printers

By the sixteenth and seventeenth centuries, commercial printing was well established in central and eastern Europe. Many of the larger communities, including Amsterdam, Frankfurt, Prague, and Krakow had active Jewish presses, producing books and other material in both Hebrew and Yiddish. Women of all ages, such as **Ella** and **Gela**, daughters of Moshe ben

Avraham, worked in family-run presses, setting type in both Hebrew and Yiddish. Some Jewish women gained prominence in the printing field. Among them were Gutel bat Yehudah Loeb ha-Kohen (1627) and **Bella Hurwitz,** both from Prague, and Rebecca and Rachel Judels (1677) of Wilmersdorf.[99] A few, such as **Roizel Fishels,** were skilled translators as well, translating prayers and Jewish literary works from Hebrew into Yiddish.

EDUCATION

While the education of girls was hardly equal to that of boys and rarely included instruction in Hebrew, the Jewish communities of Germany offer some of the earliest evidence of organized schools for girls in Europe (see chapter 4, **Education**). In the seventeenth century, Glikl of Hameln wrote that for several years she went to *ḥeder.*[100] She pointed out that "[her father] had his sons and daughters taught both religious and worldly things."[101]

This evidence notwithstanding, most of women's education was still informal, given at home by their mothers or other female relatives. Women from rabbinical families, such as **Bayla Falk** and **Laza,** were most likely to be well educated. The names of other educated women, usually from elite families, are scattered throughout the literature of the period.

Women's Education and the Yiddish Language

Jewish women, whether they resided in the great trading centers of Germany or in rural Polish villages, shared one thing in common: the Yiddish language. Yiddish had developed hundreds of years before as a dialect of German.[102] It was written using the

Hebrew alphabet, and incorporated in it were French and Hebrew words and expressions. As the Jews moved east, out of Germany, words from Slavic languages were added. Originally referred to as Judeo-German in the German-speaking areas, it eventually became Yiddish, the universal language of the Ashkenazic Jews.

Because women were not routinely given a Hebrew education, books written for an audience of women were always in Yiddish. As printing became more common, literacy among women (and men) increased and a woman interested in educating herself had a large variety of Yiddish books available to her. These included books of psalms, biblical translations and commentaries, proverbs, ethical teachings and historical narratives.[103]

FAMILY LIFE

Betrothal and Marriage

The lives of Jewish women in central and eastern Europe were similar in almost every way to what they had been in the communities of northern France and western Germany, the wellspring of the Ashkenazic community. They married young, raised children, worked side by side with their fathers and then their husbands, and frequently died in childbirth.

Marriage remained a high point for a woman and was most important in deciding her future life. Parents of a daughter often took great pains to choose a husband who could support her appropriately and was reputed to be honorable and reliable. When Glikl was making arrangements for the marriage of her daughter Esther to Moshe Schwab she heard some criticism of his character. Concerned for her daughter's future, she wrote to the young

---

> **PRAISE FOR A WOMAN HEALER**
>
> The obituary notice of this woman from Metz described her medical activities: "The estimable Blimelen, daughter of Eliezer Levi, 'she spared herself no trouble in healing the painful sores of poor children. . . .' Died on the 9th of Adar, [5]403 [March 1, 1643]."[104]

---

man's mother stipulating that if it were true, the betrothal would be canceled.

The wedding celebration itself varied according to the financial status of the couple, and most weddings were modest affairs. When a family could afford an expensive wedding, however, they did not hesitate to spend lavishly. When Glikl's daughter Tzipporah married the son of the rich and powerful R. Elia Cleve, an elaborate wedding entertainment was presented.

As in earlier times, once married, women were expected to serve their husbands, obey them, and try to please them in every way. Love was not a prerequisite, but some married couples, such as Glikl and her first husband, Hayyim, did grow to love each other. Glikl confessed in her autobiography that she never loved her second husband even though he was kind to her. She had married him for financial security in her old age.

Children

Family relationships were the most significant in a Jewish woman's life, defining her position in the world and her connection to Judaism and the Jewish people. The strength and persistence of the mother-child bonds and the involvement, or attempts at involvement, in their children's lives, are vividly shown through women's letters.

One example of strong bonds between mother and daughter is revealed in a letter from the Prague ghetto written by Resel Landau to her married daughter Hannah. Resel consistently addressed Hannah as "my darling" and sent warm regards to her daughter's family. She ended with the words: "Remember me to Isaac and the dear children, may they live long, and all our dear heads and everybody who is dear to you. . . ."[105] Glikl of Hameln was devoted to her twelve children and her concern for their welfare is evident throughout her memoirs.

Divorce and Levirate Marriage

One of the results of the Chmielnicki massacres of 1648 in Poland was that large numbers of Jewish women were left widowed or abandoned with no proof of their husbands' deaths. This placed them in the status of *agunot*, unable to remarry. Such a widespread problem forced the community leaders to alleviate the plight of these women by legally freeing them from their marriage bonds without the required witness, and thus enabling them to remarry.[106]

Divorce and widowhood were frequent, and most divorced or widowed men and women quickly remarried. The exception to this general rule involved cases of levirate marriage, the marriage of a childless widow to her husband's brother (see chapter 3). Here also special allowances were made to permit remarriage.

Due to the increase in conversions and the widening gulf between the Christian and Jewish communities, a new custom developed. If a Jewish man had a brother who had already converted, he (the husband) was

---

A MOTHER'S CONCERN

Glikl of Hameln recounted the details of a letter to her future son-in-law's mother concerning the character of the bridegroom.

"I wrote to the young man's mother, Mistress Jachet. I can still remember the very words I used. I first, as is customary, wished her a hearty *mazel tov* and then continued: as we had received several letters informing us that the young man had many faults, which we assumed to be lies, we begged her to send the bridegroom to the betrothal feast to meet the bride; and if we saw that what these denouncers, these retailers of lies, these mischief-makers, as we hoped,

had said was false, we would receive him with much joy and give him precious gifts, and he would lack no honour. If, however—God forbid!—what they said was true, we begged her not to send him, for our child must not be so cruelly deceived. If she intended, all the same, to send her son, thinking that, as we were already closely related by birth and marriage, we would disregard any faults because the first stage of the betrothal was completed, she must not do so. In the latter event—God forbid!—the betrothal must be cancelled and forgotten on both sides, and so on. . . ."[107]

AN ELABORATE WEDDING

Glikl recounted the details of her daughter's wedding with pride and relish. Although very few were as rich as Elia Cleve, the bridegroom's father, he was certainly not unique. This description shows the extent to which some in the Ashkenazic Jewish community had prospered, especially in the last half of the seventeenth century.

"After the ceremony all the guests were led into a great hall, the walls of which were lined with gilded leather. A long table crowded with regal delicacies stood in the center, and each guest was served in order of rank. My son Mordecai was then about five years old; there was no more beautiful child in the whole world and we had dressed him becomingly and neatly. The courtiers nearly swallowed him for very admiration, especially the prince, who held his hand the whole time. After the royal visitors and other guests had consumed the confects and drunk well the wine, the table was cleared and removed. Masked dancers entered and presented different poses quite nicely and suitably to the entertainment. They ended with the Dance of the Dead. It was all very splendidly done."[108]

THE TEN COMMANDMENTS FOR A GOOD WIFE

A book on marriage, written in Yiddish in 1620 and directed at Jewish women, stipulated ten guidelines for a Jewish wife:

1. The first, my dear daughter, is to beware of his anger, lest you enrage him. . . .
2. The second . . . search and consider and reflect about his food, about that which he likes to eat. . . . Try to have his meals ready at the proper time, for hunger does nobody any good. . . .
3. When he sleeps, guard his sleep so that he may not be awakened. . . .
4. Try to be thrifty and careful with your husband's money and make an effort not to bring any loss to him. . . .
5. If you should know anything of his secrets, don't confide them to anyone. . . .
6. Find out whom he likes and like that person too, and him whom he dislikes, you dislike, too. . . .
7. Don't be contrary to him. Do everything he tells you. . . .
8. Don't expect anything of him that he considers difficult. . . .
9. Heed the requests that he may make of you, awaiting in turn that he will love you if you do so. . . .
10. Be very careful to guard against jealousy. Don't make him jealous in any way.

—Lev Tov, *by Isaac ben Eliakim*[109]

Written from Petershagen, Germany, on May 6, 1562, these are the earliest examples of women's correspondence from the central European area. They were addressed to two young sons of the family who were studying in another town. Hendl, the mother of the boys, wrote:

"Have a healthy year my dear Lob and my dear Hirz, be pious and do what is right. You couldn't give me any greater pleasure. Don't run out of the house. If your uncle allows you to go somewhere be obedient. Don't fight with any young men, remain outside the school yard and don't play in front of the ditch, my dear sons. You will be well-advised, with God's help, to take my cautions to heart. I can't be with you all the time. If you act in this way I could not experience any greater joy and I will not desert you, if God wills it. And I will always send you money and clothes so that you, if God wills it, will not suffer any want even if I would have nothing myself to wear and will have to eat once and fast once. . . . A very good night from your mother Hendl. Give my regards to everybody and write me back a long letter."[110]

The boys' sister, Mele, added a letter of her own. She advised: ". . . Now know dear brothers that I will be very pleased if you study hard. If I hear that, I will send you something nice, so learn well. . . ."[111]

required to write a clause into his marriage contract: "Should the husband die childless, the marriage was to be considered as having been annulled."[112] This clause made the performance of *ḥalitzah* unnecessary and freed the woman immediately upon the death of her spouse.

Although there is no evidence that any well-known authority promulgated such a law, it was already noted as an accepted fact by R. Israel Isserlein (d. 1460) in his work *Terumot ha-Deshen* and also by Israel Bruna (d. 1480), both of whom encouraged the practice under certain conditions.[113] Such a usage was not advocated solely in order to give women more rights or freedom; rather it marked the realization that conversion was usually final and converts were lost to Judaism.

Women's Sexuality

Although modesty was the general rule, this did not preclude individual women from sexual thoughts or deeds. One rare poem, written by an unnamed German woman of the sixteenth century, reveals her feelings of lust and suggests that open flirtations among young people did occur (see p. 157, "Love Song").

Distrust of women was as prevalent in Ashkenazic lands as it had been in places like Italy, Spain, and France. R. Moshe ben Yaakov of Kiev wrote at the end of the fifteenth century: "Just as it is impossible to find a white raven, so it is impossible to find a virtuous woman. . . . If there is no real adultery, there is something akin to it."[114]

LEGAL RIGHTS

According to both Jewish and secular law, everything a wife earned was the property of her husband, who was the head of the family. He was recognized as the family spokesperson in all secular as well as religious affairs; he paid the taxes and usually represented his wife in court. Even if she ran a business of her own, she was considered his agent (see chapter 4, **Economic Activities**).[115] It was only when a husband died that his widow became a legal entity in the community and in the courts (see chapter 5, **Rights of Widows**).

Despite some legal latitude for women in the economic sphere, society continued to view them as requiring supervision, and laws were passed restricting them socially. In sixteenth-century Poland, where gambling was a common vice among Jews, it was only women who "were strictly forbidden to play cards, even without money."[116] For the Jewish community of Krakow, women's manner of dress became a concern and an ordinance was passed in that city regulating "against ostentatious dress and precious ornaments."[117]

Women's Wills

A woman's possessions were technically inherited by her husband if she predeceased him. If she was a widow, the money usually went to her children or grandchildren. This was the case for Ryke of Frankfurt, a widow who, in 1470, left all her possessions, including gold, silverwork, and gems, to her orphaned grandson Isaak[118] and gave orders concerning his education.

Some women, in order to circumvent the limits of Jewish law, registered their wills in a non-Jewish court, as they had done in earlier centuries and in other places. Jewish women could also bequeath gifts to others if

---

LOVE SONG

Once I felt enticed
to woo a young man
as I wanted to become a woman.
Then the thought occurred to me
what fun a young woman has
here on earth.

I constantly thought by myself
how I might for once,
and soon, enjoy love
and become a bride
to be wed with a young man
to live together with him in
   happiness.

Whenever I go to sleep alone
painful thoughts always come to me
that I have to be alone;
if only I had a young man
with whom I could go to bed
to have a good time with him

When I see the lads
dance like young deer
on the open meadow
I think that one of them
might want to come home with me
to give me pleasure for once.

When I wake up
at midnight
I can no longer lie in bed
because of the wonderful lovers
of whom I always fantasize
yet who cause me much frustration.

      . . . . . .

Now I want to make it happen
and constantly ponder in my mind
how I should approach it
soon to make a catch
of a young man
who is alert and joyful.[119]
                              —Anonymous

they left specific instructions before they died and if their husbands agreed. Such was the case for Rivkah bat Avraham Halfon, wife of Ḥayyim Sintzheim of Mannheim, Germany.[120]

Rivkah wrote her will in 1713, stating that since she had been a frugal wife, not spending her husband's money on frivolous things, she was certain he would accede to her wishes in giving money to charity. She then outlined the amounts and recipients of her largesse. Most of her money went to the poor, orphans, brides in need of dowries, people who needed clothing, and also to "the children of my brothers and sisters who are not wealthy." She also set aside money for a group of ten men to study in her honor for one hour each day.

After listing her bequests, she gave ethical advice to her sons and daughters, advising them not to fight with each other; to go to synagogue, educate their children, and give to charity; and above all, not to forget her.

PUBLIC POWER

The female court Jews in German cities were among the very few women who wielded some measure of public power and whose influence extended beyond their families or local communities. Although Esther Liebmann was an outstanding example, she was not the only one.

Issaḥar Homburg was the court factor in Mainz (Germany), extending credit to the ruler and accepting unpaid debts as surety. When he died in 1759, Blümele, his wife, continued Homburg's work of supplying the army. In southern Germany, Madame Kaulla (1739–1809), matriarch of the influential Kaulla family, was considered the most important female court factor in Württemberg and "exercised a beneficial influence on Jewish society."[121]

Other Jewish women like Rachel (or Rashka) of Krakow gained a variety of privileges through their connections in court but never exerted leadership or had an official public role.

RELIGIOUS PARTICIPATION

Writings of this period show the centrality of religion for the Jews of Ashkenazic lands, and women's letters especially are permeated with religious phrases such as "God forbid," "God willing," or "May the Lord, may He be praised." Quotations from religious texts are also frequently found. Referring to these letters, the authors of one anthology note: "Although not focusing exclusively on spirituality, they [the letters and memoirs] reveal the importance that many of the authors attached to God, religious observance, and the preservation of Jewish identity."[122]

Women and the Synagogue

Documents and gravestones point to the fact that by the sixteenth century, almost every synagogue in Germany and eastern Europe had its own woman precentor who was able to lead the prayers and sometimes translated them into Yiddish for the women. Female precentors had several names in Yiddish. They were called *firzogerins* (literally, those who said the words "before") or *zugerkes*. Both these words mean "prayer leader" and both assume a feminine gender. Although women functioned as prayer leaders throughout the Ashkenazic world and a few are documented as early as the Middle Ages (see chapter 4), that role became institutionalized in eastern Europe in the eighteenth century. Some *firzogerins* were inspired to add to the liturgy for women by offering their own translations or creating original prayers.

Women also recited and wrote prayers specifically for the three positive commandments that they were required to perform at home. These were: lighting candles on Sabbaths and holidays, breaking off a piece of the dough when baking bread, and going to the ritual bath after menstruation. Many of the women's collections included such prayers, as well as others that were designed to bring women closer to God while doing what was expected of them. Often, the prayers were addressed not to the God of our Fathers but to the God of our Mothers: Sarah, Rebecca, Leah, and Rachel, with whom the women identified. Although God was always referred to as "Father," sometimes with the masculine pronoun, more often the pronoun was "You." Sometimes a prayer was directed to specific ancestors as intermediaries to God. Most often, women made their

---

OBITUARY NOTICES OF WOMEN FROM METZ

Many of the obituary notices illustrate the religiosity and charity of Ashkenazic Jewish women. For example:

- "The estimable and generous Sarah Jocabed [Yokheved], daughter of Meir Eldad Levi, for she devoted herself to the living and the dead, went to the synagogue morning and night and prayed with devoutness. She spun tzitzit [and gave them to poor men] without payment and gave a gift of a hundred francs to the charity fund of the community of Metz. Her husband gave a gift in her name to the poor house. Died Monday night and was interred Tuesday the 17th of Tammuz 5419 [July 8, 1659]."

- "The just and pious Cherele, daughter of Mechoulam [Meshullam] Abraham, who lived in righteousness, helped everybody, especially women in childbirth. She went to the synagogue morning and evening one hour before the service, reading each day the entire Book of Psalms with the commentary. She sacrificed herself and fasted three days per week. . . . Her sons and daughters gave a gift to the hospice in her name." She died and was buried on Tuesday the 12th of Tevet, 5458 [February 1, 1698]."

- "The pious, distinguished, upright Minelen, daughter of Isaie [Isaiah] Jacob, she lived with integrity. . . . she fasted for several years, and resolved to go with her husband, the pious rabbi Feivouch [Feibush] Halphen, in Elul 5410 (September 1650) to Jerusalem. Yonder, in Jerusalem, as here in Metz, she did not spare herself [in caring for] the women giving birth and the sick. . . . Her sons gave a gift in her name. She died and was buried in Jerusalem the Holy City, the 24th of Elul, 5430 [September 9, 1670]."[123]

appeals as individuals, not in the name of the Jewish people or their own community, and they addressed themselves to the Matriarchs, or to the God of the Matriarchs.

Many of the prayers authored by these *firzogerins* suggest that they were produced for recitation in the synagogue before a female congregation. A good many of the synagogues had a separate women's room, including the one at Worms (Germany) and, later,

---

A SIMḤAT TORAH PRAYER

This poem was composed as a prayer to be sung on Simḥat Torah while the women decorated the *sefer Torah* for the holiday.

Our God is one—You are my God
Who created my soul and body—
Hallelujah
You created Heaven and Earth,
Therefore is your praise eternal—
Hallelujah!
You were and will be eternally
You created us all—Hallelujah
All things are in Your power:
Therefore we praise You day and
night—Hallelujah!
True and pure is Your Command
Therefore we thank You, O True
God, Hallelujah!
Living and Eternal, You are our
Consolation
As You did promise us—Hallelujah!
You live eternally on Your heavenly
throne,
For the prayers, You keep their
reward, Hallelujah!
Take as Your help the heavenly
Host;
Everything will prove true—
Hallelujah.[124]
*   —Rivkah bat Meir Tiktiner*

Prague. Some even contained a separate ark in which a Torah was kept.[125]

Ashkenazic Women and Spirituality

Among the Ashkenazim of the seventeenth century, spirituality was rooted more in traditional texts—the Torah, the Talmud, and the newer kabbalistic literature—than in esoteric experiences. Scholars could then go beyond the texts, striving to find secret meanings in the words themselves. Through those secrets, they could harness God's power and achieve a spiritual state. Because most women did not learn classic texts, they were effectively barred from participation in any attempt at enhanced spirituality.[126] Nor is there any definitive record of women as a group trying to participate in such activities until the seventeenth century.

By that time, Ashkenazim were beginning to be affected by the ideas inherent in Lurianic Kabbalah and the Messianic movement that followed it. One of those ideas was that *tikkun olam* could be accomplished by pious acts and by the addition of specific rituals and prayers recited with intensity and commitment (*kavanah*). As these beliefs spread among a larger group of men, more women also learned about them. Gradually, women, too, came to believe that they might be able to contribute to *tikkum olam* by good deeds, prayer, and ritual activities. Their writings became even more prolific during the late eighteenth and nineteenth centuries.

Up until this time, even when a woman did manage to experience what she believed was a mystical connection with God, rarely could she share either her belief or her methods with large numbers of women. This was due to two specific limitations: Women rarely studied in groups, and they had no disciples who would write down what they said and disseminate it. But the development of printing and the ability to reproduce prayer books, instructional literature, and even formulae for charms and magical cures offered women a doorway into a previously inaccessible world. For the first time, women had an opportunity to share with others what they knew or believed. The first evidence of this attempt to introduce women *as a group* to a previously all-male experience appeared in the middle of the seventeenth century.

The Early Prayer Collections for Women

Large-scale publication of women's prayers in Yiddish followed on the heels of some of the major Yiddish folk literature that began to appear by 1600 (see **Education**). These prayers, unrelated to the daily prayer regimen, were first compiled by a man and printed in Amsterdam in 1648. In explaining the purpose for his collection, titled simply *Tkhines*, the unknown compiler wrote: ". . . when the heart does not know what the mouth speaks, the prayer helps but little."[127] The goal of these prayers, then, was to expand the realm of spirituality beyond the narrow, male, esoteric circles of former times and encourage women, by acts of prayer and piety, to join in efforts to hasten the redemption through their merit.

The next Yiddish collections, including a work called *Seder Tkhines*, were more connected to the Hebrew liturgy and aspired to expand women's venue beyond the home, the cemetery, and

the *mikveh* and bring them into the synagogue.[128] Other similar collections, also written or compiled by men, appeared throughout central Europe. The *Seder Tkhines* was printed and reprinted from 1650 until 1720 and was widely available to Jewish women.[129] In addition, other, similar collections were published in Prague, Hamburg, and Fürth.

Tkhines Written by Women

Yiddish *tkhines* were very likely in existence among Ashkenazic women quite early. In the privacy of their own homes, in their own language, women surely must have whispered appeals to God or made secret bargains. Many of the *tkhines* continued in that tone, concentrating on specific holidays or situations, such as "Tkhine for When One's Husband Is Traveling" or "Tkhine for a Pregnant Woman Who Is About to Give Birth."[130] The first *tkhine* to appear in print was for women to recite when they went to the *mikveh*.[131]

An early *tkhine*, an eight-page booklet entitled *Eyn gor sheyne tkhine (A Very Beautiful Tkhine)*,[132] was printed and published in approximately 1600 in Prague. Chava Weissler suggests that it may have been written jointly by several women, for on the first page, under the title, it states, "[This *tkhine*] was for a long time kept secret among a group of pious women; they let it remain among themselves, and let no one copy it. Now they have rethought the matter, and have brought it for publication."[133]

The *Very Beautiful Tkhine* invoked the prayers of almost all the major female biblical characters: Eve, Sarah, Rebecca, Leah, Rachel, Miriam, Hannah, Deborah, Bathsheva, Esther, and the apocryphal figure Judith. The authors' sources included both biblical material and details from the Midrash, the early post-biblical writings. Each character was linked to a specific problem with which the woman reciting the *tkhine* might identify. For example, a woman facing

---

THE LEGEND OF YENTE

Yente's name appears among the many Hasidic legends associated with the Baal Shem Tov. Married to Yosef Spravedliver, a simple Galician Jew, she not only encouraged him to join the Hasidic movement, but was herself also drawn to it. After a visit to the Baal Shem Tov with her husband, Yente was so impressed with this charismatic leader that she directly emulated his practices, abstaining from sexual relations with her husband, immersing herself frequently in the *mikveh*, and fasting. She wore a tallit when she prayed and, in general, displeased her husband, who returned to R. Yisrael Baal Shem Tov to complain. Contrary to Yosef's expectations, the Baal Shem Tov declared Yente a prophet. Her fame spread, and Hasidim, both men and women, supposedly came to her for her curative powers and her blessings. It was said that she refused all money offered to her, even though it was customary for a *tzaddik* to accept a *pidyon* (redemption money) from someone bringing a request. As engaging as this legend is, there is no authentication for it.[134]

---

danger alone might call on Sarah, who went alone to the court of Abimelekh. If she had trouble conceiving, she would petition Rachel, who had been barren for a long time.

Such appeals, however, although speaking directly to women's concerns, fell far short of the type of mystical experience that some of the women endeavored to achieve. Counteracting this popular, more simplistic trend, by the middle of the seventeenth century a few women sought to connect the female petitioner with a higher level of spirituality by means of translations of esoteric formulae and prayers originally written in Hebrew for men. They learned the concepts of Kabbalah, of redemption through *devekut* (mystical communion with God) and *tikkun olam*, and translated them for audiences of women. At last, the mystical methods that for so long had been a closed book to most women because they were not taught Hebrew were now open to them. The Yiddish translations empowered still more women, and by the beginning of the eighteenth century individual prayers and collections of prayers and psalms in the Yiddish language multiplied. They were personal prayers of petition that appealed to God, either directly or through ancestral intermediaries.

The prayers of **Sarah bat Tovim** and **Leah Dreyzl** show an awareness of mysticism. **Ellus bat Mordecai of Slutsk** translated some of the practices of the kabbalists into Yiddish in 1704. Another woman translated *Sha'arei Tziyyon*, a collection that included prayers for midnight and other kabbalistic rituals of the Lurianic school. The book was originally written by the kabbalist Nathan Nata Hannover (d. 1683). Because she considered herself a modest woman, this translator never allowed her name to be used.[135]

Hasidic Women

With the establishment of Hasidism and the sharp division between the Hasidim and the *Mitnagdim*, Jewish life became divided and the women who followed the Baal Shem Tov took a different path to spirituality. The Hasidim were a rebel group in their early years, and for a woman, urging a husband or son to join them was no casual decision. Yet some women did. In the mid-1700s Sarah (Soreh), wife of the aged scholar R. Yosef, bore a son named Leib. Shortly after his birth, Yosef died and the widowed Soreh brought her son up by herself and steered him to Hasidism. While still in his teens, Leib joined the circle of the Baal Shem Tov. As an honor to his mother, he was called Leib Soreh and is still known by that name.[136]

CHAPTER 7

A Different Voice:

Jewish Women in the Lands of Islam (1492–1750)

OVERVIEW

Once a strong and united territory, the lands of the Islamic Empire had begun to separate and weaken even before the year 1000 (see chapter 3). The separation of Spain and then North Africa from the Abbasid Empire was only the beginning of this trend. In the West, the Spanish Caliphate divided into small principalities, ruled by warring potentates. In the East, the Mongol invasion of 1258, the Bedouin attacks in North Africa, and the Crusades hastened disintegration.[1] By the end of the thirteenth century, what had been a strong and glorious empire was fragmented and weak; power and prestige were passing to western European Christian leaders.

The Jews in Muslim lands suffered severely as wars and persecutions wreaked havoc with once thriving economies. Many Jews left the Middle East altogether. Then, in the middle of the fifteenth century, the Ottomans appeared, offering a chance for a better life.

The Ottoman Empire

The Ottoman Empire began with one Turkish tribe that established a bridgehead in Anatolia in approximately 1300. They "expanded relentlessly" from there, north into the Balkans as far as the Danube River, finally capturing Constantinople, the seat of the Christian Byzantine Empire, in 1453.[2] As part of their policy of populating cities with groups of people who were favorable to them, the Ottomans forcibly transferred Jews from the Balkans into Constantinople, now called Istanbul, as well as into other newly conquered areas such as Salonika and Rhodes. This demographic policy, coupled with the immigration of Spanish Jews, caused the Jewish populations of Istanbul and Salonika to double and triple.[3] With the expulsion of all Jews from Spain in 1492 and the forced conversion of Portuguese Jews in 1497, the steady trickle became a flood.

The hundreds of thousands of Jews who were expelled from Spain were turned away from one port after another. Thousands died on the ships without ever reaching a safe haven. Some went to the land of Israel, still under Mameluke rule, but a great number of these refugees, sometimes alone, sometimes in family groups, were welcomed into the newly ascendant Ottoman Empire throughout the sixteenth century.[4] Known variously as New Christians, *conversos*, or crypto-Jews, many had lived a full generation pretending to be believing Catholics, waiting for an opportunity to escape Catholic Spain and Portugal to a more tolerant environment.

The Ottomans were Muslims and believed in separating and secluding women. Many Jews tended to follow this custom. However, a few Jewish women found broadened opportunities in Ottoman lands, in service to the women of the sultan's court. This handful of women, called *kieras*,[5] became well known and, depending on the power of their noble patrons, sometimes exercised considerable **public power** themselves.

After the Ottomans conquered the Mamelukes in 1516–17, the Empire expanded still further to include Iraq, Syria, and the land of Israel, making the Jewish population of this growing empire one of the largest in the world and certainly the most heterogeneous.[6] Ottoman Jews could be divided into several groups, each with its own language, distinctive culture, and customs.

Throughout the sixteenth century, waves of *conversos* (converted Jews and their descendants) who managed to escape from Christian Spain and Portugal followed the initial Sephardic immigration. They viewed the lands of the Ottoman sultan as a place "where the gates of liberty are always wide open for you that you may fully practice your Judaism."[7]

THE VARIED JEWISH POPULATION IN THE OTTOMAN EMPIRE

- *Romaniot:* Greek-speaking Jews of the Balkans and western Asia Minor.
- *Musta'rabs:* Indigenous, Arabic-speaking Jews of the Middle East, living in Syria, Iraq, Egypt, and the land of Israel.
- *Ma'aravis* (Maghrebis): Jews of North Africa.
- Ashkenazim: Yiddish-speaking Jews from Germany and central Europe. A small number had settled in Egypt and the land of Israel.
- Sephardim: the Jews from Spain and Portugal who spoke their own language (Ladino) and established Sephardic customs wherever they went.
- Kurdish- and Aramaic-speaking Jews from eastern lands.

For their part, Ottoman sultans, eager to expand, hailed Jewish immigration and Jewish skills as an unexpected but welcome benefit. Sultan Bayezit II (1481–1512) was quoted as saying: "Can you call such a king [as Ferdinand of Spain] wise and intelligent? He is impoverishing his country and enriching my kingdom."[8] During the early sixteenth century, when the Ottoman Empire was at the peak of its success militarily, politically, and economically, a positive attitude toward immigration continued.

The vast migration of Sephardim changed the composition of all the Jewish communities of the Islamic world. Quickly outnumbering the original Jewish inhabitants, the Spanish- and Portuguese-speaking Jews assumed leadership roles wherever they settled, and their rabbis produced collections of responsa and law codes that spread Sephardic traditions and usage throughout the empire.[9] Although initially each congregation of Jews remained separate, within two or three generations, the Sephardic rite was adopted in most of the synagogues of the Ottoman lands.[10] The Sephardim revived education and secular interests as well as the study of Jewish law, which had been neglected among the original inhabitants.[11]

Decline of an Empire

This favorable climate for Jews lasted about one hundred years. Suleiman I, the Magnificent (1520–1566), was the last sultan to win military victories. Subsequent sultans were weak and less successful. The empire sustained military losses, and the economy went into a downward slide. In the land of Israel, the towns of Safed, Jerusalem, and Tiberius, which had enjoyed considerable prosperity, began to weaken economically. Trade, both foreign and domestic, steadily gave way to increasing competition from the West. Safed, once the eastern center of the Ottoman textile industry as well as a religious and intellectual center of Jewish learning and mysticism, began losing its population. The Jews of Salonika, the largest center of the cloth industry in the empire, managed to maintain and keep control of the commerce in textiles through the eighteenth century, but lost most of their foreign trade.[12]

By 1574, when Murad III became sultan, he curtailed the power of the women in his court. At the same time, he put new laws in place that accentuated a separation of Jews and Christians from the Muslim majority, and the status of the Jews throughout the empire declined sharply. It was under the rule of Sultan Murad III that the *kieras*, the female and usually Jewish liaisons between the sultanas and the outside world, lost power. Under Murad's successor Mehmed III, **Esther Handali,** the best known and most powerful of the *kieras*, was brutally executed.

By the time of Mehmed III's death in 1623, the sultanate was considerably weakened and could not maintain its power in face of the increasing strength of political interest groups. These groups, especially the Janissaries, or *Spahis* (a powerful part of the Turkish military), began to demand some of the commercial concessions that once belonged to Jews.[13]

The slow decline of the Ottoman Empire, beginning just as the sixteenth century came to an end, was never reversed, and the effects were evident among Jews as well. Where Jewish communities were once united, signs of social unrest appeared by the seventeenth century, and from the mid–eighteenth century onward, the number of poor people increased. Jewish communities fell into debt, and "many were on the bread line."[14]

The poverty and hardship endemic to the Ottoman Empire in those later years was felt by women even more than men, and women's names appear in the Jewish communal charity rolls far more often than men's names. Evidence of women's poverty is reflected in the letters that they wrote—or had others write—to send to relatives. One example of this is the letter written by **Rachel Sussman,** originally of Prague, who lived in the land of Israel.[15]

For both Jews and gentiles, educational decline followed the weakening of the economy. The standard of rabbinical learning, of great importance in the sixteenth century, began to deteriorate. Although scholars continued to write in Hebrew and Ladino, and their works were printed by the many Jewish presses that the Sephardim had brought with them from Spain and Portugal, the literature had only a limited appeal.[16] As the seventeenth century progressed, mysticism and the study of Kabbalah took precedence, spreading out from its center in Safed to other communities. Responding to this heightened interest in the miraculous, fostered in part by the persecution of Jews occurring in eastern Europe (see chapter 6) as well as in Turkey itself, many Jews began to believe that the End of Days was imminent.[17] They waited for a messiah to come and redeem them.

The Rise and Fall of Messianic Hopes

Shabbetai Zevi, a highly unstable young Jew born in Izmir (Smyrna) into a middle-class family, came to believe that he was the Messiah. He traveled throughout the empire, preaching his own brand of mysticism and gaining a large following, especially among the *conversos*. Women also flocked to him.

Shabbetai married and divorced several times. Facts about his first marriage are obscure but according to Gershom Scholem, it occurred when he was twenty-two or twenty-four years old.[18] Then in 1664, he married **Sarah,** a Polish orphan. Shabbetai returned to Izmir with her and officially announced that he was God's anointed one. Following this proclamation, Turkish officials had him arrested and gave him a choice between conversion to Islam or death. He chose conversion.

By opting to convert, Shabbetai Zevi stunned Jews throughout the Ottoman Empire and beyond. Most, completely disillusioned, turned away from a belief in the Messiah. But Shabbetai's wife, Sarah, and a small band of Turkish Jews also converted to Islam. Some of these converts later formed a Judeo-Muslim sect known as the Doenmeh.[19]

Although later Jewish scholars tried to remove all mention of Shabbetai Zevi from the records, this proved impossible. As conditions worsened for Jews in the lands of Islam, the concept of messianism, as well as mystical methods to encourage the coming of the Messiah, remained appealing. In the face of rabbinical disapproval, many who had believed in Shabbetai Zevi continued to have faith in his message and practiced his rites in secret. Some women, too, found an appeal in this new system of messianic beliefs and would make their mark in the new religious movements that developed throughout the eighteenth century.

BIOGRAPHIES

ABERLIN, RACHEL MISHAN OF SAFED, MYSTIC
(16th century)

Born into a family of mystics, Rachel was the sister of R. Yehudah Mishan, one of Isaac Luria's disciples. Rachel Mishan married Yehudah Aberlin of Salonika after he immigrated to the land of Israel in the mid–fifteenth century and settled in Safed. Yehudah became head of the Ashkenazic community there and was close to the rabbis and their mystical circle. When he died in 1582, his widow, Rachel, enjoyed a certain amount of prestige, and by 1590 she had established her own court either in Safed or Jerusalem. She had long been an admirer of Isaac Luria, and after his death, she allied herself with his closest disciple, Ḥayyim Vital. Vital and Aberlin were close associates for many years and appeared together in Jerusalem and Damascus. Vital held her in the highest regard and

---

THE ROLE OF THE MAGGID

The concept of a *maggid*, a supernatural being who communicated directly with one individual, had been introduced into Judaism by the Sephardic scholar Yosef Taitazak, and was an accepted phenomenon in the kabbalistic circles of Safed. The famous Yosef Caro, author of the Shulḥan Arukh, claimed that his *maggid* spoke to him, advised him on the law, gave him the words to write, and offered personal advice.[20]

---

lived in her home for some time, together with his wife and children.

It is mainly through Vital's writings that we know about Rachel Aberlin. Beginning in 1578, Vital reported her visions and her prophetic words. She first saw a pillar of fire hovering over Vital's head as he preached in the synagogue. At other times, Vital wrote, she saw visions of the prophet Elijah.

Aberlin acted as an advisor to other women mystics, including the daughter of Raphael Anav, a young, unnamed girl whose mystical prowess is also reported by Ḥayyim Vital.[21]

FRANCESA SARAH OF SAFED, MYSTIC
(16th century)

This pious woman lived in Safed, the center of the kabbalistic movement, during the sixteenth century and had a personal *maggid*, a spiritual guide who spoke with her and foretold future events. She may have been the only woman in Safed who communicated with such a spiritual advisor, although the phenomenon was known among men.

Even though most women in the Middle East were not even expected to pray regularly, reports about Francesa Sarah refer to her as a holy woman and authenticate her personal revelations. Ḥayyim Vital, one of the principal disciples of Isaac Luria, in his book *Sefer ha-Ḥezyonot* (*Book of Visions*, 1594), wrote: "I was in Safed. . . . A woman was there, Francesa Sarah, a pious woman, who saw visions in a waking dream and heard a voice speaking to her, and most of her words were true."[22] She predicted a plague and insisted that the community leaders ordain a fast to prevent the catastrophe. They did as she demanded, and there is no record of plague coming to Safed at that time.

FREḤA BAT AVRAHAM OF MOROCCO, POET AND SCHOLAR
(18th century)

Freḥa bat Avraham was born in Morocco and lived in Tunisia. A member of the prominent Moroccan Bar Adiba family,[23] Freḥa was probably born in the 1730s. She moved with her father and brother to Tunis, Tunisia, because of the persecutions of the Jews of Morocco that occurred from 1728 to 1757.

She wrote in Hebrew, and one of her poems, expressing hope for redemption, is among those that have been preserved. For the Bar Adiba family, however, the safety and redemption for which Freḥa yearned were elusive. In 1756, Tunis was attacked and conquered by the Algerians, and many in the Jewish community were forced to escape the subsequent persecutions. Freḥa's father and brother also fled but, for some unknown reason, Freḥa did not accompany them. When her father and brother returned to Tunis they searched for her but she was never found. It was assumed that she died or was killed during the disturbances.

To honor her memory, Freḥa's father, R. Avraham, built a synagogue in her name. He located the ritual bath on the site where her bed once stood, and the Holy Ark marked the place of her library. The fact that she possessed her own library (although it might have included only a few books) indicates that Freḥa was educated. Yosef Benjoie, an early twentieth-century writer, called her *rabbanit*, a word that usually implies a very learned

FRANCESA SARAH, MYSTIC OF SAFED

In those days there was a wise woman who did great deeds in the upper Galilee, in Safed—may it be rebuilt and reestablished quickly in our time—and her name was Francesa and she had a *maggid* to tell her and to announce to her what will happen in the world. And the sages of Safed tested her several times to know if there was substance in her words and of all that she would say not one [of her prophecies] was left unfulfilled. Once she sent to the sages of Safed and said to them that they should enact a fast day and they should stand up for their lives with prayers and entreaties, and do charitable work, "perhaps God will be kind to us and we will not perish [Jon. 1:6] in the plague, God willing." . . . Immediately the rabbis decreed a fast day . . . from the small to the large, from man to woman, from the baby to the nursling, and R. Moshe de Koriel stood up to preach to the community, and she, even she [Francesa] sat with part of the worthy women who were, in that generation, in a second story at the back of the synagogue to pray with the community. . . .[24]

woman.[25] Another writer stated: "She was well-versed in Torah and wrote Hebrew compositions and poetry."[26]

Freḥa's synagogue became a place of pilgrimage for the Jewish women of

> ## LIFT UP MY STEPS
>
> One of Freḥa's poems, written in Tunis, alluded to the Moroccan persecutions. It is a poem of redemption, expressing a hope for a return of the Jewish people and of Freḥa herself to the Land of Israel.
>
> *Lift up my steps, O Lord, my savior,*
> *I'd go to my country with a placid*
> *   joy;*
> *an ignorant people pursues me*
> *   now,*
> *and taunts me with a thunderous*
> *   noise.*
> *Take me, quickly, to a Galilee*
> *   mountain,*
> *and send your anger across their*
> *   skies;*
> *there I'll see your light, my crown,*
> *and say: Now I can die.*[27]

Tunis. "The women of the community turned to Freḥa as to a holy person (*kedoshah*) and they mentioned her name in times of distress."[28] In 1936, with the renovation of the Jewish quarter of Tunis, the old synagogue named for Freḥa was destroyed and a new one with the same name was built. It was at this time that the first article about Freḥa appeared, written by Yosef Benjoie. Although she is relatively unknown in the West, the name of Freḥa bat Avraham, the Moroccan-Jewish poet, was preserved in Tunis until modern times.

HANDALI, ESTHER OF TURKEY, KIERA IN THE SULTAN'S HAREM
(16th century)

Esther Handali began her working life as a peddler, selling trinkets and jewelry together with her husband, Elijah, to the women of the royal harem. After her husband's death, Esther proved useful to these royal women by purchasing cosmetics, jewelry, and clothing for them and, in general, creating a link between the harem and the outside world. There were other Jewish women who performed similar functions during this time, but it is Esther *Kiera* Handali, as she was known, whose name later historians associated with the job itself.[29] This was partly due to confusion, as many of the documents referring to a *kiera* mention no names.

Esther Handali, a favorite among the sultanas at court, was especially close with the sultan's mother and was also the confidante of Sultana Safiyah Baffa, a Venetian woman and Sultan Murad's favorite wife.[30] Safiyah exerted a powerful influence on the affairs of the Ottoman Empire, and it was through Esther Handali's friendship with the sultana and her own official role as *kiera* that she was able to suggest appointments and obtain trading concessions. It was alleged that Handali became so powerful that people approached her directly, offering bribes for her intervention on their behalf.[31]

Because of Safiyah's ties to the Venetian Republic, Esther Handali was especially involved with Venice. In 1584, Catherine de Medici, Queen Mother of France, wrote to Sultana Baffa seeking the support of the Turkish fleet against Spain.[32] Esther *Kiera* was employed either to make sure of the accuracy of the Turkish translations accompanying the Italian texts, or as a spy, bringing copies of correspondence to Venice. She was apparently a linguist as well as a trustworthy associate.

As a reward for her services, in 1587 Handali was given a letter of recommendation and approval to start a lottery in the Venetian Republic. This was the first time that a foreigner, and especially a Turkish Jew, was allowed this privilege in Venice,[33] which had only recently become allied with the Ottoman Empire after years of warfare.

Between 1580 and 1590, Esther Handali's wealth and privileges were supposedly at their height. Diplomatic observers considered her one of the most influential persons at court but also one who freely accepted gifts and bribes in return for her favors. At the same time, she gained a reputation among the Jews for charity and good works. In response to anti-Jewish riots, she helped Jewish merchants whose shops were looted by Muslims. When the Jewish area of Constantinople was reduced to ashes after the great fire of 1569, it was reputedly Esther *Kiera* who assisted in its rebuilding. She fed the poor, supported scholars, and financed the printing of Jewish books. After Sultan Murad III threatened to destroy the Jewish community, she prevented the decree from being enforced.[34]

Sultan Murad died in 1595, leaving a troubled empire on the verge of civil war.

In face of this crisis, the new sultan, Mehmed III, tried to assert his dominance. He began by establishing his own authority over his influential mother, Safiyah. Sultana Safiyah was used to controlling many of the court appointments, but now lost whatever authority she had held and could offer no meaningful royal protection even to her favorites at court.

One of the competing factions that were especially resentful of

FIG. 17. This portrait of a Turkish *kiera* shows her with elegant dress, holding a staff of office. (Courtesy of The British Museum)

the sultana's power was a group called the Janissaries *(Spahis)*, the feudal horsemen and warriors of the Turkish provinces. According to a contemporary report by an English ambassador, Safiyah "had begged of her sonne the turke a certen yeerely revenue . . . which was used to be bestowed . . . among the Spahies this revenue she gave unto a Jew woman which was her . . . favorite and cheiff councellor."[35] Angered by this latest interference, the *Spahis* plotted to take their revenge on the sultana's favorite, the *Kiera*. With the consent of the young sultan, Mehmed III, the *Spahis* seized "the Jew woman" and killed her.[36] The report explained that the queen mother and even the sultan at first tried to protect her, but feared for their own lives if the *Spahis* did not get their way.

Esther *Kiera*'s oldest son was killed also. A second son converted to Islam, and the third, still a young boy, was allowed to live. Thus ended the life of a complicated and powerful Jew,

---

THE MURDER OF A KIERA

A report from an English eyewitness told a slightly different story than the one reported by the English ambassador. According to this traveler:

"A Juishe woman of the greatest credett and welth in Constantinople was brought out of hir house and stabbed to death in the Viseroys yeard; thence, by a window in the Serraglio wall, where the Grand Signior, Sultan Mahomet, stood to see, she was drawne with ropes to the publiquest place in the citie. . . . At that spot, [she was dismembered and her head] "caried uppon a pike throughe the citie."[37]

---

once considered the most influential woman at the Turkish court.

Was Esther Handali the same *Kiera* who had worked with the sultana when she was still the young and favored wife? Until recently, it was assumed that all the records mentioning a *kiera* referred to Esther Handali, since hers was the only name specified in the documents. With current research, however, new questions have been raised, suggesting that we may have here a historical construct rather than a single individual. Neither the English ambassador's report nor the documents collected by the French historian Abraham Galanté, covering a period of sixty years, mentions the names of any of the *kieras*. The introduction to the ambassador's report calls her "the Jewess Kera or Keranuk."[38] Keranuk may have been her name, or it may have been another form of her title, *kiera*. Whichever *kiera* was executed that day, her enormous fortune was confiscated by the Turkish government.

Much later, a document issued in 1618 by Osman II, successor to Mehmed III, granted to the grandchildren of "the *kiera*" the privileges she once enjoyed.[39] Again, no name is given and it is unclear whether these were the grandchildren of the *kiera* who was executed in 1600, or those of Esther Handali (if she was a different *kiera*), or of another *kiera* altogether.

MALCHI, ESPERANZA OF TURKEY, *KIERA* IN THE SULTAN'S HAREM
(late 16th century)

The name of Esperanza Malchi appears in a letter written in 1599 to Queen Elizabeth I of England. Esperanza was described as a "lady-in-waiting" at the

Turkish court, and as "chief ladies' maid" to the sultan's harem. Undoubtedly, she was a *kiera* also, one of the successors to **Esther Handali**. She wrote the letter at the request of her mistress, the sultana, and described herself as "a Hebrew by law and nation."

Esperanza's name, plus the fact that the letter was written in Italian, suggests that this *kiera* was a Spanish or Portuguese *converso* who, like so many others, came through Venice before finding a haven in Turkey. In her letter, she sets forth the gifts that her employer, "the Serene Queen Mother," is sending to Queen Elizabeth through the ambassador. She enumerates: ". . . a robe and a girdle, and two kerchiefs wrought in gold, and three wrought in silk . . . a necklace of pearls and rubies . . . a wreath of diamonds from the jewels of her Highness, which she says she hopes your Majesty will be pleased to wear for her and give information of the receipt."

In return, Esperanza requests on behalf of her employer "distilled waters of every description for the face and odiferous oils for the hands" along with some cloths of wool and silk from England.[40] It was through services such as these that women like Esperanza Malchi endeared themselves to the noblewomen of the royal courts and were in a position to request—and sometimes to receive—important concessions.

MIRIAM BAT BENAYAH OF YEMEN, SCRIBE
(late 15th century)

Miriam bat Benayah, born into a family of scribes living in San'a, the capital of Yemen, is the only educated Yemenite woman known to us from

that time. Miriam worked in the late fifteenth and early sixteenth centuries in a family workshop. This might explain how, in a culture where women were rarely taught to read, let alone to write, Miriam could have become a scribe. She worked with her two brothers David and Yosef, and her father, who signed himself as *Safra* (the scribe) Benayah ben Sa'adiah b. Zekhariah.[41] She was apparently a wonder to the Jews of that city, perhaps not least because she continued working in the family business even after her marriage.

Benayah's family was well respected for their work and is credited with copying four hundred books, including copies of the Torah, collections of *haftarot*, and prayer books, all in Hebrew. Of those that remain extant, not all are signed by a single family member and may very well have been cooperative efforts. One Torah scroll was unmistakably the work of Miriam's hands, however, for at the end she wrote: "Do not condemn me for any errors that you may find, as I am a nursing woman."[42]

The existence of this scroll was first reported in 1859 by a Jewish traveler to Yemen,[43] but Miriam the Scribe was held up not as an example for women, but as a curiosity.

MIZRAHI, ASENATH BARAZANI OF AMADIYA, SCHOLAR AND TEACHER
(16th century)

As with so many educated women, Asenath Barazani came from a learned family. Her father, Shmuel ha-Levi Barazani, had no sons and taught his daughter Bible, Talmud, and other religious subjects. She probably helped him in running his yeshivah in

Amadiya (Kurdistan) until she married.

At the time of her marriage to R. Yaakov ben Yehudah Mizraḥi, her father insisted that she continue her studies. She reported this unusual demand in one of her letters, explaining: ". . . he made my husband swear that he would not make me perform work, and he [her husband] did as he [her father] had commanded him."[44] The work to which he alluded was, of course, housework, the accepted chores enumerated in the Mishnah that women were required to perform. Instead, Asenath Barazani studied and taught, first in Amadiya in her father's yeshivah, and later in Mosul, another city in Kurdistan, helping her husband to administer his school. "At the beginning," she wrote, "my husband

THE LEGEND OF ASENATH BARAZANI MIZRAḤI:

The Jews of Kurdistan greatly esteemed the Rabbanit Asenath. Her name is used until today [1950s] as a charm. They tell different stories about her. One story states, "Asenath daughter of haRav Shmuel Adonai [Barazani] was a very wise woman and learned in Torah. She learned the wisdom of the Kabbala and had a great reputation in [performing] miracles and wonders. After she gave birth to one son and one daughter[45] she prayed to God that she should stop menstruating[46] in order that she could work at learning, holiness, and purification. And God granted her request."[47]

was very busy with his own studies and didn't have time to teach the students. And I was teaching them in his place."

After her husband's death Asenath Barazani Mizraḥi became the titular, as well as the actual, head of the school. As she pointed out: ". . . I remain the teacher of Torah and she who reproaches and demands that [they observe] the immersion, and the Sabbath, and the menstrual impurity, and the prayer, and the like."[48]

Asenath Barazani was respected as a wise woman and was called *Tannit* by the Jews of Kurdistan. (*Tannit* is the feminine form of *Tanna*, the same title used for her father.)[49] Her numerous letters, written in Hebrew at the beginning of the seventeenth century,[50] show an excellent facility with a language rarely mastered by Jewish women in her time. Most of the letters were sent from Mosul to the Jews of Amadiya soliciting funds for the upkeep of her school. She also described her financial difficulties and the despair that she felt at her situation.

Letters written by her son after her death indicate that Asenath Barazani was never completely successful in gaining support for her yeshivah. Nevertheless, she lived on in the folklore of her people.

NASI, GRACIA OF PORTUGAL AND TURKEY, MERCHANT AND PHILANTHROPIST
(16th century)

Gracia Nasi, known at first as Beatrice de Luna, was born in Portugal in 1510 into a family of New Christians or *conversos*, the result of the mass conversion of Portuguese Jews in 1497. However, as so many others had done, her family secretly retained their ties to Judaism and gave her the Hebrew

FROM THE CORRESPONDENCE OF ASENATH BARAZANI MIZRAḤI

The excerpts below were written partly in poetry and partly in prose. In Hebrew verse she wrote:

To whom can I turn?
To the generous people that can cure my ills.
You righteous ones, please spare me,
And remember my deeds and the Torah of my God.
Not for my pleasure or my personal benefit am I crying here.
Not for the need of my household, my clothes, or my food.
But only to preserve the Midrashot [academies],
That my valor will not be shattered. . . .
. . . If the students of God will be scattered,
What will become of my world,
Of my days and my nights?
Therefore, listen, pious and religious people. . . .

The writer continued in prose, relating her personal story:

". . . And here is where I am going to tell you about my own problem. They caught me and hit me. . . . They sent a judgment with people that took over my house and they sold everything: my clothes and my daughter's clothes. They even took the books that were before me! And in addition they told me that I owed them one hundred *grush*. And I have no place to run or find shelter. Only from your mercy and the mercy of God. For the grave of my father and the rabbi [her husband], that their Torah may not be abolished, and their names will not disappear from the congregation. . . . And this is my problem: because I fell into debt because of the interest that I mentioned before and I have nothing left to sell. And I don't have a grown son or a messenger that can solicit for us in the community. Because it is not the custom of a woman to solicit in the community. Her honor is to be the daughter of a king, sitting on a throne, wearing gold and rubies.

I, in my day, was the key to my household. 'The beauty of the king's daughter is within.' I was raised on the knees of the greatest scholars, the pride and joy of my father. And no work did he teach me except the ways of heaven. And I studied day and night. He didn't have any sons and he even had my husband swear that he wouldn't make me do any work. At the beginning my husband was very busy with his own studies and didn't have time to teach the students. And I was teaching them in his place. I was his helpmate. And now, because of our many sins, he went to his rest and left me and the children to our sorrows. . . ."

Once more in verse, Asenath Barazani made her final appeal:

. . . And it will be known in Israel that I am tender,
And carry the burden of these orphans [her children]
Woe is me from them, and from my husband.
You, the congregation, perhaps you can lift your prominent hands,
And you will receive this letter with kindness and mercy,
And you will again be eating at my table. . . .
With great humility,
Your servant who kisses your hand. . . .[51]

—*Asenath Barazani Mizraḥi*

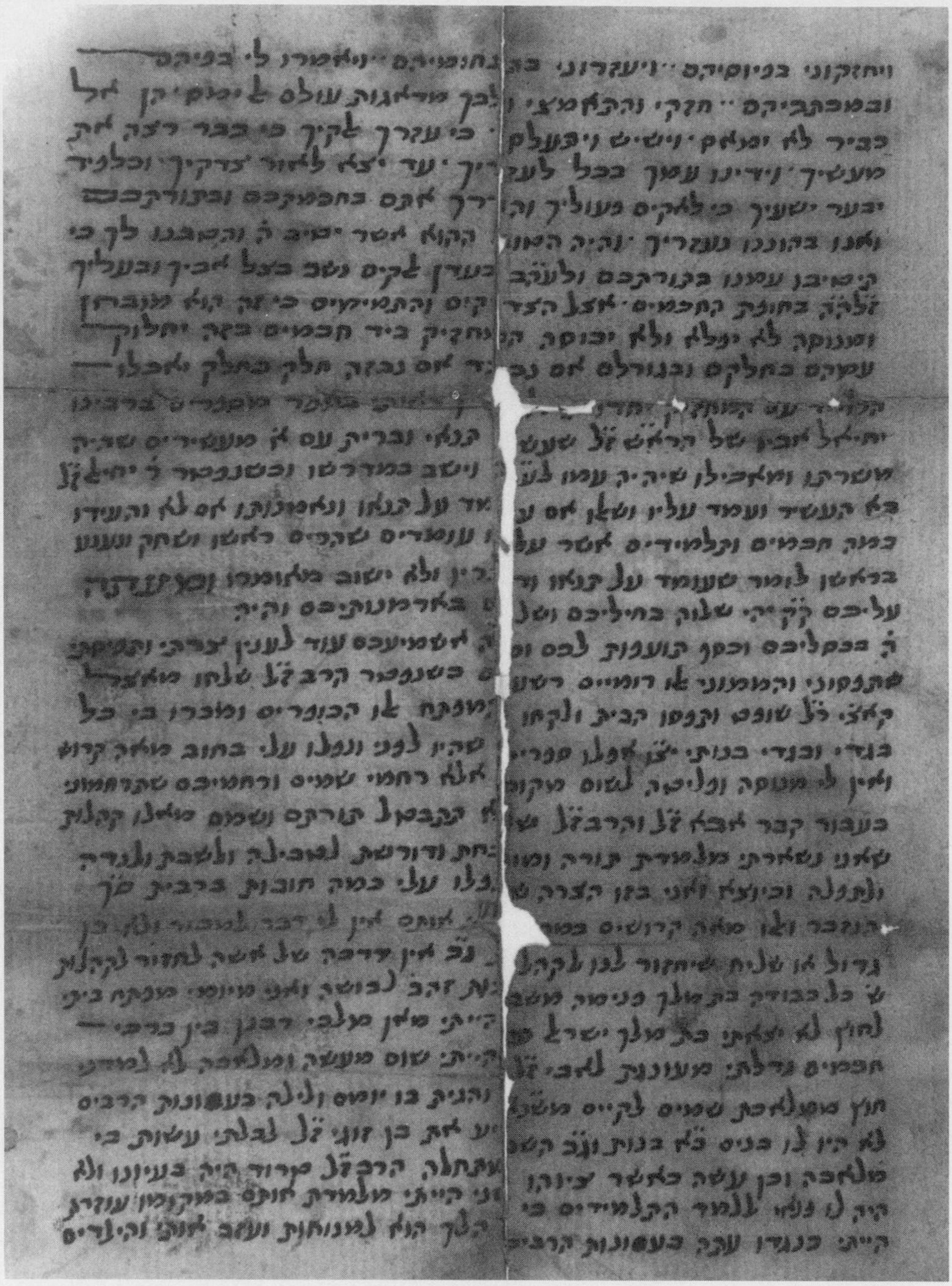

FIG. 18. The sixteenth-century letter pieced together for this photograph was written by Asenath Barazani Mizraḥi to the Jewish community of Amadiyah, pleading for funds for her late husband's yeshivah in Mosul, Kurdistan. (Courtesy of the Jacob Rader Marcus Center of the American Jewish Archives, Cincinnati, Ohio)

name Hannah. Beatrice married another *converso*, Francisco Mendes, a wealthy trader in gems and spices.

Beatrice/Hannah de Luna Mendes and her husband, Francisco, had one child, a daughter named **Reyna**. In 1536, when Reyna was five years old, Francisco died, and Beatrice, now a twenty-six-year-old widow, was heir to one half of his enormous fortune.[52]

That same year, the Inquisition was reestablished in Portugal and all *conversos* were threatened, but Beatrice de Luna, who up until that time had escaped suspicion, was allowed to leave Lisbon. Together with her daughter, Reyna, and her sister Brianda,[53] she fled to Antwerp, the capital of Flanders. Two years later, Joao Migues, Beatrice's nephew (later renowned as Joseph Nasi), joined them.[54]

Diogo Mendes, Francisco's brother and business partner, already lived in Antwerp, and after the arrival of the two women, he married Beatrice's sister Brianda. Diogo had inherited the other half of Francisco's fortune and had already extended the family business to include not only trading in spices and precious stones, but also banking.

Banking as it was practiced in the sixteenth century involved the transmission of money from country to country and the arrangement of bills of exchange. Once Beatrice de Luna Mendes and her family were safely settled in Antwerp, they became skilled in these procedures and Beatrice created a secret network, enabling Jewish *conversos* to leave Portugal, transferring their money through bills of exchange so they could make new lives elsewhere.[55]

Prosperous and respected, the Mendes family established themselves in luxurious fashion, but as long as Flanders remained part of the Spanish Empire and the Inquisition remained active, they were still not able to live without fear of discovery. The decision was made to transfer the Mendes assets to a more tolerant country, where they could live openly and practice Judaism. But before these plans could be carried out, Diogo died. Now Beatrice not only retained her half of the capital in the Mendes business, but she was also appointed administrator for the other half, which she was to manage for his widow (her sister Brianda) and their infant daughter. This assignment caused a bitter fight between Beatrice and Brianda that had ramifications for many years afterward.[56]

Beatrice de Luna Mendes now controlled one of the largest fortunes in Europe, and through her business acumen she forged connections to rulers throughout the Western world.

Despite her growing power, however, she could not protect the family from all outside dangers, and soon a new threat presented itself. In 1536, a Catholic nobleman, Don Francisco d'Aragon, sought Reyna's hand in marriage.

Beatrice Mendes took immediate action. With no warning, she, her daughter, Reyna, and her sister Brianda with her young daughter (also named Beatrice) left the Mendes mansion. Packing only their jewels and as many personal possessions as possible, they fled to Italy and before long appeared in Venice. Forty boxes filled with valuables were left behind in Antwerp.[57]

Still regarded as New Christians, the Mendes family was not required to live in the Venetian ghetto.[58] Although Beatrice continued supervising her

---

IN PRAISE OF
DOÑA GRACIA NASI

Gracia Nasi was described in many different ways. Joshua Soncino, the famed Jewish printer, praised her as:

". . . the crowned gentlewoman, the glorious diadem of Israel's multitudes, stately vine, crowning glory, beautiful garland and royal miter, the wisest of women built Israel's house in pure holiness; with her strength and treasures she extended a hand to the poor in order to rescue them and make them content in this world and in the next."[59]

Moses de Trani, at the end of his responsum dealing with Gracia Nasi and the legality of her claims against her sister, wrote: "Many women have been extremely successful but Gracia has surpassed them all. . . ."[60]

---

business and lived in luxury, those years (1545–1549) were not peaceful ones. Beatrice's sister Brianda, the widow of Diogo Mendes, challenged her for control of the family fortune, and as long as the matter remained undecided, neither of them was permitted to leave Venice.[61]

When the case was finally settled in 1549, Beatrice Mendes went to the court of Ercole II d'Este in Ferrara. The Duchy of Ferrara, already the home of **Benvenida Abrabanel**[62] and her family, was more hospitable to Jews, and it was here that Beatrice began using her Hebrew name, Hannah, or Gracia, and

took on the family name of Nasi, the Hebrew word for prince.[63] Other Portuguese Jews simply called her La Signora or La Doña.

From Ferrara, Doña Gracia continued to help crypto-Jews leave Portugal. In addition, she contributed to the printing of Hebrew books in Spanish translations for the benefit of the *conversos*. In 1553 the Hebrew Bible was translated into Spanish and published in two editions, one for Christians and one for Jews. It became known as "The Ferrara Bible" and was dedicated to the noble-hearted "Doña Gracia Naci, the Very Magnificent Lady."[64] Samuel Usque's *Consolation for the Tribulations of Israel*, a prose-poem in Portuguese, was also dedicated to Gracia, whom Usque called "the heart of her people."

In 1554, Gracia and her daughter returned to Venice and began to make plans to relocate to Istanbul.[65] Joao, now called Don Joseph Nasi, again followed Gracia. He arrived in Istanbul with his own retinue of bodyguards and servants, had himself circumcised in 1554, and returned to Judaism. He subsequently married Gracia's daughter, Reyna Nasi.[66]

In Turkey, Doña Gracia became the leading force in the Jewish community. She lavishly supported synagogues, schools, and hospitals all over the Ottoman Empire and carried on extensive trade in spices, grain, and wool with Italian cities, utilizing her own ships.[67] When she pulled her fleet out of Ancona during the Jewish boycott of that city, there were international repercussions.[68]

Finally secure in Turkey, with close ties to the sultan's court, Doña Gracia sought to acquire some place of safety for other Jews. With that goal in mind,

FIG. 19. Long believed to be a portrait of Doña Gracia Nasi, this coin actually depicts her niece, Beatrice. (Courtesy of the Library of the Jewish Theological Seminary of America)

she leased land in Tiberius, a town in Palestine, then under Ottoman control. Her hope was to encourage a self-sufficient Jewish community there. For a short time, Jewish settlement in the Galilee was increased and Tiberius became a successful city. Although a mansion was prepared there for La Signora herself, she died before she could occupy it.[69]

This settlement, one of the earliest to attract Jews to return to Zion, has usually been credited to Gracia's nephew, Don Joseph Nasi, conceding only that "she was at his right hand, serving as his inspiration."[70] However, the idea was first envisioned by Gracia, who, taking advantage of her influence at court, conceived of the plan, leased the land for a high yearly rental that she

---

LITTLE GRACIA

Gracia Nasi's niece Beatrice, daughter of Gracia's sister Brianda, joined the family In Istanbul in 1558, together with her husband, Joseph Nasi's brother Bernardo (Shmuel). At that time, Beatrice and Shmuel also openly professed Judaism.[71] Beatrice was known as "Little Gracia" because of her striking resemblance to her aunt. The coin or medal that was struck by Pastorino de Pastorini is believed to be of Little Gracia the younger, not her aunt Doña Gracia Nasi.[72]

paid herself, and briefly turned Tiberius into a thriving Jewish city. After she died, Joseph never visited the town and it deteriorated. Finally, the lease was allowed to lapse.[73]

The exact date of Gracia Nasi's death is not known, but it probably occurred in the summer of 1569 when she was fifty-nine or sixty years old. By that time, she had achieved power, fame, and riches beyond most people's imagination.

NASI, REYNA OF ISTANBUL, PRINTER AND PHILANTHROPIST
(16th century)

Born in Portugal, Reyna Nasi, daughter of **Gracia Nasi,** was taken to Antwerp at the age of five, fled to Italy when she was twelve, and finally settled with her mother in Istanbul where she married her first cousin, Joao (Joseph Nasi). Eclipsed by her outstanding mother and her powerful and influential husband, Reyna never achieved the fame or the adulation of either. Joseph became highly influential at the sultan's court and was named Duke of Naxos and the Cyclades in 1566. After his death in 1579, Reyna established and financed a printing press for the publication of Hebrew and other Jewish books. Her first press functioned from 1592 to 1594 in Belvedere, near Constantinople. A second enterprise began in 1597 and operated for two years at Kuru Tschechme. Reyna died in 1599 at the approximate age of sixty-nine. She had outlived her husband by twenty years, but there seem to have been no children.

SARAH OF PODOLIA, WIFE OF SHABBETAI ZEVI
(17th century)

Sarah was a Polish orphan, a refugee from the 1648 massacres in Poland who had a varied career and whose life story as she told it was certainly suspect. Reports claimed that she had been a prostitute, wandering from Poland to Amsterdam and then to Italy, where she worked as a servant. Sarah had once announced that she was going to marry the Messiah. How Sarah and Shabbetai Zevi met is unclear, but the couple was married in Cairo in March 1664,[74] probably a second or third marriage for Shabbetai.

After Sarah and Shabbetai Zevi returned to Izmir, Shabbetai came under the threat of death by the Turks because of his pretensions to be the Messiah. To save himself, he

---

FROM THE PRINTING HOUSE OF REYNA NASI

Examples of some of the printed inscriptions inside these books give a clue to the esteem in which the Nasi name was still held in the community.

"Printed in the palace of the Honored woman Reyna Nasi, widow of the Duke Don Joseph Nasi, at Belvedere, which is near Constantinople, under the rule of Sultan Murad."

"Printed in the house and with the type of the Crowned Lady, crown of descent and excellency, Reyna (may she be blessed of women in the tent!), Widow of the Duke, Prince, and Noble in Israel, Don Joseph Nasi of Blessed Memory . . . near Constantinople, the great city which is under the rule of the great and mighty King Sultan Mohammed (may his might increase!)."[75]

A LETTER TO A SON

The excerpts below were written by Rachel Sussman to her son, Moshe, on October 3, 1567. In between the paragraphs revealing a general parental concern, her anxiety that he had not written, and the traditional, effusive blessings common to all these letters, she reported on the serious financial problems suffered by family members.

" . . . I have also been worried by the removal of thy daughter, may she live. Her husband considered it right that she did not want to stay with her mother-in-law; she herself is in need. And I was not able, because of our many sins, to maintain her. If I could have done so, I certainly would have taken her to me.

My dear son, do the best you can for them, but avoid doing harm to thyself. Thy son-in-law is, because of our many sins, heavily indebted to the non-Jews. . . . I cannot describe to thee what foolish things he has done. He offered guarantees for his brother and to get Moses and thy mother-in-law out of their difficulties. He was, however, unable to pay, and therefore he was obliged time and again to pay interest after interest. . . . Therefore, my dear son, be careful that he may not drag thee into his affairs, and by no means agree to be a guarantor for him or for anybody else. And be watchful that he may not go away and leave thy daughter destitute, God forbid! I would have preferred her to have stayed here, and would have obtained from him the letter of divorce. But she did not want to do so.

Thy mother Rachel, who writes in great haste."

Written on the 29th of Tishrei.[76]

announced his conversion to Islam in 1666, and Sarah converted a short time later. Following his conversion, Sarah gave birth to a son and a daughter. There was a great deal of suspicion about whether these were indeed Shabbetai's children, "as her licentious behavior in Smyrna was no secret."[77] However, the records do not contest the existence of the two children. The son, Ishmael Mordecai, was circumcised in 1671 (at the age of four) and died during his adolescence.

Shortly before the circumcision of their son, Sarah was pregnant again, but nevertheless, Shabbetai divorced her and arranged a marriage with another woman, known only as the daughter of Aaron Majar. Then he changed his mind and took Sarah back, but whether he would have married the second wife as well remains unclear. Aaron Majar's daughter died before final arrangements could be made.[78] Sarah herself died in 1674.

SHAMA'AH SHABAZI OF YEMEN, POET
(17th century)

Reports of Shama'ah Shabazi, daughter of the famed Yemenite poet Shalem Shabazi, tell of her poetic skills, but these are not confirmed.[79] Legends suggest that she died young.[80] Her poetry, if there was any, is most likely immersed in the Shabazi family collections.

SUSSMAN, RACHEL BAT AVRAHAM OF JERUSALEM, POOR WIDOW
(16th century)

Rachel Sussman and her husband, Eliezer, immigrated to Jerusalem in 1546, and almost immediately their economic position deteriorated. "Outside the country we did well," Rachel complained; "in Jerusalem not as well."[81] About eighteen years after they moved to the land of Israel her husband died.[82] Her only child, Moshe, had moved with his family to Cairo, and Rachel Sussman remained alone in Jerusalem, in charge of the family's possessions.

Sussman's economic condition steadily worsened, and at times she resorted to pawning her possessions. She alternately borrowed, lent, and depended on the goodwill of several people. Occasionally, she even received money from the community welfare fund.[83] She wrote to her son: "I must degrade [myself by using] the fund for my many sins and I don't have enough. Since the first of Kislev they give me fourteen *maydin* each month and I haven't had a good bite to eat."[84]

YOHEVED/A'ISHA OF SALONIKA, WIFE OF SHABBETAI ZEVI
(17th century)

Yoheved (A'isha in Arabic) was the daughter of a respected rabbi, Yosef Philosoph of Salonika. She married Shabbetai Zevi in 1674, after his conversion to Islam, and shortly after the death of **Sarah**. The marriage lasted only two years. In 1676, Shabbetai Zevi died and Yoheved proclaimed her brother, Yaakov Philosoph (known as Jacob Querido), to be his reincarnation.

Along with her father and brother, Yoheved converted to Islam. Her brother began the sect of the Doenmeh,[85] a secret group of believers in Shabbetai Zevi who continued to have faith in his message.

THE WORLD OF JEWISH WOMEN

ECONOMIC ACTIVITIES

There were many types of work for Jewish women, especially during the sixteenth century when the Ottoman economy was thriving. One historian claimed that "no economic field was barred to the Jews, and no trade, profession or occupation of any kind was closed either to them or to the Christians."[86] Women, of course, had some limits based on what the community considered proper for their sex, but the parameters were surprisingly liberal.

One of the factors encouraging women's substantial commercial activities was the clause in many of the *ketubbot* of the *Musta'rabs* (Arabic-speaking Jews) stipulating that the profit of a wife's labor belonged to her and was not the property of her husband. In return for this right, the husband was only obligated to give a fixed amount for food and clothing. This contrasted with the standard clause in the *ketubbot* of Sephardic and Ashkenazic wives whose husbands had the right to retain all the profit from their wives' labor but had to provide complete maintenance. Women's right to keep what they earned gave *Musta'rab* women a certain amount of economic independence not available to other Jewish women.[87]

Money Lending

Lending money was considered an acceptable profession for women, as it did not require that they leave their homes. Widows and divorced women, consonant with their condition in all other Jewish communities, often had an advantage in this field because they had the capital from their *ketubbot* and they could lend it out at interest. In Jerusalem, many Jews lent small sums to Christian clerics. Not only Jewish widows, but also orphans who had the benefit of a small legacy might lend money through the medium of a guardian. A question addressed to R. Eliezer ben Arḥa (d. 1652) relates how the priests and monks of Jerusalem sometimes borrowed money from Jews, thereby providing a livelihood not only for Torah scholars, merchants, and ordinary families, but also for widows and orphans. He wrote: "For any man or woman who owned 100 *grushos* [silver coins] could start up in the money lending business. . . . In this city there is no other way of making a profit. There have been moneylenders here from time immemorial, and none of the city's great rabbis saw fit to prohibit this activity in any way whatsoever."[88]

But not every woman who made loans at interest was a widow or divor-cée. A married woman who lived in Cairo lent out money on interest and received pledges or pawns in return. Her partner for some of these loans was her son-in-law Moshe,[89] whose own mother, **Rachel Sussman** of Jerusalem, advised him: "When your mother-in-law brings good pledges, then lend, and write it down right away. When they redeem them then erase it immediately."[90]

Trade and Commerce

Jewish women who did not have enough assets to lend money on interest could also participate in economic life. From a responsum of R. David ibn Abi Zimra (d. 1573) we learn of a Jewish woman who owned real estate and was an expert in business and investment. Another woman rented a building to a group of Jews who needed a place for a synagogue.[91]

Large numbers of women were involved in local trade, sometimes functioning as intermediaries, selling the handiwork of Muslims. This occupation would put them in a similar category to the *kieras* of Istanbul, such as **Esther Handali** or **Esperanza Malchi,** who also acted as intermediaries although on a much grander scale.

Jewish women who sold goods in the marketplaces of the land of Israel, Syria, and Egypt dealt, in the main, in cloth of wool, linen, and silk; also in grain, wine, olive oil, and spices. They sold foodstuffs such as yoghurt and pita (flat bread) in the marketplace.[92] One woman even went out to the villages on business activities, perhaps to buy vegetables or other products to sell.[93] In Anatolia, women owned or leased shops.[94]

Manual Skills and Handicrafts

Many Jewish women were artisans; they spun, embroidered, and sewed,[95] not only for their families' use, but also to offer for sale. Rachel Sussman of Jerusalem wrote of her granddaughter: "Beile, may she live, has clever hands; she embroiders very nice things from silver and gold."[96] Since the family was poor, the sale of these items would make a contribution to their income. In Salonika, where almost all the Jews were involved in the making of textiles and clothing, women were active workers, dyeing the cloth, preparing it for market, and selling it.[97]

An interesting trade for a woman was welding. A question came before R. Moshe Alshekh (d. 1593) concerning Leah, a Jewish widow of Aleppo who "during the lifetime of her husband has learned the trade of steel welding.[99] No one else in the whole country knew how to do it. She obtained a permit from the ruler to work at that trade. . . ."[100]

Doctors

A small group of women in the lands of the East practiced some form of medicine. In Jerusalem, Jewish women were mentioned as *kaḥḥala*, a title specific to eye doctors. Amnon Cohen suggests that these women might have originally been cosmeticians who were proficient in the use of antimony (kohl) for eye makeup and thus became skilled in treating eye diseases.[101] Jewish women in Germany (see chapter 4) also practiced this medical specialty. In the early modern era (1500–1700), Jewish women doctors were also found in the Turkish court, especially in the harem, as doctors and midwives to the sultan's wives and other women attached to the court. Prominent among these women doctors was the widow of Shlomo Ashkenazi who, in 1603, cured the young Sultan Achmed I.[102]

Wives of physicians sometimes gained a certain amount of proficiency and often helped their husbands. We have one example of this in eighteenth-century Rhodes, where the widow of a doctor claimed that she had performed bloodletting, delivered medicines to both Jewish and gentile patients, and generally assisted her husband "in his performances of medical services." As a result of this claim, she refused to settle only for her *ketubbah* and demanded the right to all her husband's property. Although the court ruled against her, she managed

---

WOMEN IN THE MARKETPLACE

Pierre Belon visited Turkey and the Balkans in the mid–sixteenth century and described some Jewish women's commercial activities.

"The Jewish women who could go around with their faces uncovered are commonly found in the Turkish markets selling needlework. Since Islamic law does not allow Turkish women to sell and buy, they sold their [products] to Jewish women. . . . They [the Jewish women] ordinarily sold towels, kerchiefs, headgear, white belts, cushion covers, and other such products of much greater value, like bed canopies and other bed fittings of varying kinds that the Jews bought to sell to strangers."[98]

to keep the bulk of the estate from the other heirs, who did not collect their inheritance until after she died.[103]

Teachers

Women teachers were not uncommon in the Middle East. This is evidenced in earlier times by documents from the Cairo Genizah (see chapter 3) as well as by later records. In the 1560s Moshe Sussman from Cairo wrote to his mother, Rachel, in Jerusalem that, "Zvi-ele,[104] may He preserve him and redeem him, is with the teacher [*mu'allima*] Marhavah."[105] Another teacher of children, this one in Hebron, is mentioned in a travel document from the 1650s. R. Moshe ben Eliahu ha-Levi, the Karaite from Krim, stated, "I saw a woman teaching children, for we were sitting in the second story and under it was that woman teacher."[106] There is also a report about a teacher of children in Amadiya (Kurdistan) in the seventeenth century[107] known only as "the wife of R. Simon."

Other Occupations

Disputes brought before Muslim courts occasionally offer evidence of other occupations practiced by Jewish women. In 1558–1559 and again in 1565 Klara bint Shmu-il worked as an independent seamstress, as did Stiya in 1577.[108] Jewish women also worked as public criers, proclaiming what was being sold and where. In Jerusalem "there are records of a North African Jewish woman, A'ira bint 'Abd-Allah, who was a crier in 1558." In 1595 Maryam bint Ya'qub and Hanna bint Shuba were criers, and later that year Kalala bint Ibrahim the Maghrebi and Simha bint Yusef are also mentioned in the same context.[109]

Domestics and Slaves

There were always a certain percentage of poorer women who were employed as domestics in Jewish homes. Biblical law, however, forbids Jews from enslaving other Jews for more than a set period of time (Exod. 21:2–12). In compliance with this law, Jewish communities routinely redeemed Jewish captives,[110] and Jewish women who were enslaved by others eventually were freed. The records of the Muslim court of Jerusalem mention Sarah bint David, a former slave. In 1557, she stated before the court that she was redeemed in Alexandria for forty *sultani* by Yusuf ibn Ya'qub ibn Yahuda, known as Karpas, who freed her from bondage to Europeans (probably pirates). In return she paid him one quarter of the sum and hired herself out to him for ten years as his wife's servant.

While living in Istanbul, Doña **Gracia Nasi** employed many Jewish servants in her household, most of

---

IN THE HOME OF A NOBLE LADY

A report from a German merchant residing in Turkey in the sixteenth century described Doña Gracia's lifestyle in these words:

"[She] was waited on by an elaborate train of attendants, many of whom had come with her from Flanders, or even from Portugal, those who were New Christians like herself adopting Judaism on their arrival if they had not done so already."[111]

whom were Spanish or Portuguese exiles.

EDUCATION

Everywhere in the Ottoman Empire, formal education was extended exclusively to boys, a system that was certainly not foreign to Jews in all the other lands of their settlement. Most Jewish boys were taught to read and to pray, and academies were organized to teach Jewish men the law. The educational level for women was lower in Anatolia and the Balkans than in Europe, still lower in the lands of the Middle East and North Africa.

Travelers' reports from various lands sometimes attest to an extreme lack of education for women that contrasted unfavorably even with the minimum education received by women in the West. The women of Salonika were "kept in complete ignorance."[112] In Rhodes, there was no school for girls and "Jewish women, like their non-Jewish counterparts, could seldom read or write."[113] In the highlands of Yemen, most women remained uneducated and, like Muslim women in that society, did not attend religious services.[114] In Ottoman Syria, it was reported that girls did not go to school until the Alliance Israélite opened mission schools for them in 1889.[115] But as always, there were exceptions.

Miriam Benayah the Yemenite scribe is one notable exception, as was **Asenath Barazani Mizraḥi,** a scholar and teacher in Kurdistan. Mizraḥi's letters reveal not only fluency in Hebrew texts, but also a depth of knowledge in both Bible and Talmud that was surely well beyond the scope of most other learned women in Kurdistan and many men as well. **Shama'ah Shabazi,** also of Yemen,

supposedly had poetic skills, although this is not confirmed. Jewish women in Islamic lands sometimes worked as teachers of young children, indicating that they were literate at the very least.

Exceptions could also be found in North Africa. Samuel Romanelli, an eighteenth-century Jewish traveler to North Africa, while decrying women's lack of education, mentioned a woman from Tangiers, one of three wives all married to a single Jewish man. This woman, who remains unnamed, could speak Spanish. "She even knew how to pray which is a marvel!"[116] Another woman "proved the equal of a man, writing Spanish and Arabic in Hebrew characters."[117] Romanelli never mentioned—and perhaps did not know of—the poet **Freḥa bat Avraham** of Tunisia, another rare instance of a learned woman who lived earlier in the eighteenth century.

FAMILY LIFE

Betrothal and Marriage

Customs concerning betrothal and marriage in the eastern Mediterranean and the Middle East continued to be practiced according to long-standing traditions. Families arranged marriages, and neither daughters nor sons had much say in whom they would marry. Once the match was set, the groom had to contribute the standard *ketubbah* payment and the bride brought a dowry of a more or less equivalent amount. These financial arrangements enabled the couple to establish a household or a business.

Rich families might start their children off with more than the standard *ketubbah* payment, and if one of the couple was wealthier or considered a more desirable match, allowances might be made. In one of her letters Rachel Sussman described the marriage arrangement made for the daughter of a certain R. David. In this case, R. David gave the couple lavish gifts including "his house and all his books, furniture and fine clothing" because "he wishes to have an Ashkenazi [as a son-in-law] at any cost."[118]

Further on in the same letter, Sussman reported on another marrige. "R. Benjamin . . . has married his daughter to a young man, an orphan, the grandson of Isaac Cohen, a Hungarian of fifteen years. He will study with him and keeps him in his house."

Once married, the husband was obligated to support his wife and provide for all her needs unless otherwise stipulated in the *ketubbah*. One male writer, discussing whether or not religious scholars should work, pointed out: ". . . even a man who has no daughters and no need to give dowries . . . must earn in order to satisfy the needs of this wife who is consumed with jealousy and a passion for her appearance."[119]

Although such negative stereotypes persisted, husbands often took pleasure in providing ornaments for their wives, and there were old and fixed traditions surrounding women's adornments. In Rhodes, for example, it was the custom for men to give their wives gold bracelets and other jewelry as "public evidence of their devotion," and women wore them as "a point of pride."[120]

Children

Although children had no rights and child marriages for girls were common, especially in eastern Mediterranean lands, there is much evidence to confirm a close bond between mothers and children, even after they were grown. Some of this evidence comes from letters written by mothers to their daughters and sons.

A REPORT ON THE JEWISH WOMEN OF MOROCCO

Samuel Romanelli, an Italian Jew who traveled to North Africa as late as 1786 and 1790 reported that in Tangier "women are good looking and robust but totally uneducated." He noted that they did not speak, read, or write in Hebrew, Arabic, or standard Spanish, but rather, in a "mixed language" (probably Ladino). Romanelli seems to have disapproved. He wrote: "The women do not even pray, despite the fact that this was imposed upon them by the sages of the Mishnah." This traveler explained: "The Moroccan Jews [i.e., men] counter this by citing the mishnaic dictum: 'Whoever teaches his daughter Torah it is as if he teaches her wantonness.' They also counter that a woman is impure during her menstrual infirmity and the days of her menses can fall quite suddenly. This ancient custom has its roots in olden times and was adopted by them from gentile practice, for indeed, the Arab women do not pray either."[121]

FIG. 20. Jewish women of sixteenth- and seventeenth-century Turkey wore elaborate and stylish clothing and adorned themselves with jewelry. (Courtesy of Bibliotèque des Arts Décoratifs, Collection Maciet)

Divorce and Levirate Marriage

Divorce remained the prerogative of the husband, and examples of *ketubbot* in which the wife was specifically granted the right of initiating a divorce seem to have disappeared by the twelfth century. Cases where the wife wanted a divorce and the husband refused created serious problems, and Jewish courts, especially those in Syria, Egypt, and Palestine that had once recognized an alternative tradition (see chapter 3), tended to view any women wanting a divorce as a *moredet* (a rebellious woman).[122] Some of these cases eventually came before Muslim courts.

Jewish communal leaders attempted to restrict the use of non-Jewish courts, especially in matrimonial cases, but were not always successful in doing so. Divorces were often simpler if carried out by a Muslim court, and the rabbis were powerless to reverse such decisions if both the husband and wife consented. However, women usually wanted validation by a Jewish court as well, since they knew that without a Jewish divorce, they could not remarry.[123]

When parts of families converted or when members were killed or missing and their fates unknown, Jewish divorce laws were often stretched to the limit. Among the Sephardic refugees of the late fifteenth and sixteenth centuries, the burden on individuals was tremendous. As a Portuguese-Jewish exile described it: "Men arrived without their wives and women without their husbands. And they were beset by poverty and travail, want and famine and loneliness."[124] These difficult circumstances impacted on women even more than on men. One historian explained, "the results of the major demographic and social changes . . . [cut off] women from the homogeneous, protective environments into which they were born."[125] The situation was compounded still further for women due to the legal rulings that prevented them from initiating divorce proceedings and also because of their obligations in levirate marriage. Some of those problems were overcome, at least temporarily, by rabbinical rulings. Some rabbis of Salonika declared that any woman who married while she had resided in "the lands of forced conversion" and whose husband had subsequently converted and remained there, was free to remarry "any Jew who wishes to marry her, whether in the lands of forced conversion or following the

escape." The rabbis ruled that since there were no qualified witnesses, the previous marriage was not binding; the woman need not obtain a divorce, nor, in the case of a widow, was she required to be released by a *levir*.[126]

Not all rabbis were that lenient. Some, hoping that the converts would return to Judaism and worried about the repercussions of women having more than one husband, were very strict. There is much evidence, however, that in the generation after the expulsion, Jews arriving in the lands of the Ottoman Empire remarried quickly and created new families, sometimes accepting matches that would have been considered inappropriate back in Spain and Portugal. But this situation was short-lived, and once the

---

ONE MAN'S OBSERVATIONS ON THE JEWISH WOMEN OF TURKEY

On his visit to Istanbul, the well-known Rabbi Aboab of Venice commented disapprovingly on women's extravagance.

". . . Certain dames are not content to go about with the silken robes and jewels which rightly appertain to Jewish matrons, but they indubitably endeavor to emulate princesses and the highest nobility, carrying in their head-dress, plumes worth thousands of *ducats* and wearing bracelets and jewels of excessive value, with furs and skins of enormous price. Thus, besides ruining their husbands' fortunes, they place their honor in manifest danger. . . ."[127]

LETTERS FROM LOVING MOTHERS

Rachel Sussman expressed her maternal feelings for her grown son, Moshe, and other family members in this letter, written on October 3, 1567. After reporting on the serious financial problems suffered by family members, she added this postscript:

"Come hither with thy children . . . everything here is cheap. I have prepared half a measure of wine for thee. And let me know fully about thy health. The saying "Out of sight, out of mind" is not always correct. For a mother . . . does not forget the pain she suffered with her child. It was my wish to send something for thy child, but, because of our many sins, I do not possess anything. . . . My dear, write me what thou hast heard about the children. . . ."[128]

The following letter, also written to a grown son, takes a similar tone and alludes to economic hardship as well as other family issues. It was written by Doña Jamila, widow of R. Yom Tov Shalom, to her son R. Abraham Shalom (d. 1577) who was the head of a yeshivah in Safed. It is clear that Doña Jamila dictated her letter to the scribe, R. Khalifia Aguman, as he includes his own greetings at the end.

"My dear and beloved son, strings of my heart:

Know, as it pleases you, that Esther married. May you marry your sons with greater advantage, may they never be orphans. Shavuot. And more tears flowed from my eyes than from a fountain, for I found myself with no other relative to support than the Lord, blessed be He, and your brother-in-law who came. And you do not even send me two lines with him. . . .You could have done so, not for me, but for your sister who . . . does nothing but cry from your lack of affection. Were it not for your aunt, who sent me what she sent me, I would not even have had enough for the dowry. . . . may she have her repayment, may her son have many sons and great good. Amen, thus may it be willed before our Father who is in Heaven."

Doña Jamila went on to discuss a rift between her and her son and tried to justify her actions:

"And I know full well that you are angry on account of the *sini* [china or porcelain].[129] Do you not remember that the year you pawned it and I redeemed it, you pawned the *sarko* for three quarters and I redeemed it. And I sold everything on account of hunger and nothing was left. And you, all your anger is on account of the *sini*. May I never see you, nor your wife nor the children if I have ever laid eyes on any of it.

In any case, I pray for your life; you will attain this and more. . . . May you all live and be healthy, all of you. Regards to your wife and kiss the children from us. . . .

The Lord be praised, and now that your sister is wed, praise the Lord, I beg of you to concern yourself with my shroud and send me an old [*unclear*] to see (or 'read') the Torah.

And Shalom, from me, the immature Rabbi Khalifia Aguman who kisses your hands. And Shalom from your mother Doña Jamila, widow of the perfect scholar, Rabbi Yom Tov Shalom, may his soul rest in Eden.

And Esther kisses your hands and also your wife's. And do send word about the children's welfare, may they live forever. Amen. So be His Will."[130]

Sephardim felt secure, they quickly reverted to their old customs and reestablished elite families who only intermarried with each other and scorned matches with the *Romaniot* or *Musta'rab* Jews.[131]

Monogamy

The Ashkenazim of northern Europe had been monogamous for five centuries, following the ban (*ḥerem*) of Rabbenu Gershom (see chapter 4). This was at least partly due to the influence of their Christian neighbors. Most Sephardim, on the other hand, living in Muslim countries where having multiple wives was an unquestioned practice, accepted polygyny in principle. It was not uncommon for Jewish men in eastern lands to take additional wives if they could afford to. Even Ashkenazim who lived in the Ottoman Empire began to practice the local custom of polygyny, and records indicate that some Ashkenazic Jews received permission to take a second wife if there had been no children during the first ten years of marriage or if the first wife was rebellious. Ultimately, "there was not one of the sages of the land of Israel and Egypt who did not find a way to lessen [the impact] of the ban of Rabbenu Gershom in certain circumstances."[132]

It was widely understood, however, that monogamy was an advantage to women. In communities where having multiple wives was permitted, some fathers, especially among the Sephardim, tried to safeguard their daughters' futures by having conditions written into the marriage contract. There might be a clause preventing the husband from taking a second wife without his first wife's permission; or the bride's father might demand an oath by the husband, swearing that he would not marry another woman without a similar permission. But these methods were not always effective. Even if the husband had sworn or had agreed to conditions in the *ketubbah*, if he desired a second wife he could appeal to one of the prominent rabbis. Generally, if the rabbi felt that the husband had a good enough reason to marry again, the appropriate clause in the *ketubbah* could be overlooked. Sometimes this resulted in the first wife's leaving. This seems to have been the case with Sultana bint Ibraham of Jerusalem, who left her husband to live with her brother in 1582–1583. Her husband appealed to a Muslim court to demand her return, but she refused, claiming she left him when he took another Jewish wife.[133] The outcome of this case is not known.

In the event that a rabbi would not permit a second marriage, the man was told to divorce his first wife and give her the amount of her *ketubbah* before he married again.[134] The standard *Musta'rab* marriage contract routinely gave the husband both the right to divorce his wife and to take another wife without her consent,[135] although this often led to trouble. In fact, in Hebrew and Arabic a second wife was called *tzara*, a word that may come from the root *tza'ar* or "trouble."[136]

Women's Sexuality

Concubines were fairly common in Mediterranean and Middle Eastern Jewish families. Often these women began as servants and became concubines, sometimes even wives. This caused a certain amount of upheaval in families. R. David ben Shlomo ibn Abi Zimra (Radbaz) complained many times that "this generation has broken the bounds of forbidden sex" and bemoaned the fact that even Jewish communal officials were transgressing in this way.[137]

LEGAL RIGHTS

Jewish women in the Ottoman Empire, like Muslim women, were generally under male authority. The most notable exceptions here, as everywhere, were widows and divorcées, who enjoyed certain rights unavailable to married women or those not yet married. When a widow or divorced woman remarried, she was not required to give all her assets to her second husband as part of her dowry. For example, Leah, a divorcée from Jerusalem, included only half her *ketubbah* from her first husband in her dowry to her second husband. She kept the other half "to dispose of as she wished, without her husband having a say in the matter."[138]

In contrast to the relative rights of divorced or widowed women in marriage, young girls entering a first marriage had few rights and child marriages continued to be commonplace. A Jewish father enjoyed total legal authority over his minor daughter and could contract a marriage in her name without her permission.[139] This often resulted in marital problems that subsequently came before the Jewish courts. Many involved physical or emotional abuse of the young woman.

Women and the Courts

A Jewish woman could be appointed as guardian for her children and appear in court on her own recognizance. Women could also sue and be sued. In Bursa (Turkey) in the early seventeenth century, records show many cases of Muslim women suing members of their own families, often over inheritance claims.[140] Jewish women may have done the same, either in their own Jewish courts or in the Muslim courts, although they would certainly have been represented by a male advocate. Women could also be sued by others and were held responsible for their actions. If punishment was decreed, whether physical or monetary, it was administered equally to both sexes.[141]

Although there was strong disapproval of individual Jews resorting to Muslim courts, the Jewish community retained that prerogative for itself, using Muslim courts to enforce their own rulings. This might occasionally work in the woman's favor. When a Jewish man from Beirut deserted his wife and refused to send her money or food, the Jewish community's leaders tracked him down and took him to the Muslim court. In response to the Jews' request, Muslim officials forced him to divorce his wife and give her the promised *ketubbah* payment. In another instance, a widow whose brother-in-law refused either to release her or to marry her according to the law of the levirate, was freed when her relatives appealed to a Muslim court.[142]

Other cases were not so simple. In a responsum of the mid– to late–sixteenth century, R. Yosef ben David of Salonika discussed the case of a father who sought to prevent the marriage of his daughter by having the prospective groom's father thrown into jail by Muslim officials on a spurious charge.[143] In another instance in that same century, a Jewish man used the Muslim court to force a young woman to marry him. She was especially vulnerable, as her father had just died.[144] In many such cases, the woman was at the mercy of the male litigants and had little say over how the men would dispose of her.

The Legality of Slave Ownership

Custom and law regarding the ownership of gentile slaves, whether Muslim or Christian, was not always clear-cut. The Pact of Omar, originally issued by the second Caliph (634-644), specified the safeguards extended to the *dhimmis* (protected people) and also the limits imposed on them. One of those limitations forbade Jews from owning Muslim slaves and later expanded that ruling to include any slaves.[145] However, this law seems to have been widely ignored by Muslim officials, who routinely took bribes from Jewish owners of servant girls and looked the other way.[146]

Throughout the sixteenth century, slave ownership was as normative for Jews in the Ottoman Empire as it was for Christians and Muslims. Many women left Spain and Portugal and arrived in Turkey and other parts of the Empire with their own serving women. Others brought maidservants into the marriage as part of their dowries or acquired a servant to help them with housework when officials relaxed the enforcement of the traditional restrictions.[147]

PUBLIC POWER

As a group, women had no say in the rulings made by their communities and generally wielded no power. Individual women, however, occasionally did have considerable influence, especially if they were wealthy and well connected. Among Jewish women, Gracia Nasi, the rich and influential merchant and philanthropist,

was perhaps the most eminent, but she was not the only woman who enjoyed a position of power in Turkey.

A small number of women, referred to as *kieras* or *kyras*, had the potential for holding and using power as well. This was because the sultan's wives and daughters and the queen mother, although sometimes enjoying unusual amounts of power,[148] were confined to harems and forbidden to be seen in public. They therefore required agents to act on their behalf. The agents conducted business for them, brought goods to the women's apartments for purchase, arranged for or gave medical advice and treatment, and delivered letters to family members outside the royal residence. These chores were best managed by a non-Muslim, unhampered by the religious restraints of Islam. Most often it was Jewish women who performed these services.[149]

SLAVE GIRLS IN JEWISH FAMILIES

Jewish families could not always retain their slave girls, especially if they were Muslim. In a record of the court dated June 19, 1579, Marḥaba bint Yusef, wife of Ashaq, an Egyptian Jew, was accused of employing "a white Muslim woman slave" called Fatimah. Marḥaba claimed that this slave was a Christian. When the woman proved she was a Muslim by reciting *shahada*, a Muslim prayer, "she was taken away from the Jewish owner" (who had paid 60 *sultani* for her) and entrusted to the "commander of the Citadel."[150] What became of her was not noted in the records.

Records seem to indicate that there were many *kieras*. The first document, dated 1548, does not give a name but notes that in recognition of her services, Suleiman I rewarded *Kiera* with a grant of tax exemption for her and her descendants. This was done by means of an imperial decree *(firman)* confirming special privileges and exemption from "the *jiziah* [tax on non-Muslims], land tax, tax on vineyards and gardens, army tax," etc. Although this particular *kiera* converted to Islam, the privileges were issued prior to the conversion.[151] The tax exemption was granted to all her descendants, both Jews and non-Jews, and for generations after, the heirs of Kord, grandson of this *Kiera*, maintained that privileged status.[152]

The policies of Suleiman's liberal reign were continued by his son Selim II (1566–1574), and the women of the court maintained considerable power. Selim's successor, Murad III (1574–1594), did little to change that, and the sultan's mother, Nur Banu, as well as his wife Safiyah Baffa, were strong and influential.

During the rule of Murad III, a *kiera* named **Esther Handali** was among the women who served the sultanas in the palace.[153] She was the best known of the *kieras* and the one who seems to have exercised power openly. Although she was eventually killed, her murder did not lead to the discontinuation of the position of *kiera*. Jewish women continued to serve in that capacity for several centuries.

RELIGIOUS ACTIVITIES

Women in the Synagogue

Despite the fact that women's religious feelings and beliefs are evident from letters and other writings of this period, the norm was that Jewish women in Islamic countries rarely prayed in an organized fashion the way men did. Sometimes they did not even enter the synagogue. This was consistent with Muslim customs.

In Yemen and parts of North Africa women often congregated outside the synagogue, as was the custom in Jerusalem where "these righteous [Ashkenazic] women stand outside [of the study hall] and listen to the teaching and read the prayers in Yiddish until they say *Kaddish*."[154] Two Karaite widows did actually enter their synagogue in Jerusalem. R. Moshe ben Eliahu ha-Levi, the Karaite from Krim, stated that "two widows are assiduous in prayer and know all matters concerning prayer and are always present at the time of prayer when they open the doors of the synagogue."[155] This activity on the part of women was unusual enough to be worthy of comment by a traveler.

It was more common for Ashkenazic women to attend synagogue and pray. They were also accustomed to read from the Bible in Yiddish, and R. Moshe Poryat of Prague (1650) advised women traveling to the land of Israel to take along a Bible, a prayer book, *tkhines*,[156] and other Yiddish books when immigrating.[157] In Safed, there is evidence that women in a Sephardic synagogue sat "in a second story at the back of the synagogue to pray with the community."[158] **Francesa Sarah** was one of the women participating in communal prayers at the Safed synagogue and is one of the rare women acknowledged by male religious leaders to have had extraordinary religious powers. **Rachel Aberlin** (the Ashkenazi) also attended synagogue services. It was in the synagogue during a sermon delivered by

Ḥayyim Vital, the famous kabbalist and disciple of Isaac Luria, that Aberlin had her first vision.

Women, Mysticism and Magic

In Safed and the surrounding areas, women mystics who analyzed dreams, saw visions, and predicted the future were an accepted part of life. Ḥayyim Vital reported in his journal, *Sefer ha-Ḥezyonot (Book of Visions)*,[159] that he visited them regularly and relied on their advice. Francesa Sarah, Rachel Aberlin, and the young daughter of Raphael Anav all shared their visions with Vital, and he himself acknowledged their religious powers. Aberlin had dreams and visions and enjoyed a considerable following among women and even some men.

Vital also visited special diviners who predicted the future from oil drippings. Such women were called lecanomancers, and many of them were named in Vital's writings. Among them were Soñadora, Mazel Tov, and Mira.

Despite these mainly female areas of religious practice, men remained dominant in religion and especially in Kabbalah throughout this period. While Ḥayyim Vital did not hesitate to consult holy women, many of whom were recognized in the community, these women never succeeded in maintaining their fame and authority beyond their immediate environment.

Shabbetai Zevi and Women

The Sephardic women in the larger, more cosmopolitan cities of the Ottoman Empire, such as Istanbul, Izmir (Smyrna), and Salonika, attended services but certainly had a separate section or perhaps even a separate room. When Shabbetai Zevi, the false messiah, visited the synagogues, he actively appealed to women with the promise of additional privileges. In a reversal of long years of tradition, he allowed them to be called up to the Torah and promised that he would lift "the curse of Eve" from women.[160]

Despite Shabbetai's avowed goal, no individual Turkish-Jewish women stand out as examples of spirituality during his lifetime as they did during the previous century in the land of Israel. There was one isolated incident of Shabbetai's wife, **Sarah,** prophesying and two additional reports of women prophets. The first of these included ten women as part of a mixed group in Safed in 1665, and a year later "the daughters of the arch-infidel Ḥayyim Peña" were reported to have prophesied in Smyrna in 1666.[161]

Shabbetai's attempt to change women's traditional status must have been shocking, even for his followers, many of whom were *conversos* who had only returned to Jewish practice after arriving in Turkey. In this group, women had often taken a leading role in secretly teaching and maintaining the family's religious practices and educating the children. Records indicate that they sometimes took even greater risks than men to maintain Jewish practices.[162] However, once they arrived in the Ottoman Empire where Judaism could be practiced openly, the dominant role reverted to men.

CHAPTER 8

Opening Doors:

Jewish Women During and After Haskalah (1750–1900)

OVERVIEW

While the battle between the Hasidim and the Mitnagdim was threatening to destroy Jewish unity in eastern Europe, some Jews were migrating westward. Many had fled the religious wars of the seventeenth century and the anti-Jewish pogroms and persecutions in Poland, Lithuania, and the less stable German principalities. They began returning to Holland, France, and England, where religion now seemed less of an issue and where the Industrial Revolution had opened up new opportunities for trade.

Changes in the West

In these western lands, Jews confronted very different lifestyles. Concepts of freedom, religious tolerance, and reliance on reason were being openly discussed. Humanism and Deism were now acceptable, and Jews, while sometimes viewed as superstitious and more often as simply undesirable, no longer seemed so threatening. Forward-looking individuals reasoned that if Jews were allowed to mix with the rest of society to learn what gentiles knew and understood, they would become like everyone else. Jews had a different agenda, but many sought to fit into a changing world. This new intellectual climate was called the Enlightenment. Jewish historians named it, in Hebrew, Haskalah.[1]

By 1700, France already had small communities of Jews, *conversos* who had practiced their religion secretly for generations but now felt freer to practice openly. Jews from the Alsatian region, once part of Germany, found themselves in France when the borders between those two countries were altered in 1648. They suffered many disabilities, but by the end of the 1700s, the French Revolution introduced the concept of individual rights to each man and woman living within its borders.[2] In return, the government demanded primary allegiance to the State, including direct payment of taxes. This new system effectively eliminated the power of the Jewish community over its members and caused a considerable weakening of Jewish life.

In the Netherlands and Belgium, similar developments were occurring. Sephardic Jews who had been living in the cities of Amsterdam, Antwerp, and Brussels since the expulsion from Spain found a new freedom. In Amsterdam, several prosperous Jews had become principals in the Dutch West India Company. Through that influential group of merchants, they exerted pressure on behalf of their co-religionists both in the Netherlands and in the New World. But as more immigrants crossed the borders into tiny Holland, the Dutch Jews looked to England as another alternative.

From 1290 to the mid-1650s, Jews had been barred from settling in England. Individual Jews, famous physicians from Italy and France, and a few groups of New Christians had quietly managed to enter the country. (New Christians had Jewish origins and were sometimes called *Marranos*, a derogatory word meaning swine.) Only after the English (Puritan) Revolution (1646–1649) did Manasseh ben Israel, a famous Amsterdam rabbi, succeed in negotiating with Oliver Cromwell to permit the Jews to return to England. Although there was no formal cancellation of the original medieval edict of expulsion and the legal status of the Jews remained uncertain, Cromwell, then Lord Protector of England, must have given some assurances in 1655. Almost immediately, the new Jewish community acquired a cemetery and a house for public worship. Not long after, immigrants began arriving from Holland.[3]

The Revival of English Jewry

The Jews, unknown in England for four hundred years, were looked on with suspicion but were tolerated because of the benefits they brought for increased trade. There was no official Jewish community recognized by the government to negotiate privileges for Jews as there still was in eastern Europe. A Jew with enough influence or money might get considerable rights, but such personal arrangements would not necessarily benefit other Jews. For the English, the primary motivation for this new liberalization was the advancement of commerce.

By the eighteenth century, Jewish women arriving in England from eastern Europe, and even from Amsterdam, found themselves in a fairly tolerant, heterogeneous society. There was no ghetto, and Jewish community life was merely one of many options. Communal officials did not impose Jewish Law, and Jews, especially affluent ones such as Moses and **Judith Montefiore** often moved in gentile circles and interacted easily with Christians.

The Enlightenment and the Jews of Central Europe

German Jews were in a different position than Jews in England or France. Their numbers were larger, and they had a long, ambivalent history of cooperation with Christians alternating with periods of discrimination and expulsion. Another difference in their status lay in the nature of the country itself. While England and France were cohesive nations, united under single rulers, Germany remained divided until late in the nineteenth century. Each of its different territories had a separate government and a different policy toward the Jews.

The Jews of Prussia, most living in Berlin, held substantial economic and financial positions. This handful of elite Jews campaigned to acquire equal rights and eliminate the discriminating laws against them. Their unofficial leader in this cause was Moses Mendelssohn (1729–1786), a well-known and respected Jewish philosopher and author.

Mendelssohn became a key figure in the Enlightenment movement in Germany and Austria and was supported by distinguished Christian scholars. He exemplified the new Jew: religiously observant but also secularly well educated and ruled by reason. This Jewish scholar's push for education, combined with Prussia's policy of reeducating its Jewish subjects, was to have far-reaching effects on German Jews and on Jewish women throughout Europe.

The number of Jews in the Austro-Hungarian Empire remained small, with most living in Vienna, the capital city and a center for the Enlightenment Movement. When Galicia, a territory with a large Jewish

---

MOSES MENDELSSOHN AND THE JEWISH ENLIGHTENMENT

One of Mendelssohn's primary goals was to ensure "liberty of conscience" within the State, because "men's convictions are not amenable to any coercion."[4] Another goal was to help Jews live in both the world of the modern state and the world of the Jewish community. He advised Jews: "Adapt yourself to the morals and the constitution of the land to which you have been removed; but hold fast to the religion of your fathers, too. Bear both burdens as well as you can."[5]

population, was annexed in 1772, the empire found itself with significant numbers of new Jewish subjects, many of whom had not yet been exposed to enlightened ideas. Emperor Joseph II (1780–1790) attempted to improve the status of these Jews by offering them free education and full rights if they would abandon their traditional practices and stop speaking Hebrew and Yiddish. Although the Galician majority saw this offer as a danger to their culture and way of life,[6] the more prosperous Viennese Jews embraced the new opportunities.

Following the French Revolution and Napoleon's subsequent advance into Germany in the opening years of the nineteenth century,[7] the new laws of the French Revolution were imposed and all Jews were emancipated and made citizens with full rights. These reforms were short-lived, however. After the fall of Napoleon, the French edicts were rescinded and Jews were required to earn their emancipation by reeducating themselves. The total emancipation of German Jews was not accomplished until 1869.

The Salon Women

The few German- and Austrian-Jewish women who enjoyed some prominence in the late 1700s were those who embraced Enlightenment values. They are sometimes called salon Jewesses or salon women.[8] All from prosperous Jewish families, this small coterie of women became hostesses to literary and political society. Their living rooms (or salons) provided a venue for people of diverse backgrounds, occupations, and financial status to meet on a casual basis, without the rigidity of the usual German social protocol. A salon simply required a private—and preferably wealthy—home, and a cultivated hostess who encouraged lively, intellectual conversation.[9]

Prominent among the salon women was **Dorothea Mendelssohn Veit Schlegel,** daughter of Moses Mendelssohn of Berlin. Others included **Henriette Lemos Herz** and **Rahel Levin Varnhagen**, also Germans, and **Fanny von Arnstein** of Vienna. These women and a few others attained a high level of celebrity as hostesses, a role unknown in traditional Jewish life.

The Jewish salon women came from rich families and had a broad secular education, but in almost all instances, their Jewish education was neglected.[10] They were also ambitious, and often witty and charming. The wealth of their families had been acquired by means of the financial skills of fathers or husbands. The men offered services that were in demand in this era of expanding mercantilism, especially in textiles and publishing,[11] but often had little understanding or respect for the world of arts and letters. Their wives and daughters looked to their new Christian friends for appreciation and for a chance to use and enlarge their social skills, artistic understanding, and talents.

Salon society lasted just a few decades at the end of the eighteenth century and represented only the intellectual elite of the German and Austrian populations. A total of about one hundred persons attended salons, and one-third of the participants were women (both Jewish and Christian).[12] Nevertheless, it marked the first time that Jewish women enjoyed such a prominent and public place in European gentile society.

Beyond the Salons

The Jewish women of the salons, the elite families of Vienna and Berlin, and perhaps a few women of some substance like **Fani Wolf** of Eisenstadt, Hungary, made up glittering but isolated islands of upper-class culture and style. During the eighteenth century and even into the nineteenth century, most Jewish women in Germany and Austria followed a way of life that remained remarkably similar to what it had been for several hundred years. They lived in modest economic circumstances, in traditional homes, with little opportunity to participate in the majority culture.

Even as the bulk of Europe's Jews clung to their insular communities, however, the foundations of those communities were disappearing. Throughout the cities of Alsace, Austria, and Germany and, gradually, even in the most isolated towns of eastern Europe, the official, government-endorsed Jewish communities became weaker and lost their authority. More forward-looking, secular governments now offered Jews freedom from ghetto life and new privileges.

The Enlightenment Moves East

In the 1700s, Russia, Poland, Lithuania, and the Ukraine still comprised some of the largest and most creative Jewish communities in the world, with many towns and villages populated almost completely by Jews. And here, the Enlightenment movement, or Haskalah, took a slightly different turn than it did in western and central European lands. While some, especially those from the cities, certainly did assimilate, embracing the cultures of their respective lands at the expense of Judaism,[13] many Jews experienced a cultural renaissance of their own. The Hasidic movement expanded and developed a vibrant philosophy that continued to attract many Jews who were religiously inclined. More secular Jews promoted both Hebrew and Yiddish literature and developed and encouraged their own thinkers and writers, who introduced such philosophies as Cultural Judaism, Jewish Socialism, and Zionism. Some women found their place in these movements.

BIOGRAPHIES

AGUILAR, GRACE OF LONDON, AUTHOR

(19th century)

Grace Aguilar was born in London in 1816. An English Jew of Sephardic origin and a descendant of crypto-Jews, she wanted Jewish women to take pride in their faith. It was Jewish captivity and persecution, she claimed, that distorted the purity of Jewish life. In lands such as England or America, Jews were now "free to become mentally and spiritually elevated."[14]

Although her knowledge of Judaism could not be compared with that of an educated male, she was well versed in the Jewish religion and the Hebrew language. While still young, she helped her mother run a girl's school to support the family. Through her contact with these young women, she became aware of the turmoil among Jewish youth, particularly girls, and how modern thinking undermined traditional Jewish life. Women, she believed, needed a "religion of the understanding" rather than a "religion of tacit belief." Aguilar insisted that young girls "must know what they believe and why, or they will be lost in the fearful vortex of contending opinions."[15] The many books she wrote were directed toward that goal.

In her book *The Jewish Faith*, written in the form of letters to a young girl with little Jewish education, she tried to offer what she considered the "spiritual consolation, moral guidance and immortal hope of Judaism."[16] In *Women of Israel: Characters and Sketches from the Holy Scriptures*, Aguilar addressed the need of Jewish women to understand the Hebrew Bible and know the great women in biblical stories and the part they played in Jewish history.

Aguilar particularly encouraged mothers to teach their children the "religion of the heart." She felt that women, even more than men, needed a closeness to God, and that religious feeling would help them through the many trials they faced in life.

Despite poor health, Grace Aguilar wrote and studied assiduously until her death on September 16, 1847, at the age of thirty-one. In the short span of seven years, from 1840 until she died, Aguilar produced eight books as well as articles and poetry, and translated the works of others from

---

AGUILAR'S ADMONITION TO JEWISH WOMEN

In the final chapter of *Women of Israel*, Grace Aguilar wrote:

"We have gone further to draw forth every mention of our noble ancestors, that we might learn their domestic and social position at a time when inspired historians were silent; we have scanned every statute, every law, alike in the words of Moses, and in their simplifying commentary by our elders, and the result of such examination has been, we trust, to convince every woman of Israel of her immortal destiny, her solemn responsibility, and her elevated position, alike by the command of God, and the willing acquiescence of her brother man."[17]

FIG. 21. Grace Aguilar was an educator and a prolific writer. This portrait is from her book *The Women of Israel* (1878).

Hebrew into English. She penned every word of her lengthy books herself and rewrote one manuscript completely after it was lost in transit.[18] One of her works, *Home Influence*, went through forty-one editions.[19]

Grace Aguilar had a loyal following in England and also in America. She corresponded with Rabbi Isaac Leeser, leader of the Jews of Philadelphia and founder of The Jewish Publication Society, who arranged to have her books published in the United States. After her death, a branch of the New York Public Library was named in her honor.[20]

ARNSTEIN, FANNY VON OF VIENNA, SALON HOSTESS
(late 18th century)

Fanny von Arnstein, daughter of the prosperous Itzig family of Berlin and wife of Nathan Adam von Arnstein, was one of the most famous of the salon women of Vienna. Born in 1757, she was well educated in secular subjects and had many cultural and

---

A LETTER TO GRACE AGUILAR

The following excerpt from a letter written just before she died shows the grateful reaction of the women who read Aguilar's books.

"You, dearest Sister . . . have taught us to know and appreciate our dignity. . . . You have vindicated our social and spiritual equality with our brethren in the faith. . . . Your writings place within our reach those higher motives . . . which flow from the spirituality of our religion."[21]

---

artistic interests. After her marriage, she moved to Vienna with her husband and there presided over the leading salon in that city, attended by the most respected members of high society, including the emperor himself. She was co-founder of the Music Society of Austria, an organization that helped to support promising musicians. One of these was Mozart.[22]

EIDELE OF BELZ AND SOKOLOV, COMMUNITY LEADER
(19th century)

Eidele was the daughter of **Malkah** and Sholem Rokeaḥ. Born into a Hasidic family, she married a Ḥasid, R. Isaac Rubin of Sokolov. His reluctance to take on the role of rebbe gave her an opportunity to use her considerable talents. Eidele delivered sermons on the Sabbath, distributed food to the poor, and played a leading role in that community. "All Eidele needs is a rabbi's hat," her father was quoted as saying.[23]

FRANK, EVA OF OFFENBACH, RELIGIOUS LEADER
(19th century)

Eva Frank was the only daughter of Jacob Frank, head of the highly controversial Frankist movement, a late form of Sabbateanism. Although the movement was not widespread, Frank did have several thousand followers. He set up a quasi-royal court, first in Bruenn and later in Offenbach, where believers came to serve him and his family. Frank demanded that his followers worship his wife Hannah as the *gevirah* (great lady). When Hannah Frank died in 1770, Eva became the new *gevirah*.

Even more than her two brothers, Eva Frank was said to be very close to her father and faithfully followed his beliefs and his transgressive practices. At one time, Jacob claimed that Eva was actually not his true daughter but a Russian Romanov princess, and some even accepted that claim. After Jacob's death, Eva and her two brothers, Joseph and Rochus, assumed leadership of the movement, but they could not command the authority of their father. Joseph died in 1807 and Rochus in 1817, leaving Eva Frank as the sole head of the Frankists. In face of enormous debts and a continuous decline in her following, she persisted in her beliefs and in the mystical but controversial religious rites that her father had initiated. During her last fifteen years, she conducted herself as if she were a royal princess of the house of Romanov, accepting the adoration of her few remaining loyal followers.

Frankists produced very few writings, most of which were deliberately concealed by Jews opposed to the extreme beliefs of the sect, or by Frankists themselves, who feared persecution. One book taken from the court in Offenbach included a list of the dreams and revelations of Eva Frank and her brothers.[24] When that, too, was destroyed by a rabbinical court in Fürth, any hope of understanding Eva Frank's religion, or judging its sincerity, vanished. Part religious leader, part mystic and revolutionary, and part charlatan, Eva Frank remains unknown, and Jewish women have resisted her inclusion in their history.

FRANKEL, SARAH BAT JOSHUA HESCHEL TEUMIM OF CHENCINY, REBBE

(19th century)

Born in 1838, Sarah, or Sereleh, was the daughter of the famous Hasidic rabbi Joshua Heschel Teumim Frankel. She married the *tzaddik* Ḥayyim Samuel of Chenciny and after her husband's death, functioned as the rebbe in that town. Believed to be the only woman in Poland who actually "conducted herself as a rebbe,"[25] she became known for her wise parables and was consulted by famous rabbis. Sereleh lived until the age of ninety-nine and by that time could boast 250 grandchildren and great-grandchildren. When she died in 1937, it was reported that "ten thousand people attended her funeral."[26]

Sarah's daughter Hannah Brakhah, the wife of R. Elimelekh of Grodzinsk, also participated in the life of the Hasidic court and is one of the few women who were active while married.[27]

GOLDSCHMIDT, HENRIETTE BENAS OF LEIPZIG, EDUCATOR AND WRITER

(19th century)

Henriette Benas was born in Krotoschin, a small Polish town, in 1825. She married her cousin,

R. Abraham Meir Goldschmidt, a liberal rabbi and a widower with three sons, and moved to Leipzig (Germany) with her new family. There, in February 1865, the Goldschmidts became part of a movement interested in improving education for girls. The Leipzig Women's Educational Organization quickly led to a broader conference at which the German Women's League was formed, with a goal of higher education for young women and credit-granting institutions for working women.[28]

Henriette Goldschmidt was a spokesperson for the League for forty years. She was also one of the founders of a society that established municipal kindergartens and vocational schools for girls, including teacher training.[29] A follower of the pioneer German educator, Friedrich Froebel, Goldschmidt was a leader in child care and early childhood education. She spoke and wrote on the subject of education throughout her later years, but most of her work was published anonymously.

Goldschmidt died in 1920, convinced that the maternal role should be the source of women's primary satisfaction and that "the claim for political rights [for women] is very premature, and what is worse, unwarranted."[30]

GOLDSCHMIDT, JOHANNA SCHWABE OF HAMBURG, WRITER, EDUCATOR, AND SOCIAL ORGANIZER

(19th century)

Born in 1806 into a liberal German family, Johanna's father, Marcus Hertz Schwabe, was one of the founders of the first Reform temple in Hamburg (1817).[31] Johanna herself was part of its first confirmation class for Jewish boys and girls.

In 1827, Johanna married Moritz Goldschmidt and during the next twenty years was occupied with raising her eight children. In 1847, she published her first book, *Rebekka and Amalia*. Written as a series of letters between Rebekka, a Jew, and Amalia, a Christian aristocrat, the book focused on problems of Jewish conversion and assimilation.[32] Outlined in the fifth letter was a plan for an organization through which rich women would help poorer women to improve themselves by means of lectures and instruction.[33] This proposal resulted in the Women's Association to Combat and Reduce Religious Prejudice. Founded by Goldschmidt together with a Christian friend, Amalie Westendarp, in 1848, the Women's Association promoted the early, nonsectarian education of children.

In a second book, *Mothers' Worries and Mothers' Joys*, Goldschmidt formulated the idea for a nondenominational kindergarten to include poor children. Soon afterward, she helped to establish a seminary to train teachers in the new methods pioneered by educator Friedrich Froebel. Johanna Goldschmidt remained active in these organizations until her death in 1884.

HERZ, HENRIETTE LEMOS OF BERLIN, LINGUIST AND SALON HOSTESS
(late 18th–19th century)

Henriette Lemos was a talented linguist who spoke more than eight languages. Her father, Dr. Benjamin Lemos, a physician and hospital director, was descended from a wealthy Portuguese family that had emigrated from Amsterdam more than a century earlier. He had encouraged Henriette's education and particularly her language skills.

When Henriette, at fifteen years old, married Markus Herz, a prominent and wealthy physician more than twice her age, the couple expanded their home, turning some rooms into what became a double salon. There, in the 1780s, Henriette Lemos Herz began a practice of hosting an open house, a social event to which not only invited friends could come, but also scholars and intellectuals without formal invitations.[34] Markus gave lectures in the natural sciences in one room, and Henriette entertained the literary scholars, landowning nobles, Jewish merchants, and professors in an adjacent area. A dinner preceded the occasion, and the Herz salon became known as a social event in Berlin society.

When Markus died suddenly in 1803, this life came to an abrupt end. The couple had been spending beyond their means and now Henriette, with no income forthcoming, was no longer able to afford the extravagance of a salon. She opened her home to board students and girls who came from the country to find jobs in Berlin, and did some work as a translator and teacher of languages.[35] Only a few weeks after her mother died in 1817, with no one left to hold her to the Jewish community, she converted to Christianity.[36]

MALKAH OF BELZ, LEADER AT A HASIDIC COURT
(19th century)

Malkah, wife of Sholem Rokeaḥ (1779–1855), urged her husband to become a Hasid, and in accordance with her wishes, he went to study with R. Shlomo of Lutzk. Sholem was eventually named the rabbinical head of Belz (Galicia) and established a Hasidic court there. Through all this, his wife, Malkah, did not remain in the background. She was a leader in her own right at the court of Belz, and prominent men were counted among her spiritual devotees.[37]

MARKEL-MOSESSOHN, MIRIAM OF RUSSIA, HEBREW WRITER AND POET
(19th century)

Miriam Markel-Mosessohn, born in 1839 to Ḥayah and Shimon Wierzbolowski, was one of the first eastern European Jewish women to write in Hebrew. She married Anshel Markel-Mosessohn of Kovno in 1863, and the two remained happily married for forty years. The couple had no children, and Anshel encouraged Miriam to write, probably funding her early efforts as well.

In 1868, Markel-Mosessohn began a correspondence with Yehudah Leib Gordon, a noted poet and advocate of education for women, tentatively expressing her trepidation at entering "the sanctuary of Hebrew letters." Gordon encouraged her and she began translating German works into Hebrew. After many years of translating, she began to write articles in Hebrew and then to compose original Hebrew poetry, one of the few women in her century to be recognized as a *maskelet* (an author of the Enlightenment).[38]

MONTEFIORE, JUDITH COHEN OF LONDON, PHILANTHROPIST
(18th–19th century)

Judith Cohen, born in 1784, was the daughter of Levi Barent Cohen and Lydia Cohen, prosperous Ashkenazim who had come from Holland in 1773. The family was observant and regularly attended Sabbath services in the Great Synagogue of London.

Judith was educated with private tutors, and in addition to learning English literature, music, and singing, was taught French, Italian, German, and Hebrew. In 1812 she was married to Moses Montefiore and moved next door to her sister Hannah, who was already married to Nathan Mayer Rothschild.

Moses Montefiore (1784–1885), or Monte as Judith fondly called him, was of Sephardic descent, a member of a family that had emigrated from Leghorn, Italy. In 1815 his uncles purchased a broker's medal for him, paying 1,200 British pounds, about ten times the usual fee. By the time of his marriage to Judith Cohen, Moses was a successful and respected businessman.

EXCERPTS FROM JUDITH MONTEFIORE'S DIARY

Judith Cohen marked her wedding day in a typical, understated manner:

"I was this day united in the holy bonds of matrimony to Moses Montefiore, whose fraternal and filial affection . . . joined to many other good qualities and attention toward me, ripened into a more ardent sentiment."[39]

Concerning her husband's religious observance, Judith had written in her diary:

"I do not know any circumstance more pleasing to me than to perceive that my dear Monte is religiously inclined. It is that sort of religion which he possesses that in my opinion is most essential—a fellow-feeling and benevolence."[40]

JUDITH MONTEFIORE'S TRIPS TO THE LAND OF ISRAEL

Reporting on her first journey to the land of Israel, Judith only hinted at the hardships involved in this journey.

"Only six European females are said to have visited Palestine during the course of a century . . . I can never be sufficiently thankful to Almighty God for suffering us to reach this city in safety. The obstacles that presented themselves, the dangers with which we were threatened, the detentions and vexations which had actually to be endured, all rose in my mind as I gave way to the feeling of delight with which I at length saw the fulfillment of my dear husband's long-cherished wish. Nor was my satisfaction a little increased at the recollection that I had strenuously urged him to pursue the journey, even when his own ardour had somewhat abated and when I had to oppose my counsel to the advice and wishes of our companions."[41]

Reacting to a group of poor Jews lining up for financial aid in the land of Israel, Judith wrote:

"May the Almighty grant that the plan which my dear husband contemplates, may succeed, so that these poor creatures may be enabled to gain an independent livelihood instead of relying on the assistance of other countries, whose contributions are so precarious."[42]

He would become one of the richest and most influential Jews in England.

Like other upper-class English Jews, the Montefiores emulated the fashionable dress of the gentry and were not strictly observant in religious ritual. They never had any children, and Judith was therefore free to travel with her husband once he retired from business. The couple also participated in the lively social life of early–nineteenth-century London, enjoying games of whist, charity and state balls, and operas, all activities that were frowned on by more traditional Jews. However, they remained firmly attached to Judaism and the Jewish people.

A devoted diarist, Judith Montefiore recorded her impressions of several journeys to the land of Israel. She first accompanied her husband there in 1827, taking an arduous trip by coach and horses, crossing mountains and deserts where no roads had been built. Highwaymen preyed on travelers, and not only were the lodgings rat infested, but there was also an ever-present risk of plague. Nevertheless Judith Montefiore returned to the Middle East several times.

The Montefiores' generosity to the Jewish inhabitants of the land of Israel was well known, and their visits were much anticipated. They encouraged and financially supported the first agricultural settlement outside the walls of Jerusalem. Named *Yemin Moshe* in honor of Moses Montefiore, it enabled Jews to become self-sufficient and not depend on charity.

On their second trip to the Middle East in 1838, Judith was asked to light the four lamps in front of the altar in a Jerusalem synagogue and put the bells on the *sefer Torah*. This was a singular honor in a traditional house of prayer,

FIG. 22 Judith Montefiore traveled with her husband and worked with him on many charitable projects. This portrait is from volume 2 of *Diaries of Sir Moses and Lady Montefiore* (1890).

where men and women were seated separately and women were generally not permitted even to touch the Torah.

In addition to traveling with and helping her husband, Judith was devoted to her own causes. She served as an officer of the Jews' Orphan Asylum, was a patron of the Jewish Ladies' Loan and Visiting Society, and was responsible for having girls edu-

cated and taught "cookery" at the Jews' Hospital.

The *Jewish Manual*, written by "a Lady," appeared in 1846. It was the first Jewish cookbook to be published in England and it was believed—though never confirmed—that Judith Montefiore was the author.[43] The book also contained extensive advice for care of the skin, and recommended modest dress. Judith held the title of lady after her husband was knighted by Queen Victoria, sometime during the late 1830s, and was one of the first Jews to hold that title.

Judith Montefiore set an example of how a Jewish woman could live in two disparate worlds. Acculturated into Christian high society, she chose to direct her major efforts to Jewish philanthropic activities. She was a dedicated Jew, a fearless traveler, and even a fine horsewoman. One of her companions, Jemima Guedalla,

---

A DEBT OF GRATITUDE TO JUDITH MONTEFIORE

When a blood libel accusation was made against Jews in Damascus, Syria, Sir Moses Montefiore was asked to intervene. Once again, Judith accompanied him. The couple went to Egypt and successfully persuaded Mehemet Ali, Pasha of Egypt and ruler of Syria, to dismiss the ritual murder charges. The success of this mission led to recognition of Moses Montefiore as the most important Jewish statesman of his time,[44] but Moses had not done it alone. In a public speech given after this event, he acknowledged the role of his wife, claiming:

"To Lady Montefiore I owe a debt of gratitude; her counsels and zeal for our religion and love to her brethren were at all times conspicuous. They animated me under difficulties and consoled me under disappointments."[45]

---

remembered how Lady Montefiore, already well advanced in years, "got on her horse and rode for a couple of hours."[46] She died in 1862, shortly after celebrating her fiftieth wedding anniversary.

As a memorial to his wife, Sir Moses founded the Judith Lady Montefiore College at Ramsgate, England, where the couple had made their home. Long after her death, he continued to credit her for his own achievements, telling an admirer: "The little good I have accomplished, or rather that I intended to accomplish, I am indebted for it to my never-to-be-forgotten wife, whose enthusiasm for everything that is noble and whose religiousness sustained me in my career."[47]

MORGENSTERN, LINA BAUER OF BRESLAU AND BERLIN, SOCIAL WORKER AND EDUCATOR
(19th century)

Lina Bauer was born in 1830 into a prosperous family in Breslau. She received a religious education from the well-known liberal rabbi Abraham Geiger and a secular education in primary and middle school. She then followed a path to social activism through involvement in charitable causes and education. When only eighteen years old, Lina, together with her mother, organized the Penny Club to Support Poor School Children, distributing shoes, clothes, schoolbooks, and writing supplies to poor children at Christmas. This fund lasted for eighty years.[48]

After her marriage in 1854 to Theodor Morgenstern, a Russian Jew, the Morgensterns moved to Berlin. Theodor soon encountered financial difficulties, and Lina searched for a way to earn money. Among the few opportunities open to middle-class women at that time were social work and writing. Morgenstern, already a mother, organized the Society for the Promotion of Froebel Kindergartens and wrote a widely published handbook explaining this educator's ideas. She later wrote and published several children's books.[49]

By 1869 a newly united North German Federation guaranteed civil and political rights to all. For the next forty-five years, the Jews of Germany enjoyed a period of liberalism and integration, enabling Jewish women like Lina Morgenstern to utilize their energies beyond the narrow field of children's education. Lina was soon organizing soup kitchens for the poor[50] and, at the request of the Prussian government, also set up kitchens providing meals for soldiers in transit during the Franco-Prussian War of 1870.

Morgenstern expanded her interests still further, founding the Berlin Homemakers Association in 1873 for the purpose of educating women and safeguarding their welfare. This association ran a free employment agency and an old-age pension fund and taught women to cook, using texts written by Morgenstern herself.[51] She also fought for women's right to study medicine, and in 1895, during a period of increasing nationalism and arms buildup, she joined the executive committee of the Women's League for World Peace.[52]

Although she firmly advocated that women remain at home and care for husbands and children, she herself pursued her social-work activities, leaving the care of her family to her older daughter and a maid.

Morgenstern remained active until she died in 1909.

MORPURGO, RACHEL LUZZATTO OF TRIESTE, POET
(19th century)

Rachel Luzzatto was born on April 8, 1790, just five years after the gates of the old ghetto of Trieste were torn down. The Luzzattos came from a long line of Italian-Jewish scholars, and her parents were prosperous and respected in the community. Rachel received the same excellent education as her brother and her male cousins, studying Hebrew and Aramaic and being introduced to the Talmud and other medieval texts at an early age.[53] She also studied Italian literature, mathematics, Rashi's commentaries, and the Zohar. Somewhat of a mystic, Rachel Luzzatto began writing poetry when she was eighteen and continued to do so until her death sixty-three years later.

Despite a life steeped in tradition and Jewish scholarship, Rachel Luzzatto was not oblivious to the new ideas swirling outside—and sometimes even inside—the Jewish community. As a young woman, Rachel refused all the suitors approved by her family and insisted on a man of her own choosing. He was Jacob Morpurgo, an Austrian-Jewish merchant. Her parents at first refused to permit the match but finally consented when Rachel was twenty-nine years old.[54]

Accounts of their married life differ. One of Morpurgo's biographers said that she and Jacob were blissfully happy. She reported that Morpurgo cared for her four children, attended to all her household duties, and still found time to write and publish her poetry, meet and correspond with Jewish scholars, and lecture to young men who sought her wisdom.[55] Other researchers contended that she lived in near poverty and could find time for her writing only at night or on new moons, customarily celebrated as a half-holiday for women.[56] According to information collected from her daughter Perla, Jacob Morpurgo took little interest in his wife's writing and was surprised to find that people came to solicit her opinion.[57]

Like that of the entire Luzzatto family, Rachel Morpurgo's goal was to revive Hebrew poetry in Italy.[58] While she followed the tradition of earlier Italian-Jewish poets, Morpurgo is considered the first woman to have written modern poetry in the Hebrew language, including poetry on secular subjects not meant to fit into syna-gogue liturgy. Her poems were published in a Hebrew journal called *Kokhavei Yitzhak (Stars of Isaac)* and were signed with the initials of the three words, Rahel Morpurgo *hake-tanah* (the small one). In Hebrew these initials spell out *Rimah* (worm), a symbol of extreme modesty.[60]

As she grew older, Rachel Morpurgo began to believe that the soul could be united with God through contemplation and love. Her poems are filled with images of this conceptual union and with messianic hopes.

Rachel Morpurgo died in 1871 at the age of eighty-one. In 1890, one hundred years after her birth, Vittorio Castiglioni—a noted scholar, native of Trieste, and chief rabbi of the Jewish community of Rome—published a volume of her poems and letters. He named the collection *Ugav Rahel (Rachel's harp)*.

Just a few generations after Castiglioni's book was published, Nina Davis Salaman, one of the foremost English-Jewish scholars and poets of her time, rediscovered Rachel Morpurgo's work and rendered it into English. With these translations, Morpurgo was brought to life for a new generation.[61]

A POEM BY RACHEL MORPURGO

This poem, one of Morpurgo's later works, illustrates her use of metaphors from nature and her spiritual inclinations.

From a distance, I look upon the eternal hills,
Their face covered with glorious flowers.
I rise high, as if on eagle's wings, to cast a glance,
Raising my head to view the sun.
Heaven! How beautiful you stream forth,
Winds sweeping across your stage,
Revealing the place where freedom ever lives.
Who, who can express its sweetness![59]

PERELE BAT YISRAEL OF KOZIENICE, ASCETIC AND RELIGIOUS LEADER
(late 18th century)

Perele, the daughter of Israel ben Shabbetai of Kozienice (1733–1814), was an ascetic who had her own disciples. It was reported that Perele bat Yisrael wore tzitzit (ritual fringes) and regularly fasted on Mondays and Thursdays. Her large following supported her with money, most of which she distributed to the poor.[62]

RAKOWSKI, PUAH OF BIALYSTOK, HEBREW TEACHER AND PIONEER EDUCATOR
(19th century)

Puah Rakowski was born in Bialystok, Poland, in 1865. Her family traced its lineage back through thirty-six generations to the medieval sage Rashi (Shlomo ben Yitzhak of Troyes), and her father was a traditionally observant Polish Jew. Puah, like other girls of her background, attended *heder* with boys for a few years. The intention was to teach her Hebrew before she was sent to a private school for girls where she would learn Russian. However, Rakowski showed such interest and promise in the study of Hebrew texts that she begged her father to allow her to continue. He agreed, telling her wistfully: "It's a shame you were born a girl and not a boy."[63]

By the age of thirteen, Puah Rakowski had already begun to question the existence of God. She abandoned the prayers and strict observance of her Orthodox girlhood,[64] but when the time came for her to be married, she acceded to the long-standing tradition of the community and was betrothed to a man of her parents' choosing.

Rakowski's arranged marriage was a disaster. The young bride threatened suicide in order to obtain her husband's consent to study midwifery, one of the few professions open to women, and went off to school, leaving her two children with her mother. Although she completed her education, she never worked as a midwife. Instead, Puah set up a millinery workshop to maintain herself and help other women become independent. Later, she became the principal of a school for Jewish girls. Finally, at

twenty-six, after threatening to convert, she obtained a divorce from her husband and moved to Warsaw, where she accepted a post as teacher of Hebrew in another girls school.[66]

That initial teaching job led to a full-time career in Jewish education, and Rakowski eventually established the first middle school for Jewish girls in Warsaw, Poland. Known as Puah Rakowski's First Hebrew School, it was an institution devoted to the serious education of girls.[67] Rakowski believed that if Jewish daughters were educated exactly like sons, in Torah as well as cultural and moral doctrines, fewer women would be lost to the Jewish people through assimilation.[68]

Always a rebel, Rakowski insisted on her own independence. She supported her children and herself, embraced the Zionist cause, and established a Jewish women's association. As she told the first group of founders: "It was high time for us to stop being errand girls for our male comrades."[69]

A TRIBUTE TO RACHEL MORPURGO

In the foreword to his book, *Ugav Rahel*, Castiglioni wrote the following of Rachel Morpurgo:

"She is dear to us in three ways. From the point of view of our faith, because she is an Israelite; from the point of our city, because she was a native of Trieste and from the point of view of literature, because she is an exalted poetess. She is a ready writer, who by her pleasant writings added beauty and glory to our holy language."[65]

Despite Puah Rakowski's rejection of religious principles, she was an active Zionist. She eventually immigrated to Israel and died in Haifa in 1955 at the age of ninety.

RAPPOPORT, SEREL SEGAL OF DUBNO AND OLEKSINIEC, WRITER OF PRAYERS
(18th–19th century)

Serel was the daughter of R. Yaakov (Yankev) Segal, known as the *Maggid* of Dubno (1741–1804). She married R. Mordecai Katz Rappoport, rebbe at Oleksiniec in southern Poland in the late 1700s. Often referred to as Rebbetzin Serel, she was most likely the *firzogerin* in her husband's synagogue, leading the women in prayer. She also wrote original prayers, highlighting specific lines from the siddur (the order of prayers used in the syna-

gogue) as well as biblical verses, and using them as inspirations for new meditations and appeals to God. Her best-known prayers were "Tkhine of the Matriarchs for the New Moon," containing an appeal to God in Aramaic and in Yiddish,[71] and "Tkhine of the Matriarchs for the Blowing of the Shofar."[72]

SCHLEGEL, DOROTHEA MENDELSSOHN VEIT OF BERLIN, SALON HOSTESS
(late 18th–19th century)

Dorothea (originally Breindel) Mendelssohn, born in 1765, was the oldest daughter of the noted scholar and philosopher Moses Mendelssohn. In his diary, Moses described his daughter Dorothea as "not at all comely but clever and well-behaved."[73] She received a thorough secular education with private tutors, and even though it was a definite break from tradition, Dorothea was also included in her father's regular morning sessions with his own students.

But the Mendelssohns were not ready to give up all the old ways. When it came time for Dorothea to marry, tradition prevailed, and the groom, Simon Veit, was a man of her father's choosing. Much older than her, Veit was kind, loyal, and successful but hardly up to her intellectual level. During her years as Simon's wife (1783–1798), Dorothea organized a literary reading group, the Jewish Lecture Society, that she held in her home one evening a week. Then in 1798, after more than a decade of marriage and two children, she met and fell in love with a gentile literary critic, Frederich Schlegel.

In a daring act that created a scandal among Jewish and Christian acquain-

---

EXCERPT FROM A *TKHINE*

In the following excerpt from "Tkhine of the Matriarchs for the New Moon" Rebbetzin Serel Segal Rappoport chose the Hebrew words from Psalms 6:2, "Do not rebuke me in Your wrath," and examined deeper levels of meaning:

"Do not punish me with Your anger for Your Name is the True Judge. Your judgment is true and You act with grace and truth when You forgive our sins. Therefore, I rejoice in my hope that You will forgive my sins, for I regret them. I will not sin any more; rather, I will praise You and serve You with all my heart. Amen."[70]

tances, Dorothea Mendelssohn Veit left her husband and children and moved to a small apartment. Rumors that she was living with Schlegel circulated throughout the community, and the two were ostracized and isolated. Dorothea suffered even more than her lover, since her abandonment of her family was considered a rebellious act of defiance against Jewish tradition.

Eventually both Frederich and Dorothea were forced to move out of Berlin. In 1804 Dorothea officially converted. The couple married shortly after and moved to Paris, but Dorothea, although a serious person of intellect, was never able to achieve the financial resources, stability, or social acceptance that would have permitted her to preside at another salon.

Dorothea's younger sister, Henriette, never married. She became a governess in Vienna and then headed a boarding school in Paris. After her parents' death she, too, converted. Of the two Mendelssohn brothers, Abraham converted in 1822, and Joseph remained Jewish but had his children baptized. [74]

SCHWERIN, JEANETTE ABARBANELL OF BRESLAU, SOCIAL ACTIVIST
(19th century)

Jeanette, born in 1852 in Breslau, was a descendant of the famous Abrabanel family of Sephardic Jews. Her father, Edouard, was a physician, and her mother had already been active in some of the organizations founded by **Lina Morgenstern.** At seventeen, Jeanette spent a year at one of Morgenstern's schools, where she learned several languages and served as a committee member in one of the

soup kitchens. Jeanette married Dr. Ernst Schwerin when she was twenty years old. Because her children were sickly, she was house bound while they were young but continued her studies and had a circle of prominent, liberal friends. [75]

At the age of forty, with her children grown, she entered the larger world, becoming one of the original founders of the German Society for Ethical Culture in 1892. Four years later she was chosen as the organization's second president. Part of the program of the Ethical Culture society was the proposed use of libraries and reading rooms so that people of all classes and religions could read together and discuss ethical topics. [76]

Schwerin was also active in women's issues and in 1893 was one of the four founders of the Girl's and Women's Groups for Social Service Work. She directed the organization until her untimely death in 1899 at the age of forty-seven. However, Jeanette Schwerin, like **Henriette Goldschmidt** and **Lina Morgenstern** a generation earlier, never espoused women's political rights. She believed in greater professionalism for women social workers and saw social work as a "path to women's emancipation." [77]

SEGAL, SHIFRAH OF BRODY, WRITER OF PRAYERS
(late 18th century)

Shifrah Segal was the wife of Ephraim Segal, a judge at the rabbinical court of Brody (Ukraine). She was the only woman writer of *tkhines* who viewed women's rituals as equal in importance to men's and with the same potential to effect the universe and God's actions. She totally rejected the accepted male opinion that women were required to light candles to atone for Eve's sin "because she [Eve] extinguished the light of the world and made the cosmos dark."[78] Instead, she advanced her own theory of women's commandments, giving women's observance an independent spiritual significance that most Jews did not concede. In Shifrah Segal's view, women had an equivalent role in bringing redemption to the Jewish people.

Segal wrote her "New Tkhine for the Sabbath" in approximately 1770. Using kabbalistic texts as a direct source, she compared a woman's duty of candlelighting to the holy activities of God and the *Shekhinah*. Just as the High Priest lit the seven-branched candelabra in the Temple in Jerusalem, which in turn "caused the seven lamps above to shine," so when the woman lights the Sabbath candles she "awakens great arousal in the upper world."[79] For Shifrah, a woman's ritual acts, then, were symbolic, not only of those once performed in the ancient Temple, but also of similar rituals performed in heaven.

TWERSKY, HANNAH ḤAVA AND MALKAH OF CHERNOBYL, PIOUS WOMEN
(19th century)

Hannah Ḥava was the daughter of the noted Hasidic rabbi Mordecai Twersky (1770–1837) of Chernobyl, a town in the Ukraine. She was active in her father's court, and Mordecai himself believed she was endowed with the holy spirit.[80]

Twersky's granddaughter Malkah, the daughter of his fifth son, R. Abraham Twersky of Trisk (1806–1889) followed her aunt's example. Well known as "Malkeleh the Triskerin,"

she sponsored public meals, distributed food, and received petitions from Hasidim twice a day.[81]

VARNHAGEN, RAHEL LEVIN OF BERLIN, SALON HOSTESS
(late 18th–19th century)

Rahel Levin, born in Berlin in 1771, was more rebellious than most young Jewish women of her time and did not follow the same path into a traditional marriage. While still in her teens, she refused a proposed match arranged by her family and defied the restrictions of the Jewish community. Wealthy and single, she insisted on riding in an open carriage with an actress friend, flaunting traditional Jewish behavior.[82] Although subsequently engaged to two different Christian men, she did not marry until much later.

Levin was not formally educated by her parents. Instead, she studied on her own and attended theater and the opera. During a summer vacation at a spa, she met a group of non-Jews, diplomats and noblewomen, with whom she became friends. With this group as her base, she formed a salon in 1790.

Living freely as a single woman, she occupied rooms on the upper floor of her family's home. Her guests, many of them influential and famous, regularly climbed the stairs to gather and discuss the novels, plays, and politics of the day. Rahel Levin became known as the leading hostess, presiding over the premier salon in Berlin. She is credited with having encouraged many artists, including the famous poet Goethe.[83]

Until the French invasion of Prussia by Napolean's troops in 1806, Levin's salon continued to meet, but by the end of that year, the height of salon influence and prestige was ended.[84] After the war, when she was forty-two, she converted to Christianity and married Karl Varnhagen von Ense, a much younger gentile literary critic and diplomat.[85]

WENGEROFF, PAULINE EPSTEIN OF BELORUSSIA, AUTHOR
(19th century)

Pauline Epstein was born in Belorussia in 1833 into a middle-class home where tradition was important and female ritual and spirituality were integrated into family life.[86] She learned the customs of Judaism and also studied secular subjects, including German, the language of the Enlightenment. Her father, a wealthy merchant and a scholar, betrothed her to Ḥanan Wengeroff, a businessman from Minsk. Although the arrangement was a traditional one, a concession was made to the new mores of society: Pauline and Ḥanan were permitted to meet before the marriage.[87]

The Wengeroffs had five children, and Pauline did not work outside her home. As was common in that period, she kept a diary. It was this diary, written in German, that formed the basis of her book, *Memoirs of a Grandmother*, and made the details of her life available for future generations. An excerpt, translated into Russian, first appeared in *Voskhod (Sunrise)*, an important Russian-Jewish periodical.[88] The complete *Memoirs*, a history of her family and the society of mid-nineteenth-century Russia and Poland, was published six years later, shortly before her death, and brought her some measure of recognition.

In this memoir, Pauline related how she and Ḥanan began life as an observant and pious Jewish couple and

gradually left the practice of Judaism. "Little by little," she wrote, "he began to neglect his religious observances. Then he decided to cut his beard." When she quarreled with him about these matters he reminded her that as the man of the house, he was entitled to obedience. As time went on, Ḥanan Wengeroff demanded "not only assent . . . but also submission." Reflecting on the situation in many Jewish households of the time, she noted: "They [the men] preached freedom, equality, fraternity in public, but at home they were despots."[89]

Ḥanan, like many Jewish men at that time, saw tradition and the woman's active role in maintaining it as culturally regressive. He also insisted on being the sole breadwinner and rejected his wife's help even after he had lost her entire dowry in a failed

---

PAULINE WENGEROFF'S SAD DEPARTURE FROM JUDAISM

In her autobiography, Pauline Wengeroff described how she was forced to abandon the traditions that she loved.

"Little by little, I had to drive each cherished custom from our home. 'Drive' is not the right word, for I accompanied each to the door with tears and sobs. I loved my husband intensely and as faithfully as in the first days of our marriage, yet I could not submit without resistance. I wanted to preserve this cherished tradition for myself and my children, and I fought a battle of life and death."[90]

business venture.[91] Although his own grandmother had been active in the economy of her household, the new bourgeois society wanted to keep women at home. But even in the kitchen, his decisions were paramount. Pauline Wengeroff and her contemporaries "were contained in homes whose course they could not set."[92]

Regretfully, at her husband's insistence, Pauline Wengeroff abandoned one Jewish tradition after another. She no longer wore her wig, the mark of a pious Jewish woman; she stopped maintaining a kosher kitchen and sent her children for a secular education. When the two Wengeroff sons converted to Christianity, it was "the hardest blow of my life," and she mourned not only as a mother, but also as "a Jewess mourning for the Jewish people that has lost so many of its noblest sons."[95]

Pauline Wengeroff died in 1916, just one year before the Communist Revolution ended tzarist rule in Russia. At that time, large numbers of Jewish youth embraced the nonreligious culture of the new Soviet Union, and the struggles of families like the Wengeroffs lost their meaning. But Wengeroff, as she herself wrote, "was in a position to see the transformation which European education wrought on Jewish family life."[96] *Memoirs of a Grandmother* remains the only Russian-Jewish work of this period written by a woman.

REMEMBERING THE MAID OF LUDMIR

Ephraim Taubenhaus, a younger contemporary of Hannah Rachel Werbermacher who knew her in Jerusalem when he was still a child, reported that she conducted herself as a "Polish rebbe" and had her own following. He wrote:

"[She was] a short woman, her hair sprinkled with gray, but her face radiated a holy beauty. Many of the important people [living in] Jerusalem know of her. . . . In the morning, she walked to the Western Wall, dressed like an Arab woman, her hands holding her tallit and tefillin and old women and men walked after her, all of whom gathered to ask for her blessing."[93]

According to this same report, the Maid of Ludmir collected prayer petitions from her followers and once a month on Rosh Hodesh (the New Moon), brought them to Rachel's Tomb and prayed on their behalf.[94]

WERBERMACHER, HANNAH RACHEL OF LUDMIR, REBBE
(19th century)

Hannah Rachel Werbermacher, an only child, was born in 1815 in the town of Ludmir (Poland). Anxious to learn, her pursuit of knowledge led her to the study of Midrash, Aggadah, halakhic works, and ultimately, to Kabbalah.

Werbermacher's mother died young, and from that time, Hannah Rachel became consistently more depressed and isolated, gradually withdrawing from the world. One day, at her mother's grave, she fell into unconsciousness and had a mystical experience that changed her life. When she awoke, she declared that she had "been to Heaven at a sitting of the highest court and there they gave me a new and sublime

FIG. 23. Hannah Rachel Werbermacher has captured the attention of twentieth- and twenty-first-century writers, artists, and performers. Actress Rachel Botchan, played the role of Hannah Rachel in the 1996 production of *The Maid of Ludmir* by Miriam Hoffman. (Courtesy of the Folksbiene Yiddish Theater, New York, NY)

soul."[97] From that time, Hannah Rachel Werbermacher wore tzitzit, prayed with tallit and tefillin and spent her days studying. An early betrothal was broken off, and Werbermacher did not marry until she was forty years old. For this reason she came to be known as the Maid of Ludmir.

When her father died, Werbermacher used her inheritance to build her own synagogue, called *die Grüne Schule* (the green synagogue) where people congregated regularly to hear her preach sermons on the Sabbath from an adjacent apartment.[98] Rabbis and scholars from other towns made pilgrimages to

---

A WILL FROM A "CAREFUL MOTHER"

Frumet Wolf's will is a rare example of an ethical will written by a woman. The document includes her instructions for the distribution of her personal wealth. Following this, she wrote:

". . . it is unjust and unreasonable to part from one's dear ones without having made a last will. . . . But do not bear a grudge against a careful mother who could not content herself until she had secured the ultimate execution of her will."

This "careful mother" instructs her grown children to be virtuous and fear God and to live together in peace. She advises:

"You must hold together ever more closely and firmly. You need such closeness, and you will need it more than ever, once the sad event occurs—so much sadder for you than for me—your mother's being torn from you, and thus, as it were, the center disappearing from the circle.

Farewell, and accept the blessing of your always faithful mother, Fani Wolf."[99]

---

hear her wisdom.[100] Some say she was somewhat of a recluse who rarely emerged to see her followers, while other accounts report that she traveled to nearby communities, where she preached to the women.[101]

After many years, Hannah Rachel Werbermacher and her followers were threatened with excommunication by Ludmir's rabbis. To resolve the conflict, R. Mordecai of Chernobyl came and tried to persuade her to marry. "The argument was stormy," but finally Werbermacher agreed "to be married according to the way of a Jewish maiden, and to maintain a kosher and upright home in Israel."[102] Although this first marriage lasted only a few days, and a second was equally disastrous, the influence of the "Maid" waned. She could no longer focus all her attention on prayer and communion with God. Werbermacher's two marriages were rumored never to have been consummated, and her following dropped off.

Because of the continued conflict about her activities in Ludmir, she left Poland and settled in Jerusalem. There she concentrated on kabbalistic studies and, together with a male kabbalist, became involved in mystical plans to help speed the coming of the Messiah.[103] She left no writings of her own and made no significant impact on the Hasidic world. She died in Jerusalem in 1892 or 1895.

WOLF, FRUMET BEILIN OF EISENSTADT, REBEL AND CONCERNED MOTHER
(late 18th–19th century)

Frumet, or Fani, Wolf was born in the late 1700s into the Beilin family of Eisenstadt, Hungary, and was well known and well thought of in her town. One small introductory passage in a collection of writings and letters gives us a frustratingly inadequate glimpse of a pamphlet written by her, but no source is cited.[104] According to this report, Frumet Wolf was a young wife when she composed a political tract, allegedly of a controversial nature, and published it anonymously.

There is no hint of the subject matter, but it was said to have been "full of acid invectives against the communal heads of Eisenstadt."[105] The result was a rabbinical ban issued against the anonymous writer and its distributors, a fact that suggests she had allies in this endeavor.

Not content to let the issue die, Frumet Wolf admitted her authorship of the controversial material and spent several years trying to have the ban lifted and the item removed from the minutes of the communal records. Wolf's success resulted in the absence of any tangible information about the event. The only piece of writing available from this determined woman is her will, written in 1829, twenty years before her death.

THE WORLD OF JEWISH WOMEN

ECONOMIC ACTIVITIES

During the early modern period, most Jewish wives still worked alongside their husbands as shopkeepers or in small businesses. Some organized, as did the women peddlers in Kazimierz near Krakow.[106] In Bialystok, **Puah Rakowski**'s grandmother ran a flour mill and was known as a clever businesswoman.[107] The grandmother of Ḥanan Wengeroff (husband of **Pauline Wengeroff**) ran an inn and worked as a midwife in Minsk.[108]

Unmarried Jewish girls remained at home, helping with household chores or working in a family business. Poorer young women worked as seamstresses or dressmakers, or they might simply have tended younger children until a marriage was arranged for them.

Although women continued working well into the 1800s, managing a household and caring for children was becoming more of a primary activity. As the nineteenth century neared its end, the Jewish middle class was embracing the new standard: Women remained at home and men supported them. This was common in the West, but evidence does suggest that Jewish women in central Europe were increasingly home-centered and remained at home perhaps even more than their Christian counterparts.[109] **Henriette Lemos Herz** did not work until her husband's sudden death in 1803. Ḥanan, husband of Pauline Wengeroff, considering himself a modern, middle-class person, refused to allow his wife to work even though he had suffered serious business reversals and lost her entire dowry.

Teachers, Writers, and Social Workers

Educated women such as **Grace Aguilar** might become teachers or make a living writing. **Rachel Morpurgo** was a prolific writer but earned little or no money for her efforts. With no source of income or commercial experience, Henriette Herz first opened her home to board young students and working girls but soon used her skills as a linguist, translating and teaching languages.

Puah Rakowski fought against her husband to be allowed to earn an independent living. She finally divorced him. After working briefly as a milliner, she became a professional educator.

A WARNING ABOUT WOMEN

Despite what seemed like increased emancipation for women throughout this period, many men still echoed the ideas adhered to by rabbis as far back as ancient times. One popular writer warned:

"The women of Israel and their daughters sit and sell all kinds of silk and linen and everyone who comes to buy wants to taste the taste of a virgin and possess her. . . . Commerce was the midwife of female promiscuity."[110]

Later in the nineteenth century, many middle-class women were involved in charity work but did not expect money for their efforts. **Johanna Schwabe Goldschmidt** was one of the few exceptions. She attained sufficient professional status to establish a seminary for the training of kindergarten teachers. **Lina Bauer Morgenstern**, searching for a way to earn money when her husband met with financial difficulties, published a handbook promoting the Froebel kindergarten movement and wrote several children's books. In the 1870s, she earned money by organizing and running soup kitchens under the auspices of the Prussian government.

Midwives

One of the necessary and ever-present occupations for women was midwifery, and women continued to work as independent midwives despite the growing interest of university-trained male doctors in this field. Female obstetrical practitioners could be found in many of the smaller towns and villages, especially in the Russian Pale of Settlement. Most were formally trained in the schools for midwives that had been established from 1757. Upon graduation, they were called *feldshers* or *feldsher*-midwives and were often highly respected members of the community.[111]

EDUCATION

The Education of Girls

With the beginning of the Enlightenment movement there are signs of a marked improvement in the education of girls, especially in western Europe. As always, upper-class women and women from learned families had a distinct advantage both in secular and

---

BEILA OF THE BLESSED HANDS

The description of this midwife reveals the esteem in which the community held her.

"[Beila was] respected as the 'mother' of the majority of the town's children. She was always busy and whenever attending a delivery, had to prepare with her own hands all the necessary requirements; in many cases she had not been paid for her work at the birth of the previous child, but nevertheless would carry on quietly and efficiently. She continued to work until old age . . . when she died . . . all the mothers lit candles at her deathbed and around her house. Thus, there were thousands of candles, a sight that no one would soon forget."[112]

FIG. 24. Rachel Luzzatto Morpurgo was educated equally with her brother and male cousins.

Hebrew subjects. Rachel Luzzatto Morpurgo was an exceptional example of a woman steeped in all aspects of Judaism, certainly because she came from a long line of respected Italian-Jewish scholars. In England, **Judith Cohen Montefiore** and her sister Hannah Cohen Rothschild were educated with private tutors. Although their Jewish education was not on the same level as Morpurgo's, they received general instruction in the humanities, studying English litera-ture, music, and singing as well as languages, including Hebrew. Grace Aguilar also learned Hebrew and Jewish religion, subjects not routinely taught to women in central and eastern Europe.

In Germany, many enlightened Jews were anxious to enter the modern world and take advantage of some of the rewards offered by governments, but the obligation to educate sons in Jewish Law was not always easily relin-quished. Often, successful families that wanted to assimilate would compromise. Since girls were neither required nor expected to learn Hebrew or participate in synagogue ritual, daughters were sent to the new secular schools where they were educated in arts and languages. Sons were given a Jewish education and apprenticed in business.

Small numbers of women in Germany, especially among the middle classes, did learn some Hebrew, but for the most part, the Jewish education they received was grossly inadequate. Many were literate only in Yiddish and were offered "a mixture of morals, religion, reading and writing,"[113] while their secular education in state-sponsored schools taught them that Jews were backward and deficient in moral values. This left women little incentive to participate in any aspect of Jewish life. When enlightened Jews rejected the traditional Yiddish literature written for women, few alternatives were available for them within Judaism.

IDEAS ON EDUCATING GIRLS

Even when education for girls had become more accepted, many parents objected to educating their daughters in Hebrew and Jewish studies. As Puah Rakowski wrote in her memoirs:

"The more observant parents held to the rule that 'he who teaches his daughter Torah is like teaching her obscenity.' As for the more progressive, they were eager to teach their daughters foreign languages, but certainly not Hebrew. Jewish fathers argued that the sacred tongue was for boys."[114]

The salon Jewesses were all well educated in secular studies but with little Jewish education. Moses Mendelssohn broke with tradition enough to permit his daughter **Dorothea Mendelssohn (Schlegel)** to attend his morning study sessions together with his male students, but it was her brother Joseph who was given lessons in Talmud, Hebrew language, and Bible.[115] **Rahel Levin Varnhagen** pursued her own course of study. She learned French and mathematics and frequently attended cultural events but never received a formal education. In fact, German universities did not open up to women until 1908.[116]

By the mid-1800s, a few well-educated German-Jewish women were writing books directed to a nondenominational audience of women. Lina Morgenstern was the only one among these women writers who had any significant Hebrew education, but she nevertheless chose to concentrate on social activism. In Berlin, she devoted her efforts to secular education for all women and fought for women's right to study medicine. Both Morgenstern's and Johanna Goldschmidt's books focused on the problems of secular education.

Henriette Benas Goldschmidt devoted her energies to providing higher education for young women and attempted to establish credit-granting institutions for working women.[117] **Jeanette Schwerin** worked in a program that sponsored the use of reading rooms and libraries for all classes of people. Yet none of these women ever developed schools to teach Judaism to Jewish girls as Puah Rakowski did in Poland.

Puah Rakowski believed that religious, cultural, and ethical education would reduce the loss of Jewish women to assimilation.[118] Although Rakowski's ideas on Jewish education for girls were not always accepted, equal secular education did slowly spread in eastern Europe. This sometimes led to assimilation and conversion for the Jews in Russia, Poland, Lithuania, and the Ukraine just as it had in Germany. But Jews in the East actively promoted Hebrew and Yiddish literature as well. Philosophies and movements such as Cultural Judaism, Jewish Socialism, and Zionism were all introduced in eastern Europe, and these ideas opened up opportunities for women as well as men. In the mid- to late-1800s, a few women became writers for the burgeoning Russian-Jewish press or wrote separate volumes either in Hebrew, Yiddish, or Russian for a growing audience of Jews. **Miriam Markel-Mosessohn** wrote poetry in Hebrew. In 1869 Maria Saker published an article about Jews living on the western border of Russia.[119] It was the first article about Jews to appear in the Russian language.

FAMILY LIFE

As long as the Jewish community was the all-embracing framework for Jewish life, the home was less vital. Children attended Jewish schools, marital problems and divorces were handled in Jewish courts, and male officials representing the community judged women's behavior. Once individual emancipation was a real option, however, communal authority gradually eroded, even in the smaller Jewish *shtetls* of Poland and Russia. Community officials, no longer possessing real power, could only watch as growing numbers of Jews defected and chose to turn their backs on the Jewish community.

LYDIA COHEN'S CONCERNS FOR HER CHILDREN

Like many English-Jewish women in the nineteenth century, Judith Montefiore's mother, Lydia Cohen, was concerned with her daughters' Jewish identity and with preventing them from intermarrying. In 1819, she wrote in her will:

"I beg and pray for you not to forget that you are Jews and keep your religion and always have in your memory your Father in Heaven and take example from him."[120]

With communal authority on the decline, the home now became the center of Jewish identity, and the woman in that home gained a more significant role. While men went into the secular world to earn a living, women presided over homes that were sometimes a last bastion of Jewish tradition.

Betrothal and Marriage

Despite Enlightenment ideas, traditional betrothals and marriages remained common in most of the Jewish communities of Europe throughout the eighteenth century. Although assimilation and intermarriage threatened the old customs, and enlightened, secular Jews were more likely to abandon the tradition, change was slow. It began in the West and moved eastward.

In England, courtship and the agreement of both partners gradually replaced arranged marriages. Germany maintained the old traditions awhile longer but could not prevent change indefinitely. Both Dorothea Mendelssohn (Schlegel) and Henriette Lemos (Herz) married much older men, chosen by their fathers, but Rahel Levin (Varnhagen), more of a rebel, refused a proposed match arranged by her family while she was still in her teens. She remained unmarried for many years. When she did marry, her husband was a man of her own choosing, a Christian literary critic and diplomat, much younger than she.[121] As did all the women who married Christian men, Rahel converted. There was no civil marriage in Germany at that time.

A WIFE'S PRAYER

An Alsatian prayer book, written in the mid–nineteenth century, included a prayer to be recited by a wife. It echoed the same sentiments as earlier rules, assuming that the husband's happiness was the responsibility of the female partner.

"Oh my God, enlighten me that I may judge myself with severity; perhaps my husband's conduct is the result of my faults and my defects . . .

Teach me to read his soul, to divine his thoughts, to anticipate his desires, to please him, and to overcome his indifference through my love, his anger through my gentleness. . . . Keep me, my God from every feeling of hatred . . . and if my husband is inaccessible to pity . . . make my heart never change in his regard."[122]

In Trieste, Rachel Luzzatto (Morpurgo) also stood up to her parents, refusing to marry a man they had chosen for her. She had already decided on Jacob Morpurgo, a middle-class Austrian-Jewish merchant. Her parents preferred a wealthy and scholarly husband for their only daughter, one of Italian rather than Austrian descent. When Rachel was twenty-nine years old, the Luzzattos finally and reluctantly consented to her marriage with Jacob.[123]

In eastern Europe, arranged marriages were adhered to well past the mid–nineteenth century. Both Puah Rakowski and Pauline Wengeroff accepted mates chosen by their parents, although Wengeroff was permitted to see her future husband before the wedding took place—a sign of modernity. At the age of sixteen, **Ernestine Rose** of Poland (see chapter 9) defied her father's authority to arrange her marriage, even taking her plea to the secular courts. She won her case, left Poland and her father for the West, and married a Christian.

By 1800, the median age of marriage for girls in western and central Europe was twenty or more, considerably higher than it had been in the Middle Ages,[124] although some were still married younger. Henriette Lemos Herz was fifteen when she became a wife.

Once married, the young bride and her husband might still maintain the tradition of boarding with parents or other family members for a few years. This custom, called *kest*, gave the husband a chance to complete his studies if necessary, and the wife gained more training in household management, usually in her mother-in-law's home.

While many young women now lived in an environment that allowed them more choice of education and more opportunity to participate in activities outside the home, their roles as wives remained similar to that of their grandmothers and great-grand-mothers. Pauline Wengeroff was expected to obey her husband. In her case, she did obey, even though it meant abandoning Jewish tradition. Puah Rakowski was more assertive and coerced her husband into agreeing to allow her to study midwifery. She never practiced, but used it as a means to financial independence. The couple later divorced. But Rakowski was a maverick. The ten rules for a Jewish wife, written in Yiddish in 1620 by Isaac ben Eliakim of Posen (see chapter 6), remained a familiar standard even among the more educated and were repeated in more modern versions.

Children

By the late 1700s, caring for children and educating them had become a higher priority for both the Christian and Jewish population of Europe. This was reflected in the increasing number of state-run schools that all children, including Jews, were expected to attend. Jewish girls and boys were rou-tinely sent to both secular schools and *heders* (although lessons were different for girls and boys). The kindergarten movement became popular in the nineteenth century and was supported by many Jewish women.

More and more, mothers were expected to be at home, to care for their children and give them a moral education. **Frumet Wolf** acknowl-edged the importance of her own role as mother in her ethical will, pointing out that her children would need to be close after her death when "the center [disappeared] from the circle." Jeanette Schwerin was "housebound" because

her children were sickly and she did not enter the larger world until they were grown. By contrast, when Dorothea Mendelssohn Veit Schlegel ran off with another man and left her husband and children, her behavior was considered disgraceful and even her friends turned their backs on her.

Divorce

Divorce was accepted as an unfortu-nate event but was allowed by the Jewish community and always remained an option for men. A woman could not sue for divorce, but she could appeal to the Jewish court to force her husband to grant a divorce if the court felt she had legitimate grounds. Jewish Law had not changed in this regard since the early Middle Ages. By the nineteenth century, what had changed was the Jewish community.

The weakening of the Jewish com-munity worked both in favor of women and against them. Women, rarely financially independent, were often forced by circumstances to remain in an unhappy marriage. For those who could leave, it became easi-er than ever to go outside the commu-nity for a divorce with or without a husband's consent. But women who still wanted to adhere to tradition and receive a legal Jewish divorce (*get*) sometimes faced even more obstacles than before. If the husband no longer concerned himself with Jewish tradi-tion, the Jewish court had no real power to coerce him into granting the divorce. If he chose, he could continu-ally refuse to free his wife, keeping her in the state of an *agunah*, an abandoned wife who could never remarry. Puah Rakowski managed to force her hus-band to divorce her by threatening to convert, but such tactics were certainly not common. If a husband stubbornly refused to grant his wife a divorce, the Jewish community, deprived of its authority in this new age of emancipation, was helpless.

Women's Sexuality

Judaism viewed women first and foremost as sexual creatures, meant to be wives and mothers, enabling men to fulfill the commandment to be fruitful and multiply. Accordingly, girls were expected to remain virgins until marriage and to be faithful to husbands after marriage. Although in Christianity women who remained virgins could overcome the weakness and disability believed to be inherent in their sex and concentrate on a spiritual or scholarly life, there was no model in Jewish tradition for such an option. This lack of choice for women persisted and is evident in the life of **Hannah Rachel Werbermacher** (the Maid of Ludmir). Werbermacher resisted marriage until she was forty years old and was finally coerced to marry by rabbis who threatened her and her followers with excommunication. Once married, her obligation was toward her husband; she lost her aura of spirituality and her following declined. Only after rejecting two husbands and leaving for Jerusalem was she able to regain some of her previous standing as a religious leader.

Promiscuity and prostitution represented another extreme unacceptable in Judaism. Although there were always a few prostitutes who were recognized in the Jewish community, toward the end of the nineteenth century, mass immigration and family dislocation greatly increased their number. In western Europe and North America this problem was called "white slavery." Jewish women such as Bertha Pappenheim of Germany (1859–1936), dismayed by the neglect of this issue, organized in order to rescue women and their children from a life of prostitution.[125]

LEGAL RIGHTS

With Enlightenment came emancipation and the recognition of Jews as individual citizens. Subject to the same laws as Christians, and finding new opportunities in the secular world, many Jews set aside Jewish Law and embraced the laws of the countries in which they lived. Under these new laws, women may have felt freer to engage in activities outside the realm of family, but legally, their rights were not improved, especially once they married.

Most European nations had law codes similar to the English common law, which held that a married woman was a *femme couverte*. This meant that legally, her husband was responsible for her debts and represented her in court. He owned everything that was hers, including her wages and the property she inherited. This legal disability was not much different than it was under Jewish Law, but here again, as in the case of divorce, it was the community that had changed. Until the 1700s, Jews, whether men or women, had few rights and looked to the Jewish *kehillah* (community) and the Jewish courts for legal recourse. As emancipation spread, however, male Jews obtained additional rights from the secular community while their female counterparts were left behind.

As governments changed and became more democratic, especially after the 1848 revolutions in central

Europe, some Jewish men obtained the right to vote and became involved in secular government. Most European countries did not grant women the right to vote until well into the twentieth century. Nor did Jewish women fight for that right. Although many became active in social issues and had public careers, they did not publicly advocate women's suffrage. Lina Morgenstern, Jeanette Schwerin and Bertha Pappenheim firmly believed that women should remain at home and care for husbands and children. Henriette Benas Goldschmidt insisted that it was premature, if not wholly unnecessary for women to have political rights.[126]

PUBLIC POWER

During the 1800s we see more evidence of women's influence in the public sphere. Besides the traditional route of working behind the scenes to persuade husbands and fathers, women openly attempted and often succeeded in influencing public policy, especially in the areas of education and help for children and the poor. Women organized orphan asylums, established homes for underprivileged women, ran soup kitchens, and wrote books advocating a variety of programs and outlining plans for public institutions. In a few instances, their advocacy may have led to trouble, as it did for **Frumet Wolf**. In most cases their work was valued and often made a small but important impact within their own circles.

While women active in social work had considerable influence, they still had little public power. Not permitted to run for office or organize women to vote, they did not take on political roles; nor did they advocate them for other women. The situation was simi-

---

ASSERTIVE JEWISH WOMEN

Both Moses Montefiore and his brother-in-law Nathan Rothschild were susceptible to pressure from their wives, Judith and Hannah, especially on the subject of the political rights of Jews. In reporting a discussion on "liberty for the Jews" in his diary, Moses Montefiore wrote:

"He [Nathan] said he would shortly go to the Lord Chancellor and consult him on the matter. Hannah said if he did not, she would. The spirit manifested here by Mrs. Rothschild, and the brief but impressive language that she used, reminded me most strikingly of her sister, Mrs. Montefiore."[127]

---

lar for those women active in Jewish life as well. Many of these women, like their counterparts in the past or in North America, were unmarried or were older women whose children were grown and who were widowed. Grace Aguilar never married. **Sarah Frankel** acted as a rebbe in her town only after her husband died. Puah Rakowski became a successful educator after she divorced her husband and moved away.

RELIGIOUS PARTICIPATION

Because religion was becoming more voluntary in the age of Enlightenment, women's participation in it varied depending on where a woman lived, the family she was born into, the family she married into, and for the first time, her own inclinations. Women who followed tradition still had little involvement in the religious life of the community. No matter what her level of **education**, a woman was still excluded from most rituals except those specifically intended for her: lighting candles, separating the dough when baking *ḥallah*, and attendance at the ritual bath (*mikveh*). But by the nineteenth century, many of these customs had lapsed, leaving women with even fewer ways to express their Judaism.

Except for a scattering of Reform synagogues in a few German cities, women who came to pray were relegated to the women's section. While there might have been a prayer leader there to help her follow the liturgy, the inattention of the women present at the service was, by this time, notorious.[128]

The Call of Spirituality

In opposition to the rote ritual to which many Jews clung and which largely excluded women, and also to

---

WOMEN IN THE FRANKIST
MOVEMENT

Just as the early Christians honored women believers and allowed them an important place in Church hierarchy, so Jacob Frank tried to honor women. Emulating the apostles of early Christianity, he appointed twelve brothers and twelve sisters to his court[129] and demanded that his followers worship his wife, Hannah, as the *gevirah* (the lady). In 1770, when Hannah died, that honor was transferred to their daughter, Eva.

---

disprove the accusation that Judaism was mere superstition and devoid of spirituality, many women searched for a new kind of religious feeling. Grace Aguilar called it the "religion of the heart" and wrote: "If we are reawakening to its [spirituality's] sublime call, it is not from association with them [i.e., Christians]."[130] It was Jewish captivity and persecution, she claimed, that distorted the purity of Jewish life. In lands such as England or America, Jews were now "free to become mentally and spiritually elevated."[131]

Judith Montefiore was well aware of such ideas. She came from an observant English home and attended services regularly in the Great Synagogue of London. After her marriage and especially after she began traveling extensively, she must have participated less in the regular rituals of Judaism, but maintained strong ties to the broader ideals of the religion as she had learned them. Her essential religious feeling clearly overrode the details of observance, for the Montefiores ate non-kosher meat at the seaside inn where they spent their honeymoon. The young Mrs. Montefiore reported the menu of "soles and peas and beefsteaks and potatoes" without comment.[132]

In central Europe, the search for spirituality took different forms. Some German-Jewish women either ignored religious feelings or found spiritual fulfillment in community activisim, specifically in areas of social work, helping the poor and disadvantaged. Others found a new kind of home-centered Judaism.

Home-Centered Judaism

Jewish home life flourished everywhere in Europe, becoming stronger as

Jewish community life declined. The woman who ran such a home often became the backbone of the Jewish life of her family. From the 1800s on, we begin to see the Jewish home and the Jewish mother praised and sentimentalized as the last and most important bastion of Judaism. The writers of women's *tkhines* wrote prayers associated with home life and the rituals that women were required to perform. Writers like **Shifrah Segal,** following earlier women writers of *tkhines* such as **Sarah bat Tovim** and **Leah Horowitz** (see chapter 6), emphasized the importance of women's home rituals and helped enhance women's spirituality through this medium. "The informal transmission of religious feelings and identification through observance in the home was women's domain," said historian Marion Kaplan,[133] and often women fought hard to maintain it. One example of such a woman was Pauline Wengeroff, whose memories are "the epic tale of Jewish modernity as it emerged in eastern Europe."[134]

Wengeroff lost her battle, and her children converted. However, many eastern European women sought and found spiritual fulfillment in areas both inside and outside the home. A few continued in kabbalistic, mystical circles, combining an inner spirituality with involvement in women's prayers both inside and outside of traditional synagogues. Others fulfilled their spiritual needs in the growing Hasidic movement.

Women in Hasidic Circles

As Hasidism spread, it gradually changed, placing more emphasis on classical texts. However, a person's emotional response to God remained a crucial component for a Hasidic leader. As long as a group of people believed that a particular person, whether through wisdom, righteousness, or piety, could intervene with God on their behalf, that person acquired a reputation for holiness. Occasionally that person was a woman.

Most women in Hasidic circles who were considered holy were the wives, daughters, or mothers of *tzaddikim*. Usually it was these women who were the best educated. Women's names are scattered throughout Hasidic literature, sometimes even with a few details about their accomplishments. Many of them possessed an aura of spirituality that attracted other women to them and occasionally other men as well. **Perele bat Yisrael** had a large following who supported her with money. The advice of **Hannah Ḥava Twersky** was sought by many women, and even her father claimed she was endowed with the holy spirit.[135] R. Shneur Zalman's wife, Shterna, was depicted as an outspoken woman who defended her own knowledge of spirituality against her son, Dov Ber, proclaiming: "I know more about spirituality than you . . . and can pray on behalf of a *hasid* better than you."[136] A few other women who possessed a special spirituality were named in connection with male relatives. Rachel, daughter of R. Avraham Joshua Heschel of Opatow, "had a holy spark," and many Hasidim came to receive the blessings of Merish, daughter of R. Elimelekh of Lizhansk, who was known as a scholar.[137]

Despite this handful of women in the inner circle of Hasidism, however, ordinary women did not fare as well. By the end of the eighteenth century, the Hasidic courts had become magnets for the male followers of the movement. Hasidim made pilgrimages to these courts to see the great *tzaddikim* in person and learn from their example; they sat at the *tzaddik's* table, heard his teachings, and benefited from his advice. For the most part, the Hasidic court was an all-male world, and men might spend weeks or even months there, away from family, leaving their wives and children alone for the Sabbath and holidays.[138]

Women did occasionally come to these courts, usually with special requests for the rebbe. Although the Baal Shem Tov was said to believe that the prayers of women were especially meaningful to God, only some of the *tzaddikim* welcomed them and they were never included as disciples along with the men.[139] For the most part, women came requesting advice or to plead with the rebbe to intervene with God on their behalf. They would take their written appeal or prayer petition *(kvitlekh)*, together with a small sum for a *pidyon* (redemption money) to offer the *tzaddik*, who might give them an amulet or promise to pray for them. Some *tzaddikim* accepted these requests, while others refused to see women at all. Sometimes they would be directed to the wife, sister, or daughter of the *tzaddik*, who might have her own sphere of influence at the court and be considered a holy or righteous woman.

Almost all the women who were active in rabbinical courts benefited by association with notable men. The only woman who became independently famous in the Hasidic movement, and in later years maintained a court of her own, was Hannah Rachel Werbermacher.[140]

The Beginnings of Reform

The Reform movement was officially established in Hamburg, Germany, in 1818. Their original goal was to make Judaism more relevant to modern life, and much of their inspiration for change came from the Christian society around them. They changed the aesthetics of the service and allowed women and men to sit together. By the mid–nineteenth century a small number of Reform synagogues could be found outside of Germany in England, France, Hungary, and the United States,[141] but women's position in Judaism was not the focus of their attempts at modernization.

German women who had contact with the developing Reform philosophy in its early years were never active in the movement, although it might have had some impact on their personal lives. Johanna Schwabe Goldschmidt, whose father was a founder of the original Reform temple in Hamburg, was part of the first confirmation class for Jewish boys and girls. Although her adult activities concentrated on areas outside religion, her first book was a series of letters between a Christian and a Jewish woman and concentrated on problems of Jewish conversion and assimilation. Lina Bauer Morgenstern received her religious education from the well-known liberal rabbi Abraham Geiger but followed the already familiar path to social activisim through involvement in charitable causes and education.

As the nineteenth century came to a close, the Reform movement became stronger and more widespread and many women found in it the opportunity to develop their own spiritual feelings. Lily (Lilian Helen) Montagu (1873–1963), seeking a more meaningful "religion of the heart," first shared her ideas with the young, working-class Jewish women whom she taught. She went on to found Liberal Judaism in England together with Claude Montefiore.[142]

Conversion

Conversion to various forms of Christianity was a phenomenon that could be found everywhere in Europe and the Americas during the Enlightenment period. Women and men, finding Judaism irrelevant, either drifted away from their own traditions and assimilated, or converted for economic or social reasons. Conversion often freed them from the legal and social disabilities inflicted on Jews throughout Europe.

Most educated Jewish women who converted did so in order to marry Christians, to get a better education, or to satisfy their spiritual needs. Disraeli's father had his children bap-

tized so they could advance in politics and society,[143] and Moses Mendelssohn's grandchildren were baptized for the same reason. Pauline Wengeroff's sons converted in order to be accepted into Russian universities. The upper-middle-class Jewish women of Germany often sought spirituality in other religions, as did Henriette Lemos Herz, Rahel Levin Varnhagen, and the Mendelssohns' younger daughter, Henriette.

Historians can only surmise whether or not these women found fulfillment in their new religions. Rahel Varnhagen, in spite of her conversion, could never forget her Jewish identity and agonized over society's rejection of Jews. She was still struggling with those contradictions when she died in 1833. Her deathbed statement was reported to be: "My Jewish birth which I long considered a stigma, a sore disgrace, has now become a precious inheritance of which nothing on earth can deprive me."[144]

CHAPTER 9

Jewish Women in the New World:

From the First Settlement until 1900

OVERVIEW

In 1492, a sailor from Genoa named Christopher Columbus set sail for "The Indies"[1] and discovered a new world. Shortly after, Jews began arriving. Most were Sephardim who had originated in Spain and Portugal, where they had lived as Christians but secretly practiced Judaism. Others came via Amsterdam, a city that had become a haven for Spanish-Jewish exiles in the sixteenth century. Columbus left Spain on the last day that Jews were allowed to live there. Included among his crew were many *conversos*,[2] and it is probable that other participants in the Spanish and Portuguese exploration of the Americas were New Christians, probably crypto-Jews (Marranos) as well.[3]

Not long after Christopher Columbus's discovery of the New World, Spain claimed the lands that are now the southwestern United States, Mexico, Central America, the Caribbean Islands, and all of South America except for Brazil, an area controlled by Portugal. Because the main purpose of developing these new territories was trade and commerce, it is not surprising that the first Jews to arrive in the Western Hemisphere were merchants and traders. Records kept by the Spanish Inquisition give further evidence of early Jewish settlement in the lands of New Spain.

The Jews of New Spain

From 1541 Judaism was practiced openly in New Spain, although there was no official Jewish community. Then in 1571, the Church inaugurated the Inquisition in the New World as well. Between 1589 and 1605, the officials of the Inquisition waged a relentless war against "judaizers," the New Christians and their descendants suspected of secretly following Jewish traditions.[4]

Judaizing behavior might be deduced from the most basic activities, such as wearing a clean shirt or refusing to light a fire or work on the Sabbath, abstaining from food or drink on the Day of Atonement, blessing a cup of wine before drinking, washing the hands before eating, and especially, refusing to eat pork. In a repetition of the horrors perpetrated in Europe (see chapters 4–6), those who were convicted of the crime of judaizing were burned at the stake at public events called autos-de-fé (acts of faith). One auto-da-fé occurred in 1596, and among its victims were the women from the **de Carvajal** family.

The Inquisition remained active throughout the seventeenth century, not only in Mexico, but in parts of South America as well. Nevertheless, New Christians continued to be attracted to these territories, partly because the familiar culture and language of Spain and Portugal had preceded them. The economic and social opportunities in the new lands were also a significant inducement to emigrate. In Peru, Bolivia, and Mexico some were involved in silver mining. In Argentina and Chile individual Jews became farmers or merchants. Most of these crypto-Jews assimilated completely, but the long hand of the Church continued to search for them. When found, they were convicted and punished in a variety of ways. Records show that forty-six women were condemned to work as charwomen for five years as penance for the crime of judaizing.[5]

By 1700, however, there was no one in all of New Spain who was openly practicing Judaism. Some, fleeing north across the Rio Grande River to less inhabited lands far from the reach of the Church, managed to evade the Inquisition. They maintained some of their crypto-Jewish practices but, for the most part, forgot their origins.

The open practice of Judaism did not appear in Mexico until the mid-1800s, some twenty-five years after Mexican independence. The first organized congregations developed in 1885.

The Jews of Brazil

Jews initially came to Brazil from the Netherlands. They were part of a group of merchants, both Christian and Jewish, who had founded the Dutch West India Company. In 1630, when the Dutch conquered a large part of Brazil including Recife (originally a Portuguese penal colony), there was relative tolerance in that territory and Jews tentatively began to practice their religion.[6] In 1637 a small group of Brazilian merchants, including nine with Jewish or Marrano names, signed a petition requesting freedom to trade. From that year, there is evidence that Jewish refugees began to arrive from Hungary, Poland, Turkey, and Germany, as well as Spain, Portugal, and Holland.

The years from 1637 to 1654 were a period of prosperity for the Jews and crypto-Jews of Brazil. Some became owners of sugar plantations. They also traded in precious and semi-precious stones. But then, the more tolerant Dutch lost control of Recife. The land again reverted to the Portuguese, and the Inquisition was reestablished.

The Jews Arrive in North America

In September 1654, twenty-three Jewish refugees from Recife, intending to return to Europe, arrived in New Amsterdam after a long and perilous sea voyage. During a storm, pirates captured their ship and robbed them of all their valuables. A French vessel rescued the Jews and, with the expectation of a reward, agreed to take them back to Amsterdam. When the captain realized they were penniless, he put the small band ashore in New Amsterdam.[7] Although the group met with initial hostility from the Dutch colonial governor, Peter Stuyvesant,[8] this turned out to be one of the most fortuitous landings in Jewish history.

In 1729, a synagogue was erected on Mill Lane in lower Manhattan. By that time, New Amsterdam had become New York and was under the control of the English. Congregation *Shearith Israel* was the first synagogue in the colonies, but within a short time, other congregations were established in Newport, Rhode Island; Philadelphia, Pennsylvania; and Charleston, South Carolina. In 1776, when the American Revolution began, 2,500 Jews were living openly and freely in the thirteen colonies.[9] They were free not only from anti-Jewish rulings, but also from the traditional Jewish communal structure.

In Europe and the Middle East, a Jewish legal and religious framework remained, even though by the 1700s it had been considerably weakened.

THE FIRST JEWS TO SETTLE IN NORTH AMERICA

The twenty-three refugees who landed on the shores of New Amsterdam in 1654 included four married couples, two women who were probably widows, and thirteen younger people. The heads of the families were Asser Levy, Abraham Israel De Piza, David Israel Faro, and Mose Lumbroso. The two women listed separately were Judith Mercado (or De Mercado) and Ricke (or Rachel) Nuñes. They were the first known Jews to settle in what would later become the United States of America.[10] From these small beginnings, a Jewish community was built.

There were a large number of Jewish scholars to explain the law, and Jewish officials continued to exercise considerable power over parts of the Jewish population. In eastern Europe, Jews were still judged in Jewish courts, according to Jewish law. By contrast, in the New World, there was a total absence of Jewish communal authority. Without these controls, Jews were free to do as they wished. They paid their taxes as individuals and dealt with the secular courts. Jewish women were also able to act more freely, and because society was expanding into new areas, they had the opportunity to fill roles not customarily open to them.

Very little information about the lives of ordinary women has been documented for the first century of Jewish settlement. We can assume that Jewish women's physical lives paralleled those of Christian women who lived in the colonies of North America. They paid the taxes imposed by the British and sent their children to the same schools, when there were schools available. Although many Jewish women crossed the line and were assimilated out of the Jewish community, most maintained a traditional life as best they could and formed the backbone of Jewish life in North America.

Among the Jewish patriots we know about are Ḥaym Salomon, who helped supply the Continental army during the American Revolution, and David Franks and Philip Minis, who actively worked for the cause of revolution. But several Jewish women of the period left a legacy as well. They included **Abigail Franks, Abigail Minis, Esther Etting Hays,** and a handful of others.

With the Revolution over, the thirteen colonies began the struggle to become a viable nation. Because of the freedom experienced by the early Jewish settlers, more were encouraged to come, and by 1800 there were Jewish communities in many cities and towns throughout the original colonies. This was very different from the early Jewish experience in other parts of North America such as Mexico (see above) or eastern Canada.

The first Jew to appear in Canada, then called New France, was a woman named **Esther Brandeau,** but as a Jew and a woman, she was not

---

FIRST RECORD OF CIRCUMCISION IN CANADA

[This report of a New York rabbi is from the 1700s.]

Tuesday 4th Iyar, 5570. Circumcised a son of Mr. Ezekiel and Mrs. Frances Hart of Canada, aged eight months and two weeks and named him Ira James Craig. . . .[11]

[A similar archival notation indicates that one of the Harts' daughters, Catherine, later married Bernard, the son of Samuel Judah.][12]

wanted in this French colony and was sent back to France. Other Jews made their appearance in Canada from time to time, but no community was formed until 1759, when the British conquered New France and Montreal became a center for the handful of Jews scattered throughout eastern Canada.

Some Jews, British loyalists, fled north during the Revolution. One of these was Rachel Myers, a widow with nine children. The entire family left Rhode Island with the retreating British troops. After a short time in New York, she joined other refugees who were evacuated to the safety of Canada. She settled in Gagetown in New Brunswick, where a married daughter, Judith, was already living, and remained there for four years before returning to the now independent United States.[13]

As the nineteenth century progressed, the names of more Jewish women appear, principally in the thirteen American colonies. Called the "Era of Good Feeling" by historians, there was not too much opportunity for heroism of any sort in this period. After the Revolutionary War, normal life was reestablished, institutions and schools were founded, and Jews, grateful for the freedom officially granted them by President George Washington, began to organize.[14] One of the first and most necessary services required in the Jewish community was a school, and the Jew credited with establishing the first Sunday School specifically for educating Jewish children of both sexes was a woman, **Rebecca Gratz**.

Jews and the Civil War

The scattered Jewish communities of the newly independent colonies worked hard to fit into a developing American culture. At the same time, they struggled to strengthen their own ties with Judaism. They built synagogues and schools, imported rabbis from abroad, and tried to educate their own communal leaders. The Gratz family, the Seixas family, the Ettings, the Sheftalls, the Hays, the Franks, and the Benjamins are just a few of the names that surface among the early Jewish settlers. The women and the men in those families often distinguished themselves by their efforts for Judaism and for their new country. Their deeds, letters, and papers dominate the history of the Jews of early America. Few, however, were actively involved in the issue of slavery, which grew ever more contentious as the United States settled into its new role as a nation.

Only a handful of Jewish traders were active in the infamous triangle trade that brought West African slaves to the United States, and an even smaller number of Jews were plantation owners, but some Jews did own slaves and mentioned them routinely in their letters, papers, and wills.[15] By 1860, the Jewish population throughout the United States had nearly tripled,[16] but these new arrivals were hardly in a position to become involved in the Abolitionist cause or even to take sides in the growing controversy between North and South. Nor was there yet any single body that could set a Jewish policy. Divisions between Orthodox and Reform, between Sephardim and Ashkenazim, and between the older settlers and the new immigrants plagued every community.

While some Jewish leaders and journalists did actively speak out against slavery, there were others who claimed that it was permitted by the Bible and therefore was not a sin.[17] When the southern states seceded and the war broke out, Jews living in the South, even those who owned no slaves, usually remained loyal and shared the fate of all Americans in that war-torn area. Judah Benjamin, one of the few Jewish plantation owners, became a member of the Confederate cabinet in Richmond. Young Jewish men fought and died for both sides, and Jewish women and children, whatever their opinion, were forced to find safety and to sustain themselves. Among them was **Penina Moise** of Charleston. Although she was a prolific writer, we have no hint of her feelings on the slavery issue. We do know, however, that she and her family did not leave the South during the war years and suffered severe poverty afterward.

In 1860 the Emancipation Proclamation ended slavery, and shortly after the Civil War, Congress amended the Constitution to give all African-American men the right to vote. Although women had hoped to gain this right for themselves at the same time, legislators did not agree to include women's suffrage in the amendment. Only gradually did legislation allow women increased civil rights, and national women's suffrage did not come until 1920.

At the Close of the Century

As succeeding waves of Jewish immigration arrived in the New World, the Jewish communities of North America grew and changed. German Jews, who began coming to the United States and Canada in large numbers in the mid–nineteenth century, altered the image of the Jew. No longer only prosperous Sephardic merchants and importers, Jews might now be peddlers, petty tradesmen, and shopkeepers. Then in 1880, the influx of Jews from Russia and the Pale of Settlement presented yet another image of the Jew: as poor laborer and socialist activist.

Each of these immigrant groups exerted an influence on the existing society and made an important contribution to it. The early Sephardim laid the groundwork for Jewish community life and established the first relationships with the gentiles in North America. Jewish colonial women forged a middle road between assimilation and isolation. Although there was a great deal of intermarriage, the methods that they developed to honor and preserve Judaism in America were, on the whole, successful.

German-Jewish immigrants, mostly from the middle class, established themselves as entrepreneurs and achieved prominence and sometimes wealth. As they had in the Old World, German-Jewish wives and daughters worked alongside the men. In addition, they founded philanthropic and service societies to help the poor, setting up educational and health facilities such as hospitals, milk stations, and Jewish community centers and launching Jewish publications of all kinds, immigrant aid societies, and women's clubs. Hannah G. Solomon and Rebecca Kohut, founders of the National Council of Jewish Women; Lillian Wald, who originated and organized the Visiting Nurse Service and the Henry Street Settlement; Rosa Sonneschein, journalist and publisher of *The American Jewess* are just a few of the women who came out of the German-Jewish tradition of philanthropy and commitment that had begun with Rebecca Gratz.

After 1888, eastern European Jews poured into the United States and Canada. Most were poor and had little secular education, although many were well versed in Judaism. The women were hardworking and ambitious and active in labor-union organizing and the cause of social justice, leaving their mark on the history of the working classes. Theresa Malkiel, Rose Schneiderman, Clara Lemlich Shevelson, Mary Dreier, and Emma Goldman all became well known in the labor movement in the twentieth century.

Thousands of Russian-Jewish immigrant women participated in strikes, demonstrations, and boycotts, pushing for a reasonable wage, an eight-hour day, and better working conditions. Jewish women's names filled the rosters of early union membership lists.

By the close of the nineteenth century, the Jewish communities of North America were radically different than they had been when Jews first settled in the thirteen original colonies. There were more Jewish organizations and a new generation of American Jewish rabbis and communal officials, but North America never developed the kind of strong, centralized community life that Jews had known in Europe or in the Middle East. In this New World, women and men were always free to observe or not, to assimilate or remain Jewish without the authority of the Jewish community to impose its will.

In such an open atmosphere Jewish women distinguished themselves in all segments of Jewish and secular life. As they became more comfortable and well established they worked for Jewish acceptance into the general society as well as for the strengthening of the Jewish community. They also became more involved in the cause of women's rights. The most recent wave of feminism in the United States was introduced by Betty Friedan, a Jewish woman born in 1921 whose father, an immigrant from eastern Europe, began his life as an itinerant peddler and eventually became a successful merchant.

BIOGRAPHIES

BRANDEAU, ESTHER OF FRANCE, SAILOR
(18th century)

The first Jew to appear in Canada, then called New France, was a woman. Her name was Esther Brandeau, and she had traveled by ship from La Rochelle in France disguised as a boy. Under the name of Jacques La Frague, Esther found work on a ship bound for North America. Upon her arrival in Quebec in 1738, "this passenger had attracted considerable attention until the remarkable discovery was made that the comely, spirited youth whose manners were so refined was in fact no 'Jacques' but 'Esther.'"[18]

With no Jewish community and no known Jews living in New France, the Quebec authorities could think of nothing better to do with Esther Brandeau than to arrest her and send her to the local hospital since there were no suitable prison facilities for women. There, officials made efforts to convert her so that she might be enabled to remain in Canada. Despite the prisoner's confession that she had lived as a man for five years and did not want to return to her parents' home where she would be unable "to enjoy the same liberty as the Christians,"[19] she steadfastly refused to convert.

Efforts to find suitable lodgings for Esther Brandeau as well as continued attempts to convert her, became an *affaire officielle*, with a continuous stream of letters being sent back and forth across the Atlantic for several years. A final report to the Minister in France informed him that "her conduct has not been wholly bad, but she is so frivolous . . . with regard to the instruction the priests desired to give her [that] I have no other alternative than to send her back."[20] Esther Brandeau was returned to France at the expense of the French government, and we hear no more about her.

DE CARVAJAL, FRANCISCA OF SPAIN AND NEW SPAIN
(16th century)

Francisca de Carvajal was a member of a large family that followed Luis de Carvajal to the New World. Luis, a New Christian, was appointed governor of the province of León in New Spain, a territory that stretched from present day Tampico to San Antonio (now in Texas). He encouraged his family, including his sister Francisca, to follow him to New Spain, but gave them only a small amount of financial help once they arrived.

Luis was a practicing Catholic, but Doña Francisca had been raised by their aunt, a crypto-Jew, who betrothed her at the age of nine to Francisco de Matos, also a secret Jew.[21] The couple was already married and had several children when they arrived in New Spain. Francisco de Matos worked as an itinerant peddler, and the family lived for many years on the edge of poverty. After Don Francisco died, that poverty became more severe,[22] but in spite of it, marriages were arranged. In 1586 two of Doña Francisca's daughters married two of the wealthiest New Christians in Mexico.[23] The bridegrooms themselves provided their brides with dowries and bought costly gifts and sumptuous clothing for their new family.

Although outwardly all were practicing Catholics, several members of the family remained loyal to Judaism,

FIG. 25. Doña Francisca de Carvajal was brought before the Inquisition on charges of judaizing. She was stripped and tortured to force her to confess. (Courtesy of the Hispanic Society of America, New York, NY)

including a son, also named Luis de Carvajal and referred to as *el Mozo* (the Younger). In Mexico City, where they lived, they met regularly on the Sabbath for prayer and Bible discussion. Doña Francisca and her daughters prepared for the Sabbath by cleaning and cooking; on the Sabbath itself, they wore their best clothes. They kept the Passover by slaughtering a goat (sheep were not available) and smearing the blood on the doorposts of their rooms. By the end of 1588, however, the pressures of the Inquisition were worsening and New Spain was growing more dangerous for crypto-Jews. Luis el Mozo, once destined to become heir to his uncle's titles and lands, decided to take the family to a safer place; but before these plans could be undertaken, his sister Isabel was denounced by a relative, Captain Felipe Nuñez, on March 7, 1589.

Accused of attempting to convert Nuñez to Judaism, Isabel was tortured and perhaps at that time gave the names of others in her family. The Inquisition accused members of the De Carvajal family and one by one, Isabel's mother, Francisca, her brother Gaspar (a priest), Luis el Mozo, and two other sisters, Catalina and Leonor, were arrested.

FRANCISCA DE CARVAJAL'S CONFESSION

Reminding the Inquisitors that she was a woman of stature and dignity, Doña Francisca said:

"Kill me but do not undress or disgrace me, even if you give me a thousand deaths. You can see I am a woman and an honest widow, to whom things like this cannot be done in this world; especially where there is so much sanctity. I said that I believe in the law of Moses and not in Christ and there is nothing more, other than that. I am a forlorn, sad widow with children who shall clamor to God."[24]

Doña Francisca was a fifty-year-old widow when the Inquisition took her. The order from the Inquisitors was: "arrest Doña Francisca de Carvajal, widow of Francisco Rodriguez de Matos . . . removing her . . . from any protected or privileged place where she may be."[25] Determined to save her family, Francisca tried to defend herself and hide her faith, but the Inquisitors had excellent methods for obtaining information. Stripped to the waist, with her arms bound, Doña Francisca was placed on the torture rack and finally confessed to the court.

The court found Francisca de Carvajal guilty of Jewish practices. Her daughters and her son Luis el Mozo were also convicted and burned on December 8, 1596.[26] Luis de Carvajal, while still governor of the province, was arrested for his failure to denounce his niece for judaizing. He was stripped of his title and sentenced to six years of exile, but died before he was released from prison. Francisca's remaining two daughters were also burned, Mariana in 1601, and Ana, the youngest, in 1648.[27]

FRANKS, BILHAH ABIGAIL LEVY OF LONDON AND NEW YORK, COLONIAL SETTLER
(17th–18th century)

Bilhah Abigail Levy Franks was not actively involved in the greater politics of the time; she died before the Revolution had begun. However, she was a well-educated woman and a committed Jew who struggled against tremendous odds to keep Judaism alive for her family. Born in 1688 in London, of German-Jewish parentage, the Levy family moved to New York City in 1695. Sometime thereafter,

FIG. 26. Bilhah Abigail Franks was an early Jewish settler in colonial New York City. A well-educated woman, her ideas are preserved through her correspondence. (Courtesy of the American Jewish Historical Society, Waltham, Mass. and New York, N.Y.)

Abigail married Jacob Franks, a young man of similar background. Abigail and Jacob had nine children, born between 1715 and 1742.[28]

With her aristocratic manner and broad education, Abigail Levy Franks moved freely in New York society, comfortable with Christian as well as

Jewish friends and sharing a similar lifestyle. The Franks family was one of the founding members of Congregation Shearith Israel, the synagogue on Mill Lane. Although socially prominent in the community, they never prospered as much as the English branch of the family, and several of their children were sent back to London to join the business there. This separation resulted in a vivid legacy in the form of letters written by Abigail Franks, mostly to "HeartSey," her pet name for her son Naphtali Hart, who resided in England from 1733 to 1748.

Her thirty-four letters reflect the social conditions of that period but often have a very contemporary sound. Besides chiding "HeartSey" for not writing to her and scolding him for spending too much money on presents and social activities, she also expressed her own discontent with her world. She was distressed at the split between the Sephardic and Ashkenazic commu-

nities, complained of too much horse-drawn traffic in the city, and confided that the female members of the synagogue were "a stupid set of people."[30]

Abigail's letters also reflect the breadth of her own reading. She quoted from the novels of Fielding and Smollett; the essays and poems of Dryden, Addison, and Pope; and alluded to Shakespeare's plays.[31]

Even though Naphtali was living with a relative, his mother openly worried that her son was not keeping kosher in London and that he was not being as observant as he had been taught at home. Through her letters, she attempted to keep the family close—in thought, if not geographically. On December 5, 1742, she wrote: "I Should be glad if you would take care and Write offtener to y[ou]r brother david he thinks himself Ill Used and Slighted for he very Seldom has a Letter. . . ."[32]

Always a concerned mother, Abigail Franks tried to find suitable marriage partners for her sons and daughters. She even enlisted "HeartSey" in the search. Her extended correspondence with her son documents her feelings and thoughts and reflects the value she placed on family integrity and on the continuity of the Jewish religion. When her oldest daughter, Phila, eloped and married a Christian, she was devastated and considered her inability to imbue her children with her faith to be a major failure. However, in the open society of the colonies, without a traditional Jewish communal organization, the price of individual freedom was often the loss of Jewish life and tradition.

Although Abigail felt that she had failed to communicate her concept of Judaism to some of her descendants, the letters she left have passed her

---

A LETTER FROM ABIGAIL FRANKS TO HER SON

In a letter dated June 9, 1734, Franks wrote:

"I Observe You Give me an Acc[oun]t how you Spend your time I find noe fault in it but your not takeing more time for your Studying of books for If You Don't doe it now you will hardly fallow it when you grow oulder and will have An Excuse that buissness is a hindrance My advice Should be that two mornings In a Week Should be intirly Untill diner time Dedicated to Some Usefull book Besides an hour Every morning throughout the Year to the Same Purpose. . . ."[29]

views on to succeeding generations. Her insistence on the importance of adhering to tradition and maintaining family cohesion were views very similar to those held by European Jewish women in the eighteenth century (see chapter 6).

GRATZ, REBECCA OF PHILADELPHIA, EDUCATOR AND PHILANTHROPIST

(18th–19th century)

The sixth of ten children, Rebecca Gratz was born in Philadelphia in 1781, just after the Revolutionary War ended. She was raised by her parents Michael and Miriam Gratz in a refined, upper-class home where the children were all educated in secular as well as Jewish subjects. Michael Gratz's family had originated in Poland but immigrated to America from England. He was a prosperous merchant and one of the founders of Mikveh Israel, the first synagogue in Pennsylvania.

Rebecca Gratz never married but moved freely in the well-bred Philadelphia society of teas and dances, mingling with men and women. Many people believed she was the model for the Jewish character, Rebecca, in Sir Walter Scott's popular novel *Ivanhoe*.[33] Gratz had read the book and mentioned in a letter to her sister-in-law: "I am glad you admire Rebecca, for she is just such a representation of a good girl as I think human nature can reach."[34] Scott had heard of Rebecca Gratz through a mutual acquaintance, Washington Irving, who was part of her circle of friends.

In addition to social activities, however, Gratz was also active in many philanthropic organizations. Beginning at the age of eighteen, she was a founder of the Female Association for the Relief of Women and Children in Reduced Circumstances. In 1815, Rebecca Gratz also helped establish the Philadelphia Orphan Asylum, a facility for orphaned children under the auspices of the Presbyterian Church, and held the post of secretary of that organization until her death.

Gratz's managerial experience, developed in the course of her work for these two nonsectarian organizations, gave her the knowledge to establish the Female Hebrew Benevolent Society in 1819, the first Jewish charity that functioned independently of a synagogue.[35] Such charitable organizations, created by upper-class women seeking to do good works, filled a critical need for indigents who had no other place to live and found themselves without resources. Charity work was also one of the few highly approved activities for wealthier women who did not need to work for a living.

By 1838, with the encouragement of Isaac Leeser, *hazzan* of Mikveh Israel, Rebecca Gratz established the first Hebrew Sunday school in the United States, enlisting the services of two other synagogue members, Simha Peixotto and Rachel Peixotto Pyke.

Modeled after the format of the Christian Sunday school, this new institution offered Jewish education to children of poor families who could not afford private tutors. Girls and boys studied religion together in these Sunday classes, and Gratz hired women as teachers, a radical change from traditional Jewish education. Rebecca Gratz was the superintendent of the Philadelphia Sunday School for more than twenty-five years, and it became a model for similar Jewish schools throughout the country, especially those in Baltimore, Charleston, and Savannah.

Continuing her concerns for Jewish children, Gratz was instrumental in creating the Jewish Foster Home in the 1850s. This institution met the needs of the Jewish community in that period of increasing immigration, when large numbers of German Jews, often fleeing from persecution, were beginning to settle in cities throughout the New World.

Gratz lived a public life, deeply committed to the Jewish community, but she always found time to correspond regularly with family and friends. Many of the details of her activities and opinions are known from her letters.

GRATZ WRITES ABOUT AGUILAR

In this excerpt from a letter addressed to her brother Benjamin's second wife, Ann, Rebecca Gratz discussed Grace Aguilar's book, *Home Influence*, and sighed over the death of this "gifted author."

September 15, 1848

"I see that they have just published a new novel, *Home Influence* by Grace Aguilar. I wish you would read it and give me your opinion of its merits because I see many excellences in it, and found it deeply interesting. I know nothing as touching as the distresses and difficulties of childhood, and am glad to see them treated with consideration and sympathy by matured intellects . . . it is to be lamented the gifted author did not live to complete her design of continuing her subject through another work. . . .[36]

One such letter, addressed to her nephew Solomon Cohen, discussed her anxiety over the recent blood libel charge that had occurred in Damascus in 1840 and praised Moses Montefiore for mediating the affair. In addition to her interest in the Damascus Affair, Rebecca Gratz displayed knowledge of other world events and a commitment to Jewish concerns. For example, she was well acquainted with the writings of **Grace Aguilar,** a prominent Anglo-Jewish writer (see chapter 8).

Rebecca Gratz made her mark primarily as a social philanthropist. However, through her writings we can gain some insights into the feelings and experiences of educated American-Jewish women of the 1800s, as well as a sense of her own commitment to the Jewish people. A recent scholar of this period views Gratz as having "promoted an Americanized Jewish domesticity." Totally accepting of her world and her role, Rebecca Gratz, like most of the women of that period, was not a rebel. She used charitable institutions as a vehicle for strengthening her belief in Judaism and Jewish religious education. "By thus adapting Judaism to American conditions, Gratz invigorated Jewish life for generations to come."[37]

At the time of her death on August 29, 1869, the eighty-eight-year-old Rebecca Gratz was considered the foremost Jewish woman in America.

HAYS, ESTHER ETTING OF PHILADELPHIA AND NEW YORK, REVOLUTIONARY HERO
(18th century)

Esther Etting was a member of one of the pioneer Sephardic families that came to Philadelphia in 1758. She met her future husband, David Hays of New York, through their common social connections. Their marriage united the Philadelphia, New York, and Rhode Island Jewish communities, as Hays was related to Judah Touro of Newport.[38]

As a bride, Esther Etting went to live on her husband's farm in northern Westchester County, near present-day Bedford, New York. The family wholeheartedly backed the Revolution, and David Hays and their eldest son fought in the colonial army. In 1779, with the colonists surrounded by British forces, and food supplies perilously low, David Hays, together with one of his sons, secretly drove a herd of cattle through enemy lines to the troops. He had blindfolded the cows' eyes and muffled their hoofs and mouths so they would not be heard.

When some of their Tory neighbors learned of this clever ploy, they came to the Hays home and threatened Esther Hays who was in bed after the birth of her sixth child, ill with fever. She refused to give the mob any information, even when they tried to intimidate her and her small children. After continued resistance to their demands, she was pulled outside and her home was set on fire. Esther and the children took shelter with the family's slaves, who protected them in the slave quarters until David Hays returned.

At a later time, Esther Hays passed through enemy lines, alone and undetected, carrying large quantities of salt that she had sewn into her petticoats. Salt was an indispensable item for the hard-pressed Revolutionary army.[39]

JOSEPH, RACHEL SOLOMONS OF CANADA, PIOUS WOMAN
(19th century)

Rachel, the daughter of Levy Solomons, was married to Henry Joseph, the first ritual slaughterer (*shoḥet*) in Canada. She was reported to have been a very religious woman who attempted to educate her children in Judaism. With neither teachers nor textbooks available to her, she insisted they "listen attentively to their father while he recited his prayers" and herself "taught them the lessons of Judaism."[40]

LAZARUS, EMMA OF NEW YORK, POET
(19th century)

When Emma Lazarus was born, on July 22, 1849, the Women's Rights movement was just emerging, and the Civil War would soon threaten the very existence of the United States. But Emma was born into a comfortable, sheltered life in New York City, far from the politics raging at the time. She would become the first American Jewish writer whose poetic voice came to symbolize freedom and opportunity for immigrants.

Emma Lazarus was one of seven children born to Moses and Esther Nathan Lazarus, both assimilated Sephardic Jews from prosperous families. Her mother was of English descent, but her father, Moses, a successful sugar merchant, traced his ancestry back to the first twenty-three Jews who settled in New York in 1654. Raised in the rich society of Manhattan, spending summers at Newport, Rhode Island, Emma was part of an elite world of private education, elegant homes, and literary salons.[41]

Always considered by her family to be fragile and sickly, Lazarus studied at home with private tutors and began writing poetry while still a child. Her father, who dominated the family, encouraged her. When he retired, he involved himself closely in Emma's education, and she soon read and translated Italian, French, and German poets.[42] In 1866, when she was seventeen years old, Moses Lazarus privately published a collection of her work, *Poems and Translations: Written Between the Ages of Fourteen and Sixteen*. It included translations from Victor Hugo, Alexandre Dumas, Heinrich Heine, and Friedrich Schiller.

"THE PROPHET"

One of the poems written by Emma Lazarus reflects her growing idealism and commitment to Jewish welfare. The work begins with a description of some of the great Jews of the past and present: Moses ben Maimon, Judah HaLevi, Moses Mendelssohn, Isaac Abrabanel, and Heinrich Heine. It continues:

. . . *These need no wreath and no trumpet; like perennial asphodel blossoms,*
their fame, their glory resounds like the brazen-throated cornet.
But thou—hast thou faith in the fortune of Israel? Wouldst thou lighten the anguish of Jacob?
Then shalt thou take the hand of yonder caftaned wretch with flowing curls and gold-pierced ears;
Who crawls blinking forth from the loathsome recesses of the Jewry;
Nerveless his fingers, puny his frame; haunted by the bat-like phantoms of Superstition is his brain.
Thou shalt say to the bigot, "My Brother," and to the creature of darkness, "My Friend . . ."[43]

Lazarus's poems were intended to be read primarily by her family, but they caught the attention of others. This early success encouraged her to continue writing, and a second book was issued and was well received in the United States and England. Emma never married. Coming from an affluent family, she did not need to support herself and chose to devote her time to literature and writing poetry and essays.

Lazarus's sister Josephine wrote that Emma was extremely shy and had few friends of her own age except for her sisters. More recent scholars have challenged that view, pointing out that she was friendly with some of the leading intellectuals in New York and attended many musical and cultural events, as well as political discussion groups.[44] Rumors that she loved her handsome and wild cousin, Washington Nathan, were never confirmed, and Lazarus herself made no mention of him in any of her writings, but speculations persisted.[45]

At a gathering in New York in 1866, Emma met the noted American essayist and philosopher Ralph Waldo Emerson, and the two began a correspondence. Emerson became a mentor of sorts, reading the work that she sent him and making suggestions. Her relationship with Emerson was so vital to her that when the latter edited a comprehensive anthology of American poetry, *Parnassus*, and did not include any of her poems, she was devastated by this public neglect. Despite her disappointment, Lazarus continued to write, publishing a successful novel, *Alide: An Episode of Goethe's Life*.

In 1880, Lazarus began one of her most productive periods, using Jewish themes as inspiration for her poetry. Her dramatic play in verse, "The

Dance to Death," part of her collection *Songs of a Semite*, had its origin in the accounts of the slaughter of Jews accused of spreading bubonic plague in the Middle Ages. Although the poem ended with the hope that Jews would not continue to be victims, political events in Europe were precipitating just such an outcome for the Jews of Russia. These events proved to be the wake-up call for Emma Lazarus.[46]

Lazarus was thirty-two years old when she first saw the Russian-Jewish refugees who had escaped the pogroms of eastern Europe. Overcoming her initial reticence, she visited immigrants at a holding facility on Ward's Island, a U.S. immigration station. Here, Jewish refugees along with thousands of others were housed in overcrowded barracks because they were too sick or poor to be admitted into the United States. These people were very different from the Jews of her upper-class, Sephardic world, but she was moved by their plight and organized a relief effort to alleviate their conditions.

Lazarus championed Jewish unity and experienced a growing commitment to the Jewish people. Through her own initiative, she studied Hebrew and became a leading translator of the medieval Hebrew poets Judah HaLevi and Solomon ibn Gabirol, as well as Heinrich Heine.[47] She also became interested in the cause of Zionism.

In 1882, Lazarus wrote a response to a negative portrayal of the Russian Jews by Zenaide Ragozin, a Russian expatriate, that appeared in *The Century*. In the article, Ragozin maintained that the Jews had brought their troubles on themselves. Outraged, Lazarus defended her people and

---

THE BANNER OF THE JEW

In this fragment of a poem from Emma Lazarus' collection *Songs of a Semite*, Lazarus urged Jews to work for a return to the Jewish homeland in Palestine.

Wake, Israel, wake! Recall today
The glorious Maccabean rage . . .
. . . Oh, for Jerusalem's trumpets now
To blow a blast of shattering power,
To wake the sleepers high and low,
And rouse them to the urgent hour![48]

---

wrote "I am all Israel's now. I have no thought, no passion, no desire save for my own people."[49]

Lazarus, accompanied by her youngest sister, Annie, made her first trip to Europe in 1883. Her book of poetry, *Songs of a Semite,* was well received in England, and she met Robert Browning, Mary Ann Evans (known by her literary name, George Eliot), and William Morris, intellectuals who were very sympathetic to the Jewish plight. She had hoped to enlist support for the Zionist cause from among the influential Jews and non-Jews in England but did not succeed.[50] On her return to New York, Emma began to experience increased fatigue, the beginning of the Hodgkin's disease that would end her life.

A few years later, Lazarus returned to Europe. Although seriously weakened from cancer by this time, she visited the great art museums of London, Amsterdam, Rome, and Paris. Now aware of her diagnosis, she tried to ignore the pain and fatigue and make the most of this last trip. That July,

---

"THE NEW COLUSSUS"

This sonnet, written by Emma Lazarus, compares the Statue of Liberty with an ancient statue of the Greek god Helios called "Colossus," once located in the harbor of ancient Rhodes.

*Not like the brazen giant of Greek
    fame,*
*With conquering limbs astride from
    land to land;*
*Here at our sea-washed sunset gates
    shall stand*
*A mighty woman with a torch,
    whose flame*
*Is the imprisoned lightning, and her
    name*
*Mother of Exiles. From her beacon-
    hand*
*Glows world-wide welcome; her
    mild eyes command*
*The air-bridged harbor that twin
    cities frame.*
*Keep, ancient lands, your storied
    pomp! Cries she*
*With silent lips. Give me your tired,
    your poor,*
*Your huddled masses yearning to
    breathe free,*
*The wretched refuse of your teem-
    ing shore.*
*Send these, the homeless, the
    tempest-tossed to me.*
*I lift my lamp beside the golden
    door.*

---

however, just after her thirty-eighth birthday, she had to return home.

One of Lazarus's most familiar poems is also one of her last. Written shortly before her premature death, it was donated to an auction to raise funds for a pedestal for the Statue of Liberty, sculptured by Bertholdi and donated by France to the American people. Lazarus's contribution to this effort was a sonnet called "The New Colussus."

Emma Lazarus was not present when her poem, along with the works of other American poets, was auctioned off. She died in 1887, a victim of cancer at the age of thirty-eight. In 1903, when one of Lazarus's admirers, Georgiana Schuyler, found the manuscript, she arranged to have the poem inscribed on a bronze plaque, and attached to the pedestal of the Statue of Liberty. Since then, it has been memorized by countless schoolchildren, translated into many languages, put to music, and recited everywhere. With this poem, Emma Lazarus helped create the image of America as a haven for the oppressed.[51]

MINIS, ABIGAIL OF SAVANNAH, BUSINESSWOMAN AND PATRIOT
(18th century)

Born in 1701, Abigail Minis arrived in Savannah, Georgia, in 1733, a few months after the founding of that colony by James Oglethorpe. With her were her husband, Abraham; her two daughters, Leah and Esther; and a brother-in-law. They were among the first forty Jews to settle in Savannah. The Minis family had sailed from England, but there is no specific evidence of their origins.[52]

Records show that Abigail was thirty-two years old when she arrived in this new colony. In the next twenty-four years, she would give birth to seven more children, a total of five daughters and four sons. When her husband died, Abigail was fifty-six years old, but she still had eight children to support, some of whom were

THE OFFICIAL REPORT OF
ABIGAIL MINIS' DEATH

An entry in the Jewish community records on the day Minis died
noted:

"1794 October the 11th corre-
sponding with the first day of
Halamoad Succoth 5555 departed this life Mrs. Abigail Minis
aged 93 years and 2 months. This
ancient lady arrived into this
country on the 11th day of July
1733 and was buried on the 2nd
day of Halamoade Succoth in
the New burial ground. . . ."[53]

quite young. Although she had little
formal education, she took control of
the family interests, including a farm
and a retail business, and became an
astute businesswoman. She acquired
considerable property, real estate, and
cattle, as well as slaves for her plantation.[54] In addition, Abigail Minis and
her five daughters operated a tavern in
Savannah for sixteen years. It was a
very popular gathering place, not only
for local merchants, but also for
judges, assemblymen, and leading
politicians.

When the Revolutionary War broke
out, Abigail was already quite
advanced in years, but she actively
supplied the Continental army and the
Georgia Militia with much needed
goods and arranged to give them a
personal loan at considerable risk.[55]
When the British army captured
Savannah, Abigail and her family were
forced to flee. Although her life and
property were threatened, she was
able to obtain a guarantee of safe pas-

sage to Charleston from the British
governor and to avoid confiscation of
her property.[56] Her son Philip helped
the Americans recapture Savannah by
providing information to the com-
manding officers.

When the war ended, Abigail Minis
returned to Savannah and continued
to be active in her various businesses
until her death in 1794 at the age
of ninety-three. An enterprising
and hardworking Jewish immigrant,
Abigail was highly regarded in her
community. Today she is still remembered and respected as a patriot and as
the mother of Savannah's Jewish
community.

MOISE, PENINA OF CHARLESTON, POET
(19th century)

Penina Moise, the fifth of nine offspring, was born in Charleston, South
Carolina, on April 12, 1797. Charleston
was home to a growing and active
Jewish community, established in the
mid–eighteenth century.[57] The Moise
family fled there after a slave insurrec-
tion that took place in 1791 in Santo
Domingo (West Indies).

Penina's father, Abraham, a
Sephardic Jew from Alsace, had settled
in the West Indies and married a
Jewish woman there. The couple
owned a sugar plantation, but once in
the United States they never recouped
their financial losses. When Penina
was twelve years old, her father died,
leaving the family with few resources.

Although not the oldest, Penina
assumed part of the task of caring for
her sick mother and her younger siblings.[58] She left school and helped support her family by doing needlework,
but always made time to study and
write.[59] By the time she was thirty

years old, Penina Moise was a well known and respected poet. Her work appeared regularly in the *Charleston Courier* and also in publications such as the *Boston Daily Times*, the *New Orleans Commercial Times*, and *Godey's Lady's Book*.

In 1833, *Fancy's Sketch Book*, a collection of Moise's poetry, was issued, making her the first Jew to publish lyric poetry in the United States.[60] She was a member of Charleston's literary circle and a cultural leader among Christians and Jews, with a salon in her home where writers met regularly.

Like many other notable women of this period, Penina Moise never married. She devoted her life to poetry and to good works, committing herself to many Jewish causes. When Temple Beth Elohim installed an organ, she began composing hymns for the congregation.[62] In 1843 she became superintendent of the temple's Sunday school, modeled after the Philadelphia school founded by **Rebecca Gratz**. Moise was the second woman to hold that post in Charleston.[63]

When an epidemic of yellow fever raged through South Carolina in 1854, she accepted the traditional role of so many women, Jewish and gentile, and nursed victims of the disease.

Along with other Jews of Charleston, Moise was forced to flee the Union attack on the city during the Civil War. She escaped to Fort Sumter but returned when the war was over and the South defeated.[64] In order to support herself, Penina Moise, together with her widowed sister Rachel and her niece Jacqueline Levy, ran a girls school.

Shortly before the war her eyesight, always poor, had begun to fail, and she gradually became blind. Despite this handicap, she continued her writing, using her niece to transcribe the words she dictated. She wrote 190 hymns for the Beth Elohim religious service, which were set to music. The synagogue published a collection of her hymns, and selections from this hymnal were subsequently included in the *Union Reform Prayer Book*.[65]

In more recent times, poetic fashion has relegated Moise's once-popular work to obscurity, but in her own day she was loved and admired. She con-

---

TO PERSECUTED FOREIGNERS

In 1820, this poem by Penina Moise was printed in the *Southern Patriot*. It is an invitation for all those fleeing oppression to come "to the homes and bosoms of the free." The theme is startlingly similar to a later poem written by **Emma Lazarus**, but whether or not Lazarus actually saw Moise's poem is not known.

Fly from the soil whose desolating creed,
Outraging faith, makes human victims bleed,
Welcome! Where every muse has reared a shrine,
The respect of wild freedom to refine . . .
Rise then, elastic from Oppression's tread,
Come and repose in Plenty's flowery bed.
Oh, not as Strangers shall welcome be
Come to the homes and bosoms of the free.[61]

FIG. 27. Penina Moise, a colonial poet from Charleston, S.C., is best known for her hymns, still sung in synagogues today. (Courtesy of Temple Beth Elohim, Charleston, S.C.)

tinued to write poetry until she died in 1880 at the age of eighty-three. Referred to as "the blind poetess" or as Charleston's "gentle poetess,"[66] her poetry reflects intelligence, piety, and resilience to whatever life had to offer. In spite of hardships and difficulties she "always seemed content and cheerful"[67] and remained committed to education and to Judaism.

At her death, she was totally blind, and her last words were reported to have been: "Lay no flowers on my grave. They are for those who live in the sun, and I have always lived in the shadow."[68]

TWO HYMNS BY PENINA MOISE

These two poems, set to music, were among the most popular of Moise's works.

"Aspiration"

O God all gracious! In Thy gift
Though Countless blessings lie,
My voice for One alone I lift,
In pray'r to Thee on high.
Let wisdom of the heart, O Lord!
Be now and ever mine;
Naught else is life's sublime reward,
We love Thy law divine.[69]

"Praise Ye The Lord"

Praise ye the Lord! For it is good
His mighty acts to magnify
And make those mercies under-
stood,
His hand delights to multiply.
Praise ye the Lord! Praise ye the
Lord!

Let hallelujah loudly rise!
Let hallelujah softly fall
Until on angel lips it dies,
As they unto each other call,
Praise ye the Lord! Praise ye the
Lord![70]

PHILLIPS, REBECCA MACHADO OF PHILADELPHIA, ORGANIZER OF CHARITIES
(18th–19th centuries)

Rebecca was born in New York to Tzipporah and David Machado, crypto-Jews who had fled from Portugal. In 1762, at the age of sixteen, she married an Ashkenazic man, Jonas Phillips. The couple had twenty-one children, of whom sixteen survived. She also raised two grandchildren after the death of one of her daughters. One of these grandchildren, Mordecai Emanuel Noah, wrote about her favorably in his memoirs and reported that the Philadelphia community held her in high regard.

During her later childbearing years, Rebecca Phillips was already active in fund-raising and in philanthropic circles. In 1782 she helped raise money for ritual objects for the Mikveh Israel synagogue. In 1801, along with Rebecca Gratz and others, Phillips founded the Female Association for the Relief of Women and Children in Reduced Circumstances. In 1820, she was the first director and one of the managers on the board of the Female Hebrew Benevolent Society, the first non-synagogue-related charitable organization in the United States, founded by Gratz.

Rebecca Machado Phillips died in 1831 at the age of eighty-five.[71]

ROSE, ERNESTINE POTOWSKI OF POLAND AND NEW YORK, ACTIVIST
(19th century)

Ernestine was born in Piotrkow, an obscure little town in Poland, on January 13, 1810, to the family of a pious rabbi. An only child, Ernestine was a rebel from her earliest years. She insisted on studying the Bible in the original Hebrew, probably the only girl in her town to do so.[72] After her mother's death, her father, without consulting her, arranged for Ernestine to marry a much older man. Although only sixteen years old, Ernestine refused, standing up to her father despite his recognized authority as the leader and final arbiter of Piotrkow's Jews.

Despairing of a positive outcome from any appeal to a higher Jewish court, Ernestine Potowski turned to the secular courts. Young and alone, she made the journey to the Polish Regional Tribunal in Kalisz and presented her case before a Christian judge. He ruled that the contract her father had made was not binding and Ernestine Potowski need not marry the man of his choosing. Furthermore, she, and not her intended husband, had the right to her mother's inheritance. With this legal vindication of her rights, Ernestine returned home but did not stay long. In 1827, taking only part of the money that was rightfully hers, she left Poland and her father forever and turned her face westward.

Arriving first in Prussia, Ernestine taught herself German and, to support herself, invented a type of perfumed paper that acted as a room deodorizer, a discovery that assured her financial independence.[73] She passed through Holland in 1829 and France in 1830, but her ultimate goal was England.

England was in a ferment of activism during this period. Socialist groups called Utopians were springing up everywhere, anxious to repair the social ills of their time. Ernestine Potowski, only twenty-two years old, joined such a group headed by Robert Owen, who believed that ordinary people, working together, could create a perfect society, a utopia. She spoke at meetings that Robert Owen organized and was such a passionate speaker that her forcefulness and conviction overcame her Polish accent and limited English.

While still in England, Ernestine met her future husband, William Rose. He was a silversmith, a non-Jew, and also an Owenite. In 1836, soon after their marriage, Ernestine and William left for the United States.

Within a year of their arrival, Ernestine Rose was traveling and giving lectures throughout the country.

Although not yet a citizen—and in any case, prevented from voting because of her sex—Rose drew up a petition to elicit support for recently proposed legislation giving new **legal rights** for married women to own property. Going from house to house for signatures, at first doors were slammed in her face. After five months she had obtained the signatures of only five women. But she became part of a small group of women and men struggling to pass the Married

---

AN INTERESTING POLISH LADY

A newspaper article written on March 13, 1838, by Gilbert Vale, the editor of the *New York Beacon,* gives a clue to the working life of both Ernestine and William Rose. He wrote:

"Mrs. Rose, an interesting Polish lady of education and accomplishments, and who is already partially known to the readers of the *Beacon* from the part she has taken in some liberal public meetings, now manufactures Cologne and other German waters. This is a bold and dignified step. Cologne waters are imitated by novices; they are bad. . . . Mrs. Rose has similar bottles . . . but she assures that her Cologne water is genuine . . . and infinitely superior. Mr. and Mrs. Rose keep a small Fancy and Perfumery store, 9 Frankfurt Street . . . he repairs jewelry, watches . . . while she manufactures German waters and offers them for sale. . . ."[74]

Woman's Property Act. From this time on, Rose, along with Elizabeth Cady Stanton, Lucretia Mott, Susan B. Anthony, and a handful of others, was part of the Suffragist movement, working indefatigably for women's rights.[75]

AN ANTI-SEMITIC CONTROVERSY

Horace Seaver, editor of the *Boston Investigator*, wrote that the ancient Jews "were a troublesome people to live in proximity with . . ." and continued: "Even the modern Jews are bigoted, narrow, exclusive and totally unfit for progressive people like the Americans, among whom we hope they may not spread."[76]

Ernestine recognized anti-Semitism from her girlhood experiences in Poland and Germany and was dismayed to find it here in a newspaper devoted to free thought, and to which she herself had been a contributor. In reply, Rose wrote a long letter to the newspaper, bitterly demanding: "Now suppose you had the power . . . Would you drive them out of Boston, out of progressive America, as they were once driven out of Spain?" She went on to say: "The nature of the Jew is governed by the same laws as human nature in general . . . all in all the Jews are as good as any other sect. . . . Do not add to the prejudice already existing toward the Jews." She signed it "Yours for justice, Ernestine L. Rose."[77]

Not until April 7, 1848, was the Married Woman's Property Act finally passed, one of the first legal steps taken in support of a woman's independence.

Ernestine Rose gave up practicing Judaism when she left her father's house in Poland but never denied her Jewish origins. In the fall of 1863, when she read an anti-Semitic article in the *Boston Investigator* written by its editor, Horace Seaver, she was quick to respond. The *Boston Investigator* was a weekly newspaper that had frequently included articles about Rose's lectures and debates. She herself had written an occasional letter or article and considered Horace Seaver a friend. Now she countered his anti-Semitic attacks with a spirited rebuttal. Seaver printed the letter, and the exchange between the two continued for ten weeks. In her letters, Ernestine Rose took the opportunity to educate readers about the Jews and Jewish history.

Ernestine Rose continued to travel the country widely, often together with Susan B. Anthony, and became known as the "Queen of the Lecture Platform."[78] She is quoted as saying: "Emancipation from every kind of human bondage is my principle."[79] Finally, exhausted from a rheumatic illness, she returned with William to England in 1869. Before she left the United States, Rabbi Jonas Bondi, the editor of the Jewish newspaper *The Hebrew Leader*, paid tribute to her, praising "Mrs. Rose [as] the earliest and noblest among the workers in the cause of human enfranchisement."[80] She lived the remainder of her life in England, where she died peacefully in 1892. She was eighty-two years old.

SALOMON, RACHEL FRANKS OF PHILADELPHIA, WIFE OF A PATRIOT

(18th century)

Rachel was the daughter of Moses Franks of Philadelphia. She was only fifteen years old when she married the much older Ḥaym Salomon on July 6, 1777. Salomon had already allied himself with the patriots' cause against the British and had been arrested as a spy a year earlier. Because of his fluency in several languages, he was turned over to the Hessian commander to purchase commissary supplies for German troops and allowed to continue his own business, trading in ships' provisions.[81] This relative freedom allowed him to marry Rachel and even to secretly assist American and French prisoners in their plans to escape, while he openly supplied the British and Hessian commissaries.

Rachel Franks Salomon gave birth to their first child in 1778, just two weeks before the British ordered her husband's arrest again. He managed to escape to Philadelphia, leaving Rachel and her new baby behind in New York. There he appealed to Congress for some means of support, as he had lost between five and six thousand pound sterling due to his activities as a spy and through his aid to the American cause. Finally he managed to bring Rachel and their son to Philadelphia, where he advertised himself as a foreign exchange broker.

By 1781, Ḥaym Salomon was one of only two Jews (Moses Cohen was the other) among the twenty-five brokers in Philadelphia. Although he was charitable to Jewish causes and guaranteed his endorsement on American bills of exchange (essentially worthless), Salomon was delinquent in his

own taxes, and Rachel and their four children never had economic security. Although part of the Franks family was rich, her parents were not, and none of her cousins seem to have given her any financial help.

When Ḥaym died in 1785, despite his "skill and integrity,"[83] his assets, consisting of Loan Office certificates and Continental currency of inflated value, barely covered his debts. His loans to the fledgling government went unpaid, and his wife and children were almost destitute. Possibly because she had no visible means of support, Rachel remarried within two years to David Heilbrun (Hilborn). Leaving her older children behind, she resettled in Holland with her new husband.[84]

Rachel Franks Salomon was among the Jewish women who got caught up in the turmoil of revolution and had little control over their lives. Although her husband is remembered as a patriot, her personal and financial struggles have been forgotten.

SUFFRAGETTE MOVEMENT

Ernestine Rose was already crippled by disease and hardly able to use her hands when she responded to a request by Susan B. Anthony. Asked to contribute an entry for a history of the Women's movement, she penned a brief reply and added: "All I can tell you is that I used my humble powers to the uttermost, and raised my voice in behalf of human rights in general, and the elevation of women in particular, nearly all my life."[82]

SHEFTALL, FRANCES HART OF SAVANNAH, PIONEER AND DEVOTED MOTHER
(18th century)

Frances Sheftall, a strong pioneering woman, was born in 1740 in the Netherlands to Moses and Esther Hart, both Ashkenazim. She first immigrated to Charleston with her brother, who soon became a successful merchant. In October 1761, Frances, or Fanny, married Mordecai Sheftall and

---

FRANCES SHEFTALL WRITES TO HER HUSBAND IN PRISON

While struggling through the war years, Frances Sheftall corresponded regularly with her son and husband, held in a British prison, and sent countless petitions to General Benjamin Lincoln to intercede on their behalf. On March 3, 1780, she wrote to Mordecai:

". . . But [I] was verry miserable to hear that you and my dear child was in so much distress. I would have endeavoured to have sent something for your reliefe, but the enemy now lay off of the bar, so that it is not in my power to do any thing for you at present, but the first safe opportunity you may depend on my sending you whatever is in my power. . . ."

She continued with reports of other news, mentioning that "Old Mrs. Mines [**Abigail Minis**] is here with all her family and is settled here. They all desire to be kindly remembered to you."[85]

---

the couple moved to Savannah, Georgia. Mordecai's family was among the first settlers in Savannah,[86] and Fanny and Mordecai made their place in the center of the small Jewish community, even holding religious services in their home.[87]

When Savannah fell in December 1778, the British captured Mordecai and their eldest son, and Fanny Sheftall fled to British-controlled Charleston with their four younger children. Unable to obtain access to any of their funds, she managed to support them all for a year and a half by taking in sewing. As she wrote to her husband: "I am obliged to take in needle worke to make a living for my family, so I leave you to judge what a livinge that must be."[88] The family also suffered from epidemics of smallpox and yellow fever, diseases common at that time in the southern colonies.

After the war, the Sheftalls were reunited in Philadelphia. They had so little money that in order to pay for their passage from Charleston, their clothes were impounded. In 1782, the family finally returned to Savannah.[89]

Following Mordecai Sheftall's death in 1792, his wife once again became a petitioner. On behalf of her children, she tried to obtain compensation for the family's financial losses, suffered as a result of Mordecai Sheftall's service to his country, but the struggling colonial government had little money to give and Fanny Sheftall died in Beaufort, South Carolina, without succeeding in this last effort.

In another place and time, Sheftall might have been a very ordinary woman, but circumstances forced her to be strong, even heroic, in her devotion to her family. She serves as one example of many women who faced similar dangers and challenges.

THE WORLD OF JEWISH WOMEN

ECONOMIC ACTIVITIES

In colonial America, with few institutions yet in place, women sometimes found more opportunity than they would in later centuries. **Abigail Minis** of Savannah, widowed in 1756 with eight children to support, ran the family farm and retail business. She was successful enough to purchase additional property, including cattle, slaves, and real estate. She and her five daughters also operated a tavern.[90]

Not all women were as successful, however. **Frances Hart Sheftall,** in serious economic straits during the Revolutionary War, made a meager living by taking in sewing,[91] always an acceptable way for poor women to earn money.

By the nineteenth century, it was well established that the place of middle-class women was primarily in the home. They were discouraged from pursuing an education or entering business (except to help husbands or fathers) and were limited to the professions of teaching and nursing. Women with even a moderate education often opened private schools for girls. In Philadelphia in the 1830s, Simha Peixotto and Rachel Peixotto Pyke ran a private school in their home. With their teaching experience, they were able to help write the texts for the first Hebrew Sunday school, founded by **Rebecca Gratz**, and to teach some of the classes.[92]

As a young girl, **Penina Moise** contributed to the family income by doing needlework. After she was grown, she supported herself by running a school with her sister Rachel and her niece Jacqueline Levy.

Poorer or less-educated women had even fewer choices and could obtain employment only as domestics or in factories. Rose Schneiderman's mother worked as a laundress, but factory work was usually preferable because it offered more money. By the end of the nineteenth century, large numbers of women were employed as sewing-machine operators in factories and doing piecework at home. Some of those women went on to become leaders of the Labor Union movement. They included Theresa Serber Malkiel, who was already working in a garment factory in the 1890s at the age of seventeen. Rose Schneiderman was thirteen when she began her working life in 1895 as an errand girl in a department store and, three years later, found employment as a cap maker for a higher wage.

EDUCATION

Education for girls continued to be informal and unstructured in colonial America, but most Jewish women in the eighteenth century seem to have acquired the rudiments of English literacy. Only very slowly were secular schools beyond the elementary level introduced for women. However, there were a handful of Jewish women in the New World who were fairly well educated. **Bilhah Abigail Franks** carried on an extensive correspondence with her son Naphtali and many other relatives. In her letters she quoted from novels, essays, and poems as well as the plays of Shakespeare; encouraged her son to study regularly; and was aware of Jewish rituals and laws.

Many other letters to family and friends indicate a basic education. Some Jewish women acquired enough education to teach professionally. However, the extent of their Jewish learning was usually more limited. The Franks children were raised in a traditional Jewish home and given Hebrew lessons. **Rachel Solomons Joseph**, wife of the first Canadian *shoḥet*, taught Judaism to her own children without the aid of books. Grace Seixas Nathan (1752–1831), sister of Gershom Seixas, the first cantor in New York, came from a family well versed in Judaism. She wrote poetry on Jewish themes and may have known some Hebrew.

Rebecca Gratz was one of the few women whose knowledge included both secular and Jewish subjects. She established a Hebrew school in her home to teach her nieces and nephews and then organized a Hebrew school for poor Jewish children in Philadelphia. Hers was the first such school to teach Jewish subjects to girls and boys at no charge and to employ female teachers.

Emma Lazarus, exceptionally well educated in secular subjects, learned Hebrew independently in her adult years. Formal Jewish education for girls was rare in North America until well into the twentieth century. Rosa Sonneschein, founder and editor of *The American Jewess*, the first English-language magazine for Jewish women in the United States (published from 1895–1899), was the daughter and wife of Reform rabbis and was learned in Jewish subjects. She urged greater religious observance, but her own education was obtained informally from her family and not in a Jewish school.

FAMILY LIFE

Betrothal and Marriage

With no established Jewish community in the New World, the institutions surrounding marriage and betrothal were virtually impossible to follow. This had both advantages and disadvantages. On the one hand, there were few arranged marriages such as the one **Ernestine Rose**'s father tried to impose on her. On the other hand, a lack of partners made selecting a mate very difficult, sometimes even impossible, for young people. In Savannah, Abigail Minis's five daughters had no choice of husbands. Of the five eligible young Jewish men in that city, three were their brothers and the other two were too young for the older sisters. Four of the five remained single. Hannah was the only one who married, and she was divorced after sixteen months.[93]

The more upper-class, financially successful families had even fewer choices. Bilhah Abigail Franks bemoaned the fact that there were no suitable marriage partners for her sons and daughters, and urged her son "HeartSey," living in England, to help in the search. She wrote: ". . . pray Tell me doe you Expect Your Sisters to be Nuns for Unless they can Meet with a Person that Can keep them a Coach & Six I supose they must not think of Changeing there Condition."[94]

In a community with so few Jews, and even fewer among their social class, matchmaking was not always successful. Several of the Franks children did not marry at all. One daughter, Richa, remained unmarried until after her father's death when she moved to England. Naphtali ("HeartSey") married his first cousin

Phila Franks, in England. This was undoubtedly considered a good match. Another son, Moses, also married an English cousin, but Phila Franks, Abigail and Jacob's oldest daughter, eloped in 1742. She secretly married a Christian, General Oliver de Lancey, and was baptized. Abigail Franks was so hurt by this marriage that she never spoke to her daughter again.

The Franks's son David also intermarried. His wife was Margaret Evans, a Christian woman from Philadelphia. The couple had two daughters, Rebecca and Abigail.[95]

Abigail Minis's daughter Esther had a Christian admirer, a sailor named John Robinson. She refused to marry him, but in spite of this rejection he left her his entire estate when he died in 1758.[96] Many other Jewish men and women did intermarry and assimilated into the new American landscape.

The easy acceptance of Jews by some parts of the gentile community led to even more intermarriage in the nineteenth century.[97] When Rebecca Gratz's aunt, Shinah Simon, married a non-Jew named Dr. Joseph Schuyler, Shinah's father, Joseph (Rebecca's grandfather), broke with her completely as Abigail Franks did with her daughter Phila. Whether this rejection within her own family influenced Rebecca's decision not to marry can only be surmised.

When Rebecca was a young woman of twenty-one, a Christian, Samuel Ewing, had courted her. Ewing was a prominent lawyer, son of the provost of the University of Pennsylvania and a good friend of the Gratz family. Samuel praised Rebecca in a letter, saying: "She will . . . as a wife . . . render anyone happy."[98] But Ewing eventually married another woman, confessing to her that he had previously loved Rebecca.

> ### ABIGAIL FRANKS LAMENTS FOR HER DAUGHTER
>
> On June 7, 1743, after discovering that her oldest daughter had eloped with a Christian man, Abigail Franks was distraught. She wrote to her son Naphtali ("HeartSey"):
>
> ". . . the Severe Affliction I am Under on the Conduct of that Unhappy Girle Good God Wath a Shock it was when they Acquainted me She had Left the House and Had bin Married Six months. I can hardly hold my Pen whilst I am a writting it Itts wath I Never could have Imagined Especially Affter wath I heard her Soe often Say that noe Consideration in Life should Ever Induce her to Disoblige Such good parents."[99]

Rumors that Rebecca returned his love were never confirmed.

Rebecca Gratz certainly had her difficulties with intermarriage. While two of her brothers married Christian women and she maintained a warm relationship with at least one of those gentile sisters-in-law, Marie Gist Gratz, she also expressed a feeling that it was impossible to reconcile two different creeds in a marriage. In a letter dated 1817, she wrote about the lack of harmony among her relatives when her Aunt Shinah converted.[100] But this was not the whole story. As she explained to her friend Peggy Ewing, she was "never one of the numerous train of worshippers [to] the Goddess of romance."[101] In fact, Rebecca Gratz, who never married, had many male friends but claimed that "she was a stranger to love" and "had her doubts about the happiness of most marriages."[102]

Five siblings of the Gratz family remained unmarried. Rebecca lived with her three bachelor brothers and her single sister, Sarah, but was involved with the children of her married brothers and sisters. After her sister Rachel's death in 1823 Rebecca Gratz took the responsibility of raising those six nieces and nephews.[103]

In the period from 1800 to 1875 some of the most creative and productive Jewish women living in the United States were unmarried. Educated, enlightened, and with opportunities available to them outside the Jewish community, many devoted themselves to charity work and lived lives similar to those of upper-class gentile women. As succeeding waves of immigrants arrived in the New World, the Jewish communities of North America grew and the availability of marital partners increased.

The majority of Jewish women continued to have traditional marriages and bear children. In 1869, Reform rabbi Isaac Mayer Wise, urged the adoption of a more active role for women in the ceremony itself. This included a declaration of marriage vows by both partners and an exchange of rings.[104]

Children

All evidence indicates that the small Jewish communities in the New World valued children, and the ideal family was large. Although **Rebecca Machado Phillips**'s family of twenty-one children was more numerous than most, it was certainly not unheard of. Cantor Gershom Seixas of New York

had three children from his first wife. When she died and he remarried, he and his second wife, Hannah, had eleven children. She cared for all fourteen of them. Abigail Minis had eight children and Abigail Franks had nine.

Divorce

In the early colonial period, with no rabbis and no traditional Jewish courts, divorces, when they occurred, were usually filed and granted through civil courts. Hannah Minis, when she was divorced, certainly did not have a Jewish court *(beit din)* with three rabbis available in Savannah to grant her a *get*.

As German Jews entered the United States in the mid-1800s, they brought the practices of Reform Judaism with them and quickly adopted Reform ideas concerning divorce. Religious divorce was rejected in favor of civil divorce, and the secular courts might declare husbands who had deserted their wives legally dead, thus avoiding the problem of the *agunah*.[105] Traditional rabbinical courts were not established in North America until the nineteenth century, and then only on a voluntary basis.

Women's Sexuality

Extreme modesty and circumspection in sexual matters was a hallmark of eighteenth- and nineteenth-century England, and this fit in well with the traditions of Jewish life with its emphasis on modesty for women. In the early period, departures from the norms of decency were kept secret and most Jewish women were protected within middle- or upper-class families.

In the later part of the nineteenth century, however, with the influx of poor immigrants from eastern Europe, many young women came alone and were hard-pressed to find employment that would enable them to support themselves. A significant number of these immigrant women resorted to or were lured into prostitution. By the 1890s there were a growing number of Jewish prostitutes and unwed mothers.[106] Middle-class German Jews were concerned enough about this problem to organize institutions to help them, and homes for "wayward girls" began to appear, especially in the larger cities. The official stance of the Jewish community was that prostitution was rare, but there is much evidence to indicate that it was a serious and growing problem in America and Europe that lasted into the twentieth century.

LEGAL RIGHTS

The Civil Rights of Women

Jewish women's legal rights in the American colonies and in Canada, Mexico, and South America paralleled the legal rights of all women and usually followed the laws of the colonial government in power. The early Canadian settlements lived first under French rule. When the English gained control, English common law was the standard as it was in the American colonies. Under English law, an unmarried woman had the right to her own wages and property. She could sue and be sued and was responsible for herself as an adult. Although her family could exert pressure on her, they could not force her to marry against her will.

A married woman, however, was not a legal entity; she was subsumed into the legal person of her husband. As a result, once married, a woman

had no right to her own wages, could not own or bequeath property, or sue in court.

These disabilities remained in place after the Revolution and after the United States had gained its independence from England, but as the nineteenth century progressed, some Americans began working for change. In 1836, Judge Thomas Hertell, a social reformer and a member of the New York legislature, introduced a resolution allowing married women to own property. Despite opposition, he pressed his case and finally, in 1840, introduced a third version of his bill. It was titled "An Act For the More Effectual Protection of the Right of Property of Married Women, and to Enable Them To Devise Their Estate."[107]

It took many years for the Married Women's Property Act to become law.

AN ACT FOR THE PROTECTION AND PRESERVATION OF THE RIGHTS AND PROPERTY OF MARRIED WOMEN

Resolved: That a select committee be appointed to inquire and report to this house, at the present or succeeding session of the legislature, what provisions, if any, will be proper and necessary to be made by law, the better to protect the rights and property of married women from injury and waste by means of improvident, prodigal, intemperate and dissolute habits and practices of their husbands. The law shall take effect immediately after the passage thereof.[108]

With the help of women activists like Ernestine Rose, who carried petitions from door to door collecting signatures, it was finally passed in 1848. Within the next two decades, many other new laws helped women toward equality. Working women were given the right to keep their own salaries. Married women were also granted the right to sue in court, even to sue their husbands. New laws gave women joint guardianship over their children, a right that up until then belonged only to fathers. But although the women of many of the western territories were given the right to vote when those areas became states,[109] on the national level women were not granted suffrage easily.

The heroic battle to gain the franchise for all women was won only in 1920, after World War I had already "made the world safe for democracy"[110] and after women had chained themselves to the gates of the White House. While few Jewish women's names appear in the leadership lists for this cause, many supported it. For the most part, however, Jewish women activists chose priorities more consonant with the needs of the American Jewish community. Women's suffrage was largely a middle-class movement, and at the end of the nineteenth century, most Jews were immigrants and identified with the working class.

Wills

Under English common law, as under Jewish law, unmarried women who owned property could make bequests to others but married women were not legally permitted to leave a will, as they technically owned no property. However, women found ways to avoid those limits in every age and place, and the New World was no exception.

In the eighteenth and nineteenth centuries, several wills of Jewish women show their continued interest in charity and in support of the Jewish community. Judith Baruch Alvares left thirty pounds to an orphan, and one hundred pounds was set aside to make a pathway to the Jewish cemetery "in order to the more commodious carrying my own and other corps [sic] to the grave." Rachel Luis of New York ordered her executor to sell her household goods and, with the money, to buy a *sefer Torah* for the synagogue. Simja de Torres, who died in New York, left five pounds each to the synagogues of New York and Kingston, Jamaica, where she was born and five pounds "to the poor of my nation in New York."[111]

Husbands also continued leaving their estates to their wives in spite of Jewish laws to the contrary. In his will, Judah Hays left his wife "absolutely all my plate and linnen and all my household furniture."[112]

PUBLIC POWER

In the United States, one of the ways that women found to exert influence on society was from the lecture platform. However, women were not widely accepted as public speakers. Ernestine Rose was the only Jewish woman who became well known as a speaker against slavery, but like other female abolitionists, she was often confronted by social constraints that disapproved of women speaking to mixed audiences.

In spite of this, within a year of her arrival from England, Rose was invited to lecture by the Society for Moral Philanthropists, a group that organized programs and debates on current social issues. She traveled the country speaking on women's rights, better education for the children of the masses, and later, against slavery, frequently paying her own expenses. She continued to speak out despite the fact that her appearance in any public venue was often criticized and actively discouraged by conservative leaders and newspapers.[113]

Through the power of their words, women like Ernestine Rose managed to be successful in influencing the passage of the Married Women's Property Act, in abolishing slavery, and in sensitizing the country to a variety of injustices. When women combined forces, as they did in the Women's Suffrage movement, they sometimes could wield considerable power.

Jewish women also learned to use organizational skills. In 1893, the first Congress of Jewish Women, held under the umbrella of the Parliament of Religions, was convened in Chicago. Speakers included Henrietta Szold, Josephine Lazarus (Emma Lazarus's sister), Rebekah Kohut, and Hannah G. Solomon. All of these women became important leaders in the twentieth century. From that first meeting came the National Council of Jewish Women.

Immigrant women also organized to exert pressure on their local communities. Some joined forces temporarily, organizing boycotts and protests. Their efforts were often successful in bringing about change.

In addition to fighting legal injustices, many Jewish women developed a fine sense of social responsibility that grew out of their commitment to Judaism. While still a young woman, Rebecca Gratz joined her mother, Miriam, and her sister Richea, along

---

THE LAST WILL AND TESTAMENT OF REBECCA GRATZ

Rebecca Gratz's will included the *Shema*, a statement taken from Deuteronomy (6:4–7) expressing the centrality of the belief in one God, and is one more piece of evidence showing her devotion to Judaism. It read it part:

"I Rebecca Gratz, of Philadelphia, being in sound health of body and mind, advanced in the vale of years, declare this to be my last will and testament. I commit my spirit to the God who gave it, relying on His mercy and redeeming love, and believing with a fine and perfect faith in the religion of my fathers. Hear O Israel, the Lord our God is one Lord."[114]

---

with twenty other women, including **Rebecca Machado Phillips,** in organizing the first women's charity in Philadelphia. Gratz was only twenty years old in 1801, when the Female Association for the Relief of Women and Children in Reduced Circumstances was founded. This organization was devoted to helping poor women and orphaned children of all religions. The group was made up of women who were all in a similar financial and social position. They distributed food and clothing and operated one of the first public soup kitchens.[115] When Gratz got older, she was involved in several other charitable causes, including the Philadelphia Orphan Asylum and the Female Hebrew Benevolent Society.

FIG. 28. *Los Conversos,* a painting by artist Billie Hutt of New Mexico, depicts descendants of crypto-Jews surrounded by symbols of both Christianity and Judaism. One woman is lighting the Sabbath candles, while another, sitting at the table, is wearing a crucifix. (Courtesy of the Collection of Ron and Barbara Balser)

Frances Wisebart Jacobs, known as Denver's "Mother of Charities," organized the Hebrew Ladies' Relief Society in Denver, Colorado, in 1872 to deal with problems of illness and poverty in her city. Begun as a charity for Jews, it quickly expanded to the broader community, and Jacobs was the official speaker for the group. With her help, the first free kindergarten for poor children was established.[116]

Emma Lazarus brought money, food, and clothing to Jewish refugees from eastern Europe and soon organized groups to train Jews in industrial trades. This project developed into the Hebrew Technical Institute for the purpose of vocational training. She attended rallies to raise money, improve the food, and provide running water and washing facilities. She wrote about the Russian Jews in poems and essays, pointing out that "[u]ntil we are all free, we are none of us free."[117] Hers was a courageous stand. In 1881 many American Jews were reluctant to associate with these poor immigrants, fearing the newcomers would reflect badly on their own community.

In an age when women could neither vote nor hold political office, they succeeded in creating social and legal changes by public speaking and by uniting and organizing women for specific goals. Through these methods, Jewish women also gained limited power in the Labor Union movement and in immigrant aid, causes that represented the greatest needs of the Jewish community.

RELIGIOUS PARTICIPATION

In locations where no Jewish community existed, it was often the women who maintained tradition in the home. This was certainly the case with the crypto-Jews of New Spain and the colonies of South America. The customs that remained the longest among them were those that the women practiced, and recent reports confirm that some Mexican-American women in the southwestern United States still retire to a shed behind the house on Friday evenings, where they secretly light candles.[118]

In the American colonies, where freedom of religion was widely accepted, Jews practiced openly and quickly built their own synagogues. Although men invariably assumed leadership positions here, women often were involved in fund-raising and other synagogue activities. Rebecca Machado Phillips and Grace Seixas Nathan were active in fund-raising drives for Mikveh Israel Synagogue in Philadelphia. Many women left money to synagogues in their **wills**.

Jewish women, responsible for the home environment, often were expected to teach the children about Judaism without a formal education themselves. Abigail Franks ran a traditional and kosher Jewish home in colonial New York, as did most of the families involved with the synagogue. Those who left the established Jewish community for the more isolated regions

---

A WOMAN WRITES TO HER PARENTS

Rebecca Alexander, wife of Hyman Samuel, wrote a letter in Yiddish to her parents in Europe telling of her life in a remote part of Virginia. She explained:

"We are completely isolated here. We do not have any friends . . . There is no cemetery in the whole of Virginia. In Richmond, which is twenty-two miles from here, there is a Jewish community consisting of two quorums. . . . One can make a good living here, and all live at peace. . . . There is no rabbi in all of America to excommunicate anyone. This is a blessing here; Jew and Gentile are as one. There is no *galut* here. In New York and Philadelphia there is more *galut*."

In a second letter, however, Rebecca Alexander seems to have changed her mind. Explaining that the family was moving to South Carolina, she wrote:

"I know quite well you will not want me to bring up my children like Gentiles. Here they cannot become anything else . . . [In Charleston] there is a blessed community of three hundred Jews. You can believe that I crave to see a synagogue to which I can go."[119]

---

of the country were not able to do so. While this was a hardship for some, others may have found it liberating.

The Reform movement gained a wide acceptance in the United States in the nineteenth century. According to Reform theology, women were allowed to sit together with men in synagogue services, were considered equally obligated to perform commandments, and were included in some synagogue choirs. Young girls were educated together with boys for confirmation, a rite that was meant to replace Bar Mitzvah. Temple Beth Elohim in Charleston, South Carolina, was the first Reform synagogue in the United States, and Penina Moise ran the Sunday school there in her later years.

Even within the well-populated areas, however, many Jews had little interest in synagogue life. During her early years as a writer, Emma Lazarus, from a prosperous and assimilated family, was distant from her Jewish heritage. She admitted: "my religious convictions . . . and the circumstances of my life have led me somewhat apart from my people."[120] But in 1880, Lazarus began one of her most productive periods, using Jewish themes as inspiration for her poetry.

Strong Jewish communities that observed Jewish law with all its intricacies did not develop in the New World until the very end of the nineteenth century, when the large immigration of traditional Jews from eastern Europe reestablished many of the Old World practices. Even then, there was never an official recognition of the Jewish community that compelled Jews to abide by communal decisions. Jewish practices always remained voluntary.

EPILOGUE

In this book, we have attempted to highlight a sampling of representative women, considering each one in the context of her time and, as a background, discussing the generalities of life for each period. Our sources have been varied and numerous.

European women such as Licoricia, Kandlein, and Venguessone came to us from Christian records. From Christian sources we also found mention of Jewish women doctors, teachers, and moneylenders. Islamic writings gave us information on a few Jewish women poets like Sarah and Qasmuna and a scattering of otherwise unknown individual women who were involved in lawsuits, divorces, or loans and whose cases came through the Muslim courts.

Women such as Rashi's female relations as well as Dolce of Worms, Rabbi Isserles's mother, and some Hasidic women were part of prominent families, and details about them were preserved through the writings of their male relatives. Data about other women were gleaned from Jewish historical writings, including rabbinic responsa and a variety of books and articles, both old and new. Sometimes the name of a Jewish woman came from a footnote or casual comment that we were able to trace to an original Hebrew source. Information concerning additional Jewish women may still be buried in archives or in unpublished manuscripts waiting to be discovered.

As printing and literacy spread, historical sources became so numerous that we had to carefully select whom and what would be included in this volume. But the multiplication of sources concerning Jewish women was not only the result of the spread of literacy. The Enlightenment movement (Haskalah) was another important factor. It removed individual restrictions and made it possible for Jews to function as citizens outside the Jewish community. In the process, it transformed Judaism and Jewish women everywhere.

Even in Middle Eastern lands, where women had long remained without formal education, the ideas of the Enlightenment slowly spread. New organizations like the Alliance Israélite Universelle, founded in France in 1860, moved into less developed Jewish communities, including the Balkans, Greece, Turkey, Iran, Morocco, and Egypt. Aimed at improving the social and legal status of all Jews, the Alliance opened schools for girls where both secular and Jewish subjects were studied. Whether reluctantly or enthusiastically, whether inside the fence of Jewish law and community or in opposition to it, women moved into the modern world.

Many made their mark on Jewish life, actively and creatively using the new outlook to serve Jewish causes while at the same time asserting their own independence. So Bertha Pappenheim (1865–1938) created the Jüdische Frauenbund in Germany, insisting that by becoming active in charitable causes Jewish women could be fulfilled. Lily Montagu (1873–1963) took advantage of the new religious openness by advancing the cause of Liberal Judaism in England. Golda Meir (1898–1978) asserted her independence from her parents and then from her husband, to follow a greater goal, working to help found and then lead the new State of Israel.

Still others abandoned Judaism. Rosa Luxemburg of Poland (1871–1919) embraced Socialism. Fighting the battle to create a classless society, she died in prison. Large numbers of eastern European Jews became political rebels in the wake of the Haskalah and the growth of democratic movements. They fought against the government of tzarist Russia and for individual rights for all people. Many were imprisoned or killed. Manya Shoḥat (1880–1961) also began her adult life as a Russian revolutionary but found her way to Jewish Socialism and ultimately immigrated to the land of Israel, where she helped establish the kibbutz movement.

In the past, power was available only to a small number of Jewish women, in very specific and limited circumstances. Today, Jewish women constitute an important and growing part of the secular, political world and also hold seats of power in official Jewish community organizations. Jewish women are prominent politicians, teachers, writers, philosophers, and rabbis as well as wives, mothers, and grandmothers. They are no longer required to choose between career and family as they were forced to in the earlier years of the twentieth century.

Although beyond the scope of this work, women entering the twenty-first century have crossed all the boundaries that once existed in Jewish life. They have reexamined and sometimes challenged Jewish law itself and broken the hegemony of men in the synagogue. They have created a place for themselves in the Jewish academy, in the public realm of power, and in the private realm of spirituality.

Rarely is this generation of Jewish women aware of the legal and social limitations their ancestors experienced. But hopefully, those who create and continue the history of women will begin with a fuller knowledge of all that has gone before and not have to discover it once again, as so many had to do in the past, when women were "written out of history." Today, we have extensive records and documents, biographies and autobiographies, diskettes, microfilms, and computer chips at our fingertips. Even as we write, others are recording the lives of contemporary Jewish women, the famous and infamous, the remarkable and the not so remarkable, for a posterity as yet unborn.

APPENDIX

A Brief Review of Women's Religious Participation in the Twentieth Century

The twentieth century represents the first time Jewish women as a group openly challenged their tradition and pushed for full participation in Jewish religious and communal life. The more liberal denominations of Judaism, especially those in North America, were the first to introduce such change. Rabbi Mordecai Kaplan, founder of the Reconstructionist movement in the United States, initiated the Bat Mitzvah ceremony for girls. In 1922, he called his own daughter, Judith, up for an *aliyah* to the Torah on her twelfth birthday, a bold move that went relatively unnoticed by the Jewish world until it was later adopted by Reform and Conservative congregations.[1]

In 1956, the Committee on Law and Standards, the legal body of Conservative Jewry in the United States, quietly ruled that it was not against Jewish law to call women to the Torah for an *aliyah*.[2] This ruling cleared the way for adopting the ritual of Saturday Bat Mitzvah, but remained unnoticed and with little effect on older women for twenty years.

Sally Priesand broke the barrier for women in the rabbinate in 1972 and became the first (Reform) rabbi ordained by a rabbinical seminary.[3] Although women such as Lily Montagu in England and Ray Frank and Paula Ackerman in the United States[4] had fulfilled a rabbinical role in the late nineteenth and early twentieth centuries, they had done so without official ordination by a community of rabbis. Regina Jonas, the first Jewish woman to become a Reform rabbi in Germany, was privately ordained in 1931 after being refused ordination by the Berlin Academy for the Science of Judaism. She worked for a short time as a hospital chaplain but died in Auschwitz in 1942.[5]

By the 1970s, at least parts of the established Jewish community were ready to accept women clergy, and other women, already studying for the rabbinate in the Reform and Recon-structionist movements, soon followed Priesand. In this same decade, individuals in the Conservative movement were agitating for change in different areas. A small group of women, all yeshivah educated, had been studying Jewish law together. They came to the conclusion that it was not illegal for women to fulfill commandments and take public roles. Within the talmudic statements concerning these issues, they claimed, there was room for interpretation and different understandings.

With the encouragement of a burgeoning feminist movement, this group, calling itself *Ezrat Nashim* (the Women's Section), arrived at the Conservative Rabbinical Convention in 1973 and made their demands. Women should be given full membership in Conservative synagogues, called up to the Torah, counted in a prayer quorum (minyan), and ordained as rabbis.[6] The Conservative Committee on Jewish Law and Standards undertook investigation into those demands, and over the course of ten years all were accepted by the Conservative movement in theory.[7] The implementation of these rulings was left to individual rabbis and congregations, however, and by the opening of the twenty-first century, many still had not accepted them.

The Orthodox movement has resisted such changes and remains steadfastly attached to the older traditions that have been in place for centuries. However, reflecting their own sensitivity to changing times, they have made important concessions to women.[8] A significant rise in the education of girls is opening up new doors of opportunity to Orthodox women to study in yeshivahs organized and run especial-

ly for them. This has resulted in increasing numbers of women scholars who are learned in Jewish law. Women advocates *(to'anot batei din)* are now operating in Israel to help women through the intricacies of the rabbinical court system.[9] Many women scholars have written responsa on legal issues pertinent to women.[10] In addition, the Women's Tefilla Network, operated primarily by Orthodox women in cities throughout the United States, holds all-female services and gives women a chance to lead and participate fully in the traditional rituals. Even more recent is the Jewish Orthodox Feminist Alliance (JOFA), which promotes activisim and supports women's rights in Orthodox circles.[11]

All these developments may be innovations in Judaism, but the concept of change itself has been ongoing throughout Jewish history and continues even in the most conservative bastions of tradition. In Israel, despite continued opposition, a small number of women from all denominations gather once a month for a Torah service at the Western Wall in Jerusalem. Calling themselves "Women of the Wall," they insist on their right to pray together. They have taken their case through the Israeli court system to the Supreme Court, where they obtained a favorable ruling in late 1999. Orthodox groups in Israel, who bitterly resent women organizing and challenging the law, are still opposing this ruling.

Once, public religious ritual was a male sphere. Today, women rabbis and cantors are molding and reshaping the rabbinate, offering different approaches and fresh perspectives on old issues.[12] In past centuries, mystical methods to enhance spirituality were never completely mainstream and women's role in Jewish spirituality was even more marginal. Today, it is women who have often shown a greater interest in spiritual life. Healing services, group meditation, and mysticism, all designed to help Jews enter into God's presence, are being introduced and led by male and female rabbis and prayer leaders. These attempts to redefine spirituality and make it relevant to contemporary life may serve to reintroduce this aspect of the Jewish religion and, in the process, to enhance Judaism.

NOTES

CHAPTER ONE

1 H. Tadmor, "The Period of the First Temple, the Babylonian Exile and the Restoration," pt. 2 in *A History of the Jewish People*, ed. H. H. Ben-Sasson (Cambridge, Mass.: Harvard University Press, 1976), 182.

2 Naḥman Avigad, *Corpus of West Semitic Stamp Seals*, revised by Benjamin Sass (Jerusalem: Israel Academy of Sciences and Humanities, 1997), 30.

3 Ezra 1:2–4; 6:3–5. James B. Pritchard, *The Ancient Near East, An Anthology of Texts and Pictures*, vol. 1 (Princeton, N.J.: Princeton University Press, 1958), 206–208.

4 Bezalel Porten and Ada Yardeni, eds. and trans., *Textbook of Aramaic Documents from Ancient Egypt*, vol. 2 (Jerusalem: Hebrew University Press, 1989).

5 Victor Tcherikover, *Hellenistic Civilization and the Jews*, trans. S. Applebaum (New York: Atheneum, 1977), 39–51.

6 Tcherikover and Fuks, *Corpus Papyrorum Judaicarum*, vol. 1 (Cambridge, Mass.: Magnes Press, Hebrew University Press, Harvard University Press, 1957), 1–3.

7 Jean Baptiste Frey, *Corpus Inscriptionum Judaicarum: Jewish Inscriptions from the Third Century B.C. to the Seventh Century A.D., (CIJ)*, vol. 1, *Europe* (reprinted and with a new introduction by Baruch Lifshitz) (New York: K'tav, 1975); this work is a collection of all these ancient inscriptions with French translations.

8 Emil Schürer, *A History of the Jewish People in the Time of Jesus*, ed. with an introduction by Nahum N. Glatzer (New York: Schocken, 1961), 176–184.

9 Josephus, *The Jewish Wars*, vol. 6 of Josephus Flavius, *The Complete Works of Josephus*, trans. H. St. J. Thackeray (Cambridge, Mass.: Harvard University Press, 1925), 351–358; 479.

10 Yigael Yadin, *Bar Kokhba: Rediscovery of the Legendary Hero of the Last Jewish Revolt against Rome* (New York: Random House, 1971).

11 Yigael Yadin, "Expedition D: The Cave of Letters," *Israel Expedition Journal* 12 (1962): 235–238.

12 Jacob Neusner, *There We Sat Down: Talmudic Judaism in the Making* (New York: Ktav, 1972), 13.

13 Yadin, "Expedition D: The Cave of Letters," 235–238; Yadin, *Bar Kokhba*, 233.

14 Naphtali Lewis, *Greek Papyri*, vol. 2 of the *Documents from the Bar Kokhba Period in the Cave of Letters* (Jerusalem: Israel Exploration Society and Hebrew University, 1989), 29.

15 Tcherikover and Fuks, *Corpus Papyrorum*, vol. 2, 246–247.

16 Lewis, *The Documents*, 47–64.

17 H. J. Poletsky, "The Greek Papyri from the Cave of Letters," *Israel Exploration Journal* 12 (1962): 261.

18 Tcherikover and Fuks, *Corpus Papyrorum*, vol. 2, 246–247.

19 Tal Ilan, *Integrating Women into Second Temple History* (Tübingen: Mohr Siebeck, 1999), 217–233.

20 Tcherikover and Fuks, *Corpus Papyrorum*, vol. 2, 22–24.

21 Ibid.

22 Bezalel Porten, *The Elephantine Papyri: Three Millennia of Cross Cultural Continuity and Change* (Leiden: Brill, 1996), 177–183, Doc. B28. Note that Mibtahiah's name is spelled with a *p* in this document.

23 Bernadette Brooten, *Women in the Ancient Synagogue* (Atlanta, Ga.: Scholar's Press, 1982; Brown Judaic Studies, Brown University).

24 Ross S. Kraemer, *Her Share of the Blessings: Women's Religions Among Pagans, Jews and Christians in the Greco-Roman World* (New York: Oxford University Press, 1992), 118, 122–123. For a copy of the original inscription see Frey, *CIJ*, vol. 1, #741.

25 For information on Shelamzion, see Tal Ilan, *Jewish Women in Greco-Roman Palestine* (Tübingen: J. C. B. Mohr, 1995), 69; Ross Kraemer, "Jewish Mothers and Daughters in the Greco-Roman World," *The Jewish Family in Antiquity*, ed. S. Cohen (Atlanta, Ga.: Scholars Press, 1993), 100–101; Lewis, *The Documents*, 71–82.

26 Frey, *CIJ*, Rufina, #741.

27 Frey, *CIJ*, Sophia #731c.

28 Porten and Yardeni, *Textbook of Aramaic Documents*, vol. 2, *Contracts*, 60–63, Doc. B3.3.

29 Frey, *CIJ*, #738; Kraemer, *Her Share of the Blessings*, 84; 108; 119.

30 Tcherikover and Fuks, *Corpus Papyrorum*, vol. 2, 16–18.

31 Kraemer, *Her Share of the Blessings*, 118.

32 Bonnie S. Anderson and Judith P. Zinsser, *A History of Their Own*, vol. 1 (New York: Harper & Row, 1988), 41.

33 Tcherikover and Fuks, *Corpus Papyrorum*, vol. 2, 16–18.

34 Ibid., vol. 2, 19–20; includes an annulment of a contract for a wet nurse named Martha from 14 B.C.E.

35 Kraemer, *Her Share of the Blessings*, vol. 1, 171–173.

36 Ilan, *Jewish Women in Greco-Roman Palestine*, 192.

37 Leonie Archer, *Her Price Is Beyond Rubies: The Jewish Woman in Graeco-Roman Palestine* (Sheffield, England: Journal for the Study of the Old Testament Press, 1990), 161–162. But see Michael Satlow, "Reconsidering the Rabbinic *Ketubah* Payment," in *The Jewish Family in Antiquity*, ed. Shaye J. D. Cohen (Atlanta, Ga.: Scholars Press, 1993), 137. Satlow believes that in Babatha's marriage contract, as well as a few others of that same period, the word *ketubbah* means dowry. The definition of *ketubbah* as a future promise of payment by the husband in case of divorce or death did not evolve until later.

38 Lawrence Fine, in "The Role of Women at the Rituals of Their Infant Children," in *Judaism in Practice*, ed. Lawrence Fine (Princeton, N.J.: Princeton University Press, 2001), 101, believes that the two terms "the law of Moses and the Jews" and "the law of Moses and Israel" were interchangeable and did not mark any political difference in Jewish status.

39 For a discussion of the evolution and formulation of the marriage contract and *ketubbah*, see Ilan, *Jewish Women in Greco-Roman Palestine*, 192–193 and n.113.

40 Ilan, *Integrating Women*, 236.

41 N. Lewis, R. Katzoff, and J. C. Greenfield, "Papyrus Yadin 18," *Israel Exploration Journal* 37 (1987): 240–241.

42 Ilan, *Jewish Women in Greco-Roman Palestine*, 69, disagrees with the supposition that Shelamzion was a minor but gives other, rabbinic sources for child marriages. See also

Judith Hauptman, *Rereading the Rabbis: A Woman's Voice* (Boulder, Colo.: Westview Press, 1998), 92–94.

43   Porten, *The Elephantine Papyri*, 177–183, Doc. B28.

44   Ilan, *Integrating Women*, 258.

45   John J. Collins, "Marriage, Divorce and Family in Second Temple Judaism," in *Families in Ancient Israel*, ed. Leo G. Perdue et al. (Louisville, Ky.: Westminister John Knox Press, 1997), 116. See also Satlow, "Reconsidering the Rabbinic *Ketubah* Payment," 146; and Reuven Yaron, *Introduction to the Law of the Aramaic Papyri* (Oxford: Clarendon Press, 1961), 100. Yaron states that while both ancient Elephantine and medieval Egypt follow common prototypes, a direct connection "can nevertheless not be regarded as established."

46   The more common word *polygamy/polygamous* implies the possibility of having many mates and could apply to men or women. *Polygyny/polygynous* applies only to men having more than one wife and is therefore more accurate.

47   Lewis, *The Documents*, 24.

48   H. J. Poletsky, "The Greek Papyri," 261.

49   Poletsky, "The Greek Papyri," 261; Yadin, *Bar Kokhba*, 249; Lewis, *The Documents*, 113–114, Doc. 26.

50   Yadin, "Expedition D: The Cave of Letters," 247.

51   Ilan, *Integrating Women*, 210.

52   Philo, *The Special Laws*, 3:175, as cited by Ross Kraemer, ed., *Maenads, Martyrs, Matrons, Monastics* (Philadelphia: Fortress Press, 1988), 30.

53   Porten and Yardeni, *Textbook of Aramaic Documents*, vol. 2, *Contracts*, 126–127, Doc. B5.5.

54   Yadin, "Expedition D: The Cave of Letters," 244.

55   Yadin, *Bar Kokhba*, 236.

56   Ibid., 233; Ilan, *Jewish Women in Greco-Roman Palestine*, 51.

57   Porten and Yardeni, *Textbook of Aramaic Documents*, vol. 2, *Contracts*, 126–127, Doc. B5.5.

58   Yaron, *The Law of the Aramaic Papyri*, 42–43.

59   Lewis, *The Documents*, 85, Doc. 19.

60   See Yadin, *Bar Kokhba*, 244.

61   Lewis, *The Documents*, 71–82.

62   Avigad, *West Semitic Stamp Seals*, 30.

63   Ibid., 31.

64   Brooten, *Women in the Ancient Synagogue*, was a pioneer in this field. Others have followed her lead.

65   Kraemer, *Her Share of the Blessings*, 118.

66   Ibid., 121.

67   Brooten, *Women in the Ancient Synagogue*, 143.

68   Rebecca Lesses, "Exe(o)rcising Power: Women As Sorceresses, Exorcists, and Demonesses in Babylonian Jewish Society of Late Antiquity," *Journal of the American Academy of Religion* 69, no. 2 (2001): 346. An alternative translation is in James Alan Montgomery, *Aramaic Incantation Texts from Nippur* (Philadelphia: University of Pennsylvania Press, The Museum Publications of the Babylonian Section, Vol. 3, 1913), 190–191.

69   Joseph Naveh and Shaul Shaked, *Magic Spells and Formulae: Aramaic Incantations of Late Antiquity* (Jerusalem: Magnes Press, 1993), 101–105, from an amulet in the collection of the Metropolitan Museum of Art, New York City.

70   For a full discussion of these inscriptions and their possible meanings, see Kraemer, *Her Share of the Blessings*, 23–29; Brooten, *Women in the Ancient Synagogue;* and Frey, *CIJ,* nos. 400, 581, 590, 597, 692, 731c.

71 Theodore Schrire, *Hebrew Amulets: Their Decipherment and Interpretation* (New York: Behrman House, 1982), 13–19. Schrire claims that the use of amulets was common during the period of the Maccabees (2 Macc. 12:40).

72 Ross S. Kraemer, "Jewish Women in the Diaspora World of Late Antiquity," in *Jewish Women in Historical Perspective* (Detroit: Wayne State University Press, 1991), 50, gives the text from a papyrus amulet. T. Schrire, *Hebrew Amulets*, 5–10, discusses amulets and bowls of metal and clay, and also a few made from bones.

73 *Alphabeta de-Ben Sira* (reprint ed., Warsaw: n.p., 1927), 13–14. Theodore H. Gaster, "A Canaanite Magical Text," *Orientalia*, n.s. 11 (1942): 41–79.

CHAPTER TWO

1 A significant group of Jews in Palestine favored hellenization, and the Maccabees fought simultaneously against these Jews and the Syrians. See 1 Maccabees 7:1–30; 2 Maccabees 5:1–10; Victor Tcherikover, *Hellenistic Civilization and the Jews*, trans. S. Applebaum (New York: Atheneum, 1977), 124.

2 1 Maccabees is an account of the events in the land of Israel from the ascent of King Antiochus in 175 B.C.E. to the death of Simon, the last Maccabee brother. It was originally written in Hebrew but survives only in a Greek translation. 2 Maccabees concentrates mainly on the exploits of Judah the Maccabee and was written by Jason of Cyrene. See *Encyclopaedia Judaica*, 1st ed., s.v. "Maccabees I"; "Maccabees II." 3 and 4 Maccabees, although lumped with the first two books, deal with different subjects.

3 Flavius Josephus, *Jewish War*; *Jewish Antiquities*. The translations in this chapter all refer to *The Complete Works of Josephus* (Cambridge, Mass.: Harvard University Press, 1925).

4 These dates are given in *Encyclopaedia Judaica*, 1st ed., s.v. "Hasmoneans," which dates the reign of Jannai's wife and successor as 76–67 B.C.E. But see Schürer, *A History of the Jewish People in the Time of Jesus*, ed. Nahum N. Glatzer (New York: Schocken, 1961), 82 and 92, which gives 78 B.C.E. as the date of Alexander Jannai's death and the reign of his wife as 78–69.

5 Tcherikover, *Hellenistic Civilization and the Jews*, 256.

6 Sources for Sambathe and other Greek sybils include Ralph Marcus, "Hellenistic Jewish Literature," in *The Jews: Their History, Culture and Religion*, vol. 2, ed. Louis Finkelstein (New York: Harper and Bros., 1955), 764–765; H. W. Parke, *Sibyls and Sibylline Prophecy in Classical Antiquity* (London & New York: Routledge, 1988), 5, 13.

7 Philo, *De vita contemplative (On the Contemplative Life)*, trans. F. H. Colson (Cambridge, Mass.: Harvard University Press, reprint 1950), verses 17–40 and 64–90; Ross Kraemer, "Monastic Jewish Women in Greco-Roman Egypt: Philo Judaeus on the Therapeutrides," *Signs* (winter 1989): 347.

8 For brief definitions of the Mishnah, Talmud, Tosefta, and Beraitot, see Judith Hauptman, *Rereading the Rabbis: A Woman's Voice* (Boulder, Colo.: Westview Press, 1998), 7–9, or *Encyclopaedia Judaica*, 1st ed., s.v. "Mishnah," "Talmud," "Tosefta," and "Baraita," for a fuller explanation.

9 Jacob Neusner, *A History of the Jews in Babylonia*, vol. 2, (Leiden: Brill, 1966), 246–249, estimates an outside figure of 1,200,000 and probably less. But see Solomon Grayzel, *A History of the Jews: From the Babylonian Exile to the Present, 5728-1968* (New York: New American Library, 1968), 212–213, who suggests the Jewish population may have reached 2 million between the second and fifth centuries.

10 Ross Kraemer, *Her Share of the Blessings: Women's Religions Among Pagans, Jews, and Christians in the Greco-Roman World* (New York: Oxford University Press, 1992), 93; Tal Ilan, *Jewish Women in Greco-Roman Palestine* (Tübingen: Mohr, 1995), 33.

11 The traditional story offered here is, in part, a synopsis from Rachel Adler, "The Virgin in the Brothel and Other Anomalies: Character and Context in the Legend of Beruriah," *Tikkun* 6 (1988): 28–32;102–106. Note that alternate spellings include *Bruria* and *Berurya*. All English translations of Talmudic sources are from *The Babylonian Talmud*, trans. and ed. L. Epstein (London: Soncino Press, 1936).

12 David Goodblatt, "The Beruriah Traditions," *Journal of Jewish Studies* 25 (1975): 68–85, esp. p. 68, note 1. The author uses this information to assert that there is insufficient evidence to maintain that Beruriah, daughter of R. Hananiah b. Teradyon, and the wife of R. Meir are one and the same person.

13 Josephus, *Jewish Antiquities*, 13:230–235.

14 Emil Schürer, *A History of the Jewish People in the Time of Jesus*, ed. with intro. by Nahum Glatzer (New York: Schocken, 1961), 67–68.

15 *Encyclopaedia Judaica*, 1st ed., s.v. "Herod I."

16 Emil Schürer, *A History of the Jewish People*, 169–173.

17 Josephus, *Jewish Antiquities*, 18:238–242.

18 Tal Ilan, "The Quest for the Historical Beruriah, Rachel and Ima Shalom, *AJS Review* 22 (1997): 11–17.

19 See Daniel Boyarin, *Carnal Israel: Reading Sex in Talmudic Culture* (Berkeley: University of California Press,1993), 47, for a completely different reading of this passage as displaying "a highly negative attitude toward sexual pleasure."

20 Moses was said to have utilized a chemical process, combining sulfur, acid salts, and mercury or lead for this purpose. See Raphael Patai, *The Jewish Alchemists: A History and Source Book* (Princeton, N.J.: Princeton University Press, 1994), 37.

21 Walter Schönfeld, *Frauen in der abendländischen Heilkunde: vom Klassischen Altertum bis zum Ausgang des 19. Jahrhunderts* (Stuttgart: Ferdinand Enke Verlag, 1947), 46–47.

22 Mary Lefkowitz and Maureen Fant, *Women's Life in Greece and Rome*, 2nd ed. (Baltimore: Johns Hopkins University Press, 1992), 299. The authors point out that since her name occurs in the New Testament and her sayings survive only in quotation, it seems probable that Marie is fiction.

23 Josephus, *Jewish Antiquities*, 15:234–240.

24 Josephus, *Jewish War,* 1:443; *Jewish Antiquities*, 15:222–6. See Tal Ilan, *Integrating Women into Second Temple History* (Tübingen: Mohr Siebeck, 1999), 105–115, for an analysis of both these stories.

25 For more information about Mariamne, see Joseph Sievers, "The Role of Women in the Hasmonean Dynasty," in *Josephus, the Bible and History,* eds. Louis H. Feldman and Gohei Hata (Detroit: Wayne State University Press, 1989); Josephus, *Jewish Antiquities*, 15:234–240; Schürer, *A History of the Jewish People*, 131–137.

26 Josephus, *Jewish War,* 1:599; *Encyclopaedia Judaica*, 1st. ed., s.v. "Mariamne II."

27 The wife of R. Akiva is never named in the Talmud. Later sources refer to her as Rachel. See Ilan, "The Historical Beruriah, Rachel and Imma Shalom," 8–10.

28 B. *Nedarim* 50a; *Encyclopaedia Judaica*, 1st ed., s.v. "Akiva."

29 Josephus, *Jewish Antiquities*, 17: 322.

30 Matt. 14:6–11; Mark 6:21–29. But see *Encyclopaedia Judaica*, 1st ed. s.v. "Herodias."

31 B. *Berakhot* 48a and Genesis Rabbah 91.3 claim that Queen Salome was not a Hasmonean. Most scholars question this family connection. See Jacob Neusner, *The Rabbinic Traditions About the Pharisees Before 70*, vol. 1 (Leiden: Brill, 1971), 86–141; Sievers, "The Role of Women," 130.

32 For information on Salome Alexandra, see Sievers, "The Role of Women," 136–137; Schürer, *The History of the Jewish People*, 92; Josephus, *Jewish Antiquities*, 13: 418–432; Neusner, vol. 1, *The Rabbinic Traditions*, 89–90. Talmudic sources include B. *Berakhot* 48a; *Midrash Tannaim al Sefer Devarim*, vol. 1 (Berlin: Tzvi H. Itzkowski, 1908–1909), chap. 11, verse 14.

33   See B. *Shabbat* 152a; B. *Megillah* 18a; B. *Mo'ed Katan* 17a.

34   B. *Rosh Ha-Shanah* 26b.

35   B. *Ketubbot* 104a. A full discussion concerning the aged serving woman of Yehudah ha-Nasi can be found in Leonard Swidler, *Women in Judaism: The Status of Women in Formative Judaism* (Metuchen, N.J.: Scarecrow Press, 1976), 107–110.

36   Miriam Peskowitz, *Spinning Fantasies: Rabbis, Gender and History* (Berkeley: University of California Press, 1997), see especially 69–72.

37   Judith Romney Wegner, *Chattel or Person? The Status of Women in the Mishnah* (New York: Oxford University Press, 1988), 74.

38   M. *Nedarim* 4:3; Tos. *Berakhot* 2:12; P. *Shabbat* 3:4. Daniel Boyarin, *Carnal Israel: Reading Sex in Talmudic Culture* (Berkeley: University of California Press, 1993), 180, believes that the text of the Tosefta shows that women were allowed to study in Palestine, but see Wagner, *Chattel or Person*, 161, who points out that the Rabbis of the Palestinian Talmud had a much more limited definition of "studying Torah."

39   M. *Shabbat* 2:6; Léonie Archer, *Her Price Is Beyond Rubies: The Jewish Woman in Graeco-Roman Palestine* (Sheffield, England: *Journal of the Study of the Old Testament*, Supplement Series, University of Sheffield, 1990), 95–100.

40   B. *Kiddushin* 29a. This passage explains that women are exempt from those things that obligate a father toward his son: to circumcise him, teach him a trade, teach him Torah, and obtain a wife for him. It goes on to stipulate that girls do not learn or study (29b) because in Deuteronomy it says "and you shall teach them to your sons."

41   For example, see B. *Kiddushin* 80b and B. *Sukkah* 51b.

42   B. *Ḥagigah* 20a. This case involves two scholarly women whose clothing got mixed up while they visited the *mikveh* (ritual bath). They sought clarification as to whether wearing someone else's clothing would make them ritually unclean.

43   B. *Yoma* 66b. This has often been translated as "Women's place is at the spinning wheel," an anachronism, since spinning wheels were not invented before the Middle Ages.

44   Judith Romney Wegner, "Women in Classical Rabbinic Judaism," *Jewish Women in Historical Perspective* (Detroit: Wayne State University Press, 1991), 88.

45   Boyarin, *Carnal Israel*, 194–195, believes that a learned woman such as Beruriah could have existed in second century Palestine but not in later centuries in Babylonia. Wegner, "Women in Classical Rabbinic Judaism," 76, points out that Beruriah is not mentioned at all in the Mishnah and her existence is highly unlikely. Goodblatt, "The Beruriah Traditions," 84–85, asserts that Beruriah is likely to have lived in third and fourth century Babylonia and not in second century Palestine.

46   B. *Nedarim* 50a; B. *Ketubbot* 62b–63a. Further discussion of Rachel, wife of Akiva, can be found in Susan Sered, "A Tale of Three Rachels or the Cultural Herstory of a Symbol," *Nashim* 1 (1998): 26–31.

47   Wegner, *Chattel or Person*, 32–34.

48   Ibid., 34.

49   P. *Ketubbot* V, 10, 30b; P. *Bava Batra* VIII, 9, 16c.

50   Josephus, *Jewish Antiquities*, 15:259–60; Ilan, *Integrating Women*, 253.

51   B. *Gittin* 49b.

52   See Mordechai A. Friedman, *Jewish Marriages in Palestine: A Cairo Genizah Study*, vol. 2 (Tel Aviv: Tel Aviv University, 1981), 321.

53   M. *Ketubbot* 7:10 contains a list of reasons for which a husband can be compelled to divorce his wife. These include infirmities that make him repulsive and occupations that create a bad odor. In B. *Yevamot* 65a, the Rabbis stipulated that a husband is forced to divorce his wife if no children have resulted from their union after ten years of marriage. If she claims her husband is impotent (if he doesn't "shoot like an arrow"), she is believed and he must divorce her.

54 B. *Ketubbot* 64a makes an ambiguous statement implying that a husband should be forced to divorce a recalcitrant or rebellious wife *(moredet)* after thirteen months, but there was no clear agreement on it. Maimonides, in *Mishneh Torah*, Ishut 14:8, says a husband should be forced to divorce her "because she is not like a captive to be forced to engage in intercourse with someone she hates," but later, R. Jacob Tam insisted that a husband should not be compelled to divorce a *moredet*. See *Tosafot* to *Ketubbot* 63b, s.v. "*aval.*"

55 Shaye J. D. Cohen, "Purity and Piety: The Separation of Menstruants from the Sancta," *Daughters of the King: Women and the Synagogue*, eds. Susan Grossman and Rivka Haut (Philadelphia: Jewish Publication Society, 1992), 103–116.

56 But see Israel Elfenbein, ed., *Teshuvot Rashi, Solomon ben Isaac* (New York: Defus Ha'Aḥim Shulzinger, 1943), #336, for a later and even stricter opinion. In this responsum, Rashi claims that a menstruant must have her own utensils and linen for the days of her *niddah*, and may not even hand her husband a cup without an intermediary. It has been assumed that the separation of the *niddah* accounts for the separation of the sexes in the synagogue, but this is not the case.

57 Wegner, *Chattel or Person*, 100.

58 Matt.14:3–5; Mark 6:17.

59 Because Herod Antipas repudiated his daughter, the King of Arabia became his enemy and declared war against Judea in 36 C.E.See Schürer, *A History of the Jewish People*, 169–173.

60 Wegner, "Women in Classical Rabbinic Judaism," 84.

61 Wegner, *Chattel or Person*, 52–53. The concern for paternity led the Rabbis of the Talmud to stipulate that a woman must wait three months after her husband's death before she could remarry. See M. *Yevamot* 4:10.

62 For a full explanation of the rules concerning the *Sotah*, see Rachel Biale, *Women and Jewish Law: An Exploration of Women's Issues in Halakhic Sources* (New York: Schocken Books, 1984), 33ff. The ordeal of bitter waters was never performed after the second Temple period, and both the mishnaic and talmudic discussions were only theoretical.

63 But see Ilan, "The Historical Beruriah, Rachel, and Imma Shalom," 14–15, who claims that this story had other, anonymous sources and is one more example of how the Babylonian Talmud adds well-known names to older traditions.

64 Sievers, "The Role of Women," 132.

65 Josephus, *Jewish Antiquities*, 13:432.

66 M. *Sotah* 3:4 and M. *Tohorot* 7:8; B. *Kiddushin* 80b ("women are temperamentally light-headed"). See also Plato, *Laws*, 6:780c–781d, as cited by Mary R. Lefkowitz and Maureen B. Fant, eds., *Women's Life in Greece and Rome: A Source Book in Translation* (Baltimore: Johns Hopkins University Press, 2nd ed.1992), who wrote: "women's natural potential for virtue is inferior to a man's," and Ovid, *The Art of Love*. In a discussion of women's "crimes," Ovid wrote: "Each one of these crimes was prompted / By woman's lust—lust that far / Outstrips ours in keenness and frenzy." This is cited in Alcuin Blamires, ed., *Woman Defamed and Woman Defended: An Anthology of Medieval Texts* (Oxford: Clarendon Press, 1992), 19.

67 Philo, *De vita contemplative (On the Contemplative Life)*, trans. F. H. Colson (Cambridge, Mass.: Harvard University Press, reprint 1950), 33.

68 Ibid., 68.

69 Ross S. Kraemer, "Monastic Jewish Women," 349–350, favors the view that they were previously married women.

70 Shmuel Safrai, "The Place of Women in First-Century Synagogues," *Jerusalem Perspective* 40 (September/October 1993): 5.

71 Ibid., 4.

72 Philo, *De vita contemplative*. See especially verses 17–40 and 64–90.

73 B. *Sanhedrin* 67a. See Rebecca Lesses, "Exe(o)rcising Power: Women As Sorceresses, Exorcists, and Demonesses in Babylonian Jewish Society of Late Antiquity," *Journal of the American Academy of Religion* 69, no. 2 (2001): 344–375.

74 Joshua Trachtenberg, *Jewish Magic and Superstition: A Study in Folk Religion* (reprint, New York: Atheneum, 1970), 304, n. 1.

75 Melissa M. Aubin, *Gendering Magic in Late Antique Judaism* (Ph.D. thesis, Dept. of Religion, Duke University, UMI, 1998), 122.

76 For example, see B. *Shabbat* 60a–62a; B. *Pesaḥim* 110a; B. *Bava Metzia* 107b.

CHAPTER THREE

1 Miriam Peskowitz, *Spinning Fantasies: Rabbis, Gender and History* (Berkeley: University of California Press, 1997), 157; Shmuel Safrai, "Ha-im Haita Kayemet Ezrat Nashim b'Bet haKenesset beTekufah ha-Atikah? (Was There a Women's Gallery in the Synagogue of Antiquity?)," *Tarbitz* 32 (1963): 329–338; Shmuel Safrai, "The Place of Women in First-Century Synagogues," *Jerusalem Perspective* 40 (Sept.–Oct. 1993): 5.

2 For an excellent synopsis of the new Muslim religion and its spread, see Norman A. Stillman, *The Jews of Arab Lands: A History and Source Book* (Philadelphia: Jewish Publication Society, 1979).

3 Ibid., 25–26.

4 Ibid., 9.

5 Reuben Ahroni, *Yemenite Jewry: Origins, Culture and Literature* (Bloomington, Ind.: Indiana University Press, 1986), 49.

6 Stillman, *The Jews of Arab Lands*, 14.

7 André N. Chouraqui, *Between East and West: A History of the Jews of North Africa*, trans. Michael M. Bernet (Philadelphia: Jewish Publication Society, 1968), 18, points out that there was a "natural alliance" between the Jews and the nomadic Berbers (called *Botrs*).

8 The Jews of Kairouan had been brought in from other areas by the Arab conquerors when they first established the city to replace the Roman city of Carthage that had been destroyed.

9 The English sisters Agnes Lewis and Margaret Gibson showed Schechter a few ancient, handwritten sheets that they had purchased while traveling in Egypt. This ultimately led to Schechter's decision to travel to Cairo.

10 Solomon Schechter, "A Hoard of Hebrew Manuscripts," *Studies in Judaism* (Philadelphia: Jewish Publication Society, 1938): 2–30.

11 There is some question whether his father died before their arrival or shortly after. See *Encyclopaedia Judaica*, 1st ed., s.v. "Maimonides," but compare to Moses Maimonides, *A Maimonides Reader*, ed. Isadore Twersky (New York: Behrman House, 1965), 4.

12 Ibn Almali himself married Moshe's sister Miriam. See *Encyclopaedia Judaica*, 1st ed., s.v. "Maimonides."

13 Maimonides, *Mishneh Torah*, ed. Shmuel Rubenstein (Jerusalem: Mosad HaRav Kuk, 1956), Yad Melakhim 1:6.

14 Eliyahu Ashtor, *The Jews of Moslem Spain*, vol. 1 (Philadelphia: Jewish Publication Society, 1973), 12–16.

15 Stillman, *Jews of Arab Lands*, 56. A twelfth-century source, Abraham ibn Daud, *Sefer HaQabbalah (The Book of Tradition)*, ed. and trans. Gerson D. Cohen (London: Routledge and Kegan Paul, 1967), reports that the spread of learning to Spain was the result of a shipwreck. See Gerson D. Cohen, "The Story of the Four Captives," *Proceedings of the American Association for Jewish Research*, 29 (1960–61): 55–131.

16 *Sibuv HaRav Rabbi Petahiah meRegensburg (The Travels of Rabbi Petahiah of Regensburg),* ed. L. Grunhut (Jerusalem: 1967), 9–10. See also Judith R. Baskin, "Ḥinukh Nashim Yehudiot ve-Haskalatan b'Yemei haBainayim b'Artzot ha-Islam vehaNatzrut (The Education of Jewish Women and Their Enlightenment in the Middle Ages in the Lands of Islam and Christianity)," *Pe'amim* 82 (winter 2000), 33.

17 Avraham Grossman, *Ḥasidot u-Moredot: Nashim Yehudiot be-Eropah be-Yemei ha-Benayim (Pious and Rebellious: Jewish Women in Europe in the Middle Ages)* (Jerusalem: Zalman Shazar, 2001), 182.

18 Renée Levine Melammed, "A Woman Teacher in Twelfth-Century Cairo," *AJS Review* 22 (1997): 19–35.

19 Grossman, *Ḥasidot u-Moredot*, 182. Translated from the Hebrew by Isaac Taitz with the help of Dan Blumenfeld.

20 Both her letter as well as the earlier one from her husband were written by intermediaries, as was the custom in addressing a great rabbi like Maimonides and does not imply that either were unable to write. See Melammed, "A Woman Teacher," 27, n. 21.

21 Ibid., 24.

22 H[aim] Z. Hirschberg, *A History of the Jews of North Africa*, vol. 1 (Leiden: Brill, 1974), 94–95 gives a full discussion of the possible origins and misreadings of the name *Kahina*. See also chapter 1, n. 14.

23 Ibid., 91. Chouraqui, *Between East and West*, 28, called the *Jerawa* and other Berber tribes either "Jews or semi-proselytes."

24 Hirschberg, *A History of the Jews*, vol. 1, 90, believes her sons were certainly killed with her, but see Chouraqui, *Between East and West*, 34–37, who believes the sons of *Kahina* lived to convert to Islam and join the army that conquered Spain.

25 *Sisters of Exile: Sources on the Jewish Woman* (New York: Ichud Habonim Labor Zionist Youth, 1973), 32.

26 Norman Stillman, nstillman@ou.edu, "Al-Kahina," in H-Judaic, H-Judaic@h-net.msu. edu, June 3, 1998, asserts that the argument that Ibn Khaldun, the Arab historian who first claimed she was Jewish, "had original sources available to him that were not available to the historians who were writing in the century following [Kahina's life] is simply not credible." However, Hirschberg, *A History of the Jews*, 49, presents Kahina as a Jew, or at least, as coming from a "judaized tribe."

27 Shelomo Dov Goitein, "Messianic Troubles in Baghdad," *Jewish Quarterly Review* 43 (1952–1953): 58.

28 S. D. Goitein, "Otograf shel haRambam u-Mikhtav alav me'et Aḥoto Miriam (Autograph of the Rambam and a Letter to Him from His Sister Miriam)," *Tarbitz* 32 (1962–63): 190–191.

29 Shelomo Dov Goitein, *A Mediterranean Society*, vol. 5 (Berkeley: University of California Press, 1967–1993), 123; S. D. Goitein, "Autograph of the Rambam": 184–194.

30 Abraham ibn Daud, *Sefer HaQabbalah*, 95.

31 This translation and its explanation appear in James M. Nichols, "The Arabic Verses of Qasmūna bint Ismā'il ibn Baghdālah," *International Journal of Middle East Studies* 13 (1981): 156. He has supplied the word "woman" that was missing in the manuscript.

32 Both these poems can be found in the original Arabic in Jalal al-Din al-Suyuti, *Nuzhat al-julasa' fi ash'ar al-nisa' (Entertaining the Company with Poems by Women)*, ed. S. Munajjid (Beirut:Dar al-Kitab al_Jadid, 1978), 86–87. These translations are from Nichols, "The Arabic Verses of Qasmūna," 155. A less literal translation of these same poems appears in Gustav Karpeles, "Women in Jewish Literature," in *Jewish Literature and Other Essays* (Philadelphia: Jewish Publication Society, 1895), 118.

33 Nichols, "The Arabic Verses of Qasmūna," 156, never mentions his source for this, but says "the sources record . . ."

34   James A. Bellamy, "Qasmuna the Poetess: Who Was She?" *Journal of the American Oriental Society* 103 (1983): 423–424, claimed she was the daughter of Shmuel ha-Nagid, and that the original reading of her name, as the daughter of Ismail ibn Bagdala, was a misreading of Ismael ibn Nagrela, the Arabic name of Shmuel ha-Nagid. Goitein accepted Bellamy's claim, although there is no definitive proof of this. Shmuel ha-Nagid was a renowned talmudic scholar and poet. He was head of the Jewish community of Granada as well as vizier to the king of Granada. See also Goitein, *Mediterranean Society*, vol. 5, 470.

35   Norman Roth, *Jews, Visigoths and Muslims in Medieval Spain: Cooperation and Conflict* (Leiden: E. J. Brill, 1994), 174–175.

36   David S. Margoliouth, *Relations Between Arabs and Israelites* (London: Oxford University Press, 1924), 76, concedes that Sarah is the one Jewish poet whose name is "at least plausible" but claims that all the Arabian poets labeled as Jewish are highly suspect, not least because their names appear only in Arabic but not Jewish sources.

37   Meyer Waxman, *Blessed Is the Daughter* (New York: Shengold Publishers, Inc., 1968), 39, alleges these facts but gives no source for them.

38   T. Carmi, ed. and trans., *The Penguin Book of Hebrew Verse* (New York: Penguin Books, 1981), p. 97.

39   Goitein, *Mediterranean Society*, vol. 5, 468 assumes Hasdai was the moving force behind Dunash's hasty departure from Spain. But see Ezra Fleischer, "Al Dunash ben Labrat ve-Ishto u-Veno (Dunash ben Labrat and His Wife and Son)," *Meḥqerei Yerushalayim beSifrut Ivrit* 5 (1983–84): 189–202, who claims there is no evidence for this assumption and that he seems to have left of his own free will.

40   The poem is included in the Arabic collection *Kitab-l-Aghani*, ed. Abu al-Faraj al-Isbahani (10th century), and was first published in the West in Theodor Nöldeke, *Beitrage zur Poesie der Alten Araber* (Hannover: n.p., 1864), 53–54. It was translated from the Arabic by Aliza Arzt.

41   For a full explanation of the oral poetic tradition of Arabia and Yemen, see Michael Zwettler, *The Oral Tradition of Classical Arabic Poetry, Its Character and Implications* (Columbus, Ohio: Ohio State University Press, 1978). See also Nissim B. Gamlieli, *Ahavat Teman* (Tel Aviv: Afikim, 1975).

42   Goitein, *Mediterranean Society*, vol. 3, 347.

43   Translation by Goitein, *Mediterranean Society*, vol. 5, 468.

44   Ibid., 350, gives a translation of the complete document.

45   Shelomo Dov Goitein, "New Revelations from the Cairo Genizah: Jewish Women in the Middle Ages," *Hadassah Magazine* (October 1973): 15, 38–39.

46   Goitein, *Mediterranean Society*, 349.

47   Ibid., 347

48   Emily Taitz, "Kol Ishah—The Voice of Women: Where Was It Heard in Medieval Europe?" *Conservative Judaism* 38 (spring 1986): 52–53.

49   Goitein, *Mediterranean Society*, vol. 1, 127–130. In the case of families with no servants, it was more common for the man to go to market, since it was not considered proper for respectable women to be wandering about the streets.

50   Maimonides, *Mishneh Torah*, Ishut 14:23.

51   Mark R. Cohen, "Four Judaeo-Arabic Petitions of the Poor from the Cairo Geniza," *Jerusalem Studies in Arabic and Islam* 24 (2000): 457.

52   Goitein, *Mediterranean Society*, vol. 2, 170.

53   Goitein, *Mediterranean Society*, vol. 5, 355.

54   Moshe Gil, ed., Documents of the Jewish Pious Foundations from the Cairo Genizah (Leiden: Brill, 1976), doc. 90.

55 H. S. HaLevi, "Ḥayyei HaMishpaḥah b'Yisrael beTekufat HaGeonim (Family Life in Israel in the Period of the Geonim), *HaHed* 10 (1935): 16–22. Our thanks toTzvi Howard Adelman for this reference.

56 HaLevi, "Ḥayyei HaMishpaḥah," 17.

57 Goitein, *Mediterranean Society*, vol. 2, 184. See also idem, "The Jewish Family in the Days of Moses Maimonides," *Conservative Judaism* 29:1 (1974): 27.

58 Jacques Hassoun, "Un Judaisme au feminin," *Les nouveaux cahiers* 86 (autumn 1986): 7.

59 Goitein, *Mediterranean Society*, vol. 5, 201. See below for a partial text of this letter.

60 Goitein, "New Revelations from the Cairo Genizah," 39.

61 Ben-Zion Dinur, *Yisrael ba-Golah (Israel in Exile)*, vol. 1, book 4: *MeHaDorah Shniah* (Jerusalem, Tel Aviv: Devir and Mosad Bialik, 1962), 34, #13.

62 Goitein, *Medierranean Society*, vol. 3, 122.

63 B. M. Lewin, ed., *Ozar HaGeonim* (Jerusalem: 1938), *Ketubbot* 169, #428.

64 Dinur, *Yisrael ba-Golah*, 33, #10, citing from Rav Hai Gaon, *Hemdah Genuza*, #162.

65 Abraham Elihu Harkavy, *Zikhron leRishonim vegam leAharonim*, vol. 4 (Berlin: 1887), 87, #194. This is a collection of the rulings of Rav Sherira Gaon and his son Rav Hai and dates from the late tenth century. It is reprinted in Dinur, *Yisrael ba-Golah*, vol. 1, book 4, 31, #1.

66 Lewin, ed., *Ozar HaGeonim*, *Yevamot* 154, #351. A man could always have more than one wife, but sometimes the first wife had a right to refuse to tolerate it. In that case, he was free to divorce her.

67 Melammed, "A Woman Teacher," 23.

68 Mordecai Friedman, *Jewish Marriages in Palestine: A Cairo Genizah Study*, 2 vols. (Tel Aviv: Tel Aviv University Press, 1981), vol. 1, 312–346; vol. 2, 56.

69 Ibid., vol. 2, 56.

70 B. *Ketubbot* 63a–b; Lewin, *Ozar HaGeonim*, 193, #470.

71 Hai Gaon, *Hemdat Genuzah*, in *Kovetz Sifre ha-Geonim, Teshuvot u-Fesakim (Ge'onika)* (B'nei Brak: Masorah, 1984–85), #140.

72 Goitein, *Mediterranean Society*, vol. 5, 201.

73 Goitein, *Mediterranean Society*, vol. 3, 265.

74 Mordechai A. Friedman, "The Ransom-Divorce: Divorce Proceedings Initiated by the Wife in Medieval Jewish Practice," *Israel Oriental Studies* 6 (1976): 288–307.

75 Maimonides, *Mishneh Torah*, Ishut 14:8.

76 Simḥa Assaf, *Teshuvot HaGeonim* (Jerusalem: HaMadpis, 1926), #42.

77 Azriel Hildesheimer, ed., *Sefer Halakhot Gedolot*, 3 vols. (Jerusalem: Meqsey Nerdamim, 1971–88), 2:83; Hai Gaon, *Hemdat Genuzah*, in *Kovetz Sifre ha-Geonim*, #85, for R. Netronai's ruling. Rav Sherira's response, including all the previous rulings, both favorable and unfavorable, can be found in David Cassel, ed., *Teshuvot Ge'onim Qadmonim* (Berlin: Fridlendersche Buchdrukerei, 1847–48), #91.

78 Assaf, *Teshuvot HaGe'onim*, #58.

79 Ruth Langer, "The *Birkat Betulim*: A Study of the Jewish Celebration of Bridal Virginity" *Proceedings of the American Academy for Jewish Research* 61 (1995): 53–85.

80 Ibid., 67–69.

81 Harkavy, *Zikhron leRishonim vegam leAharonim*,, vol. 4, 230, #438. It was part of a response to a North African rabbi.

82 Maimonides, *Mishneh Torah*, ed. Shmuel Rubenstein (Jerusalem: Mosad HaRav Kuk, 1956), Ishut 21:3 and 10. See also *Encyclopaedia Judaica*, 1st ed., s.v. "Woman."

83 Ashtor, *The Jews of Moslem Spain*, vol. 1, 316.

84 Yom Tov Assis, "Sexual Behavior in Medieval Hispano-Jewish Society," in *Jewish History: Essays in Honour of Chimen Abramsky*, eds. Ada Rapoport-Albert and Steven J. Zipperstein (London: Peter Halban, 1988), 25–59.

85 Yehudah ben Asher, *Zikhron Yehudah, v'Hu Sefer She'elot u'Teshuvot l'Rabbenu Yehudah ben HaRash v'Sh'ar Gedolei Zmano,* eds. Yehudah Rosenberg and David Cassel (Berlin: Daniel Friedlander, 1846; reprint, Jerusalem: 1967), #17, acknowledged the existence of Jewish prostitutes in his response to a letter asking if it was not better that Jewish men use Jewish women for that purpose rather than "mix the holy seed in gentile women."

86 For a rather lewd poem by a thirteenth-century Spanish-Jewish poet comparing Arab women to Spanish women, see R. Brann, *The Compunctious Poet: Cultural Ambiguity and Hebrew Poetry in Muslim Spain* (Baltimore: Johns Hopkins University Press, 1991), 145.

87 Assis, "Sexual Behavior," 36.

88 Ibid., 38.

89 Shelomo Dov Goitein, "The Jewish Family in the Days of Moses Maimonides," *Conservative Judaism* 29:1 (1974): 28–29.

90 Goitein, *Mediterranean Society,* vol. 3, 348–349.

91 Goitein, "New Revelations from the Cairo Genizah," 14–15, 38–39.

92 Lawrence H. Schiffman and Michael D. Swartz, *Hebrew and Aramaic Incantation Texts from the Cairo Genizah* (Sheffield, England: Sheffield Academic Press, 1992), 73.

93 Goitein, *Mediterranean Society,* vol. 5.

CHAPTER FOUR

1 Esra Shereshevsky, *Rashi, the Man and His World* (New York: Sepher-Harmon Press, 1982), 21.

2 Jonathan Riley-Smith, *The Crusades: A Short History* (New Haven: Yale University Press, 1987), 128–129, 177–178, 204–207.

3 Jacob R. Marcus, *The Jew in the Medieval World: A Source Book: 315–1791* (1938; reprint, New York: Atheneum, 1979), 43.

4 Jocelyn N. Hillgarth, *Readers and Books in Majorca, 1229–1550* (Paris: CNRS, 1991), 449, #127; and 1001. The "Five Books of Genesis" was most likely the "Five Books of Moses."

5 David Nirenberg, "A Female Rabbi in Fourteenth-Century Zaragoza?" *Sefarad* 15 (1991): 179.

6 Ivan G. Marcus, "Mothers, Martyrs, and Moneymakers: Some Jewish Women in Medieval Europe," *Conservative Judaism* 38 (1986): 41–42.

7 Judith Baskin, "Dolce of Worms: Women Saints in Judaism," in *Women Saints in World Religions,* ed. Arvind Sharma (Albany, N.Y.: SUNY Press, 2000), 52.

8 Louis Stouff, "Isaac Nathan et les siens: Une famille juive d'Arles des XIV et XV siècles," *provence historique* 37 (1987): 508.

9 A. Cardoner Planas, "Seis mujeres hebreas practicando la medicina en el reino de Aragon," *Sefarad* 9, no. 2 (1949): 443.

10 Hermann Zotenberg, *Catalogue des manuscrits hébreux et samaritains de la bibliotèque Impériale* (Paris: Impremerie impériale, 1866), 55, #408.

11 Joseph Shatzmiller, *Jews, Medicine, and Medieval Society* (Berkeley: University of California Press, 1994), 112.

12 Moritz Stern, *Regensburg im Mittelalter,* vol. 5 of *Die israelitsche Bevölkerung der deutschen Städte: ein Beitrag zur deutschen Stadtgeschichte* (Frankfurt am Main: J. Kaufmann, 1935), 173.

13 *Calendar of the Liberate Rolls, Henry III,* vol. 1 (Westminster: January 12, 1240), 440.

14 For information on Kandlein, see Franz Bastein and Joseph Wideman, eds., *Monumenta Boica Regensburger Urkundbuch,* vol. 54 (Munich: C. H. Beck, 1956), 45, 83; Arye Maimon, Mordecai Breuer, and Yakov Guggenheim, eds., *Germania Judaica,* vol. 3, pt. 2 (Tübingen: J. C. B. Mohr, 1995), 1191.

15 Information on Licoricia can be found in Barrie Dobson, "The Role of Jewish Women in Medieval England," *Christianity and Judaism: Studies in Church History* 29 (1992); Henry P. Stokes, "A Jewish Family in Oxford in the 13th Century," *Jewish Historical Society of England: Transactions* 10 (1921–23); Cecil Roth, "The Jews of Medieval Oxford," *Oxford Historical Society*, New Series 9 (Oxford: Clarendon Press, 1951), 56–57; Michael Adler, "The Jewish Woman in Medieval England," in idem, *The Jews of Medieval England* (London: Edward Goldston, 1939), 39; Zefira Entin Rokeah, "The Jewish Church-Robbers and Host-Desecrators of Norwich (ca. 1285)," *Revue des études juives* 141 (1982): 331–362.

16 Michael Adler, "The Jewish Woman in Medieval England," in idem, *The Jews of Medieval England* (London: Edward Goldston, 1939), 39.

17 Zefira Entin Rokeah, "Crime and Jews in Late Thirteenth Century England," *Hebrew Union College Annual* 55 (1984): 126–127.

18 Rokeah, "Crime and Jews," 126–127. The "goods and chattels" mentioned were probably pledges left with her when the money was borrowed. By law, at least part of this bounty belonged to the king.

19 Shirley Kaufman, Galit Hasan-Rokem, and Tamar S. Hess, eds., *The Defiant Muse: Hebrew Feminist Poems from Antiquity to the Present* (New York: Feminist Press, 1999), 65.

20 Ibid.

21 Shlomo Noble, "The Jewish Woman in Medieval Martyrology," in *Studies in Jewish Bibliography, History and Literature in Honor of T. Edward Kiev*, ed. Charles Berlin (New York: Ktav, 1971), 349, quoting from A. Neubauer and M. Stern, *Hebräische Berichte über die Judenverfolgungen wärhend der Kreuzzüge* (Berlin, 1892), 50–51.

22 Ibid.

23 Michael Toch, "Selbstdarstellung von mittelalterlichen Juden," *Bild und Abbild von Menschen im Mittelalter*, ed. Elisabeth Vavra (Klagenfurt: Wieser Verlag, 1999), 173–192.

24 Daniele Iancu-Agou, "Une vente de livres hébreux à Arles en 1434: Tableau de l'élite juive arlesienne au milieu de XVe siècle," *Revue des études juives* 146 (1987): 43–44.

25 Marcus, *The Jew in the Medieval World*, 128.

26 Ibid.

27 Susan Einbinder, "Pulcellina of Blois: Romantic Myths and Narrative Conventions," *Jewish History* 12, no. 1 (1998): 34–35.

28 Daniele Iancu-Agou, "Une vente de livres hébreux à Arles en 1434: Tableau de l'élite juive arlesienne au milieu de XVe siècle," *Revue des études juives* 146 (1987): 43–44.

29 Habermann, *Sefer Gezerot Ashkenaz v'Zarfat* (Jerusalem: Mosad Rav Cook, 1945), 143.

30 Marcus, *The Jew in the Medieval World*, 128; see also Einbinder, "Pulcellina of Blois," 35, who suggests that the countess hated Pulcellina because she owed her money.

31 For information and theories concerning Raquel of Toledo, see Edna Aizenberg, "Una Judía Muy Fermosa: The Jewess As Sex Object in Medieval Spanish Literature and Lore," *La Corónica* 12 (spring 1984):187–194. See also Salo Baron, *A Social and Religious History of the Jews*, 2nd ed., vol. 4 (New York: Columbia University Press, and Philadelphia: Jewish Publication Society, 1957; 4th reprint, 1971), 31, 37, 252, n. 45.

32 *Encyclopaedia Judaica*, 1st ed., s.v. "Casimir III"; Chone Shmeruk, *The Esterke Story in Yiddish and Polish Literature* (Jerusalem: Zalman Shazar, 1985).

33 Siegmund Salfeld, ed., *Das Martyrologium des Nürnberger Memorbuches* (Berlin: Leonhard Simion, 1898): 16–17, and reprinted in *Revue des études juives* 26 (1893). Other documents have reported 32 or 33 victims.

34 Robert Chazan, *European Jewry and the First Crusade* (Berkeley: University of California Press, 1987), 2.

35 Avraham Grossman, *Ḥasidot u-Moredot: Nashim Yehudiot be-Eropah be-Yemei ha-Benayim (Pious and Rebellious: Jewish Women in Europe in the Middle Ages)* (Jerusalem: Zalman Shazar, 2001), 339.

36   Moritz Güdemann, *Ha-Torah veha-Ḥayyim be-artzot ha-Ma'arav (Torah and Life in the Lands of the West)* (Jerusalem: Makor, 1971–72/1896–97), 189–90; Ephraim Urbach, *Ba'alei HaTosafot, Toldoteihem, Ḥibboreihem, Shitatam (The Tosafists: Their Lives, Writings and Methods)*, vol. 1 (Jerusalem: Mosad Bialik: 1980), 61; vol. 1, 18–19.

37   Information about Rashi's daughters can be found in Urbach, *Ba'alei haTosafot*: 228; Shmuel Teich, *The Rishonim: Biographical Sketches of the Prominent Early Rabbinic Sages and Leaders from the Tenth–Fifteenth Centuries*, ed. Hersh Goldwurm (Brooklyn, N.Y.: Mesorah Publications, 1982); Shereshevsky, *Rashi*, 22 and n. 15.

38   The text that had been used to prove that Rashi's daughter helped write a responsum was *Shibbolei HaLeket*, a thirteenth-century work. The misprint was pointed out by Dan Rabinowitz, "Rayna Batya and Other Learned Women: A Reevaluation of Rabbi Barukh HaLevi Epstein's Sources," *Tradition* 35:1 (spring 2001): 57. In an e-mail message to the e-mail list H-Judaic, H-Judaic@listserve.msu.edu, August 16, 1999, David Berger, DVBBC@cunyvm.cuny.edu, "Rashi's daughters," concurred with Rabinowitz and stated that the relevant text should be read the *grandson* of Rashi rather than his daughter, thus making the grandson the person writing the reply to the query.

39   Franz-Josef Zives, "Reynette—eine jüdische Geldhändlerin im spätmittelalterlichen Koblenz (Reynette: A Jewish Moneylender in Late Medieval Koblenz)," *Koblenzer Beiträge zur Geschichte und Kultur* 4 (1994): 32. Our thanks to Christoph Cluse, University of Trier, Germany, for this reference.

40   This anti-Jewish action is sometimes referred to as the Rhindfleisch pogrom. Salfeld, ed., *Das Martyrologium des Nürnberger Memorbuches* (Berlin: Leonhard Simion, 1898), 178. Information on Richenza's death was also obtained from an e-mail message from Moshe N. Rosenfeld.

41   L. L. Barthelamy, *Les médecins à Marseilles avant et pendant le moyen âge*, as quoted in Harry Friedenwald, "Jewish Doctoresses in the Middle Ages," in *The Jews and Medicine: Essays*, vol. 1 (New York: Ktav, 1944), 217.

42   Steven Bowman, *The Jews of Byzantium: 1204–1453* (Tuscaloosa, Ala.: University of Alabama Press, 1985), 277, citing a Greek document.

43   Bowman, *Jews of Byzantium*, 277; Yale Strom, *The Expulsion of the Jews: Five Hundred Years of Exodus* (New York: SPI Books, 1992), 38; *Encyclopedia of the Jewish Diaspora* (Jerusalem: 1967), s.v. "Bulgaria"; *Encyclopaedia Judaica*, 1st ed., s.v. "Bulgaria"; Solomon Rosanes, *Divrei Yemei Yisrael be-Togarmah* (Husiatyn: 1907), 6. For information about Sarah's daughter Tamar, see Franz Babinger, *Mehmed the Conqueror and His Time* (Princeton, N.J.: Princeton University Press, 1978), 11.

44   Irving Agus, *Urban Civilisation in Pre-Crusade Europe*, vol. 2 (New York: Yeshiva University Press, 1965), 607.

45   Rashi to *Ketubbot* 66a, s.v. "V'shalosh ve'arba bevat eḥad."

46   Meir ben Barukh, *She'elot u-Teshuvot ha-Maharam, (The Responsa of the Maharam)* (Prague), ed. M. Bloch (1893; reprint Tel Aviv: n.p., 1969–70), #941.

47   Michael Adler, "The Medieval Jews of Exeter," *Devonshire Association for the Advancement of Science, Literature and Art: Transactions* 68 (1931): 221–240. The quote is on pp. 236–237.

48   Meir ben Barukh, *She'elot u-Teshuvot*, nos. 876, 880.

49   Ibid., #502.

50   Israel Abrahams, ed. and trans., *Hebrew Ethical Wills* (2nd ed., 1926; reprint, Philadelphia: Jewish Publication Society, 1926; 2nd ed., 1976), 165–166.

51   Walther Schönfeld, *Frauen in der abländischen Heilkunde: von klassischen Altertum bis zum Ausgang des 19. Jahrhunderts* (Stuttgart: Ferdinand Enke V, 1947), 75.

52   Isadore Loeb, "Le rôle des juifs de Paris en 1296 et 1297," *Revue des études juives* 1 (1880): 71; Schönfeld, *Frauen*, 75–76. The old French word for a woman doctor was *miresse* or *mirgesse*.

53 Grossman, *Ḥasidot u-Moredot*, 204.

54 "Sketches from Early History," in *Sisters of Exile* (New York: Ichud Habonim; Labor Zionist Youth, 1973), 35.

55 Richard Emery, *The Jews of Perpignan in the Thirteenth Century* (New York: Columbia University Press, 1959), 26.

56 William Chester Jordan, "Jews on Top: Women and the Availability of Consumption Loans in Northern France in the Mid–Thirteenth Century," *Journal of Jewish Studies* 29 (1978): 56.

57 Isaac ben Moses, *Sefer Or Zarua*, pt. 1 (Zhitomir, n.p., 1862), #762.

58 David Cassel, *Teshuvot Geonim Qadmonim*, (Berlin: n.p., 1848), 14a, #66.

59 Louis Finkelstein, *Jewish Self-Government in the Middle Ages* (New York: Philipp Feldheim, 1964), 201, j. 20, for R. Gershom's ruling. For R. Tam's ruling, 168–170.

60 Michael Toch, "Die jüdische Frau im Erwerbsleben des Spätmittelalters (The Jewish Woman in the Working World of the Late Middle Ages)," in *Zur Geschichte der jüdischen Frau in Deutschland*, ed. Julius Carlebach (Berlin: Metropol-Verlag, 1993), 39.

61 A. Landgraf, ed., *Commentarius Cantabrigiensis in Epistolam ad Ephesios in Commentarius Cantabrigiensis in Epistolas Pauli e Schola Petre Abaelardi*, vol. 2 (Notre Dame, Ind.: University of Notre Dame Press, 1937), 434.

62 Erika Uitz, *Women in the Medieval Town*, trans. Shiela Marnie (London: Barrie and Jenkins, 1990), 98. Although the quote from the record does not make it explicit, it is clear from Uitz's discussion just prior to the quote that she believes the school would have also been for girls.

63 Abrahams, *Hebrew Ethical Wills*, 211.

64 Judith Baskin, "Some Parallels in the Education of Medieval Jewish and Christian Women," *Jewish History* 5 (1991): 43.

65 Yosef ben Moshe, *Sefer Leket Yoshar: Orekh Ḥayyim*, ed. Jacob Freimann (Berlin: 1903) part b, 19–20.

66 Simḥa of Vitry, *Maḥzor Vitry* (Berlin: 1889), pars. 610, 635.

67 Yom Tov Assis, "Sexual Behavior in Mediaeval Hispano-Jewish Society," *Jewish History: Essays in Honour of Chimen Abramsky*, eds. Ada Rapoport-Albert and Steven J. Zipperstein (London: Peter Halban, 1988), 45.

68 Joseph Dan, *Iyunim beSifrut Ḥasidut Ashkenaz* (Ramat Gan: 1975), 140, and translated by Judith R. Baskin, "The Problem of Women in *Sefer Hasidim*," *AJS Review* 19 (1994): 6–7. The original MS is *Sefer ha-Kavod*, Opp. 111, fol. 178, in Bodleian Library.

69 Bowman, *The Jews of Byzantium*, 123.

70 *Sefer HaYashar leRabbenu Tam* (Koenigsburg: 1847), chap. 7, 27b.

71 Abrahams, *Hebrew Ethical Wills*, 211.

72 R. Ḥayyim Or Zarua, *Responsa* 69, 126, 191, as translated by Finkelstein, *Jewish Self-Government*, 67–68.

73 Ibid.

74 Finkelstein, *Jewish Self-Government*, 142–143.

75 Y. Y. Yuval, "Takkanot Neged Ribui Gerushin beGermaniah beMeah HaḤamesh-Esrei (An Appeal Against the Proliferation of Divorce in Fifteenth-Century Germany)," *Zion* 48:2 1983): 177–216, with English summary, xvi–xvii.

76 Ibid.

77 *Sefer HaYashar leRabbenu Tam*, ed. S. F. Rosenthal (Berlin: 1898; reprint, Jerusalem: Private, 1972), 80, 45b.

78 Bowman, *The Jews of Byzantium*, 124.

79 Meir ben Barukh, *She'elot u-Teshuvot*, #1022. See also Biale, *Women and Jewish Law*, 50.

80 But see Avraham Grossman, "The Historical Background to the Ordinances on Family Affairs Attributed to *Rabbenu* Gershom *Me'or Ha-Golah*," in *Jewish History: Essays in*

Honour of Chimen Abramsky, eds. Ada Rapoport-Albert and Steven J. Zipperstein (London: Peter Halban, 1988), 3–23, for a possible exception to this trend.

81   See Avraham Grossman, "Medieval Views on Wife-Beating: 800–1300," *Jewish History* 5 (spring 1991): 53–62; Abrahams, *Jewish Life in the Middle Ages*, 89.

82   Assis, "Sexual Behavior in Medieval Hispano-Jewish Society," 34.

83   Finkelstein, *Jewish Self-Government*, 216–217.

84   R. Joseph Kimhi, *Sefer HaBerit (The Book of the Covenant)*, trans. Frank Talmage (Toronto: 1972), 32–35.

85   E. E. Urbach, "Etudes sur la littérature polémique au moyen-âge," *Revue des études juives* 100 (1935): 49–77.

86   Yom Tov Assis, "Sexual Behavior," 45.

87   Eliezer ben Natan, *Sefer Raban: Hu Sefer Even ha-Ezer,* eds. Aryeh Loeb Rashkes and Louis Ginzberg (Jerusalem: 1915), #115.

88   Additional responsa concerning this issue include: Cassel, *Teshuvot Geonim Kadmonim,* #107 (R. Yosef Tov-Elem); Rashi's Commentary to *Bava Kamma* 87a; Rashi, *Teshuvot Rashi, Solomon ben Isaac,* ed. Israel Elfenbein (New York: Defus Ha-Aḥim Shulzinger, 1943), #230; and Finkelstein, *Jewish Self-Government*, 378 (R. Avraham ben Naḥman). The material in the preceding three paragraphs is taken from "Pegi'atan Ra'ah: Their Touch is Evil: The Medieval Transformation of a Talmudic Idea", an unpublished paper by Emily Taitz.

89   Judith Hauptman, *Rereading the Rabbis: A Woman's Voice* (Boulder, Colo.: Westview Press, 1998), 179–191.

90   Burns, *Jews in the Notarial Culture: Latinate Wills in Mediterranean Spain, 1250–1350* (Berkeley: University of California Press, 1966), 114.

91   This definition is quoted from Mary Erler and Maryanne Kowaleski, eds., *Women and Power in the Middle Ages* (Athens, Ga.: University of Georgia Press, 1988), 2.

92   Habermann, *Sefer Gezerot*, 97.

93   Suzanne Bartlet, "Chera and Co.: Three Jewish Businesswomen of the Thirteenth Century," *Jewish Culture and History* 3, no. 2 (2000): 7.

94   Andrée Courtemanche, "Les femmes juives et le crédit à Manosque au tournant du XIVe siècle," *Provence historique* 37 (1987): 555–556.

95   All these women are mentioned in Stouff, "Isaac Nathan et les siens," 508.

96   See Tos. B. *Ḥagigah* 16b, s.v. "ha."

97   Tos. to B. *Rosh ha-Shanah* 33a, s.v. "ha Rabbi Yehudah."

98   Grossman, *Ḥasidot u-Moredot*, 321.

99   Ze'ev Falk, "Ma'amad ha-Ishah be-Kehillot Ashkenaz be-Yemei ha-Beinayim,(The Status of Women in the Jewish Communities of Germany in the Middle Ages)." *Sinai* 48 (1960–61): 62; Isadore Epstein, "The Jewish Woman in the Responsa: 900 C.E.–1500 C.E.," in *Response: The Jewish Woman* 18 (summer 1973), 23–31.

100 See Tos. B. *Berakhot* 45b, s.v. "she-ani hatam."

101 For a variety of opinions permitting women to pray and perform commandments, see: R. Nissim's commentary to B. *Megillah,* chap. 2, s.v. "v'hakol"; Irwin H. Haut, "Are Women Obligated to Pray," *Daughters of the King: Women and the Synagogue,* eds. Susan Grossman and Rivka Haut (Philadelphia: Jewish Publication Society, 1992), 93—97; Emily Taitz, "Women's Voices, Women's Prayers: The European Synagogues of the Middle Ages," *Daughters of the King*, 59–71; Epstein, "The Jewish Woman in the Responsa," 25.

102 Meir ben Barukh, *She'elot u-Teshuvot*, #108.

103 George Jochnowitz, ". . . Who Made Me a Woman," *Commentary* 71, no. 4 (April, 1981): 63–64. See chap. 5 for another version of this prayer in Italy. But see Joseph Tabory, "The Blessings of Self-Identity and the Changing Status of Women and of Orthodoxy,"

Kenishta 1 (2001): 124, who questions whether "this form of the blessing was actually adopted out of a sense of pride in being a woman." He suggests it may well be that this was just a mechanical adjustment.

104 R. Yosef ben Moshe, *Sefer Leket Yoshar*, 7. This author was a disciple of R. Isserlein. See also Shlomo Ashkenazi, "Meḥaberot, Piyyutim, Teḥinot u-Tefillot," *Maḥanayim* 109 (1966): 86.

105 Ashkenazi, "Meḥabrot, Piyyutim, Teḥinot, u-Tefillot," 109.

106 Abrahams, *Jewish Life in the Middle Ages*, 26.

107 Yitzḥak ben Yosef of Corbeil, *Sefer Mitzvot Qatan*, attributes this statement to R. Yitzḥak of Dampierre. See Judith Baskin, "Medieval Jewish and Christian Women," 46, 51 n. 46.

108 *Mordecai, Pesaḥim* 108, s. v. "Nashim ḥashuvot."

109 Yaakov ben Moshe ha-Levi Moellin, *She'elot u-Teshuvot Maharil*, new ed. (Jerusalem: Mifal Torat Ḥakhmei Ashkenaz; reprint, Makhon Yerushalayim, 1977), nos. 45, 57, and 58.

CHAPTER FIVE

1 Adolph Neubauer, "The Early Settlement of the Jews in Southern Italy," *Jewish Quarterly Review* 4 (1892): 606–608. The entire article contains excellent data on Jewish settlements in ancient Rome through the Middle Ages.

2 Ahimaaz ben Paltiel, *The Chronicle of Ahimaaz*, trans. and intro. by Marcus Salzman (New York: AMS Press, Inc., 1966), 61.

3 Robert Bonfil, *Jewish Life in Renaissance Italy*, trans. Anthony Oldcorn (Berkeley: University of California Press, 1994), 20. German Jews began migrating into Italy after the plague of 1348 resulted in their persecution and expulsion.

4 Shlomo Simonsohn, ed., *The Jews in the Duchy of Milan*, vol. 1 (Jerusalem: Israel Academy of Sciences and Humanities, 1982), xvi–xvii. These charters were modeled after the earlier charters issued in the ninth century by the French king Louis the Pious. "Chartae Ludovici Pii Imperatoris," in Dom Martin Bouquet, *Receuil des historiens des Gaules et de la France*, vol. 6, 649–651, charters xxxii–xxxiv.

5 Parts of Italy, including Sicily and Sardinia, were under Spanish rule in 1492, and their Jews were included in the Spanish expulsion. See *Encyclopaedia Judaica*, 1st edition, s.v. "Italy."

6 Kenneth R. Stow, *Alienated Minority: The Jews of Medieval Latin Europe* (Cambridge, Mass.: Harvard University Press, 1992), 7. This was a small number compared to the Jewish populations of France or the Holy Roman Empire, which were double that amount.

7 See, for example, Jacob Burckhardt, *The Civilization of the Renaissance in Italy*, trans. S. G. C. Middlemore, vol. 2 (New York: Harper Torchbooks PB, 1958), 389. But compare with the more recent opinion of Joan Kelly-Gadol, "Did Women Have a Renaissance?" in *Becoming Visible: Women in European History*, eds. Renate Bridenthal, Claudia Koonz, and Susan Stuard (Boston: Houghton, Mifflin, 1977; 2nd ed., 1987), 175–201, and Howard Adelman, "Rabbis and Reality: The Public Roles of Jewish Women in the Renaissance and Catholic Restoration," *Jewish History* 5 (1991): 36.

8 Bonfil, *Jewish Life in Renaissance Italy*, 133; Shalom Sabar, "Bride, Heroine and Courtesan: Images of the Jewish Woman in Hebrew Manuscripts of the Renaissance in Italy," *Tenth World Congress of Jewish Studies*, Div. D, vol. 2 (1989), 64.

9 Moses A. Shulvass, *The Jews in the World of the Renaissance*, trans. Elvin I. Kose (Leiden: E. J. Brill, 1973), 46–47.

10 See Sandra Debenedetti Stow, "The Etymology of 'Ghetto:' New Evidence from Rome," *Jewish History* 6 (1992): 79–85.

11 Don Harràn, "Jewish Musical Culture: Leon Modena," in *The Jews of Early Modern Venice*, eds. Robert C. Davis and Benjamin Ravid (Baltimore: Johns Hopkins University Press, 2001), 212–213.

12 This role was originally laid out in M. *Sotah* 3:4; See also Howard Adelman, "The Educational and Literary Activities of Jewish Women in Italy During the Renaissance and the Catholic Restoration," *Shlomo Simonsohn Jubilee Volume* (Tel Aviv: Tel Aviv University Press, 1993), 9–23; Adelman, "Rabbis and Reality," 27–40.

13 Immanuel ben David Frances, *Kol 'Ugab* #15, as cited by A. Rhine, "The Secular Hebrew Poetry of Italy," *Jewish Quarterly Review*, n.s., 1 (1910–1911): 386.

14 Benzion Netanyahu, *Don Isaac Abravanel: Statesman and Philosopher*, 2nd ed. (Philadelphia: Jewish Publication Society of America, 1968), 25. The author notes that some earlier sources have mistakenly assumed that Jacob, Samuel's father-in-law, was Isaac's brother. Jacob was Isaac's nephew, and thus Samuel and Benvenida were second cousins. See 287, n. 65.

15 David Malkiel, "Jews and Wills in Renaissance Italy: A Case Study in the Jewish-Christian Cultural Encounter," *Italia: Studi e ricerche sulla storia, la cultura e la letteratura degli ebrei d'Italia* 12 (1996): 22.

16 Salo W. Baron, *A Social and Religious History of the Jews* (Philadelphia: Jewish Publication Society, 1957), vol. 14, 75, 88.

17 Malkiel, "Jews and Wills," 22.

18 Malkiel, "Jews and Wills," 13.

19 David Reubeni, "The Travel Diary of David Reubeni," in *Masterpieces of Hebrew Literature: A Treasury of 2,000 Years of Jewish Creativity*, ed. Curt Leviant (New York: K'tav, 1969), 515.

20 Renée Levine Melammed, "Medieval and Early Modern Sephardi Women," *Jewish Women in Historical Perspective*, ed. Judith Baskin (Detroit: Wayne State University Press, 1991), 123.

21 Jacob Marcus, *The Jew in the Medieval World: A Sourcebook* (New York: Atheneum, 1974), 399–400.

22 This quote from the Portuguese rabbi Immanuel Aboab was translated and quoted by Cecil Roth, *The House of Nasi: Doña Gracia* (Philadelphia: Jewish Publication Society, 1947), 67–68.

23 Kenneth Stow and Sandra Debenedetti Stow, "Donne ebree a Roma nell'eta del ghetto: affeto, dipendenza, autonomia (Jewish Women in Rome at the Time of the Establishment of the Ghetto)," *Rassegna Mensile di Israel* 52 (1986): 81.

24 This synagogue was organized by Jews from the province of Catalonia, Spain, when they first came as refugees to Italy. See Abraham Berliner, *Geschichte der Juden in Rom* (Frankfurt am Main: J. Kaufmann, 1893), 192.

25 Shulvass, *The Jews in the World of the Renaissance*, 229; Berliner, *Geschichte der Juden in Rom*, 194.

26 Berliner, *Geschichte der Juden in Rom*, 194; Howard Adelman, "Italian Jewish Women," in *Jewish Women in Historical Perspective* (Detroit: Wayne State University Press, 1991), 140.

27 Debora Ascarelli, *Debora Ascarelli, Poetessa* (Rome: Sindicato Italiano Arti Grafiche, 1925).

28 Don Harràn, "Madama Europa, Jewish Singer in Late Renaissance Mantua," *Festa Musicologica: Essays in Honor of George J. Buelow*, eds. Thomas J. Mathiesen and Benito V. Rivera (Stuyvesant, N.Y.: Pendragon Press, 1995), 204, n. 20, citing Andrea Calmo, *Lettere Piacevoli*, 2:33.

29 Translated by Dr. Vladimir Rus from the original, located in microfilm in the Biblioteca Angelica, Rome.

30 Ahimaaz ben Paltiel, *Chronicle of Ahimaaz*, 82–83.

31 David Amram, *Makers of Hebrew Books in Italy* (Philadelphia: Julius Greenstone, 1909), 32.

32 Ibid.

33 Ibid.

34 Henri Bresc, *Livre et société en Sicilie (1299–1499)* (Palermo: Centro di Studi Filologici e Linguistici Siciliani, 1971), #177. Bresc also lists other Sicilian Jewish women who owned books, including two sisters who inherited two medical books.

35 For basic information concerning Paula dei Mansi, see *Encyclopedia Judaica: Das Judentum in Geschichte und Gegenwart* (Berlin: 1928), s.v. "Anau"; and *Jewish Encyclopedia* (New York: Funk & Wagnalls, 1912), s.v. "Anaw."

36 Gustav Karpeles, *Jewish Literature and Other Essays* (Philadelphia: Jewish Publication Society, 1895), 116–117.

37 Berliner, *Geschichte der Juden in Rom*, 116–117. It is interesting to note that besides herself, Paula includes no women's names in her family tree.

38 Leon Modena, *The Autobiography of a Seventeenth-Century Venetian Rabbi: Leon Modena's Life of Judah*, ed. and trans. Mark Cohen (Princeton, N.J.: Princeton University Press, 1988), 79. See also Adelman, "The Educational and Literary Activities of Jewish Women in Italy," 13.

39 Aaron Berekhiah da Modena, *Ma'avar Yabbok* (Zhitomir: 1851), 14, 7b.

40 Berliner, *Geschichte der Juden in Rom*, 116–117. It is interesting to note that besides herself, Paula includes no women's names in her family tree. This and the following quotation were translated from the Hebrew by Emily Taitz.

41 Ibid., 117–118.

42 Aaron Berekhiah da Modena, *Ma'avar Yabbok* (Zhitomir: 1851), 13–14, 7a–b. This is also repeated in Simḥah Assaf, *Meqorot leToldot ha-Ḥinukh be'Yisrael*, vol. 4 (Jerusalem: Devir, 1930–1943), 54.

43 Reubeni, "The Travel Diary," in *Masterpieces of Hebrew Literature*, 514.

44 Gino Luzzatto, *I Banchieri Ebrei in Urbino Nell'eta Ducale* (Padua: Arnaldo Forni, 1902), 27; Harry Friedenwald, *The Jews and Medicine* (Baltimore: Johns Hopkins University Press, 1944), vol. 1, 217.

45 Harràn, "Jewish Musical Culture," 213.

46 David Jacoby, "New Evidence on Jewish Bankers in Venice and the Venetian Terraferma, 1450–1550," *The Mediterranean and the Jews: Banking, Finance and International Trade (XVI–XVII Centuries)*, eds. Ariel Toaff and Simon Schwarzfuchs (Ramat Gan: Bar Ilan University, 1989), 170–172.

47 Howard Adelman, "Servants and Sexuality: Seduction, Surrogacy and Rape: Some Observations Concerning Class, Gender and Race in Early Modern Italian Jewish Families," *Gender and Judaism: The Transformation of Tradition*, ed. Tamar M. Rudavsky (New York and London: New York University Press, 1995), 92. See chap. 4 for similar examples in northern Europe.

48 Harràn, "Madama Europa," 200.

49 Ibid.

50 Jacob Mann, *The Jews in Egypt and Palestine Under the Fatimid Caliphs*, vol. 1 (New York: K'tav Publishing Co., 1970), 242. But see Joel L. Kraemer, "Spanish Ladies from the Cairo Geniza," Mediterranean Historical Review 6:2 (1991): 247–8, who believes this letter was written by a Spanish woman from Egypt in a later century.

51 Franz Kobler, ed., *A Treasury of Jewish Letters: Letters from the Famous and Humble*, vol. 2 (Philadelphia: Jewish Publication Society, 1978), 233. The original letter can be found

in the Taylor-Schechter Collection (Cambridge, England), document 13J 21 (10), and was reproduced by Mann, *The Jews in Egypt and in Palestine*, 309.

52 Don Harràn, "Doubly Tainted, Doubly Talented: The Jewish Poet Sara Copio (d. 1641) As a Heroic Singer," in *Musica Franca: Essays in Honor of Frank A. D'Accone*, eds. Irene Alm, Alyson McLamore, and Colleen Reardon (Stuyvesant, N.Y.: Pendragon Press, 1996), 378.

53 Yisrael Yaakov Yuval, *Ḥakhamim beDoram: HaManhigut HaRuhanit shel Yehudei Germania (Sages in Their Time: The Spiritual Activities of the Jews of Germany)* (Jerusalem: Hebrew University Press, 1988), 249. See also *Encyclopaedia Judaica*, 1st edition, s.v. "Luria;" Meyer Kayserling, *Die jüdischen Frauen in der Geschichte Literatur und Kunst* (Leipzig: 1879; reprint, Hildesheim: Georg Olms Verlag, 1991), 180; and Leo Jung, *The Jewish Library*, vol. 3, *The Jewish Woman* (New York: Soncino Press, reprint, 1970), 152. Both repeat the same traditional but unverified story.

54 Sara's name is variously spelled *Sarah* or *Sarra*. Copio is the masculine form of her family name, sometimes spelled *Coppio*. At times the feminine form is used, as *Coppia* or *Copia*.

55 Helen Leneman, "Sara Coppio Sullam: Seventeenth-Century Jewish Poet in the Ghetto of Venice," *Response* 15 (spring 1987): 15.

56 This and much of the subsequent information is from several articles by Carla Boccato, including "Sara Copio Sullam, la poetessa del ghetto di Venezia: episodi della sua vita in un manoscrito del secolo XVII," *Italia* 6 (1987): 104–218.

57 Leneman, "Sara Coppio Sullam," 16.

58 Adelman, "The Educational and Literary Activities of Jewish Women in Italy," 18–20.

59 Harràn, "Doubly Tainted, Doubly Talented," 372.

60 See for example the dedication by Leon Modena in his tragedy *L'Ester* (Venice: Giacomo Sarzina, 1619), 3–7.

61 Kobler, *A Treasury of Jewish Letters*, vol. 2, 436.

62 Ibid., 442–447.

63 Adelman, "Jewish Women in Italy," 20.

64 Leneman, "Sara Coppio Sullam," 17. These lines were written by Sara's friend and admirer, Leon Modena, who also wrote the epitaph for her baby daughter.

65 *Codice di Giulia Soliga* is believed to have been authored by Leon Modena. See Carla Boccato, "Un altro documento inedito su Sara Copio Sullam: il 'codice di Giulia Soliga,'" *Rassegna mensile di Israel* 40 (1974): 303–316.

66 Leneman, "Sara Coppio Sullam," 16.

67 But Leneman, "Sara Coppio Sullam," 16, agrees with Boccato, who says the date could have been an approximation or even completely wrong. Her birth date also remains unverified.

68 Fabio Oliveri, "Jewish Women in Ancient and Medieval Sicily," *Eleventh World Congress of Jewish Studies*, Div. B, vol. 1 (1994), 133.

69 Avraham Grossman, *Ḥasidot u-Moredot, Nashim Yehudiot be-Eropah be-Yemei haBenayim (Pious and Rebellious: Jewish Women in Europe in the Middle Ages)* (Jerusalem: Zalman Shazar Center, 2001), 318–319; Marcel Poorthuis and Chana Safrai, "Fresh Water for a Tired Soul: Pregnancy and Messianic Desire in a Mediaeval Jewish Document from Sicily," *Women and Miracle Stories: A Multidisciplinary Exploration*, ed. Anne-Marie Korte (Leiden: Brill, 2001), 129–131, gives a full English translation of the document.

70 Baron, *A Social and Religious History of the Jews*, vol. 4, 158–164.

71 The Third Lateran Council of 1179 forbade Jews from employing Christian servants and repeated those rulings continually throughout the next century, a fact that sug-

gests they were not being followed. There were certainly instances of Christians work-ing for Jews after 1179, but as pressure increased, those instances became less common. See Solomon Grayzel, *The Church and the Jews in the XIIIth Century*, vol. 1 (Philadelphia: Jewish Publication Society, 1933), 296–297.

72 See Adelman, "Italian Jewish Women," 143, who says some women taught Italian and sometimes Hebrew to young girls and were referred to with the title *rabbit* or *rabbanit*.

73 See Stow and Debenedetti Stow, "Jewish Women in Rome," 66–67.

74 Adelman, "Rabbis and Reality," 35.

75 Stow and Debenedetti Stow, "Jewish Women in Rome," 66.

76 Adelman, "Rabbis and Reality," 36, citing Meir Katzenellenbogen, *She'elot u-Teshuvot meha-Ri Mintz u-mehaRam Padua* (Krakow: 1882), #26.

77 Adelman, "The Educational and Literary Activities," 16–17.

78 Harràn, "Jewish Musical Culture," 212–213.

79 Ibid.

80 Barbara Sparti, "Jewish Dancing Masters and 'Jewish Dance' in Renaissance Italy," *Jewish Folklore and Ethnology Review* (spring 2000), n. 28.

81 Robert. Bonfil, "The Historian's Perception of the Jews in the Italian Renaissance: Towards a Reappraisal," *Revue des études juives* 143 (January–June 1984): 71–72.

82 Adelman, "Rabbis and Reality," 33; Jeremiah J. Berman, *Shehitah: A Study in the Cultural and Social Life of the Jewish People* (New York: 1941), 83–136.

83 Adelman, "Servants and Sexuality: Seduction, Surrogacy and Rape," 82.

84 Adelman, "Italian Jewish Women," 143.

85 Bonfil, *Jewish Life in Renaissance Italy*, 135.

86 Barbara Sparti, "Dancing Couples Behind the Scenes: Recently Discovered Italian Illustrations, 1470–1550," *Imago Musicae* 13 (1996): 22–33, cites the source for this as a miniature from a manuscript of the *Arba'a Turim*, found in the Biblioteca Apostolica Vaticana, Codice Rossiano 555, fol. 220r.

87 Rothschild Miscellany, Israel Museum, MS 180/51, fol. 246v, as cited by Sparti in "Dancing Couples," 26–28.

88 Bonfil, *Jewish Life in Renaissance Italy*, 133, points out that the secular course of study for Jews paralleled that of Christians. See also Sabar, "Bride, Heroine and Courtesan," 64.

89 Benjamin Richler, "Ḥinukhan v'Siḥatan shel B'not Ashirim b'Italia b'yemei haRenesans (The Education and Conversation of Rich Italian Daughters During the Renaissance)," *Asufot Kiriyat Sefer* (Jerusalem: Bet HaSefarim HaLeumi vehaUniversitai, 1997–1998), 276.

90 Ibid., 275.

91 David Kaufmann, "The Dispute about the Sermons of David del Bene of Mantua," *Jewish Quarterly Review*, o.s., 8 (1896): 516.

92 Shulvass, *The Jews in the World of the Renaissance*, 166. But see Adelman, "Jewish Women in Italy,"139, who writes: "Women's public activities were not an aspect of Renaissance values . . . or the liberation of women but reflections of the normal give and take . . . [reflecting] the ongoing needs of the Jewish community."

93 Ahimaaz ben Paltiel, *Chronicle of Ahimaaz*, 83.

94 Howard Adelman, "Finding Women's Voices in Italian Jewish Literature," in *Women of the Word: Jewish Women and Jewish Writing*, ed. Judith Baskin (Detroit: Wayne State University Press, 1994), 57–58.

95 Adelman, "Rabbis and Reality," 36, citing *She'elot u-Teshuvot mehaRi Mintz u'mehaRam Padua* (Krakow: 1882), 60, #26.

96 Adelman, "Women's Voices in Italian Jewish Literature," 58–59.

97 Howard Adelman, "Custom, Law and Gender: Levirate Union among Ashkenazim and Sephardim in Italy after the Expulsion from Spain," *The Expulsion of the Jews: 1492 and After*, eds. Raymond B. Waddington and Arthur H. Williamson (New York: Garland Publishing, Inc., 1994), 118.

98 The problem of *agunot* still remains in the Orthodox Jewish community, where a Jewish woman may not remarry without the religious *get*, which she can receive only from her husband. For a full review of this ongoing problem, see Jack Nusan Porter, ed., *Women in Chains: A Sourcebook on the Agunah* (Northvale, N.J.: Jason Aronson, 1995).

99 Howard Tzvi Adelman, "Jewish Women and Family Life, Inside and Outside the Ghetto," *The Jews of Early Modern Venice*, eds. Robert C. Davis and Benjamin Ravid (Baltimore: Johns Hopkins University Press, 2001), 153.

100 Ibid., 160–161.

101 Malkiel, "Jews and Wills," 15–26.

102 Azriel Diena, *She'elot u-Teshuvot*, ed. Yaacov Boksenboim, vol. 1 (Tel Aviv: University of Tel Aviv, 1977), 11, #6.

103 Ariel Toaff, *Love, Work and Death: Jewish Life in Medieval Umbria*, trans. Judith Landry (Portland, Ore.: Vallentine Mitchell & Co., 1996), 32, n.74.

104 Howard Adelman, "Wife Beating among Early Modern Italian Jews," *Eleventh World Congress of Jewish Studies, Proceedings* (1993), Div. B, vol. 1, 135–138.

105 A. Rhine, "The Secular Hebrew Poetry of Italy," 352.

106 Stow and Debenedetti Stow, "Jewish Women in Rome," 82.

107 Adelman, "Jewish Women and Family Life," 153.

108 Louis Finkelstein, *Jewish Self-Government*, 294.

109 Bonfil, *Jewish Life in Renaissance Italy*, 243; Cecil Roth, *The Jews in the Renaissance* (Philadelphia: Jewish Publication Society, 1977), 48.

110 Diena, *She'elot u-Teshuvot*, vol. 1, 541–548, nos.137–138.

111 Diena, *She'elot u-Teshuvot*, 12, #6, as cited by Adelman, "Italian Jewish Women," 139.

112 Malkiel, "Jews and Wills," 12–14.

113 Adelman, "Jewish Women and Family Life," 151–153; Stow and Debenedetti Stow, "Jewish Women in Rome," 78–81.

114 See chap. 4 for examples of this in Spain.

115 Sally McKee, ed., *Wills from Late Medieval Venetian Crete (1312–1420)*, 3 vols. (Washington, D.C.: Dumbarton Oaks Library and Collection, 1998), vol. 1, 170–171 #134.

116 Ibid,. vol.1, 141–142, #108; 155–156, #121; vol. 2, 605–609, #471, #475.

117 Ibid, vol. 2, 595–596, #463.

118 Stow and Debenedetti Stow, "Jewish Women in Rome," 80.

119 Ibid., 70. But see Toaff, *Love, Work and Death*, 52, who shows that women who became administrators of their husband's wills in the 15th century were much more closely supervised.

120 Stow and Debenedetti Stow, "Jewish Women in Rome," 77, mentions both Dolcebella and Rachel Corcos.

121 Bonfil, *Jewish Life in Renaissance Italy*, 108.

122 Finkelstein, *Jewish Self-Government*, 292–293.

123 Toaff, *Love, Work and Death*, 176–178.

124 Bonfil, *Jewish Life in Renaissance Italy*, 243.

125 Benjamin Ravid, "From Yellow to Red: On the Distinguishing Head-Covering of the Jews of Venice," *Jewish History* 6 (1992): 180–181, 188. The distinguishing color for both Jews and Christians in Muslim lands was always yellow and this remained so in Italy.

Perhaps the negative connotation of that color did not have similar associations for those living under Islam.

126 Diane Owen Hughes, "Distinguishing Signs: Ear-rings, Jews and Franciscan Rhetoric in the Italian Renaissance City," *Past & Present* 112 (1986): 3–50. The earrings that Jewish women wore were eventually adopted by the aristocracy and then were forbidden to others, including Jews.

127 See Yirmiyahu Yovel, *The New Otherness: Marrano Dualities in the First Generation* (San Francisco: Swig Judaic Studies Program at University of San Francisco, 1999), 5.

128 Sabar, "Bride, Heroine and Courtesan," citing MS Heb. 8' 5492, fol. 7r, in Jewish National and University Library, Jerusalem. See chap. 4 for other examples of this variation.

129 Nina Beth Cardin, ed. and trans., *Out of the Depths I Call to You: A Book of Prayers for the Married Jewish Woman* (Northvale, N.J.: Jason Aronson, 1992), 100.

130 Howard Adelman, "The Literacy of Jewish Women in Early Modern Italy," *Women's Education in Early Modern Europe: A History, 1500–1800*, ed. Barbara J. Whitehead (New York & London: Garland Publishing, 1999), 133–158. These quotes are on p. 136 and are from Yagel's commentary on Proverbs, *Eshet Ḥayyil* 18b–19a.

131 Adelman, "The Literacy of Jewish Women," 139.

CHAPTER SIX

1 See Jonathan I. Israel, *European Jewry in the Age of Mercantilism 1550–1750* (Oxford: Clarendon Press, 1985), 23.

2 Ibid., 23.

3 Ibid., 40.

4 Bernard D. Weinryb, *The Jews of Poland: A Social and Economic History of the Jewish Community in Poland from 1100–1800* (Philadelphia: Jewish Publication Society, 1982), 28–29, 114, notes that immigrants to eastern Europe came principally from Germany, and German rabbis remained the principal authorities for eastern European Jews until the sixteenth century.

5 *Encyclopaedia Judaica*, 1st ed., s.v. "Court Jew."

6 Donald Kagan, et. al., eds., *The Western Heritage: Since 1300*, 6th ed. (Upper Saddle River, N.J.: Prentice Hall, 1998), 441ff.

7 Weinryb, *The Jews of Poland*, 190.

8 But see Moshe Idel, "One from a Town, Two from a Clan," *Jewish History* 7, no. 2 (fall 1993): 79–104, who believes there was no direct cause and effect between Lurianic Kabbalah and Sabbateanism. Lurianic Kabbalah was a closely guarded secret among small groups of men and was not widespread. See especially pp. 84–89.

9 Glückel of Hameln, *The Life of Glückel of Hameln, 1646–1724, Written by Herself*, trans. and ed. Beth-Zion Abrahams (New York: Thomas Yoseloff, 1963), 46. This woman's name has been spelled many ways since her book came into prominence about one hundred years ago. We have chosen the form used by Natalie Zemon Davis in her book, *Women on the Margins: Three Seventeenth-Century Lives* (Cambridge, Mass.: Harvard University Press, 1995), 9.

10 Gershon G. Scholem, *Major Trends in Jewish Mysticism*, 1st ed., 1941; 3rd ed. (New York: Schocken Books, 1954), 333–334.

11 Baal Shem Tov, meaning "Master of God's good name," is a title that dates back to the first centuries of the common era. It had been used for mystics and practitioners of magic up until the time of Yisrael ben Eliezer. Once the name became attached to this most famous mystical leader, it disappeared as a general title. See *Encyclopaedia Judaica*, 1st ed., s.v. "Baal Shem."

12 Scholem, *Major Trends*, 330.

13 Ada Rapoport-Albert, "On Women in Hasidism: S. A. Horodecky and the Maid of Ludmir Tradition," *Jewish History: Essays in Honor of Chimen Abramsky*, eds. Steven J. Zipperstein and Ada Rapoport-Albert (London: Halbam, 1988), 507. However, see Naftali Loewenthal, "Women and the Dialectic of Spirituality in Hasidism," *BeMagle Hasidim: Kovetz Mehkarim leZikhrono shel Professor Mordecai Wilensky (In Hasidic Circles: Collected Research in Memory of Professor Mordecai Wilensky)*, ed. Emanuel Etkes, et. al. (Jerusalem: Bialik Institute, 1999), 22–25, who suggests that two works written in Yiddish in the early nineteenth century may have assumed a readership of both men and women.

14 Israel, *European Jewry*, 119.

15 Weinryb, *The Jews of Poland*, 120; Israel, *European Jewry*, 120.

16 Israel Eisenstadt, *Da'at Kedoshim* (Peterburg: Behrmann, 1897–1898), 217. See also Chava Weissler, *Voices of the Matriarchs: Listening to the Prayers of Early Modern Jewish Women* (Boston: Beacon Press, 1998), 229, n. 22; and Solomon Freehof, *The Responsa Literature* and *A Treasury of Responsa* (New York: K'tav, 1973).

17 Eisenstadt, *Da'at Kedoshim*, 217.

18 Dan Ben-Amos and Jerome R. Mintz, eds., *In Praise of the Baal Shem Tov (Shivhei ha-Besht)* (Bloomington, Ind.: University of Indiana Press, 1970), 136, #114: "The Interruption of the Besht's Vision."

19 *Encyclopaedia Judaica*, 1st ed., s.v. "Adel."

20 Solomon Feffer, "Of Ladies and Converts and Tomes: An Essay in Hebrew Book Lore," in *Essays in Jewish Book Lore*, ed. Philip Goodman (New York: K'tav, 1971), 365–378. The poem is on p. 371. Note that Ella claims she is the only girl among six children. However, a short time later another girl, Gela, was born, and we see her working in her father's shop fourteen years later.

21 Feffer, "Of Ladies and Converts and Tomes," 371.

22 Weissler, *Voices of the Matriarchs*, 12, 197, note 24; Israel Zinberg, *A History of Jewish Literature*, trans. and ed. Bernard Martin (New York: Ktav, 1975), vol. 7, 242.

23 Marcia Spiegel and Deborah Kremsdorf, *Women Speak to God: The Prayers and Poems of Jewish Women* (San Diego: Woman's Institute for Continuing Jewish Education, 1987), 17.

24 Dan Rabinowitz, "Rayna Batya and Other Learned Women: A Reevaluation of Rabbi Barukh HaLevi Epstein's Sources," *Tradition* 35:1 (spring 2001), 62.

25 Meyer Kayserling, *Die jüdischen Frauen in der Geschichte, Literatur, und Kunst* (Leipzig: 1879), 177–178; Batya Bromberg, "Nashim Mehadshot Dinim ba'Halakhah (Women Who Make New Law)," *Sinai* 59 (1966): 248–250.

26 Rapoport-Albert, "On Women in Hasidism," 516–518, n. 36. See also Jacob S. Minkin, *The Romance of Hassidism* (New York: Thomas Yoseloff, 1955), 233, 345–346.

27 This translation is from Zinberg, *A History of Jewish Literature*, vol. 7, 242–243.

28 Converts were routinely given the name "ben Avraham" to indicate their new identity as sons of Abraham.

29 Glückel, *Life*, 13.

30 Ibid., 11–12.

31 Ibid., 11–12.

32 Ibid., 32–33.

33 Ibid., 11–12.

34 Ibid., 109–110.

35 This excerpt from the memoir of a young Jew from Moravia is reprinted in Jacob R. Marcus, *The Jew in the Medieval World: A Source Book: 315–1791* (New York: Atheneum, 1979), 432.

36 Leah Horowitz may have been married twice, as a few sources give her husband's name as Shabbetai HaKohen Rappaport. See Weissler, *Voices of the Matriarchs*, 228, n. 9.

37 Weissler, *Voices of the Matriarchs*, 105, citing Ber of Bolechow, *Zikhronot R. Dov mi-Bolikhov*, ed. N. Vishnitzer (Berlin: Klal Verlag, 1922), 44.

38 Weissler, *Voices of the Matriarchs*, 124.

39 Ellen Umansky and Dianne Ashton, eds., *Four Centuries of Jewish Women's Spirituality: A Source Book* (Boston: Beacon Press, 1992), 52.

40 Franz Kobler, ed., *A Treasury of Jewish Letters: Letters from the Famous and Humble*, vol. 2 (Philadelphia: Jewish Publication Society, 1978), 479, note 47.

41 The original of this letter can be found in Alfred Landau and Bernhard Wachstein, *Jüdische Privatbriefe aus dem Jahre 1619* (Wien und Leipzig: Wilhelm Braunmuller, 1911), 89–92. It was translated from the German by Alice Morawetz.

42 Weissler, *Voices of the Matriarchs*, 113. In n. 42, p. 232, Weissler points out that Leah Horowitz used a source from the *Zohar* for this passage.

43 Umansky and Ashton, *Four Centuries*, 52.

44 Avraham Habermann, *Nashim Ivriot b'tor Madpisot, Mesadrot, Motzi'ot le'Or veTomkhot bemehabrim (Hebrew Women as Printers, Editors, Publishers and Financial Backers)* (Berlin: 1945), 11, 14. See also Zinberg, *A History of Jewish Literature*, vol. 7, 242.

45 Ezra Korman, *Yidishe Dikhterins* (Chicago: Farlag L. M. Stein, 1928), 22.

46 Ibid., 347.

47 Kayserling, *Die jüdischen Frauen*, 178; *Encyclopaedia Judaica*, 1st ed., s.v. "Jacob ben Mordecai of Schwerin."

48 Weissler, *Voices of the Matriarchs*, 28.

49 Selma Stern, *The Court Jew: A Contribution to the History of the Period of Absolutism in Central Europe* (1950; reprint, New Brunswick, N.J.: Transaction Books, 1985), 47–50.

50 Aron Liebmann's marriage to Esther had been a second marriage also. His first wife was the daughter of Samuel Hameln and sister of Hayyim Hameln, who was the husband of Glikl. Jost Liebmann had been Hayyim Hameln's business partner, so both men were connected through marriage or business. See Glückel of Hameln, *Life*, 44, 59.

51 Stern, *The Court Jew*, 50.

52 Ibid., 53.

53 *Encyclopaedia Judaica*, 1st ed., s.v, "Jost Liebmann."

54 Stern, *The Court Jew*, 54–55.

55 David Gans, *Tzemah David*, as cited and translated in Marcus, *The Jew in the Medieval World*, 323–325.

56 *Encyclopaedia Judaica*, 1st ed., s.v. "Meisel, Mordecai."

57 Eli Valley, *The Great Jewish Cities of Central and Eastern Europe: A Travel Guide and Resource Book to Prague, Warsaw, Crakow, and Budapest* (New York: Jason Aronson Press, 1999), 111; *Encyclopedia Judaica*, 1st ed., s.v. "Meisel, Mordecai."

58 Korman, *Yidishe Dikhterins*, 350.

59 Ibid., 8. Translated by Cheryl Tallan.

60 Weinryb, *The Jews of Poland*, 99.

61 Habermann, *Nashim*, 17.

62 Simon Schwarzfuchs, trans., *Un obituaire israelite: Le "Memorbuch" de Metz, vers 1575–1724* (Metz: Société d'histoire et d'archéologie de la Lorraine, 1971), 29, #366. The *Memorbuch* is a list of obituary notices written for the confraternity of the grave diggers of Metz between 1575 and 1724.

63 It is assumed that the word *bat*, meaning "daughter of" was pronounced *bas* in the Yiddish-speaking areas. Since there is no proof of exactly how sixteenth-century Yiddish was pronounced, in the interests of consistency we are using the Modern Hebrew *bat* throughout.

64 *Tkhines* is the current Yiddish pronunciation of the Hebrew *Teḥinot* .

65 Weissler, *Voices of the Matriarchs*, 126.

66 Umansky and Ashton, *Four Centuries*, 54.

67 Ibid., 55.

68 Translated from the Yiddish by Joseph Adler for Sondra Henry and Emily Taitz, *Written Out of History: Jewish Foremothers* (reprint, New York: Biblio Press, 1996), 191.

69 Weissler, *Voices of the Matriarchs*, 132.

70 Her father probably came from Tiktin (Tykocin), near Bialystock, in northeast Poland. The birthplace of Rivkah herself is not known, but she lived in Prague at least some of her life and is buried there.

71 Chone Shmeruk, *Sifrut Yiddish be-Polin* (Jerusalem: Magnes Press, 1981), 59.

72 We thank Frauke von Rohden for this reference.

73 A critical edition of *Meneket Rivkah* with a translation into modern German is being prepared from this copy by Frauke von Rhoden, in Berlin.

74 Rivkah's gravestone is located in the Jewish cemetery of Prague. The inscription has been recorded by Otto Muneles, *Ketuvot mi-Beit ha-Almyn haYehudi ha-Atik be-Prague* (Jerusalem: Ha-Akademiah ha-Leumit ha-Yisraelit leMada'im, 1987–88), 161, and was translated by Cheryl Tallan with the help of Dr. Tirzah Meacham. Thanks to Frauke von Rhoden for drawing our attention to this reference.

75 See Shmeruk, *Sifrut*, 58.

76 Korman, *Yidishe Dikhterins*, XLIV.

77 Parts of *Meneket Rivkah* are quoted by J. C. Wagenseil in *Sota. Hoc. est: Liber Mischnicus, De Uxore Adulterii Suspecta* (Altdorf: 1674). Her book is also the subject of a dissertation by J. C. Luft, *De Rebecca Polona, Eruditam in Gente Judaica Foeminorum Rariori Exemplo* (Altdorf: 1719).

78 Simḥa Assaf, *Mekorot le-Toldot ha-Ḥinukh be-Yisrael (Sources on the History of Education in Israel)*, vol. 4 (Tel Aviv: Dvir, 1930–1954), 45–46. This passage was translated into English from Assaf's Hebrew translation from the Yiddish.

79 Shmeruk, *Sifrut*, 61.

80 Assaf, *Mekorot*, 46. This passage is translated from Assaf's Hebrew translation.

81 This ideal can already be found in the Talmud (B. *Berakhot* 17a) but was particularly emphasized among Ashkenazic families.

82 Joseph Katz, *She'erit Yosef* (Krakow: 1893), 75.

83 Louise Tilly and Joan W. Scott, *Women, Work and Family* (New York: Holt Rinehart, 1978), 50.

84 Michael Toch, "Die jüdische Frau im Erwerbsleben des Spätmittelalters," *Zur Geschichte der jüdischen Frau in Deutschland,* ed. Julius Carlebach (Berlin: Metropol Verlag, 1993), 38.

85 Weinryb, *The Jews of Poland,* 99.

86 Myer S. Lew, *The Jews of Poland: Their Political, Economic, Social and Communal Life in the Works of Rabbi Moses Isserles* (London: Edward Goldston, 1944), citing *Jahrbuch,* XI, 100–101.

87 Weinryb, *The Jews of Poland*, 99, citing Shlomo Luria, *She'elot u-Teshuvot Maharshal* (Lemberg: 1859), #99.

88 Jacob Katz, *Out of the Ghetto: The Social Background of Jewish Emancipation* (1973; reprint, New York: Schocken Books, 1978), 17.

89 Marcus, *The Jew in the Medieval World*, 86, quoting from a list of the tolerated communal officials in Berlin, dating from 1750.

90 Toch, "Die jüdische Frau," 40.

91 Shlomo Luria, *She'elot u-Teshuvot*, #99.

92 Glückel of Hameln, *Life*, 125.

93 Marcus Brann, *Geschichte der Juden in Schlesien: Jahresbericht des jüdisch-Theologischen Seminars*, vol. 6 (Breslau: 1896–1910), anhang (appendix) 3: "Verzeichniss der Juden, die von den ältesten Zeiten bis zur Mitte des 16 Jahrhunderts in Schlesien gelebt haben." See especially xli–lxvii for individual entries of women in business either alone or with husbands, brothers, or sons. See also Weinryb, *The Jews of Poland*, 99.

94 Walther Schönfeld, *Frauen in der abendländischen Heilkunde* (Stuttgart: Ferdinand Enke Verlag, 1947), 75.

95 Harry Friedenwald, "Jewish Doctoresses in the Middle Age," In idem, *The Jews and Medicine* (Baltimore: The Johns Hopkins Press, 1944), 220.

96 Metz, an important town in Lorraine (Lothir) was originally part of the Holy Roman Empire and considered German territory, although French influence was strong. The ruling bishops of the area allowed no Jews to settle there after the French expulsions of the fourteenth century. In 1567, when Lorraine was reclaimed by France, Jews came back. See Abraham Cahan, "Le Rabbinat de Metz pendant la période française (1567–1871)," *Revue des études juives* 7 (1883): 103–116.

97 Schwarzfuchs, *Le "Memorbuch" de Metz*, xi.

98 See Israel Zinberg, *Old Yiddish Literature from Its Origins to the Haskalah Period*, vol. 7 of *A History of Jewish Literature*, trans. and ed. Bernard Martin, vol. 1 (Cincinnati and New York: Hebrew Union College Press and Ktav, 1975/1938), 150–151.

99 Habermann, *Nashim*, 11, 14. See also Zinberg, *A History of Jewish Literature*, vol. 7, 242.

100 *Heder* is a primary school for Jewish children. The word itself derives from the Hebrew for "room," but it was in Ashkenaz that it first developed the meaning of "school." See Max Weinreich, *History of the Yiddish Language*, trans. Shlomo Noble (Chicago: University of Chicago Press, 1980), 212. (He uses the spelling *kheyder*.) During the medieval and early modern period it was attended almost entirely by boys. Glückel of Hameln, *Life*, 14.

101 Glückel of Hameln, *Life*, 13. But this translation includes the correction made by Davis, *Women on the Margins*, 233, n. 67. The quote in Abrahams says: "[h]e had his daughters taught religious and worldly things."

102 Weinreich, *History of the Yiddish Language*, 6, points out that the first written sentence in Yiddish is from 1272 in the Worms *Mahzor*. However, it was certainly used as a spoken language long before that time.

103 Davis, *Women on the Margins*, 23.

104 Schwarzfuchs, *Le "Memorbuch" de Metz*, 11, #153.

105 Kobler, *Treasury of Jewish Letters*, vol. 2, 473.

106 *Encyclopaedia Judaica*, 1st ed., s.v. "Chmielnicki, Bogdan."

107 Glückl of Hameln, *Life*, 99. The marriage of Esther and Moses Schwabe alias Krumbach did take place. It was this daughter with whom Glikl lived in her old age, and she praised her son-in-law for his generosity and his honorable behavior.

108 Ibid., 79.

109 Isaac ben Eliakim of Posen, *Lev Tov*, as cited and translated by Marcus, *The Jew in the Medieval World*, 443–444.

110 Bernd-Wilhelm Linnemeier and Rosemarie Kosche, "Jüdische Privatkorrespondenzen des mittleren 16. Jahrhunderts aus dem nordöstlichen Westfalen." *Aschkenas* 8, no. 2 (1998): 288–289 (German translation, 295–296).

111 Ibid., 289 (German translation, 296).

112 Jacob Katz, *Exclusiveness and Tolerance: Studies in Jewish-Gentile Relations in Medieval and Modern Times* (New York: Behrman House, 1983), 149–150.

113 Ibid., 149 and note 2, citing *Terumot HaDeshen*, 223.

114 Weinryb, *The Jews of Poland*, 99. R. Moshe of Kiev was born in Lithuania and wandered throughout eastern Europe for most of his life. See *Encyclopaedia Judaica*, 1st ed., s.v. "Moses ben Jacob of Kiev."

115 Eliezer ben Natan, *Sefer Raban: Hu Sefer Even ha-Ezer* eds. Aryeh Loeb Rashkes and Louis Ginzberg (Jerusalem: 1915), #115.

116 Lew, *The Jews of Poland*, 132, citing *Jahrbuch der jüdisch-literarischen Gesellschaft*, XI, 88–89. This and subsequent rulings from Poland reflect the decisions of R. Moshe Isserles, a Jewish scholar and rabbi of the late sixteenth century.

117 Ibid., 102–103. This is a sixteenth-century ruling.

118 I. Kracauer, "Ein jüdisches Testament aus dem Jahre 1470," *Monatsschrift für Geschichte und Wissenschaft des Judentums* 60 (1916): 295–301.

119 This love song was found in the *Hebräische Liederbuch,* no. 3, a late 16-century songbook housed in the Bodleian Library, Oxford MS opp. add. 4o 136. For further information on the songbook, see Albrecht Classen, *Deutsche Frauenlieder des fünfzehnten und sechzenten Jahrhunderts* (Amsterdam, Atlanta Ga.: Rodopi, 1999), chap. 12, 195–211. We thank Dr. Classen for this translation into English.

120 Joseph Bloch, "Le testament d'une femme juive au commencement du XVIIIe siècle," *Revue des études juives* 90 (1931): 146–160.

121 Mordechai Breuer, "The Early Modern Period," in *Tradition and Enlightenment: 1600–1780*, vol. 1 of *German-Jewish History in Modern Times*, ed. Michael Meyer (New York: Columbia University Press, 1996), 187.

122 Umansky and Ashton, eds., *Four Centuries*, 5.

123 Schwarzfuchs, *Le Memorbuch*, 16, #212, #550, #292. These entries were translated from Hebrew into French and therefore the spellings reflect a French pronunciation. Where these may be unclear, they are rendered in the more common English spelling in brackets.

124 Meir Wunder, *Ateret Rivkah* (Jerusalem: HaMakhon leHantzaḥat Yahdut Galicia, 1991–1992), 154, contains the original poem in Hebrew. The English translation can be found in Zinberg, *Old Yiddish Literature*, vol. 7 of *A History of Jewish Literature*, 285.

125 Valley, *The Great Jewish Cities*, 74, notes that the *Altneuschul* had an *Aron haKodesh* in the women's section, which was separated from the main synagogue by a thick wall.

126 Weissler, *Voices of the Matriarchs*, 89.

127 Ibid., 18.

128 Ibid., 19–20.

129 Devra Kay, "An Alternative Prayer Canon for Women: The Yiddish *Seyder Tkhines*," *Zur Geschichte der Jüdischen Frau in Deutschland*, ed. Julius Carlebach (Berlin: Metropol-Verlag, 1993), 49–85.

130 See Tracy Guren Klirs, comp., *The Merit of Our Mothers* (Cincinnati: Hebrew Union College, 1992), for many other examples.

131 Shulamith Z. Berger, "Teḥines: A Brief Survey of Women's Prayers," *Daughters of the King: Women and the Synagogue*, eds. Susan Grossman and Rivka Haut (Philadelphia: Jewish Publication Society, 1992), 74.

132 This *tkhine* has not yet been published. For information on it, see Weissler, *Voices of the Matriarchs*, 2ff, and Yitshak Yudlov, "'Sheyne Tkhine' ve-'Orah Ḥayyim': Shnei Sifrei Yiddish bilti Yedu'im ('Sheyne Tkhine' and 'Orah Ḥayyim': Two Unknown Yiddish Books)," *Kiryat Sefer* 62 (1989): 457–458.

133 Weissler, *Voices of the Matriarchs*, 24.

134 Tzvi Rabinowicz, *Hasidism: The Movement and Its Masters* (Northvale, N.J.: Jason Aronson, 1988), 342; but see also Rapoport-Albert, "On Women in Hasidism," 519–520, n. 54, citing M. Feinkind, *Froyen Rabbonim un barimte perzenlekhkeiten in Poylen* (Warsaw: 1917), 20–25, for the original information. Rapoport-Albert believes that Yente's story "is almost certainly apocryphal."

135 Weissler, *Voices of the Matriarchs*, 12.

136 Milton Aron, *Ideas and Ideals of the Hasidim* (New York: Citadel Press, 1964), 110–111.

CHAPTER SEVEN

1   Jane S. Gerber, "My Heart Is in the East," *The Illustrated History of the Jewish People*, ed. Nicholas de Lange (New York: Harcourt, Brace & Co., 1997), 179.

2   Ibid., 184.

3   Joseph Hacker, "The Sephardim in the Ottoman Empire in the Sixteenth Century," *The Sephardi Legacy*, ed. Ḥaim Beinart, vol. 2 (Jerusalem: Magnes Press, 1992), 110.

4   Ibid., 113.

5   *Kiera* (sometimes *kyra*) seems to have been a title and can be found in a few documents and tombstones before this period. See Mordechai Friedman, *Jewish Marriage in Palestine: A Cairo Geniza Study*, vol. 1 (Tel Aviv: Tel Aviv University Press, 1980), 79. Friedman notes that a Greek word "*kyra* or *kyria* meaning 'lady' appears before a proper name in several Greek tomb inscriptions in Beth She'arim (Israel) and elsewhere. *Kyra* does appear before a proper name in several early Hebrew and Aramaic inscriptions . . ." but has not been found in any other legal documents prior to its use in the Palestinian *ketubbot* discovered in the Genizah. Thanks to Dr. Ruth Lamdan, Tel Aviv University, for this reference.

6   J. S. Gerber, "My Heart Is in the East," 183.

7   Samuel Usque, *Consolation for the Tribulations of Israel*, trans. Martin A. Cohen (Philadelphia: Jewish Publication Society, 1965), 231.

8   Walter F. Weiker, *Ottomans, Turks and the Jewish Polity: A History of the Jews of Turkey* (Lanham, Md., New York and London: The Jerusalem Center for Public Affairs and University Press of America,1992), 32, citing Abraham Galanté, *Histoire des juifs d'Istanbul depuis la prise de cette ville en 1453 par Fatih Mehmet II jusqu'à nos jours* (Istanbul: Isis Yayimeilik, 1986), vol. 1, 123.

9   Historians draw much of the knowledge of Jewish life under Islam from these collections. Among the most famous are David ben Solomon ibn Abi Zimra (1479–1573), known as RaDBaZ, author of *Teshuvot haRadbaz*; and Joseph ben Ephraim Caro (1488–1575), author of *Bet Yosef, She'elot u-Teshuvot Avkat Rochel* and the *Shulḥan Arukh*, his most famous compendium on Jewish law. This latter became a definitive code for all Jews. The Ashkenazim added their own gloss to reflect their differing traditions. See *Encyclopaedia Judaica*, 1st ed., s.v. "Caro, Joseph ben Ephraim" and "Shulḥan Arukh."

10 Hacker, "The Sephardim in the Ottoman Empire," 115–116.

11 Joseph Hacker, "The Intellectual Activity of the Jews of the Ottoman Empire During the Sixteenth and Seventeenth Centuries," *Jewish Thought in the Seventeenth Century*, eds. Isadore Twersky and Bernard Septimus (Cambridge, Mass.: Harvard University Press, 1987), 96–99; idem, "The Sephardim in the Ottoman Empire," 115.

12 Jacob Barnai, "The Jews of the Ottoman Empire in the Seventeenth and Eighteenth Centuries," *The Sephardi Legacy*, ed. Ḥaim Beinart, vol. 2 (Jerusalem: Magnus Press, 1992), 152–153.

13 Weiker, *Ottomans, Turks and the Jewish Polity*, 35–36.

14 Ibid., 155.

15 These excerpts are part of a collection of seven letters all written in Yiddish between 1565 and 1570. They were found among the Genizah letters and most are in the Taylor-Schechter collection at Cambridge University library. They have been reprinted and translated by Chava Turniansky, "Tzaror Iggarot biYiddish meYerushalayim, meShmot haShishim shel Meah haShesh-Esrei (A Correspondence in Yiddish from Jerusalem, Dating from the 1560s)," *Shalem* 4 (1984): 149–210.

16 Bernard Lewis, *The Jews of Islam* (Princeton, N.J.: Princeton University Press, 1984), 128–129.

17 J. S. Gerber, "My Heart Is in the East," 194.

18 Gershom G. Scholem, *Sabbatai Sevi, the Mystical Messiah, 1626–1676,* trans. R. J. Zwi Werblowsky (Princeton, N.J.: Princeton University Press, 1973), 105, n. 2.

19 Scholem, *Major Trends in Jewish Mysticism* (1946; reprint, New York: Schocken, 1961), 303–304; J. S. Gerber, "My Heart Is in the East," 196.

20 *Encyclopaedia Judaica,* 1st ed., s.v. "Maggid."

21 Morris M. Faierstein, trans. and ed., *Jewish Mystical Autobiographies: Book of Visions and Book of Secrets* (New York and Mahwah: Paulist Press, 1999). For a full analysis of Aberlin and other women mystics, see Yosef Chajes, "Derekh lo meqabelet: mystiqa-ot yehudiot b'aspaqlariat shel 'Sefer HaHezzionot' leRabbi Hazzim Vital," *Zion* 67:2 (2002): 139–162. This information was brought to our attention through an unpublished paper delivered by Yossi Chajes of Haifa University at a conference at the Jewish Theological Seminary, November, 2001.

22 Faierstein, *Jewish Mystical Autobiographies,* 50.

23 Joseph Chetrit, "Freḥa bat Yosef—Meshoreret Ivriyah be-Morocco be-Meah ha-18" (Freḥa bat Yosef—A Hebrew Poetess in Eighteenth-Century Morocco), *Pe'amim* 4 (1980): 84–93. Information on the Bar-Adiba family on p. 86, footnote 11. Note that Chetrit refers to her in this early article as "bat Yosef" rather than "bat Avraham." In his later article he corrected her name.

24 Yosef ben Yitzhak Sambari, *Sefer Divre Yosef,* ed. Shimon Shtober (Jerusalem: Makhon Ben Zvi, 1994), 364.

25 Joseph Chetrit, "Freḥa bat Rabbi Avraham," *Pe'amim* 55 (1993): 128, citing Yosef Benjoi.

26 Chetrit, "Freḥa bat Rabbi Avraham," 124–130.

27 Freyha Bat Avraham Bar-Adiba, "Lift up my Steps," trans. Peter Cole, in *The Defiant Muse: Hebrew Feminist Poems from Antiquity to the Present, A Bilingual Anthology,* eds. Shirley Kaufman, Galit Hasan-Rokem, and Tamar S. Hess (New York: The Feminist Press, 1999), 74–77. This poem was first published in Hebrew, in Tunis, in the newspaper *Alyahudi* (26 November 1936): 1, in an article authored by Yosef Benjoi, and republished in *Pe'amim* 55 (1993): 128.

28 Chetrit, "Freḥa bat Rabbi Avraham," 126.

29 Ḥaim Gerber, *Yehudei ha-Imperiah ha-Otomanit be-me'ot ha-16–17: Kalkalah ve-Ḥevrah (The Economic and Social Life of the Jews in the Ottoman Empire in the Sixteenth and Seventeenth Centuries)* (Jerusalem: Merkaz Zalman Shazar, 1982), 64, believes that there were at least three women *kieras* in the court at this time. Two were named Esther.

30 Stanford J. Shaw, *The Jews of the Ottoman Empire and the Turkish Republic* (New York: New York University Press, 1991), 91.

31 Cecil Roth, *The House of Nasi: The Duke of Naxos* (Philadelphia: Jewish Publication Society, 1948), 201; John Sanderson, *The Travels of John Sanderson in the Levant, 1584–1602, with His Autobiography and Selections from His Correspondence,* ed. Sir William Foster (London: Hakluyt Society, 1931), 86.

32 *Jewish Encyclopedia,* 1st ed., "Kiera (Esther)."

33 Roth, *The House of Nasi: The Duke of Naxos,* 121.

34 Roth, *The House of Nasi: Doña Gracia,* 107.

35 Orhan Burian, *The Report of Lello, 3rd English Ambassador to the Sublime Porte* (Ankara: Türk Tarih Kurumu Basimeri, 1952), 4–5.

36 Burian, *The Report of Lello,* 5. See also Abraham Galanté, *Documents officiels turcs concernant les juifs de Turquie: Recueil de lois, règlements, firmans, bérats, ordres et décisions de tribunaux* (Istanbul: Ḥaim Rozio & Co., 1931), 180, who claims that the *kiera's* execution was carried out with the consent of the Sultan.

37 Sanderson, *Travels of John Sanderson,* 85.

38 Burian, *The Report of Lello,* viii.

39 Galanté, *Documents officiels,* 181–183.

40   Franz Kobler, ed., *A Treasury of Jewish Letters: Letters from the Famous and Humble*, vol. 2 (Philadelphia: Jewish Publication Society, 1978), 391.

41   *Encyclopaedia Judaica*, 1st ed., s.v. "Benayah."

42   Shlomo D. Goitein, *Jews and Arabs: Their Contact Through the Ages* (New York: Schocken Books, 3rd ed., 1974), 86.

43   *Encyclopaedia Judaica*, 1st ed., s.v. "Benayah."

44   Erich Brauer, *The Jews of Kurdistan* (Detroit: Wayne State University Press, 1993), 177.

45   Asenath had more than one daughter. See Jacob Mann, *Texts and Studies in Jewish History and Literature*, vol. 1, pt. 2 (Cincinnati: Hebrew Union College Press, 1931), 483.

46   The exact words this author used are: ". . . it should stop being with her as the way of women."

47   Abraham Ben-Jacob, *Kehillot Yehudei Kurdistan (The Communities of the Jews of Kurdistan)* (Jerusalum: Makhon Ben Zvi, 1961), 37.

48   Brauer, *The Jews of Kurdistan*, 177.

49   Ben-Jacob, *Kehillot* , 35. A *Tanna* was the name given to a scholar who took part in the discussions and rulings of the Mishnah.

50   Some scholars think that the date should be earlier. See Uri Melammed and Renée Levine Melammed, "Ha-rabbanit Asenath—Rosh ha-Yeshivah Kurdistan" (Rabbi Asenath—Yeshivah Director in Kurdistan), *Pe'amim* 82 (winter 2000): 164.

51   Sondra Henry and Emily Taitz, *Written Out of History: Our Jewish Foremothers*, 2nd ed. rev. (Fresh Meadows, N.Y.: Biblio Press, 1990), 112–113. Translated from the Hebrew by Isaac Taitz. The original Hebrew is in Mann, *Texts and Studies*, vol. 1, pt. 2, 507–515.

52   The original source for this information, as well as reports on all of Gracia's legal records, is Moses de Trani, *Avqat Rokhel*, #80, and *She'elot u-Teshuvot haRashdam* (Lemberg: 1862), nos. 327–332. These are cited by Libby Garshowitz, "Gracia Mendes: Power, Influence and Intrigue," in *Power of the Weak: Studies on Medieval Women*, eds. Jennifer Carpenter and Sally-Beth MacLean (Urbana and Chicago: University of Illinois Press, 1995), 94–125; Roth, *The House of Nasi: Doña Gracia*, 28.

53   Abraham David, "New Jewish Sources on the History of the Members of the Nasi-Mendes Family in Italy and Constantinople," *Henoch* 20 (1998): 179–187. See p. 180 for this information.

54   Leah Bornstein-Makovetzky, "Yehudim Portugezim baHatzar ha-Malkhut ha-Otomanit be-Meah ha-Shesh-esrei: Don Yosef Nasi" (The Jews of Portugal at the Sultan's Court of Constantinople in the Sixteenth Century: Don Joseph Nasi), in *Me-Lisbon le Saloniki ve-Kushta* (From Lisbon to Salonika and Constantinople), ed. Zvi Ankori (Tel Aviv: University of Tel Aviv, 1986), 74. Note that Joao Migues, the son of Gracia's brother, is variously referred to in historical sources as Joao Micas, Giovanni Miches, and Joseph Nasi. See also Shaw, *The Jews of the Ottoman Empire*, 88–89.

55   Lucien Wolf, "Jews in Tudor England," in *Essays in Jewish History*, ed. Cecil Roth (London: Jewish Historical Society, 1934), 77–78, reports that the House of Mendes maintained agents in London who helped the fugitive *conversos* and "provided them with bills of exchange on Antwerp." The agents were named as Christopher Fernandes and Antonion della Rogna.

56   Moses de Trani, *Avqat Rokhel*, #80, as cited by Abraham David, "New Jewish Sources," 180, and Garshowitz, "Gracia Mendes," 99.

57   The money was finally returned due to the efforts of Beatrice's nephew, Joao. See Garshowitz, "Gracia Mendes," 100–101, and Roth, *The House of Nasi: Doña Gracia*, 46–48.

58   Riccardo Calimani, *The Ghetto of Venice: A History*, trans. Katherine Silberblatt Wollfthal (New York; M. Evans & Co. 1987), 90–96.

59   Joshua Soncino, *Nahalah li-Yehoshua*, nos. 12, 12b. Translated from the Hebrew by Garshowitz, "Gracia Mendes," 108.

60 Moses de Trani, *Avqat Rokhel*, #80, 73a. Translated from the Hebrew by Gershowitz, "Gracia Mendes," 110.

61 Renata Segre, "Sephardic Settlements in Sixteenth-Century Italy: A Historical and Geographical Survey," in *Jews, Christians and Muslims in the Mediterranean World after 1492* (London: Frank Cass & Co., Ltd., 1992), 132.

62 Ibid., 132, who writes that although Gracia Nasi and Benvenida Abrabanel briefly lived in the same city, "there is no evidence that the families ever saw eye to eye."

63 David, "New Jewish Sources," 180–181.

64 Roth, *The House of Nasi: Doña Gracia*, 73–74, quoting from the Ferrara Bible, translated from Hebrew into Spanish and signed "Yom Tob Athias and Abraham Usque."

65 Brianda Mendes seems to have remained in Italy, and one report says that she lent money at interest to the Republic of Venice and remained a Christian, at least for a short while. See Joel L. Kraemer, "Spanish Ladies from the Cairo Geniza," in *Mediterranean Historical Review* 6 (1991): 239. But see also David, "New Hebrew Sources," 184.

66 Bornstein-Makovetzky, "Yehudim Portugezim ba-Ḥatzar ha-Malkhut," 74.

67 Ibid., 83.

68 Ruth Lamdan, "Parashat Ḥerem Ancona" (The Episode of the Ancona Boycott), in Ankori, *Me-Lisbon le Saloniki ve-Kushta (From Lisbon to Salonika and Constantinople)*, 184–185.

69 Kraemer, "Spanish Ladies from the Cairo Geniza," 239.

70 Bornstein-Makovetzky, "Yehudim Portugezim ba-Ḥatzar ha-Malkhut," 83.

71 David, "New Hebrew Sources," 184. David claims that Beatrice's mother, Brianda (Gracia's sister), died in Ferrara as a practicing Jew in spite of reports to the contrary. His source for this is "Responsa Mattanot ba'Adam," JTS MS Rab. 1355, sign 223, 254a–b.

72 Bornstein-Makovetzky, "Yehudim Portugezim ba-Ḥatzar ha-Malkhut," 74.

73 Ibid.

74 Scholem, *Sabbatai Sevi*, 192–196.

75 Roth, *The House of Nasi: The Duke of Naxos*, 218.

76 This letter was translated from the Yiddish by Franz Kobler, ed., *A Treasury of Jewish Letters*, vol. 1, 364–367. It is also found in Ellen M. Umansky and Dianne Ashton, eds., *Four Centuries of Jewish Women's Spirituality: A Sourcebook* (Boston: Beacon Press, 1992), 39–41.

77 Scholem, *Sabbatai Sevi*, 413.

78 Ibid., 851.

79 This woman was first brought to our attention through personal correspondence with S. D. Goitein in 1978. Dr. Goitein also mentioned her in "The Social Structure of Jewish Education in Yemen," in *Jewish Societies in the Middle East: Community, Culture and Authority*, eds. Shlomo Deshen and Walter P. Zenner (Lanham, Md.: University Press of America, 1983), 226.

80 Uziel Alnadaf, ed., *Zakhor le'Avraham*, pt. 2 (Jerusalem: Sh. Ben A. H. Alnadaf, 1991), 4a.

81 Turniansky, "Tzaror Iggarot" 194, letter d, lines 50–51, in Yiddish; 195, in Hebrew.

82 Ibid., 152.

83 Ibid.

84 Ibid., 194, letter d, lines 51–53, in Yiddish; 195, in Hebrew.

85 For a full discussion of Shabbetai Zevi and his movement, see *Encyclopaedia Judaica*, 1st ed., s.v. "Shabbetai Zevi" and "Doenmeh"; and Scholem, *Sabbatai Sevi*, who gives a closely detailed account of his entire life from 1626 to 1676.

86 Barnai, "The Jews of the Ottoman Empire," 150.

87   Ruth Lamdan, *A Separate People: Jewish Women in Palestine, Syria, and Egypt in the Sixteenth-Century* (Leiden: Brill, 2000), 117.

88   Ibid., 117, quoting from Eliezer ben Arḥa, *She'elot u-Teshuvot*, ed. E. Basri (Jerusalem: Mifal Or ha-Mizraḥ, 1977–78), siman 13(2). R. Eliezer lived in Hebron and Gaza, and by that time, the flourishing Ottoman economy was in a serious decline.

89   Turniansky, "Tzaror Iggarot," 156.

90   Ibid., 198, letter d, lines 96–97, in Yiddish; 199, in Hebrew.

91   R. David ben Solomon ibn Abi Zimra, *She'elot u-Teshuvot haRadbaz*, vol. 1, nos. 67, 146, as cited by Marc D. Angel, *The Jews of Rhodes* (New York: Sepher-Hermon Press, Inc., 1978), 99.

92   Lamdan, *A Separate People*, 118.

93   Lamdan, *A Separate People*, 118, quoting Moshe Gallanti, *She'elot u-Teshuvot* (Jerusalem: Y. D. u-beno Z. Shtaitsberg, 1959–60), siman 31.

94   Ḥaim Gerber, "Social and Economic Position of Women in an Ottoman City—Bursa, 1600–1700," *International Journal of Middle-East Studies* 12 (1980): 236.

95   Lamdan, *A Separate People*, 121.

96   In a letter dated 1567 and written to her son in Egypt. It is translated in Umansky and Ashton, eds., *Four Centuries of Jewish Women's Spirituality*, 40.

97   Aryeh Shmuelevitz, *The Jews of the Ottoman Empire in the Late Fifteenth and Sixteenth Centuries* (Leiden: E. J. Brill, 1984), 139; Barnai, "The Jews of the Ottoman Empire," 152.

98   Pierre Belon du Mans, *Les obseruations de plusiers singularitez & choses memorables, trou- uées en Grèce, Asie, Iudée, Egypte, Arabie, & autres pays estranges, Redigées en trois livres* (Paris: 1555), 323.

99   For the identification of *aziro* with welding, see Lamdan, *A Separate People*, 121, n. 36.

100 R. Moshe Alshekh, *She'elot u-Teshuvot ha-Maharam Alshekh*, ed. Yom Tov Porges (Safed: Sifriyah Toranit Bet Yosef, 1975), 117, siman 57.

101 Amnon Cohen, *Jewish Life under Islam: Jerusalem in the Sixteenth Century* (Cambridge, MA: Harvard University Press, 1984), 176.

102 Walther Schönfeld, *Frauen in der abendländischen Heilkunde: vom klassischen Altertum bis zum Ausgang des 19. Jahrhunderts* (Stuttgart: Ferdinand Enke Verlag, 1947), 151. The reporter claimed that the sultan's disease was leprosy; however, to date, there is no known cure and it may have been some other skin disease.

103 Angel, *The Jews of Rhodes*, 99, citing R. Ezra Malkhi (d. 1768), *Ein Mishpat* (Konstandinah: 1770), Even Ha-Ezer 2.

104 His young son. The name is a diminutive of Zvi.

105 Turniansky, "Tzaror Iggarot," 188, letter g, lines 9–10, in Yiddish; 190, for Hebrew translation.

106 Avraham Yaari, *Masa'ot Eretz Yisrael shel Olim Yehudim (Journeys of Jewish Immigrants to the Land of Israel)* (Tel Aviv: Modan, 1996/1976), 317.

107 Brauer, *The Jews of Kurdistan*, 177.

108 Cohen, *Jewish Life under Islam*, 183.

109 Ibid., 197.

110 Redemption of captives was considered obligatory for Jews. See Maimonides, *Mishneh Torah*, Mattanot Ani-im 8:10–15; and Joseph Caro, *Shulḥan Arukh, Yoreh Deah*, 252.

111 Cecil Roth, *The House of Nasi: Doña Gracia*, 103, quoting from a report by Hans Dernschwam, the factor of the Fugger banking house.

112 Josef Nehama, *Histoire des Israelites de Salonique*, vols. 6–7 (Thessalonique: Commu- nauté Israelite de Thessalonique, 1978), 395.

113 Angel, *The Jews of Rhodes*, 78.

114 Stephen Sharot, "Judaism in Pre-Modern Societies," *Jewish Societies in the Middle East*, eds. Shlomo Deshen and Walter P. Zenner (Washington, D.C.: University Press of America, 1982), 54.

115 Walter P. Zenner, "Jews in Late Ottoman Syria: Community, Family and Religion," in *Jewish Societies in the Middle East*, eds. Shlomo Deshen and Walter P. Zenner (Washington, D.C.: University Press of America, 1982), 194.

116 Samuel Romanelli, *Travail in an Arab Land*, trans. and ed. Norman A. Stillman (Tuscaloosa, Ala.: University of Alabama Press, 1989), 103.

117 Ibid., 39.

118 Translation of this and the following quotes can be found in Kobler, *A Treasury of Jewish Letters*, vol. 1, 364–367.

119 Hacker, "The Sephardim of the Ottoman Empire," 132, citing R. Shlomo ben Yitzhak Beit ha-Levi, *Responsa, Hoshen Mishpat* 24.

120 Angel, *The Jews of Rhodes*, 93.

121 Romanelli, *Travail in an Arab Land*, 29.

122 Ruth Lamdan, "The Mercies of the Court: Jewish Women Seeking Divorce in Sixteenth-Century Palestine, Syria and Egypt," *Nashim* 1 (winter 1998): 52.

123 Shmuelovitz, *The Jews of the Ottoman Empire*, 49, 72.

124 Hacker, "The Sephardim in the Ottoman Empire," 126, as cited from the writings of R. Abraham Shamsolo, who reached Greece from Portugal after 1508.

125 Lamdan, "The Mercies of the Court," 52.

126 Minna Rozen, *Jewish Identity and Society in the Seventeenth Century: Reflections on the Life and Work of Refael Mordekhai Malki*, trans. Goldie Wachsman (Tübingen: J. C. B. Mohr, 1992), 99; Lamdan, "The Mercies of the Court," 61–62, gives other similar rulings including *Responsa of R. Samuel de Medina* (Rashdam) (New York: 1959), *Even Ha-Ezer* 10.

127 Cecil Roth, "Immanuel Aboab's Proselytization of Marranos," *Jewish Quarterly Review* 23 (1932 33): 138.

128 This letter was translated from the Yiddish by Franz Kobler, ed., *A Treasury of Jewish Letters*, vol. 1 (Philadelphia: Jewish Publication Society, 1978), 364–367. It is also found in Umansky and Ashton, *Four Centuries of Jewish Women's Spirituality*, 39–41.

129 Joel L. Kraemer, "Spanish Ladies from the Cairo Geniza," *Mediterranean Historical Review* 6 (1991): 252, n. 53, explains the meaning of this word.

130 Eliezer Gutwirth, "A Judeo-Spanish letter from the *Genizah*," in *Judeo-Romance Languages*, eds. Isaac Benabu and Joseph Sermoneta (Jerusalem: The Hebrew University and Misgav Yerushalyim, 1985), 127–138, and in English, 131, 135–136. The original document is now in the Taylor-Schechter collection of Genizah documents in the Cambridge University Library.

131 Hacker, "The Sephardim of the Ottoman Empire,"126.

132 Ruth Lamdan, "Ribui haNashim be-Hevrot ha-Yehudit be-Eretz-Yisrael u-be-Mitzrayim be-Dorot ha-Smukhim le-Gerush Sepharad" (Polygamy in Jewish Societies in the Land of Israel and in Egypt in the First Generations after the Expulsion from Spain), *Sefer ha-Yovel le-Daniel Carpi (Daniel Carpi Jubilee Volume)*, eds. Dina Poret, Mina Rozen, and Anita Shapira (Tel Aviv: University of Tel Aviv, 1995–96), 118.

133 Amnon Cohen, *A World Within: Jewish Life As Reflected in Muslim Court Documents from the Sijill of Jerusalem (XVI Century)*, pt. 1: *Texts* (Philadelphia: University of Pennsylvania Center for Judaic Studies, 1994), 171, #226(d).

134 Lamdan, "Ribui haNashim be-Hevrot ha-Yehudit," 73–89.

135 Zenner, "Jews in Late Ottoman Syria," 195.

136 This connection is suggested by Cohen, *Jewish Life under Islam*, 135.

137 Ruth Lamdan, "Hahzakat Shefahot beHevrah haYehudit be-Eretz-Yisrael, Suriah u-Mitzrayim be-Me'ah ha-Shesh-Esrei (Female Slaves in the Jewish Society of Palestine,

Syria and Egypt in the Sixteenth Century)," *Yemei HaSahar: Perekim beToldot HaYehudim be-Imperiah HaOtomanit (Days of the Cresent: Chapters in the History of the Jews of the Ottoman Empire)*, ed. Minna Rozen (Tel Aviv: Tel Aviv University, 1996), 366, citing *She'elot u-Teshuvot haRadbaz*, pt. 4, siman 1000.

138 Lamdan, *A Separate People*, 114. She is quoting from Yom Tov Zahalon, *She'elot u-Teshuvot ha-Maharitaz ha-Hadashot* (Jerusalem: Makhon Or haMizrah, 1980–1981), siman 54. The woman and her second husband are called Leah and Reuben at the beginning of this responsum. Later, when the will of the woman is being discussed, her real name, Rivkah Esther bat Yitzhak ha-Levi, and his, R. Yitzhak Yizak ben R. Yisrael Moshe, are mentioned.

139 Ruth Lamdan, "Child Marriage in Jewish Society," *Mediterranean Historical Review* 11, no. 1 (1996): 40. Lamdan points out that a father had no such rights over a son, who could not be married before the age of thirteen and had to give his own informed consent.

140 H. Gerber, "Position of Women," 232.

141 Cohen, *Jewish Life under Islam*, 127.

142 Shmuelovitz, *The Jews of the Ottoman Empire*, 74, citing R. Moshe ben Yosef Trani of Safed's collection of responsa: *She'elot u-Teshuvot HaMabit*, #80; #130.

143 Ibid., 67, citing *She'elot u-Teshuvot HaRival* (R. Joseph ben David), vol. 2, #77.

144 Ibid., 68, citing *She'elot u-Teshuvot Maharashdam*, (R. Samuel ben Joseph de Medinah), vol. 3, #101.

145 Lamdan, "Hahzakat Shefahot," 355.

146 Ibid., 368.

147 Ibid., 368.

148 Minna Rozen, "Influential Jews in the Sultan's Court in Istanbul," *Michael* 7 (1981): 395. Thanks to Dr. Ruth Lamdan, Tel Aviv University, for this source.

149 Rozen, "Influential Jews," 395.

150 Cohen, *Jewish Life under Islam*, 216–217.

151 H. Gerber, *Yehudei ha-Imperiah ha-Otomanit*, 65, 108–109 (the quote is on p. 109). A number of Jews were given tax exemption by the Ottoman sultans, including Joseph Hamon, royal physician to Suleiman's son and successor, Selim II. See Shaw, *The Jews of the Ottoman Empire*, 87; Shmuelevitz, *The Jews of the Ottoman Empire*, 93–103.

152 H. Gerber, *Yehudei ha-Imperiah ha-Otomanit*, 109. Gerber believes that a group of Jews subsequently referred to as "Kords" are this *Kiera*'s descendants, but this is not proven.

153 Rozen, "Influential Jews," 395, states: "Jewish women also attained positions of power in the Sultan's court. Many of them were doctors, midwives, providers of clothing, perfumers, jewelers, and [sellers of] other products to the women of the palace."

154 Yaari, *Masaot Eretz Yisrael*, 299.

155 Ibid., 313.

156 *Tkines* are women's supplicatory prayers in Yiddish, usually collected into small books. For more information on *tkines*, see chap. 6.

157 Yaari, *Masaot*, 278.

158 Faierstein, *Jewish Mystical Autobiographies*, 50.

159 Faierstein, *Jewish Mystical Autobiographies*, passim.

160 Scholem, *Sabbatai Sevi*, 403–404.

161 Ibid., 254. In these reports, "prophesy" consisted of falling into a trancelike state and acknowledging that Shabbetai Zevi was the messiah, and/or reporting visions of him as king and ruler.

162 Renée Levine Melammed, *Heretics or Daughters of Israel: The Crypto-Jewish Women of Castile* (New York: Oxford University Press, 1999), 32, 173.

CHAPTER EIGHT

1 For a general background, see Jacob Katz, *Out of the Ghetto: The Social Background of Jewish Emancipation, 1770–1870* (Cambridge, Mass.: Harvard University Press, 1973; reprint New York: Schocken Books, 1988), 108.

2 Paula E. Hyman, *The Emancipation of the Jews of Alsace* (New Haven: Yale University Press, 1991), 11.

3 Todd Endelman, *The Jews of Georgian England 1714–1830: Tradition and Change in a Liberal Society* (Philadelphia: Jewish Publication Society, 1979), 14–17.

4 Allan Arkush, *Moses Mendelssohn and the Enlightenment* (Albany, N.Y.: SUNY Press, 1994), 1–13.

5 Ibid., 221.

6 See *Encyclopaedia Judaica*, 1st ed., s.v. "Trieste" and "Austria," for a general background. See also Katz, *Out of the Ghetto*, 2. Galicia had formerly been a part of Poland.

7 Prussia fell to Napoleon in 1806/7. The Edict of 1812 granted full rights to the Jews and abolished any special taxes on Jews. See *Encyclopaedia Judaica*, 1st ed., s.v. "Germany: Effects of French Revolution."

8 Paula Hyman, *Gender and Assimilation in Modern Jewish History: The Roles and Representation of Women* (Seattle: University of Washington Press, 1995), 20–21.

9 Deborah Hertz, *Jewish High Society in Old Regime Berlin* (New Haven: Yale University Press, 1988), 104.

10 Deborah Hertz, "Intermarriage in Old Berlin," *Jewish Women in Historical Perspective*, ed. Judith R. Baskin (Detroit: Wayne State University Press, 1991), 186, points out that one source records that "girls were not even allowed to be in a house where tutors were training the community's boys in these subjects" (referring to Hebrew and Talmud).

11 Ibid., 221.

12 Ibid., 113.

13 Carole B. Balin, *To Reveal Our Hearts: Jewish Women Writers in Tsarist Russia* (Cincinnati: Hebrew Union College Press, 2000) p. 12, points out that the educated women of eastern Europe "resembled far more their sisters in Berlin and Vienna than those in the *shtetls* of the Pale."

14 Grace Aguilar, *The Women of Israel; or Characters and Sketches from the Holy Scriptures* (London: Groombridge & sons, 1878), 565.

15 Grace Aguilar, *The Jewish Faith* (Philadelphia: Sherman & Co., 1864), 14.

16 Ibid. 7–19. This quote is part of the full title of her work. It appears on the title page and is elaborated in the introduction.

17 Ibid. *Women of Israel*, 566–567.

18 Isaac Leeser, "Editor's Preface," in Grace Aguilar, *Spirit of Judaism* (Cincinnati: Bloch Publishing Co., n.d.), 1.

19 Naomi Shepherd, *A Price below Rubies: Jewish Women As Rebels and Radicals* (Cambridge, Mass.: Harvard University Press, 1993), 19.

20 *Jewish Encyclopedia* (New York: Funk and Wagnalls, 1901–1906), s.v. "Aguilar, Grace." The library was established with funds donated by the noted American Jewish philanthropist, Jacob Schiff. It is located on 110th St. in Manhattan.

21 Gustave Karpeles, *Jewish Literature and Other Essays* (Philadelphia: Jewish Publication Society, 1895), 136–137.

22 *Encyclopaedia Judaica*, 1st ed., s.v. "Arnstein."

23 Harry M. Rabinowicz, *Hasidism: The Movement and Its Masters* (Northvale, N.J.: Jason Aronson, 1988), 344.

24 *Encyclopaedia Judaica*, 1st ed., s.v. "Frank, Jacob and the Frankists."

25   Naftali Loewenthal, "Women and the Dialectic of Spirituality in Hasidism," in *BeM'aglei Hasidim: Kovetz Meḥkarim shel Professor Mordecai Vilensky (In Hasidic Circles: Collected Research in Memory of Professor Mordecai Wilensky)*, ed. Emanuel Etkes, et al. (Jerusalem: Bialik Institute, 1999), 14.

26   Ibid., 12.

27   Ada Rapoport-Albert, "On Women in Hasidism: S. A. Horodecky and the Maid of Ludmir Tradition," *Jewish History: Essays in Honor of Chimen Abramsky*, eds. Steven J. Zipperstein and Ada Rapoport-Albert (London: Halbam, 1988), 518, n. 39.

28   Irmgard Fassmann, *Jüdinnen in der deutschen Frauenbewegung* (Hildesheim, Zürich, New York: Georg Olms Verlag, 1996), 163. Many thanks to Dr. Maria Baader for this reference and for other information on nineteenth-century German-Jewish women.

29   *Encyclopaedia Judaica*, 1st ed., s.v. "Goldschmidt, Henriette."

30   Fassmann, *Jüdinnen*, 177.

31   Ibid., 133.

32   Meyer Kayserling, *Die jüdischen Frauen in der Geschichte, Literatur und Kunst* (1879; reprint, Heldesheim, Zürich, New York: Georg Olms Verlag, 1991), 255; Fassmann, *Jüdinnen*, 140.

33   Kayserling, *Jüdischen Frauen*, 256.

34   Hertz, *Jewish High Society*, 98.

35   *Encyclopaedia Judaica*, 1st ed., s.v. "Herz, Henriette."

36   Hertz, *Jewish High Society*, 99–100.

37   Milton Aron, *Ideas and Ideals of the Hassidim* (New York: Citadel Press, 1964), 190–194.

38   Balin, *To Reveal Our Hearts*, 13–50.

39   Sonia L. Lipman, "Judith Montefiore—First Lady of Anglo-Jewry," *Jewish Historical Society of England, Transations, Sessions 1962–1967* 21 (1968): 290, quoting from Louis Loewe, *Diaries of Sir Moses and Lady Montefiore*, vols. 1, 2.

40   Lucien Wolf, "Lady Montefiore's Honeymoon," in Lucien Wolf, *Essays in Jewish History*, ed. Cecil Roth (London: Jewish Historical Society of England, 1934), 242.

41   Lipman, "Judith Montefiore," 294.

42   Ibid., 297.

43   *The Jewish Chronicle* (October 10, 1862), in their report on a Yom Kippur sermon by Dr. Nathan Marcus Adler, quoted him with this statement. See also Lipman, "Lady Montefiore," 300. A facsimile of this cookbook, with an introduction by Chaim Raphael, was published by Nightingale Books, Cold Spring, N.Y., in 1983.

44   Azriel Eisenberg, ed., *Eyewitnesses to Jewish History, from 586 BCE to 1967* (New York: Union of American Hebrew Congregations, 1973), 184–186, citing *Diaries of Sir Moses and Lady Montefiore*, vol. 2, ed. Dr. L. Loewe.

45   Wolf, "Lady Montefiore's Honeymoon," 240.

46   Lipman, "Judith Montefiore," 288. Lady Montefiore was either sixty-one or seventy-one at the time.

47   Wolf, "Lady Montefiore's Honeymoon," 240.

48   Marion A. Kaplan, *The Making of the Jewish Middle Class: Women, Family, and Identity in Imperial Germany* (New York and Oxford: Oxford University Press, 1991), 207.

49   Fassmann, *Jüdinnen*, 185.

50   Kaplan, *Making of the Jewish Middle Class*, 207.

51   *Encyclopaedia Judaica*, 1st ed., s.v. "Morgenstern, Lina"; *Jewish Encyclopedia*, 1912, s.v. "Morgenstern, Lina."

52   Kaplan, *Making of the Jewish Middle Class*, 207.

53   Trude Weiss-Rosmarin, *Jewish Women Through the Ages* (New York: Jewish Book Club, 1940), 87; Nina Davis Salaman, *Rahel Morpurgo and Contemporary Hebrew Poets in Italy* (London: George Allen & Unwin, 1924), 35.

54 Salaman, *Rahel Morpurgo*, 38; Yael Levine Katz, "Rachel Morpurgo," *Judaism* 49 (winter 2000): 15.

55 Dora Kobler, "Four Rachels" (London: 1945), a pamphlet available at YIVO Institute for Jewish Research in New York City.

56 Salaman, *Rahel Morpurgo*, 47; see also Nahida Remy, *The Jewish Woman*, trans. Louise Mannheimer (New York: Block Publishing, 1916), 169; Weiss-Rosmarin, *Jewish Women Through the Ages*, 87.

57 Vittorio Castiglioni, ed., *Ugav Raḥel (Rachel's Harp)* (Hebrew and Italian) (Krakow: Joseph Fisher, 1890), 7–8.

58 Salaman, *Rahel Morpurgo*, 20.

59 Translated from the Hebrew with the help of Daniel Blumenfeld. These verses are part of a three-stanza poem titled "Desolate Valley" that appears in Hebrew in Castiglioni, ed., *Ugav Raḥel*, 96.

60 Salaman, *Rahel Morpurgo*, 20.

61 Nina Davis Salaman's translations appear in the following anthologies: Nathaniel Kravitz, *3,000 Years of Hebrew Literature* (Chicago, Swallow Press, Inc. 1972), 595; Leo W. Schwarz, ed., *A Golden Treasury of Jewish Literature* (New York, Farrer and Rinehart, 1937), 595.

62 Harry M. Rabinowicz, *The World of Hasidism* (Hartford, Conn.: Hartmore House, 1970), 202–210.

63 Hyman, *Gender and Assimilation*, 56, citing Puah Rakowski, *Zikhroynes fun yiddisher revolutsionerin* (Buenos Aires: Tsentral-Farband fun Poylishe Yidn in Argentine, 1954), 19. For a new and complete translation of Rakowski's memoir, see Puah Rakowski, *My Life As a Radical Jewish Feminist in Poland*, ed. Paula Hyman (Bloomington and Indianapolis: University of Indiana Press, 2002).

64 Hyman, *Gender and Assimilation,* 55, 64, citing Rakowski, *Zikhroynes*, 22–23.

65 Castiglioni, *Ugav Raḥel*, 1–4, translated by Elisa Blankstein.

66 Shepherd, *Price below Rubies*, 66.

67 Hyman, *Gender and Assimilation*, 161; Lucy S. Dawidowicz, *The Golden Tradition: Jewish Life and Thought in Eastern Europe* (Boston: Beacon Press, 1967), 391.

68 Hyman, *Gender and Assimilation*, 58, citing Rakowski, *Zikhroynes*, 19. The educational experience of Yiddish-speaking women in the nineteenth century continues to be explored as more memoirs and autobiographies are translated into English.

69 Rakowski, *Zikhroynes*, as translated by Dawidowicz, *The Golden Tradition*, 392.

70 Tracy Klirs, ed., *The Merit of Our Mothers (Bizkhus imohes): A Bilingual Anthology of Jewish Women's Prayers* (Cincinnati: Hebrew Union College Press, 1992), 52.

71 Chava Weissler, *Voices of the Matriarchs: Listening to the Prayers of Early Modern Jewish Women* (Boston: Beacon Press, 1998), 145.

72 Full texts of these two prayers in Yiddish and English can be found in Klirs, *Merit of Our Mothers*, 46–77. See also Weissler, *Voices of the Matriarchs*, 145–146; 176–177.

73 Alexander Altmann, *Moses Mendelssohn: A Biographical Study* (Tuscaloosa: University of Alabama Press, 1973), 98.

74 See *Encyclopaedia Judaica*, 1st ed., s.v. "Mendelssohn family."

75 Fassmann, *Jüdinnen*, 234–236.

76 Ibid., 236–239.

77 Ibid., 243.

78 Weissler, *Voices of the Matriarchs*, 62–63.

79 Ibid., 62.

80 Rapoport-Albert, "On Women in Hasidism," 501; Rabinowicz, *Hasidism: The Movement and Its Masters* (Northvale, N.J.: Jason Aronson, 1988), 344–345; Rabinowicz, *The World of Hasidism*, 205.

81 Rabinowicz, *The World of Hasidism*, 205 and *Hasidism: The Movement*, 345.

82 Hertz, *Jewish High Society*, 101.

83 Hannah Arendt, *Rahel Varnhagen: The Life of a Jewish Woman* (New York: Harcourt, Brace Jovanovich, 1974), 203.

84 Ibid., 229.

85 Arendt, *Rahel Varnhagen*, 175; Hertz, *Jewish High Society*, 102.

86 Shulamit Magnus, "Pauline Wengeroff and the Voice of Jewish Modernity," in *Gender and Judaism: The Transformation of Tradition*, ed. T. M. Rudavsky (New York: New York University Press, 1995), 184.

87 Shepherd, *A Price below Rubies*, 64–65.

88 Balin, *To Reveal Our Hearts*, 203 note 5 referring to Paulina Vengerova, *"Iz dalekavo proshlavo" (From the Distant Past)*, *Voskhod* (October 1902): 28–41; (November 1902): 70–82.

89 All the above quotes are from Wengeroff, *Memoirs*, as translated by Dawidowicz, *The Golden Tradition*, 164.

90 Ibid., 165.

91 Magnus, "Pauline Wengeroff," 186.

92 Ibid., 188.

93 Eiphraim Taubenhaus, "BaHatzer Beitah shel Ishah 'Tzaddik'" (In the Courtyard of the Woman *Tzaddik*), in *BeNativ HaYahid: Hayyei Holem veLohem ba-Ir HaMekubalim (One Man's Way: A Dreamer and Fighter in the City of the Kabbalists)* (Haifa: Metzuda, 1959), 37.

94 Ibid., 38.

95 Wengeroff, *Memoirs*, as translated by Dawidowicz, *The Golden Tradition*, 168.

96 Ibid., 161.

97 S. A. Horodezky, *Leaders of Hassidism*, trans. Maria Horodezky-Magasanik (London: "Hasefer" Agency for Literature, 1928), 115.

98 But see Taubenhaus, *BeNativ HaYahid*, 39, who refers to it as "the green house" and never mentions that it was a synagogue.

99 Franz Kobler, *Her Children Call Her Blessed* (New York: Stephen Daye Press, 1955), "Excerpts from the Will of Frumet (Fani) Wolf," 143–144.

100 Taubenhaus, *BeNativ HaYahid*, 40, claimed that when R. Mordecai of Chernobyl came to see her "he was the first man who was permitted to enter the holy of holies of the Maid of Ludmir."

101 This last account comes from eyewitness reports offered to S. A. Horodecky by "old women" who still remembered her visit to their town of Staro-Konstantinow. See Rapoport-Albert, "On Women in Hasidism," 504.

102 Taubenhaus, *BeNativ HaYahid*, 40.

103 *Encyclopaedia Judaica*, 1st ed., s.v. "Ludomir, Maid of."

104 Kobler, *Her Children Call Her Blessed*, 143–144.

105 Ibid.

106 Gershon David Hundert, "Approaches to the Jewish Family in Early Modern Poland-Lithuania," in *The Jewish Family: Myths and Reality*, eds. Steven M. Cohen and Paula E. Hyman (New York: Holmes and Meier, 1986), 22.

107 Shepherd, *A Price below Rubies*, 65–66.

108 Magnus, "Pauline Wengeroff," 188.

109 Marion A. Kaplan, "Priestess and Hausfrau," in *The Jewish Family: Myths and Reality*, eds. Steven M. Cohen and Paula E. Hyman (New York: Holmes and Meier, 1986), 74.

110 Ibid., 55, citing Yiddish novelist Ayzik Meyer Dik.

111 Michael Nevins, *The Jewish Doctor: A Narrative History* (Northvale, N.J.: Jason Aronson, 1996), 100.

112 Edward Kossoy and Abraham Ohry, *The Feldshers* (Jerusalem: Magnes Press, 1992), 162.

113 Marion A. Kaplan, "Jewish Women in Imperial Germany," *Jewish Women in Historical Perspective*, ed. Judith Baskin (Detroit: Wayne State University Press, 1991), 210. Hyman, *The Emancipation of the Jews of Alsace*, 65, points out that in Alsace, where the Jews had close ties to Rhineland culture, both women and men might be literate only in Yiddish. But it remained the case for women in many areas, and for longer periods, since they did not need to deal with outsiders as much as men did.

114 Rakowski, *Zikhroynes*, as translated by Dawidowicz, *The Golden Tradition*, 390.

115 Altmann, *Moses Mendelssohn*, 98.

116 Kaplan, "Jewish Women in Imperial Germany," 215.

117 Fassmann, *Jüdinnen*, 163.

118 Hyman, *Gender and Assimilation*, 58, citing Rakowski, *Zikhroynes*, 19.

119 Maria Saker, "Ob evreiakh v zapadnomkrae (About Jews on the Western Border)" *Den'* 7 (1869), as cited by Balin, *To Reveal Our Hearts*, 203, note 8.

120 Lipman, "Judith Montefiore—First Lady of Anglo-Jewry," 288.

121 Arendt, *Rahel Varnhagen*, 175; Hertz, *Jewish High Society*, 102.

122 Hyman, *The Emancipation of the Jews of Alsace*, 62–63, citing Arnaud Aron, *Prières d'un coeur israelite: écueil de prières et de méditations pour toutes les circonstances de la vie* (Strasbourg: Société consistoriale des bons livres, 1848), 266–267.

123 Salaman, *Rahel Morpurgo*, 38; Yael Levine Katz, "Rachel Morpurgo," *Judaism* 49 (winter 2000): 15.

124 Jacob Katz, "Family, Kinship and Marriage among Ashkenazim in the Sixteenth to Eighteenth Centuries," *Jewish Journal of Sociology* 1 (1959): 16.

125 Kaplan, "Jewish Women in Imperial Germany," 212–213.

126 Fassmann, *Jüdinnen*, 177.

127 Louis Loewe, *Diaries of Sir Moses and Lady Montefiore*, vol. 1 (Oxford: 1983), 61.

128 M. Kaplan, "Jewish Women in Imperial Germany," 210.

129 *Encyclopaedia Judaica*, 1st ed., s.v. "Frank, Jacob, and the Frankists." The author, Gershom Scholem, suggests that the main distinction of the sisters was "to serve as Frank's concubines." However, both men and women were believed to be sexually promiscuous and women certainly could have done that without the official title.

130 Aguilar, *The Women of Israel*, 572.

131 Ibid., 565.

132 Ibid., 248; Endelman, *The Jews of Georgian England*, 133. In his later life, Montefiore was said to have traveled with his own *shohet*.

133 Kaplan, "Jewish Women in Imperial Germany," 206.

134 Magnus, "Pauline Wengeroff," 181.

135 Rapoport-Albert, "On Women in Hasidism," 501.

136 Loewenthal, "Women and the Dialectic of Spirituality," 21–22.

137 Rabinowicz, *The World of Hasidism*, 203–204; Rapoport-Albert, "On Women in Hasidism," 518, n. 39.

138 Loewenthal, "Women and the Dialectic of Spirituality," 12–13; Rapoport-Albert, "On Women and Hasidism," 497, 511, n. 16.

139 Rapoport-Albert, "On Women and Hasidism," 498, 514, n. 21.

140 Ibid., 503, cites one article written by S. A. Horodecky that preceded his book on Hasidism. He based the report on interviews with people who still remembered her. Another important source was Ephraim Taubenhaus, *BeNativ HaYaḥid*, 37–41, who knew her in Jerusalem.

141 *Encyclopaedia Judaica*, 1st ed., s.v. "Reform Judaism."

142 Ellen Umansky, ed., *Lily Montagu: Sermons, Addresses, Letters, and Prayers* (Lewiston, N.Y.: Edwin Mellon Press, 1985).

143 One of his sons, Benjamin Disraeli, later became prime minister of England, a post he could never have held if he had remained a Jew.

144 Karpeles, *Jewish Literature and Other Essays*, 132, citing *Rahel, ein Buch des Andenkens für ihre Freunde*, vol. 1, 43. See also Arendt, *Rahel Varnhagen*, 216–228.

CHAPTER NINE

1 There is some evidence that Columbus himself was a *converso*. He was known as Christobal Colon, a name possibly of Spanish-Jewish origin, common among Jews living in Italy. It was said that his command of the Italian language was poor and his Castilian good. For a full review of the evidence of Columbus's possible Jewish origins, see Meyer Kayserling, *Christopher Columbus and the Participation of the Jews in the Spanish and Portuguese Discoveries* (New York: Longmans, Green, 1894); and Jonathan D. Sarna, "The Mythical Jewish Columbus and the History of America's Jews," in *Religion in the Age of Exploration: The Case of Spain and New Spain*, eds. Brian F. Le Beau and Menachem Mor (Omaha, Neb.: Creighton University Press, 1996), 81–95, who points out that Columbus associated with Jews, signed with a mystical signature suggestive of the *Kaddish*, and searched for a biblical basis for his voyages to the New World. However, these links to Judaism are highly conjectural and remain unproven.

2 Columbus was guided by the astronomical tables of Abraham Zacuto, known as Diego Roderigo, a physician and astronomer who was a New Christian. Luis de Torres, the official interpreter for Columbus's voyage, spoke both Hebrew and Arabic and was also a recently baptized Jew.

3 *Encyclopaedia Judaica*, 1st ed., s.v. "Mexico," reports that "a number of *Marranos* who were known as New Christians went to Mexico with Cortes who conquered the country in 1521." New Christians had Jewish origins and were called Marranos, meaning swine. This term was initially applied to them derisively but later adapted by the *conversos* themselves. Jewish historians often refer to them as "crypto-Jews." Crypto-Judaism implies the existence of hidden religious activities but is different from normative Judaism.

4 Seymour Liebman, *The Jews in New Spain: Faith, Flame and the Inquisition* (Coral Gables, Fla.: University of Miami Press, 1970), 130.

5 *Encyclopaedia Judaica*, 1st ed., s.v. "Mexico."

6 Herbert I. Bloom, "Brazilian Jewish History," *American Jewish Historical Society* 33 (1934): 47–57.

7 Abram Vossen Goodman, *American Overture: Jewish Rights in Colonial Times* (Philadelphia: Jewish Publication Society, 1947), 76–77.

8 The original letter from Peter Stuyvesant to the Dutch West India Co. requesting that the Jews be forced to leave New Amsterdam was sent on September 22, 1654. Nine months later, on April 25, 1655, the reply came. The Jews would be permitted to stay. See Samuel Oppenheim, "Early History of the Jews in New York," *American Jewish Historical Society Proceedings* 18 (1909): 1–99. The letters are discussed on pp. 4–8.

9 Rufus Learsi, *The Jews in America: A History* (New York: Ktav, 1972), 29.

10 Stephen Birmingham, *The Grandees: America's Sephardic Elite* (New York: Harper & Row, 1971), 56, offers this list of names. However, other names are also mentioned as part of this early group. One, Solomon Pieterson, is noted in court proceedings as speaking for the Jews. Oppenheim, "Early History of the Jews in New York," 52–53, claims that a full record of names "do not exist prior to 1673–74 and this list may be incomplete or only partially correct."

11 Rev. Jacques Judah Lyons, ed., "Items Relating to the Congregation Shearith Israel, New York," *American Jewish Historical Society Publications* 27 (1920): 76–77.

12   Ibid., 76–77.

13   Sheldon J. Godfrey and Judith C. Godfrey, *Search Out the Land: The Jews and the Growth of Equality in British Colonial America 1740–1867* (Montreal: McGill-Queens University Press, 1995), 124.

14   George Washington sent a letter to the Jews of Philadelphia, New York, Richmond, and Charleston in 1790, welcoming them to live freely in the newly independent country. The original letter is in the archives of Congregation Mikveh Israel in Philadelphia.

15   Bertram W. Korn, *American Jewry and the Civil War* (New York: Atheneum, 1970), xxvii–xxxiii.

16   Ibid., 1.

17   Ibid., 32–55.

18   Benjamin G. Sack, *History of the Jews in Canada,* vol. 1 (Montreal: Canadian Jewish Congress, 1945), 22.

19   Sack, *History of the Jews in Canada*, vol. 1, 23, citing *Public Archives of Canada: Archives Nationales, Archives des Colonies,* series F, vol. 70, 66–69.

20   Ibid., vol. 1, 23–24, citing *Public Archives of Canada*, series F, vol. 71, 132.

21   Liebman, *The Jews in New Spain*, 164–165.

22   Martin A. Cohen, *The Martyr: The Story of a Secret Jew and the Mexican Inquisition in the Sixteenth Century* (Philadelphia: The Jewish Publication Society, 1973), 76–77.

23   Ibid., 120–121. Rather than money, part of the girls' dowry may have been the potential influence they had with their uncle, the acting governor.

24   Liebman, *The Jews in New Spain*, 165.

25   Cohen, *The Martyr*, 18.

26   Ibid., 253; Liebman, *Jews in New Spain*, 308.

27   Ibid.

28   Paula E. Hyman and Deborah Dash Moore, eds., *Jewish Women in America: An Historical Encyclopedia* (New York: Routledge, 1998), s.v. "Franks, Bilhah Abigail Levy."

29   Abigail Franks, *The Lee Max Friedman Collection of American Jewish Colonial Correspondence: Letters of the Franks Family (1733–1748),* eds. Leo Hershkowitz and Isidore S. Meyer (Waltham, Mass.: American Jewish Historical Society, 1968), 27.

30   Ibid., 100.

31   Ibid., xv, 45.

32   Ibid., 110.

33   Gratz Van Rensselaer, "The Original of Rebecca in Ivanhoe," *The Century* 24, no. 9 (1882), 682.

34   Rebecca Gratz, *Letters of Rebecca Gratz,* ed. David Philipson (Philadelphia: Jewish Publication Society, 1929), 32.

35   Hyman and Moore, *Jewish Women in America*, s.v. "Gratz, Rebecca."

36   Gratz, *Letters of Rebecca Gratz*, 351.

37   Both quotations are from Diane Ashton, *Rebecca Gratz: Women and Judaism in Antebellum America* (Detroit: Wayne State University Press, 1997), 256.

38   Birmingham, *The Grandees*, 159.

39   All the material about Esther Etting Hays can be found in Solomon Solis-Cohen, "Notes Concerning David Hays and Esther Etting Hays," *American Jewish Historical Society Proceedings* 1 (1894): 63–72. See also Birmingham, *The Grandees*, 158–160. The slaves the couple possessed were brought into the marriage by Esther when she left Philadelphia.

40   Sack, *History of the Jews in Canada*, vol. 1, 96.

41   Carole S. Kessner, "Matrilineal Dissent: The Rhetoric of Zeal in Emma Lazarus, Marie Syrkin and Cynthia Ozick," *Women of the Word: Jewish Women and Jewish Writing*, ed. Judith R. Baskin (Detroit: Wayne State University Press, 1994), 199. See also Birmingham, *The Grandees*, 4, 12.

42 Hyman and Moore, *Jewish Women in America,* s.v. "Lazarus, Emma"; Bette Roth Young, *Emma Lazarus in Her World: Life and Letters* (Philadelphia: Jewish Publication Society, 1995), 7.

43 As reproduced in H. E. Jacob, *The World of Emma Lazarus* (New York: Schocken Books, 1949), 197.

44 Emma's sister Josephine perpetuated an image of Emma as a frail and reclusive person, but the recent discovery of new letters written by Lazarus contradicts that opinion. See Young, *Emma Lazarus,* 12, 20–23.

45 Young, *Emma Lazarus,* 18.

46 Emma Lazarus, *Emma Lazarus: Selections from Her Poetry and Prose,* ed. Morris M. Shappes (New York: Cooperative Book League, 1944), 23.

47 Kessner, "Matrilineal Dissent," 220. These two great Spanish-Hebrew poets of the Middle Ages had previously been translated into German, and this may have helped Lazarus in her translating work.

48 Lazarus, *Emma Lazarus: Selections,* "The Banner of the Jew," 27.

49 Zenaide Ragozin, "Russian Jews and Gentiles, from a Russian Point of View," *The Century* 23 (1882): 919. The rebuttal, "Russian Christianity versus Modern Judaism," appeared in *The Century* the following month. Later that year Lazarus published a series of essays in the *American Hebrew* that appeared from November 3, 1882, to February 1883, under the general title: "An Epistle to the Hebrews," attacking anti-Semitism.

50 Kessner, "Matrilineal Dissent," 203.

51 Young, *Emma Lazarus,* 3.

52 Malcolm H. Stern, "The Sheftall Diaries: Vital Records of Savannah Jewry (1733–1808)," *American Jewish Historical Quarterly* 54 (March, 1965), 243–277. The list of original Jewish immigrants is on p. 246; Julie L. Oliver, "The Life of Abigail Minis: An Original Georgia Settler," (Savannah, Ga.: Georgia Historical Society, 1993, photocopied), 2.

53 Stern, "The Sheftall Diaries," 266.

54 Jacob R. Marcus, *The American Jewish Woman, 1654–1980* (New York: Ktav, 1981), 17. See also Hyman and Moore, *Jewish Women in America,* s.v. "Abigail Minis."

55 Levy, *Savannah's Old Jewish Community Cemeteries* (Macon, Ga.: Mercer University Press, 1983), 76.

56 Some reports claim that Abigail Minis was briefly kept under house arrest by the British before being allowed to leave, but this report is not confirmed. See Levy, *Savannah's Old Jewish Community Cemeteries,* 76; and Marcus: *The American Jewish Woman,* 26.

57 Charles Reznikoff with Uriah Z. Engleman, *The Jews of Charleston* (Philadelphia: Jewish Publication Society, 1950), 17.

58 Reznikoff, *The Jews of Charleston,* 82. Hyman and Moore, *Jewish Women in America,* s.v. "Moise, Penina."

59 From correspondence with Solomon Breibart, Archivist of Temple Beth Elohim, Charleston, S.C., 1998.

60 Hyman and Moore, *The Jewish Woman in America,* s.v. "Moise, Penina."

61 Louis Harap, *Image of the Jew in American Literature: From Early Republic to Mass Immigration* (Philadelphia: Jewish Publication Society, 1974), 261.

62 *Encyclopaedia Judaica,* 1st ed., s.v. "Moise, Penina."

63 The first superintendent was Sally Lopez, who received the weekly lessons from Rebecca Gratz in Philadelphia. She in turn made copies to distribute to the teachers. Reznikoff, *The Jews of Charleston,* 150.

64 Korn, *American Jewry and the Civil War,* 112

65 *Union Hymnal: Songs and Prayers for Jewish Worship* (New York: The Central Conference of American Rabbis, 1948). Moise's hymns include nos. 8, 45, 50, 55, 65, 73,93, 140, 156, 157, 209, 212, 219.

66 Reznikoff, *The Jews of Charleston*, 84; *Encyclopaedia Judaica*, 1st ed., s.v. "Moise, Penina."

67 Reznikoff, *The Jews of Charleston*, 83.

68 Charlotte Adams, "A Hebrew Poet of the South," *The Critic* (December 28, 1899): 328.

69 *Union Hymnal*, 49.

70 Ibid., 65.

71 See Aviva Ben-Ur, "The Exceptional and the Mundane: A Biographical Portrait of Rebecca (Machado) Phillips (1746–1831)" in *Women and American Judaism: Historical Perspectives*, eds. Pamela S. Nadell and Jonathan D. Sarna (Hanover, N.H.: New England University Press, 2001), 46–80, for a fuller biography of Phillips's life.

72 Yuri Suhl, *Ernestine L. Rose: Women's Rights Pioneer* (New York: Biblio Press, 1990), 9–10.

73 Ibid., 22.

74 Ibid., 73–74.

75 Hyman and Moore, *Jewish Women*, s.v. "Rose, Ernestine"; Miriam Gurko, *The Ladies of Seneca Falls: The Birth of the Woman's Rights Movement* (New York: Schocken Books, 1974), 89.

76 Yuri Suhl, *Eloquent Crusader: Ernestine Rose* (New York: Julian Messner, 1970), 54, 154–55.

77 Ibid., 221.

78 Hyman and Moore, *American Jewish Women*, s.v. "Rose, Ernestine"; and Gurko, *The Ladies of Seneca Falls*, 89.

79 Hyman and Moore, *American Jewish Women*, s.v. "Rose, Ernestine."

80 Suhl, *Ernestine L. Rose*, 244.

81 Edwin Wolf II and Maxwell Whiteman, *The History of the Jews of Philadelphia from Colonial Times to the Age of Jackson* (Philadelphia: The Jewish Publication Society, 1975), 103, 171, 429, 430.

82 Suhl, *Ernestine L. Rose*, 247.

83 This is quoted from Salomon's obituary in the *Independent Gazetteer*. See Wolf and Whiteman, *History of the Jews of Philadelphia*, 171.

84 *Encyclopaedia Judaica*, 1st. ed., s.v. "Salomon, Haym."

85 Marcus, *The American Jewish Woman*, 30.

86 *Encyclopaedia Judaica*, 1st. ed., s.v. "Sheftall."

87 Hyman and Moore, *Jewish Women in America*, s.v. "Frances Hart Sheftall."

88 Marcus, *The American Jewish Woman*, 30.

89 Stern, "The Sheftall Diaries," 252.

90 Marcus, *The American Jewish Woman*, 17.

91 Ibid., 30.

92 Hyman and Moore, *Jewish Women in America*, s.v. "Gratz, Rebecca" and "Hebrew Teachers Colleges," for details of the establishment of the Sunday school.

93 Holly Snyder, "Queens of the Household," in *Women and American Judaism: Historical Perspectives*, eds. Pamela S. Nadell and Jonathan D. Sarna (Hanover, N.H.: University Press of New England , 2001), 28.

94 Hershkowitz and Meyer, *Letters of the Franks Family*, 109–110.

95 Ibid., 116, n. 4. Thomas Sully, a popular Philadelphia society portrait painter, painted Rebecca Franks's portrait.

96 Holly Snyder, "Queens of the Household," 28.

97 Sidney M. Fish, "The Problem of Intermarriage in Early America," *Gratz College Annual of Jewish Studies* 4 (1975): 85–95.

98 Ashton, *Rebecca Gratz*, 67.

99   Hershkowitz and Meyer, *Letters of the Franks Family*, 116.
100 Wolf and Whiteman, *History of the Jews of Philadelphia*, 239–240, letter to Maria Fenno Hoffman dated 1817.
101 Ashton, *Rebecca Gratz*, 82.
102 Ibid., 57–58, 67.
103 Hyman and Moore, *Jewish Women in America*, s.v. "Gratz, Rebecca."
104 Charlotte Baum, Paula Hyman, and Sonya Michel, *The Jewish Woman in America* (New York: Dial Press, 1976), 27.
105 Ibid.
106 Ibid., 170.
107 Suhl, *Ernestine L. Rose*, 63.
108 Ibid., 53.
109 Wyoming was the first, in 1869, followed by Utah in 1870 and Colorado in 1893. See M. Gurko, *The Ladies of Seneca Falls*, 314–315.
110 President Woodrow Wilson coined this phrase to justify U.S. entrance into World War I, but feminists complained that there was no democracy in the U.S. until women got the vote.
111 All these quotes are from Snyder, "Queens of the Household," 31.
112 Anita Libman Lebeson, *Recall to Life: Jewish Women in American History* (New York: Thomas Yosoloff, 1970), 43.
113 Suhl, *Ernestine L. Rose*, 48.
114 Gratz, *Letters of Rebecca Gratz*, xxiv.
115 Ashton, *Rebecca Gratz*, 60–64, 70; and Wolf and Whiteman, *History of the Jews of Philadelphia*, 271–277. Both of these books outline all of Gratz's philanthropic activities.
116 Hyman and Moore, *Jewish Women in America*, s.v. "Jacobs, Frances Wisebart."
117 Baum, Hyman, Michel, *The Jewish Woman in America*, 39.
118 Henry J. Tobias, *A History of the Jews in New Mexico* (Albuquerque, N.M.: University of New Mexico Press, 1990), 15–20. Tobias also discusses other crypto-Jewish practices among the older inhabitants. Candlelighting is reported among some natives of Bolivia. See *Encyclopaedia Judaica*, 1st ed., s.v. "Bolivia."
119 Lebeson, *Recall to Life*, 44–45.
120 Hyman and Moore, *Jewish Women in America*, s.v. "Lazarus, Emma."

APPENDIX

1   Ira Eisenstein, *Reconstructing Judaism: An Autobiography* (New York: Reconstructionist Press, 1986), 96.
2   Judith Hauptman, "Women and the Conservative Synagogue," in *Daughters of the King: Women and the Synagogue* (Philadelphia: Jewish Publication Society, 1992), 171.
3   Annette Daum, "Language and Liturgy," in *Daughters of the King*, 189.
4   Ellen Umansky and Diane Ashton, *Four Centuries of Women's Spirituality: A Sourcebook* (Boston: Beacon Press, 1992), 115 (Montagu); 108 (Frank); 122 (Ackerman).
5   Ellen Umansky, "Spiritual Expressions: Jewish Women's Religious Lives in the United States in the Nineteenth and Twentieth Centuries," in *Jewish Women in Historical Perspective*, ed. Judith R. Baskin (Detroit: Wayne State University Press, 1999), 361–362, n. 35.
6   "Conservative Jews Vote for Women in Minyan," *New York Times* (September 11, 1973): sec. A, p. 1.
7   Hauptman, "Women and the Conservative Synagogue," in *Daughters of the King*, 169–176.
8   Rela Geffen Munson, "The Impact of the Jewish Women's Movement on the American Synagogue," in *Daughters of the King*, 231–233.

9   Rochelle Furstenberg, "Israeli Life: Orthodox Women: A Progress Report," *Hadassah* (May 2000), 12–14.

10 Micah D. Halpern and Chana Safrai, *Jewish Legal Writings by Women* (Jerusalem: Urim Publications, 1998).

11 This organization is located in New York City and can be contacted through the Internet at *jofa@rcn.org* or *www.jofa.org*.

12 Based on a conversation with Rabbi Renni Altman, Associate Rabbi of Temple Beth-El, a Reform temple in Great Neck, N.Y.

BIBLIOGRAPHY

Abraham ibn Daud. *Sefer Ha-Qabbalah (The Book of Tradition)*, ed. and trans. Gerson D. Cohen. London: Routledge and Kegan Paul, 1969.

Abrahams, Israel, ed. and trans. *Hebrew Ethical Wills*. 2nd ed. 1926. Reprint, Philadelphia: Jewish Publication Society, 1976.

—————. *Jewish Life in the Middle Ages*. 1896. Reprint, New York: Atheneum, 1981.

Adams, Charlotte. "A Hebrew Poet of the South." *The Critic* (December 28, 1899): 328.

Adelman, Howard Tzvi. "Rabbis and Reality: The Public Roles of Jewish Women in the Renaissance and Catholic Restoration," *Jewish History* 5 (1991): 27–40.

—————. "The Educational and Literary Activities of Jewish Women in Italy During the Renaissance and the Catholic Restoration." In the *Shlomo Simonsohn Jubilee Volume*, eds. Aharon Oppenheimer et al. 9–23. Tel Aviv: Tel Aviv University Press, 1993.

—————. "Wife-Beating among Early Modern Italian Jews, 1400–1700." *Eleventh World Congress of Jewish Studies: Proceedings (1993)*. Division B, vol. 1 (1994): 135–142 (English section).

—————. "Finding Women's Voices in Italian Jewish Literature." In *Women of the Word: Jewish Women and Jewish Writing*, ed. Judith R. Baskin. 50–69. Detroit: Wayne State University Press, 1994.

—————. "Custom, Law and Gender, Levirate Union among Ashkenazim and Sephardim in Italy after the Expulsion from Spain." In *The Expulsion of the Jews: 1492 and After*," eds. Raymond B. Waddington and Arthur H. Williamson. 107–125. New York and London: Garland Publishing, Inc. 1994.

—————. "Servants and Sexuality: Seduction, Surrogacy and Rape: Some Observations Concerning Class, Gender and Race in Early Modern Italian Jewish Families." In *Gender and Judaism: The Transformation of Tradition*, ed. Tamar M. Rudavsky. 81–97. New York and London: New York University Press, 1995.

—————. "Italian Jewish Women." In *Jewish Women in Historical Perspective*, ed. Judith Baskin. 2nd ed. 150–168. Detroit: Wayne State University Press, 1998.

—————. "The Literacy of Jewish Women in Early Modern Italy." In *Women's Education in Early Modern Europe: A History, 1500–1800*, ed. Barbara J. Whitehead. 133–158. New York and London: Garland Publishing, 1999.

—————. "Jewish Women and Family Life, Inside and Outside the Ghetto." In *The Jews of Early Modern Venice*, eds. Robert C. Davis and Benjamin Ravid. 142–165, 176–179. Baltimore and London: The Johns Hopkins University Press, 2001.

Adler, Michael. "The Medieval Jews of Exeter." *Devonshire Association for the Advancement of Science, Literature and Art: Transactions* 68 (1931): 221–240.

—————. "The Jewish Woman in Medieval England." In *The Jews of Medieval England*, ed. Michael Adler, 17–42. London: Edward Goldston, 1939.

Adler, Rachel. "The Virgin in the Brothel and Other Anomalies: Character and Context in the Legend of Beruriah." *Tikkun* 6 (1988): 28–32; 102–106.

Aguilar, Grace. *The Jewish Faith*. Philadelphia: Sherman & Co., 1864.

—————. *The Women of Israel or Characters and Sketches from the Holy Scriptures and Jewish History*. London: Groombridge & Sons, 1878.

—————. *Spirit of Judaism*, ed. Isaac Leeser. Cincinnati: Bloch Publishing Co., n.d.

Agus, Irving. *Urban Civilization in Pre-Crusade Europe*. 2 vols. New York: Yeshiva University Press, 1965.

Ahimaaz ben Paltiel. *The Chronicle of Ahimaaz*, trans. and intro. by Marcus Salzman, 1924. Reprint, New York: AMS Press, Inc., 1966.

Ahroni, Reuben. *Yemenite Jewry: Origins, Culture, and Literature*. Bloomington, Ind.: Indiana University Press, 1986.

Aizenberg, Edna. "Una Judía Muy Fermosa: The Jewess As Sex Object in Medieval Spanish Literature and Lore." *La Corónica* 12 (1984): 187–194.

Alnadaf, Uriel, ed. *Zakhor le-Avraham*. Jerusalem: Sh. ben A. H. Alnadaf,1991.

Alshekh, R. Moshe. *Sefer She'elot u-Teshuvot ha-Maharam Alshekh (The Responsa of R. Moshe Alshech)*, ed. Yom Tov Porges. Safed: Sifriyah Toranit Bet Yosef, 1975.

Altmann, Alexander. *Moses Mendelssohn: A Biographical Study*. Tuscaloosa, Ala.: University of Alabama Press, 1973.

Amram, David. *Makers of Hebrew Books in Italy*. Philadelphia: Julius Greenstone, 1909.

Anderson, Bonnie S., and Judith P. Zinsser, *A History of Their Own*. New York: Harper & Row, 1988.

Angel, Marc D. *The Jews of Rhodes*. New York: Sepher-Hermon Press, Inc., 1978.

Archer, Léonie. *Her Price Is Beyond Rubies: The Jewish Woman in Graeco-Roman Palestine*. Sheffield, England: Sheffield Academic Press, 1989.

Arendt, Hannah. *Rahel Varnhagen: The Life of a Jewish Woman*. New York: Harcourt, Brace Jovanovich, 1974.

Arkush, Allan. *Moses Mendelssohn and the Enlightenment*. Albany, N.Y.: SUNY Press, 1994.

Aron, Milton. *Ideas and Ideals of the Hassidim*. New York: Citadel Press, 1964.

Ascarelli, Debora. *Debora Ascarelli, Poetessa*. Rome: Sindicato Italiano Arti Grafiche, 1925.

Ashkenazi, Shlomo. "Meḥabrot Piyyutim, Teḥinot u-Tefillot," *Maḥanayim* 109 (1966–1967): 75–82.

—————. "Rof'ot yehudyot me-fursamot (Famous Jewish Women Doctors)." *Meḥanayim* 123 (1969–1970): 146–157.

—————. *Ha-Ishah be-Aspaqlariat ha-Yahadut* (The Woman in the Mirror of Judaism). 2nd ed. 2 vols. Tel Aviv: Zion, 1979.

Ashton, Dianne. *Rebecca Gratz: Women and Judaism in Antebellum America*. Detroit: Wayne State University Press, 1997.

Ashtor, Eliyahu. *The Jews of Moslem Spain*. 3 vols. Philadelphia: Jewish Publication Society, 1973–1984.

Assaf, Simḥa. *Teshuvot Ha-Geonim*. Jerusalem: HaMadpis, 1926.

—————. *Mekorot leToldot ha-Ḥinukh be-Yisrael*. 4 vols. Jerusalem: Devir, 1930–1954.

Assis, Yom Tov, "Sexual Behaviour in Mediaeval Hispano-Jewish Society." In *Jewish History: Essays in Honour of Chimen Abramsky*, eds. Ada Rapoport-Albert and Steven J. Zipperstein. 25–59. London: Peter Halban, 1988.

Aubin, Melissa M. *Gendering Magic in Late Antique Judaism*. Ph.D. thesis, Dept. of Religion, Duke University, UMI, 1998.

Avigad, Naḥman. *Corpus of West Semitic Stamp Seals,* revised by Benjamin Sass. Jerusalem: Israel Academy of Sciences and Humanities, 1997.

Babinger, Franz. *Mehmed the Conqueror and His Time.* Princeton: Princeton University Press, 1978.

Babylonian Talmud, trans. and ed. Rabbi I. Epstein. London: Soncino Press, 1936.

Baer, Yitzhak. "Ha-Yesodot ve-ha-Hathalot shel Irgun ha-Kehillah ha-Yehudit be-Yemei ha-Benayim (The Origins of the Organization of the Jewish Community of the Middle Ages)." *Zion* 15 (1950): 1–41.

——————. *A History of the Jews in Christian Spain,* trans. L. Schoffman. 2 vols. Philadelphia: Jewish Publication Society, 1961–1966.

Balin, Carole B. *To Reveal Our Hearts: Jewish Women Writers in Tsarist Russia.* Cincinnati: Hebrew Union College Press, 2000.

Barnai, Jacob. "The Jews of the Ottoman Empire in the Seventeenth and Eighteenth Centuries." In *The Sephardi Legacy,* vol. 2 of *Moreshet Sepharad: The Sephardi Legacy,* ed. Haim Beinart. 2 vols. 134–165. Jerusalem: Magnus Press, 1992.

Baron, Salo. *A Social and Religious History of the Jews,* 2nd ed. 1952. New York: Columbia University Press, and Philadelphia: Jewish Publication Society, 4th reprint, 1971.

Bartlet, Suzanne. "Chera and Co.: Three Jewish Businesswomen of the Thirteenth Century." *Jewish Culture and History* 3, no. 2 (2000): 1–20.

Baskin, Judith R. "Some Parallels in the Education of Medieval Jewish and Christian Women." *Jewish History* 5 (1991): 41–51.

——————. "The Problem of Women in *Sefer Hasidim.*" *AJS Review* 19 (1994): 1–18.

——————. "Hinukh Nashim Yehudiot ve-Haskalatan be-Yemei ha-Benayim be-Artzot ha-Islam ve-ha-Natzrut (The Education of Jewish Women and Their Enlightenment in the Middle Ages in the Lands of Islam and Christianity)." *Pe'amim* 82 (2000): 31–49.

——————. "Dolce of Worms: Women Saints in Judaism." In *Women Saints in World Religions,* ed. Arvind Sharma. 39–69. Albany, N.Y.: SUNY Press, 2000.

Bastein, Franz, and Joseph Wideman, eds. *Monumenta Boica,* vol. 54. Munich: C. H. Beck, 1956.

Baum, Charlotte, Paula Hyman, and Sonya Michel. *The Jewish Woman in America.* New York: Dial Press, 1976.

Bellamy, James A. "Qasmuna the Poetess: Who Was She?" *Journal of the American Oriental Society* 103 (1983): 423–424.

Belon du Mans, Pierre. *Les obseruations de plusiers singularitez & choses memorables, trouuées en Grèce, Asie, Iudée, Egypte, Arabie, & autres pays estranges, Redigées en trois livres.* Paris: 1555.

Ben-Amos, Dan, and Jerome R. Mintz, eds. *In Praise of the Baal Shem Tov* (*Shivhei ha-Besht*). Bloomington, Ind.: University of Indiana Press, 1970.

Ben-Jacob, Avraham. *Kehillot Yehudei Kurdistan (The Communities of Jews of Kurdistan).* Jerusalem: Makhon Ben Zvi, 1961.

Ben Sira. *Alphabeta deBen Sira (im ha-Perush ha-Yashan ha-Kolel Mishlim Ma'asiot u-Midrashot ve-Rasha).* Warsaw: Troklin, 1927.

Ben-Ur, Aviva. "The Exceptional and the Mundane: A Biographical Portrait of Rebecca Machado Philips (1746–1831)." In *Women and American Judaism: Historical Perspectives,* eds. Pamela S. Nadell and Jonathan Sarna. 46–80. Hanover, N.H.: New England University Press, 2001.

Berger, Shulamith A. "*Tehines*: A Brief Survey of Women's Prayers." In *Daughters of the King: Women and the Synagogue,* eds. Susan Grossman and Rivka Haut. 73–83. Philadelphia: Jewish Publication Society, 1992.

Berliner, A[braham]. *Geschichte der Juden in Rom.* Frankfurt am Main: J. Kaufmann, 1893.

Berman, Jeremiah J. *Shehitah: A Study in the Cultural and Social Life of the Jewish People.* 83–136. New York: n.p., 1941.

Biale, Rachel. *Women and Jewish Law: An Exploration of Women's Issues in Halakhic Sources.* New York: Schocken, 1984.

Birmingham, Stephen. *The Grandees: America's Sephardic Elite*. New York: Harper & Row, 1971.

Blamires, Alcuin, ed. *Woman Defamed and Woman Defended: An Anthology of Medieval Texts*. Oxford: Clarendon Press, 1992.

Blau, Joseph L., and Salo W. Baron, eds. *The Jews of the United States, 1790–1840: A Documentary History*. New York and London: Columbia University Press, and Philadelphia: Jewish Publication Society, 1963.

Bloch, Joseph. "Le testament d'une femme juive au commencement du XVIIIe siècle." *Revue des études juives* 90 (1931): 146–160.

Bloom, Herbert I. "Brazilian Jewish History." *American Jewish Historical Society* 33 (1934): 47–57.

Boccato, Carla. "Un altro documento inedito su Sara Copio Sullam: Il 'codice di Giulia Soliga.'" *Rassegna mensile di Israel* 40 (1974): 303–316.

——————. "Sara Copio Sullam, la poetessa del ghetto di Venezia: Episodi della sua vita in un manoscrito del secolo XVII." *Italia* 6 (1987): 104–218.

Bonfil, Robert. "The Historian's Perception of the Jews in the Italian Renaissance: Towards a Reappraisal." *Revue des études juives* 143 (1984): 59–82.

——————. *Jewish Life in Renaissance Italy*, trans. Anthony Oldcorn. Berkeley: University of California Press, 1994.

Bornstein-Makovetzky, Leah. "Yehudim Portugezim ba-Ḥatzar ha-Malkhut ha-Otomanit be-Meah ha-Shesh-Esrei: Don Yosef Nasi (Portugese Jews at the Sultan's Court of Constantinople in the Sixteenth Century: Don Joseph Nasi)." In *Me-Lisbon le Saloniki ve-Kushta (From Lisbon to Salonica and Constantinople)*, ed. Zvi Ankori. 69–94. Tel Aviv: University of Tel Aviv, 1986.

Bouquet, Martin, ed. *Receuil des historiens des Gaules et de la France*. Vol. 6. Paris: V. Palmé, 1840.

Bowman, Steven B. *The Jews of Byzantium (1204–1453)*. Tuscaloosa, Ala.: University of Alabama Press, 1985.

Boyarin, Daniel. *Carnal Israel: Reading Sex in Talmudic Culture*. Berkeley: University of California Press, 1993.

Brann, Marcus. *Geschichte der Juden in Schlesien: Jahresbericht des jüdisch-Theologischen Seminars*. Vol. 6, anhang (appendix) 3: "Verzeichniss der Juden, die von den ältesten Zeiten bis zur Mitte des 16 Jahrhunderts in Schlesien gelebt haben." Breslau: 1910.

Brann, Ross. *The Compunctious Poet: Cultural Ambiguity and Hebrew Poetry in Muslim Spain*. Baltimore: Johns Hopkins University Press, 1991.

Brauer, Erich. *The Jews of Kurdistan*. Detroit: Wayne State University Press, 1993.

Breger, Jennifer. "Three Women of the Book: Judith Montefiore, Rachel Morpurgo, and Flora Sassoon." *AB Bookman's Weekly* 101 (March 30, 1998): 853–864.

Bresc, Henri. *Livre et Société en Sicile (1299–1499)*. Palermo: Centro di Studi Filologici e Linguistici Siciliani, 1971.

Breuer, Mordechai. "The Early Modern Period." In *German-Jewish History in Modern Times*, ed. Michael Meyer. Vol. 1, *Tradition and Enlightenment: 1600–1700*. 79–260. New York: Columbia University Press, 1996.

Bright, John. *A History of Israel*. 2nd ed. Philadelphia: Westminster Press, 1974.

Bromberg, Batya. "Nashim Meḥadshot Dinim ba-Halakhah (Women Who Make New Law). *Sinai* 59 (1966): 248–250.

Brooten, Bernadette J. *Women Leaders in the Ancient Synagogue: Inscriptional Evidence and Background Issues*. Atlanta, Ga.: Scholars Press, 1982.

Burckhardt, Jacob. *The Civilization of the Renaissance in Italy*, trans. S. G. C. Middlemore. 2 vols. New York: Harper Torchbooks PB, 1958.

Burian, Orhan. *The Report of Lello, 3rd English Ambassador to the Sublime Porte*. Ankara: Türk Tarih Kurumu Basimeri, 1952.

Burns, Robert I. *Jews in the Notarial Culture: Latinate Wills in Mediterranean Spain, 1250–1350.* Berkeley: University of California Press, 1996.

Cahan, Abraham. "Le Rabbinat de Metz pendant la période française (1567–1871)." *Revue des études juives* 7 (1883): 103–116.

Calendar of the Liberate Rolls. 6 vols. London: His Majesty's Stationery Office. 1916–1964.

Calimani, Riccardo. *The Ghetto of Venice: A History,* trans. Katherine Silberblatt Wollfthal. New York: M. Evans & Co. 1987.

Cardin, Nina Beth, ed. and trans. *Out of the Depths I Call to You: A Book of Prayers for the Married Jewish Woman.* Northvale, N.J.: Jason Aronson, 1992.

Cardoner Planas, A. "Seis mujeres hebreas practicando la medicina en el reino de Aragon." *Sefarad* 9 (1949): 441–445.

Carmi, T., ed. and trans. *The Penguin Book of Hebrew Verse.* New York: Penguin Books, 1981.

Cassel, David, ed. *Teshuvot Geonim Qadmonim (Replies of Early Geonim).* Berlin: Fridlendersche Buchdrukerei, 1847–48.

Chazan, Robert. *European Jewry and the First Crusade.* Berkeley: University of California Press, 1987.

Chetrit, Joseph. "Freha bat Yosef—Meshoreret Ivriyah be-Morocco be-meah ha-18 (Freha bat Yosef—a Hebrew Poetess in Eighteenth-Century Morocco)." *Pe'amim* 4 (1980): 84–93.

————. "Freha bat Rabbi Avraham," *Pe'amim* 55 (1993): 124–130.

Chouraqui, André N. *Between East and West: A History of the Jews of North Africa*, trans. Michael M. Bernet. Philadelphia: Jewish Publication Society, 1968.

Classen, Albrecht. *Deutsche Frauenlieder des fünfzehten und sechzenten Jahrhunderts.* Amsterdam, Atlanta, Ga.: Rodopi, 1999.

Cohen, Amnon. *Jewish Life under Islam: Jerusalem in the Sixteenth Century.* Cambridge, Mass.: Harvard University Press, 1984.

————. "Texts." Pt. 1 of *A World Within: Jewish Life As Reflected in Muslim Court Documents from the Sijill of Jerusalem (XVI Century).* Philadelphia: University of Pennsylvania Center for Judaic Studies, 1994.

Cohen, Gerson D. "The Story of the Four Captives." *Proceedings of the American Association for Jewish Research* 29 (1960–61): 55–131.

Cohen, Martin A. *The Martyr: The Story of a Secret Jew and the Mexican Inquisition in the Sixteenth Century.* Philadelphia: The Jewish Publication Society, 1973.

Cohen, Shaye J. D. "Women in the Synagogues of Antiquity." *Conservative Judaism* 34 (1980): 23–29.

————. "Purity and Piety: The Separation of Menstruants from the Sancta." In *Daughters of the King: Women and the Synagogue*, eds. Susan Grossman and Rivka Haut. 103–115. Philadelphia: Jewish Publication Society, 1992.

Collins, John J. "Marriage, Divorce and Family in Second Temple Judaism." In *Families in Ancient Israel*, eds. Leo G. Perdue, Joseph Blenkinsopp, John J. Collins, and Carol Meyers. 104–162. Louisville: Westminister John Knox Press, 1997.

Courtemanche, Andrée. "Les femmes juives et le crédit à Manosque au tournant du XIVe siècles." *provence historique* 37, no. 150 (1987): 545–558.

Daum, Annette. "Language and Liturgy." In *Daughters of the King: Women and the Synagogue*, eds. Susan Grossman and Rivka Haut. 183–202. Philadelphia: Jewish Publication Society, 1992.

David, Abraham. "New Jewish Sources on the History of the Members of the Nasi-Mendes Family in Italy and Constantinople." *Henoch* 20 (1998): 179–187.

Davis, Natalie Zemon. *Women on the Margins: Three Seventeenth-Century Lives.* Cambridge, Mass. and London: Harvard University Press, 1995.

Dawidowicz, Lucy. *The Golden Tradition: Jewish Life and Thought in Eastern Europe.* Boston: Beacon Press. 1967.

Diena, Azriel. *She'elot u-Teshuvot,* ed. Yaacov Boksenboim. 2 vols. Tel Aviv: University of Tel Aviv, 1977.

Dinur, Ben-Zion. *Yisrael ba-Golah (Israel in Exile).* 2 vols. Jerusalem, Tel Aviv: Devir and Mosad Bialik, 1958–1972.

Dobson, R. Barrie. "The Role of Jewish Women in Medieval England." In *Christianity and Judaism: Studies in Church History* 29, ed. Diana Wood. 145–168. Oxford: Blackwell, 1992.

Einbinder, Susan. "Pucellina of Blois: Romantic Myths and Narrative Conventions." *Jewish History* 12 (1998): 29–46.

Eisenberg, Azriel, ed. *Eyewitnesses to Jewish History, from 586 B.C.E. to 1967.* New York: Union of American Hebrew Congregations, 1973.

Eisenstadt, Israel. *Da'at Kedoshim.* Peterburg: Bermann, 1897–1898.

Eisenstein, Ira. *Reconstructing Judaism: An Autobiography.* New York: Reconstructionist Press. 1986.

Eliezer ben Natan. *Sefer Ravan: hu Sefer Even ha-Ezer,* eds. Aryeh Loeb Rashkes and Louis Ginzberg. Jerusalem, 1915.

Emery, Richard. *The Jews of Perpignan in the Thirteenth Century.* New York: Columbia University Press, 1959.

Encyclopaedia Britannica, 200th Anniversary ed.

Encyclopaedia Judaica. 16 vols. Jerusalem and New York: Keter and Macmillan, 1971–72.

Encyclopaedia Judaica: Das Judentum in Geschichte und Gegenwart. 10 vols. Berlin: Eschkol, 1928–1934.

Encyclopedia of the Jewish Diaspora. Jerusalem: 1967

Endelman, Todd. *The Jews of Georgian England, 1714–1830: Tradition and Change in a Liberal Society.* Philadelphia: Jewish Publication Society, 1979.

Ephraim of Bonn. *Sefer Zekhirah,* ed. A. M. Habermann. Jerusalem: Mosad Bialik, 1970.

Epstein, Isidore. "The Jewish Woman in the Responsa (900 C.E.–1500 C.E.)." *Response* 18 (summer 1973): 23–31. This issue of *Response* is also called *The Jewish Woman: An Anthology,* ed. Liz Koltun.

Erler, Mary, and Maryanne Kowaleski, eds. *Women and Power in the Middle Ages.* Athens, Ga.: University of Georgia Press, 1988.

Faierstein, Morris M., trans. and intro. *Jewish Mystical Autobiographies: Book of Visions and Book of Secrets.* New York and Mahwah: Paulist Press, 1999.

Falk, Ze'ev. "Ma`amad ha-Ishah be-Kehillot Ashkenaz be-Yemei ha-Benayyim (The Status of the Woman in the Communities of Germany in the Middle Ages.)" *Sinai* 48 (1960–61): 61–67.

Fassmann, Irmgard. *Jüdinnen in der deutschen Frauenbewegung.* Hildesheim, Zürich, New York: Georg Olms Verlag, 1996.

Feffer, Solomon. "Of Ladies and Converts and Tomes: An Essay in Hebrew Book Lore." In *Essays on Jewish Book Lore,* ed. Philip Goodman. 365–378. New York: Ktav, 1971.

Fine, Lawrence. "The Role of Women at the Rituals of Their Infant Children." *Judaism in Practice,* ed. Lawrence Fine. 99–114. Princeton, N.J.: Princeton University Press, 2001.

Finkelstein, Louis. *Jewish Self-Government in the Middle Ages.* New York: Philip Feldheim, 1964.

Fish, Sidney M. "The Problem of Intermarriage in Early America." *Annual of Jewish Studies* 4 (1975): 85–95.

Fleischer, Ezra. "Al Dunash ben Labrat ve-Ishto u-Veno (Dunash ben Labrat and His Wife and Son)." *Mehqerei Yerushalayim be-Sifrut Ivrit* 5 (1983–84): 189–202.

Frankel, Ellen. *The Five Books of Miriam: A Woman's Commentary on the Torah.* New York: G. P. Putnam, 1996.

Franks, Abigail. *The Lee Max Friedman Collection of American Jewish Colonial Correspondence: Letters of the Franks Family (1733–1748)*, eds. Leo Hershkowitz and Isidore S. Meyer. Waltham, Mass.: American Jewish Historical Society, 1968.

Freehof, Solomon. *The Responsa Literature* and *A Treasury of Responsa.* New York: Ktav, 1973.

Frey, Jean Baptiste. *Europe.* Vol. 1 of *Corpus Inscriptionum Judaicarum: Jewish Inscriptions from the Third Century B.C. to the Seventh Century A.D.* 1936. Reprinted, with a new introduction by Baruch Lifshitz. New York: Ktav, 1975.

Freyha (or Freḥa) Bat Avraham Bar-Adiba. "[Lift up my Steps]; Hear My Voice in the Morning", trans. Peter Cole. In *The Defiant Muse: Hebrew Feminist Poems from Antiquity to the Present, A Bilingual Anthology*, eds. Shirley Kaufman, Galit Hasan-Rokem, and Tamar S. Hess. 74–77. New York: The Feminist Press, 1999.

Friedenwald, Harry. "Jewish Doctoress in the Middle Ages." In *The Jews and Medicine: Essays*, ed. Harry Friedenwald. 2 vols. 1944. Reprint, New York: Ktav, 1967. 1: 217–220.

Friedman, Mordechai A. *Jewish Marriage in Palestine: A Cairo Geniza Study.* 2 vols. Tel Aviv: Tel Aviv University Press, 1980.

Frymer-Kensky, Tikva. *In the Wake of the Goddesses: Women, Culture, and the Biblical Transformation of Pagan Myth.* New York: Free Press, 1992.

Furstenberg, Rochelle. "Israeli Life: Orthodox Women: A Progress Report." *Hadassah* (May 2000): 12–14.

Galanté, Abraham. *Documents officiels turcs concernant les juifs de Turquie: Recueil de lois, règlements, firmans, bérats, ordres et décisions de tribunaux.* Istanbul: Etablissements Ḥaim Rozio & Co., 1931.

Gamlieli, Nissim B. *Ahavat Teman (Love of Yemen).* Tel Aviv: Afikim, 1975.

Garshowitz, Libby. "Gracia Mendes: Power, Influence, and Intrigue." In *Power of the Weak: Studies on Medieval Women*, eds. Jennifer Carpenter and Sally-Beth MacLean. 94–125. Urbana and Chicago: University of Illinois Press, 1995.

Gaster, Theodore H. "A Canaanite Magical Text." *Orientalia*, n.s. 11 (1942): 41–79.

Gerber, Ḥaim. "Social and Economic Position of Women in an Ottoman City—Bursa, 1600–1700." *International Journal of Middle East Studies* 12 (1980): 231–244.

—————. *Yehudei ha-Imperiah ha-Otomanit be-me'ot ha-16–17: Kalkalah ve-Ḥevrah (The Economic and Social Life of the Jews in the Ottoman Empire in the Sixteenth and Seventeenth Centuries).* Jerusalem: Merkaz Zalman Shazar, 1982.

Gerber, Jane S. "'My Heart Is in the East. . . .'" In *The Illustrated History of the Jewish People*, ed. Nicholas de Lange. 141–197. New York: Harcourt, Brace & Co., 1997.

Gershenzon, Shoshanna, and Jane Litman. "The Bloody 'Hands of Compassionate Women': Portrayals of Heroic Women in the Hebrew Crusade Chronicle." In *Crisis and Reaction: The Hero in Jewish History*, ed. Menachem Mor. 72–91. Omaha, Neb.: Creighton University Press, 1995.

Gil, Moshe, ed. *Documents of the Jewish Pious Foundations from the Cairo Genizah.* Leiden: Brill, 1976.

Glückel of Hameln. *The Life of Glückel of Hameln, 1646–1724, Written by Herself*, trans. and ed. Beth-Zion Abrahams. New York: Thomas Yoseloff, 1963.

Godfrey, Sheldon J., and Judith C. Godfrey. *Search Out the Land: The Jews and the Growth of Equality in British Colonial America 1740–1867.* Montreal: McGill-Queens University Press, 1995.

Goitein, Shelomo D. "A Report on Messianic Troubles in Baghdad." *Jewish Quarterly Review* 43 (1952–1953): 57–76.

—————. "Otograf shel ha-Rambam u-Mikhtav alav me'et Aḥoto Miriam (Autograph of the Rambam and a Letter to Him from His Sister Miriam)." *Tarbiz* 32 (1962–63): 184–194.

——————. "New Revelations from the Cairo Geniza: Jewish Women in the Middle Ages." *Hadassah Magazine* (October 1973): 14–15, 38–39.

——————. "The Jewish Family in the Days of Moses Maimonides." *Conservative Judaism* 29 (1974): 25–35.

——————. *Jews and Arabs: Their Contact Through the Ages.* 3rd ed. New York: Schocken Books, 1974.

——————. "The Social Structure of Jewish Education in Yemen." In *Jewish Societies in the Middle East: Community, Culture and Authority*, eds. Shlomo Deshen and Walter P. Zenner. 211–233. Lanham, Md.: University Press of America, 1983.

——————. *A Mediterranean Society: The Jewish Communities of the Arab World As Portrayed in the Documents of the Cairo Geniza.* 6 vols. Berkeley: University of California Press, 1967–1993.

Goldfeld, Anne. "Women As Sources of Torah in the Rabbinic Tradition." *Judaism* 24 (1975): 245–256.

Goodblatt, David. "The Beruriah Traditions." *Journal of Jewish Studies* 26 (1975): 68–85.

Goodman, Abram Vossen. *American Overture: Jewish Rights in Colonial Times.* Philadelphia: Jewish Publication Society, 1947.

Graetz, Heinrich. *History of the Jews.* 6 vols. Philadelphia: Jewish Publication Society, 1902.

Gratz, Rebecca. *Letters of Rebecca Gratz*, ed. David Philipson. Philadelphia: Jewish Publication Society, 1929.

Grayzel, Solomon. *The Church and the Jews in the XIIIth Century.* 2 vols. Philadelphia: Jewish Publication Society, 1933.

——————. *A History of the Jews: From the Babylonian Exile to the Present, 5728–1968.* New York: New American Library, 1968.

Grisebach, Eduard. *Die Wanderung der Novelle von der trülosen Wittwe durch die Weltliteratur*, 2nd ed. Berlin: Verlag, F & P. Lehmann, 1889.

Gross, Henri. "Étude sur Simson ben Abraham de Sens." Pts. 1 and 2. *Revue des études juives* 6 (1882):167–186; 7 (1883): 40–77.

Grossman, Avraham. "The Historical Background to the Ordinances on Family Affairs Attributed to Rabbenu Gershom Me'or Ha-Golah." In *Jewish History: Essays in honour of Chimen Abramsky*, eds. Ada Rapoport-Albert and Steven J. Zipperstein. 3–23. London: Peter Halban, 1988.

——————. "Medieval Views on Wife-Beating: 800–1300." *Jewish History* 5 (1991): 53–62 .

——————. *Ḥasidot u-Moredot: Nashim Yehudiot be-Eropah be-Yemei ha-Benayim (Pious and Rebellious: Jewish Women in Europe in the Middle Ages).* Jerusalem: Zalman Shazar, 2001.

Güdemann, Moritz. *Ha-Torah veha-Ḥayim be-Artzot ha-Ma'arav* (Torah and Life in the West). 1896–97. Reprint, Jerusalem: Makor, 1971–72.

Gurko, Miriam. *The Ladies of Seneca Falls: The Birth of the Woman's Rights Movement.* New York: Schocken Books, 1974.

Gutwirth, Eliezer. "A Judeo-Spanish letter from the *Genizah*." In *Judeo-Romance Languages*, eds. Isaac Benabu and Joseph Sermoneta. 127–138. Jerusalem: The Hebrew University and Misgav Yerushalyim, 1985.

Habermann, A[braham] M[eir]. *Nashim Ivriot be-tor Madpisot, Mesadrot, Motzi'ot le-Or ve-Tomkhot be-Meḥabrim* (Hebrew Women as Printers, Editors, Publishers and Financial Backers). Berlin: Reuben Mas, 1932–33.

——. *Sefer Gezerot Ashkenaz ve-Tzarfat.* Jerusalem: Mosad Rav Cook, 1945.

——. *Iyyunim ba-Shirah u-va-Piyyut shel Yemei ha-Benayim (Studies in Sacred and Secular Poetry in the Middle Ages).* Jerusalem: Reuben Mas, 1972.

Hacker, Joseph. "The Intellectual Activity of the Jews of the Ottoman Empire During the Sixteenth and Seventeenth Centuries." In *Jewish Thought in the Seventeenth Century*, eds. Isadore Twersky and Bernard Septimus. 95–135. Cambridge, Mass., and London: Harvard University Press, 1987.

———. "The Sephardim in the Ottoman Empire in the Sixteenth Century." In *The Sephardi Legacy*. Vol. 2 of *Moreshet Sepharad: The Sephardi Legacy*, ed. Ḥaim Beinart. 109–133. Jerusalem: Magnes Press, 1992.

HaCohen, Yosef. *Emek haBakha*. Toronto: n.p., 1981.

HaLevi, H. S. "Ḥayyei ha-Mishpaḥah be-Yisrael be-Tekufat Ha-Geonim (Family life in Israel in the Period of the *Geonim*)." *Ha-Ḥed* 10 (1935): 16–22.

Halpern, Micah D., and Chana Safrai. *Jewish Legal Writings by Women*. Jerusalem: Urim Publications, 1998.

Harap, Louis. *Image of the Jew in American Literature: From Early Republic to Mass Immigration*. Philadelphia: Jewish Publication Society, 1974.

Harkavy, Abraham Elihu. *Zikhron Kamah Geonim*. Vol. 4 of *Zikhron le-Rishonim ve-gam le-Aharonim*. Berlin: Ittskovski, 1887.

Harrán, Don. "Madama Europa, Jewish Singer in Late Renaissance Mantua." In *Festa Musicologica: Essays in Honor of George J. Buelow*, eds. Thomas J. Mathiesen and Benito V. Rivera. 197–231. Stuyvesant, N.Y.: Pendragon Press, 1995.

———. "Doubly Tainted, Doubly Talented: The Jewish Poet Sara Copio (d. 1641) As a Heroic Singer." In *Musica Franca: Essays in Honor of Frank A. D'Accone*, eds. Irene Alm, Alyson McLamore and Colleen Reardon. 367–422. Stuyvesant, N.Y.: Pendragon Press, 1996.

———. " Jewish Musical Culture: Leon Modena." In *The Jews of Early Modern Venice*, eds. Robert C. Davis and Benjamin Ravid. 211–230, 289–295. Baltimore: Johns Hopkins University Press, 2001.

Hassoun, Jacques. "Féminin singulier: En Egypte, du Xe au XVe siècle: Un Judaisme au feminin." *Les nouveaux cahiers* 86 (1986): 6–14.

Hauptman, Judith. "Women and the Conservative Synagogue." In *Daughters of the King: Women and the Synagogue*, eds. Susan Grossman and Rivkah Haut. 159–181. Philadelphia: Jewish Publication Society, 1992.

———. *Rereading the Rabbis: A Woman's Voice*. Boulder, Colo.: Westvlew Press, 1998.

Haut, Irwin H. "Are Women Obligated to Pray." In *Daughters of the King: Women and the Synagogue*, eds. Susan Grossman and Rivka Haut. 93–97. Philadelphia: Jewish Publication Society, 1992.

Hemdat Genuzah (1862–63), reprinted in *Kovetz Sifre ha-Geonim, Teshuvot u-Fesakim (Ge'onika)*. B'nei Brak: Masorah, 1984–85.

Henry, Sondra, and Emily Taitz. *Written Out of History: A Hidden Legacy of Jewish Women Revealed Through Their Writings and Letters*, New York: Bloch Publishing Co., 1978. Reprinted as *Written Out of History: Our Jewish Foremothers*. Fresh Meadows, N.Y.: Biblio Press, 1982; 1986; 1990; 1996.

Hertz, Deborah. *Jewish High Society in Old Regime Berlin*. New Haven: Yale University Press, 1988.

———. "Emancipation Through Intermarriage? Wealthy Jewish Salon Women in Old Berlin." In *Jewish Women in Historical Perspective*, ed. Judith R. Baskin. 2nd ed. 193–207. Detroit: Wayne State University Press, 1998.

Heyd, Ariel. "Te'udot Turkiot al Binyanah shel Tiveriah be-me'ah ha-16 (Turkish Documents on the Rebuilding of Tiberius in the Sixteenth Century)." *Sefunot* 10 (1966): 193–210.

Hildesheimer, Azriel, ed. *Sefer Halakhot Gedolot*. 3 vols. Jerusalem: Meqsey Nerdamim, 1971–88.

Hillgarth, Jocelyn N. *Readers and Books in Majorca, 1229–1550*. Paris: CNRS, 1991.

Hirschberg, H[aim] Z. *A History of the Jews in North Africa*. 2 vols. 1974. Reprint, Leiden: E. J. Brill, 1981.

Horodezky, S[amuel] A. *Leaders of Hassidism*, trans. Maria Horodezky-Magasanik. London: "Hasefer" Agency for Literature, 1928.

Hughes, Diane Owen. "Distinguishing Signs: Ear-rings, Jews and Franciscan Rhetoric in the Italian Renaissance City." *Past & Present* 112 (1986): 3–50.

Hundert, Gershon David. "Approaches to the Jewish Family in Early Modern Poland-Lithuania." In *The Jewish Family: Myths and Reality*, eds. Steven M. Cohen and Paula E. Hyman. 17–28. New York and London: Holmes and Meier, 1986.

Hyman, Paula E. *The Emancipation of the Jews of Alsace.* New Haven: Yale University Press, 1991.

———. *Gender and Assimilation in Modern Jewish History: The Roles and Representation of Women.* Seattle: University of Washington Press, 1995.

Hyman Paula E. and Deborah Dash Moore, eds. *Jewish Women in America: An Historical Encyclopedia.* New York: Routledge, 1997.

Iancu-Agou, Danièle. "Une vente de livres hébreux à Arles en 1434: Tableau de l'élite juive Arlesienne au milieu du XVe siècle (The Sale of Hebrew Books in Arles in 1434: A Picture of the Elite Jewish Woman of Arles at the Middle of the Fifteenth Century)." *Revue des études juives* 146 (1987): 5–62.

Ichud Habonim."Sketches from Early History." In *Sisters of Exile: Sources on the Jewish Woman.* 31–39. New York: Ichud Habonim; Labor Zionist Youth, 1973.

Idel, Moshe. "One from a Town, Two from a Clan."*Jewish History* 7 (1993): 79–104.

Ilan, Tal. *Jewish Women in Greco-Roman Palestine.* Tübingen: J. C. B. Mohr, 1995.

———. "The Quest for the Historical Beruriah, Rachel and Ima Shalom. *AJS Review* 22 (1997): 1–17.

———. *Integrating Women into Second Temple History.* Tübingen: Mohr Siebeck, 1999.

Isaac ben Moses . *Sefer Or Zarua.* Zhitomir, 1862.

al-Ishbahani, Abu al-Faraj, ed. *Kitab-al-Aghani* (10th century). In Theodor Nöldeke, *Beitrag zur Poesie der Alten Araber,* 53–54, Hannover, 1864.

Israel, Jonathan I. *European Jewry in the Age of Mercantilism 1550–1750.* Oxford: Clarendon Press, 1985.

Jacob, H[einrich] E. *The World of Emma Lazarus.* New York: Schocken Books, 1949.

Jacoby, David. "New Evidence on Jewish Bankers in Venice and the Venetian Terraferma, c. 1450–1550." In *The Mediterranean and the Jews: Banking, Finance and International Trade (XVI–XVIII Centuries),* eds. Ariel Toaff and Simon Schwarzfuchs. 151–178. Ramat Gan: Bar Ilan University, 1989.

Jewish Encyclopedia. New York: Funk & Wagnalls, 1912.

Jochnowitz, George. ". . . Who Made Me a Woman." *Commentary* 71, no. 4 (1981): 63–64.

Jordan, William Chester. "Jews on Top: Women and the Availability of Consumption Loans in Northern France in the Mid–Thirteenth Century." *Journal of Jewish Studies* 29 (1978): 39–56.

Josephus, Flavius. *The Complete Works of Josephus,* trans. H. St. J. Thackeray. Cambridge, Mass.: Harvard University Press, 1925.

Jung, Leo, ed. *Woman.* Vol. 3 of *The Jewish Library*, ed. Leo Jung. Reprint, London and New York: The Soncino Press, 1970.

Kagan, Donald, et. al., eds. *The Western Heritage: Since 1300.* 6th ed. Upper Saddle River, N.J.: Prentice Hall, 1998.

Kanarfogel, Ephraim. *Jewish Education and Society in the High Middle Ages.* Detroit: Wayne State University Press, 1992.

Kaplan, Marion A. "Priestess and Hausfrau: Women and Tradition in the German-Jewish Family." In *The Jewish Family: Myths and Reality*, eds. Steven M. Cohen and Paula E. Hyman. 62–81. New York and London: Holmes and Meier, 1986.

———. *The Making of the Jewish Middle Class: Women, Family, and Identity in Imperial Germany*. New York and Oxford: Oxford University Press, 1991.

———. "Tradition and Transition: Jewish Women in Imperial Germany." In *Jewish Women in Historical Perspective*, ed. Judith R. Baskin. 2nd ed. 227–247. Detroit: Wayne State University Press, 1998.

Karpeles, Gustav. *Jewish Literature and Other Essays*. Philadelphia: Jewish Publication Society, 1895.

Katz, Jacob. "Family, Kinship and Marriage among Ashkenazim in the Sixteenth to Eighteenth Centuries." *Jewish Journal of Sociology* 1 (1959): 4–22.

———. *Out of the Ghetto: The Social Background of Jewish Emancipation, 1770–1870*. 1973. Reprint, New York: Schocken Books, 1988.

———. *Exclusiveness and Tolerance: Studies in Jewish-Gentile Relations in Medieval and Modern Times*. New York: Behrman House, 1983.

Katz, Joseph. *She'erit Yosef*. Krakow: n.p., 1893.

Katz, Yael Levine. "Nashim Lamdaniyot bi-Yerushalayim." *Mabu'a* 26 (1994): 98–125.

———. "Rachel Morpurgo." *Judaism* 49 (winter 2000): 13–29.

Katzenellenbogen, Meir. *She'elot u-Teshuvot me-ha-Ri Mintz u-me-ha-Ram Padua*. Krakow: n.p., 1882. Reprint, Jerusalem: 1980.

Kaufman, Shirley, Galit Hasan-Rokem, and Tamar S. Hess, eds. *The Defiant Muse: Hebrew Feminist Poems from Antiquity to the Present*. New York: Feminist Press, 1999.

Kaufmann, David. "The Dispute About the Sermons of David del Bene of Mantua." *The Jewish Quarterly Review*, o.s. 8 (1896): 513–524.

Kay, Devra. "An Alternative Prayer Canon for Women: The Yiddish *Seyder Tkhines*." In *Zur Geschichte der Jüdischen Frau in Deutschland*, ed. Julius Carlebach. 49–85. Berlin: Metropol-Verlag, 1993.

Kayserling, Meyer. *Die jüdischen Frauen in der Geschichte, Literatur und Kunst*. 1879. Reprint, Hildesheim: Georg Olms Verlag, 1991.

———. *Christopher Columbus and the Participation of the Jews in the Spanish and Portuguese Discoveries*. New York: Longmans, Green, 1894.

Kelly-Gadol, Joan. "Did Women Have a Renaissance?" In *Becoming Visible: Women in European History*, eds. Renate Bridenthal, Claudia Koonz, and Susan Stuard. 2nd ed. 175–201. Boston: Houghton Mifflin, 1987.

Kessner, Carole S. "Matrilineal Dissent: The Rhetoric of Zeal in Emma Lazarus, Marie Syrkin and Cynthia Ozick." *Women of the Word: Jewish Women and Jewish Writing*, ed. Judith R. Baskin. 197–215. Detroit: Wayne State University Press, 1994.

Kimhi, Joseph. *The Book of the Covenant of Joseph Kimhi*, trans. Frank Talmage. Toronto: Pontifical Institute of Mediaeval Studies, 1972.

Klepfitz, Irene. "Die mames, dos loshn / The mothers, the language: Sarah Schnirer." *Bridges* (winter/spring 1994): 19–24.

Klirs, Tracy G., comp. and introd. *The Merit of Our Mothers (Bizhus imohes): A Bilingual Anthology of Jewish Women's Prayers*. Cincinnati: Hebrew Union College Press, 1992.

Kobler, Dora. "Four Rachels." (London: 1945.) A pamphlet available at YIVO Institute for Jewish Research in New York, N.Y.

Kobler, Franz, ed. *A Treasury of Jewish Letters: Letters from the Famous and Humble*. 2 vols. Philadelphia: Jewish Publication Society, 1978.

———, ed. *Her Children Call Her Blessed: A Portrait of a Jewish Mother*. New York: Stephen Daye Press, 1955.

Korman, Ezra. *Yidishe Dikhterins: Antologye*. Chicago: Farlag L.M. Stein, 1928.

Korn, Bertram W. *American Jewry and the Civil War*. New York: Atheneum, 1970.

Kossoy, Edward, and Abraham Ohry. *The Feldshers*. Jerusalem: Magnes Press, 1992.

Kovetz Sifre ha-Geonim, Teshuvot u-Fesakim (Ge'onika). 1857–58—1960. Reprint, Bnei Brak: Masorah, 1984–85.

Kracauer, I. "Ein jüdisches Testament aus dem Jahre 1470." *Monatsschrift für Geschichte und Wissenschaft des Judentums* 16 (1916): 295–301.

Kraemer, Joel L. "Spanish Ladies from the Cairo Geniza." *Mediterranean Historical Review* 6 (1991): 237–267.

Kraemer, Ross S., ed. *Maenads, Martyrs, Matrons, Monastics*. Philadelphia: Fortress Press, 1988.

———. "Monastic Jewish Women in Greco-Roman Egypt: Philo Judaeus on the Therapeutrides." *Signs* (winter 1989): 342–370.

———. *Her Share of the Blessings: Women's Religions among Pagans, Jews, and Christians in the Greco-Roman World*. New York and Oxford: Oxford University Press, 1992.

———. "Jewish Mothers and Daughters in the Greco-Roman World." In *The Jewish Family in Antiquity*, ed. Shaye J. D. Cohen. 89–112. Atlanta, Ga.: Scholars Press, 1993.

———. "Jewish Women in the Diaspora World of Late Antiquity" In *Jewish Women in Historical Perspective*, ed. Judith Baskin. 2nd ed. 46–72. Detroit: Wayne State University Press, 1998.

Kravitz, Nathaniel. *3,000 Years of Hebrew Literature*. Chicago: Swallow Press, Inc. 1972.

Lamdan, Ruth. "Parashat Herem Ancona—Ha-Tzad ha-Sheni shel ha-Matbe'a (The Boycott of Ancona—Viewing the Other Side of the Coin)." In *Me-Lisbon le Saloniki ve-Kushta (From Lisbon to Salonica and Constantinople)*, ed. Zvi Ankori. 135–154. Tel Aviv: Tel Aviv University Press, 1986.

———. "Ribui HaNashim bi-Hevrot ha-Yehudit be-Eretz-Yisrael u-be-Mitzrayim be-Dorot ha-Smukhim le-Geyrush Sepharad (Polygamy in Jewish Societies in the Land of Israel and in Egypt in the First Generations after the Expulsion from Spain)." In *Sefer ha-Yovel le-Daniel Carpi (Daniel Carpi Jubilee Volume)*, eds. Dina Poret, Minna Rozen, and Anita Shapira. 73–89. Tel Aviv: University of Tel Aviv, 1995–96.

———. "Child Marriage in Jewish Society in the Eastern Mediterranean During the Sixteenth Century." *Mediterranean Historical Review* 11 (1996): 37–59.

———. "Hahzakat Shefahot be-Hevrah ha-Yehudit be-Eretz-Yisrael, Suriah u-Mitzrayim be-Me'ah ha-Shesh-Esrei (Female Slaves in the Jewish Society of Palestine, Syria and Egypt in the Sixteenth Century)." In *Yemei Ha-Sahar: Perekim be-Toldot ha-Yehudim be-Imperiah ha-Otomanit (The Days of the Crescent: Chapters in the History of the Jews of the Ottoman Empire)*, ed. Minna Rozen. 355–371. Tel Aviv: Tel Aviv University, 1996.

———. *Am Bifnei Atzman: Nashim Yehudiot be-Eretz Yisrael, Suryah, u-Mitzrayim be-Me'ah ha-Shesh-Esrei (A Separate People: Jewish Women in Palestine, Syria, and Egypt in the Sixteenth Century)*. Tel Aviv: Bitan, 1996.

———. "The Mercies of the Court: Jewish Women Seeking Divorce in Sixteenth-Century Palestine, Syria and Egypt," *Nashim* 1 (winter 1998): 51–69.

———. *A Separate People: Jewish Women in Palestine, Syria, and Egypt in the 16th Century*. Leiden and Boston: E. J. Brill, 2000.

Landau, Alfred, and Bernhard Wachstein, eds. *Jüdische Privatbriefe aus dem Jahre 1619*. Vienna and Leipzig: Wilhelm Braunmüller, 1911.

Landgraf, A. ed. *Commentarius Cantabrigiensis in Epistolam ad Ephesios in Commentarius Cantabrigiensis in Epistolas Pauli e Schola Petre Abaelardi*. Notre Dame, Ind.: University of Notre Dame Press, 1937.

Langer, Ruth. "The *Birkat Betulim*: A Study of the Jewish Celebration of Bridal Virginity." *American Academy for Jewish Research, Proceedings* 61 (1995): 53–85.

Lazarus, Emma. "An Epistle to the Hebrews." 14 essays. *American Hebrew* (November 1882 to February 1883).

———. *Emma Lazarus: Selections from Her Poetry and Prose*, ed. Morris U. Shappes. New York: Cooperative Book League, 1944.

Learsi, Rufus. *The Jews in America: A History*. New York: Ktav, 1972.

Lebeson, Anita Libman. *Recall to Life: Jewish Women in American History*. New York: Thomas Yosoloff, 1970.

Leeser, Isaac. "Editor's Preface." In *The Spirit of Judaism*, ed. Grace Aguilar. Philadelphia: 5–8. Jewish Publication Society, 1849.

Lefkowitz, Mary R., and Maureen B. Fant, eds. *Women's Life in Greece and Rome: A Source Book in Translation*. 2nd ed. Baltimore: Johns Hopkins University Press, 1992.

Leneman, Helen. "Sara Coppio Sullam: Seventeenth-Century Jewish Poet in the Ghetto of Venice." *Response* 15, no. 3 (1987): 13–22.

Lesses, Rebecca. "Exe(o)rcising Power: Women As Sorceresses, Exorcists, and Demonesses in Babylonian Jewish Society of Late Antiquity." *Journal of the American Academy of Religion* 69, no. 2 (2001): 343–375.

Leviant, Curt, ed. *Masterpieces of Hebrew Literature: A Treasury of 2,000 Years of Jewish Creativity*. New York: Ktav, 1969.

Levine, M. Herschel. "Three Talmudic Tales of Seduction." *Judaism* 36 (1987): 466–470.

Levy, B. H. *Savannah's Old Jewish Community Cemeteries*. Macon, Ga.: Mercer University Press, 1983.

Lew, Myer S. *The Jews of Poland: Their Political, Economic, Social and Communal Life in the Works of Rabbi Moses Isserles*. London: Edward Goldston, 1944.

Lewin, Benjamin M. ed. *Otzar Ha-Geonim*. Haifa: n.p., 1928.

Lewis, Bernard. *The Jews of Islam*. Princeton, N.J.: Princeton University Press, 1984.

Lewis, Naphtali. *Greek Papyri*. Vol. 2 of *The Documents from the Bar Kokhba Period in the Cave of Letters*. Jerusalem: Israel Exploration Society and Hebrew University, 1989.

Lewis, Naphtali, R. Katzoff, and J. C. Greenfield. "Papyrus Yadin 18." *Israel Exploration Journal* 37 (1987): 229–250.

Liebman, Seymour. *The Jews in New Spain: Faith, Flame and the Inquisition*. Coral Gables, Fla.: University of Miami Press, 1970.

Linnemeir, Bernd-Wilhelm, and Rosemarie Kosche. "Jüdische Privatkorrespondenzen des mittleren 16. Jahrhunderts aus dem nordöstlichen Westfalen (Jewish Private Correspondence of the Mid–Sixteenth Century from North-east Westfalen)." *Aschkenas* 8 (1998): 275–324.

Lipman, Sonia L. "Judith Montefiore—First Lady of Anglo-Jewry." *The Jewish Historical Society of England, Transactions* 21 (1968): 287–303.

Loeb, Isidore. "Le rôle des Juifs de Paris en 1296 et 1297." *Revue des études juives* 1 (1880): 61–71.

Loewe, Louis, ed. *Diaries of Sir Moses and Lady Montefiore, Comprising Their Life and Work As Recorded in Their Dairies from 1812 to 1883*. 2 vols. 1890. Reprint, Oxford: Jewish Historical Society of England, 1983.

Loewenthal, Naftali. "Women and the Dialectic of Spirituality in Hasidism." In *Be-Magle Hasidim: Kovetz Meḥkarim leZikhrono shel Professor Mordecai Wilensky* (In *Hasidic Circles: Collected Research in Memory of Professor Mordecai Wilensky)*, ed. Emanuel Etkes, et al., 7–65 (English section). Jerusalem: Bialik Institute, 1999.

Lowenthal, Marvin. *The Jews of Germany: A Story of Sixteen Centuries*. New York: Longmans, Green & Co., 1936.

Luria, Shlomo. *She'elot u-Teshovot Maharshal*. Lemberg, 1859.

Luzzatto, Gino. *I Banchieri Ebrei in Urbino Nell'eta Ducale*. Padua: Arnaldo Forni, 1902.

Lyons, Jacques Judah, ed. "Items Relating to the Congregation Shearith Israel, New York." *American Jewish Historical Society Publications* 27 (1920): 76–77.

The Lyons Collection: American Jewish Historical Society, Publications #27. 1–125. Baltimore: American Jewish Historical Society, 1920.

Magnus, Shulamit S. "Pauline Wengeroff and the Voice of Jewish Modernity." In *Gender and Judaism: The Transformation of Tradition*, ed. Tamar M. Rudavsky. 181–190. New York and London: New York University Press, 1995.

Maimon, Arye, Mordechai Breuer, and Yacov Guggenheim, eds. "Band III (1350–1519)." Third band of *Germania Judaica*. Tübingen: J. C. B. Mohr, 1987–1995.

Maimonides, Moses. *Maimonides Reader*, ed. Isadore Twersky. New York: Behrman House, 1965.

———. *Mishnah Torah*, ed. Shmuel Rubenstein. Jerusalem: Mosad ha-Rav Kook, 1956.

Malkiel, David. "Jews and Wills in Renaissance Italy: A Case Study in the Jewish-Christian Cultural Encounter." *Italia: Studi e ricerche sulla storia, la cultura e la letteratura degli ebrei d'Italia* 12 (1996): 7–69.

Mann, Jacob. *Texts and Studies in Jewish History and Literature*. 2 vols. Cincinnati: Hebrew Union College Press, 1931.

———. *The Jews in Egypt and Palestine under the Fatimid Caliphs*. 2 vols. 1920–1922. Reprint, New York: Ktav Publishing Co., 1970.

Marcus, Ivan G. "Mothers, Martyrs, and Moneymakers: Some Jewish Women in Medieval Europe." *Conservative Judaism* 38 (1986): 40–77.

Marcus, Jacob R. *The Jew in the Medieval World: A Sourcebook: 315–1791*. 1938. Reprint, New York: Atheneum, 1974.

———. *The American Jewish Woman, 1654–1980*. New York: Ktav, 1981.

Marcus, Ralph. "Hellenistic Jewish Literature." In *The Jews: Their Religion and Culture*, ed. Louis Finkelstein. Vol. 2 of *The Jews*, ed. Finkelstein. 43–81. 1949. Reprint, New York: Harper and Bros., 1971.

Margoliouth, David S. *The Relations Between Arabs and Israelites prior to the Rise of Islam*. London: Oxford University Press for the British Academy, 1924.

McKee, Sally, ed. *Wills from Late Medieval Venetian Crete (1312–1420)*. 3 vols. Washington, D.C.: Dumbarton Oaks Library and Collection, 1998.

Meir ben Barukh. *She'elot u-Teshuvot ha-Maharam, defus Prague (The Responsa of the Maharam, Prague Edition)*, ed. M. Bloch. 1893. Reprint, Tel Aviv: n.p., 1969–70.

Melammed, Renée Levine. "A Woman Teacher in Twelfth-Century Cairo," *AJS Review* 22 (1997): 19–35.

———. "Medieval and Early Modern Sephardi Women." In *Jewish Women in Historical Perspective*, ed. Judith Baskin. 2nd ed. 128–149. Detroit: Wayne State University Press, 1998.

———. *Heretics or Daughters of Israel: The Crypto-Jewish Women of Castile*. New York: Oxford University Press, 1999.

Melammed, Uri, and Renée Levine Melammed. "Ha-Rabbanit Asnat—Rosh ha-Yeshivah Kurdistan (Rabbi Asnat—Yeshivah Director in Kurdistan)." *Pe'amim* 82 (2000): 163–178.

Meyers, Carol. *Discovering Eve: Ancient Israelite Women in Context*. New York and Oxford: Oxford University Press, 1988.

Midrash Tannaim leDevarim, ed. David Tzvi Hoffman. 2 vols. in 1. Berlin: Tzvi H. Itzkowski, 1908–1909.

Minkin, Jacob S. *The Romance of Hassidism*. New York: Thomas Yoseloff, 1955.

Mirrer, Louise. "The Beautiful Jewess: Marisaltos in Alfonso X's *Cantiga* 107." In *Women, Jews and Muslims in the Texts of Reconquest Castile*, ed. Louise Mirrer. 31–44. Ann Arbor, Mich.: University of Michigan Press, 1996.

Modena, Aaron Berekhiah da. *Ma'avar Yabbok*. Zhitomir, 1851.

Modena, Leon. *L'Ester*. Venice: Giacomo Sarzina, 1619.

———. *The Autobiography of a Seventeenth Century Venetian Rabbi: Leon Modena's Life of Judah*. Ed. and trans., Mark R. Cohen. Princeton: Princeton University Press, 1988.

Moellin, Yaacov ben Moshe ha-Levi. *She'elot u-Teshuvot Maharil*. Reprint, Jerusalem: Makhon Yerushalayim, 1979.

Montagu, Lilian. *Lily Montagu: Sermons, Addresses, Letters, and Prayers*, ed. Ellen M. Umansky. Lewiston, N.Y.: Edwin Mellen Press, 1985.

Montefiore, Judith. *The Jewish Manual or Practical Information in Jewish and Modern Cookery with a Collection of Valuable Recipes and Hints Relating to the Toilette, Edited by a Lady*. London: T. & W. Boone, 1846; Reprint, Cold Spring, N.Y.: Nightingale Books, 1983.

Montgomery, James A. *Aramaic Incantation Texts from Nippur*. Philadelphia: University Museum, 1913.

Mordecai ben Hillel. *Mordecai, Pesaḥim* 108, s.v. *"Nashim ḥashuvot."* Mordecai's commentary can be found in all standard editions of the Babylonian Talmud.

Morpurgo, Rachel. *Ugav Raḥel (Rachel's Harp)* (Hebrew and Italian), ed. Vittorio Castiglione. Krakow: Joseph Fisher, 1890.

Muneles, Otto. *Ketuvot me-Beit ha-Almyn ha-Yehudi ha-Atik be-Prague*. Jerusalem: Ha-Akademiah ha-Leumit ha-Yisraelit le-Mada'im, 1987–88.

Munson, Rela Geffen. "The Impact of the Jewish Women's Movement on the American Synagogue." In *Daughters of the King: Women of the Synagogue*, eds. Susan Grossman and Rivka Haut. 227–236. Philadelphia: Jewish Publication Society, 1992.

Naveh, Joseph, and Shaul Shaked, *Magic Spells and Formulae: Aramaic Incantations of Late Antiquity*. Jerusalem: Magnes Press, 1993.

Nehama, Josef. *Histoire des Israelites de Salonique*. 7 vols. 2nd ed. Thessalonique: Communauté Israelite de Thessalonique, 1978. Vols. 6–7.

Netanyahu, B[enzion]. *Don Isaac Abravanel: Statesman and Philosopher*. 2nd ed. Philadelphia: Jewish Publication Society of America, 1968.

Neubauer, A[dolf]. "The Early Settlement of the Jews in Southern Italy." *Jewish Quarterly Review*, o.s. 4 (1892): 606–624.

Neusner, Jacob. *A History of the Jews in Babylonia*. 5 vols. Leiden: E. J. Brill, 1966.

———. *The Rabbinic Traditions about the Pharisees Before 70*. 3 vols. Leiden: E. J. Brill, 1971.

———. *There We Sat Down: Talmudic Judaism in the Making*. New York: Ktav, 1972.

———. *Invitation to the Talmud: A Teaching Book*. 1973. Reprint, San Francisco, Harper and Row, 1973.

Nevins, Michael. *The Jewish Doctor: A Narrative History*. Northvale, N.J.: Jason Aronson, 1996.

Nichols, James M. "The Arabic Verses of Qasmūna bint Ismā'il ibn Baghdālah." *International Journal of Middle East Studies* 13 (1981): 155–158.

Nirenberg, David "A Female Rabbi in Fourteenth-Century Zaragoza?" *Sefarad* 51 (1991): 179–182.

Noble, Shlomo. "The Jewish Woman in Medieval Martyrology." In *Studies in Jewish Bibliography, History and Literature in Honor of T. Edward Kiev*, ed. Charles Berlin. 347–355. New York: Ktav, 1971.

Nöldeke, Theodore. *Beitrage zur Poesie der Alten Araber*. Hannover, 1864.

Oliver, Julie L. "The Life of Abigail Minis: An Original Georgia Settler." Savannah, Ga.: Georgia Historical Society, 1993.

Oliveri, Fabio. "Jewish Women in Ancient and Medieval Sicily," *The Eleventh World Congress of Jewish Studies (1993), Proceedings*. Division B, vol. 1 (1994): 130–134.

Oppenheim, Samuel. "Early History of the Jews in New York." *American Jewish Historical Society, Proceedings* 18 (1909): 1–99.

Parke, Herbert W. *Sibyls and Sibylline Prophecy in Classical Antiquity*. London & New York: Routledge, 1988.

Patai, Raphael. *The Jewish Alchemists: A History and Source Book*. Princeton, N.J.: Princeton University Press, 1994.

Peskowitz, Miriam. *Spinning Fantasies: Rabbis, Gender and History*. Berkeley: University of California Press, 1997.

Petaḥiah of Regensburg. "Rabbi Petachiah of Ratisbon (1170–87)," trans. Elkan Nathan Adler. In *Jewish Travellers*, ed. Elkan Nathan Adler. 64–91. London: George Routledge & Sons, 1930.

———. *Sibuv Ha-Rav Rabbi Petaḥiah me-Regensburg (The Travels of Rabbi Petaḥiah of Regensburg)*, ed. L. Grünhut. Jerusalem: n.p., 1967.

Philo. All citations of Philo are from the Loeb Classical Library edition of the *Works of Philo* in 10 volumes and 2 supplements.

Philo Judaeus. *Supplement I: Questions and Answers on Genesis*, trans. Ralph Marcus. Cambridge, Mass.: Harvard University Press, 1929.

———. *On the Special Laws and Allegorical Interpretations*. Vol. 3, trans. F. H. Colson. Reprint, Cambridge, Mass.: Harvard University Press, 1950.

———. *De vita contemplative (On the Contemplative Life or Suppliants)*, trans. F. H. Colson. Reprint, Cambridge, Mass.: Harvard University Press, 1950.

Poletsky, H. J. "The Greek Papyri from the Cave of Letters." *Israel Exploration Journal* 12 (1962): 258–262.

Poorthuis, Marcel, and Chana Safrai. "Fresh Water for a Tired Soul: Pregnancy and Messianic Desire in a Mediaeval Jewish Document from Sicily." In *Women and Miracle Stories: A Multidisciplinary Exploration*, ed. Anne-Marie Korte. 123–144. Leiden: Brill, 2001.

Porten, Bezalel. *The Elephantine Papyri: Three Millennia of Cross-Cultural Continuity and Change*. Leiden: E. J. Brill, 1996.

Porten, Bezalel, and Ada Yardeni, eds. and trans. *Contracts*. Vol. 2 of *Textbook of Aramaic Documents from Ancient Egypt*. Jerusalem: Hebrew University Press, 1989.

Porter, Jack Nusan, ed. *Women in Chains: A Sourcebook on the Agunah*. Northvale, N.J.: Jason Aronson, 1995.

Pritchard, James B., ed. *The Ancient Near East: An Anthology of Texts and Pictures*. Princeton, N.J.: Princeton University Press, 1958.

Rabinowicz, Harry M. *The World of Hasidism*. London: Valentine, Mitchell, 1970.

———. *Hasidism: The Movement and its Masters*. Northvale, N.J.: J. Aronson, 1988.

Rabinowitz, Daniel. "Rayna Batya and Other Learned Women: A Reevaluation of Rabbi Barukh HaLevy Epstein's Sources." *Tradition* 35, no. 1 (2001): 55–69.

Ragozin, Zenaide. "Russian Jews and Gentiles, from a Russian Point of View." *Century Magazine* 23 (1882): 905–920.

Rapoport-Albert, Ada. "On Women in Hasidism: S. A. Horodecky and the Maid of Ludmir Tradition." In *Jewish History: Essays in Honor of Chimen Abramsky*, eds. Steven J. Zipperstein and Ada Rapoport-Albert. 495–525. London: Halbam, 1988.

Rashi, Solomon ben Isaac. *Teshuvot Rashi, Solomon ben Isaac (The Responsa of Rashi)*, ed. Israel Elfenbein. New York: Defus Ha'Aḥim Shulzinger, 1943.

Ravid, Benjamin. "From Yellow to Red: On the Distinguishing Head-Covering of the Jews of Venice." *Jewish History* 6 (1992): 179–210.

Remy, Nahida. *The Jewish Woman*, trans. Louise Mannheimer. New York: Bloch Publishing, 1916.

Reubeni, David. "The Travel Diary of David Reubeni," In *Masterpieces of Hebrew Literature: A Treasury of 2,000 Years of Jewish Creativity*, ed. Curt Leviant. 503–520. New York: Ktav, 1969.

Reznikoff, Charles. *The Jews of Charleston: A History of an American Jewish Community*, with the collaboration of Uriah Z. Engleman. Philadelphia: Jewish Publication Society, 1950.

Rhine, A. B. "The Secular Hebrew Poetry of Italy." *Jewish Quarterly Review,* n.s. 1 (1910–1911): 341–402.

Richler, Benyamin. "Ḥinukhan veSiḥatan shel B'not Ashirim be-Italia beYemei haRenesans (The Education and Conversation of Rich Italian Daughters During the Renaissance)." *Asufot Kiriyat Sefer.* 275–278. Jerusalem: Bet HaSefarim HaLeumi vehaUniversitai, 1997–98.

Riley-Smith, Jonathan. *The Crusades: A Short History.* New Haven: Yale University Press, 1987.

Rokeah, Zefira Entin. "The Jewish Church-Robbers and Host-Desecrators of Norwich (ca. 1285)." *Revue des études juives* 141 (1982): 331–362.

———. "Crime and Jews in Late Thirteenth-Century England: Some Cases and Comments." *Hebrew Union College Annual* 55 (1984): 95–157.

Romanelli, Samuel. *Travail in an Arab Land,* trans. and ed. Norman A. Stillman. Tuscaloosa, Ala.: University of Alabama Press, 1989.

Rosanes, Solomon. *Divrei Yemei Yisrael be-Togarmah.* Husiatyn: n.p., 1907.

Roth, Cecil. "Immanuel Aboab's Proselytization of Marranos." *Jewish Quarterly Review* 23 (1932–33): 121–162.

———. *The House of Nasi: Doña Gracia.* Philadelphia: Jewish Publication Society, 1947.

———. *The House of Nasi: The Duke of Naxos.* Philadelphia: Jewish Publication Society, 1948.

———. *The Jews of Medieval Oxford (Oxford Historical Society, New Series 9).* Oxford: Clarendon Press, 1951.

———. *Jews in the Renaissance.* Philadelphia: Jewish Publication Society, 1964.

Roth, Norman. *Jews, Visigoths and Muslims in Medieval Spain: Cooperation and Conflict.* Leiden: E. J. Brill, 1994.

Rozen, Minna. "Pe'ulatam shel Yehudim Rabi Hashpa-ah be-Ḥatzer ha-Sultan be-Kushta le-ma'an ha-Yishuv ha-Yehudit be-Yerushalyim be-Me'ah ha-yud-zayin (Influential Jews in the Sultan's Court in Istanbul in Support of Jerusalem Jewry in the Seventeenth Century)." *Michael* 7 (1981): 394–430.

———. *Jewish Identity and Society in the Seventeenth Century: Reflections on the Life and Work of Refael Mordekhai Malki,* trans. Goldie Wachsman. Tübingen: J. C. B. Mohr, 1992.

Sabar, Shalom. "Bride, Heroine and Courtesan: Images of the Jewish Woman in Hebrew Manuscripts of the Renaissance in Italy." *The Tenth World Congress of Jewish Studies (1989), Proceedings.* Division D, vol. 2 (1990): 63–70.

Sack, Benjamin G. *History of the Jews in Canada.* 2 vols. Montreal: Canadian Jewish Congress, 1945.

Safrai, Shmuel. "Ha-im Haita Kayemet Ezrat Nashim be-Beit ha-Knesset be-Tekufah ha-Atikah? (Was There a Women's Gallery in the Synagogue of Antiquity?)." *Tarbiz* 32 (1963): 329–338.

———. "The Role of the Women in the Temple." *Jerusalem Perspective,* vol. 2, no. 9 (1989): 5–6.

———. "The Place of Women in the First-Century Synagogues." *Jerusalem Perspective,* no. 40 (September/October 1993): 3–6.

Salaman, Nina Davis. *Rahel Morpurgo and Contemporary Hebrew Poets in Italy.* London: George Allen & Unwin, 1924.

Salfeld, Siegmund, ed. *Das Martyrologium des Nürnberger Memorbuches.* Berlin: Leonhard Simion, 1898.

Sambari, Yosef ben Yitzhak. *Sefer Divre Yosef,* ed. Shimon Shtober. Jerusalem: Makhon Ben Zvi, 1994.

Sanderson, John. *The Travels of John Sanderson in the Levant, 1584–1602, with his Autobiography and Selections from His Correspondence,* ed. Sir William Foster. London: Hakluyt Society, 1931.

Sarna, Jonathan D. "The Mythical Jewish Columbus and the History of America's Jews." In *Religion in The age of Exploration: The Case of Spain and New Spain*, eds. Brian F. Le Beau and Menachem Mor. 81–95. Omaha, Neb.: Creighton University Press, 1996.

Satlow, Michael. "Reconsidering the Rabbinic *ketubah* Payment." In *The Jewish Family in Antiquity*. ed. Shaye J. D. Cohen. 133–151. Atlanta, Ga.: Scholars Press, 1993.

Schechter, Solomon. "A Hoard of Hebrew Manuscripts." *Studies in Judaism*. 2ⁿᵈ series. 1–30. Philadelphia: Jewish Publication Society, 1908.

Schiffman, Lawrence H., and Michael D. Swartz. *Hebrew and Aramaic Incantation Texts from the Cairo Genizah*. Sheffield, England: Sheffield Academic Press, 1992.

Scholem, Gershom G. *Major Trends in Jewish Mysticism*. 1941. 3ʳᵈ ed., New York: Schocken Books, 1954.

———. *Sabbatai Sevi, the Mystical Messiah, 1626–1676*, trans. R. J. Zwi Werblowsky. Princeton, N.J.: Princeton University, 1973.

Schönfeld, Walther. *Frauen in der abländischen Heilkunde von klassischen Altertum bis zum Ausgang des 19. Jahrhunderts*. Stuttgart: Ferdinand Enke Verlag, 1947.

Schrire, Theodore. *Hebrew Amulets: Their Decipherment and Interpretation*. New York: Behrman House, 1982.

Schürer, Emil. *A History of the Jewish People in the Time of Jesus*, ed. with an introduction by Nahum N. Glatzer. New York: Schocken, 1961.

Schwarz, Leo W., ed. *A Golden Treasury of Jewish Literature*. New York: Farrer & Rinehart, 1937.

Schwarzbaum, Ḥayyim. *The Mishle Shualim (Fox Fables) of Rabbi Berechiah haNakdan*. Kiron: Institute for Jewish and Arab Folklore Research., 1979.

Schwarzfuchs, Simon, trans. *Un Obituaire israélite: le "Memorbuch" de Metz, vers 1575–1724*. Metz: Société d'histoire et d'archéologie de la Lorraine, 1971.

Sefer Hemdah Genuzah. In *Kovez Sifre ha-Geonim, Teshuvot u-Fesakim (Ge'onika)*. 1857–58— 1960. Reprint, Bnei Brak: Masorah, 1984–1985.

Segre, Renata. "Sephardic Settlements in Sixteenth Century Italy: A Historical and Geographical Survey." In *Jews, Christians and Muslims in the Mediterranean World after 1492*, ed. Alisa Mehuyas Ginio. 112–137. London: Frank Cass & Co., 1992.

Sendry, Alfred. *The Music of the Jews in the Diaspora (up to 1800)*. New York: Thomas Yoseloff, 1970.

Sered, Susan. "A Tale of Three Rachels or the Cultural Herstory of a Symbol." *Nashim* 1 (1998): 26–31.

Sharot, Stephen. "Judaism in Pre-Modern Societies." In *Jewish Societies in the Middle East: Community, Culture, and Authority*, eds. Shlomo Deshen and Walter P. Zenner. 49–83. Washington, D.C.: University Press of America, 1982.

Shatzmiller, Joseph. *Jews, Medicine, and Medieval Society*. Berkeley: University of California Press, 1994.

Shaw, Stanford J. *The Jews of the Ottoman Empire and the Turkish Republic*. New York: New York University Press, 1991.

Shepherd, Naomi. *A Price below Rubies: Jewish Women As Rebels and Radicals*. Cambridge, Mass.: Harvard University Press, 1993.

Shereshevsky, Esra. *Rashi, the Man and His World*. New York: Sepher-Harmon Press, 1982.

Shmeruk, Chone. "Ha-Soferet ha-Yehudit ha-Rishonah be-Polin—Rivkah bat Meir Tiktiner ve-Ḥiburiah (The First Jewish Author in Poland—Rivkah bat Meir Tiktiner and Her Work)." *Gilad* 4–5 (1978): 13–27.

———. *Sifrut Yiddish be-Polin*. Jerusalem: Magnes Press, 1981.

———. *The Esterke Story in Yiddish and Polish Literature*. Jerusalem: Zalman Shazar, 1985.

———. "Ha-Soferet ha-Yehudit ha-Rishonah be-Polin—Rivkah bat Meir Tiktiner ve-Ḥiburiah (The First Jewish Author in Poland—Rivkah bat Meir Tiktiner and Her Work)." In *Ataret Rivkah*, ed. Meir Wunder. 148–160. Jerusalem: "Hed" Press, 1991–92.

Shmuelevitz, Aryeh. *The Jews of the Ottoman Empire in the Late Fifteenth and Sixteenth Centuries*. Leiden: E. J. Brill, 1984.

Shulvass, Moses A. *The Jews in the World of the Renaissance*, trans. Elvin I. Kose. Leiden: E. J. Brill, 1973.

Sievers, Joseph. "The Role of Women in the Hasmonean Dynasty." In *Josephus, the Bible and History*, eds. Louis H. Feldman and Gohei Hata. 132–146. Leiden: E. J. Brill, 1989.

Simḥa of Vitry. *Maḥzor Vitry*. Berlin: n.p., 1889.

Simonsohn, Shlomo, ed. *The Jews in the Duchy of Milan*. 4 vols. Jerusalem: Israel Academy of Sciences and Humanities, 1982.

Slouschz, Nahum. *The Renascence of Hebrew Literature (1743–1885)*. Philadelphia: Jewish Publication Society, 1909.

Snyder, Holly. "Queens of the Household." In *Women and American Judaism: Historical Perspectives*, eds. Pamela S. Nadell and Jonathan Sarna. 15–45. Hanover, N.H.: University Press of New England, 2001.

Solis-Cohen, Solomon. "Notes Concerning David Hays and Esther Etting Hays." *American Jewish Historical Society, Proceedings* 1 (1894): 63–72.

Sparti, Barbara. "Dancing Couples Behind the Scenes: Recently Discovered Italian Illustrations, 1470–1550." *Imago Musicae* 13 (1996): 22–33.

———. "Jewish Dancing Masters and 'Jewish Dance' in Renaissance Italy." *Jewish Folklore and Ethnology Review* (Spring 2000): 11–23.

Spiegel, Irving. "Conservative Jews Vote for Women in Minyan." *New York Times* (September 11, 1973): section A, p. 1.

Spiegel, Marcia, and Deborah Kremsdorf, eds. *Women Speak to God: The Prayers and Poems of Jewish Women*. San Diego: Woman's Institute for Continuing Jewish Education, 1987.

Stampfer, Shaul. "Gender Differentiation and Education of the Jewish Woman in Nineteenth-Century Eastern Europe." *Polin* 7 (1992): 63–87.

Stern, Malcolm H. "The Sheftall Diaries: Vital Records of Savannah Jewry (1733–1808)." *American Jewish Historical Quarterly* 54 (1965): 243–277.

Stern, Moritz. *Regensburg im Mittelalter*. Vol. 5 of *Die israelitsche Bevolkerung der deutschen Stadte*, ed. Moritz Stern. Berlin: Verlag Hausfreund, 1935.

Stern, Selma. *The Court Jew: A Contribution to the History of the Period of Absolutism in Central Europe*, trans. Ralph Weiman. 1950. Reprint, New Brunswick, N.J.: Transaction Books, 1985.

Stillman, Norman A. compiler. *The Jews of Arab Lands: A History and Source Book*. Philadelphia: Jewish Publication Society, 1979.

Stillman, Norman. nstillman@ou.edu, "Al-Kahina." In H-Judaic, H-Judaic@h-net.msu.edu: June 3, 1998.

Stokes, Henry P. "A Jewish Family in Oxford in the Thirteenth Century." *Jewish Historical Society of England, Transactions* 10 (1921–23): 193–206.

Stouff, Louis. "Isaac Nathan et les siens. Une famille juive d'Arles des XIVe et XVe siècles." *provence historique* 37, no. 150 (1987): 499–512.

Stow, Kenneth. *Alienated Minority: The Jews of Medieval Latin Europe*. Cambridge, Mass., and London: Harvard University Press, 1992.

Stow, Kenneth, and Sandra Debenedetti Stow. "Donne ebree a Roma nell'eta del ghetto: affeto, dipendenza, autonomia (Jewish Women in Rome at the Time of the Establishment of the Ghetto)." *Rassegna Mensile di Israel* 52 (1986): 63–116.

Stow, Sandra Debenedetti. "The Etymology of 'Ghetto': New Evidence from Rome." *Jewish History* 6 (1992): 79–85.

Strom, Yale. *The Expulsion of the Jews: Five Hundred Years of Exodus*. New York: SPI Books, 1992.

Suhl, Yuri. *Eloquent Crusader: Ernestine Rose*. New York: Julian Messner, 1970.

———. *Ernestine L. Rose: Women's Rights Pioneer*. New York: Biblio Press, 1990.

al-Suyuti, Jalal al-Din. *Nuzhat al-julasa' fi ash'ar al-nisa (Entertaining the Company with Poems by Women)*, ed. Salah al-Din al-Munajjid. 86–87. 1958. Reprint, Beirut: Dar al-Kitab al Jadid, 1978.

Swidler, Leonard. *Women in Judaism: The Status of Women in Formative Judaism*. Metuchen, N.J.: Scarecrow Press, 1976.

Tabory, Joseph. "The Benedictions of Self-Identity and the Changing Status of Women and of Orthodoxy." *Kenishta* 1 (2001): 107–138.

Tadmor, H. "The Period of the First Temple, the Babylonian Exile and the Restoration." In pt. 2 of *A History of the Jewish People*, ed. H. H. Ben-Sasson. 91–182. Cambridge, Mass.: Harvard University Press, 1976.

Taitz, Emily. "Kol Ishah—The Voice of Woman: Where Was It Heard in Medieval Europe?" *Conservative Judaism* 38 (1986): 46–61.

———. "Women's Voices, Women's Prayers: The European Synagogues of the Middle Ages." In *Daughters of the King: Women of the Synagogue*, eds. Susan Grossman and Rivka Haut. 59–71. Philadelphia: Jewish Publication Society, 1992.

———. *The Jews of Medieval France: The Community of Champagne*. Westport, Conn.: Greenwood Press, 1994.

Tam, Yaakov ben Meir. *Sefer ha-Yashar le-Rabbenu Tam*. Königsburg: n.p., 1847.

———. *Sefer ha-Yashar le-Rabbenu Tam*. Berlin, 1898. Reprint, Jerusalem, n.p., 1972.

Tanakh, The Holy Scriptures. The New JPS Translation According to the Traditional Hebrew Text. 1985. 4th reprinting. Philadelphia: Jewish Publication Society, 1988. All biblical references and quotations are from this edition.

Taubenhaus, Ephraim. "BaHatzer Beitah shel Ishah 'Tzaddik' (In the Courtyard of the Woman *Tzaddik*)." In *Be-Nativ HaYahid: Hayyei Holem ve-Lohem ba-Ir HaMekubalim (One Man's Way: A Dreamer and Fighter in the City of the Kabbalists)*. 37–41. Haifa: Metzuda, 1959.

Tcherikover, Victor. *Hellenistic Civilization and the Jews*, trans. S. Applebaum. New York: Atheneum, 1977.

Tcherikover, Victor (Avigdor), and Alexander Fuks, eds. *Corpus Papyrorum Judaicarum*. Vol. 1. Cambridge, Mass.: Harvard University Press for The Magnes Press, 1957.

Teich, Shmuel. *The Rishonim: Biographical Sketches of the Prominent Early Rabbinic Sages and Leaders from the Tenth–Fifteenth Centuries*, ed. Hersh Goldwurm. Brooklyn, N.Y.: Mesorah Publications, 1982.

Tiktiner, Rebecca. *Meneket Rivkah*. Krakow, 1619. Available at the Rare Book Division of the Jewish Theological Seminary Library, New York, N.Y.

Tilly, Louise, and Joan W. Scott. *Women, Work and Family*. New York: Holt Rinehart, 1978.

Toaff, Ariel. *Love, Work and Death: Jewish Life in Medieval Umbria*, trans. Judith Landry. Portland, Ore.: Vallentine Mitchell, 1996.

Tobias, Henry J. *A History of the Jews in New Mexico*. Albuquerque, N.M.: University of New Mexico Press, 1990.

Toch, Michael. "Die jüdische Frau im Erwerbsleben des Spatmittelalters (The Jewish Woman in the Working World of the Late Middle Ages)." In *Zur Geschichte der jüdischen Frau in Deutschland*, ed. Julius Carlebach. 37–48. Berlin: Metropol-Verlag, 1993.

———. "Selbstdarstellung von mittelalterlichen Juden (Self-Portrayal of Medieval Jews)." In *Bild und Abbild von Menschen im Mittelalter*, ed. Elisabeth Vavra. 173–192. Klagenfurt: Wieser Verlag, 1999.

Trachtenberg, Joshua. *Jewish Magic and Superstition: A Study in Folk Religion*. 1939. Reprint, New York: Atheneum, 1970.

Trible, Phyllis. *Texts of Terror: Literary-Feminist Readings of Biblical Narratives*. Philadelphia: Fortress Press, 1984.

Turniansky, Chava. "Tzaror Iggarot bi-Yiddish me-Yerushalayim, me-Shmot ha-Shishim shel Meah ha-Shesh-Esreh (A correspondence in Yiddish from Jerusalem, Dating from the 1560s)." *Shalem* 4 (1984): 149–210.

Uitz, Erika. *Women in the Medieval Town*, trans. Sheila Marnie. London: Barrie & Jenkins, 1990.

Umansky, Ellen M. "Spiritual Expressions: Jewish Women's Religious Lives in the United States in the Nineteenth and Twentieth Centuries." In *Jewish Women in Historical Perspective*, ed. Judith R. Baskin. 2ⁿᵈ ed. 337–363. Detroit: Wayne State University Press, 1998.

Umansky, Ellen M., and Dianne Ashton, eds. *Four Centuries of Jewish Women's Spirituality: A Sourcebook*. Boston: Beacon Press, 1992.

Union Hymnal: Songs and Prayers for Jewish Worship. New York: The Central Conference of American Rabbis, 1948.

Urbach, Ephraim E. "Études sur la littérature polémique au moyen-âge." *Revue des études juives* 100 (1935): 49–77.

———. *Ba'alei haTosafot: Toldoteihem, Ḥibboreihem, Shitatam (The Tosafists: Their Lives, Writings and Methods)*. 2 vols. Jerusalem: Mosad Bialik, 1980.

Usque, Samuel. *Consolation for the Tribulations of Israel*, trans. Martin A. Cohen. Philadelphia: Jewish Publication Society, 1965.

Valley, Eli. *The Great Jewish Cities of Central and Eastern Europe: A Travel Guide and Resource Book to Prague, Warsaw, Crakow, and Budapest*. New York: Jason Aronson Press, 1999.

Waxman, Meyer. *Blessed Is the Daughter*. New York: Shengold Publishers Inc., 1968.

Wegner, Judith Romney. *Chattel or Person? The Status of Women in the Mishnah*. New York and Oxford: Oxford University Press, 1988.

———. "Philo's Portrayal of Women—Hebraic or Hellenic?" In *"Women Like This": New Perspectives on Jewish Women in the Greco-Roman World*, ed. Amy Jill Levine. 41–66. Atlanta, Ga.: Scholars Press, 1991.

———. "Women in Classical Rabbinic Judaism." In *Jewish Women in Historical Perspective*, ed. Judith R. Baskin. 2ⁿᵈ ed. 73–100. Detroit: Wayne State University Press, 1998.

Weiker, Walter F. *Ottomans, Turks and the Jewish Polity: A History of the Jews of Turkey*. Lanham, Md.; New York; and London: The Jerusalem Center for Public Affairs and University Press of America, 1992.

Weinreich, Max. *History of the Yiddish Language*, trans. Shlomo Nobel. Chicago: University of Chicago Press, 1980.

Weinryb, Bernard D. *The Jews of Poland: A Social and Economic History of the Jewish Community in Poland from 1100–1800*. Philadelphia: Jewish Publication Society, 1982.

Weiss-Rosmarin, Trude. *Jewish Women Through the Ages*. New York: Jewish Book Club, 1940.

Weissler, Chava. "Prayers in Yiddish and the Religious World of Ashkenazic Women." In *Jewish Women in Historical Perspective*, ed. Judith R. Baskin. 2ⁿᵈ ed. 169–192. Detroit: Wayne State University Press, 1998.

———. *Voices of the Matriarchs: Listening to the Prayers of Early Modern Jewish Women*. Boston: Beacon Press, 1998.

Weitstein, P. H. "Kadmoniot me-Pinkasaot Yeshanim: le-Korot Yisrael be-Polin be-Klal u-ve-Krakow be-Prat (Antiquities from the Old Notebooks of the Communities of Israel in Poland in General and in Krakow Specifically)." *Otzar HaSifrut* 4 (1892): 577–642.

Wolf, Edwin II, and Maxwell Whiteman. *The History of the Jews of Philadelphia from Colonial Times to the Age of Jackson*. Philadelphia: Jewish Publication Society, 1975.

Wolf, Lucien. "Jews in Tudor England." In *Essays in Jewish History*, ed. Cecil Roth. London: Jewish Historical Society of England, 1934.

―――. "Lady Montefiore's Honeymoon." In *Essays in Jewish History*, ed. Cecil Roth. 231–258. London: Jewish Historical Society of England, 1934.

Wunder, Meir, ed. *Ateret Rivka*. Jerusalem: Ha-Makhon le-Hantzaḥat Yahadut Galicia, 1991–1992.

Yaari, Avraham. *Masa'ot Eretz Yisrael shel Olim Yehudim (Journeys of Jewish Immigrants to the Land of Israel)*. 1976. Reprint, Tel Aviv: Modan, 1996.

Yadin, Yigael. "Expedition D: The Cave of Letters." *Israel Exploration Journal* 12 (1962): 227–257.

―――. *Bar Kokhba: Rediscovery of the Legendary Hero of the Last Jewish Revolt Against Rome*. London: Weidenfeld and Nicolson, 1971.

―――, Jonas C. Greenfield, and Ada Yardeni. "Babatha's Ketubba." *Israel Exploration Journal* 44 (1994): 75–101.

Yaron, Reuven. *Introduction to the Law of the Aramaic Papyri*. Oxford: Clarendon Press, 1961.

Yehudah ben Asher. *Zikhron Yehudah ve-hu Sefer She'elot u-Teshuvot le-Rabbenu Yehudah ben ha-Rosh ve-She'ar Gedolei Zemano*. 1845–46. Reprint, Jerusalem, n.p., 1967–68.

Yitzḥak ben Yosef of Corbeil, *Sefer Mitzvot Qatan*. Ladi, 1805.

Yosef ben Moshe. *Sefer Leket Yoshar: Orekh Ḥayyim*, ed. Jacob Freimann. 1903–1904. Reprint, Jerusalem: n.p., 1963–64.

Young, Bette Roth. *Emma Lazarus in Her World: Life and Letters*. Philadelphia: Jewish Publication Society, 1995.

Yovel, Yirmiyahu. *The New Otherness: Marrano Dualities in the First Generation*. San Francisco: Swig Judaic Studies Program at the University of San Francisco, 1999.

Yudlov, Yitshak. "'Sheyne Tkhine' ve-'Orah Ḥayyim': Shnei Sifrei Yiddish bilti Yedu'im ('Sheyne Tkhine' and 'Orah Ḥayyim': Two Unknown Yiddish Books)." *Kiryat Sefer* 62 (1989): 457–458.

Yuval, Yisrael Yaakov. "Takkanot Neged Ribui Gerushin be-Germaniah ba-Meah ha-Ḥamesh-Esrei (An Appeal Against the Proliferation of Divorce in Fifteenth-Century Germany)." *Zion* 48 (1983): 177–216.

―――. *Ḥakhamim be-Doram: Ha-Manhigut ha-Ruḥanit shel Yehudei Germaniah be-Shilḥei Yemei ha-Benayim (Sages in Their Time: The Spiritual Activities of the Jews of Germany in the Middle Ages)*. Jerusalem: Hebrew University Press, 1988.

Zenner, Walter P. "Jews in Late Ottoman Syria: Community, Family and Religion." In *Jewish Societies in the Middle East*, eds. Shlomo Deshen and Walter P. Zenner. 187–209 Washington, D.C.: University Press of America, 1982.

Zinberg, Israel. *Old Yiddish Literature from Its Origins to the Haskalah Period*. Vol. 7 of *A History of Jewish Literature*, 1938. Reprint, trans. and ed. by Bernard Martin. Cincinnati and New York: Hebrew Union College Press and Ktav, 1975.

Zives, Franz-Josef. "Reynette–eine jüdische Geldhändlerin im spätmittelalterlichen Koblenz (Reynette—a Jewish Moneylender in Late Medieval Koblenz)." *Koblenzer Beiträge zur Geschichte und Kultur* 4 (1994): 25–40.

Zolty, Shoshana. *And All Your Children Shall Be Learned*. Northvale, N.J.: Jason Aronson, 1993.

Zotenberg, Herman. *Manuscrits orientaux: Catalogue des manuscrits hébreux et samaritains de la Bibliotèque Impériale*. Paris: Imprimerie impériale, 1866.

Zwettler, Michael. *The Oral Tradition of Classical Arabic Poetry, Its Character and Implications*. Columbus, Ohio: Ohio State University Press, 1978.

INDEX

Seals, 1, 2, 15, 16–17
Sephardim, definition of, 166–167
Segal, Shifrah, 217–218, 233
segregation of sexes, 42, 124, 166
    in synagogues, 4, 47, 196, 272, 285 n. 56
servants (Christian), 117, 124, 299 n. 71
Shama'ah Shabazi of Yemen, 183–184, 188
Shapira-Luria, Miriam, 114
Sheftall, Frances Hart, 262, 263
Shelamzion of Southern Israel, 6, 9, 14,
        16, 280 n. 25, 280 n. 42
Shevelson, Clara Lemlich, 243
Shoḥat, Manya, 274
Shondlein, 91
Shulḥan Arukh, 307 n. 9
slaves (Jewish)
    Elephantine, 8, 9, 10, 12
    under Islam, 49–50, 187
    Rome, 103
    sale of daughter by father, 40
slave ownership
    antiquity, 8, 9
    Ottoman Empire, 195
    United States, 241
slave trade, 241
Solomon, Hannah G., 243, 269
Sonneschein, Rosa, 243, 264
Soreh, mother of Leib, 163
Spanish Jewry,
    expulsion, 53, 76, 104, 166
    under Islam, 52–53
subordination of women
    Bible, 1
    Talmud, 37–39, 45, 47
    Geonic period, 47
    Italy, 121–122, 123
    Europe, 157, 230
    United States, 267–268
Sophia of Gortyn, 9, 17
sotah, see "bitter water" ordeal
suffrage movement
    early modern Europe, 231
    United States, 261, 268, 269
sukkah, participation in, 100
Sullam, Sara Copio, 106, 114–117, 121
sumptuary laws, 123–124, 126
Sussman, Rachel bat Avraham, 168, 183,
        184, 185, 192
synagogue benefactors and fund-raisers
    antiquity, 17–18
    Islamic era, 71
    United States, 271
synagogue officials
    Christian Europe, 102
    Italy, 127
synagogue leaders, antiquity, 8, 9, 10,
        17–18

Szold, Henrietta, 269

T

Talmud, Babylonian, definition of, 24, 25
Talmud, Palestinian, definition of, 24
Tamar, 86, 292, n. 43
Tamet of Elephantine, 6, 9–10, 12
Tation of Kyme, 10, 18
testamentary capacity of women
    Elephantine, 8, 15
    Fatimid Egypt, 70
    Christian Europe, 98
    Italy, 124–125
    early modern Europe, 158–159
    United States, 268, 269, 271
Theodote of Alexandria, 10, 11
Theopempte of Myndos, 10, 17, 18
Therapeutrides, 23, 45, 46
Tiktiner, Rivkah bat Meir, xi, 147–149, 160
tkhines, 161–162, 196, 233
de Torres, Simja, 268
Tosefta, definition of, 24
Twersky, Ḥannah Ḥava, 218, 233
Twersky, Malkah, 218

U

umarried women, 44, 264–266
unwed mothers
    Italy, 124
    United States, 267
Urania of Worms, 101

V

Varnhagen, Rahel Levin, 202, 218–219,
        226, 234
Virdimura of Sicily, 117
virginity, value of, 42, 68, 230
Vital, Ḥayyim, 170, 197

W

Wald, Lillian, 243
welders, Ottoman era, 186
Wengeroff, Pauline Epstein, 219–220, 223,
        226, 229, 233, 235
Werbermacher, Ḥannah Rachel, 220–222,
        230, 234
wet nursing, 10, 13
Wife of Dunash ben Labrat, 58–59, 60, 63
Wife of Ḥayyim of Sicily, 117, 128
wifely duties, 67–68, 228, 229
wills, *see* testamentary capacity of women
Wolf, Frumet/Fani Beilin, 203, 222–223,
        229, 230
Women of the Wall, 276
Women's Tefilla Network, 276
Wuhsha of Egypt, 59–61, 67, 68, 69, 70